STRANGE ATTRACTOR

STRANGE ATTRACTOR

The Hallucinatory Life of Terence McKenna

Graham St John

foreword by Erik Davis

The MIT Press
Cambridge, Massachusetts
London, England

The MIT Press
Massachusetts Institute of Technology
77 Massachusetts Avenue, Cambridge, MA 02139
mitpress.mit.edu

© 2025 Graham St John

All rights reserved. No part of this book may be used to train artificial intelligence systems or reproduced in any form by any electronic or mechanical means (including photocopying, recording, or information storage and retrieval) without permission in writing from the publisher.

The MIT Press would like to thank the anonymous peer reviewers who provided comments on drafts of this book. The generous work of academic experts is essential for establishing the authority and quality of our publications. We acknowledge with gratitude the contributions of these otherwise uncredited readers.

This book was set in Stone Serif and Pangram by Westchester Publishing Services. Printed and bound in the United States of America.

Library of Congress Cataloging-in-Publication Data

Names: St John, Graham, 1968– author. | Davis, Erik, writer of foreword.
Title: Strange attractor : the hallucinatory life of Terence McKenna / Graham St John ; foreword by Erik Davis.
Description: Cambridge, Massachusetts ; London, England : The MIT Press, [2025] | Includes bibliographical references and index.
Identifiers: LCCN 2024034434 (print) | LCCN 2024034435 (ebook) | ISBN 9780262049573 (paperback) | ISBN 9780262382069 (pdf) | ISBN 9780262382076 (epub)
Subjects: LCSH: McKenna, Terence K., 1946–2000. | Hallucinogenic drugs. | Ethnobotany—United States—Biography. | LCGFT: Biographies.
Classification: LCC GN21.M35 S7 2025 (print) | LCC GN21.M35 (ebook) | DDC 581.6/3092 [B]—dc23/eng/20241224
LC record available at https://lccn.loc.gov/2024034434
LC ebook record available at https://lccn.loc.gov/2024034435

10 9 8 7 6 5 4 3 2

EU Authorised Representative: Easy Access System Europe, Mustamäe tee 50, 10621 Tallinn, Estonia | Email: gpsr.requests@easproject.com

In memory of Rick Watson

CONTENTS

FOREWORD BY ERIK DAVIS ix

PREFACE xvii

INTRODUCTION 1

I 7

1 EDGE RUNNERS 9

2 BERKELEY 35

3 TERRY INCOGNITA 65

4 LA CHORRERA 95

5 RETURN TO PARADISE 121

6 GROWMANCE 143

7 LUX NATURA 179

8 STAND-UP PHILOSOPHER 211

II 257

9 TIMEWAVE ZERO 259

10 PSYCHEDELIC GURU 297

11 ZONE GHOST 337

12 METAMORPHOSIS 365

APPENDIX A: ACKNOWLEDGMENTS AND SOURCES 399
APPENDIX B: THE McKENNAVERSE 413
NOTES 417
INDEX 491

FOREWORD

Erik Davis

After Terence McKenna was diagnosed with brain cancer in 1999, one of his quips was that, if the lump in his skull was really going to kill him, he hoped it would have the good graces to wait until after the big odometer click—which it did, with McKenna shuffling off this mortal coil in April 2000. But the witticism draws its depth and poignancy from the fact that temporal themes and millennialist patterns stretch and echo throughout his career. In a word, Terence was *untimely*. He named and called for an archaic revival, a return to mushroom-munching orgies under the moon, but he was also a McLuhanite man of technology who described, and conceptually minted, apocalyptic engines of futurity. Case in point is his famous Timewave theory, which was less a theory than another occult device, this one managing to transform the profoundly cyclical patterns of the *I Ching* into a mathematical map of the novelty waves rippling back through history from a Singularity planted in the near future and sucking us forward like a Death Star tractor beam.

McKenna's speculative riffs themselves possessed tractor-beam power, and one of those magnetizing forces was the wrinkling of time. His rants and riffs, almost invariably consumed live or in the simulated Now of recorded audio, can lead us on *Time Bandits*–like romps through the archives of the ages, ranging through literature, anthropology, esotericism, natural history, and comparative religion. Or they might invoke, through joke or looping syntax or the occasional bout of glossolalia, the blazing all-time Eternal Return at the center of the DMT flash.

Terence's untimeliness makes him a curious object for a biography, a literary form that is by definition wedded to linear history and yet, in this case, and like its subject, must wage a certain agon against and through the march of time. On the one hand, then, *Strange Attractor* gives us another exemplar of the boomer tale, for although Terence was no hippie, he was most definitely a head—better yet, a freak. As such, the arc of his relatively short life follows a familiar sixties pattern: buttoned-up 1950s upbringing, a liberating move to California, anti-authoritarian rabble-rousing, exotic voyages East and South, active participation in the drug trade, and eventually, and less commonly, the rejection of assimilation and the pursuit of a long strange underground struggle through the late 1970s and '80s. Graham St John tracks these adventures with thoroughness and sympathy, and pays particularly valuable attention to McKenna's family life, and the highs and lows of his creative and psychedelic partnership with his remarkable wife, the artist and independent ethnobotanist Kat Harrison. There is much that St John turns up here that will surprise and please even knowledgeable Terence McKenna obsessives.

But it is during the following era that McKenna's untimeliness comes to the fore, because the last decade of the twentieth century was an untimely time. The 1990s saw the publication of McKenna's most significant books, the birth of his electric celebrity, and the solidification of his unusual gig as a tireless if sometimes exhausted psychedelic circuit rider. In other words, Terence McKenna peaked not during the revolutionary sixties of his youth but during the millennialist nineties of his early middle age. And though he became popular among heads and weirdos of all ages, he also resonated with the era's most youthful subculture, as his words, thoughts, and gawky frame shuttled through the clubs, tracks, and mindstreams of the rave scene. And this is the scene that was nurturing a youngish Graham St John, who now tracks and refracts Terence's biography from a psychedelic perspective forged in the digital millennialism of psytrance and global electronica.

More than any other figure of the nineties, Terence articulated, at least for me, the strange timeslip slide of it all, the exciting and foreboding sense of acceleration and mutation that characterized those times, or at least many of its subcultures, in ways we have yet to assimilate or even really understand. With his intoxicating tales of DMT elves, Rosicrucian rebels, gnostic astronauts, heroic doses, and the mighty Eschaton, Terence single-handedly weirded the times. However seriously you took his raps, he was voicing the ambient air of expectancy, destabilization, and discarnate virtuality produced by the world-changing media developments of the decade. Terence's fascination with the imaginative potential of technology, something that always separated him from the bucolic hippies and Luddites of his generation, perfectly tuned him into the rising times, when subcultures traded roots for wires, when samples, hyperlinks, and remix culture catalyzed bold chimeras, and when crude datagloves and dial-up bulletin boards summoned spaces of possibility far more hallucinatory and transformative than their tepid baud rates and clunky pixels would suggest.

All eras have their signature drugs, compounds that carry associations and aspirations beyond the statistics of their consumption patterns. LSD was the drug of the 1960s; ketamine, I fear to say, is the drug of the 2020s. And while the exoteric signature drug of the 1990s was most certainly MDMA, the tiger in the tank of rave, the esoteric drug of the era was without doubt DMT. Talk about untimely! As St John covered in an excellent book *Mystery School in Hyperspace* (2015), DMT was very much around in the hippie days. Nick Sand cooked it up before he started making LSD; Robert Hunter and the Dead were fans; Alan Watts took it and didn't like it, while Timothy Leary took it and did (in a 1966 trip report, he even anticipates one of McKenna's most famous images by describing "elf-like insects merrily working away"). But though DMT was part of the '60s pharmacopeia, it did not really register until the '90s, when it became an arcane icon of the era's own transformative and accelerated energies. The resonance makes sense. Smoked DMT is at once faster, denser, brighter, and more packed with "information" than LSD, which is no slouch in any of those departments. But DMT was also the most fantastic possibility that Terence described that was also unquestionably real. It was the smoke rising from McKenna's pied pipe. I will never forget an encounter I had at a Bay Area rave in 1994, when I saw a scrawny kid wearing a T-shirt with "DMT" emblazoned across it in large block letters. The drug was still fairly recondite stuff back then, at least in my scene, and I approached him as a fellow initiate of the chrysanthemum hypercube. But the kid had never taken the stuff. DMT was a wish, a prayer, a vector of possibility.

And that's how I have come to see many of Terence's ideas: as wishes, prayers, and vectors of possibility. Again, Terence was untimely. His sixties turned out to be nineties; he was growing grizzled when he became a youth-culture celebrity, and then he died way too young. Even his position in psychedelic history is liminal. He looms as the last great spokesperson and avatar of the tripster underground before that underground was colonized by the corporate, regulatory, journalistic, and pharmaceutical forces of the so-called "psychedelic renaissance." "Great," here, signifies many things, including Terence's formidable if furtive impact on culture, his matchless and entrancing tongue, and his outstanding and outlandish visionary panache. Great, too, were the implications of his peculiar thoughts and narratives, their oracular ability to charge mundane history with fantastic implications. But players in the psychedelic renaissance don't know what to do with such powers. Stan Grof they can embrace, and Leary they can do battle with, but McKenna? In many ways, the new professionals have just left him for the kids.

Terence often said that his function was simply to give permission. But it wasn't just permission to take psychedelics, sometimes in heroic doses; it was permission to match the growing novelty of the times with a mode of speculation that combined dream-text, book learning, comedy, science fiction, and a profound if sometimes absurd affirmation of the imagination, literary and esoteric, human and posthuman. McKenna was a true Imagineer, at once a world-builder, a way-finder, and a psychoactive in his own right. That's what's so cool about the structure of *Strange Attractor*. While honoring McKenna's history and its unfolding network of influences, events, and encounters, St John also honors the transhistorical (and untimely) reach and substance of Terence's "funny ideas." In the second half of this book, St John offers one of the deepest and most extensive maps of the McKennaverse we possess—ideas, concepts, and clusters of associations that, even divorced from the charismatic power of Terence's leprechaun drawl, still possess the power to puzzle, to intrigue, to amuse, and to compel. Terence minted mind candy that delivers.

I still remember the force these ideas had on me when I was a young freelance writer covering the weird. As one of the few druggy journalists outside of *High Times*, I found Terence's model of sharp and amusing speculation invaluable and inspiring. I also found him a pretty fun guy to hang around. Though we were colleagues more than friends—he called me a "fellow grunt in the culture wars" in one book inscription—I saw him on his trips to New York and later San Francisco. It was not until the final year of his life that I spent more time with him. I flew to Hawaii one week for a *Wired* magazine profile, staying with him and Christy, interviewing him sober in the day and stoned at night, and guzzling some of his drain-O ayahuasca alone one evening in a lawn chair outside. That year we also crossed paths in San Francisco, where he and Christy sometimes stayed at our apartment, which was conveniently located near the gamma knives of UCSF, where his cancer was being treated.

My favorite memory of Terence, which I have related elsewhere, was minted during one of those San Francisco visits. Though he was very frail, I took him to see an occult bookseller who lived half a block away in a tiny bedroom stuffed to the gills with rare and marvelous tomes. We spent about an hour picking through the marvels, and at one point, with shocked glee, Terence plucked out a plain black musty tome entitled *The Cult of the Peacock Angel*. The book concerned the Yezidi, a Kurdish sect in northern

Iraq who worship an angel named Melak Taus, who Christians and Muslims identify with Satan. Terence said he first heard about the book through the California poet Robert Duncan, though I have never been able to track down the reference. He had thought the book was mythical, like H. P. Lovecraft's *Necronomicon*. And now the thing was in his hands, like a faerie gift that survives the dispersion of pixie dust. He peeled off a stack of twenties and simply asked, "Don't tell my girlfriend."

It was difficult to spend much time with Terence and not wind up righteously stoned. Though he served as the nuncio for the mushroom, and the emissary of the machine elves, cannabis was his true and abiding power plant and ally. That night at our place he cracked out some powerful THC oil as Jennifer and I introduced him to the small museum of traveler's bric-a-brac that packs our abode. I pulled down a decorative silver pipe that a friend of ours had recently given us as a wedding gift: a fluted, rather flimsy ornamented tube with a nonfunctional bird-like bowl. Terence's eyes bugged out as he grasped the inexpensive tchotchke. "That's it, that's the peacock angel!" He dragged out his recent purchase and showed us the frontispiece, which indeed showed an extraordinarily similar peacock pipe. Given how high we were, it was like a revelation from Melak Taus himself.

I have often considered the strange fact that I got to know Terence most intimately when he was dying. It's not the only time that I have made a deep connection with someone—a Zen teacher, my best therapist—shortly before they prematurely left the earth. But with Terence there is the additional sense that death and dying lie at the heart, or the abyss, of the psychedelic mystery. Trippers are often confronted, sometimes again and again, with the phantasmagoria of their own personal demise, but a demise that sometimes also invokes the immense scale and significance of cosmic end times.

In his influential midcentury account of gnosticism, which McKenna no doubt absorbed as a young man, Hans Jonas described how the gnostic individual transformed and psychologized cosmic metaphysics by turning such models into personal experience. The mythic story, in other words, became a mystical apocalypse that you actually undergo. Such a gnostic visionary doesn't just immanentize the eschaton, in the phrase made popular by William F. Buckley Jr. (and Robert Anton Wilson); they *internalized* it, so that, as Jonas wrote in a 1969 essay, "the eschaton is taken into the range of the subject's own faculties of self-modification and becomes a supreme possibility of existence." Whatever "the gnostics" were really doing, I do believe that psychedelics also can and do enact this supreme possibility. All manner of millennial armageddons can unfurl in the visions of the heroically dosed, which is why so many unfortunately turn into self-obsessed prophets.

I first smoked DMT in the early 1990s, right around the time I first discovered McKenna's mind-popping *Archaic Revival*. Coming up alone in a friend's darkened living room, I experienced an overwhelming insight as hyperspace bloomed in my brainstem: *now I know why people spend their entire lives preparing for the moment of death*. This gnostic grok has proven far more lasting than the snow-globe shake-up that followed it that night, and more than most other journeys as well. This conviction, or the experience of the conviction, motivates my continual devotion to spiritual teachings and practices, while also helping me come to understand psychedelics as bardo flight simulators. But it also fundamentally shaped my sense of Terence, whose raps I still hear as a kind of stand-up eschatology. Indeed, I believe there is a special pressure on psychedelic people to try to practice dying in an enlightened and courageous way, at least publicly. Leary did it, Ram Dass did it, Ann Shulgin did it, albeit more privately. And as St John shows in one of the best chapters in the book, Terence did it too, facing and discussing his process candidly and wittily in interviews and often in person.

What then of Terence's legacy? The biography you hold, written with tremendous gusto and kaleidoscopic detail, gives us a rich and resonant portrayal of the man and his mind. It lays a crucial foundation for any serious assessment of a fellow who was too witty to settle on the serious, even as he reached for the profound. This question of McKenna's ultimate impact is of course confused in part by the anomalous character of his path. His style, concerns, and career all blurred the line between entertainer and intellectual, stoner and poet, and the untimely aura of his pronouncements—at once cosmic prophecy and eschatological comedy—render his contributions fundamentally out of joint.

How and why and by whom will Terence be remembered, discussed, and appreciated? Right now, somewhere on the planet, someone is probably listening to one of his hundreds of recorded raps, but how do you measure such influence? What of the Timewave, Terence's biggest idea and most outsized silliness, which returned with a vengeance during the 2012 craze? Sure, this idea does not stand the test of time, at least on the surface. But meanwhile the times themselves have accelerated in ways that recall nothing so much as Terence's formalized "ingression of novelty." Did this guy produce knowledge or not? What about McKenna's forceful articulation of the "stoned ape" thesis, which claims that organic psychedelics helped bootstrap consciousness in early hominids—a possibility that was mocked or ignored when McKenna published *Food of the Gods* in 1992, and that today is a considered a legitimate if minority position among paleontologists and other scholars? What to do with this strange liminal man?

One thing is for sure: he is not done with us. Like many friends and admirers of Terence, I often wonder how he would react to the bizarre, frightening, and mind-melting world we find ourselves in. Where would he stand on SpaceX, or commercial VR, or trans activists, or the ketamine industry? Here technology may well swoop in to offer a suggestion. The depth of McKenna's recorded archive, to say nothing of the rapidly accelerating technology of large language models, may well supercharge his legacy. I have already seen a few reasonably compelling AI McKennabots, and far mightier ones are no doubt in the works, haunted artifacts whose "hallucinations" may actually, as was the case of Terence's talks, enhance the value of the final product. There would be more than a little poetic justice to such an algorithmic half-life. McKenna loved psychedelic technology, and the wide distribution of McKenna's sampled voice in electronic dance music long ago made him a man who lives on in memes. More to the point, there was always something encyclopedic about Terence, something superhuman about his speech and the cosmic database it drew from, the way he unpacked his Akashic library into the foyer of your own mind with the grace of a dancer, the mischief of an elf. As consensus reality continues to break down—a process that Terence voiced and prophesied as well as anyone—the magnetism of his attractor may only grow in force.

PREFACE

Terence Kemp McKenna (1946–2000) had a gifted ability to weave the world with words. An unremitting zeal and an outrageous sense of humor coincide in one of the most enigmatic figures of the late twentieth century. In an insistent weave by which the cryptic, the Delphic, and paradox itself are embraced as guiding principles, psychedelics not only drive the conversation but are pivotal to McKenna's rugged philosophy. As an intellectual seer and reluctant ambassador, McKenna grew to become one of the most imposing characters to emerge from the psychedelic sixties. Among the most compelling yet misunderstood and remarkably undocumented figures in the psychedelic movement, he continues to haunt the present. Today, his voice is likely the most sampled in the history of electronic music compositions, a circumstance evident by the late nineties, and therefore predating his demise. Echoing like cybernetic quicksilver through the tendrils of the early electronic surround, his voice grew legion with the birth of the internet. McKenna's embrace of the Net and persistent romance with cyberspace ensured that his voice would be digitally embalmed for future generations.

Biographies are works of nonfiction as much as they are works of the biographer's imagination. For this project, my mind has been shaped by a litany of people, archives, and primary materials that are, for those readers interested in my sources, explained and annotated in appendix A ("Acknowledgments and Sources"). As vast as my sources are, this work is not intended to be a complete account. Gaps in the record, absent and muffled voices, distorted information, destroyed documents, competing opinions, estranged relationships, divided kin—the obstacles to any such endeavor are many. This work is simply *my* lens on McKenna, an approach combining historical document with incisive analysis. Throughout, the work not only addresses the life of our subject, but begins to tackle the content, impact, and significance of his life's work. I could scarcely have imagined a more daunting task. As McKenna's life and output are not a simple story, I chose an approach that consists of two integrated parts (i.e., chronological and thematic), maintaining an overall faithfulness to the cradle-to-grave journey. While far from comprehensive, the work is *comprehensive enough*—evoking McKenna's phrase, apropos of Wittgenstein, "true enough."

The closest extant biographical account is *The Brotherhood of the Screaming Abyss: My Life with Terence McKenna*. Self-published by Terence's younger brother, Dennis, *Brotherhood* was first published in 2012.[1] While they diverged in important ways, the brothers shared formative experiences and common interests. Their passions infamously converged in the 1971 "experiment at La Chorrera," a series of anomalous occurrences in the Colombian Amazon that marked a transition in both of their lives, with Terence ultimately becoming a stand-up philosopher and cheerleader for tryptamines, and Dennis an ethnopharmacologist of renown.

While *Brotherhood* documents Dennis's life *with* Terence, there were long periods—such as the last two decades of Terence's life—in which Dennis had limited involvement with his brother. That many of Terence's friends, family, colleagues, and lovers were not consulted compounds the book's problems. Setting these issues and the resentments typical of fraternal biographical works aside, *Brotherhood* is a valuable resource—all the more so given the adverse circumstances curbing the documentation of Terence.

The biographical treatment of McKenna remains patchy, imprecise, and incomplete, certainly compared with other figures in the psychedelic pantheon, notably Timothy Leary. If McKenna was the "Timothy Leary of the 1990s," as Leary himself averred, there is no veritable bibliotheca on the nineties "Leary," as there is on the original.

But the adversities faced by biographers of Terence McKenna are many. The chief setback is that, aged fifty-three, he died in the aftermath of a massive seizure caused by glioblastoma multiforme, the most aggressive form of brain cancer. If we depict the cluster headaches suffered throughout his life as brain tremors, McKenna was violently rocked by the Big Kahuna on May 22, 1999, a tragic episode from which he would not recover, despite the surgical interventions.[2] Achieving a new plateau after completing the construction of his Hawaiian hideaway shared with Christy Silness, with whom he had settled down, McKenna's life came to an abrupt halt on April 3, 2000, leaving in his wake Silness, his son Finn (twenty-one), and daughter Klea (nineteen). In doing so, he checked out some dozen years before the "concrescence" of his Timewave Zero model, predicted to fall, quite conveniently, within his own lifetime (December 21, 2012). Had he conformed to the average life expectancy, he would have been sixty-six.

A further tragedy is the incineration of McKenna's library and archives, in three separate incidents. In the first, a brush fire swept through the Berkeley Hills in the summer of 1970, razing the family home of close friend Michael Malcolm, in whose garage was stored the already voluminous library of a ravenous book hound. Fortunately, Malcolm managed to rescue his mother and a couple of *thangkas* (Tibetan scroll paintings) on the day of the fire. McKenna's trove went up in smoke. A second, more devastating, blaze broke out on February 7, 2007, seven years after McKenna's death. The library, ostensibly including rare and irreplaceable first edition volumes among approximately 3,000 books, had been bequeathed to the Esalen Institute and was eventually kept in a multistory building in downtown Monterey. The fire was reported to have started in a sandwich shop on the lower floor, consuming several businesses along with McKenna's library, housed on the upper floor. The loss was lamented far and wide by those associating the library with his legacy—"a kind of second body," writes Erik Davis, "for Terence's fabulous and fascinating mind."[3] It is unclear what plans Esalen had for McKenna's library, but the outcome of such a terrible effacement is that a Terence K. McKenna Research Archives does not exist. The third fire occurred in 2019, when McKenna's remnant digital archive, stored in Capetown in the home of Mike Kawitzky, was engulfed in a blaze destroying Kawitzky's house. In the final chapter, I return to the flames licking at McKenna's legacy.

Biographers must contend with the loss of material records that these blazes signal. The devastation is especially frustrating when addressing McKenna's relationships. Of particular note is his friendship with Rick Watson.[4] Hitting it off at Awalt High School, Mountain View, California, in 1963–1964, the two corresponded over decades, sharing their dreams, highs, and disappointments through the sixties and beyond. During McKenna's senior year (1964–1965) in Lancaster, California, when the teens were separated, Watson recalls that they exchanged extensively, occasionally with missives stretching over more than twenty pages. The writing was sporadic: "long hiatuses, followed by bursts of epistolary activity."[5] Much of this material has not likely survived. McKenna's early mail to Watson was discarded by Watson's parents in the late sixties (when he lived in Kathmandu). Other letters did not survive Watson's travels. In turn, his sixties mail to McKenna is likely to have been destroyed in the Berkeley Hills blaze. Given Watson's own unique talents as a writer, the loss of this material is especially lamentable. We are, however, fortunate that he retained letters from his friend written between 1968–1996, a three-decade correspondence conveying an infrangible bond.

These misfortunes aren't the only factors obstructing the effort. McKenna's involvement in the cultivation, extraction, supply, consumption, and promotion of banned or controlled drugs explain equivocal communications, if not silence and outright secrecy. From the age of eighteen, in his final year of high school, McKenna became "devoted" to smoking cannabis, which, as a nervous and hyperactive child, allowed him to self-medicate toward "normalcy."[6] Not unaccustomed to rolling 25 bombers a day, smoking weed became the central practice of his life. Given the criminalizing of the herb, along with morning glory seeds, LSD, hashish, hallucinogenic mushrooms, and DMT, among other allied albeit illicit and maligned botanicals, we must inhale a cloud of half-truths. Under the rarely sighted early to mid-seventies business name Omega Associates, a business card from the era evokes an exotic tableau of possible trading goods—a cornucopia of antiquities, butterflies, and flora (see figure 0.1). As a self-identified mushroom "consultant" into the mid-eighties, McKenna's life was a shadowy fuzz of covert behavior and paranoia, precipitating strange, false, and incomplete memories. Adding to the haziness, associates, friends, and family potentially implicated in unlawful activities and fearful of incrimination are guarded, selectively forgetful, if not silent.

The subterfuge is notable in the wake of an India supply-side hashish importing operation uncovered by customs officials in 1969. McKenna behaved like a fugitive over the next three years, presuming that his name was registered with Interpol and paranoid enough to use the passport of at least one acquaintance to cross borders. He remained in virtual incognito for months while hunting butterflies in remote locations across the

FIGURE 0.1
Business card for Omega Associates, ca. 1973. Art design by, and courtesy of, Kathleen Harrison.

Indonesian archipelago, finally reentering the United States in 1971. There is rich irony in the lepidopterist's technique of capturing (and killing) insects for the purposes of preservation, when our white-robed practitioner was himself evading capture, as consistent with his belief that there was "a price on my head."

McKenna's activities between 1968 and 1971 (aged twenty to twenty-four) are consequentially crepuscular, and documentation is scarce. One document that has survived, what I call the "Boulder Statement," was apparently composed when residing in Boulder, Colorado, in 1972, and possibly part of a plea to clear his name. The three-page document features a detailed timeline, a statement of purpose, and a rationale of movements and financial activities from 1965 to 1972. While its detailed itinerary is invaluable for its probable accuracy, the document is of ambiguous utility.[7] Dates of travel and places visited are consistent with details provided elsewhere, and an awareness that international agencies share border-crossing records may have encouraged accuracy. And yet, for all the intel it delivers, the document is a cloaking device. The statement outlines how its author secured a financial base for his travels, ostensibly through the sale of *thangkas* and exotic insect specimens. Given questionable statements accounting for movements over the period in question, and what is known about other clandestine income sources—hashish—I treat the document with caution.

In addition to retracing sojourns in India and Nepal trading in Tibetan artworks, the Boulder Statement also addresses the 1969–1970 trek through Indonesia, where, McKenna wrote, "it was my intent to secure my financial position by the sale of specimens of exotic butterflies to collectors in various parts of the world. This I was able to do." That McKenna collected and traded in *thangkas* and butterflies over this period is beyond question. Yet, since the timeline includes a period (approximately March 1968 to August 1969) in which he shipped hash from India to the United States, the document serves as plausible cover for more clandestine, and lucrative, activities.

While Terence was an amateur entomologist, and had a passion for collecting lepidopterans, as Dennis knew, "the persona of the collector" also provided good cover for a fugitive in the tropics. "When you show up in a village with a butterfly net," Terence is said to have recollected, "you are immediately tagged as a harmless eccentric." At a spidery six-foot-three, in loose, white, Nehru-collared garb, and sporting a telescoping net, he cut a striking figure among the diminutive locals. All the more practical was such an open camouflage for a user of cannabis and a blazer of sheesh in a country—Indonesia—where drug possession could attract severe penalties.

Dennis further noted how the same cover was affected in Colombian Amazonas, "when our real quest was for exotic hallucinogens."[8] Such deceptions, disguises, and ambiguities were necessary to avoid scrutiny and incrimination. Terence would, after all, avoid the fate of Leary, who saw the inside of thirty jails and prisons. McKenna was never incarcerated, beyond being a "prisoner of mundane obligation."[9]

Condensing a pivotal life phase, the Boulder Statement is revealing for what it conceals. It is a portrait of a life staged, exaggerated, and wrangled. It also demonstrates that McKenna had a style of communicating that he reserved for straights, boors, and unbearable types who never doubt themselves. This was evident in a chance encounter with Dr. Karl Heintz of "Far Eastern Mining and Minerals, Inc.," in Timor, in February 1970. The story is recounted in McKenna's memoir *True Hallucinations*. Whether this meeting happened at all, or if Heintz actually existed, there can be little doubting the substance of the self-description reserved for squares:

> I am an art historian turned biologist. I went to Nepal to study Tibetan but found that I am no linguist when it comes to Asian languages. I have returned to biology, my first love. Specifically, I am an entomologist. I am collecting butterflies here in Indonesia retracing the route of Alfred Russel Wallace. Wallace was the real discoverer of the theory of natural selection, but Darwin got all the credit. I identify with his underdog status. Wallace was shafted by Victorian science because he was of the wrong class and didn't know how to play politics the way Darwin did. Wallace explored the Amazon Basin as well and if all goes well, I hope to travel and collect there too. Eventually I will write a monograph on speciation among the butterflies of Amazonas and Eastern Indonesia, which will get me a degree. Then, who knows. Teaching perhaps. Hard to say.[10]

The grift was honed and convincing, and not so remote from the truth. The conviction of a budding lepidopterist following his calling is undeniable. McKenna was impeccably polite and very persuasive. What's more, he had developed the skills and perfected the stylizations of a cataloguer through his lab assistant work for the entomology department at the University of California, Berkeley, where he prepared specimens for the California Insect Survey. As Sara Hartley recalled, "Old World in his movement and manner," McKenna styled himself on nineteenth-century naturalist Alfred Russel Wallace, if not Jules Verne's Phileas Fogg.[11]

Cultivating *Psilocybe* mushrooms—a chief source of income for a decade from the mid-seventies—was also subject to masking. After Terence returns from the Amazon with *Psilocybe cubensis* (then known as *Stropharia cubensis*) spores, conspires with Dennis on a cultivation method, and builds a business model and distribution community with his wife Kathleen Harrison, mushrooms become a vital source of income into the eighties. Just as they were familiar with the overground, McKenna, Harrison, and their kids were at least part-time inhabitants of an underworld necessitating secrecy and silence. The US Psychotropic Substances Act (1978), an amendment to the Controlled Substances Act (1970), made psilocybin a federally prohibited Schedule I drug (and therefore classified with heroin, alongside LSD and DMT), with the result that *Psilocybe* mushrooms were illegal to grow, sell, and possess. While the operation could be lucrative, the cycle was laden with risk. The wake-up call arrived when an acid distributor friend and neighbor was busted. "They fucked him so terrifyingly that I saw I couldn't do this anymore," Terence reflected. "I had to work something else out." The solution was "Terence McKenna," a charismatic talking head successfully marketed to the early adopters.[12] Coming in from the cold, he grew increasingly brazen, apace with his public persona. Many performances were extended endorsements on the value of substances that were, and remain, classed by the Drug Enforcement Administration as prohibited substances with "no currently accepted medical use and a high potential for abuse."[13] It was risk-laden high theater. Often acting as a spokesperson recruited by a hyperdimensional agency for whom the mushroom is the medium, McKenna comported himself as "their" agent on Earth.

The effort to obtain the straight line on McKenna must confront an inescapable obstacle. He was a master *bullshitter*. Which is to say, he was an epic storyteller. As an ebullient orator, Terence staked his credibility on intriguing audiences with new material. He grew uncommonly dedicated to finding novel ways to craft old stories before new audiences. As Dennis relates, Terence acquired his capacity as an entertainer from their father, Joe McKenna. "Dad was an Irish storyteller. . . . His wild accounts were usually well worn, if never told the same way twice." His oldest son inherited Joe's "talent, or flaw, for never letting facts get in the way of a good story." Considering this inheritance both a skill *and* a handicap, Dennis weighs his own task as an auto/biographer: "I haven't always been sure where the yarn spinning ends and the family history begins."[14]

While McKenna's raps represent a rich resource, containing a litany of tall tales and outlandish embellishments, they are at the same time a banquet of potential embarrassments for the biographer. Determining where the truth ends and the hallucination begins is no simple feat, notably as the archive of recorded content is replete with unverifiable anecdotal material. McKenna had a meticulous facility for recall, but what *was* retrieved was not always factually accurate. Take, as just one example, reference to Frank Herbert's *Dune*. In a 1989 Esalen rap, the sci-fi epic is stated to be the source of the drug "stroon," which permits protagonists "to see forward and backward into time" and conquer fear.[15] This is one of many occasions that evince a conflation of the fictional drugs "melange" (from *Dune*) and "stroon" (from Cordwainer Smith's *Norstrilia*), which feature similar qualities (they both extend life and are the most valuable commodities in their respective universes). While erroneous, such detail is hardly mendacious, notably given its appearance in a rap invoking disciplined efforts to breathe through anxiety and overcome one's fear of dying in high-dose tryptamine sessions.

That such misquoted or misremembered sources are not infrequent is not unconnected to the off-the-cuff tenor of the output. In other cases, audiences are lavished with impressive albeit specious detail. As a garrulous polymath, McKenna not infrequently dispensed glib Polyfil that served to charm an already captive audience. Whether namedropping, strategically placed obscurantism, or padding the rap with atavistic esoterica, the technique impacted his audience not unlike the effect obtained as a teen when slipping obscenities into fast-paced classroom discussions, a linguistic subterfuge that amused the unlettered athletes for whom he acquired jester-like virtue. As conversation bristled with the "26n rule" of Whorf's law, Chomsky's "rules of grammar," or skewed lines from *Finnegans Wake*, with occasional invocations of Wittgenstein or Merleau-Ponty, the hedge was that no one would mount a challenge amid the vociferous dispensation. I do not imply insincerity as a prevailing trait. Persistently knocking himself off his own podium, with barbed sidebars that invariably registered decibels on the laughometer, McKenna was riotously unassuming. Neither pretentious nor superficial, his public-facing career reveals an urge to win approval from an early age.

While reliably entertaining, remarkably eloquent, and syntactically precise, McKenna was an unreliable handler of information. Punctuality is a characteristic for which he is often remembered, as a feature of his consummate dedication to show up at the appointed time, and as evident in the timely execution of his delivery. Punctiliousness is another thing altogether, given the laissez-faire attitude to details more characteristic of the tout than the technician. Truth becomes a casualty in the hallucinatory showman's determination to land the story. Imprecision appeared most overt vis-à-vis dates, figures, and quanta, a circumstance not only ironic for someone so committed to being *on time*, but somewhat puzzling for a figure convinced that he had received a precise mathematical revelation about the structure of the nature of time itself.

To give an example of this loose affair with temporality, Exhibit A is McKenna's first encounter with DMT—or when he "got elves" at 2894

Telegraph Avenue, Berkeley—which, as this book illustrates, was a pivotal moment in his life, and integral to the time-fated trip to Colombia in 1971. And yet, as profound as the Elf Event was, there is remarkable confusion about the exact date (even the year) of occurrence in McKenna's testimony. Given the consequence of an event that amounted to something of a rebirth day, a short discussion justifying the date I use in this book (February 1966) is necessary. The earliest recorded public remark dating this event was stated at Esalen Institute in Big Sur, California, in December 1982, where the year of the formative DMT experience was said to be 1965.[16] But perplexity reigns, for on multiple occasions the episode is stated to have occurred on "one rainy February evening, in 1967,"[17] while elsewhere it is February 1966 when "the compass of my life was set."[18] For a figure seeking to forge a reputation in the field of temporal precision—indeed, making claims to a "map of time"—such fluctuations around this decisive event are surprising. Since 2015, I have joined Rick Watson (who was present on the evening in question) in dialogue on this subject. In corroboration with an unnamed "third man" present that night, Watson is adamant that his friend's protean interlude with "machine elves" must have happened in the months following his arrival at Telegraph Avenue in the fall of 1965 and no later than the spring (i.e., before March) of 1966. In fact, McKenna corroborates this timeline himself, elsewhere stating that his original DMT event took place on a rainy night in February 1966, adding that this was "six months after I took LSD."[19] This is consistent with what is known about the period of McKenna's first LSD experience (i.e., the summer of 1965). Despite muddying the temporal terrain of his own psychedelic birthday, the weight of evidence, then, suggests February 1966 as the likely window.

That this event, according to the memories of those present, notably McKenna himself, is thought to have transpired in the period between the fall of 1965 and February 1967 may be a blazing testament to the haze that blankets that period. Prevarication around the timing may also be a projection of the weird temporality of the DMT trance itself. But the inexactitude inherent to the dating of this critical moment on the path toward his "map of time" should serve to prompt wariness toward McKenna's own treatment of time, whether pivotal dates in his own timeline, conniptions with quanta, or a dada-like approach to data.

On the subject of time, and if you like, Exhibit B, the most elaborate yarn woven by the trickster of temporality was his novelty-charting Timewave mythos. It is a subject treated at length in this book, but it is sufficient to relate here that, predicting history coming to a head on December 21, 2012, McKenna devised a "formal proposition" that was pluckishly tendered as "a revision of the mathematical description of time used in physics."[20] It was all rather self-consciously improbable for a figure who failed Algebra 2, and who conceded that he was "not even into long division." There was an uncanny finish to it that rendered the Timewave not a discovery or an invention, but an artifact of some *other* order. It was a device that had about it "the ozone-stench of otherworldliness."[21] This puzzling artifact positioned his labors, in his own candid review of this unlikely circumstance, alongside Pythagoras or Plato, notably the Myth of Er, the concluding legend to the *Republic*. "I would never have come to this idea myself," McKenna blanched, hinting at the influence of the mushroom. "I mean, it's too irrational for me."[22]

Back in the "real world," these breathtaking claims did not go unchallenged. When young mathematician Matthew Watkins observed that McKenna's model of novelty was arbitrary and involved little math, effectively disproving the claim that a fractal map of temporal resonance is encoded in the King Wen sequence of the *I Ching*, McKenna disingenuously rebranded this critique the "Watkins Objection," which his model withstood. The theater of "real science" in action.[23] Watkins relates the good-natured character of his meeting with McKenna in Palenque. But as has been observed, McKenna's attitude toward Watkins was "not always so good-humored or even particularly honest," but even somewhat "underhanded."[24] Ultimately, the Timewave appeared to be less a falsifiable scientific model than an instrument of his faith in "the concrescence," and, beyond that, an open window on its architect's soul.

Nothing if not insistent, McKenna would sooner hoover up ideas into a synthesis than dispense with his model. The response to Watkins is consistent with the strategy of the bricoleur. The art of improvising was most evident when McKenna told stories about himself. As Rick Watson explained,

> Terry was a magpie, picking bits and pieces here and there, and fashioning an extraordinary bricolage which was his self. That is, beyond the normal postmodernist notion, he constructed himself quite consciously out of other peoples' experiences. He would sometimes tell a story about his days in Colorado which later turned out to have been lifted out of a book about a zoologist's encounter with whip scorpions in Africa!

An unreliable source of information about himself, Terence was, as Dennis put it, prone to "mince facts." This might be said about anyone, Watson knows, but his friend developed mincing facts into an art-form. "His ability to immediately grasp something and weave it into his fabric was quite extraordinary; I never knew anyone else who had that ability."[25]

McKenna crafted his identity, editing his own memories, reconstructed before ever-widening audiences. Spiced with the oeuvre of Thomas Pynchon, spliced with the history of religion, sprinkled with insights on nanotechnology, his storytelling was remixed and repackaged in improv theater as metaphysical as it was antinomian. Thought-forms, verse, chaos theory, lines from *I Love Lucy*, Heideggerian existentialism, the poetry of Anne Waldman, Gödel's incompleteness theorem, Ilya Prigogine's nonequilibrium thermodynamics were all effortlessly retrieved to clarify a position or affirm experience, with the outcome mirthful and provocative in equal measure.

That Watson refers to the way his friend remixed the experience of others to embellish his own myth is a more than curious aside since this was a strategy McKenna deployed vis-à-vis Watson's own storytelling. I'm thinking of Watson's short story "DMT, or, Spider Woman Comes to Town," aspects of which, as we will see, McKenna appeared to lift and twist to entertain his audience. As a restless intellect, McKenna modified tales related in his public life, echoing in fashion strategies adopted to kill boredom in Paonia, his hometown in Colorado. If this depicts an impatient, beguiling persona, he was also among his own greatest critics. Often self-deprecatory but rarely self-defeating, he was a nomad perpetually "on the run."

That McKenna walked a fine line between truth and fiction is inscribed in *True Hallucinations*, where the reader is as uncertain as the author about where reality and illusion part ways. The memoir casts the author as an actor in a movie, reading his own script on the fly. With chapters recounting high adventure in Timor, Nepal, Colombia, and the United States, the work offers some debt to *The Hasheesh Eater* of Fitz Hugh Ludlow, whose readers embark on a rapid traversal of inner locales. World-travels between 1968 and 1972 emerge as a riotous passage in which the young McKenna adopts the subjunctive traits and actual trajectory of his hero Wallace. Later he identifies with Billy Pilgrim from *Slaughterhouse-Five*, seemingly on account of Vonnegut's signature absurdism, but presumably also because of Pilgrim's abduction by the Tralfamadorians, who exist in all times simultaneously, and who are privy to knowledge of future events, including the destruction of the universe at the hands of a Tralfamadorian test pilot. An eccentric stranger through his Southeast Asian and Amazonian theaters of operation, McKenna pursued a life stranger than fiction. "Something happened back there in the Amazon jungle," he reflected in later years, "and it turned my life into literature."[26]

I want to return to the strange episode in *True Hallucinations* involving the enigmatic Karl Heintz, a story featuring the hallmarks of a true hallucination.

Whether events happened as related or are instances of creative nonfiction, it is a revealing episode in which McKenna verbally agrees to participate in a bio-extraction project for "a band of renegade Nazi scientists"[27] in Amazonas—a project that would benefit from the legitimacy of an entomologist. The account reveals the state of exception common among travelers meeting in locations remote from home. The "standards for dinner conversation in the warm tropics leave room for the self-aggrandizing traveler's tale." In the field, removed from domestic routines, where boundaries defining one's identity are relaxed, memories are garnished with embellishments tacitly accepted among co-liminars. Amid the extended travails of a coming-of-age world adventure, no longer the person he was at the point of debarkation, and not yet he who arrived at his destination—a figure who came to embrace the sensibility of The Wanderer (the *I Ching*'s hexagram 56, Lü)—McKenna operates in accord with the logic of *the road*. He capitulates to Heintz's enthusiastic offer, agreeing to a "well paid" but ambiguous corporate-sponsored trip to the Amazon, with two weeks of tennis in Singapore thrown in to get him physically in shape. The position never materializes. But that isn't the point I want to make here. What happens when life "on the road" is extended upon one's return? What if one hardly returns to any form of stable life and standard discourse where a traveler's hyperbole is shelved? Where and with whom in this mode of constant departure while always arriving will there be occasion for authentic, unvarnished communications?

An elusive chameleon like this proves exasperating to the historian. Determining whether reported incidents and events did "undergo the formality of actually occurring," to adopt McKenna's favorite phrase from Alfred North Whitehead, or if they were an amalgam of events that never actually occurred in the way they were presented poses a challenge for the biographer. Out of all the many variations on the truth—with stories told and retold with a concern for reception over veracity—the reader is asked to recognize that the story that is awarded narrative precedence is sometimes simply that which is the best bit.

Further confounding for us is an obsessiveness with enigmata. From a young age, McKenna's penchant for the cryptic, the obscure, and the gnomic was apparent to Laddie Livingston. "Terry's life was an all out war," claimed his older cousin-in-law, who later became superintendent of schools in Delta County, Colorado, "a scorched earth war with acumen's razor. It just couldn't be simple because that would mean way too many people could understand."[28] Signature to his capacity to live the mystery, Terence embraced the Neo-Platonic principle of the *coincidentia oppositorum*, the unity of opposites. Adapted from Mircea Eliade and Carl Jung, implicit to alchemy, and augmented by psychedelics, this concern serves as something of an organizing principle. As mooted in early public oration, it is in the union of opposites, in a world that does not "strive for closure," that "cultural sanity" may be achieved. Tryptamines (notably DMT and psilocybin) were integral to this effort since they "raise paradox to a level of intensity" essential to the emergence of civilized culture.[29] Dialogue between the inner and outer, past and future, the fallen and the sublime, animates *True Hallucinations*, dubbed a rhetorical "admixture text" in *Darwin's Pharmacy* where Richard Doyle observes that the uncanny, surreality, and noesis are implicit to McKenna's rhetoric—as faithful to the psychedelic experience itself.[30] The workings of the unconscious, the Oversoul, or *logos*, manifest as UFOs and other concretizations of opposites recur throughout McKenna's oratory and textual output. The psychedelic state amplifies conditions in which opposites attract. As applied in the pages of this book, the alchemized symbolic materials surfacing in McKenna's oeuvre are worthy of closer inspection. A wide variety of objections may be expressed— from hypocrite to misanthropist—where this consistent mythopoetics is misrecognized or misunderstood.

The *coincidentia oppositorum* is not always obvious, lest resolved, in a uniquely iconoclastic metaphysics, where the prophet and trickster collide. Contrary positions compete for attention in the McKennaverse. Humanity is "caught up in a cosmic drama of fall and redemption," he declares in *True Hallucinations*.[31] In a modern world fallen from grace, salvation remains a consistent trope, as, for example, implicit to the historiography of his opus *Food of the Gods*. Tied to a mythos of "the Fall," then, is a countervailing commitment to the sublime stature of humanity as redeemed. As the super-agents of this incongruity, shamans are embraced in the brothers' book *The Invisible Landscape*, where psychedelic shamanism embodies a kind of time bridge to the "archaic" associated with a pre-Fall "paradisiac condition."[32] An anti-materialist, neo-gnostic current permeates this metaphysics, as evidenced by the Timewave, which evokes an accelerated *fall* that is at the same time the spirit's release from matter—a kind of falling upward—a process that intuits human divinity. While we may have fallen from paradise, the advocacy for an "archaic revival" holds the promise of a future "Eden," vouchsafed by plant hallucinogens.

A final issue frustrates the biographer. Though they pursued dramatically different lives with quite distinct profiles, the brothers McKenna are often conflated and entangled. The task of determining where Terence ends and Dennis begins is complicated by two coauthored books in which individual authorship is often indistinct, and memoirs wherein the siblings are commonly of "one mind." For example, as documents of the experiment at La Chorrera, in both *The Invisible Landscape* and *True Hallucinations*, it is unclear how much of Dennis's thoughts and behavior have been transferred from his influential older brother. And further, to what extent are these obsessions then transferred back to Terence? In *True Hallucinations*, cross-transferences build to absurd heights in which the brothers suspect each other of being the messiah.

The untimely demise, the fires, the secrecy, the embellishment, the theater, the elusiveness, the penchant for the gnomic, and the fraternal transference are among the factors thwarting a biography in the twenty-five years since McKenna's death. Fortunately, in addition to candid input from a multitude of interlocutors, historians have at their disposal a substantial oeuvre, from which this book has benefited. For an entrée to the McKennaverse, go to the back of the book (see appendix B).

INTRODUCTION

It is October 18, 1987, and a buzz overtakes the auditorium in Los Feliz, California. The occasion: a high-water mark in the career of an upstart thinker. Standing against the era's "beige fascism," fashioning on the fly a vintage exposition of his own spoken wordcraft, the speaker delivers a rap in equal measure genuine wisdom and amusing verve. The capacity crowd at the Philosophical Research Society in Los Angeles is exposed to what this virtuoso orator knows as the "felt presence of the other," a presence with which he has been intimate since a "born again" mid-sixties episode with an alien dimension. At that juncture two decades prior, our wordsmith entered the "auric equivalent of the Pope's private chapel," where "insect elf machines proffered strange little tablets with strange writing." Smoking the obscure potent molecule N,N-dimethyltryptamine (DMT) in Berkeley in 1966 was like "being struck by noetic lightning." At the center of the freak universe in time and space, all expectations of the nature of the world were turned on their head.

The capacity crowd in the auditorium built by mystic maven Manly P. Hall is exposed to the *feeling of knowing*, a hallmark of Terence McKenna, the ascendent Oracle of the Weird who stands before them. The performance is a whistle-stop tour of the *calling* of a figure who, as a teenaged existentialist, had recovered from the "theological fiddle-faddle" of Roman Catholicism. But while LSD confirmed Freud's dynamics of the psyche, the DMT trance was seismic: "It not only had the quality of a miracle as I imagined it, it had the quality of a miracle as I could *not* have imagined it." Searching for an explanation for his life's quantum leap, McKenna came to understand that psychedelics are "enzymes for the imagination," a realization affirmed in 1971 when hunting an orally active form of DMT in the Amazon basin.[1]

The event is an occasion for the on-brand logic upon which McKenna's renown grew. The Tarzan of epistemology leaps from one branch of logic to another with remarkable ease: Gödel's incompleteness theorem, the

Eleusinian Mysteries, the new nanotechnological frontier, and the cephalopods imagined as totemic to the coming cybernetic society in which we'll participate in a "telepathic aquarium" where our neighbors will *see what we mean*. Whether the human enterprise is to launch into "the realm beyond history" or whether we'll upload ourselves into another dimension, high adventure was afoot. Not fated to the cultural wastelands of the eighties, audience members are invited to recognize themselves as pioneers of "a truly moral and ethical human society." By some "strange quirk of the metaphysical machinery," they were privileged to live through an extraordinary symmetry break. Not mute bystanders to a cosmic accident, they were proactive participants at the leading edge of the millennium.

And with this revelation, like a blues trumpeter, McKenna blazons the kernel of his exulted routine, "the transcendental object at the end of time"—an unknowable, inevitable, and yet thoroughly designable future transformative event. With the challenging remit of making hope cool, such is the recurring climax of McKenna's rap, as brought home in the encore. Strapped in for the ride, the audience accelerates through a breach in time that, according to the fractal charts, recapitulates the fall of the Roman Empire, presaging a new Dark Age, and an ultra-novel event. "A 10,000 year rush, from chipping of stone flint to walking through the violet doorway of a self-generated, hyper-dimensional vehicle that carries us to our true home. No *wonder* it leaves an explosive set of eddies in its wake! . . . This is what happens when a culture prepares to depart for the stars."[2]

Escaping the mediocrity of the times, at performances like this, the audience placed themselves in the hands of a metaphysical tour guide who channels a bardic tradition while undermining all pretense of tradition. They submit before an uproarious orator whose freak raves disclose a fabulous mythopoetics in which gnosis collides with the surreal. They turn themselves over to a competent navigator who cribs with ease from genetic science and modernist literature while performing the vocal equivalent of sleight of hand to convey the message that the mystery is available, if you "take it easy, but take it."

In over 250 recorded lectures, workshops, and nightclub appearances throughout his career, McKenna left a staggering impression on the cultural underground. And yet, despite this prodigious output, he remains today an enigma. McKenna's life has received scarce attention from biographers, and as a result, accounts remain riddled with half-truths and jammed with riddles. The resultant sketchiness might well be consistent with a figure who self-identified as "anarcho-cryptic" and "half-baked," who was mercurial, a fugitive, a freak nomad, a disguise artist, an "edge runner." The perplexity isn't surprising. After all, McKenna has been labeled altered statesman, psychoactivist, Magellan of hyperspace, Omega Man, holy fool, and cosmic triggerman, among many other epithets. And yet, the effort to transpose his life ought to respect the scale of the man's impact. It is fitting that this Sphinx-like figure was drawn to an enigmatic class of serotonergic hallucinogens, notably DMT and *Psilocybe* mushrooms. These psychotropic compounds were the tools pivotal to decades-long navigations in psychedelic hyperspace, widely celebrated psychonautical travails that exposed as much about the *other* as they revealed about himself.

Inhabiting a life that blurred truth and fiction, McKenna's magnetic psychedelic antagonism compels comparison drawn from an unlikely source: the fictional character of Col. Walter E. Kurtz, as portrayed in Francis Ford Coppola's 1979 classic *Apocalypse Now* (and performed by Marlon Brando). Based on the cowritten screenplay of Coppola and John Milius—which at an early stage was titled "Psychedelic Soldier"—and partly inspired by a character in Joseph Conrad's 1899 novella, *Heart of Darkness*, Kurtz is a portrait in transgression. The film offers curious parallels adjacent to McKenna's life. With its screenplay contemporaneous with his East Asian adventure, *Apocalypse Now* depicts an accursed war waged in the background of McKenna's prime. The confluence of the film and the life of our subject aside, what strikes me is that, as masters in breaking convention—true experimentalists—Kurtz and McKenna offer contrasting careers in boundary dissolution.

A career officer in the US Army, Kurtz was a West Point graduate destined for a top post within the Pentagon. He was sent to Vietnam to compile a report on the failings of military policies—producing an incisive rebuke of army hypocrisy. In the mid-sixties, Kurtz insisted on joining the Special Forces, seeking adventure and denying himself further career advancement. Kurtz returned to Vietnam as a Green Beret in 1966–1967, went rogue, raised an army of "Montagnards" near the Cambodian border, and became a ruthless killer, a "God-King," and something of a cult leader. Intimate with the limits of human civilization, the estranged Colonel was driven mad by the atrocities of war.

A radical argonaut of the sixties, resisting conscription and evading the war in Vietnam while running hash from India to the United States, McKenna also knew something about boundary transgression. A proclivity to test boundaries from an early age was embodied in what he called "edgerunning"—"the oldest books, the forgotten countries, the unpronounceable islands."[3] While he applied to Berkeley's Experimental College around the same time that the fictional Kurtz applied for Special Forces (i.e., 1964),

McKenna eventually elected a path anterior to academia and to the privileges of academic rank. On another timeline, he could have made full professor, just as Kurtz could have made full general. But, fighting a war of his own, McKenna underwent a "heroic" career in ontological guerrillahood, growing scornful of academic science, with shades not dissimilar to Kurtz's educated (the fictional character had a master's degree in history from Harvard) and idealistic contempt for military command.

As contentious as it may be, the point of comparing McKenna with Kurtz is to illuminate their differences. Bearing little resemblance to the bloodlusty Col. Kurtz or Conrad's greedy demi-god colonial model, McKenna was no rogue agent for enterprises commercial or military. Quite unlike the maddened and corrupted Kurtz, who is eventually claimed by the jungle, it was McKenna's objective, as is ostensibly accomplished in the Amazon by way of tryptamine "mediators," to get "in touch with the living mind of the tropical forest."[4] Like Kurtz, McKenna is obsessed with death, with final things, but their own *ends* offer a distinct contrast. While McKenna had an animate shadow, he ought to be remembered, according to his old friend Douglas Hansen, for his great compassion and genuine core values.[5] Rick Watson clarified the sentiment vis-à-vis his friend's everyday persona. When in Terence's company, his close friends became the center of his attention: "He made you feel special." In those moments, beyond the public penchant for showmanship and being a "know-it-all guru," he was relaxed and receptive. "There was this really nice quality of respect."[6] Ultimately, the McKenna known to his late-nineties lover, Christy Silness, was not a man with a heart of darkness, but "a kind human being with a sensitive heart."[7]

The figures of Walter and Terence present contrasting stories on the condition the human condition is in: one growing more alienated from his humanity, the other applying radically empirical methods to "be the alien"—to explore the limits of his humanness. If psychedelics facilitate access to the wide spectrum of human being, then they amount to a right of birth. Such was the tenor of rousing commentary at the Scottish Rite Temple in Los Angeles on October 2, 1988—an event held to honor Swiss chemist Albert Hofmann. "In the future it will be unimaginable," emcee McKenna declared deep inside the lines of the War on Drugs, "that governments once regulated the substances that people use to explore personal growth. It is the mark of a barbarous culture. Truth is not so easily swept aside. One doesn't 'Just Say No' to truth."[8] In response to the assault on truth, McKenna was dedicated to promoting his own brand of radical empiricism, a kind of *freak habitus* composed of ethnobotanical knowledge, repurposed tools, and techniques by which explorers were empowered to interface with nature, with mystery, with their *other* selves, while at the same time directly observing the powerful artifice of culture. With success from the mid-seventies promulgating *Psilocybe cubensis* cultivation techniques, and through a public road show mounted from the mid-eighties, audiences were regaled with tales of the "N,N-unspeakable," its sourcing, and its methods of administration. As apparent throughout a protean career in ethnobotanical knowledge transfer, and as a tireless font of information for hackers of consciousness in the networked underground, McKenna augmented the capacity for his audience to grow independent from dominant sources of cultural conditioning—to enhance the means of perception. Since his untimely demise, with his extemporizations resounding within the echo chambers of the "post electric society" forecast, his ideas have had extraordinary currency in psychedelic culture.

* * *

The book's twelve chapters are organized into two parts, the first tracing a chronology of McKenna's life, and the second charting a course through the McKennaverse, with each chapter addressing thematic episodes in the evolution of his thought. Commencing with the momentous elven eureka moment that triggered a cascading sequence of events, in part I the story pans back to McKenna's upbringing in Colorado and passes through the Californian escapade; education at UC Berkeley; world travels in India, Southeast Asia, and the Amazon; the co-discovery (with Dennis) of a popular means of psilocybin cultivation; marriage (and divorce); and the emergence of an underground celebrity. From "metapolitical" exilehood to the freak expedition to La Chorrera, from the business of selling mushrooms to the craft of moving "Terence McKenna," from self-effacing stoner to raving shamanologist, from altar boy to freak icon, from the commitment to a family to the demands of fame, the story uncovers tensions signature to an enigmatic life.

While retaining a chronological perspective, part II illuminates McKenna's intellectual development, with thematic chapters addressing the Timewave opus, the ambivalent mantle of "psychedelic guru," and the long search for a "visible language" within a prescient *cyber* space, before ultimately approaching his demise and fiery metamorphosis. While final matters and last things—eschatology—permeate McKenna's psychedelic philosophy, enchantment with the end was at the same time a fascination with new beginnings. The story of his death is also one of cyberdelic resurrection. Turning to his posthumous career in the disembodied "mind space" and cyber promised land he long envisioned, the book begins to address McKenna's immortalization in the imagination, where he remains animate.

I

1 EDGE RUNNERS

ORANGE MOTHBALLS

It is a cold, damp evening on Telegraph Avenue, Berkeley, in February 1966. A strange young man in a little black suit buttoned up to the throat mounts the steps and raps on the door at 2894. A wiry freak bids him entry. Held by his host as his great inspiration, the visitor is cast as "always the one to get there first, whatever it was, to do it, to reject it, and to be absolutely contemptuous of it by the time anybody else even arrived at the scene of the crime." On this occasion, the guest has arrived with a little glass pipe and stuff that looks like orange mothballs.

"Something that might interest you."

"What is it?"

Rick Watson, who subscribes to the credo that they must live as if the apocalypse has already happened, replies. "It's called DMT."

"How long does it last?"

"Ten minutes."

"Let the good times roll."[1]

Settling in to take hits from a mothball, Terence McKenna is soon transported into another dimension. He sinks to the floor. Tumbling forward into a fractalized geometric space, he finds himself in the company of "insect elf machines" proffering strange little tablets with improbably recombinant inscriptions:

> I was aghast, completely appalled. Because the transition had been a matter of seconds. And my entire expectation of the nature of the world was just being shredded in front of me. I've never actually gotten over it. . . . These self-transforming machine-elf creatures were speaking in some kind of colored language, which condensed into these rotating machines that were like Fabergé eggs, but crafted out of luminescent super-conducting ceramics and liquid crystal gels. And all this

stuff was just so weird and so alien and so unEnglishable that I felt like it was a complete shock. I mean, the literal turning inside out of the intellectual universe.

The late teen who had recently commenced studies in the Experimental College at Berkeley considered himself intellectually prepared for anything. He was an art history nerd who painted in the style of Pollock, had a keen interest in Tibetan *thangkas*, was a Hieronymus Bosch fan, could recite Coleridge, and read Melville, Burroughs, Lovecraft, and the complete works of Huxley. Moreover, in the months preceding, he had been exposed to, and taken apart by, LSD, a psychedelic odyssey and rite of passage that inaugurated a feeling of being *experienced*. And having now achieved the ranks of the experienced, he undertook this new task with a confident nonchalance. Yet the immediate outcome was so unexpected, and so un-Englishable, he was cast into a state of shock. "I can't believe it," he repeated to himself over and over, as he came up. But as it sank in, the truth was that he *could* believe it. "I couldn't stop believing it."[2]

If McKenna entered this moment a materialist, he was now "shit out of business!" His compass was set. Rocked by the impossible—and taking care of business—he would tour the globe to enunciate how "the ordinary world is almost instantaneously replaced, not only with a hallucination, but a hallucination whose alien character is its utter alienness."[3]

It was a height from which he would never descend. His eureka moment. Not unlike Burroughs, who declared to Allen Ginsberg in 1953 that "Yagé is it,"[4] McKenna understood that he had been exposed to *the* secret. "There is a secret and this is it," he remarked. "It is the secret that the world is not only not the way you think it is, it's that the world is a way that you can't think it is." Further, this secret was not "something untold," but that which "can't be told." While convinced that he'd been introduced to the most powerful of all hallucinogens, armed with the knowledge of its endogenous status, McKenna spent his remaining days in the afterglow of his Elf Event promulgating the "paradox that DMT is the most powerful yet most harmless" of all substances. And with that in mind, he became seized by "an absolutely messianic desire" to expose others to this enigma.[5]

The tale of McKenna's elves is among the more storied in psychedelic folklore. In one telling, the experience transported Terence to his childhood, a time when magic ruled the world, "from top to bottom, side to side, from first to last, atom to atom."[6] He may have left that world behind, but as he would later reflect, here *magic* was masquerading as a *drug*. That a doorway had opened on another world was an idea animated by *Aladdin's Lamp*, a favored childhood fairytale. "I felt like Aladdin," McKenna remarks a quarter-of-a-century later at a retreat at the Ojai Foundation, in Ventura

County, California. "You buy something in a junkshop, you take it home, you try to clean it up, and next thing you know a flame a mile high pours out and demands to do your bidding."[7]

The bearer of the lamp on that fateful evening on Telegraph Avenue was McKenna's lifelong pal, Rick Watson. Ricky and Terry became best friends as students in 1963 at Awalt High School, in Mountain View, California. McKenna may have been eleven months Watson's senior, but Rick was always the one to get there first. With an interest in organic chemistry; keen sensitivities across jazz, poetry, and banning the bomb; and connected to the roots of the psychedelic revolution, like the older and more experienced brother McKenna never had, Watson became a close confidante and respected companion. Rick was a living, breathing, embodiment of the conscientious and adventurous outré life to which McKenna had been drawn throughout his upbringing. Their friendship, and the accompanying period of experimentation, encapsulate a crucial phase in the passage from small-town weirdo to transnational freak. But at the start of 1963, Terence subsisted in a larval state in Colorado, biding his time like a pre-metamorphic pupa.

PAONIA

At 5,682 feet, Paonia rests at the foot of Mount Lamborn in North Fork Valley, western Colorado. There, Terence Kemp McKenna is born on November 16, 1946. Dennis follows suit in December 1950. At the turn of the sixties, the coal mining and cattle town has a population of 1,200. The brothers McKenna struggle to belong in Paonia, a rumored Guinness World Record recipient for a settlement featuring the most churches per capita.[8] Whether there is any truth to that claim, Terence grows up believing street corners are for churches. The accounts of both brothers offer stories of aspirational teenagers plotting escape from infernal boredom: the small-town mentality where success is measured by sporting prowess; a sexually repressed Catholic family; their father's suppressed creativity; and the era's darkling mood.

Born in Colorado with Irish roots, Joe McKenna was a woodsman, a World War II veteran, and subsequently a salesman of shoes and then electrical equipment. During the war, he served as a top gunner and engineer in a B-17 Flying Fortress on bombing missions over Western Europe, a subject that was never a topic for conversation. From his youth, Joe enjoyed science fiction and the adventure novels of Zane Grey and Edgar Rice Burroughs. As Dennis's recollections reveal, their father's devil-may-care attitude was replaced in the aftermath of the war with a desire for settling down to the mild-mannered life he had earned in combat. Sloan Wilson's *The Man in the Gray Flannel Suit* presented the conformist keep-your-head-down archetype to which Joe gravitated and against which his sons rebelled. A storyteller who never told a tale the same way twice, Joe was also a cipher with whom the boys were frequently in conflict.

Joe met and married Hazelle Kemp in Delta, Colorado, in 1937. A compassionate and tolerant woman, Hadie was a model of fifties motherhood. Her father's favorite daughter, she was devoted to her husband and to raising their boys, who loved her dearly and toward whom they harbored guilt, having so frequently overstepped the limits. A graduate of Paonia High School and business college in Grand Junction, during World War II, Hadie became personal secretary to Henry J. Kaiser, the founder of Kaiser Steel. Possessing a large vocabulary, with interests in classical music and literature, Hazelle McKenna was as generous with her wisdom as she was with her cooking.[9]

The bungalow in which the brothers are raised on the corner of Fourth and Orchard Avenue was half a block from Hadie's childhood home. She was the first child (of four) to Italian-born orphan Teresa Aurelia Balena ("Honey") and Joseph Kemp, known as Dad Kemp to his grandchildren. A Coloradan who worked in the local fruit industry before becoming Paonia's town clerk, and later an accountant at the local power company, Joseph had a love for books and language—a passion passed on to Hadie. Though Joe McKenna himself had a beguiling way with words, it was Dad Kemp, a master storyteller with a great command of language, from whom Terence inherited his abilities, according to Dennis, as a "skilled bullshitter." As Terence lived at Dad Kemp's house until aged three, these skills were honed from an early stage. In Dennis's telling, even though he wasn't Irish, their maternal grandfather had "a touch of the Irish bard," and many of the personality quirks the brothers shared "can ultimately be traced to that man."[10]

Encouraged to read, the boys are weaned on a steady diet of science fiction. They became fans of *Weird Tales*, H. P. Lovecraft, Ray Bradbury, Arthur C. Clarke, Jules Verne, and H. G. Wells. With his mind merging with the alternate universes of Asimov, Sturgeon, Herbert, and Heinlein, sci-fi was, as Terence averred, "the entry drug into the psychedelic world."[11] Paonia may have felt to Terence like the closed world of Diaspar to Alvin, the insatiably curious Unique in Clarke's great 1956 tale of discovery, *The City and the Stars*. "Terrible Terry," as he is early branded, was intelligent, defiant, and, as Dennis adds, more than occasionally obnoxious. Four years his junior, Dennis was never in the same school at the same time as his brother. He nevertheless had to surf the wake of his "exceptional intelligence and aggressiveness."[12]

FIGURE 1.1
Terence McKenna, aged two, ca. 1949.

Terence had a propensity to torment his younger brother. At some length in his autobiography Dennis describes the "Nobody People" whom Terence invented to maintain a "climate of fear."[13] The Nobody People are Dennis's entrée to the world of spirits and entities to which he would later gain access when drinking ayahuasca. But there is another terror whose name would go unuttered in *The Brotherhood*. This was the flesh-eating monster Terence called the "Wendigo," more than likely inspired by Algernon Blackwood's novella and in reference to a mountain creature who in First Nations Algonquin folklore descends from the forest at winter to snatch and devour its victims. According to Ron Curry, Dennis's best friend in Paonia, Terence painted a picture with canvas and oil of this monster. He kept the painting, titled "The Wendigo," in the closet of their shared bedroom, occasionally

FIGURE 1.2

Terence, age three, ca. 1950, and, from left to right, Judy Livingston, Pat MaCraken, and Jody Livingston. Photo courtesy of Judy Livingston.

pulling it out to remind Dennis that if he didn't watch out, the Wendigo would get him that night.

Painting his own picture now, Curry recalls his first encounter with Terry McKenna. It was 1956. He was six years old on his first day at Paonia Elementary.

"If you don't watch out kid, I'm gonna kick you clear from here to nowhere," the fourth grader warned him.

FIGURE 1.3
McKenna family (Hazelle, Joe, Dennis, and Terence McKenna), Easter 1954.

Curry doubled over in laughter before evading the older boy. "I couldn't imagine not being somewhere."

Dennis, who knew his brother as his "mentor and tormentor,"[14] did not have the luxury of escape. Curry believes the reign of terror to which Dennis was subjected nightly for years expressed more than a common resentment of an older toward a younger sibling. Dennis's memoir offers detail on a significant incident involving their father and Terence aged three or four. The event "drove a wedge" between them, "changing their relationship forever." The story was related by Terence to Dennis decades later, possibly in the wake of Terence's first LSD experience. Joe had discovered his son in a sandbox with a playmate, another boy, "playing with each other's genitals, and, somehow, handling each other's shit." Failing to recognize this as normal infant behavior, Joe freaked out and gave Terence a spanking. All of Joe's repressed Catholic fears about sexuality—especially homosexuality—surfaced in a blind rage. Terence never forgot his dad's vicious turn, as incomprehensible as it was. "That was it," Dennis was informed, as if the incident happened just yesterday. "That was it between us." In this primal instant, Terence resolved "to never show vulnerability, and to put his own (perceived) self-interests front and center at all times." Dennis speculates that this episode was not only the cause of Terence's subsequent hostility toward his father, but explains his own treatment at the hands of Terence. It also left him wondering if the experience affected his brother's ability to trust others. The episode may have caused the "emotional firewall" Dennis perceived in his brother.[15] Perhaps it also ignited the spirit of the prodigal outcast that Terence came to inhabit.

Their father is a continuing source of resentment, notably when it came to his eldest son's performance of the regional coming-of-age rite of passage. Pressure mounts when Terence fails to shoot an elk during the October hunting season when aged twelve. While hiding his conviction that he was a "wilted pansy" stricken with anxieties about this bloodlust rite, in the following year he shoots an elk dead. "I never had to please my father again." Home free, "everything was forgiven from that moment on." This story later helps weaponize his proposition that "culture is not your friend."[16]

His views on culture did not come from a place of material need. Thanks to Joe's success as a traveling salesman, the McKennas lived comfortably. And while they were among the wealthiest families in town, their prosperity was relative. Joe piloted his own light aircraft—a Piper Tri-Pacer—useful for covering sales territory and taking the family on weekend trips. Their father's wings ensured good contracts and afforded options unavailable to other families.[17] It also gave the boys an early means of getting high.

That he was the target of bullying furthers our understanding of a possible mean streak in Terence's early life. Skinny, nearsighted, and bug-eyed, he was intimidated by the "roving cannibal bands" of his peers sworn to get him.[18] Such was his harassment that he, as he was fond of claiming, "had to find a new way home from school every day."[19] Alternate routes of deviant latitude are long familiar to those who are threatened by the staid orthodoxies of middle America. As a wily tactician, Terry managed to avoid beatings by endearing himself to the alpha males—notably through his amiable linguistic capabilities. The daring lover of expletive puns gained in stature at school by dropping coded obscenities into his rapid-paced classroom elocution.[20] He excelled as an inventor of outrageous idiom—a compulsion later relied upon as a livelihood.

Terence also knew conflict in his role as an altar boy (until about age twelve) at Paonia's Sacred Heart Catholic Church. By the time he was nine or ten, he claims to have become an "earnest practitioner of ceremonial magic," drawing pentacles in his room and burning rosemary. One day cleaning out the sacristy, the priest discovers an old aspergillum, a holy water sprinkler, he wanted to throw out.

"I have a use for that," Terence announces.

"Oh, what is your use for this, my son?"

"Well, I'm involved in the conjuration of Azazel, the 11th General of the Mercuric sphere." This incident, he claims, "launched an investigation that has made that town unsafe for the practice of ceremonial magic to this day."[21]

Ron Curry spent a lot of time over at the McKenna house. Of Joe McKenna, Curry explains, "he wasn't mean or anything, but he commanded a lot of respect." On one occasion, Joe grabs him by the arm, looks into his eyes, and says, "Ron, you're a good boy." As two of the strangest people in town, his sons by contrast defy the boundaries of the acceptable. Terence's hyper nonconformism found expressive outlets. By the time he is a freshman at high school, aged fourteen, he swans about town in a white pair of shorts splashed with bright paints, Pollock-style. At home, Gustave Doré's etchings of *Paradise Lost* and *The Inferno* adorned the wall of the bedroom he shared with Dennis. Accustomed to standing out, he later plays Clarence Darrow in a high school play about the Scopes Trial. "He won some award for that. He was a great actor. He was always acting. Always on."[22]

Terence spent his lunchtimes in the school library, where he encountered the world of literature. He claimed to read 200 pages a day before he fell asleep at night, and Curry believes it. His friend was afflicted with a burning curiosity. "Whatever his momentary interest . . . it was an obsession until he got it out of his system."[23] The intersection of the anomalous and the fantastic made for an early domain of fascination. While Hazelle devoted countless hours reading to him from the Oz books, Terence is also exposed to *Fate*, the magazine of the paranormal to which Joe was a longtime subscriber. Though never admitting it, Joe McKenna was more bookish than most of his friends. As a child, he had suffered from rheumatic illness, during which time he acquired a private obsession with sci-fi fan fiction.[24] Featuring stories about flying saucers, Atlantis, the Bermuda Triangle, and even the "sacred mushroom" of South America (the subject of a story in August 1961), *Fate* was, and remains, a catalog of anomalies that represent what Terence came to decry as the safe limits of the unknown that boggle the minds that populate the trailer courts of America. As a kid, he pawed through his Dover reprint of D. H. Rawcliffe's *Illusions and Delusions of the Supernatural and the Occult*. The book was like an alluring literary *Wunderkammer* featuring everything from mesmers and ectoplasm to "birds that did advanced arithmetic." This Victorian-era "catalog of edges" and taxonomy of the weird opened his impressionable mind to the notion of "hallucinations."[25] By age twelve, with the aid of Plato's *Republic* and Thomas More's *Utopia*—books recommended by Bonnie Hutchins, the town librarian whom he regarded as his mentor—Terence also developed a strong awareness of the world beyond Paonia.

Terence had occasion to recall a conversation between Hutchins and a teacher about a new library acquisition that was strictly off-limits. Hazelle had been alerted to the appearance in the library of *Brave New World*, a book that Terence was determined to lay his hands on—a work he later described as "the most intelligent anti-drug book ever written." This wasn't the first time he'd entered, and won, a "First Amendment struggle" with his mother. *Frankenstein* and *Dracula* were early test cases, in the wake of which he claims to have achieved "total carte blanche." Emerging victorious from the last censorship battle of his childhood, Terence went on to devour the works of Huxley, whom he would call "the Abraham" of the psychedelic movement.[26]

The pursuit of Huxley was partly encouraged by Hazelle herself. Alarmed by the deteriorating vision suffered by her sons, she grew enthused with the Bates Method of vision improvement that Huxley endorsed in *The Art of Seeing*. She took the boys on 350-mile "visionary pilgrimages" to Denver for sessions with a specialist four times a year for a couple of years. Terence couldn't say if the techniques improved his vision, but the message in *The Art of Seeing*—that "we must begin our education by learning to actually look at the world," to pay attention to the details—honed his visionary instincts.[27] From the age of twelve or thirteen, he began meticulously making his way through Huxley's entire oeuvre.

While Huxley impressed, standing tall among Terence's favored volumes was Jung's *Psychology and Alchemy*. Inspiring a passion for hermetic thought, this work opened the door on a vast obscure literature.[28] The obsession with alchemy was never released from his system; Terence later grew dedicated to collecting hermetic, occult, and alchemical treatises, including works by Cornelius Agrippa and about magus, "intelligencer," and court astrologer to Elizabeth I, John Dee, to whom he felt great affinity, notably in the wake of historian Francis Yates, who celebrated Dee as the true Renaissance man. Book hunting was to be an expensive passion, compelled perhaps by Mercurius, the trickster spirit *familiaris* who is the alchemists' guide and their tempter, "their good luck and their ruin." He learned from Jung the dual-natured character of Hermes Psychopompos, "a chthonic god of revelation and also the spirit of quicksilver," who unites the paired opposites.[29] As a child, Terence became so fascinated with mercury that he harried his grandfather for his hearing aid batteries and smashed them with a hammer to obtain a substance that is both a metal and a liquid. Collected in little bottles he carried everywhere, mercury was a magical substance onto which he could project the contents of his mind. "A child playing with mercury is an alchemist hard at work."[30] The child playing with mercury is also exposed to toxic poisoning.

No doubt reinforced by Huxley, exposure to Jung formed awareness of "the self as a larger and more inclusive mode of being" than the ego.[31] The foundations for a spiritual métier were being laid. By his mid-teens, a questing curiosity saw exposure to scholars of mysticism like Evelyn Underhill and William James, notably James's *The Varieties of Religious Experience*, but also primary sources, like Teresa of Avila, Thomas Traherne, and Hildegard von Bingen. "I got the idea that there was this experience but I couldn't find it, I couldn't find it on my knees at the church for hour after hour. I mean, I found various forms of existential boredom ad infinitum, and I would sit in nature and I would hyperventilate." Alas, "the juice just wasn't coming."[32] As virtual billboards for LSD, mescaline, and the exploits of the late beatniks, early teenage subscriptions to the *Village Voice* and the *Evergreen Review* offered tantalizing hints of the "juice." But his early adolescence was not outwardly optimistic. While an early curiosity for the transcendent showed hints of later passions, exposure to the likes of André Michaux and Albert Camus gave shape to a dark brooding phase, with McKenna identifying as an "existentialist brat" until his late teens. Though he stored little credence in astrology, the pessimism was amplified by his stature as "a triple Scorpio with a heavy twelfth house."[33]

As illuminated by reflections late in life, McKenna's early literary choices set him apart from his peers. "There was a period in my life where I formed my taste by saying I liked what I didn't like," he later confided to Esalen workshoppers. "Inevitably these were good choices because I was raised in an ecology that valued Norman Rockwell, Rock of Ages, Silent Night, Rosemary Clooney." He was traveling the other way: Jackson Pollock, Samuel Beckett, Jean Genet, Karl Jaspers, Martin Heidegger. "I didn't know what these things meant," commenting on behavior that appears precocious beyond measure. "I just knew they were mantras that kept straight people away."[34]

Against the grain of Podunk hostility to foreigners, intellectuals, and abstract painting, he received his calling. "I will take the position that all these things are good. . . . Abstract expressionism, Jews, black people, science: good, good, good, good!" It was to be a lonely vigil. "I would look at a Pollock and think, you know, 'It is messy. It may be horse shit. But we must never admit that. We must defend the genius of Pollock unto death because we don't understand it.'" But by clinging to his obtuse convictions, Terence came to understand some of these things and make them his own. "I discovered that that was the path to wisdom: a total rejection of the culture I came up with."[35]

With such hobbies, repudiation, and precocity, it is little wonder young McKenna forged closer relationships with teachers more than his peers. Given his poor eyesight, like Dennis, he was ill-equipped for basketball and was not a top pick in school sports. To keep the coach off his back, he ran the mile, and even won a couple of ribbons at state track meets. He was often seen jogging around the park opposite their house.[36] Though not for reasons the coach will have approved, this training came in handy later on.

McKenna later reported that it was from age seven or eight that he pursued his vocation of "edge running." No reflection on his track and field prowess, the phrase revealed a penchant to collect rocks and butterflies, and his interest in amateur rocketeering. It would be the first of several transitional life phases where he could "hardly recognize who I had been before." While his peers were playing Little League baseball, Terry was "back in the hills digging out trilobites and tracking down moths."[37] Reflection on these early passions gave over to contemplating the roots of a lifelong pursuit of "a certain flash of iridescence," of the kind found when breaking open ore-bearing rock, capturing certain species of butterflies in tropical environments, or "when you mix potassium perchlorate in sugar in a hot-sauce pan and ignite it." The scintilla, the spark, the possibility, to be discovered was felt to derive from "pushing out at the edge of the permissible."[38] Further condensing how childhood set the stage for a life of questing, it was claimed that the fixation on "drugs, magic, and the more obscure backwaters of natural history and theology" afforded a profile of "an eccentric Florentine prince," rather than a kid growing up in the US heartland of the late fifties.[39] The young prince's early talent for abstract style was displayed in an eight-by-four-foot mural he hung in their bedroom.[40] "Abstract precisionism" is how art critic and close friend Michael Malcolm saw McKenna's style by the time he arrived in Berkeley. Of the few of his friend's paintings he had the opportunity to inspect, he found them well executed.[41]

In his sophomore year at Paonia High, such talents had been encouraged by geography and art teacher "RJ" Pease, whose company Terence enjoyed, to the disapproval of his parents.[42] Described as "an astronomer, pianist, guitarist, artist, judo expert and true avant-garde intellectual," RJ is introduced in a letter to Terry's old friend Tim A. Cannon (a.k.a. Solly) as "a wonderful person who shares my disgust at the common cravenness of life." Terry receives RJ as a sparkling gem in a colorless universe. "The thought that somewhere there are others like him where we may find our people has been all to keep me from the gas pipe."[43] Letters to Solly convey that Terry has been elected to the student council, and joins the art club and debating team. In the following year, after a planned trip with Solly to New York is quashed by his parents, numbed by fury, Terry reaches for lines from *Nausea* relating that even Sartre's prose fails to capture the wretchedness of his condition. "Without doubt there is in the world no more mean spot of ground to be found anywhere than this accursed clime. All here is leaden skies and the world drifts in an endless twi-lite. The air stinks of intellectual poverty and militant clodishness [sic]."[44]

Though Terence has affirmed that his first psychedelic drug was science fiction, among the other outré activities competing for his attention and instrumental to achieving early heights was rocketry, with both siblings fantasizing futures at the pointy end of aerospace engineering. Jamming potassium perchlorate and sugar into stainless steel pipes and blowing "enormous craters" in the pitcher's mound a short distance from home was a pastime they both enjoyed. Perhaps the earliest incidence of edge-running is what Terence cast as his first encounter with morning glory seeds. This episode was inspired by newspaper stories as much as it was by Leary—whose plight was followed closely in the *Village Voice*.[45] At the end of the 1963 summer, after the "high priest" had been expelled from Harvard, seeds from "bindweed," a wild morning glory found growing locally were taken home, ground up, and wolfed down. Terence later regarded this as his first trip. Though the bindweed was inactive, significance was assigned to this anxious "trip" as the source of "interesting false positives."[46] Meanwhile, he applied to participate in the International Federation for Internal Freedom, an intentional community Leary set up on a secluded beach in Mexico in 1962/63. Involving LSD training sessions, the IFIF's Zihuatanejo Project was inspired by Huxley's final novel *Island*. "Somewhere there is a letter from fifteen-year-old Terence McKenna to Ralph Metzner pleading to be taken aboard the circus, but I think they were too loaded to ever reply."[47]

Girls were another obsession. And yet, how does one satisfy one's desires as a "nervous, yammering, skinny, bespectacled Ichabod like creature"?[48]

Terence's first serious love interest appears to have been the librarian's daughter. Kris Hutchins was two years Terry's senior, and according to Dennis, she might just as well have been the "Whore of Babylon" to their father, distraught that his son might "knock her up." As such a scandal would virtually ruin his life, that outcome had to be averted, not via birth control education, but through more extreme measures. Dennis paints a portrait of a cunning sibling who sold the impression that he was having (unprotected) sex to leverage his way out of town.[49] It is possible that one rumored event was more than enough to see Terence, an altar boy of years past, run out of town. According to Watson, Terry's oft-told fable was that the teenagers were caught "making out in a graveyard." The secluded Bethlehem Cemetery was a great place to meet girls and smoke dope, Dennis recalls.[50] We know little about Kris, their affair, or if they were actually discovered working the graveyard shift.[51] And yet its possibility corresponds with an incident outrageous enough for parents to intervene and for Terence to be forced out of Paonia High School—discretely expelled, even if not officially.

Some twenty-five years later, McKenna gave a banquet address at a San Francisco ufology conference where he ranged into terrain that may offer some explanation for his strife-lain involvement with girls, and indeed older women—that is, desirable others—throughout his adolescence:

> As a species we are coming into a kind of pubescent awareness of the presence of the *other* our childish historical concerns that were self-directed and self-indulgent no longer satisfy. And a deep kind of yearning has come upon the species. A yearning for the confirmation of the presence of an other, in the same way that an adolescent child becomes aware of and develops an extremely intense, highly charged, and ambivalent attitude toward the opposite sex. I think we are discovering, in our own psychic structure, the potential, the possibility, of a relationship with an intelligent species outside ourselves, and this raises for us all the tensions, all the issues that accompany an adolescent love affair.[52]

With a built-in heteronormativity, the comments suggest how McKenna's adolescent contact experience—with all of its infatuation, fumbling, and revelation—fueled his later approach to the UFO phenomenon. Not only that; it goes some way to illuminating his evolving thought on the hyperspatial *Other* with which he thought we must reckon as a species.

Back on Earth in early-sixties Paonia, when he wasn't channeling his angst into abstract form, or obsessing over girls, McKenna marked his parents as "fascists." This, as Dennis demurs, was an unfair assessment. In fact, Joe and Hadie wanted their sons to graduate from high school and enter college, ensuring their deferment from the building Southeast Asia conflict.[53]

Defending his plan to transplant to California to complete his schooling, this trajectory stood in Terence's favor. That, and the fact that the 1963 outrage involving Kris—whom I imagine as a fellow bookish nerd and the most appealing alien in the neighborhood—gave his parents no alternative than to lube the Californian dreams of a sixteen-year-old. Channeling Clarke's Alvin, longing to break the "eternity circuits" of small-town Colorado, nothing would obstruct the trail to his El Dorado.

MOUNTAIN VIEW

In Mountain View, Terence lands in the home of local teachers Aunt Tress and Uncle Ray Somers, and his cousin Kathi. There he attends Awalt High, which, opening its doors in 1960, had been freshly engineered to accommodate the exploding population of future Silicon Valley. Proximate to Stanford Research Institute, Shockley Semiconductor Laboratory, and Xerox PARC, Awalt—which would merge with and be renamed Mountain View High School in 1981—is staffed with bright teachers whose pupils are virtually thrown together. This raw thrownness proves catalytic in Watson's mind, recalling Mountain View as a "cultural wasteland," a proving ground for the alienated. Rick's articulate classmate has a taste for the outrageous, and possesses an elocution—tone, pitch, and a strong emphasis on certain words—styled on the recordings of Dylan Thomas. The era demands mischief-making, like action painting in the style of Pollock, and reciting ad-lib poetry modeled on Ginsberg's *Howl*.[54] Contemporaneous events afford bleak amplitude. "I grew up very quickly in a single day," Terence claimed, when, on November 22, 1963, "two of my heroes, and I only had two, chose that particular moment to leave the plane. John F. Kennedy, murdered in Dallas by the government. And Aldous Huxley passing quietly into eternity, loaded to the gills in Southern California."[55]

Mischief is incited among a small cohort that includes a "devotee of the darker sides of the psyche," John Parker, identified by Watson as the most brilliant among their circle of teenage psychedelic explorers, albeit the most troubled (see figure 1.4). Usually wearing black, "never seen in the sun," as an admirer of Lovecraft, Parker witnesses "the eldritch horror . . . lurking behind the pantomime of light." A counterpoint to the optimism of the early Haight-Ashbury scene, with his Cheshire-cat grin, Parker "stood out as a grim seer, and like Kubla Khan, heard from afar 'ancestral voices prophesying war.'"[56] According to fellow Awalt alum Douglas Hansen, Parker was "an original 'beat,'" long before the term was used, "destined

FIGURE 1.4
John Parker from the 1972 film *Ceremony* (directed by George Csicsery) in which Parker portrays a mythical figure representing the Sun. Photo courtesy of George Csicsery.

to forever be outside the mainstream of society and denied participation in its material rewards and illusions." Barely finishing high school, he later "escaped into a permanent underground of his own making."[57] Despite his troubled upbringing, Parker is a boundless source of wisdom on botany and psychopharmacology, and for the remainder of the sixties he becomes an inspiration for Terence and something of a mentor to Dennis. He was the most "far out" person they knew. If Terence later became a psychonautical Magellan, Parker was Heredotus. Parker appears to have become heir to the talents of his father. A brilliant chemist who worked for NASA and the CIA, Dr. John Parker was a mysterious figure, a man who, as Hansen recalls, "allowed us to build an LSD lab in his garage in the summer of 1964," but who was, in Watson's memory, "definitely into the dark arts."

McKenna and Parker were members of the World Affairs Club, a scholastic brains trust (see figure 1.5). Among their number were jazz drummer Lee Hildebrand, who became a record producer and East Bay music critic; Gray Brechin, later historical geographer and author of urban studies classic *Imperial San Francisco: Urban Power, Earthly Ruin*; and Brechin's brother Vern, future engineer at the Stanford Linear Accelerator Center. As Hansen

FIGURE 1.5
World Affairs class, Awalt High, Mountain View, California, 1964. McKenna (standing, second from right). Other members include John Parker (standing, third from right), Lee Hildebrand (standing, fourth from right), Verne Brechin (standing, fifth from right), and Gray Brechin (in front, third from left). Photo courtesy of Rick Watson.

remarked, McKenna was a small-town boy from Colorado who stepped into "the center of the universe of technology, the cold war, psychedelics, and the emergence of a new culture." It is a step he made with conviction.[58]

As a sophomore, and member of the '64 World Affairs Club, Hansen recalls visiting McKenna's house and exploring his impressive library, noting especially his enthusiasm for the works of ethnomycologist Robert G. Wasson. As committed enthusiasts of the "other" and the means by which *it* may be contacted, the boys share an interest in the promise of psychedelics. Besides Huxley, they had their noses in Robert S. De Ropp's *Drugs and the Mind*. By this time, McKenna is not only extraordinarily well-read and displaying great erudition; his extemporizing evokes a couple of core ideas: "the new eschatology" and the "aesthetics of chaos." Foreshadowing the Timewave, these are ideas Hansen watches take off like a Saturn V rocket. While he was "looking clear-eyed at the trajectory of the human experiment and foreseeing the end," McKenna was also "looking at manifestations of a consciousness that could transcend that grim forecast and perhaps transform and extend human existence."

Hansen's friend was making his voice heard. On one occasion, McKenna pickets American Opinion, a Los Altos bookstore operated by the far right advocacy group the John Birch Society. On another, he invites William Marx Mandel to speak to the World Affairs Club. Author, broadcast journalist, and left-wing political activist, Mandel worked for Stanford's Hoover Institute and was a Soviet affairs analyst investigated in 1961 by the House Committee on Un-American Activities. The faculty obligated the club to balance this invitation by hosting a speaker representing the right. McKenna made a vociferous stand against a visiting professor from Stanford who stood before a map of Vietnam and advocated dropping small nukes in the north.[59]

It is possibly through his membership in World Affairs that McKenna forges connections with students from nearby Los Altos High, a "seedbed of weirdness" in the memory of David Wallin. Wallin, whose father was a sociologist at Stanford, and who himself becomes a clinical psychologist and author of *Attachment in Psychotherapy*, is introduced to Terence by Susan Zebroski, future wife of Rick Watson. It was at a party at Zebroski's house where Wallin likely first encountered McKenna, whom he found instantly relatable as smart and mischievous. They would not have a lasting connection, but the McKenna Wallin knew cultivated a proclivity to hold forth on the subject of "destiny"—"what somebody is made for." His magnetism prompted others to try their hand at their own versions of Terry McKenna. Immediately received as a "real artist of the spoken word," Wallin recognized Terence as "a living, breathing example of somebody who was just doing his thing, and because he was so brilliant, people enjoyed watching him do his thing."[60]

So impressive was McKenna's thing that he is invited onto the editorial board of alternative Los Altos student newsletter *Neo Etudiant*. Mimeographed on ochre paper, *Neo Etudiant* ran a few four- to six-page issues over about one month in 1963/64 before threatened by the school and shut down. The newsletter was distributed at both Los Altos and Awalt High Schools and featured World Affairs Club speakers. At this time McKenna meets another Los Altos student, and lifelong friend, Nina Wise. One or two years his junior, Wise knew him as a genius among a small circle of outsiders, bohemians, and intellectuals. As a "monologist," he was capable of "shifting from something very particular to something very global very quickly"; he also, she added, had a certain narcissistic quality. She and others were more than happy to watch him shift gears, and they became devotees of this undeniable center of fascination: "It was thrilling and fun."

With Terry sitting cross-legged, "we would sit all around him and he would go on these rants." When Wise later sought his guidance, McKenna was among her most significant influences.[61]

THE ADVENTURES OF RICK AND TERRY

McKenna's cohort had a thirst for rare, specialist, and esoteric knowledge, notably relating to psychotropic compounds. Among the formative adventures, for Rick and Terry at any rate, was an episode with morning glory seeds eaten on a day trip to San Francisco in the spring of 1964—an episode that amounted to more than "false positives." McKenna has unpacked, and minced, the long backstory to this episode. In the early nineties, he elaborated on an experience on morning glory seeds that were eaten in Paonia. Alarmists and defenders of virtue in the press had decried the abuse of morning glory seeds. Upon eating "Heavenly Blue" seeds purchased at the hardware store for thirty-five cents a packet, he began to notice that the leaves imprinted in the fabric of the living room curtains "seemed to have little faces that were dancing." The "ratty drapes" he'd been living around for years became animated in a fashion previously unnoticed. And as this happened, he began absorbing his surroundings under new, turbocharged powers of observation:

> I went outside and was looking around at everything, and then I just felt physically overcome. My knees basically gave way underneath me, and I sat down under a tree and I closed my eyes, and my life has never been the same since. Because there, waiting behind closed eyelids were ruined cities covered with creeping jeweled lichens, and inhabited by shining-eyed creatures that were I was not sure exactly what. And, much, much more. And I just spent a half an hour or so literally in trance gazing into this unfolding reverie of deserts, jungles . . . machines in orbit around alien worlds. All of this stuff. And I was stunned. I still am stunned. And that essentially set the compass for the rest of my intellectual life.[62]

In Watson's telling, this tale is an example of his friend's proclivity for garnishing the truth. The narrative offers an illustration of how, over the course of his public career, McKenna embellished and remixed his own experiences before new audiences. As Watson relates, this story constitutes an "origin myth" which incorporated the visions when he and Terence took morning glory seeds in San Francisco in 1964. It also smacks of Terence's subsequent response to DMT.[63] As Watson confirmed, McKenna did not allow facts to "get in the way of a good story."

The formative role of "Heavenly Blue" arrives by way of another of Watson's stories, "Morning Glory."[64] Written in 1990, the tale recounts in scintillating detail the adventures of the two boys in San Francisco in early 1964, in which Rick (aged sixteen) and Terence (aged seventeen) consume morning glory seeds. This is a few years after the ineffectual experiment with "bindweed" in Paonia. The boys were primed on the "solvents of conceptual sludge" that Huxley urged are essential, as he stated to *Playboy* in 1963, to "cut holes in the confining stockade of verbalized symbols." These "solvents" permit the individual to receive the world with what Plotinus described as "that other kind of seeing, which everyone has but few make use of." Huxley's silken discourse lit the path ahead.[65] In Watson's account, Rick and "Terr" gain awareness that psychedelic alkaloids are found in species of morning glory. That the seeds are an analog of LSD was knowledge obtained from a graduate psychology student, a guest scientist teaching a night class for advanced science students at Awalt. It is pre-prohibition, and the specialist had been administering low doses of LSD in controlled settings at the International Foundation for Advanced Study (IFAS) in Menlo Park. Established by Myron Stolaroff to test the potential of LSD in technical problem-solving and innovation, IFAS was introducing LSD to scientists, engineers, and figures like *Whole Earth Catalog* founder Stewart Brand.[66] The young Stanford psychologist, who was carefully focused on set, setting, and preparation,[67] was none other than psychedelics research pioneer and later president of the Association for Transpersonal Psychology, James Fadiman.

At this time, Fadiman pursued a rather delicate career as a graduate student. By day, he wore a coat and tie, and by night he absorbed *The Bhagavad Gita*, *The Tibetan Book of the Dead*, and the writings of Wasson. Fadiman had obtained intimate knowledge of the effects of morning glories himself, which he ate one glorious morning at Jasper Ridge Biological Preserve with principal investigator at IFAS, Willis Harman, after making the acquisition from a local gardening store. The greatest threat, Fadiman discovers, is to his "core beliefs." During that session he receives a formative vision in which he proudly writes "a very sophisticated analysis of reality" on a huge blackboard. But God appears and wipes the board clean, announcing: "That was just wonderful . . . I certainly hope you'll do others." Fadiman understood that he had been taught to abandon hubris, to relinquish his attachment to belief, faith, and ideology.[68]

It is reasonable to assume that Fadiman was somewhat fresh from this lesson in humility when he showed up at Mountain View. While their classmates were bored out of their skulls, the meeting proved transformative for Rick and Terry. The straight-talking grad student was received as a hip "psychopomp" from their dreamtime. At last, a veil had been lifted to reveal that "the magical world of the imagination, which we had seen glimpses of in surrealist paintings and films, and heard resonances of in music and poetry, was an actual and visit-able place, one you could experience and explore directly," with the aid of specific compounds. Their motivational speaker held the keys to a radical gnosis, and they wanted in.[69]

Enraptured, hoping to score the glory, Terr and Little Ricky make an appointment to visit the non-pompous psychopomp at his IFAS office in Menlo Park. Fadiman is ultra-cautious, declaring that morning glory seeds, like LSD, should be administered under strict clinical supervision. Caution was justified. The psychedelics research field was buckling under increased regulatory pressure and in fact the IFAS study would be shut down by the FDA in 1966. Though returning empty-handed, the boys absorb enough on sourcing, preparation, and dosage to make a start. Several dozen packets of "Heavenly Blue" (presumably *Ipomoea tricolor*, or Mexican morning glory) are soon acquired from a Los Altos nursery. They use a coffee grinder to pulverize the seeds, the powder filling dozens of large gelatin capsules. "Our normal mistrust of adults led us to double the recommended dose from 300 to 600 seeds each." Recalling that their teacher emphasized the importance of setting, they decided to swallow dozens of these little "basketballs" in San Francisco's Golden Gate Park, near the De Young Museum. On the appointed day, when two hours pass sans any sign of activity, the duo suspect they'd been had.

Ravenous, they catch a bus down Market Street, swan into a deli and order pastrami on rye sandwiches. Then something happened:

> The sandwiches glowed profoundly, and the strips of salt-beef had an iridescent, nacreous sheen to them which was exquisitely beautiful. The glass of Coke appeared as a microcosmic universe, with planets and stars forming as bubbles in the thick interstellar syrup, gradually enlarging and then suddenly flying to the surface and popping, mini super-novae, encapsulating all of cosmic history within the magnifying cylinder of the glass. We appeared to ourselves and each other as inside-out alimentary canals, equipped with this grinding demon at one end chewing up the diverse flora and fauna of our plates' contents, rending their proteins and fibers, breaking down their carbohydrate polymer chains, injecting saliva in some arcane alchemy of which our stomachs were the alembics.

Terry announces he will vomit, and is soon discovered on the stair en route to the restroom. As if pasted onto a slide under a microscope, he appears to Watson as "a six foot long amoeba . . . all his interior anatomy, at that moment very actively digesting his half-eaten pastrami sandwich." Peeling his pal from the stairs, Watson whispers in his ear: "Terry, I think we'd better get out of here."

> Out into the full chrome, neon, sun-glint glare of Market Street, cars like screaming iron boars snarling and lunging, buses like electric metal snails stuck to their tracks, antennae crackling with blue sparks from the powerlines above, and a hysterical, speed-demented angry mob swarming on the sidewalks of Market Street, a Bruegelian pandemonium, a normal Saturday afternoon of San Francisco shopping.

That day's long voyage led the now beatific duo to City Limits, the café downstairs at City Lights bookstore, North Beach: "Terry and I burst in, talking a mile a minute, a running commentary on every thing and every one about us. We were seeking out sympathetic vibes, some recognition of our Heightened Reality, some fellow beings in the multiverse." The Beat world's center of gravity had by then become iconic and touristy. The scene had moved on. And, after polishing off the apples in a large copper display bowl, so do they. "We flew down the hill, ecstatic, to the Third Street train station, both of us now chanting stream-of-consciousness ad lib poetry, inspired, intoxicated, exhilarated, full of boundless joy, for we knew we had discovered what we had both come into this world looking for, our own Lost Kingdom, and stately Pleasure Dome."

As soon as the adventure began, Terence comes crashing to earth. A rift develops, first with Aunt Tress and then his parents, triggered by his affair with a classmate's mother, consummated, no less, on morning glory seeds. The incident gains notoriety at Awalt where an account of flight on the glories circulates. Nodding toward this incident, Elizabeth Hansen speaks of the magnetism that "catapulted many into unseemly advances toward" Terence. "He needed to 'leave town' on more than one occasion because the 'wrong woman' fell in love with him."[70] Convincing his parents to keep him in school in California for his 1964/65 senior year, Terence transfers south to Antelope Valley High in Lancaster, seventy miles north of Los Angeles, a school from which Frank Zappa and Captain Beefheart had graduated. In the Mojave Desert near Edwards Air Force Base, he lodges with the family of one of Joe McKenna's old war buddies, Truman. There, experiments with the glories continue. "We'd grind up a couple hundred of these things and take them in a banana milkshake and wander out into the sagebrush."[71] Stumbling forward sans measurement or mentor, rare reminiscences indicate that "everything would appear somehow more pregnant with potential meaning."[72]

In his last semester at Lancaster, Terence travels to Berkeley for Christmas vacation, where he finally scores and smokes cannabis, the herb that is soon an essential staple. Though it is not what he expected, he reports a capacity for "incredible verbal performances and extemporaneous feats of heavy lifting." Smoking ganja affords a capacity to recite pseudo chapters of *Moby-Dick* on the fly. "I could just fall into these rhetorical things and rave," he said. "But it didn't seem to be getting me off from my own point of view."[73] We know little of his senior year, other than that a showdown with Truman seems to have deepened his contempt for authorities. In Dennis's acerbic narrative: "It was Terence against the world; adults and authority figures were the enemy. J. D. Salinger's *The Catcher in the Rye* and Ayn Rand's manifestos influenced Terence's thinking heavily at the time, and validated, for him, his anti-authoritarian stance as well as his belief that it was perfectly OK to be totally selfish."[74] Terence excels at Antelope Valley. The 1965 Annual Commencement program lists Terry Kemp McKenna among a couple of hundred graduates, awarding him "Bank of America Trophy Winner in Liberal Arts." The departmental honors recipients are listed on the final page of the program, with Terence listed under "Language Arts."

At this same juncture, Watson isn't coping so well. In the summer of 1964, Rick had left home and moved into a shared house on Bryant Street in Palo Alto. As had been his vocation over previous summers, he works at the Stanford School of Medicine. Studying fluctuations in levels of steroid hormones in cancer patients, he is skilled at extraction procedures, isotope labeling, and gas chromatography, having constructed an apparatus in the family garage. There is little desire to return to school. With Terry in "exile" down in Lancaster, what was the point?[75] Rick scores a brick of weed that he blazes to excess. As ordinary highs are no longer enough, potent THC concoctions are cooked up with solvents and lab equipment lifted from the hospital.[76] He grows paranoid. His lab work suffers. And throughout this period of home experimentation, Rick is overwhelmed with a desire to get out.

Escape is hatched on a Greyhound to New York where Rick finds an introduction to Allen Ginsberg and Peter Orlovsky, and makes an unsuccessful attempt to enroll in the Bronx School of Science. Returning to Palo Alto a few weeks later, he sets up in a house on Webster Street, while working at Stanford's Lanyon Gallery. Across this period, a troupe of characters cascade through Rick's world, among them Neal Cassady, who occasionally waltzes inside the house and hovers over a vintage Smith Corona. "I always had a sheet of paper on the platen and Neal would be standing there talking a mile a minute, hitting up on my girlfriend, trying to get the keys to her Austin-Healey 3000 and typing with one hand."[77] Among Rick's friends is Merry Prankster Robert "Papa Elf" Cullenbine, a.k.a. Cully. Later president of the Midpeninsula Free University, Cully had studied economics at

Stanford and worked at Wells Fargo where he stored his stash of weed in the bank's vaults.[78] Cully took Watson to Ken Kesey's farm up at La Honda and introduced him to LSD. Subsequent to his own exposure as part of voluntary experiments at the Menlo Park Veteran's Hospital in 1960, Kesey had acquired a supply of Sandoz acid he distributed like a pied piper. Kesey's style was "controlling and manipulative," muses Watson, unimpressed with the heavy Hells Angels vibe at La Honda. Kesey was "recording people, and lacing drinks with drugs and it just seemed pretty sordid."

This scene also moved DMT into Watson's orbit. At $100 a gram, it was a huge expense for someone pulling $120 a month. The spice was hardly the go-to high in 1965. Paraphrasing Jefferson Airplane's Grace Slick, Tom Wolfe wrote in *The Electric Kool-Aid Acid Test* that "LSD is a long strange journey; DMT is like being shot out of a cannon." At La Honda, it was the preserve of the hard core. The odd balls among eight balls. Occasionally, a Prankster would take one of the Hells Angels up into their treehouse and inject him with DMT. In Wolfe's saga, Mountain Girl informs Kesey that a good hit rendered Freewheelin Frank "as naked as an Angel is ever gonna git."[79] Watson freebased DMT a dozen times at most, but its unsettling effects, described as "profoundly disturbing, or disturbingly profound,"[80] made for a substance that was used sparingly and with great respect.

The gravity of the material was discovered by the spring of '65. In another of his stories, Watson describes an epic episode with Douglas Hansen and two other friends in Los Altos. Smoking DMT, Watson and his ripped accomplices had formed a "body-mind-being." In his description, an "intricate organism of concentric vitreous transparent spheres or nested Platonic diaphanous solids" are likened to Kepler's diagram in the *Mysterium cosmographicum*, "all spinning inside each other on axes impossible to imagine in Euclidean space." There was a problem, however. The final member of the group to take a hit, named "Jerry," appeared before Rick as "a Wrathful Deity from the Tibetan pantheon, totally black." Jerry committed a cardinal error. He tried to apply the brakes. While the minds of the other three had merged, Jerry was "holding on to some dark corner of his soul." Filled with fear and suspicion, Watson wrote, he "accused me of trying to poison him."[81]

The lesson was simple. If you surrender to the experience, chances are you will become immediately familiar with a glowing "field of pure and blissful energy." Of this alluring possibility, Watson knew his most outgoing friends will be intrigued. Among the intrepid recipients was his buddy Michael Moore, who would paint an inspired work titled "DMT-TV." As a graduate student at Yale, Moore's first dose of DMT, a pinkish-amber resin, arrived by mail in New Haven care of Watson in the early spring of 1966.

But the most celebrated of Watson's graduates was up in Berkeley. While most heads, even psychedelic connoisseurs, let DMT alone, "Terry was the one who really took it up and . . . made it his life's mission. His crusade." Watson admired his friend's DMT-inspired pursuit of the mystery, and his conviction that the tryptamine wasn't simply triggering neurological noise. "That it must bear meaning. Or be a bearer of meaning":

> From that very first experience he had this hallucination, vision, of these machine-like language elves, assembling and disassembling into hyperspatial entities. They were combination of language, multidimensional tactile visual entities and living and very communicative and chattering away, and he said: "This is such a compelling experience that I cannot believe that it's meaningless. . . . This is an extraordinary experience that it must reveal some hidden reality."[82]

As for the provenance of the stuff that moved the electric elves to romance Terr, and in turn drive him to embark on a quest for their origin, Watson is ultimately uncertain. In our exchanges he conjectures that it might have passed through Bud Mills, a Triumph-riding student in Stanford's Stegner Fellowship program where Kesey workshopped *One Flew over the Cuckoo's Nest*. The Merry Pranksters had motored across the country the year before on Kesey's bus, landing in the summer of 1964 at the mansion on the 2,500-acre Millbrook estate, in Upstate New York, where Leary established the League for Spiritual Discovery. While the convergence at Castalia of the tribal chieftains (Leary and Kesey) was anticlimactic in Wolfe's account, the rapprochement did expose the "fierce roan-mad" punks to DMT produced by underground alchemist Nick Sand.[83] Given the Pranksters returned west soon after, it is not difficult to place Watson (and McKenna) in the path of some returning crystal.

But neither Watson nor McKenna knew the origins of the "mothballs." This mystery was guaranteed given Sand's outlaw profile. A fugitive from 1974 (when he jumped bail) to 1996 (when his lab in Port Coquitlam, British Columbia, was raided), Sand was subsequently imprisoned until late 2000. He was released on parole only months after McKenna was released from his body. While these circumstances did not permit corroboration, Sand warmed to the idea that his product could have spiced the bard's vision when I raised this possibility with him at Hungary's Ozora Festival in late July 2016, eight months before his own departure.

The imagination runs wild in the absence of knowledge, and sometimes in spite of it. When McKenna spoke to those gathered at the Ojai Foundation in 1993, the audience were informed that an unnamed friend (i.e., Watson) had told him that the elf-catalyzing material he'd smoked was boosted from a US Army chemical research operation down at the Stanford

Research Institute (SRI) in Menlo Park. "Someone managed to get a fifty gallon drum of this material out of the inventory without anybody knowing." McKenna was flexing his fact-mixing muscles, since the provenance of the DMT was not Army-sourced, but, according to Watson, "ear wax" from Kesey's circle.[84] McKenna's commentary on a "fifty gallon drum"—a canard which has wormed its way into popular accounts[85]—is a spectacular embellishment on the "six-inch-high cylindrical metallic containers" featuring in Watson's story "DMT, or, Spider Woman Comes to Town." That semi-fictional account relates nefarious activities at the SRI where, in the shadows of Cold War mind-control experiments under the direction of the CIA's Project MKUltra, the US Army Chemical Corps conduct classified research with psychoactive compounds tested as interrogation drugs and psychochemical-warfare agents. Upon visiting the SRI himself, Watson confirms that he knew the government had "a purer form of DMT."[86]

Behaving like a cartoon character whose growing fan base hung on his every word, McKenna was prone to animate his own stories. By the late nineties, the tale of the fifty-gallon drum of crystalline DMT grew even more legs as it was sutured to a story about the military development of the aerosol-delivered hallucinogenic incapacitant 3-quinuclidinyl benzilate, or Agent BZ. In the mid-sixties, the US Army was "trying to develop an aerosol artillery shell that would land in a Vietnamese village," and DMT, alongside other even more debilitating psychedelics, was ostensibly the focus of intensive R&D. As this "famous story in the underground" gained mileage, a drum of this material is said to have been lifted from the military. What's more, "rumor persists," Esalenites are briefed, that the drum "is not empty yet!"[87] That elements of this story are lifted and twisted to varnish an epiphany before audiences hungry for novelty perfectly illustrates the fuzzy boundary separating fact from fiction in the McKennaverse.

2 BERKELEY

2894 TELEGRAPH AVENUE

Standing on the northwest corner of Telegraph Avenue and Russell Street in Berkeley, a large rooming house is home to towering odysseys, and even taller tales. The building at 2894 Telegraph is leased to McKenna, who sublets rooms to fellow students from fall 1965 through fall 1967 (see figure 2.1). As friends gravitate to his spacious, ground-floor room, Terence unloads his wordcraft on loaded audiences. Furniture may be sparsely appointed, but there is no shortage of sativa products. With McKenna seated cross-legged on a rug, baked guests grow spellbound by his erudition and uproarious punditry. Regulars include coinhabitants Ernie Waugh, McKenna's pal from Lancaster and a fellow scholar in Joseph Tussman's Experimental College who later obtains a doctorate in English from Berkeley, and John Yenches, a brilliant North Carolina alum. Steve Jurist from Los Angeles pays regular visits, as do other scholars from Joe's College, like Royce Kelley, and Berkeley local Michael Malcolm. Sharing McKenna's interest in Tibetan art, Malcolm later completes a degree in religious studies, mastering Tibetan and Sanskrit, and becomes a successful dealer and curator of Asian art at Doris Wiener's gallery on Madison Avenue.

Malcolm recalls McKenna's centripetal influence on this scene. Unsurpassingly quick-witted, a marvelous raconteur, and "a source of endless, Joycean pleasure."[1] As long as the hash is available, so are the roving disquisitions, and McKenna is driven to acquire the finest material. Among he and Malcolm's favored smoking dens is a curtained booth in a joint on Telegraph named "The Only Afghani Restaurant in the United States." Another Tussmanite and frequenter of Terry's bedroom is his consort Stephanie (Stefi), a charming, smart, and beautiful companion with whom he is involved for eighteen months.

FIGURE 2.1
2894 Telegraph Avenue, Berkeley, 1939. The structure seen at the front of the property is removed by 1965. Photo courtesy of Berkeley Architectural Heritage Association.

An Experimental College freshman, George Csicsery, becomes familiar with Terence's salons. For the summer of 1966, he and another Tussmanite, his girlfriend, Kevin Mahoney, sublet a ground-floor room. A student of comparative religion and later writer and filmmaker, Csicsery frequently spars with McKenna. Csicsery graduated from a boarding school in Buffalo, New York, founded by refugee Piarist priests where he acquired working knowledge of Eliade, Jung, Emile Durkheim, Max Weber, among other thinkers. That the extremely well-read McKenna was sans any formal training impresses Csicsery.[2] Disillusionment with the sociopolitical moment is never far from the surface: "Terry's political stance was always bound up with his cosmological perspective that we were in a transformative phase that marked the end of a certain kind of civilization and the beginning of something superior." While his sparring partner is preoccupied with Teilhard de Chardin and McLuhan, Csiscery cleaves to Jacques Ellul, the critic of technology whom he placed in opposition to the "polyanna-ish McLuhanism" then popular.[3]

Elizabeth Hansen admired McKenna for his mind and his humor. He was the center of social gravity. Exposed to this scene as girlfriend of Royce

Kelley, then as a student of art and philosophy at UC Berkeley, and then partner to Malcolm for eleven years, Hansen pursued interests in Sanskrit, Tibetan Buddhism, and Chinese language and calligraphy, later acquiring degrees in art and landscape architecture. She recalls the social gatherings forming at Terry's abodes, which while typically sportive, occasionally attracted drama. On one evening, Tussmanite and later writer of pulp porn Arthur Schmidt finds himself in a commotion with McKenna, and is eventually pitched off the porch. Known to some as a controlling "jerk," others defend their host against charges of control and manipulation. "A lot of people are jealous of the magnetism that Terence had and try to explain it away in all manner of psychologisms," said Hansen, rallying to her friend's side. "He was not a tyrant," and nor did he "command attendance to satisfy his ego."[4]

Elizabeth later married Douglas Hansen, McKenna's friend from Mountain View who sublet a room at 2894 in September 1966. "[We] felt like [the Telegraph house] was the center of the universe, or at least of the revolution that was exploding all around us," recalls Douglas Hansen.[5] McKenna had by then moved to Tunnel Road in the Berkeley Hills, while maintaining control of the lease on Telegraph.

Kevin Mahoney (see figure 2.2) develops a crush on Terry McKenna. He has a strong will. He is lanky, has poor eyesight, and totes a dog-eared copy of *Ulysses*. She has a standard poodle named Orpheus who follows her everywhere, including to the revolution. Terence says she is not unlike "Cassandra," she who speaks the truth but whom no one believes. Mahoney identifies with that. "No one took me very seriously intellectually . . . because I was just a young blonde fashionista." But the anthropology student and one-time manager of the Nova boutique on Telegraph Avenue—about a block up from Shambhala Books, at one time managed by Malcolm—is no vacant blonde. She would earn a BA and BSc from UC Berkeley, later an MA in accountancy, and in 1978 becomes one of the first women to enter the IT field, in which she led a successful career.

"There was a lot of things to love about Terry," Kevin recalls. The details mattered. The Rapidograph pen deftly wielded to compress text into confined spaces. The cheap black umbrella sported everywhere in these non-drought Berkeley years. The infuriating dedication to unusual words—like "declension" and "adumbration"—lifted from the dictionary and inflicted upon unassuming folks daily. The framed photograph of family hound Skelly at his desk. The pooch had been Terence's constant companion throughout his childhood. "The day that he told his parents that he was not coming back to Colorado . . . the dog died."

FIGURE 2.2
Kevin Mahoney, Berkeley, 1965. Photo by Michael Rossman, courtesy of George Csicsery.

His faithfulness is a standout too. As far as Kevin knew, if Terry "was with a woman that was the woman he was with." And then there was the radicalism. Terry owned a television, and watching the Vietnam War on the evening news became a routine spectacle, as was his gloss on the unfolding horror. Amid the escalating street protests, Kevin and Terence meet at countless demonstrations, not occasionally legging it from the cops. Not least of all, they share a conservative Irish Catholic background—from which they were both "recovering." The connection gave Mahoney the means to "get" Terence, she said. "My older brother was very much like Terry in that he would pontificate for hours and by golly you wouldn't interrupt him cause he'd put you down," she laughs.[6]

While the Telegraph House became something of a psychedelic incubator, Terence had his first, and perhaps most bizarre, acid trip in San Francisco immediately before moving to Berkeley. It was the summer of 1965. He had just moved up from Lancaster, took a job as a busboy, and was living in a flophouse in the shadows of an overpass at the edge of Tenderloin. The peculiar tenant across the hall replaced his white light bulbs with red ones and the windows were painted black. Barry "the Fish" Melton, who introduces McKenna to cannabis and LSD, will soon shoot to fame as lead guitarist of Country Joe and the Fish, later passing the bar to become a California state public defender. Melton is the source of a white capsule of Sandoz LSD McKenna drops one night at a house on Green Street. In one telling, the audience is regaled with a story of how Terence "completely came to pieces" on this virgin outing. As he reported, "I disgraced myself in several dimensions that nobody's ever been willing to explain to me fully since. I gather my sexuality, my bowels, my everything else just went into a tizzy!"[7]

Another retelling ventures more detail on the never-to-be-revisited place to which he was transported that night. When the trip set in, "the universe divided itself into two opposing concept entities." On the one hand, there were the *"losteks."* They are "profound, the very essence of solidity, meaning, and being," with their presence accompanied by the organ tone in Bach's Mass in B Minor. The antithesis to this humorless and "Godly" entity were the *"Pinkastares,"* embodying "all the silliness that fills in the cracks between the *losteks*." The *Pinkastares* were "fragmented, small, jumpy, brightly colored, and trebly." The difference between these entities was like "the contrast between Wagner and a child's music box." Terence oscillated between these polar worlds. He would announce "The *losteks*," before melting in awe. Then he'd say, ". . . and the *Pinkastares*," which issued "gales of laughter and rolling around on the floor."[8] After a couple of hours of pronouncing the two words, and enacting the disparate sensibilities of their occupants, his company grew restless. Those witness to this raw psychedelic pantomime had never seen anything like it. By 4 am, Terence was booted out onto the stoop.

Loose on the streets of San Francisco, there were eight hours before his job started in a restaurant about thirty blocks away.[9] He took the trolley up Nob Hill to Grace Cathedral, the massive Episcopal church on California Street. "I let myself in and proceeded to have a religious epiphany in the realization that they'd gotten it all wrong—it was the rose window that was God."[10] What happens next reads like screenplay inspired by Pynchon's *The Crying of Lot 49*. He wanders across the street to the Masonic Grand Lodge of California:

> The great doors stood open and I walked into the immense lobby. I walked into an elevator. There were only five floors. I pushed floor five. The elevator went up to the fifth floor. I stepped out and found myself in the foyer of a theater, a performance space. Nobody seemed to be around, so I walked through these velvet curtains into this vast theater with rows and rows of empty seats down to the proscenium. Hung over the stage was this enormous banner about twenty feet across. Emblazoned on it was the letter M.[11]

"Gee, you shouldn't have!" McKenna blushes.[12]

Later in '65, now dwelling at 2894 Telegraph Avenue, destiny takes the form of a 500-microgram Sandoz capsule. Terence embarks on this adventure holding deep resentment toward his parents and their lifestyle. "I was dark, into Jean Genet, Albert Camus—an existential brat." His politics amounted to "half-baked Marxism." But that "Terence" dissipated in "complete boundary dissolution and love." In a single trip, he claims, "all my animosity toward my parents, all my ambivalence toward my sexuality, everything was replaced with the force of revelation."[13] The incident is pivotal to a mode of thinking that he later took on the road: that psychedelics *dissolve boundaries*. "Every cultural game is about the accentuation and stress of difference, and in the absence of the perception of difference, in the absence of boundaries there is a transformative release."[14] His experience that day under that tree is explained in a later interview:

> I remember being nineteen years old, twelve hours into an LSD trip. I was sitting under a tree and I just started to weep, and I saw what my upbringing had done to me. I saw the resentment of my parents and my callowness and my immaturity and I sat there for about an hour and cried this stuff out. And got up a better person . . . and then I could call up my parents and tell them and I could accept their Catholicism and their conservatism and the differences. It was just like ten years of psychotherapy in an hour.[15]

The newfound attitude appeared to extend to his brother, toward whom Terence grows protective. Since he felt guilty about traumatizing Dennis, recalls Mahoney, "he wanted to make sure that we all treated Dennis very well." In Terence's eyes, "Dennis could do no wrong."[16]

The acid in question is likely to have again arrived care of the Fish, who is once again McKenna's neighbor. Melton now lives across the intersection next to Jabberwock, the former jazz and then psychedelic rock club favored among students on the corner of Telegraph and Russell. Having just released their debut *Electric Music for the Mind and Body*, a defining freak album of the era, Country Joe and the Fish are the house band at Jabberwock, diagonally opposite 2894 (see figure 2.3).

FIGURE 2.3
Jabberwock, 2901 Telegraph Avenue, Berkeley, 1965. Photo courtesy of Berkeley Architectural Heritage Association.

It is via Melton that a one-gram (one million micrograms) ampoule of pure Sandoz acid comes into the picture. Over one night in 1965 or 1966, Terry and Rick transfer the ampoule's contents to gelatin capsules containing milk sugar. To cap the lot, they were getting a 5–10 percent cut. Rick uses a microsyringe to drop 500-microgram doses of Hofmann's "medicine for the soul" in each capsule, while Terry does the capping. They could do a few hundred an hour. Trouble is that by morning the acid dissolved and retarded the capsules. They were midwives to nearly 2,000 crippled disasters. A fiasco it may have been, but there is nothing wrong with the quality of the material. Where Rick was careful to avoid dosing himself, Terry set caution to the wind. When they finish, he flushes out the ampoule with orange juice, gulps it down, and begins the ascent. At sunrise, Stephanie joins them for a trek up Strawberry Canyon. Watson has no precise recall of how his share of the shriveled caps were moved or where they ended up. Perhaps we shouldn't be surprised given that, at 500 micrograms a pop, precise recall is a challenging feat (Owsley Stanley's contemporaneous "Blue Cheer" tablets were 250 micrograms). There is a failed bid to move the stuff on a biker gang in Haight Street. The scene turned nasty when Watson tried to collect. "I didn't pursue it," he says. "By this time the Haight was a very bad place."[17] Over the next few years, the hip Disneyland of Haight-Ashbury is "filled with juvi-junkie consumers . . . a mini-parody of America at large."[18]

During his residence at Telegraph Avenue—September '65 through September '66—McKenna discovers that DMT can animate the psychedelic experience. While he sings its praises, LSD alone fails to deliver the visions expected upon reading classical sources like Havelock Ellis's *The Dance of Life* and S. Weir Mitchell's 1896 "Essay on Mescaline Intoxication." He craves what Ellis was on, which yielded visions of "Jeweled ruins and phosphorescent maidens in diaphanous gowns, howling demon songs beneath a violet moon."[19] However, the visions do arrive when priming DMT with LSD, as transpired in the earliest DMT phase. In fact, the combo sets the stage for one of his life's "high water weirdness events." During Easter 1966, Terence is alone in his room traversing the DMT space on a strong acid foundation when interrupted by an upstairs resident, a wild theater major named Rosemary, who came rapping on his bedroom door for what seemed like an eternity. The trip is ruptured such that, leaping out of his entranced state, the inhabitants of hyperspace are pulled back into the room with him. As he opens the door with "an elf hanging off each hand," Rosemary is greeted with a stream of alien syntax: "whey ducwham waxebo gwhani haptigo butix shning."[20]

In fall 1966, still holding the lease at 2894, Terry takes up residence at 151 Tunnel Road in Berkeley. On a steep sloping property, and accessible from the road above, his modest room is poised above three rickety flights of Escher-like stairs. Amid the lofty, bookcase-lined room sits a pool table, around which Terence dwells. An arboreal respite from the bustle of Telegraph Avenue, Tunnel Road is the perfect place to complete the first phase of his Berkeley studies. As Douglas Hansen vividly recalls, Terry always had the best hash, smoked in his brass water pipe. The scene at Chez McKenna is select. Hansen, a regular, never sees more than four people in the room at one time. He also never sees McKenna take to speed or hard liquor.[21] He was not to suffer addictions of the kind known by forebears like Ludlow (opium), Burroughs (heroin), or Watts (alcohol), although cannabis became an unassailable habit. He avoids the scene that, by 1967, devastates Haight-Ashbury, and takes a terrible toll on some Telegraph House occupants. Speed apparently turns Yenches into "a fallen angel," and compels others like Hansen to escape Berkeley altogether.[22]

The "intellectual nest in the trees" is a source of fond memories for Sara Hartley. From New York's Upper East Side, with interests in archaeology and photography, Hartley is another Tussman scholar drawn into McKenna's orbit. "Intelligent, with a slightly feral twist to her gawkish sexuality," he writes of Hartley in his memoir. "Her large brown eyes cannot hide a kitten cruelty and a mean love of puns."[23] At Tunnel Road, she recalls discussion passing from Heidegger and Husserl to McLuhan and Joyce, as the hash pipe circulated. She'd read little, and it was all quite intimidating. But she grew fond of his "brilliant shmooze," as rich and expansive as any good drug. And as Hartley elaborates, the captivating raconteur was also welcoming toward women. At a time when women were sidelined in discourse, Elizabeth Hansen similarly recalls how her contributions were received by Terry "with the full empathy that he extended to the men in the room." The "pinch of grandiosity" he assumed was never, thought Hartley, motivated by hunger for personal power.[24]

A DEGREE IN SHAMANIC STUDIES

With an intent to major in history, McKenna sought to specialize in intellectual history, taught at Berkeley by Carl E. Schorske, who had sided with the student protests during the Free Speech Movement. It's possible McKenna is among the standing-room-only audiences Schorske attracted when lecturing on European history and philosophy. "The first history teacher that I had," McKenna reminisces, "was a wonderful old man who really, now that I look back on it, taught the history of ideas."[25] Arriving in San Francisco during the heat of the Cold War, at the peak of the lunar space quest, and at the height of the era's experiments in consciousness expansion, McKenna is among an exclusive cohort accepted into the first year of a two-year Experimental College program founded by the chairman of Berkeley's department of philosophy, Joseph Tussman. In 1965, he is selected among the 150 incoming freshmen entering the College of Letters and Sciences. The two-year experiment, conducted twice between 1965 and 1969, was inspired by Alexander Meiklejohn's pioneering Experimental College at the University of Wisconsin, where Tussman was a student. In the midst of the era's campus turmoil, Tussman created a program of study as a "way of life" and, apropos the influence of classic Greek philosophy, as "an initiation into the great mandatory political role."[26]

Replacing the first two years of undergraduate study and structured as a "big questions" program divided into four semesters—Greece during the Peloponnesian Wars, seventeenth-century England, the period of the adoption of the US Constitution, and contemporary America—"Joe's College" was designed for highly motivated students. Priced at $150 per semester, the program involved two lectures a week, with many seminars and informal discussions taking place in an old fraternity house at the edge of campus.[27] Besides one course per semester, students were ungraded. According to Dennis, "evaluations were based on intense dialogues with faculty members and fellow students, and extensive, eclectic reading lists that participants were encouraged to develop on their own."[28] Given that Terence signed up for the first of the two programs, his was the "experimental" Experimental College, involving, as Tussman himself conceded, "more chaos . . . than I was happy with."[29] After completing the 1965–1967 program, Terence traveled around the world, eventually returning to Berkeley and graduating in 1975 with a BSc degree in conservation and resource management.

As Dennis observes, "Tussman did exactly what any smart philosophy professor trained in Socratic dialogue would do: He dared Terence to think for himself." As independent as his thought was, McKenna maintained the flame ignited by Tussman's understanding that humans are "so delicately poised between the bestial and the angelic."[30] Terence claims to have had an excellent relationship with Tussman, who not only possessed the same first name as his father, but apparently resembled Joe McKenna—an irony given the latter considered Berkeley "the epicenter of the degeneracy that was sweeping the younger generation."[31] Whether or not Terence saw Tussman as his "intellectual father," as Dennis claims, he was a figure with whom he, in Csicsery's recollection, "sparred regularly."[32] The impression he left is apparent in Tussman's 1967 letter of recommendation. "Mr. McKenna . . . is a person of very unusual gifts. He is intelligent and articulate, very independent, and capable of hard work. He has a great capacity for leadership . . . is quite original and widely perceptive. He is destined to do outstanding work."[33]

At Joe's College, McKenna takes a philosophy course taught by Paul Feyerabend, future author of *Against Method*, who is said to have remarked at the beginning of his Epistemology 101 course, "I will teach you to recognize the truth and I will teach you to ask the question, 'What's so great about it?'"[34] McKenna is likewise exposed to the psychohistorical teachings of political science professor Norman Jacobson. The first two years of what he eventually calls a degree in "shamanic studies" sees McKenna school himself in Eliade, phenomenology via a course offered by Hubert Dreyfus, Jungian psychology, Marshall McLuhan, hermetic philosophy, and alchemy, adding to this an interest in Asian and Renaissance art and modernist literature, whereupon he acquires a cache of tropes with which to translate in rare eloquence his navigations of the mind.

It is pivotal that McKenna is exposed to his DMT flash at the beginning of his education at UC Berkeley, the counterculture's educational headwaters where he undertakes a self-directed study in the history and philosophy of shamanism. This extraordinary research, coupled with a radical extracurricular program, makes for an unorthodox take on shamanism. With an exclusive interest in narcotic shamanism, McKenna later declares that "a shaman is a true anarchist."[35] That which he deemed *shamanic* was unlike anything taught in Anthropology 101.

The quieter Tunnel Road digs appeared suited to Terence's intellectual development in the wake of his psychedelic ground zero. He realized not only the tired cliché that "everything you know is wrong," but also that, as he stated in reflection on this mid-sixties Berkeley juncture, "whatever is true cannot even be imagined." It was a potent threshold, a moment of upheaval—socially and personally. The era was driven by inquiry, as was recollected before a rapt and cracked-up audience twenty-five years later. "Just what *is* going on?!" Decades of reflection enabled insight. "The good stuff can take pressure," McKenna came to understand. "If something is real, you can stretch it. You can test it. It doesn't require belief." Such was his great intellectual watershed. "The understanding that belief, of any sort, was a kind of encumbrance to the relationship that I was attempting to have with what I was naïvely calling 'reality.' That was the thing." What seemed revelatory in the radical psychedelic empiricism forged in this protean era of experimentalism is that this discovery was independent from any system, program, author, or body. And since he was never part of a "secret society" as such, he never felt constrained to talk about it. "Nobody swore me to silence."[36]

While quaffing from a deep and widening carafe of wisdom, McKenna's outlook upon entering UC Berkeley is shaped by a triad of intellectual inspirations. The abiding influence of Jung, Eliade, and McLuhan is evident in McKenna's final dissertation for the Tussman program, "The Future of Magic in Electronic Societies," submitted in the summer of 1966. Given the threat of "absolute destruction" observed from his perch amid the growing strife, McKenna aimed to ascertain the future role of the shaman. As a confident polemic on the nature of time, with heavy doses of prophecy and prescience, the work alludes to an "electronic media network" comprising a disembodied "world-wide symbiotic organism." Projecting thought on the coming "electronically-maintained eschatology," the effort contains the kernel of ideas on the end of history that preoccupies its author until his own end-time.[37]

How much credence should we invest in the sophomoric thoughts of a nineteen-year-old? While puzzling and grandiose, if not breathlessly utopian, "The Future of Magic in Electronic Societies" is an early layer of the

McKennan palimpsest. The work gropes its way toward a redemptive vision which, with the "electronic shaman" at the tiller, promises to escape the "terror of history."[38] Resisting the "technologized, dehumanized orgy of rationalism" and crying out for an "archetypal renewal," mythic time grows possible through the development of "solid state" electronic circuitry. And as the new "eschatological mode of existence" will enable humankind to enter an essentially "unchanging state"[39] in which we will escape not only history, but ritual and culture too, we stumble into the wet dream of a nerd-prince saturated with the raw input of his intellectual triad. Before we continue, a whistlestop tour of Jung, Eliade, and McLuhan, and their significance for McKenna, is necessary.[40]

In a 1991 address to the Carl Jung Society of greater Los Angeles, McKenna worked the crowd with the claim that his greatest desire as a young man was to become a Jungian analyst.[41] He had developed an interest in the analytical psychologist well before "the Jungians" ruined the party. Readily admitting his status as a "tin-pot" Jungian, the fascination is selective and shaped by an irresolvable contradiction. "I have to confess to you," he says to another audience, "I'm not that interested in my own personal stuff."[42] The gravitation to Jung reveals an intellectual interest in the visionary character and transpersonal weight of symbolism. Where psychotherapy and the operations of "the shadow" are of limited interest, Jung's later work holds appeal. Noteworthy are the alchemy studies the *Mysterium Coniunctionis* and *Aion: Researches into the Phenomenology of the Self*, the influence of Valentinian Gnosticism, and the work on "flying saucers."

McKenna grew ambivalent about the applicability of Jung's ideas. As much as Jung's *Collected Works* provide a lingua franca to parse the unconscious, he contended that the flood of visual imagery associated with the DMT event is not assimilable to the contents of the individual or collective unconscious.[43] Whereas for Jung, the opus involved heeding the inner voice in one's visions and dreams, for McKenna, "the work" is performed, and the inner voice beheld, downstream from one's synergistic metabolism of "hallucinogenic" plant molecules. McKenna's dialogue with the mushroom *logos* compares with Jung's commerce with the collective unconscious. If the unconscious was like a depthless ocean upon which the dreamer nightly drifts, McKenna waxed lyrical on the fisherman-like nature of the psychedelic experience, where the "creative act is to let down the net of human imagination into the ocean of chaos on which we are suspended and attempt to bring out ideas."[44] McKenna defended the psilocybean *logos*—and the broader world of psychoactively triggered hallucinatory experiences that are historically dismissed as false if not pathological—in a fashion not

FIGURE 2.4
The fisherman (Terry, about eight years old). Photo courtesy of Dennis McKenna.

dissimilar to Jung's defense of the unconscious from its dismissal as the path of error and equivocation. Just as it was difficult in the early twentieth century for Jung's contemporaries "to accept the counterweight to the conscious world," as Jung wrote in *Memories, Dreams, Reflections*, by the century's end, McKenna waged his own battles as a medium for the hallucinatory world.[45] Most compelling for the young McKenna was that the process Jung knew as "individuation" was informed by the symbolism of alchemy from antiquity to the Middle Ages. In their dissolutions, decoctions, and distillations of the *prima materia*—the transmutation of matter, ostensibly into gold—Jung saw alchemists literalizing and externalizing inner spiritual process, a transcendent function evidently transposed in McKenna's own temporal mythopoetics (i.e., the Timewave; see chapter 9).

Among the immediately jarring factors in McKenna's embrace of Jung, and a reason he avoided identifying as a Jungian, was Jung's dismissal of hallucinogens. Disparaging the use of psychedelics in psychotherapy, Jung held that LSD and mescaline initiated "ersatz" religious experiences. Influenced by the view prevailing in fifties psychiatry that these drugs were responsible for "psychomimetic" (psychosis mimicking) experiences, and compounded by their prohibition, by the late sixties Jungians largely rejected psychoactive compounds for therapeutic purposes.[46] The position could hardly have been more remote from the views McKenna began formulating—informed by Huxley, and inspired by personal experience. As tryptamines and other plant compounds are the *prima materia* metabolized in the alembics and retorts of the mind, the discourse of alchemy is adopted in the service of the objective that Jung recognized as the great redemptive work of the self: the merging of spirit and matter, the production of the "philosopher's stone." "The stone" became such a baked-in obsession that McKenna saw it everywhere. "It's the universal panacea at the end of time. It's the chocolate cake that your mother made once a week when you were a child. It is the *pana supersubstantialis*. It's all things to all men and all women."[47]

Complementary to Jung, Romanian historian of religion Mircea Eliade held appeal for McKenna, who ransacked the history of ideas to find clues to his ontological upheaval. By the time he entered college, McKenna had working knowledge of Eliade's corpus. *Cosmos and History, The Sacred and the Profane*, and *Shamanism: Archaic Techniques of Ecstasy*,[48] among other works, formed a combined resource excavated in the quest to apprehend his "N,N-unspeakable" *hierophany*. If in Eliade's philosophy of religion a *hierophany* is an awareness of "a wholly different order" transcending the profane world of the everyday, then McKenna behaved as if he had blown a new hole in the sacred.

The moment of *elf realization* was all the-more astonishing for a figure born into the *"desacralized cosmos"* of the twentieth century.[49] While cautiously eliding mention of his psychedelic path to the *other* in his earliest student work, later McKenna sought to re-establish dialogue with the "archaic" by means of the hero-shaman. In the eighties, the "archaic revival" leitmotif drew from Eliade's idea that "archaic man" resists the "terror of history" through the repetitious return to *ecstasis*. As eventually conveyed in *Food of the Gods*, the original *ecstasis* relied on a cult of Goddess, cattle, and psilocybin mushroom worship whose roots reach back to ancient rites that "dissolve the boundaries of the ego, and reunite the worshiper with the personified vegetable matrix of planetary life."[50] While Eliade serves as an early mystic theologian in McKenna's quest to comprehend his breakthrough into "hyperspace," and lent credence to his "stoned ape" hypothesis, he challenged Eliade's early views—that Eliade later modified—that shamanic ecstasies induced by inebriants are inauthentic, decadent, and corrupting. Given the growing climate of distaste—on the grounds of romanticism, Eurocentrism, and intellectual colonialism—directed toward Eliade's approach to shamanism (and religion), notably in Michael Taussig's *Shamanism, Colonialism, and the Wild Man* (1987)—of which McKenna wrote a glowing review[51]—his deference to Eliade quieted in later years.

While Jung and Eliade were colleagues in the community of religionists known as the "Eranos circle," the third scholar in the trinity, Canadian media theorist Marshall McLuhan, was outside the box. McKenna was not only drawn to McLuhan's contention that the Western mind had become, with the advent of movable type and the Gutenberg printing press, imprisoned in a kind of cultural strait-jacket of linear space and Euclidean time. The quicksilver mind who transmitted these thoughts became a permanent star in McKenna's firmament since McLuhan was identifying a "psychic impoverishment" from which humanity was now becoming liberated.

For McLuhan, the "mechanical bride" to which modern users of technology were once wed had been set free by the redeeming and retribalizing power of electricity. Such was the position in *Understanding Media*, where electrical networks are extensions of the human nervous system, externalizing human consciousness in a techno-matrix. As an expression of its presumed ability to collapse space and generate a "global village," McLuhan held that the computer promises "a Pentecostal condition of universal understanding and unity."[52] McKenna is heir to the divine providence of electronic media presaging a new "happening" where, as McLuhan held, "everything resonates with everything else," a prophesy of complete human interdependence. Catnip for McKenna, such ideas evolved as the academic restrictions on his psychedelic eschaton lifted and he bailed out of academia.

If all media are "extensions of man" that transform our environment, it was McKenna's contention that "hallucinogens" ought to be considered among such extensions. Unlike Jung and Eliade, McLuhan is early received as a "turned on" intellect. While the idea that McLuhan was "experienced" is a fantasy from which McKenna became disabused, McLuhan's enigmatic characteristics earned him honorary status. In McKenna's 1989 *Mondo 2000* review of *The Letters of Marshall McLuhan*, the curtain lifts on the "Godfather of Cyberpunk," who is remembered as a "polarizing force." While "flippant, wigged-out, and incomprehensible" for squares, McLuhan was welcomed as "one of us" by Terence and friends, who searched for telltale signs of McLuhan's personal participation in the sixties experiment. He gave permission, so it seemed to McKenna's cohort, for the emergent youth culture to "finally, mercifully dismantle linear stuffed-shirt Western Civilization." For those who cracked his cryptic code, McLuhan was leading the charge of "global tribalism and fucking in the streets."[53] Alas, study of his letters revealed an Anglo-Canadian conservative who possessed the "zeal of a Catholic convert." Indeed, McLuhan converted from his Baptist roots to Roman Catholicism as a young man. While he may have "accurately nailed the attraction of psychedelic drugs" for electrified youth "turning on" to a world of instant information, McLuhan dismissed the potential of psychedelics to augment intelligence or enable cognitive flexibility.[54] When *Playboy* forced the inquiry, McLuhan admitted he had never taken LSD. "I'm an observer in these matters, not a participant." A further clarification suggests a prescient connection with McKenna that no one saw coming: "I had an operation last year to remove a tumor that was expanding my brain in a less pleasant manner, and during my prolonged convalescence I'm not allowed any stimulant stronger than coffee."[55] Such disappointments aside, while McLuhan dismissed psychedelic prosthetics as "media," McKenna, adapting his provocative discourse, witnessed psychedelic media affording humanity a return, not to medieval "sense ratios" but to an authentic state of immediacy he associated with shamanism.

Spurred by his mid-sixties DMT experience, McKenna cherrypicked and stored Jung's "depth" approach, Eliade's "integrative" method, and McLuhan's "mosaic" style in his thought toolbox. With his mind open toward the "hyperspatial zeitgeist," their ideas formed the basic conceptual architecture for an understanding of the collective "post electric" unconscious—which is the obsessive focus of a futurist manifesto produced during the UC Berkeley interregnum (1967–1970).

ELF REALIZATION

From his early Berkeley phase, McKenna was driven by an independent course of study that becomes a preoccupation for his remaining days. He embarks on a life-long quest. It is a life of the witness who has been exposed to the unspeakable, and of the seeker whose objective ever lies beyond reach. Jung, Eliade, and McLuhan offer useful models, but each suffer from limitations and are ultimately unsatisfying, as are countless thinkers and sources digested and regurgitated over the next three-and-a-half-decades. Vividly remembering his pal's epiphany in February 1966, Watson recalls that McKenna announced how he would "devote his life" to uncovering its origins and meaning.[56] From that moment on, goofy-footing the waves breaking between the dimensions, the accidental occultist comported himself as a dimension surfer bent on accessing, decoding, and tweaking the mechanics, aesthetics, and phenomenology of hyperspace. He became a restless surfer of the surreal and medium of the impossible.

McKenna's protean zeal is reminiscent of Ludlow, who recalled his formative experience eating hashish in 1855: "Till I die, that moment of unveiling will stand in clear relief from all the rest of my existence. . . . The years of all my earthly life to come can never be as long as those thirty seconds."[57] Or we may find common ground in the drive of radical hashish evangelist Paschal Beverly Randolph. "I gained more light [from hashish] than from all the 'spiritual' experiences of my entire life—real, positive, genuine, unutterable light—nor has my soul ever parted with one jot of that light to this day."[58] Apparently unaware of this occultist proponent of "Affectional Alchemy" who is an upstream actor in an American utopian psychonaut tradition, seized by the "DMT flash" more than a century later, McKenna sought its traces in psychology, philosophy, art history, architecture, literature, cinema, and culture. Before returning to late sixties Berkeley, I take further pause to broach a (non-exhaustive) set of targets, suspects, and tropes upon which McKenna set his sights—all of which signal life after the appearance of "Terence McKenna."

Our zealous prowler of the higher dimensions searched in vain for it in the art world. "Verrocchio never saw it. Michelangelo didn't anticipate it. Yeats didn't know. Blake hadn't a clue. Melville wasn't briefed."[59] There was no wrinkle of it, "not an *atom* of the presence of this thing," in the carpets of Central Asia or in the visions of an Arcimboldo or a Fra Angelico or a Bosch.[60] If art is "a probing of the unknown," then why do painters, from Early Renaissance to Abstract Expressionists, give no hint? "We've had Beccafumi, Pollock, Piero della Francesca, but nobody got near this, not even the Surrealists." And yet, as Charles Hayes was informed, "here's this experience that leaves you absolutely quaking. It's like an aesthetic orgasm, a Niagara of beauty, but alien beauty."[61] At other times, it had the qualities of an outrageous jest and the ambiguity of a pun. And yet while it possessed the "zany, impossible, improbable, hysterical revelation of the joke,"[62] it was remote from any known amusement, and could not be pegged as any *thing* of the kind.

Dissatisfaction was felt further afield. Pushed to describe the architecture of an "other space" that is beautiful, veridical, and yet utterly bizarre, *it* is fleetingly described to Will Noffke as "an Arabian maelstrom of color and form" in which "one senses somehow the Sistine Chapel, the Kaaba and Konark. A hyperdimensional infundibulum, if you will." No further insight on this trio of sacred sites was forthcoming. Moreover, dwelling in a time before the "visionary art" that came to pervade the psychedelic art scene, the restless student of art history was astonished that the history of art is typically devoid of *it*.[63]

Typically but not absolutely. While desultory that its traces were generally absent in art, clues *were* uncovered in *Finnegans Wake*. If *Ulysses* was the "algebra" of literature, as was claimed, *Finnegans Wake* is the "partial differential equation." The work's rich seams were mined throughout McKenna's life, with the *Wake* loved not only for Joyce's depth of humor, or because it celebrates complexity and the human journey sans judgment from its author, but because reading it was not unlike a psychedelic trip. In Joyce's masterpiece, there are no fixed identities, only allegory within allegory, and resonant temporal cycles. It is as if one has "taken the entirety of the last thousand years of human history and dissolved all the boundaries." In *Finnegans Wake*, Joyce seems to have come closest among authors to "pushing the entire contents of the universe down into about fourteen cubic inches." These observations derive from "Surfing on *Finnegans Wake*," a seminal Esalen appearance which could have passed as the output of a Joycean scholar. Surfing the *Wake*, McKenna ultimately achieves a breakthrough on the nature of language. Forging a world from the word, accomplishing the distillation of our experience of "what it is to be human," no work came closer to literary alchemy.[64]

Another of McKenna's favorite authors, Russian-American novelist Vladimir Nabokov, is also plausibly evocative. As apparent in *The Gift* and *Ada*, Nabokov possesses a remarkable capacity to convey unseen realms, the *potustoronnost*, or the "otherworld."[65] There is likewise occasion for simpatico in filmmaker Federico Fellini, as the DMT event and the Italian director's films, notably *Amarcord*, are seen to hold a common undercurrent in the circus, with all of its kinky shadowiness. Scenes in *Giulietta degli spiriti* are reported to be "drenched" with the psychedelic tryptamine trance. If traces of this trance are evident in cultural form, they appear to have been located less in "high" expressions than in lower, erotic, and grotesque forms. With McKenna enjoying the opportunity to compare his experience with a great many others, and by then entering therapy himself, in the late eighties the "archetype of the circus" is felt to rule over the liminal DMT realm.[66] Of notable appearance in this ludic space are clowns, recognizable as none other than the self-transforming machine elves, who stumble over themselves to win the observer's gaze. The erotic is an undeniable feature of this archetype. Despite the earlier perception that depth psychology offers little reward for grokking the DMT space, McKenna works with an early memory, gazing on high to witness a woman acrobat in a tiny spangled costume suspended only by her teeth. "I got it," he discloses. "Death and Eros." He says he was aged three or four. "I was wrapped up in something and being held." And, confessing this "kinky undercurrent" from the underside of his youth, "I was horny as hell."[67]

There is perhaps no metaphor more fitting for DMT than the circus, which, for Terry, meant the Cherry Days festival, celebrated in Paonia on July Fourth. On Cherry Days, when the carnival was in town, he and Dennis weren't allowed to stay out after 9:30 p.m. Perverse, miscreant, alluring, some dark-skinned, the carnies were at large, unpacking their outlandish wonders, "bilking all the rubes," before moving on again. It was a seasonal perturbation of the local scene and utterly captivating. "Every kid worth his salt wants to run off with the circus."[68]

As mischievous as it was, the jest is never far from the quest, with psychedelic safaris frequently noted to inaugurate exposure to The Mysteries. As we'll see, in his earliest written account of the molecule, McKenna imagines DMT as the quickest route to "The One." While all available superlatives deriving from art, mysticism, and metaphysics came up short, the DMT event is championed in "Post Electric Thought" as the most contemporary, numinous, and productive in the perennial quest to uncover "the mystery."[69] While utopian discourse is retained throughout his life, the perennialist approach is discontinued in step with the investigation's shamanic turn—where clues were to be unearthed, even while discontent with traditional studies of shamanism and religion. On the public circuit, the compulsion, McKenna later stated, was to locate the essence of visions in Nepal (where we travel in the next chapter). Would traces of the DMT trance be tracked down in the art of the old pantheon? Central Asian Tibetan shamanism had, he conjectured, "created astronauts of inner space" who had "good recon" in this area. Enthralled by the Dharmapalas, McKenna claims to have become immersed in studies of the guardians of the Dharma, deciding, however, that ultimately there too it was inaccessible.[70]

In the wide-ranging search for an ontological engine with which to test his intuitions of the *other* and, at odds with a persistent claim that the grail will not be located in "esoteric traditions," one framework had a tenacious hold on McKenna's imagination. Interpolated through a sci-fi template, Gnosticism, notably Mandaeism, provides an enduring narrative framework deployed to articulate the tryptaminal experience associated with metabolizing DMT and psilocybin. Mandaeism is the Late Antique Mesopotamian baptismal movement that McKenna knew to be the oldest continuous Western religion with a Gnostic intent. As a New York Open Center audience were informed, "I sort of think that we all should become Mandaeans." Out of all the religions he studied, the Mandaeans were "the most psychedelic, the most ethically correct."[71] While we can't know for sure what he meant by that, the central gnosis recycled and iterated throughout McKenna's career is that humanity, having made the sojourn into history, into matter, in which we are trapped, faces a return to the light source, "coming soon." Whether in the obsession with psychedelics and hyperspace, computers and cyberspace, or with the possibilities of the imagination, his life's work illustrates this transhumanist becoming. And Mandaeanism was compelling since it promised an eschaton without judgment. While the Mandaeans hold to a peculiar apocalyptic belief in a messiah, their "Secret Adam" teaches no message and creates no moral revolution. Inspired by his reading of E. S. Drower's *The Secret Adam: A Study of Nasoraean Gnosis*, McKenna informed an East Coast workshop, without batting an eye, that the Gnostic Adam possessed the blueprints for a "soul machine" that will "pump all souls back to the light source outside the machinery of cosmic fate."[72] He wavered throughout his career on whether his psilocybin teacher was an extraterrestrial "Secret Adam" with a "phone home" setting, or something closer to a product of his own mind state. In the free-ranging workshops that were not unlike Grand Slam tournaments in which he volleyed with himself for hours, McKenna sometimes conceded the outlandish implication that he was the contactee who received the message to "call the following toll free number."[73] The settling of the score aside, this neo-gnostic manifold also provided a lens through which to parse contact with the DMT elves, those other-dimensional *doers*, crafters, and weird makers sometimes lauded in accord with Mandaean soteriology, and thought somehow implicated in the building of the soul machine.

HIGH AND DRY

In the summer of 1967 Terence was for the most part blissfully unaware of the probing inquiry that would later consume him. In October, he embarks with Stefi on his first overseas trip.[74] He wants to emigrate to the British colony of Seychelles, an archipelagic island country in the Indian Ocean at the eastern edge of the Somali Sea. There, he imagines, they will live out the war and teach English, while he completes his opus. Joe's College had been a fine incubator, but freedom is sought from the academic system. Confident of gestating a classic, the ideal hatchery was to be found in exotic climes. An "islands of the world" encyclopedia had been consulted, mindful of key criteria. The locale had to be tropical, the English language recognized, and it had to be remote.[75] The chosen destination was imagined an ideal topos for a young man jonesing to be the "crypto" apologist for the coming revolution. Geographically antipodal to the West Coast of the United States, removed from the worldly dramas of the late sixties, the plan was to forge his perennialist manifesto on the "electronic enstasis" on the island of Silhouette.

They were to arrive in Seychelles via Israel, where they disembark in mid-November. Stephanie is Jewish, and they elect to take advantage of an Israeli program entitling an open world air-ticket to those volunteering in a moshav or kibbutz for six months. They rail across Europe and sail aboard the Mediterranean cruise ship SS *Messipia*, from Brindisi, via Athens, to Haifa. Alas, the going is rough. Something dramatic goes down either en route or soon after that causes a rupture in their relationship. Upon arrival, as she planned, Stephanie joins a moshav on the Sea of Galilee, and makes plans to join Terry in paradise after six months or so.[76] He is unhappy with this turn of events. With the Summer of Love coming to an end, he will be swept by the winds of fate.

Living in the Old City and later also working on a kibbutz in the north, Kathleen Harrison planned six months in the region. She made for Israel to join her best friend and fellow UC Santa Cruz sophomore, Nina Wise, who, as we will recall, befriended McKenna in Palo Alto. Wise was now working on a kibbutz in the south, taking Hebrew lessons in an ulpan. Raised in the town of Avalon on Santa Catalina in the Channel Islands off the coast of Los Angeles, a past cheerleader and valedictorian, Harrison was "brilliant and drop dead gorgeous," says Wise, who knew her friend as an extremely independent woman who would never marry. During a year abroad on study leave,[77] the women plan to reunite on Christmas Eve in Jerusalem, Wise arriving from the south, Harrison from the north. They decided to converge at the residence of Wise's friend Gila, a local university student, who hosts McKenna, with whom Wise maintained correspondence. Christmas Eve 1967 was dark and stormy. Electricity had gone down all over the city to preserve power for the pilgrims in Bethlehem, the heights of which were captured during the recent Six-Day War. Wise and McKenna wait into the night, for Harrison had gotten lost. She knocked on doors around the neighborhood until eventually one opened to reveal a woolly-faced and goggle-eyed freak.[78]

Harrison was nineteen when she'd landed in Israel, an explorer of worlds both inner and outer. By twelve, she wanted to become a beatnik. By 1967, episodes with LSD augmented her phenomenological inquiries, and she had grown familiar with the multidimensionality of DMT. She was also a dreamer. In fact, among her more poignant dreams involved her new acquaintance the night before they met. As she had never seen his photo, she hadn't known that it was he she dreamt of. In the dream, they cross paths along a cliff edge. He gestures to a sign with an arrow informing her to follow that direction, the opposite way to his own path. They were above a shining sea, and on the horizon a black island is silhouetted in the midday sun.

Harrison is soon invited out on adventures into the Old City. "I dreamt about you last night," she says inquiringly. She describes the island in her dream, and he explains his near future plans for Silhouette Island. For two weeks over Christmas, Terry, Nina, Kat, and Gila explore the Church of the Holy Sepulchre, the Wailing Wall, and the Mosque of Omar, among other sites in a region where everyone is watchful and Israeli soldiers patrol every path. They are taken in by Palestinian shopkeepers, antiquity dealers, and Turkish hookah venders. There is a good supply of golden Lebanese hash. Jerusalem is the inception of a common future means to support travel and subsistence. He begins smuggling compressed kilo blocks of hash inside antiquities. As Harrison explains, "he'd purchase very old cast figurines, bronze I believe," sold in closet-sized shops in the alleyways of the Old City. They examine hundreds. His chosen vessels are taken to a specialist who is instructed to create small hollow pedestals at their base. With each base packed solid with hash and sealed with olive wood, the refitted antiquities are shipped to the United States.[79]

"He was so strange that I was not attracted to him, at all," Harrison says of her first impressions, "romantically or socially, or anything." And yet there is an unmistakable charm. "I loved how he worked to put things into words." She writes her mom a postcard: "I just met the strangest person I've ever met and I think he's going to have an effect on my life."[80]

McKenna rides a freight train south to the Red Sea port of Eilat. Worrying about the situation with Stephanie, and waiting for his ship to sail, he falls in with "the most amazing collection of freaks, Colombians, Danes, fed up kibbutzniks and Bedouins." Ravi and Big Yank are among the characters holding court in this scene, an itinerant fraternity whose daily dedication is to smoke as much hash as they can. In this company, Terence learns how to smoke a ghetto chillum using a Dr Pepper bottle and an *agara* (coin).[81] For a short while, he claims to have dwelt in a cave in a wadi in the Negev. "I was a poor traveling hippie, a hashishine, and a cave dweller and ne'er-do-well."[82]

In early January, he departs for Kenya. In Mombasa, he stumbles upon a library holding a bargain sale, acquires fifty kilos of Yogic, Arthur Avalon, and theosophical literature, which he then hauls to the Seychelles, along with a lid of Mombassan weed, and presumably his typewriter.[83] On January 25, he lands in Victoria, the port capital of Mahé, the main island of the Seychelles group, and resides in the islands until late March. His arrival anticipates tourists flocking to the region after the islands gain independence in the seventies. Unfortunately, realizing that remote Silhouette is protected by a barrier reef and inaccessible, he takes up residence instead in a small rented house on Ile au Cerf, two and a half miles off Mahé. As it is shared with fifty Creole-speaking families, his writerly idyll is not deserted, but the island is about as close to an inhabitable "Mars" as he could find.

For the longest hiatus since forming the habit, Terence stops smoking weed on the island. In his brother's version of this story, he plants marijuana seeds in his back garden and writes until the plants bud.[84] In his own telling, less a prisoner of circumstance, he undertakes a conscious experiment to quit smoking. "I wanted to see how much of my interior life was actually riding on this ocean of cannabis ingestion." He nails a Mombassan "bomber" above his kitchen door. According to this plan, he pledges to himself that he will light up the lid when the manuscript is done. He keeps a diligent pace, typing every day from 8 am until noon for six weeks. As part of his daily regimen, he would "take my dogs" and explore the island. He grows confident that his routine is the recipe to a master stroke, and forms a vision of himself "returning triumphantly to Berkeley like Lenin entering Moscow" with the manifesto raised high.

When the writing is finally complete, he drags his lawn chair out under the coconut palms at sunset and fires up the potent ganja. He begins to read the 220-page document, expecting to be awash with a sense of relief and accomplishment. The anticipated exaltation fails to arrive, however. Absorbing the text under his now heightened state, he sinks into "the incontrovertible, instantaneous, deep, unarguable realization that this book that I had written was *dog shit!*"[85]

He smokes day and night, desperate to breathe life into the text, but resurrecting the corpse is futile. And the moral he applies to this story? "I realized that I was a fool to try to navigate life without cannabis." His monstrous literary progeny is, by implication, the consequence of his decision to deprive himself of weed.[86] Regardless of how this went down, he neglects to inform his later audience how, in New York later that year, he attempts to hawk his sophomoric "abortion," titled "Crypto-Rap: Meta-Electrical Speculations on Culture."

Another contemporaneous factor seems to have influenced the harsh self-assessment of his "crypto-anarchist" opus. He had received word from Stephanie that she would not be joining him. It became apparent, he later recollects, that she had grown infatuated, not only with Zionism but with another man.[87] Crypto-Rap is an intellectual love letter forged during a period of lost love. Heartbroken, he remains friends with Stefi, whom he visits in Berkeley for lunch over many subsequent years.

As he forged "Crypto-Rap," I imagine Terence skulking among coco de mer palms, known as the "sex bombs" of the plant world. While male trees sprout long flamboyant catskins, as one observer reports, the huge bilibed seed of the female tree "looks uncannily like a shapely woman's bottom." For seventeenth-century sailors, the trees were "the equivalent of a porn movie."[88] It does not seem too unwarranted to speculate that, in addition to his forced dry run, McKenna's tortured text mirrored his tormented state. Insomnia, illness, and shattered dreams were his lot in paradise. While it is almost certain he intended to stay longer than two months, the split with Stephanie seems to have compelled him to weigh anchor. Forking out $35 for a berth, in early March he departs Port Victoria, and after eight days at sea, makes Bombay (Mumbai). After three days, "ill and disheartened from a personal reversal," he returns by air to San Francisco.[89] The description offered of his passage to India is of a man listless. "In the middle of my twenty-second year, in the hold of the British Steam Navigation Company liner SS Karanja, I was weak and semi-delirious, wracked with hives, heartbreak, and dysentery." All the same, his "romantic disappointment" seems to release its grip during the transit, allowing for "a clear space in which to turn toward the future and discern it." And in that cargo hold, "unbidden came the thought that I would go with Dennis to South America. Even then, I knew it for a certainty."[90] During his three days in the region—Bombay, and possibly Karachi—investments are made in cannabis indica products for quick shipment to the United States, likely including a package intended for himself.

Dated March 7, 1968, "Crypto-Rap" labored under the "battle cry of Crypto-Anarchy." As a love letter to an "electrically collectivized humanity," and designed to "stop the bullshit, the warmachine, the hatemachine, the deathmachine," the manuscript was intended to incite the revolt in progress.[91] In his analysis, Erik Davis positions the work as a radical outing in media philosophy, describing it as a "fascinating, arcane, and sometimes jejune combination of social criticism, psychedelic esotericism, and science-fiction media theory."[92] For Dennis, it was simply "the kind of polemical screed a guy writes when he's twenty, knows everything, and has bones to pick with everyone."[93] I address this manuscript, which underwent further modification, at the end of chapter 3.

1968: AT THE CROSSROADS

Returning to Berkeley in April 1968, sans Stephanie and brandishing a doubtful manuscript, Terence reoccupies his cheap digs at Tunnel Road. Soon after, Kevin Mahoney recalls "everyone" piling into a Land Rover belonging to Malcolm's girlfriend, Joan Connelly, and ferrying across the Bay Bridge to San Francisco to see *2001: A Space Odyssey*. They sit facing each other on the rear benches of the troop carrier, passing the hash pipe, Kevin in a silver metallic dress. Afterward, as Terence is dropped off, he climbs out, looks at Kevin, and asks if she wanted to come up. It is the start of their "non-relationship relationship," upon which Kevin offers further insight. He is the only man she was ever involved with whom she felt like she had to protect. On one occasion, a group of muggers approach them in a 7-Eleven parking lot. Kevin had taken karate. "I wasn't very good, but I could punch someone."[94] Terry wasn't beyond deploying his *weird* in self-defense, though. Navigating the sidewalk of Telegraph Avenue on another occasion, a random guy pulls a knife on Terry. He "just stopped and stared at him bug-eyed like, and let out a howl." The terrified assailant fled.[95]

Returned from Israel, Harrison and Wise move into a cottage near the beach in Santa Cruz. They planned to continue their studies, but the year became a blur for both women. In Harrison's parlance, in the wake of a mutually mind-blowing acid trip, it was the year of "The Great Gnostic Undoing." The experience "took everything apart to its molecules," says Harrison, who retreated from the world and didn't talk for months. The acid ascetic realized she had the opportunity to "re-construct the world piece by piece," rebuilding reality from the ground up. One day she decides to accept the sunset is real. This kind of lifestyle tended to narrow her boyfriend options. "I just mostly had to hang out with people who were really philosophical questioners too."[96] Wise confirms the wipeout. It was a state of complete dissolution of self and ego. Her consciousness expanded into a state of "non-dual awareness."[97]

"We didn't have teachers for this," recounts Wise, who knew there was only one person who could even begin to grok their cosmic funk. And so, spread across the psychedelic bardos, they drift up to Berkeley to visit the recently returned McKenna. Serving lapsang souchong tea amid his volumes, *thangkas*, and rugs at Tunnel Road, Terence "just loved to have young women coming to his feet to ask him what the heck was going on," Harrison laughs. "He was always holding court. . . . The prince with the teapot and the pipe." These receptions were absorbing affairs. It was not unusual for visitors to get bombed out and become verbally incapacitated at McKenna's court. In her case, she had taken a psychedelic vow of silence. "I didn't even begin to have language."

"Sometimes the breeze blows the curtains in just such a way that the world feels like a different place," he imparted.

"And I was like 'Oooh K.'"[98]

Meetings with McKenna at this time were rewarding for Wise, who recognized the gnostic qualities of her experience. He encouraged her to consult the *Collected Works of Jung*, the Bollingen Series, which became the foundation for her degree in religious studies and aesthetics of movement. As a later Buddhist practitioner and teacher, her first real experience of non-dual states informed Wise's career in performance art, stage writing, and directing new theater. As for McKenna, she considered him to be her "main mentor."[99]

In the early fall of 1968, clutching his dire manuscript, McKenna makes for New York. He aimed to peddle his "rambling, sophomoric, McLuhan-esque diatribe"[100] to any publisher risking the burden. "I have lost my belief in what it says," he apprises Watson, "but I continue, pre-programmed, to hope for a publisher."[101] Among the presses in play is Hart Publishing, founded by Hartley's uncle Harold Hart, who finds the manuscript unreadable.[102] The fantasy of a publisher's advance is dashed, but Terence gives Sara an antique cloisonné water pipe for the trouble. It will be twenty years before his writing is featured in the "great glass boxes along Fifth Avenue in Gotham."[103] At this time, he makes Hartley a curious proposition: an adventure to the Amazon. Her track record on archaeological expeditions and her skills in photography are impressive. She is at a crossroads, her career direction wavering between archaeology and filmmaking. She assents to a trip in a year or two. They dub their forthcoming venture "The A. R. Wallace Memorial Expedition."[104]

The East Coast visit offers brief respite from the pressure cauldron of Berkeley. Earlier in May–June 1968, Terence was drawn into the street uprisings that stirred his antifascist passions. Never tossing in with organized resistance groups like the Students for a Democratic Society, the Weathermen, or the Berkeley Commune, he is what Ron Curry names "a free agent, radical."[105] Himself radicalized, George Csicsery grew witness to a loose cannon. For his Tussmanite colleague, Terry was "a flaming radical" and "a real hotheaded barn burner." Csicsery recalls an antiwar clash on University Avenue, near the intersection with Shattuck. Joining protestors who occupied the street, McKenna violently shook his fists as he marched, chanting, "*Off* the pigs!"[106]

Ron Curry observes the zeal firsthand. He and his buddy, Bob, landed in Berkeley in mid-December 1968, in the aftershock of Nixon's victory. Fresh out of Aspen, they lodge at Tunnel Road for a week before their host notifies them that they are interfering with his love life. They arrive late in the evening, whereupon McKenna produces his pipe, they get smashed, and he raves into the night. "Tomorrow we're going to SF State to protest," he told them.

"What are you protesting?"

"We are protesting for a Black Studies Department at SF State." They are warned that the scene had grown a little edgy.

He wasn't wrong. They were about to be cast into a riot zone heavily inspired by the Black Consciousness movement. In support of demands for an ethnic studies program, a campus strike had been underway at San Francisco State University for weeks (lasting five months). The campus was under the control of the SFPD Tactical Squad, which, like an occupying force, was called in by SF State acting president Samuel Hayakawa, who opposed the Black Students Union and the Third World Liberation Front. Marches on the administration building were met with violent repression. McKenna had been rabble-rousing on campus since September. "Every day we would riot, and every day they would call out the Tac Squad and repeat this the next day, with two days off for weekends."[107]

They awake the next morning, get baked, and watch McKenna eat his soba breakfast. "I live a spartan existence here," he says. He eats buckwheat noodles every day. "That's what the Roman army marched on. That's what the Japanese soldiers marched on. If it's good enough for them, it's good enough for me."

When they arrive, a large crowd has already gathered at the Quad, at the center of SF State campus. Cops are stationed every ten feet. As McKenna walks passed one officer, beyond baton range, he turns around and flips him off. "Leather faggot!"

Moments later, as police cleared the area with mounted support, Terry and company disperse. Separated, Curry jumps through backyards to avoid tear gas, clubbing, and capture. Later, when the heat has dissipated, he returns to a now calmer scene to witness McKenna standing under his open umbrella at a church across the street where an injured protester lay. The scene makes such an impression on Curry that he is adamant that the image was carried on the front page of the *San Francisco Chronicle* soon after. While no such photograph has turned up, the vision of McKenna with umbrella, gazing wild-eyed upon an injured comrade, remained front-page news in Curry's imagination[108] (see figure 2.5).

McKenna's involvement in one of the longest student strikes in history was minor, marginal, and maybe even counterproductive, but the protest led to the founding of the departments of Black and ethnic studies at SF State. "The grip of the military-political propaganda machine must be broken," he wrote in his unpublished manifesto. "All forms of non-linear and acausal agitation should be used."[109] And, as he opined twenty years later, Berkeley had become "the sixth military district." It was surreal. "Every twelve feet there was a kid with a bayonet on a rifle." McKenna grew cynical. "That's where I learned my politics."[110]

The uncertainty of the hour is matched by personal circumstances, as conveyed in a letter to Watson, recently of Kathmandu. From his vantage in the carriage house, Terr apprises Rick of his state of mind on August 8, 1968. "I write to you from the friction heated interstices of a society locked in

FIGURE 2.5
Ron Curry, 1969. Photo courtesy of Kevin Mahoney.

obscene union with a death ridden apocalyptic consort, everywhere there is a sense of busting apart." The situation is charged and without precedent. Alluding to Robert A. Heinlein's 1952 short story "The Year of the Jackpot," in which the statistical improbabilities are synchronized in an end-of-the-world scenario, McKenna writes: "It is truly the year of the jackpot; all processes, in the microcosm and the macrocosm, skid towards collapse, explosion and the point of no return. Rioting is continuous, many predict that the elections will not be held, syncretic fragmentation on all levels is the motif of the age." He is at the crossroads. "Hectic (from Hecate?) is the mode I anticipate. . . . All is madness."[111]

The letter also divulges his motives. He sought to recruit his friend to assist him in the acquisition of *thangkas* for the purpose of resale, business intended to resolve Rick's financial straits. On his recent visit to Bombay, McKenna searched for a *thangka* of the "vintage Tantric" variety" and succeeded in locating a "magnificent specimen," only to be thwarted in its acquisition. Watson is urged to maintain vigilance for Tibetan scrolls of impressive quality. "I will pay up to $500 for an outstanding piece," he is informed.[112] Terence divulges how he has suddenly grown flush and that he seeks to further invest his funds by way of another curious proposition: "You must wonder how it is that I, always one who lived from hand-to-mouth, should be in such a fortunate financial position. . . . I must confess that if even the hint of opulence is mine," he remarks of recent business fortunes, "it is due to contrabanding of cannabis indica products acquired while I was on the sub-continent." If he desired to pursue it, Watson is assured that the arrangement will be accompanied by "a liberal outpouring of advice on how best to conceal and transport the arcanum."[113]

As we'll see, the offer to sweeten the package with his smuggling expertise thrown in has a ludicrous pedigree. The proposition arrived amid a full-blown charm offensive. The letter conveys the conceit that travels to foreign lands permit entry to a zone of exception, where alternative rules, behaviors, and, presumably, deeds of the "left hand" prevail. "People in distant places, travelers," he confides in his fellow traveler, "are inclined to overlook the niceties of karma that evolve within the closest spatial focus of a drawing room."[114]

Soon after, Watson introduces McKenna to Richard Horn and Scottish artist Scotty Dick, who will supply McKenna with hash acquired in Benares. McKenna takes over the shipment and marketing, recruiting US-based buyers in California, Colorado, and New York. Watson recalls, at least on one occasion, bricks of hash filling the concealed interior of a thirty-inch ceramic statue of Ganesha.[115]

The August '68 letter is ultimately a paean to travel, to life on the road, and to paying forward respect to his pal who had orchestrated an escape from the war machine. "I have followed your travels with attention and great interest," he began signing off, daring to suppose that he held a "deeper insight" into Watson's experiences than those not intimate with the road. After all, he had himself "recently returned from distant lands and dusty cities awash with a confusion of tongues and customs. It is the personal existential aspect of traveling that I can empathize with. . . . Fare well William Patrick Watson, I anticipate your return, our reunion. . . . All time is only an interlude, and all places, once we have left them behind are only heat mirages dancing before the eye of memory."[116]

By late 1968, McKenna dwelt inside an Orwellian nightmare. The situation had deteriorated so much that he felt he could not return to his studies at UC Berkeley.[117] On the rooftops of the Quad buildings at SF State, the intelligence agencies field observers with telescopic cameras. One morning in early January leaving Tunnel Road Terence notices a man in a car with "a funny license plate" and a mounted clipboard who seemed to be taking a lot of interest in his comings and goings. He tells Malcolm that "we've shot our wad," reminding him that "the first duty of a revolutionary is to survive." And so he and Malcolm acquire around-the-world air tickets, their minds set on Luang Prabang, Laos, via Hong Kong.[118] Beyond that, they imagine India, Seychelles, and Nepal.

Before he departs, McKenna tells his friends that 1969 will be a genuine "screechpuke."[119]

3 TERRY INCOGNITA

A NEW PERCH

Rick Watson's journey east is an accident. Always the one to get there first, he escapes the United States in February 1968 on a Yugoslav freighter. Hitching a ride from Thessalonika to Skopje, the first car that stops is commanded by a Dutch army officer going all the way to New Delhi to get married.[1] It is a genuine fork in the road. Rick climbs in and remains on board as they traverse West Asia, arriving in Kashmir 4,000 miles later. He eventually makes Kathmandu, taking a room in the city center, sleeping on a carpet he'd acquired in Kabul. Unsure of what he was doing in the Nepali capital, Watson is motivated by a vague desire for things Buddhist and Tibetan. He has hopes of writing poetry but is "overwhelmed by the sensory and pathological onslaught of this fecund, festering city."[2]

Far from getting there first, as a young American arriving in Nepal in the late 1960s, Watson had not only arrived on the heels of hippies who had in recent years made it to Kathmandu in growing numbers, but he was following travelers who had for a century romanticized the Himalaya, and notably Tibet, as a vast spiritual resource. By 1968, there was already a sizable foreign youth presence in Kathmandu, visited by the original "dharma bum," Buddhist poet Gary Snyder in 1962 and by other disenchanted Westerners descending on a place that had become synonymous with "Oriental mystique." Accessing the writings of Blavatsky, Lama Govinda, and Evans-Wentz's translation of the *Bardo Thodol* (*The Tibetan Book of the Dead*), they were drawn to the Himalayan periphery "less to find the people who resided there," writes Mark Liechty, "than to find the selves they wished to be—or imagined to have lost." By the 1960s, the closing of Tibet (resulting from Chinese occupation) coincided with the opening of Nepal, "the last home of mystery." The Western fantasies long focused on Tibet were now shifting to Nepal.[3]

Uncertain perhaps of where he was, Rick knew with great certainty where he was not. Nepal was a place conveniently remote from the America of the late sixties. Cheap, tolerant, and with quality, and legal, hashish at hand, Kathmandu amounted to a waking dream for travelers and expats. Watson eventually rents a place in Swayambhunath, west across the river from Kathmandu. There, he lives with his girlfriend, Linda, who opens a shop hawking Tibetan-style clothing to travelers. From their "gray cube" they absorb the entire valley. "Gilded pagoda roofs rising above like alien Asian antennae," he writes to a friend from his new vista. "The mountains are steep and deeply treed, furrowed and folded, orange in erosion where scattered villages cling precariously to their sides." The Monkey Temple at Swayambhu is captured with an eye and ear for detail, as are the street processions and "the cosmic cacophony" of Tibetan ceremony music. Similar such impressions would entice McKenna. "Frequently moving lights brighter than the brightest stars are seen swiftly moving through the night sky, faster than any satellite could travel." Echoing wider obsessions with the levitating monks of Tibetan Buddhism, "one suspects bodhisattvas sitting on lunar lotus disks traversing space. My place among this enchantment is a fulfillment of a karmic obligation to wander." Drawn to "the exiled Tibetans citadeled in the high places,"[4] Watson treks to Thangboche Monastery, situated beneath Everest at 13,000 feet. He begins learning Tibetan.

Shortly after arriving in the region, Watson meets avant-garde New York writer Richard Horn, who invites him to a party at Horn's house on the outskirts of town. The two-story concrete block is a modern Nepali structure that brilliantly disguises its outlandish interior. The scene he stumbles upon is one of "unimaginable mindless frenzy":

> the elite of Kathmandu freaks . . . packed, perhaps two hundred of them, in the spacious ground-floor room, all arrayed in the most fantastic rainbow motley of Asian garments intermixed with tattered Western hippie gear, saris and dhotees and sarongs and embroidered velour vests, bright orange and scarlet bolts of silk draping bodies like Grecian robes, with tons of Nepali jewelry, necklaces with enormous chunks of amber, coral and turquoise, with silver filigree work. The air, or what was left of it, was thick with hashish chillum smoke resembling an invading ground fog, with most of the assembled motionless, collapsed upon the floor as if turned to Medusan stone, while the few still-mobile wailed away on tabla drums, flutes, cymbals, gongs, strange Asian horns, and I imagine a phonograph (as they were in those days) lost in the cacophonous din, playing a heavily abraded Doors or Jimi Hendrix album.[5]

A gangly, combed-over Jew with Coke-bottle glasses and whose age appeared to far exceed his twenty-two years, Horn becomes a mesmeric figure in

Watson's world. With the rare distinction of completing a novel, the kaleidoscopic designed *Encyclopedia*, published by Grove Press in 1969, Horn was in Nepal on an advance from Grove for a second work.[6] Not unlike McKenna, Horn had little time for priests, charlatans, and other obstructors of the quest. "Like Terr, he would accost the holy of holies in its citadel and demand a demonstration, a hands-on road test of hyperreality."[7]

With the scene at home growing more grotesque by the day, Terry seeks to reunite with his friend, now stationed on top of the world. Having successfully traded in both items, *thangkas* and hashish are his chief bets to finance international travel. "After a brief visit to Laos and delays in Bangkok and Bombay," he sails with Malcolm from Bombay, in early February 1969, again bound for Seychelles.[8] Retaining dreams of settling in the antipodean paradise to repair his manifesto, McKenna's mind was fixed on the islands, now pulling Malcolm into the fantasy. They intended, it seems, to acquire property from their trading proceeds, a plot that appears to come unstuck. The Boulder Statement offers insight: "Once arrived in Mahé I surveyed the available real estate and concluded that inflation and the prospect of increased tourism had made investment there a financial

FIGURE 3.1
Postcard to Douglas Hansen, from Victoria, Seychelles, March 12, 1969. Courtesy of Douglas Hansen.[11]

impossibility for the investors I represented."[9] If there is any truth to this statement, it may explain why, in a letter to Nina Wise, the return venture is described as "disastrous" and "the Second Saga of Seychelles."[10]

Foiled again in paradise, McKenna sails from Port Victoria on March 13. "I returned then to India and after a brief illness in Delhi, continued on to Kathmandu, Nepal, in order to pursue my interest in Tibetan languages and religion."[12] They likely took advantage of the new Thai Airlines service from Bangkok to Kathmandu. From April to September, McKenna lives in Boudhanath, then a small Tamang village on the eastern outskirts of Kathmandu inhabited by a sizable population of Tibetan refugees. His small, rented apartment faced the Boudha Stupa, majestically backdropped by the Annapurna Range in the far distance. He reunites with Watson, tanned and in Asian dress, "the sympathetic effect of life amongst the Newari and Tibetans." Rick had recently returned from adventures in India, traveling with Horn and his entourage, an "extended and extensive migratory hippie family" that included Chris Jagger (brother to Mick), among other pulsating contributors to "the background cosmic radiation."[13]

In Nepal, McKenna entertained the persona of a mystic-rebel in exile. That, at least, is the self-portrait in missives to friends sent from his remote loft in Boudhanath. "My mind is as on fire as the world around me," he shared with Wise. But even as the Vietnam conflagration flared, he opens toward the "mystery." In letters over June–July 1969, in which Wise is encouraged to join him, he gives notice of an intent to step up the search for clues to a "secret" that by its own inner logic cannot be named.[14]

This correspondence occasions the grandiose flourishes of an elevated young man. High upon his world perch, he is alive to the hunt, while awaiting "the roar and carnage of our beautiful revolution to call me home."[15] Does the elevated locale assist clarity of vision or foster detachment from reality? With sentiments that read like the work of a socialist pamphleteer, in a letter to Wise sent the day before Apollo 11 astronauts amble on the moon, he ratchets up the pressure on her to drop out. "I do not think I would give you any better advice in the world than to get out of the University. It is a ball shining operation that totally co-opts real revolution." Six months of travel had convinced him that "the burden of world revolution falls on us."

> If we fail to measure up to this challenge—refuse to abandon our personalistic and comfortable little plans and pursuits for this collective chore, then it is not ourselves and our generation to which we are traitors but it is the human species and consciousness itself that we consign to ruin. And knowing that fact how much more guilty and monstrous are we than the blind fools who rush us toward planetary destruction?[16]

In the same missive, the paradox of fighting a system by withdrawing from it is addressed. Neither Marxist rhetoric nor being a "professional Jewish SDS radical" constitute revolution, he wages. "Ours is a rotten age and to die a martyr for love—and the revolution is love—is not the worst of modern fates. Better by far to die moral than to ever love Big Brother."[17]

Soon to be unfeasible for the foreseeable future, a return is contemplated. "I carry a passport stamped USA and it is a constant reminder to me that I have dues to pay and must someday use that passport as a ticket back into the eye of a hurricane of evil." And while embraced as a "metaphor," it is not insignificant that he identifies as a "criminal"—a status soon more than metaphorical.

McKenna's self-portrait in this period is that of a field researcher with a firm, if ambitious, educational program in Tibetan language and religion. He begins daily Tibetan lessons with Gelugpa Lama, Tashi Gyaltsen, a former resident of Lhasa. If there was a *program*, it is to be developed on the fly, and pieced together retrospectively. Speculation is cultivated on the influence of hallucinogens on the Bon, the indigenous pre-Buddhist religion of Tibet, understood as "a kind of shamanism closely related to the motifs and cosmology of the classical shamanism of Siberia." He arrives at the understanding that a Tibetan folk shamanism was being practiced in the mountainous region of Nepal bordering Tibet, among a group generally despised as heretics and low types by the Buddhist community in Nepal.

With visionary scroll paintings catching his eye, he obsesses over the origins of the extravagant imagery common to these works, the ferocious multi-armed, and multi-headed guardians of the Dharmapalas.[18] Having absorbed Wasson's speculation concerning the influence of *Amanita muscaria* in Vedic India, and with his knowledge of that mushroom's role in shamanic ecstasy in Siberia, McKenna hypothesizes that the pre-Buddhist shamanic tradition responsible for such outlandish images must have possessed knowledge of psychotropic plant sources. Despite well-known efforts to bridge the ancient with the nascent, there simply wasn't any comparison between Tibetan Buddhism and the hallucinogenic experience then growing popular in the West. They were familiar with *The Psychedelic Experience*, the tripping guide that adopted the *Bardo Thödol* as a programming model.[19] But as far as McKenna was aware, "one-to-one mapping between the psychedelic experience and traditional systems of esoteric thought," was absent.[20]

True Hallucinations offers a revisionist contemplation of its author's activities in Nepal. As his memoir claimed, the plan was to find evidence of any knowledge that the Bonpo retained about hallucinogens. "I wished, in my naivete, to prove my hypothesis about the influence of plant hallucinogens on Tibetan painting and then write a monograph about it." To fulfill that objective, McKenna realized he had to learn Tibetan language, an achievement that, he surmised, demanded a life of scholarly commitment. During the spring and summer of '69 in Nepal, he wrote, "I put aside all my research ideas and resolved to dedicate myself to learning as much Tibetan as I could." Despite his advanced age, Tashi Gyaltsen is identified as a kind and understanding teacher who arrived every morning at seven sharp for a two-hour lesson, commencing with penmanship and the alphabet. "I was like a child," wrote McKenna.[21] While the image of a learned scholar and mage is projected, that the pupil made little progress is a neglected feature of the distilled mythology. "Strangely, for someone so linguistically and oratorically gifted," reflects Watson, his friend was a monoglot.[22]

Unlike McKenna, Roger Williams took the study of Tibetan Buddhism seriously. As a member of the small expat community in Boudhanath, Williams was among McKenna's neighbors and friends. The future Tibetologist, tour guide, and publisher likely introduced McKenna to Gyaltsen, with whom Williams was then studying Tibetan language. Williams spent eight years in Nepal learning from HH Gyalwa Karmapa 16th, with subsequent studies reflecting a curiosity for Buddhist iconography and Himalayan history, culture, and languages. His thirst for knowledge led him to Hindu iconography, Chinese calligraphy, and Japanese and Tibetan Buddhist woodblock art, in which he specialized. Commenting on their disparate approaches, McKenna was, says Williams, a dilettante who neither had the time nor the patience required from those who seek to learn from Tibetan teachings.

> He was in a hurry. He wanted to be the smartest guy in the room all the time. He was bright, very bright and he had a great memory, which can be an advantage or a disadvantage depending on one's personality. What he lacked in knowledge he made up for with confidence or bullshit. He didn't appear to understand that the first step to knowledge (not information but knowledge) was an admission of ignorance coupled with a desire to learn. We cannot learn what we already pretend to know.[23]

During his Nepali sojourn, the novice became engaged in advanced activities to which his lama presumably remained blissfully unaware. While projecting an image in the Boulder Statement that language studies were pursued in the region from April to September 1969, as his memoir's "Kathmandu Interlude" chapter conveys the student pursued other interests. In this story, at summer solstice, the rooftop of his Boudhanath building becomes the elevated site for a sexual liaison in which a "violet psycho-fluid" dubbed *luv* emanates from his companion. It is a passing encounter with an Englishwoman, a wild-tempered and "unhealthily thin" redhead who had, upon his "facetious" suggestion, ingested the ground seed of a Himalayan datura (sometimes known as "hells bells" and a plant with notoriously unpredictable effects), while he dosed on a treasured tab of Orange Sunshine LSD. These are the foundations for the DMT they inhaled from his glass pipe. "We were both howling and singing in the glossolalia of DMT, rolling over the ground with everything awash in crawling, geometric hallucinations." Having transformed into a Kaliesque figure, "something erotic but not human," the woman who could not recall anything of the experience afterward seemed "on the edge of devouring me":

> Reality was shattered. This kind of fucking occurs at the very limit of what is possible. Everything had been transformed into orgasm and visible, chattering oceans of elf language. Then I saw that where our bodies were glued together there was flowing, out of her, over me, over the floor of the roof, flowing everywhere, some sort of obsidian liquid, something dark and glittering, with color and lights within it. After the DMT flash, after the seizures of orgasms, after all that, this new thing shocked me to the core.[24]

This translucent material, which is described, apropos Joyce, as being "all-space in a notshell,"[25] prompts interest in the purple liquid said to form on the skin of ayahuasqueros and used in divination—a theme that fired the brothers' curiosity when bound for the Amazon.[26]

Such sensational other-dimensional teachings were a distraction from the Tibetan lessons, a circumstance upon which the pupil seems to project guilt. The following provocation in his memoir compels the reader to draw closer. Within the phosphorescent *luv* smearing his and his lover's bodies on that Nepali rooftop, McKenna scries something fantastic:

> I looked into it again and now saw in it the lama who taught me Tibetan, who would have been asleep a mile away. In the fluid I saw him, in the company of a monk I had never seen; they were looking into a mirrored plate. Then I realized that they were watching me! I could not understand it. I looked away from the fluid and away from my companion, so intense was her aura of strangeness.[27]

The impression gained is that of Kassapa Buddha, who, with watchful eyes staring out from atop the stupa, fixes McKenna in a withering gaze. He may have arrived at an epic climax of paranoia and shame, but it is a moment our willful student was determined to embrace, as illustrated in the treatment of the opening scene for his memoir's proposed theatrical adaptation. The long-imagined film was envisioned to open on "a small mountain village rooftop in Northern India" where the howling liaison of which we are already familiar is in full session. Upon their climax, a ray of dawn light illuminates the couple's roost. They bear witness to a "glowing purple liquid" spilling from their groins. Thomas (the script's character based on McKenna) stares into the liquid, in which he sees "some ancient guru passing judgement on his life." Uncoupling, the pair realize from the dead silence in which they are now bathed that their screams of ecstasy have likely woken the entire village. The pair hastily repair from the roof.

The scene that never saw daylight ends with Thomas loping through the early-morning streets, naked but for a pair of scarlet silken panties. He'd pursued the disoriented redhead into the street to prevent her from coming to some unspeakable grief and to preempt any leery eyeballs drawn onto his coordinates. Little did he know that he had hurriedly pulled on her underpants in the dark before stepping out into the street in hot pursuit. This scene was imagined to be the curtain-raiser to the True Hallucinations film—with "Skateaway" by Dire Straits a possible soundtrack. She floats through the early morning, her silver satin evening gown disappearing around the corner. In the next street, a group of merchants freeze before the precession. Caught up, he takes her arm in a courtly fashion, leading her back to his quarters where he sets about making some tea. Regaining her composure, she stares at him and announces in a lucid tone, "Look, look, look at you! Cor, you've got my knickers on!!"[28] Casting himself as the central protagonist in an absurd spectacle, this event appears to signal the end of McKenna's short career as a student of Tibetan language, while also serving as the opening shot on a grander adventure.

We might note with more than passing interest that the depiction of submissiveness before his lama, and the sense of shame implicit to this story, competes with the dissonance toward, and defiance of, religious authorities otherwise maintained. By the time he arrived in Nepal, McKenna claimed to be aware that one need not put themselves "at somebody's feet for a dozen years,"[29] or "sweep the ashram" for a dozen more, to achieve a hierophany. In any case, he was bereft of the material advantages of any of his well-heeled compatriots traversing the trans-Eurasian "hippie trail." He was daily confronted with the challenges of supporting himself in the region. The student guise was a convenient conceit for the more immediately lucrative activity of hash smuggling.

It is quite possible that McKenna had more interactions with swamis as sources of hashish. While details are sketchy on this subject, there were multiple visits to Bombay's Crawford Market. Upon instruction, McKenna would arrive at a crossroads, dismiss his cab, and take the hand of a child who led him through the labyrinth to a Muslim gangster named the Baby Elephant. This was "a huge guy drenched in perfume with all of his lieutenants around him." They were always glad to see him, but these encounters were fraught with danger. He was perfectly aware that they could off him at any moment at their leisure, without consequences.[30] While there are also claims of being hauled around Karachi, Pakistan, in a rickshaw "scoring hash," possibly in 1969, details are scarce.[31] Hair-raising encounters with Indian mafia at Crawford Market, gold strapped to his body, are later co-mapped with the entities in the DMT experience. "I am your friend. I am not like all the others," they announce unreassuringly, reminiscent of "guys with shining eyes and deformed limbs" in the Crawford warrens. These characters knew that "we had enough money on our body to ransom them all for five years' income, and we would know that they knew."[32]

While Watson is certain his friend learned little, if any, Tibetan, and had no contact with Bon shamans,[33] he did invest considerable time, and finances, collecting painted scrolls. This was a key motive for traveling through the region with Malcolm, with whom McKenna shared this passion in common. Before their departure, Malcolm joined his friend on regular visits to the Avery Brundage collection of Asian art in San Francisco, with its large array of *thangkas*.[34] Later, after returning to the United States, Malcolm became a New York City–based dealer in Southeast Asian art. In Nepal, with Watson acting as advisor and negotiator, the bargain hunt was on for the "guardians of the dharma," the most bizarre expressions in Vajrayānist art. While McKenna informed Wise, among others, that the effort was part of a campaign to save Tibetan art "in danger of being lost," given many of the works were valued with estimates into the thousands, this was no simple salvage operation. The quantity of works acquired at this time is uncertain, but Watson was involved with several purchases, including pieces that had arrived in Nepal with Tibetans fleeing the Chinese occupation, while other acquisitions were made at the Chinese Department Store in Kathmandu, where antiquities were hocked next to tinned goods and luxury comestibles. The Chinese were moving Tibetan art confiscated from the monasteries. Among the museum-quality pieces acquired at the urging of Watson was a variation of the "1,000 Buddha" design with gold leaf background and red outline, a staggering work that McKenna retained. Several *thangkas* were shipped back to the United States, some possibly sold at Malcolm's New York gallery.[35]

The two sought the painted Wrathful Deities all the way to their aboriginal source, Dolpo, in remote western Nepal, thought to be the main locus of the surviving Bon practice. They even devised a harebrained project to rent a helicopter from the Nepalese army, agreeing upon a fee. Beyond that, they had grandiose plans for Samarkand and Tashkent along the Silk Road to Outer Mongolia.[36]

SCREECHPUKE

Sojourns in Nepal and further afield were supported by an India/US hashish import operation. McKenna began shipping hash to the States (from Jerusalem) from late 1967. Apparently buoyed by his success, under the supposed name "Colorado Fuel and Iron," he collaborates in 1969 with US-based associates in multiple states to receive hash shipped from India. The fledgling network collapses in the wake of a bust at Glenwood Springs, Colorado, on August 14–15. A Bombay-to-Aspen shipment of sixteen pounds of hash with an estimated street value of $54,000 (purchase value approximately $800) is intercepted by US Customs, triggering a surveillance tail and arrests.[37] The bust leaves a mark on McKenna for years to come.

The writing had been scrawled across it for at least a year before the wall came crashing down. When visiting his family en route to New York in the summer of '68, Terence had a package forwarded to the McKenna residence in Paonia. Dennis recounts the episode as they collected the package from the post office:

> Terence was agitated and insisted on checking the mail every day. He said this was his biggest shipment yet. When it finally arrived, we knew it immediately, because the entire post office was redolent with the aroma of fine Nepali hash. Terence had had the bright idea to conceal the hash in the swollen stomach of one of those "happy Buddha" statuettes.

The Buddha had broken open in transit, "scattering large balls of hash throughout the packing material." Not without a few heart palpitations, their "incense" cleared the post office.[38] With signs of carelessness already present, Terence subsequently sent his aromatic shipments "barely concealed in locked tin boxes," which Dennis thought reckless. And as he later reported first hand: "My misgivings proved correct."[39]

Kevin Mahoney was among Terence's Berkeley-based recipients. "He used me because he knew I was crushing on him," noted Mahoney, who recalls a package addressed to her arriving in Berkeley in early 1968 (probably sent from Israel). A year later, and a month after he departed for India in January '69, a Ganesha statue packed with hash is shipped to Hartley and Mahoney at their duplex on Cedar Street in Berkeley. The shipment is an unmitigated disaster. The ill-fated Ganesha was posted, it seems, with little concern for the risk to the recipients, and nor apparently were appropriate propitiations performed before Ganesha, Vighneshvara, the Lord of Obstacles. Terence wasn't a "Svengali," Mahoney reckons. He was just "a young man who had a talent for sweeping people into his plan."[40] And, she added,

"I was very naive about boys." The "plan" involved the women joining McKenna in India for future adventures, their travels sponsored by sales of the indica product. Hartley planned to trek to Ladakh with Terry and, upon his encouragement, had taken a study unit on Ladakh. The arrangement would ensure the personal delivery of his cut. "Terry needed revenue badly," said Hartley.[41]

It was a fiasco from the get-go. On the package, McKenna had been instructed to use a variation of Mahoney's name, care of the previous tenant. However, since the previous tenant had mail forwarded to a new address, the US Postal Service redirected the hash there. Reluctantly going over to collect, Mahoney freaked out when seeing her full name on the package. Terrified of being busted she left without the package.[42] Mahoney and Hartley then arranged for a male friend with fake "Kevin Mahoney" ID to collect it. The ruse succeeded, but, says Hartley, the Ganesh and most of its precious load was stolen by a local dealer. "We were a bunch of hapless coeds" and "couldn't have been dumber crooks."[43]

Mahoney never makes it to India, but she does make it to Aspen, Colorado, where she marries Ron Curry, moving into Curry's mother's house in Glenwood Springs, with his six brothers and sisters. It's not known how many shipments were made pre-bust, but as Dennis claims, Terence was "regularly sending shipments of hash to colleagues" in Aspen, and "there were several shipments that came in over the summer" before the interception.[44] At this time, Dennis was living with Bill Cole, whom Terence had recruited to receive shipments in Aspen, purchased at $100 a kilo. Cole had no reason to be diffident, but it all went Pete Tong on August 14 after he collected a package from Basalt post office. Dennis followed in his own car, eager to sample the "good shit." Cole drives to Glenwood Springs, where he says he planned to get a haircut from Mahoney. Little did he know that another tailing vehicle carries agents from US Customs and the federal Bureau of Narcotics and Dangerous Drugs, along with a postal inspector and a local police sergeant. Upon arriving at the Curry house, the unopened package remains in Cole's VW convertible. He grows paranoid when noticing a carload of guys parked nearby. He asks Curry's brother if he recognizes them. Negatory. In a desperate bid to avoid implicating the Curry household, Cole returns to his car where the agents stop him at gunpoint.[45]

Bill and Dennis are arrested and taken to the county jailhouse to face arraignment on hashish smuggling charges. Dennis protests his innocence. The police have few details, but they play the eighteen-year-old like a fiddle. It didn't help that he has a Bombay address for Terence in his wallet. Unaware of his right to remain silent, his mouth runs a marathon, admitting his brother is the supplier. "I broke down completely, and in tears I confessed: 'Yes, it's all true!'" That confession is followed by another, forty-three years later. "Looking back on this, I am still ashamed. What kind of a worm rats out his own brother? . . . I'm not proud of it. . . . I was scared out of my wits."[46] Dennis's later confession didn't go far enough for Mahoney. When the feds return to the house to interrogate her, they had written up the indictment in her name. "They accused me of being the ringleader of this drug smuggling operation. They had notes on my sex life for the last two years." Dennis, she laughs fifty-one years later, and without a hint of bitterness, "is a little bit of a squirrel."

> Dennis was a little Catholic boy. To him I was probably the Madonna Prostitute. So Dennis caved completely and gave the feds all of our names so they came back and interrogated me and they're harassing me and they're saying that I'm the leader of the gang of people who are importing hashish into the country because all of these men are my lovers, which is really untrue. But it was so salacious. And the feds like salacious things.

Dennis is released, his case dismissed, and Mahoney spends five days in jail. Cole, Mahoney, and Curry plead guilty as youth offenders. Defended by their attorney, Arthur H. Weed, the spouses get three-year probations under the Federal Youth Corrections Act. "All I did was cut Bill's hair!" Mahoney laughs.[47] Questioning Cole, the feds already knew about Terence. "When I denied knowing anyone named Terry they laughed in my face."[48] Cole is held in federal custody for a sixty-day period of observation and examination, before receiving three years' probation.[49]

Berkeley and Aspen weren't the only destinations in McKenna's ill-fated hash network. A docket involving six pounds of hash is processed in the US District Court for the Southern District of New York on November 2, 1970. A package had been received by Richard Levinson, whose place appears to have been raided, likely in the wake of the events at Glenwood Springs. Soon after Terence's name appears in this case file, a bench warrant is issued in his name, on November 6.[50] A year later, with McKenna still a fugitive, the defendants (Levinson and a local buyer) each receive two-year probations, earlier appearing before a federal grand jury where they gave testimony concerning the "prime culprit" misspelled—in the transcribed statement of prosecutor, Arthur J. Viviani, before Judge Sylvester J. Ryan—"Mr Terrence McKenna." It is further reported that the defendants were prepared to appear as government witnesses in a trial of McKenna. The trial never happens.[51]

These proceedings are two years down the pike. In Colorado in 1969, denying he knew Terence, Cole takes the rap. It is four decades before

Colorado becomes the first US state to legalize cannabis (and hash) for personal use (in 2012). Cole held no grudges, then or now. In fact, there is no resentment among the Colorado codefendants, and nor is there acrimony toward Terence, who in the immediate wake of the Glenwood Springs bust is said to have received a telegram from his father: "Interpol is looking for you, get out now!" Another message is said to have been wired from his coconspirators in Aspen: "Colorado Fuel and Iron gone down."[52] While it appears that Terence did not appear in the books until more than a year after Glenwood Springs, he goes into hiding nevertheless and is reluctant to enter the country for the next two years. It is during this time that Hazelle McKenna suffers declining health—a circumstance weighing heavily on Terence. Joe's wired warning may have served to protect his son, but it also shielded his weak and ailing wife from further distress. Given he saw all illegal drugs as "addictive, destructive, and evil," we can speculate on Joe's motivations. While his distrust is likely to have been fueled by the moral panic developing around psychedelic drugs, his fears and prejudice ran deep. He had harbored contempt for drug users ever since a bombing mission over Germany during the war. When a B-17 crewmate was badly injured by shrapnel, so the story went, they opened the medical kit only to find that "some hophead had stolen the morphine."[53]

EXPATRIATE EXPULSION

The year 1969 was a "screechpuke" shaped and colored according to McKenna's own design. The fantasy of escaping to remotest Outer Mongolia appears apt in light of the episode that magnified his cultivated exile status. But that destination is never obtained. Around this time, there is a further message to "get out." The reason for their sudden expulsion is probably related to the hash trade, and specifically to the interception in Colorado. At the same time, Sino-Nepali tensions were centered precisely on the region Watson and McKenna intended to visit. Dolpo is west of Mustang, a remote region of northern Nepal and then a base for CIA-backed Khampa rebels. The duo's express interest in this sensitive frontier may have rendered them suspect.[54] At the time, Watson was approached by a professor of Asian Studies whom he recalls tried to recruit him to perform "research" for the CIA. Did his refusal seal their fate? Regardless, they had "forty-eight hours to leave."[55]

As Watson later wrote Moore, "my citadel of dreams in the rarified Himalayan highlands collapsed beneath the ceiling of karma, and I was banished from the kingdom unto the desolate dust of India."[56] Expelled expatriates

Ricky and Terr met in Benares on the banks of the Ganges.[57] The author of the Boulder Statement claims he returned to Delhi in September to sell *thangkas*, securing a financial base for further travels. In October, he lands in Benares and rents a houseboat on the Ganges, where there are plans to rendezvous with Hartley. Working as a field assistant for the American Museum of Natural History, Hartley was en route to a dig led by Richard A. Gould in Western Australia's Gibson Desert. As he had refused her wiring him the money, Hartley carries cash in a money belt. But when he fails to meet her at the airport, after half a day she is approached by a crisply attired young Indian. He informs her that he is in the employ of the chief magistrate of Varanasi, a dignitary who is at her service. Reluctantly, she is driven to a large villa where a servant stands by every door. Upon meeting the chief magistrate, he takes off his clothes, and serves great hash. With no intention of becoming a lost girl "procured" by Mr. Magistrate, Hartley escapes that scene and cruises the Ganges on a rented boat searching for McKenna. Finally, a Dutch junkie on a houseboat directs her to him. During her stay, they take mescaline and explore Sarnath, where the Buddha had delivered his first lectures. They muse about a career together using newly portable video gear to make "travel" films with his commentary. In the end, she observes, "I think he preferred butterfly hunting."[58]

Among the exotic creatures McKenna nets at this time is a beautiful American belly dancer named Dhyana. A woman of many different names, talents, and partners (including Watson and John Parker), Dhyana Hachten, a.k.a. Languedoc, was an enchantress known for her lovemaking talents, which may be among the reasons why Mahoney regarded her as a "Valley Girl."[59] For the more panoramic view of Dhyana we are indebted to New York writer and president of Artkraft Strauss Tama Starr, a mutual friend of the couple with whom McKenna often stayed when visiting New York. Dhyana married a French chef at age fifteen, and was a fabulous cook herself. She studied fine art in Philadelphia, read music and practiced baroque pieces on a soprano recorder, drew and painted, designed clothes, invented herbal medicines, practiced botany, was a masseuse, a skilled meditator, and a belly dancer of note. She was, explains Starr, "a seeker of knowledge." Given this gallimaufry of interests, and that Dhyana's long, elaborate letters amounted to "multicolor collages, including drawings and watercolors and scientific quips and factoids tucked into the corners," Dhyana and Terence were not the unlikely duo that was otherwise apparent. They remain on and off lovers until 1972, when finally parting ways, though remaining affectionate friends. Dhyana was killed in 1992 in a car accident in Hawaii. She was making love to a nineteen-year-old man (the driver of the vehicle who survived) at the time of impact.[60]

McKenna traveled to Cambodia with Dhyana, regrouping with Watson later in Calcutta. They all travel on to Rangoon, but are pressured to leave Burma within forty-eight hours, before transiting to Bangkok. With Terry and Dhyana set on temple sightseeing, the party seek visas for Laos. Since the capital of Laos, Vientiane, was under US control, they needed visas from the embassy in Bangkok. As it was necessary to leave their passports with the embassy overnight, it was an unsettling juncture. Circulating rumors of government agents performing on-the-spot conscriptions fed their paranoia. While mulling this over, an incident at their hotel the following morning sealed their fate. As they were eating breakfast, an armored personnel carrier full of GIs firing their semi-automatics into the air drove through the hotel courtyard and careened straight into the swimming pool.

Pandemonium had caught up with them, and it was time to move on. That Terry and Rick had to cancel a meeting with British writer, Taoist, and *I Ching* translator John Blofeld, in Bangkok, adds to their disappointment.[61] The proverbial cats on a scorched tin roof leave Thailand immediately. Rick and Linda depart for Hong Kong, then Taipei. Terence departs with Dhyana on a long-planned tour of Indonesia.

LEPIDOPTERIST AT LARGE

McKenna trekked the archipelago via Singapore and Malaysia. Six months in the region from late October 1969 enables the collection of butterflies and beetles, a passion inspired by trailblazer Alfred Russel Wallace. In extensive fieldwork, first in the Amazon River Basin (1848–1852), and then in the Malay Archipelago (1854–1862), Wallace had identified the faunal divide known as the Wallace line, marking out Wallacea as a distinct biogeographic region that includes Sulawesi, Lombok, Sumbawa, Flores, Sumba, Timor, and Seram. A collector of some 126,000 exotic and many undiscovered species, from large mammals to butterflies and birds of paradise across the region, Wallace was an expansive writer and superb illustrator whose detailed journaling of his adventures made him a popular figure for aspiring natural historians.

The self-made naturalist-cum-spiritualist underdog was venerated by McKenna. Wallace's Amazonian and Far Eastern ventures were supported by the sale of collected specimens—though he later lost almost everything through unsuccessful investments. Unlike Charles Darwin and Charles

Lyell, Wallace did not inherit family wealth and never enjoyed a long-term, salaried position. Noteworthy for McKenna, Wallace was extraordinarily resourceful, supporting himself by and large from his publications. Wallace was also inclined toward marginal ideas across politics, religion, and science, not least of all the idea of the transmutation of species, a precursor to his independent theory of natural selection, for which Darwin largely received credit.

As a boy, Terence pored over *The Malay Archipelago* and other of Wallace's striking illustrated accounts. He grew captivated by the generous writing style and explorative spirit of a figure who sought exotic species of butterflies, orangutans, and birds, with a great eye for detail. As a natural history boffin, by eleven or twelve, McKenna had amassed insects, butterflies, shark's teeth, ancient seashells, and spiral ammonites from the dry arroyos and sandstone country of his youth. While other boys his age collected baseball cards and stamps, he amassed rocks and other natural ephemera. "His tarantulas, blue morpho butterflies, and gigantic horned stag beetles," Dennis recalls, "arrived via the mail-order catalogs he found listed in the back of *Science News*."[62] Before leaving the United States, he worked as a laboratory assistant in the entomology department at UC Berkeley and was engaged chiefly in the preparation of insect specimens. Collecting is so cardinal to his persona that in the wake of the 1965 psychological horror film *The Collector*—in which the protagonist is an amateur entomologist with a large collection of butterflies and a penchant for stalking beautiful women—Mahoney cheekily dubs McKenna "The Collector."[63] He later explains that, in his "pre-Buddhist incarnation," the attraction of tropical butterflies was "the exuberant expanse of color, the affirmation of the patterned richness of the universe that seemed to be thrown out like a spark by these things."[64] It is the lepidoptera that most retained his interest beyond childhood. Besides, practicing lepidopterology in remote regions happened to be a convenient activity for a man on the lam (see figure 3.2).

Roughly tracing his hero's journey, McKenna made several traversals of the Wallace line, from Sundaland in the west to Wallacea in the east, with Sulawesi as his primary objective. In Singapore, the Collector says he hired himself out to Chinese "natural product dealers" who issued him with a list of desired finds, among them butterflies, which were gathered on a commission basis. He claims to have spent months with these folks, who spoke neither English nor Indonesian.[65] McKenna trekked a month or so in Malaysia and Sumatra before returning to Singapore in December to sell his specimens. In late December, he lands in Java, busses east across the island, continues on to Bali, and travels the length of the Lesser

FIGURE 3.2
Hunting in Malaysia, 1969.

Sunda Island chain, visiting Lombok, Sumba, Sumbawa, Timor, and Flores Islands.[66] Throughout this sojourn, McKenna remained off-radar, his parents occasionally receiving postcards from "HCE," the non de guerre lifted from *Finnegans Wake* (where it designates Humphrey Chimpden Earwicker, among countless other designations, including "Here Comes Everybody") that he assumed as he slowly picked his way across the archipelago "in search of butterflies and anonymity."[67]

In one of his last public appearances, McKenna mooted a further motive for travels in the region: searching for evidence of the shamanic use of hallucinogens. He traveled from Nepal to India, and throughout Malaysia, Thailand, and Indonesia, using his guise as a professional butterfly collector "as an excuse to go to these extremely rural and tribal situations and observe what was going on."[68] While we're presented with a portrait of an amateur anthropologist, there is little evidence that McKenna had anything more than superficial dialogue with Malaysian and Indonesian culture. Very much unlike fellow autodidact, collector, and seeker of patterns Harry Smith, the anthropologist and filmmaker named by biographer John Szwed as "the ultimate bohemian," McKenna had neither the passion nor patience for native languages, Tibetan, Bahasa, Japanese, or otherwise.[69] When encounters are related, it is to highlight adversities endured, specifically of the immuno-challenging variety. Terence had, for example, occasion to recall his reception upon arrival in a village, its inhabitants assembling to watch the visitor receive a gourd of corn beer. The old women of the village, he suspected, had sat up the night before chewing the corn and spitting it out into a bowl, so it would ferment. He was repulsed, but there was nothing for him to do than raise the gourd, thank everybody, and announce: "Here it comes."[70] Unlike Wallace, or Smith, McKenna was no keen ethnologist. He preferred insect "societies" over the human variety, concluding that the shamanic use of hallucinogens in these islands lay in the remote past, having "retreated to the status of a myth."[71]

The Indonesian venture is patchy in detail. As Watson stated, Dhyana "was the only person who knew what happened in Indonesia,"[72] and those details died with her. While among the more covert episodes in McKenna's life, a rough itinerary over this period can be deduced from a composite of the Boulder Statement, the narrative of *True Hallucinations*, and the meticulous attention to dates and precise geo-locations attached to each of over 2,000 insect specimens collected on his sojourns. These specimens were carefully wrapped and folded in newspaper and other ephemeral "envelopes" and stored in a great old trunk inherited by Klea McKenna. In 2008, Klea curated an interactive photographic exhibition at PlaySpace Gallery in San Francisco, which was then compiled as a book, *The Butterfly Hunter*, a project salvaging memory fragments from an otherwise cloaked period of her father's life. Klea has stated that the catches and locations were not chosen randomly. Like an archaeologist unearthing "encoded messages from another time," she processed each item, tracing Terence's course through Singapore, Malaysia, across Indonesia, and eventually to Colombia. "I see him, each night returning to a small, sweaty, mosquito-netted room, sorting and labeling the day's boon to the hum of an electric fan. Meanwhile, the Vietnam War was raging, the Nixon administration was self-destructing, student revolts were flaring around the world and he was folding the headlines of these events into hundreds of origami-like envelopes to hold his Lepidoptera specimens."[73]

The Butterfly Hunter features eighty photographs of Lepidoptera—butterflies and moths—and beetles that McKenna collected, backgrounded by the magazine pages, comic strips, and personal documents that formed the original envelopes for the specimens. The book also includes photos of McKenna in white garb with long net against jungle backdrops that he had sent home to Paonia—with the project relating the guilt Terence had formed toward his practice by the mid-seventies. "Butterfly hunting," Klea writes, "is a conflicted activity, a desire for beauty and a small act of violence, both justified by science. Preserving something by taking its life."[74] As each "origami" envelope included the date and precise place of capture, Klea was able to chart her father's itinerary on regional maps reproduced in the book's endsheets. The first specimen presented in the book, a golden butterfly wrapped in a Malay comic, was captured in Maran, Pahang State, Malaysia, October 30, 1969. Another early capture places him at Kuah on Langkawi Island, northwest coast of Malaysia, on November 17, one day after his twenty-third birthday.

One stand-out story derives from this period. We have already met Dr. Karl Heintz of Far Eastern Mining and Minerals, a figure encountered at the Rama, "the best and only hotel" in Kupang, Timor, where McKenna was a guest for ten days in February 1970. This is a remarkable story in the life of an amateur naturalist. McKenna is suddenly presented with an unbelievable opportunity: a lucrative all-expenses-paid assignment to the Amazon as a biologist on a survey team. It is a marriage of convenience. The Singapore-based Far East Mining seeks the façade of science to lend its operations legitimacy and to avoid a tax burden. Terence, short on funds, effectively masquerades as a scientist. "I traveled and lived under the dramatic assumption that international police agencies were combing the globe looking for me. My cover, that of a graduate student in entomology doing field work for a degree—a butterfly collector."[75] Matching their conceit with a con of his own, McKenna is prepared to throw in with "a band of renegade Nazi scientists," an exercise in frontier libertarianism that, had it materialized, may have ranked among the strangest relationships to have emerged at the turn of the seventies.

McKenna traveled to Bali buoyant, sharing news with the freaks of Kuta Beach that a Waffen SS type he met in Kupang was about to send him $500 and a ticket aboard the SS *Rotterdam* embarking from Singapore, all enabling the first leg of a corporate-sponsored trip to the Amazon. He reunites with Dhyana, with whom he then splits amicably, and not for the last time. Awaiting news from Heintz, presumably, he prepares his specimens and ships them to buyers in Singapore and the United States.[76] Checking *poste restante* in Denpasar every day for a week earns him no reward. He suspects that his "false history" had been uncovered. He will not be hunting butterflies for Nazis after all. While this will not be his ticket to the Amazon, he would look back on the strange incident in Kupang as further proof that he was destined to travel to the Amazon, and that he had come "under the spell of the cosmic giggle."[77]

Meanwhile, McKenna resumes his original plan, outfitting himself for a final Wallacean tour out to Ambon and Seram in the Moluccas (Maluku),[78] via Sulawesi. He elsewhere indicates this journey took in Ternate, an island in the Malukus.[79] The oldest and largest island within Wallacea, Sulawesi (formerly Celebes) hosts a rich fauna with a large number of species unique to the island, like the dwarf cuscus, the spectral tarsier (*Tarsius tarsier*, a primate that fits in the palm of your hand), and the miniature buffaloes, the anoas. The features of Sulawesi's birds and mammals distinguished from those in other parts of the world had led Wallace to propose, in *The Malay Archipelago*, that Sulawesi represented an ancient land, with its unique fauna steeped "in a remote antiquity."[80] McKenna was a little more single-minded and yet no less infatuated with the place. In the south of Sulawesi, he remains seven weeks in "the little explored interior,"[81] his hunting grounds the forests of Bantimurung Bulusaraung National Park, a site for a rich haul over March–April. Given local specimens were on average 10–12 percent larger in wing surface than elsewhere, Sulawesi was known as the holy grail of butterfly collecting, with the falls at Bantimurung among Wallace's inspired destinations.

Despite his close proximity to butterfly paradise, McKenna appears to have had Nazis on his mind upon arrival in the region. Bussing inland from Makassar, he made his way to the district police headquarters at Maros to arrange admission to the park. There he encounters a police colonel who appeared to him unsettlingly like Erich von Stroheim in "SS drag," and who attempted, unsuccessfully, to separate him from his passport.[82] Delivered above the waterfall at Bantimurung by the police, he finds his way to the house of "the butterfly guru," Ali Baduk, "a small wiry man, with intense eyes and long, very long fingers." For seven dollars a day, he has food, lodging, and all the butterfly collecting he wants.

Baduk impresses as something of a butterfly whisperer under whose guidance the young traveler with a beard every match for Wallace's is led toward the grail. In *The Malay Archipelago*, the naturalist had written of his bounty discovered along the rock pools between the lower and the upper falls:

> The large semi-transparent butterfly, *Idea tondana*, flew lazily along by the dozens, and it was here that I at length obtained an insect which I had hoped but hardly expected to meet with—the magnificent *Papilio androcles*, one of the largest and rarest known swallow-tailed butterflies. . . . When the sun shone hottest about noon, the moist beach of the pool below the upper fall presented a beautiful sight, being dotted with groups of gay butterflies—orange, yellow, white, blue, and green—which on being disturbed rose into the air by hundreds, forming clouds of variegated colours.[83]

Since he was a child, McKenna had dreamt of the region Wallace dubbed the "Kingdom of Butterflies." McKenna observes a "swift, twice falling, cool river that cascades down to a forested chasm of porous limestone," where "the magic of this place really exceeds my ability to understand it." Under the eye of his Sulawesian swami, at the upper end of the valley, McKenna came to understand the value of the mystery. "Ornithoptera are the Great Birdwing butterflies of the Old World Tropics; they are the largest and contend as the most beautiful in the world, in the class with the Morphos of the Amazon Basin. And the Celebes form of the Genus Triodes is the most magnificent of the Birdwings." On the first day out, on which they catch two males, he is ecstatic. Later in his two-week stay they find the female *Triodes* and examples of the *Papilio androcles* Wallace had collected at this site over 130 years before.[84] Any of the "birdwings" McKenna collected from this and other sites were likely sold for a reasonable profit.

Wallace documented some 256 different species in an area then alive with butterflies. Already by the 1970s, not long after McKenna collected his specimens, the butterfly population of Bantimurung suffered a dramatic collapse at the hands of collectors and tourists. Few butterflies are today observable at Bantimurung Falls, save those pinned to boards and hawked as souvenirs. Of the nearby butterfly museum inside the national park accessible through a gate under a towering "birdwing" statue, sad commentaries now portray a virtual butterfly mausoleum.

McKenna had a singular and near-surgical dedication to extracting butterflies for sale. And while he appears to have approached the practice as a form of meditation, it held elements of the unexpected:

> In the bamboo groves of the higher valley . . . I came face to face with a small Indonesian lemur. I had watched a day-flying moth halt its flight and arrange itself on a bamboo stalk about four feet to my left. As I turned to look at it I felt a sense of motion in the background. There, gripping a swaying stem with splayed fingers, its

enormous yellow eyes peering curiously into mine, was the lemur. We had a long moment of recognition, and then it leaped backward and out of sight.[85]

After trekking out to Maluku Province, collecting on Ambon Island and Seram, from Sulawesi's capital of Makassar passage is sought to Hong Kong. There, McKenna arrives in mid-May before hurrying on to Taipei (Taiwan) to rendezvous with Watson and reunite with Dhyana. In the wake of Nepal, Rick and Linda had been living in Taipei, where they were taught Chinese philosophy and martial arts by Martin Inn, a student of T'ai Chi Ch'uan, which he learned from Chung Ta-Chen (see figure 3.3).[86]

FIGURE 3.3
Linda Underhill and Rick Watson with T'ai Chi Ch'uan instructors Chung Ta-Chen and Martin Inn, Japanese Buddhist Temple, district of Hsi-men Ting, Taipei, Taiwan, mid-1970. Photo courtesy of Martin Inn.

Plans to stop in Taiwan are thwarted, as meager finances and news of his mother's grave illness prompt a hasty flight to Japan. Terence arrives in Tokyo on June 10, and ends up residing there until late September. Upon arriving, he and Dhyana visit Expo '70 in Osaka. Australian expat, poet, and Dada-inspired visual artist Terry Reid recalls his first sighting of the man he soon befriends. Out on the plaza, tall and lanky in the company of Japanese, with his long reddish beard and full white "tropical" dress, McKenna stands out "like a Light House." Reid helps them find a tiny six-tatami room in an apartment building owned by the daughter of the Akimoto family, a teacher of tea ceremony. With the assistance of Masayasu Takayama, a fellow instructor and graduate in Spanish and international relations from Tokyo's Sophia University, McKenna teaches English at the Nakano Academy of American English for the equivalent of $5 an hour, a then tidy sum.[87] There are escapades to the mountains around Tokyo to collect butterflies, but of the Tokyo interlude, McKenna felt trapped in an inhuman work cycle. "The nights on the trains. The airless rooms of the Akihabara English language schools."[88] Work is suffocating, but *the work* was unceasing. Clive Hart's *Structure and Motif in Finnegans Wake* is carefully absorbed and doubtlessly woven into salons at the Akimoto apartment where backpacker friends and bohemian expats convene to smoke hash and bear witness to McKenna's stratospheric flights of the mind. And set against Strauss and Bach, often in Takayama's presence, a loquacious drawl drew expatriate habitués to Classic Café, hidden in a narrow side-alley to Nakano's high-roofed, glass-covered mall, hand-built from the fire-bombed remnants of postwar Tokyo.[89] McKenna maintains correspondence with Takayama throughout his life, and while he hoped one day to return to Japan, the opportunity never arose.

McKenna barely had time to apply the brakes to the decade's accelerating escape velocity. Multiple factors contributed to the sensation of "deepening alienation" he feels when finally departing tropical Asia.[90] He does not relish teaching English at Nakano. He discovers that his books have been destroyed in a fire at the Malcolm residence in the Berkeley Hills. He learns that his mother's cancer has advanced, and as her condition worsens his status as a fugitive keeps him from her. Compounding these woes, despite his collection hauls, finances remain dire.

POST ELECTRIC EXILE

The primary route of escape from these financial straits was a dog-eared manuscript hauled around Asia in the late sixties as if it were a passport to the future. As a prevailing life theme, McKenna intended to write his way out of exile. Expelled, or perhaps more accurately, propelled, from Paonia, compelled to leave Mountain View, evading Interpol in Asia, expulsion from Nepal, exile—the reality and the myth—loomed large in his imagination. Later cautiously suggesting that he "chose exile,"[91] however you carve it, McKenna behaved like a writer in exile. And despite the unverified claims—such as the graveyard sex, the "watch list"—an exiled sensibility permeates a manifesto completed while ostensibly outlawed from his homeland.

Tokyo was a convenient interlude to complete this prophetic work. A year from Glenwood Springs, McKenna wrote like a "metapolitical" exile. The "sixties" had ended. What he and his friends thought was an unstoppable freight train now seemed no more than a mayfly in Nixon's path. Under that administration, America was "locked in a death grip with a demonic consort that leads the Republic bleeding into psychosis and schizophrenia," as observed in the closing pages of "Post Electric Thought," a manuscript written in Seychelles, Berkeley, and Tokyo between 1968 and 1970.[92] With the Indochina crisis spiraling out of control, the world was "plunging toward the abyss." And with the "final cultural struggle" then being waged, the possibility of species obliteration grew perilously near. Offering an ungainly program of nonlinear solutions, McKenna imagined the work a lightning rod for the rebellion. He fantasized his anarcho-crypto tract firing the revolutionary imagination of late-sixties Berkeley. He dreamt of provoking thought on the "post electric society," with the end goal something named the "entasis of 2000," a thesis in which "electric man" was destined to dwell in the "hyperspatial plane of pure energy" that had been discovered by Einstein.[93]

The work was an exercise in perseverance. A delivery adept who captivated audiences with his memory and wit, McKenna struggled to affect his charm via the sensorially regimented world of print. The ill-fortuned "Crypto-Rap" is a testament to this struggle. A style note omitted in "Post Electric Thought" invokes the advantages of the lively rap over communication interred in text: "I would much rather be talking to you,"[94] he writes, with a preference for spirited oratory over the written word. But disparagement and rejection did not quash his desire to forge a utopian manifesto. The updated manuscript saw a title change and obliterated any mention of "crypto anarchism" (the phrase replaced with "post electric"). McKenna banishes "crypto" from his lexicon thereafter. Finding an audience for this revised esoteric polemic becomes a primary objective in the pre-Colombian phase. That and remaining aloof from authorities.

A savage garden of ideas, "Post Electric Thought" is a work its author subsequently disavowed. A lumbering document from which he grew distant, it is nevertheless an early barometer of trademark thought-forms. Outrageously naive at times, it is a provocative missive, bristling with futurist insights, notably in the realm of virtual reality, networked information, and universal connectivity.[95] As the document opens a window on the mind of its author during a long phase of uncertainty, social upheaval, and personal turmoil, I have cause to address it at some length.

"Post Electric Thought" offers a distinct echo of the rhetoric of the "electrical sublime" that, by 1970, is a century-old tradition among US commentators. In fact, media scholars James W. Carey and John J. Quirk publish a two-part article in 1970 that critically dissects the McLuhanesque rhetoric investing electricity "with the aura of divine force and utopian gift" and which is reckoned as "the progenitor of a new era of social life."[96] Like McLuhan and other cultural imagineers, McKenna's interest in technology reflects mythopoesis over engineering. In particular, the enthusiasm for "solid state" electronics exhibits intrigue with the alchemical symbolism of "the stone."

As the cloying work of a young man, it's understandable why McKenna distanced himself from "Post Electric Thought." It was likely as embarrassing to him as a love letter from his youth. An effort to define "the final, total and complete meaning of Love," a universal principle manifest as "the union of the many with the One," the "nexus of logic and intuition" considered "the primary idea of all metaphysics," and "the central mystery at the heart of all higher religions," it is more or less a love thesis.[97] Like the chorus line to a schmaltzy love song, "the One" is a personal revelation chanted ad nauseam, including in the very last lines:

> We, like the gnomes in the song by "Pink Floyd" will learn ". . . a new way to say Hurray!" It is always been there to be said: it is the exultant shout of Deity at the art and the act of eternal play within the totality of Love that is the infinite creation of the Good. Let us then, with love's pure vision insist that the river run.[98]

Allowing that to settle, the manuscript sheds light on its author's psychedelic philosophy in its protean phase, championing nonlinearity, intuition, and the "union of opposites." In this early layer of thought, a *philosophia perennis* is animated by three interwoven themes: Taoism, Neo-Platonism (the nonduality of the Plotinian One), and the psychedelic experience that facilitates access to Huxley's "Mind-at-Large." The text shows inspiration from the phenomenologies of Husserl and Merleau-Ponty and is permeated with Jung, Eliade, and McLuhan. In the first instance, alchemy, and specifically Alexandrine alchemy, is implicit to the "numinous idea complex" unpacked and pivotal to understanding the "unity of being" desired in the post electric world.[99] For the Eliadean crypto-anarchist, the "electric eschatology" is a future atemporal space to which humanity is destined. It is the perpetually refinable "enstatic" mode of "post electric" society, a concept repeated so often it is as if the repetition will trigger the electronic dispensation. And, finally, the social life of electricity is clearly inspired by McLuhan's study of the impact of print on modern consciousness.

"Post Electric Thought" welds millenarian and Gnostic insight under the aegis of an "electronic optimism"—circumstances rendering this unearthed document the Nag Hammadi of the "techgnostic" tradition.[100] Enabled by "techno-yoga" that delivers enlightenment to all who desire it, the prophesied outcome is a kind of psycho-cultural transformation. Pivotal is the mercurial power of electricity, "an emanation of divine Pneuma," and also of "Sophia," noted to be "the feminine power essence that is knowledge," the attainment of which is deemed essential to becoming liberated from "the matrix." This "feminine-electrical" current will enable the Many to be charged into the One."[101]

Following a rambling survey of successes and failures to attain "the One" within the history of religion, the work charts the transit to "holo-electric culture" in which, after 400 years of print-led oppression, universal connectivity is achievable. We learn that a kind of "electro-Aquarius" is attainable "with a little help from my friends," that is, cybernetics, electronics, holography, Tantra, and psychedelics. Ultimately, advances in miniaturization foster the potential for transcendence at the genetic level, the controlled means through which "man" becomes the "Anthropic Adam," "a sacral, telepathic race of men and women with perfect bodies sharing a mind of infinite content." In an indeterminate pantheism indebted as much to McLuhan as Arthur C. Clarke, "consciousness becomes no longer human at all but is diffused through all being."[102]

"Post Electric Thought" is a youthful libertarian work of transhumanist futurism. Resistant to rational materialism and embracing Lucien Lévy-Bruhl's subject/object-dissolving "participation mystique," dismissive of Marxism and Maoism, the manifesto is founded in a suspicion of government and faith, while projecting a future where intuition prevails over ideology.[103] The age in which it was produced is deemed equally desperate and hopeful. While America had become "a cultural Golem that must be destroyed," the ideal of America remains foregrounded. Indeed, a key passage from the US Declaration of Independence forms the manuscript's epigraph. The nation possesses "a technical, ideological and even ethical capability for cultural reformation that . . . is more than equal to its manifested destructiveness." While replete with "ego ridden corporate and pentagon bureaucrats . . . leather clad motorcycle police . . . hydrogen weapons and lobotomised politicians," America holds the "unrealized energy" of its youth-led rebellion.[103]

As a battleground upon which the world of linearity and uniformity face the collective drive to realize the One, the twentieth century is depicted as a struggle with the demiurge of Gnostic lore. The "flawed Ialdabaoth" appears unchained "wherever the blight of 'liberating' technical processes touch the earth." The narrative has shades of H. G. Wells's *War of the Worlds*, except now the omnipresent alientech—"an electrical mode [that] . . . proliferated to every corner of the earth"—holds the promise of adaptation and survival "at the darkest hour, while crematoria roared and cities that print had built—e.g. London, Berlin, Dresden—burned."[105]

If not already the strangest of documents, "Post Electric Thought" addresses the path out of this calamity via *Finnegans Wake*, described as "a kind of high-speed photograph that shows the mystery in the act of leaving literature and taking up a new abode." McKenna is obsessed with the *Wake* as a hyperspatial object. Joyce is championed as the literary hero-channeler of the Many in the One. And, as a focal point through this period, *Finnegans Wake* is identified not as a book but as "a word-blurb concretization of the One." With its multitudinous acausal narrative "coursing through the mind," the text prompts a revelation that "the individual subject/object relationship breaks down" in the face of its central perception: "that each is everything." Following McLuhan, the *Wake* approximates a sacred text. In this literary model of the post electric future in which "hyperspace and hypertime" flourish, all is "mercurial and has the capacity of becoming anything or everything."[106]

As a patchwork thesis declared bereft of value, the manuscript envisions a post electric social theory guiding the conscious creation of what is introduced as the "hyperspatial zeitgeist."[107] While *The Republic*, *Civitas Dei*, and Moore's *Utopia* are among exemplary models, the "holo-electric" utopia was to be metaphysically augmented with alchemy and Tantra—traditions of gnosis of both the Occident and the East (Northern Hindu)—as well as cybernetics and psychedelics. The work illustrates immersion in the scholarship of John Woodroffe, Chang Chen Chi, Walter Evans-Wentz, and Herbert V. Guenther on the subject of Eastern gnosis. This study began in earnest on Seychelles when absorbing the yoga and theosophical literature accumulated in Mombasa. "Post Electric Thought" features a long meditation on nondual Vedanta, especially its classical expression in the Tantra Shastras. In this philosophy, Siva-Sakti is the Oneness that appears to offer practical insight on the achievement of the "declension of the One into the Many" anticipated.[108] These are non-devotional interests. While his pre-Colombian phase demonstrates inspiration as much from Eastern as from Western esoterica, McKenna holds only partial interest in the embodiment of esoteric practices then growing popular, like yoga, meditation, and Tantra.

In a statement far ahead of its time, McKenna embraced a futurist phenomenology that Davis names "esoteritech."[109] Within this thesis, computers are considered "metaphors for a functioning universe and ubiquitous information." In this prophecy of the Net, information is envisaged to permeate a future networked topography. Any part of the "electrical matrix" in this proto-chaos vision "can manifest itself at any other part instantaneously," with the computer regarded as "a small cybernetic universe wherein the Hermetic axiom—that what is not here is nowhere and what is here is everywhere—is seen to be true—phenomenologically." In commentary predating Leary's cyberphilia, it is announced that "all of the information generated of interest and relevance to the totality of humanity could be instantaneously available to everyone through the cybernetic matrix."[110]

The most utopian sentiment in this tract is reserved for technology hailed as "the ultimate media form" that perfectly mirrors 3D reality: holography. Beholding this future-tech, McKenna embraced a contrivance deployed in science fiction since Asimov's *Foundation Trilogy*. One imagines these ideas etched out on lonely Seychelles. "The act of love in a holographic environment" builds toward a multidimensional holo-erotic climax, which transforms "a brief internal experience into an endlessly intensified and realized psychic event." In the adaptation of holography as "the means of numinous completion of the post electric revolution," McKenna appeared to be ahead of the curve of seventies sci-fi and New Age physics. His adoption is rose-colored with shades of McLuhan and Eliade, for as the medium hallmarking the return to "sacral sense ratios with a fully constellated and functioning consciousness," holography is championed as the means to "keep the new electric world soul in circulation."[111]

As declared in this remarkable document, "unimaginable dimensions of mind remain to be explored and should be investigated with all the energy that the establishment now expends on devising new ways to stun and kill civilian populations."[112] Accompanying these thoughts, the electric exegesis includes McKenna's first known statement on the role of psychedelics. Specific compounds and organic sources are reckoned to be "our way back" to a gnosis lost to print and its mechanisms. On the menu are marijuana, described as a "kind of mystery sacrament"; LSD, a "prototype of the expanded electrical information matrix"; and mescaline and psilocybin, mentioned briefly as a "direct inlet into a high energy and One-emulating world of natural vegetable gnosis."[113] Yet most profound among the emergent "third generation" psychedelics, and the main doorway into the "hyperspatial zeitgeist," is a "camphorous-smelling rose or orange crystalline waxy paste." DMT is then named in a digression unusually detailed amid an abstract text sparsely addressing empirical means to "the One":

> A fragment half the size of a pea, is placed in the pipe, vaporized and deep inhaled four or five times. A rupture of plane will occur, subjectively a trans-linguistic totally One oriented hyper-instant, objectively about five minutes. . . . So contemporary and numinous is this expression of the One that it may be seen as the current concretization of the hyperspatial zeitgeist. . . . This experience, approached in a state of karmic purity and experienced in solitude, daylight and quiet, is a model of the content of the highest expression of electronically collectivized being.[114]

Although readers could be forgiven for thinking otherwise, unlike much of the praxis described in this text—for example, holography—the "DMT flash" is not the substance of sci-fi fantasy. As his earliest known report on the DMT experience—deriving from episodes that very few had experienced in the modern context—the report illustrates how McKenna might have had his fingers (lips) on the pulse (pipe) of the zeitgeist.

The proto-psychedelic love tract was soon abandoned. Initiated in Berkeley and a product of the labor of its author's early career as a meta-exile, the exegesis did not bear fruit as the revolutionary manifesto it was conceived to be. Nonetheless, despite distancing himself from the effort, its prophesied content gave shape to a futurist career. This discussion, then, offers something of a preamble to chapter 11. For now, we embark on the next leg of the antipodean odyssey that caused McKenna to leave his esoteric love treatise behind.

4 LA CHORRERA

More than a physical place, La Chorrera is a sacred site in McKennan folklore. A wild coming-of-age drama, the "A. R. Wallace Memorial Expedition" proved transformative for both brothers, leaving lasting impressions on subsequent generations of psychedelic explorers. In early 1971, at a juncture both personal and global, vulnerable and turbulent, the brothers' Amazonian adventure turned out to be a quest into the psilocybean sublime, a place where reality and fiction merged. As would be conveyed in *True Hallucinations*, the brothers had arrived at "the history defining moment when humanity would march into the higher dimension,"[1] a cosmic venture culminating with Den tolling the mission bell, Terry encountering a flying saucer, and the explorers expelled from the jungle. An unexpected threshold where the shamanic and the psychotic grew seamless, the quest offered the source material for the bulk of Terence's epic memoir. The remote destination in the Colombian Amazon to which he made repeat sojourns in 1971 became the focal point for Terence's adventures in the psychedelic occult. This chapter commences our plunge into the terrain that triggered a legend.

PATH TO THE AMAZON

Though Terence was remote from his mid-sixties hierophany by the turn of the seventies, his elf-led graduation ceremony became the inspirational backdrop to a modern-day grail adventure with apocalyptic undertones. The spice pipe had been passed around in the long hajj to the Amazon. When Dennis visited Berkeley in 1967, Terence announced he knew what the philosopher's stone was. "It's sitting in that jar right there on the bookshelf."[2] A year later, meeting Hartley in New York, Terence shared the now compelling idea—from Dennis (and John Parker)—that some hallucinogens "fit into the DNA." The only action now worthy of attention appeared to operate not on the street level but on the molecular level. "So far, the most interesting unlikelihood in our lives is DMT, right?"[3]

At the height of resistance to the war, Terence had turned away from classical forms of organized resistance. After all, as he earlier contended in "Crypto-Rap," the answer lay neither in the political science of the New Left nor in the *San Francisco Oracle*.[4] He was convinced that the historical crisis, which is the crisis of history, demanded novelty. Traditional protest was patently ineffectual in the face of "the *lux natura*, the spiritual radiance behind organic nature,"[5] to which they had been exposed. Out of this romance, he was determined to surf the swells of novelty at its native point break.

"As forces of evil harangue the unconscious masses of the planet toward world disaster a few, young and non-linear announce alternatives to ruin." Such was the contention in "Post Electric Thought."[6] And such a band of the few soon mobilized for the Amazon, the jungle source of the DMT to which the brothers are called. Though John Parker never makes the trip, he serves as an inspiration. According to a letter from Dennis that Terence received in Taipei in May 1970, Parker wanted to join the expedition. Written almost a year before they embark, the letter reveals Parker's stature as an absent guide. Dennis pushes for an itinerary through Mexico (Mazatec highlands) and Central America. Among his reasons is that Parker, apprehensive of a South American adventure, would join them only if they first travel to Mexico, imagined to be a "proving ground for methods and equipment" in advance of the push southward. To work with Parker "on methods and specific problems would be invaluable training," wrote Dennis. "Without JP, could any of us really expect to find and process the treasures we seek in the Amazonian jungles?"[7] As Dennis explains fifty-two years later, over years of correspondence, Parker was the "genesis" of more than a few of their adopted ideas. Referring to an arcane alchemy implicit to their Amazonian odyssey, Parker appears to have been a stimulus for an idea that lay at the heart of the coming experiment: "that β-carbolines can intercalate into DNA and render it superconductive," like some kind of "radio broadcast."[8]

In the fall of 1970, Terence hauls up in Canada, where he works in chain restaurants, residing as close as possible to the United States without crossing its border. Paranoid, he had gained entry to Vancouver from Tokyo using the Canadian passport of Terry Reid, whose passport photo bore a great likeness.[9] With the Amazon an all-consuming passion, a rented clapboard house in Victoria, British Columbia, became the center of research and planning over the next three months. He is joined in Victoria by Hartley, Malcolm, Bill Cole, Dhyana, and another Berkeley friend, Michael Lasky (a.k.a. "Dave") (see figure 4.1). The group ransack articles from a

FIGURE 4.1
La Chorrera planning meeting, Victoria, Canada, fall 1970. Left to right: Michael Malcolm, Bill Cole, Michael ("Dave") Lasky, Terry, and Dhyana. Photo courtesy of Sara Hartley.

science library database and maintain correspondence with Dennis in Colorado. Terence recruits Dave—as well as Royce Kelley and Cole's younger brother Tom—to join himself, Dennis, and Sara on a trek to the Putumayo region of Colombia's interior. Under the pretense of an amateur ethnobotanical expedition, over three months they were to observe the botanical and social environment of the Witoto. They select as their goal a place where the Río Igara Paraná passes through a roaring cataract into a placid lake on the shores of which stood a Catholic mission. Intuited as a modern-day quest for "the stone," La Chorrera would become the site of an "experiment" whose legend in psychedelic folklore was earned as much from its freakish absurdity than anything remotely resembling science.

What became known as "the experiment at La Chorrera" had uncertain advance parameters. The original plan for the Amazonian quest involved an overland trek to Peru, via Mexico and Central America. Terence had proposed to make the journey with Malcolm in a Land Rover belonging to Malcolm's girlfriend Joan. The plan evaporated for reasons logistical as much as legal. Terence's problems with the law necessitated avoiding the

United States completely, that is, until circumstances compelled him otherwise. On October 25, 1970, Hazelle McKenna succumbed to her long battle with cancer. As she lay dying, in a desperate bid to see her, Terence boarded a flight from Vancouver to Grand Junction. On instruction from his father, he boarded a return flight in San Francisco. He was too late. Hazelle died while he was en route. And as Dennis related, he need not risk the remaining journey. "He was crushed," said Mahoney. "Not only was she a wonderful person, but he really loved his mother."[10] If the times weren't tough enough, within two weeks the court for the Southern District of New York issued a warrant for his arrest.

The ground had shifted. Unable to visit his dying mother, there was no genuine closure for Terence, a circumstance that had a significant bearing on his subsequent conjectures about time. Hazelle's passing appeared to coincide with the dissipation of the "post electric" élan that had consumed her son so thoroughly in the years prior. That drive morphed into something else in the jungle interior. They were stepping into the unknown, a juncture Watson marked with a "poetic talisman"—among the few poems he wrote to McKenna that survived—to safeguard their passage:

> By shores of Titicaca
> Smoke the silver hookah
> Erect your star antenna
> Broadcast the name McKenna
> In acrostics Kabbalistic
> And pun it in Mandaean
> Then surely crypto-mystic.[11]

Preparing for the jump-off, the McKennas scoured any literature they could find concerning ayahuasca. Possibly the earliest text alerting Terence to the visionary brew was *The Rivers Ran East*, the 1953 account of explorer and former OSS officer Colonel Leonard Clark's epic 1946–1947 quest into the Peruvian Amazon in search of the Seven Cities of Cibola (El Dorado). Douglas Hansen apprised Terence of *The Rivers Ran East* in 1964, and while we do not know the extent of its influence, the title is listed in McKenna's legacy library at LibraryThing. The book is notable for Clark's attention to botanical and ethnological knowledge, and his tendency toward exaggeration characterizing the author's description of a secret visionary brew made from what was known to the Asháninka (who Clark called "Campa") as *camorampi*, or the "soul vine." The mysterious brew of which Clark does not himself partake is described as "very like opium, apparently in the De Quincy–like dreams it would presently bring on." While Clark feigned interest in the "medical secrets" of the "witchmen" as his cover for entering the "high bush"—that is, locating the lost cities in the upper Marañón—the *materia medica* arguably comprised his actual El Dorado.[12]

Stories such as Clark's provided early tropes for an ethnobotanical journey of discovery. Devouring knowledge on the botanical means of entrancement favored over LSD and other lab-manufactured chemical compounds, Terence kept vigil on the research output of Richard Evans Schultes. The preeminent ethnobotanist was pivotal to earlier quests for psychoactive admixtures, decoctions, and snuffs in the northwestern Amazon. Obsessed with jungle alchemies that might cure his opiate addiction, William Burroughs had tracked down the taxonomist in Bogotá in 1953. Searching for the "final fix," the Beat pioneer embarked on a seven-month odyssey through Panama, Colombia, and Peru, a journey partly documented as an epistolary narrative in *The Yage Letters*.[13] While the straight-laced Schultes grew wary, Burroughs blagged his way onto an expedition to Puerto Leguízamo, collecting twenty pounds of the yagé vine *Banisteriopsis caapi*. He blazed a trail into the Colombian Amazon that the McKennas trekked some twenty years later. Debacle and misadventure were a hallmark of Burroughs's exploits, but as he reported to Allen Ginsberg in a letter not included in *The Yage Letters*, yagé was "the most powerful drug I have ever experienced."[14]

The intricacies of this drama were unknown to Terence and his freak expeditionary group, their attention directed at the turn of the seventies to the intoxication said to be produced by an oral preparation known among the Witoto as *oo-koo-hé*, made from the sap of *Virola theiodora* and the ashes of admixture plants.[15] They knew that *Virola* was a genus of trees in the Myristicaceae, or nutmeg, family, containing tryptamines. By the seventies, Schultes was familiar with the mind-altering effects produced from the insufflation and oral ingestion of prepared resin from the bark of species of the genus *Virola* among several groups, including the Witoto and Waiká. Curiosity grew around a remark from Schultes that the Witoto used the substance to see and speak with the "little people." Schultes maintained a legendary presence in the Amazonas for over twenty-five years. In February 1969, commissioned by pharmaceutical companies to gather *Virola* bark, he made an important discovery. When stripping the bark from *V. theiodora* on the banks of the Río Loreto Yacu near Leticia, Schultes's assistant divulged that the tree was the source of little pellets his father ate "when he wanted to speak with the little people."[16] The boy was referring to a practice, then disappearing, of ingesting *Virola* resin coated with the ashes of a variety of plants and consumed orally with inebriating effect. Since the psychoactive compounds in species of *Virola* were known to be tryptamines (especially 5-MeO-DMT), which the stomach enzyme monoamine oxidase

(MAO) typically degrades and prevents absorption in the active form, the surprising discovery that psychoactivity could result from orally ingested concoctions fueled speculations about Amazonian alchemies that rippled out of the forest to fire the imaginations of amateur ethnobotanists. Excited about the mechanism producing what would later be known as the "ayahuasca effect," Dennis declared, "This is it, . . . the orally active form of DMT we theorized must exist!"[17] They wondered if this form could facilitate a more protracted exposure to hyperspace than that to which they were accustomed. And it was no small aside that the trail left by Schultes had a scent of the diminutive tykes who'd curried such favor with Terence.

When the McKennas arrive in the Amazon on the scent of the hyperspatial little folk, the world was in turmoil. The possibility of nuclear apocalypse was a constant source of anxiety. Nixon ruled under a "law and order" platform. The Vietnam War was waged into the new year. The rainforest ecology of the Amazon was under growing threat, as were its subsistence inhabitants. Embodying the hermetic principle that the microcosm mirrors the macrocosm, the external disarray corresponded to the brothers' inner lives. They were in mourning. Terence, the nomadic persona non grata, was denied his mother's deathbed and funeral. Dennis wrote in telling terms: "So overwhelmed were we by the sense of loss, and of guilt, we were ready to tear space and time apart in order to reverse that cosmic injustice."[18] If the situation weren't bad enough, a brush fire in the Berkeley Hills had destroyed Terence's library and artworks. He was processing that loss too. At a threshold potent with death and destruction, exile and endings, crises and contact, renewal and redemption, Terence (aged twenty-four), and Dennis (twenty) land in the Putumayo in February 1971.

Armed with his telescoping net and robed in his loose, white collecting rig, Terence ranged southern Colombia since early December (see figure 4.2). The flight from Vancouver to Mexico City had "passed over my mother sleeping in her grave for the first winter. On over Albuquerque, only a pattern of freeway interchanges in the desert's night emptiness. On and on into what was then only an idea: the Amazon."[19] In Bogotá, he drops in at the Universidad de los Andes, where anthropologist Horacio Calle taught. Named "Alfredo Guzman" in *True Hallucinations*, Calle is assumed to be the only non-Indian to have taken *oo-koo-hé*, and had years earlier informed Schultes about the orally active preparation. But Calle is out with *his* Indians—the Witoto—in a village en route to La Chorrera.

The brothers are joined in Colombia by four other Americans, pseudonymized in both memoirs as "Vanessa," "Dave," "Ev," and "Solo" (see figure 4.3).[20] All are "refugees from a society that we thought was poisoned

FIGURE 4.2
Butterfly hunter, Colombia, 1971. Photo courtesy of Sara Hartley.

by its own self-hatred and inner contradictions." "We had decided," Terence reports of this party of anti-ideologues and iconoclasts, "to put all of our chips on the psychedelic experience as the shortest path to the millennium."[21] Among the outliers is Sara Hartley (a.k.a. "Vanessa" in the brothers' memoirs). Shlepping her Uher reel-to-reel tape recorder and Rolleiflex and Nikons into the jungle to record the expedition, Hartley considers it a personal travesty that mold eventually destroyed the many hours of conversations she recorded (video and audio), alongside most of her photographs. Reproduced as the frontispiece in *True Hallucinations*, a surviving plate captures Terence in the jungle with telescopic butterfly net. In memory shards, Hartley paints a portrait of a boy's own adventure stoked by shroomic millennialism. By the time they reach La Chorrera she understood that Terence was deficient in math and analytical skills, "with pockets of ignorance that made some of his speculations ungrounded."[22]

FIGURE 4.3
Beneath the big sky outside San Augustine, Colombia, February 1971. Left to right: Sara, Dennis, Terry, Kume, and Dave. Photo courtesy of Sara Hartley.

Hitchhiking in Berkeley in the summer of 1967, Terry met Lasky (a.k.a. "Dave"), a "gay meditator, a maker of pottery, an embroiderer of blue jeans," who had a degree in ethnobotany from Syracuse University. "If they sold harlequin suits off the rack [Dave] would have worn one."[23] Regarded as "our translator and newly my lover," Erica Nietfeld, known as Kume (a.k.a. "Ev") had been living in South America for several years. By Terence's side throughout much of the story, Kume is mute in the narrative. Given a passive role, she is cast as a prize won from his nemesis, "Solo Dark." That Kume eventually leaves McKenna for one of his best friends is a likely reason for the muzzling. Of his newfound relationship, Terence claims it was "no idyll for everyone. For Vanessa, who had once been my lover, it was surely a source of resentment."[24] Fifty years later, Hartley offers a competing memory. "We briefly had a sexual relationship in South America which was 'meh,'" she reveals. "We ended that mutually." For the most part, she offered, "Terry was respectful of my ideas but always in the lead."[25]

The final, albeit short-lived, participant is "Solo Dark." A mysterious fruitarian and keeper of exotic pets, Solo is described as the leader of New Jerusalem. The robe wearing sect, whose members are said to have included incarnations of Erwin Rommel and Rasputin, communicated through Ouija boards with entities they called "Beings of Light." With piercing blue eyes and "a wreath of wild long hair," Solo is portrayed as a wretched nutjob incarnating a confabulation of Christ, Hitler, and Lucifer, among others.[26] The minutiae of existence were controlled by hidden forces with which Solo claimed to be in contact. Solo insisted that his menagerie of animals remain vegetarian, including a sickly monkey, a Christ-identified Collie, and a Buddhist kitten with scurvy. While we are privileged to a version of history according to the exaggerations of the victor, depicted as a leadership rival, Solo loses his girlfriend of four years (i.e., Kume) to McKenna, before abandoning the party en route to La Chorrera. Solo, whom McKenna despised, receives a fuller description than the woman with whom he would be involved for the next four years. Solo Dark was a source of genuine paranoia. Aware of how R. G. Wasson, who, on his second journey to the remote Mazatec uplands to re-visit the sacred mushroom, was accompanied by an undercover CIA agent in a failed bid to sequester the compound for dark ops, McKenna contemplates the "irony of the situation." And yet the full nature of the irony is undisclosed in *True Hallucinations*—that is, because Solo's original self-moniker was "Cia."[27]

Upon Terence's instruction, expedition members were to be attired in loose white garb—his preferred rig worn throughout Asia. In Terence's primitive screenplay, the group are first fitted out in this clobber in Florencia, where they pause a few days awaiting the flight to Puerto Leguízamo. The "native" costume featured Nehru collars, long close-fitting sleeves, long tunic, and pants tight at the ankle. "The people will accept you dressed like this. . . . The purity of white reassures people. Besides, it suits our purposes too. We are on a quest."[28] While the colonialist luster of this style is eyebrow-raising, it is not inconsistent with the Mandaean fixation.

The "experiment at La Chorrera" first came to public attention in 1975, in *The Invisible Landscape*. That the brothers' coauthored work published with The Seabury Press ever made it into print is a remarkable feat. Although it retained some familiar content, the work broke from the "post electric" obsessions that had proven unappealing to publishers. Amid speculation on quantum mechanics, cybernetics, genetics, the "holographic mind," the *I Ching*, tryptamines, and an alternative model of time, the book gave hints of an experiment that appeared to have been tasked with purposes scientific, shamanic, and alchemical, and which was all at once divinatory, utopian, and millenarian. As the manuscript's original title, "Shamanic Investigations" (1972), suggests, the project was motivated by a romantic attachment to the shaman, figured as an Eliadean superhuman, with the authors behaving as if they were returning to a "mythic" time lost to humanity since the fall into profane history.[29] Drawing inspiration from Michael Harner's early work on ayahuasca, unlike Eliade, their investigations were neither armchair-bound nor un-intoxicated.

For the most part obscure and unobtainable until the 1994 HarperCollins edition, *The Invisible Landscape* is the literary equivalent of a *Wunderkammer*. Implicit to a work in which holographic and hermetic principles cross-fertilize is a gnostic-inflected theory of liberation: of energy released from matter, the imagination freed from the unconscious, and humanity liberated from history. Navigating the pages of this book, the reader must chart a course between prophecy and delusion. According to a 1976 review: "The authors attempted deliberately to induce in themselves a state similar to if not identical with schizophrenia. It is no personal derogation to remark that their book suggests that they succeeded."[30] *True Hallucinations* later offered a detailed backstory to the experiment, beating a wickedly erudite path into the heart of the Putumayo. As a favorable point of comparison with *The Rivers Ran East*, the reader of *True Hallucinations* is similarly treated to a blur of fact and fantasy—with the difference that, in the latter, the perplexity is by authorial design.[31]

DEVIL'S PARADISE

Alluding to Conrad's novel, the "pilgrimage" of the McKenna brothers into the "heart of darkness" was inspired, ventures Wouter Hanegraaff, "by utopian hopes of restoring paradise."[32] The Amazonian region the McKenna party traversed had been, not unlike the Congo, subject to colonial interest in rubber extraction, with similar outcomes for the indigenous population: slavery, brutality, terror. As is recognized in the opening chapter of *True Hallucinations*, the Witoto of the La Chorrera region had been decimated at the hands of the rubber industry in the early twentieth century. The party are confronted with this brutal history at Puerto Leguízamo where they make chance encounter with ninety-three-year-old John Brown (see figure 4.4), the American-born son of a slave and once the personal servant of British adventurer Captain Thomas Whiffen, who ranged the La Chorrera region in 1912. In the employ of the Peruvian Amazonian Company,

FIGURE 4.4

John Brown, Puerto Leguízamo, Colombia, February 1971. Photo courtesy of Sara Hartley.

Brown had been a crew foreman for House of Arana, the notorious force behind the ruthless exploitation of Amazonian tribes during the rubber boom. Over several days awaiting their ride down the Putumayo, the party make repeat visits with Brown, "at once near and yet ghostly and far away, a living bit of history." On his visits with El Señor Brown, known locally as "*mal y bizarro*" (bad and weird), Terence is educated on the dark history of their destination. In 1911, as many as 20,000 Indians are said to have perished pushing through the very *trocha* they will take through the jungle, where those refusing to work "had the bottoms of their feet and their buttocks removed by machete." All so that a motor vehicle could be driven the length of the trail in 1915. It was, Terence writes, "a ride from nowhere to nowhere." As for La Chorrera, it had served as a rubber-collecting depot, and was once the Peruvian Amazonian Company headquarters. As the party are informed, the "fever-haunted old town on the lowland across the lake no longer stood, but the dungeons for the Indian slaves could still be seen, crumbling iron rings set deep in sweating basaltic stone."[33]

Following this depressing portrait of their route and destination, *True Hallucinations* remains silent on the matter. As the pages turn, this dark legacy becomes a faint reminder of the world soon to be overcome. The book is hardly an account of the "rapacious and pitiless folly" of imperial exploits, apropos Conrad's narrative.[34] It appears neither of the brothers had made much advance study of the tragic backstory of the Putumayo region, whose populations had suffered 400 years of abuse at the hands of colonialists, treasure hunters, and entrepreneurs. Nor is there any serious effort to distinguish their own interests in the region's biota from those of previous expeditions, survey parties, and prospectors. If they had been better apprised of the legacy for which the region has been named the "Devil's Paradise," would they have so blithely marched forth? If Terence's experience with Far Eastern Mining and Minerals a year earlier was true, one might suppose he had few qualms. After all, despite knowing large mining corporations to be the "scourge of the earth,"[35] he had been eager to saddle up with a team of "ex-SS" fortune seekers (of oil, nickel, tin, bauxite, uranium) in the Amazon. And even if it were true, did any of it matter? After all, if the Millennium was on the horizon, one's means of arrival is surely an insignificant detail.[36]

Still, John Brown remains an enigma. While McKenna learns Brown had aided the British Consul in Rio de Janeiro, Roger Casement, to expose the abominable treatment of indigenous communities—Witotos, Boras, Ocainas—by the Arana empire, he remarks somewhat opaquely in a footnote that Colombian writer John Estacion Rivera "implicates Brown in the murders." Brown's ambiguity has been a convenient trope for historians. In a matter-of-fact account of the everyday terrors inflicted on Indians by their oppressors, Michael Taussig, in *Shamanism, Colonialism, and the Wild Man*, amplifies the ambivalence around Brown. Commissioned by the Peruvian Amazonian Company to hunt Indians at the rubber station Abisinia, "he saw hundreds killed," including men and women who were "held by their hair while their heads were hacked off with machetes."[37] We are left with a grisly portrait, one animated by McKenna, who writes of Brown's dry laugh, "like the rustle of roof thatch when tarantulas stir." Given his murky backstory, in *Colombia's Forgotten Frontier* Lesley Wylie suggests Brown embodies the "fluidity of identity in the Putumayo."[38] It is in this sense that Brown serves as an oddly ideal trailblazer for the McKenna expedition, where in the coming weeks identities would indeed become liquid.

On the morning of their embarkation downriver, the party stops by Brown's house. "His eyes and skin shone. He was the gatekeeper of the Plutonic world downriver from Puerto Leguízamo, and he knew it. I felt like a child before him, and he knew that too. 'Bye, bye, babies. Bye, bye,' was his dry farewell." Brown serves as a wizened gatekeeper to the Amazon, a role he is also cast to perform in Dennis's memoir. And yet we remain uncertain as to the precise nature of the wisdom Brown imparts. After all, concerning the 70-mile *trocha* from the Putumayo to La Chorrera, McKenna recalls that Brown's "*rambling monologues* barely prepared me for its strangeness."[39] While Brown neither appears to give his blessings nor diverts the party from their objective, the account to Terence of Brown's experience drinking ayahuasca at La Chorrera was inspiration to continue toward their goal.[40]

As they board their thatched-roof dugout pulled by the trading vessel *Fabiolita*, the brothers aren't thinking about the place of their destination in the geography of terror. Some 900 miles downriver, La Chorrera is imagined as a new frontier, "the absolute center of the geography of the secret."[41] The contemporaneous exploits of the astronauts of Apollo 14 lend a grandiose sheen to their mission. As Dennis recalls, "we, too, were impelled by the call of a mystery we felt to be no less worthy of pursuit." And, thought Terence, "the world one is leaving has been truly broken away from and the destination is still unknown," as he inhales the Santa Marta Gold while drifting out of time down the Río Putumayo.[42]

SHROOM REFUGE

If DMT seemed to define, as it did for Terence, "the most radical and flowery unfolding . . . of the hallucinogenic dimension that can occur without serious risk to psychic and bodily integrity," by the time they arrive in Colombia, the party had achieved only brief flashes of their objective. "We were in that moment the fans of the goddess, not yet her lovers." Earlier in February, at San Augustine, he had received a brief flash from an unexpected quarter. He'd gobbled down a lone golden *Psilocybe cubensis*. It is his first taste of the mushroom. In a pause in their trek a quarter hour later, he threw back his head to take in the "big" sky:

> A silent thunder seemed to shake the air before me. Things stood out with a new presence and significance. This feeling came and passed over me like a wave just as the first fury of the tropical storm burst overhead, leaving us soaked. The eerie sense that some other dimension or scale of being had intersected with the bright tropical day lasted only a few minutes. Elusive but strong, it was unlike any feeling I could recall.[43]

Terence did not alert the group to his soon fading experience, an episode that may have satisfied his impression that the "sacred mushroom" is a "mid range psychedelic"—the classification offered for *teotlnanácatl* (*Psilocybe mexicana*), as briefly footnoted in "Post Electric Thought."[44] In any case, they were chasing "bigger game," and the last thing they expected to encounter in the jungle interior was more cow shit fruiting with fantastic fungi.

And yet this is precisely their fate. In Dennis's account, the group gather and take mushrooms in Puerto Leguízamo on February 6, the effects of which prompt him to later suggest that they had stumbled upon "the perfect recreational psychedelic."[45] The party ride the Putumayo for several days, and with a couple of porters hired to bear their provisions, work the *trocha* several days more before arriving at their objective on February 21. The tiny mission of La Chorrera interrupts the jungle where a sudden drop in elevation causes the Cara Paraná to pass through a chute of roaring rapids. The cascade settles into a large placid lake surrounded by "emerald" cow pastures and hills flourishing with *P. cubensis*.

The bounty had arrived unbidden. On the following evening, the party each eat six mushrooms. "I knew only that the mushroom was the best hallucinogen I had ever had," Terence recalls, "a quality of aliveness I had never known before."[46] As he inquires on February 23, his last diary entry for weeks: "Are we indeed now in some way camped on the edge of another dimension?" *P. cubensis*, Terence later wrote in his memoir, is unclaimed "by any aboriginal people anywhere and thus is neutral ground in the tryptamine dimension we are exploring." He further claimed that through the teachings of this virgin vegetable, "one can gain entry into the world of the elf chemists." Terry was already populating this terrain with specters of his own. These familiars he appears to have spied upon the party's arrival at the mission. When first entering La Chorrera, they pass through a courtyard where the walls feature "paintings in tempera of cartoon elves with pointed ears."[47]

Once mushrooms are discovered growing in abundance at La Chorrera, the call of *oo-koo-hé* grew weaker. There were good reasons for this de-prioritization. A chief obstacle was "Marxist, misogynist, screwball" Horacio Calle. They located the paranoid coca-chewing Colombian en route at the Witoto village of San Jose El Encanto, at the mouth of the Cara Paraná. "It was a Mr. Kurtz deal," Terence later reflects in allusion to Conrad's tale. "They were his Indians, his river, his jungle, and he was way into coke."[48] Dennis recalls the anthropologist's "dismay when we showed up in our white linens, long hair, beards, bells, and beads, accompanied by Solo's menagerie of sickly dogs, cats, monkeys, and birds. We could have stepped into his scene directly off the streets of Haight-Ashbury."⁴⁹ Appalled by the sudden arrival of a troupe of freaks in loose white garb and apparently insensitive to local cultural practice, and yet who sought access to its most cherished alchemy, Calle is suspected to be behind a nocturnal incident in which a palm tree bursts into flames next to the travelers' hut.

Upon arriving at La Chorrera, Terence and Kume visit a village nine miles distant, returning with *Banisteriopsis* bark. On this side mission, Terence appears to step into Wonderland, and as he does so, his original plans rapidly dissipate:

> It was during that walk through the pasture that I noticed for the first time, or at least mentioned for the first time, that everything was very beautiful and that I felt so good that I had a strange sense of being in a movie, or somehow larger than life. Even the sky seemed to have a slight fish-eye lens effect, as though everything were cinematically exaggerated. What was this? Was it a slight distortion of space brought on by accumulating levels of psilocybin? Psilocybin can induce such perceptual distortions. I felt ten feet high; just a touch of the superhuman, or a bit like Alice, whose mushroom eating made her alternately tall and small. It was odd, but very pleasing.⁵⁰

The mushroom encounter coincides with Terence falling in love. This happenstance is aided by the fact that Kume's previous lover, Solo Dark, is now out of the picture. There had been a showdown on the trail, an incident transpiring at a fork where Terence came to understand that the unhinged and brooding Solo "was probably going to kill me." Seizing the moment, Terence stopped to observe out loud that Solo was "the world's most outrageous jackass." Suffering from an abscessed tooth, sans money, and now also sans his girlfriend, Solo bailed from the expedition.⁵¹

The departure of the dejected Solo prior to their arrival at La Chorrera animates the party's idyllic circumstance. "Our mood was one of lightness and delight," wrote Terence in response to the gently swelling euphoria induced by mushrooms in this remote paradise. "It was a very happy time." The dark pall of the late sixties lifts to reveal a beatific mood synchronized with their newfound destination. Long ruminations on this mood offer no register of the twentieth-century horrors visited upon the place in which they luxuriate. With no further thoughts about Indian slave dungeons, "each day seemed like an alchemical pearl born from the warm and starry night preceding."⁵² They had achieved an Arcadian paradise from which they would never become separated:

> It was the only time in my life when I was truly content simply to be. I had quite effortlessly formed the assumption, which I assumed was shared by all, that we

would never leave La Chorrera. Leaving seemed unimaginable since all things seemed to be perfectly present there. The sense of homecoming and of being at last where one was supposed to be was at times overwhelming.[53]

Terence's Amazon lay at a marked remove from that known to Colonel Clark, who, traversing the Andean Cordilleras some twenty-five years before, witnessed slavery, cannibals, head shrinkers, and a veritable wildlife bestiary.

La Chorrera is the perfect refuge for a man on the run. Yet trouble was brewing in Shangri-la, challenges of a variety unknown to Clark. That cavalier explorer, despite the intensity of his odyssey, did not himself taste of the exotic fruits of the jungle. Clark's perils were decidedly this-worldly, by contrast to the hazardous dimensions to be negotiated at La Chorrera. While Terence pursues his affair with the mushroom, and with Kume, the beshroomed Dennis shows signs of becoming separated from his mind. At first, there are the rants, unrelenting until his brother suggests he journal his thoughts. This he does, feverishly churning out formulations and protocols.

The mood in their bush hut grows unsettled. One night Sara recalls Dennis "hovering over me with a large knife."[54] As the situation becomes intolerable, she and Dave move their hammocks to another dwelling at the mission. The split is amicable, but the detractors lose confidence in the mission. Instead of collecting plants, Dennis raves about superconductivity, harmonic cancellation, and "the gnosis from beyond the Crab Nebula."[55] Over the coming weeks, a tussle escalates as Hartley believes Dennis is in the grip of a psychotic break. He is in danger of running off and perishing in the forest. But where Hartley, the pragmatist, witnesses a full-blown medical crisis requiring intervention, Terence sees potential. "I believe that the real cause of tension even then," he explains, "was a sense that something in the mushroom experience was pulling everyone toward it." While the estranged duo resist capitulating to the Other, the three who stay the course are prepared "to become alchemical children, ready to strip down and climb into the sophic fountain and take the measure of the thing from the inside."[56]

FREAK APOCALYPSE

With psilocybin bounteous, the brothers are unexpectedly exposed to a tryptamine source serving as the gateway to an invisible, unclaimed, landscape. Associated with an introduced pastoral culture, the source was not hedged about with proscriptions or guarded by cultural authorities. At this time, as Terence later conveys, globally, *Psilocybe* rituals were confined to the central isthmus of Mexico, where mushroom-using groups preferred the smaller endemic species, and *P. cubensis* was not known for its use in any shamanic rite in the world.[57] It was further speculated that *P. cubensis* was disdained in Mexico because it "entered the New World with the Spanish, and is to the Indians a plant of the conquest."[58] Since there was no apparent tradition of psychoactive mushroom consumption among the Witoto, the perception was that there were no cultural sensitivities to disrupt, as had occurred with the Mazatec following the spotlight that Wasson had thrown on the "Little Ones That Spring Forth" in the wake of his 1957 *Life* article "Seeking the Magic Mushroom." That report triggered hippie gravitation en masse to the Oaxacan mountain village of Huautla de Jiménez in central Mexico, where the ancient Mazateca ceremony was rapidly despoiled.[59]

The situation vis-à-vis *oo-koo-hé* was a little more complicated, with Terence later speculating that La Chorrera may have been the site of a "now defunct ookuyé cult." This possibility, he thought, might have explained the presence near their hut of *V. theiodora* and *B. caapi* showing old machete scars. Who was responsible for harvesting the source ingredients for yagé? Moreover, could the party have "somehow already lived there a long time and were now only meeting our own reflection moving backwards"?[60]

Whatever the case, upon first blush, the hunt for *the key* in its resinous form is abandoned. But while *oo-koo-hé* is struck from the menu, the unexpected abundance of hallucinogenic mushrooms—as they later learn, the most reliably potent species—at peak bloom upon arrival at their chosen objective is the clearest confirmation the brothers could have that they had achieved the center of the secret in space and time. The discovery is, in short, miraculous. And as Dennis confirmed decades later, as psilocybin is a compound with structural and functional similarities to DMT, *P. cubensis* was "the perfect orally active form of DMT" they had trekked for.[61]

Alien to today's world of satellites, cellular networks and the immediacy they enable, La Chorrera was the perfect off-grid laboratory. Dennis ran mad with ideas, fulminating with formulae, mapping the pathway toward the secret. Their destination was like a *Rough Guide* version of Hesse's Castalia, where Magistri Ludi play "the game" in complete isolation from the world. Inside their hut, Dennis's notebook begins filling with ideas he'd exchanged with his brother and Parker for years. Jung, alchemy, four-dimensional objects, eschatology, the fiction of A. C. Clarke and H. P. Lovecraft, alongside his growing enthusiasm for organic chemistry, were all stirred into the cauldron with a procedure Dennis names "hypercarbolation"—the process whereby metabolizing psilocybin will alter their neural DNA, "changing man into an eternal hyper-dimensional being."[62]

This is the novum of "Den's opus," and the idea that fired his brother's imagination. Perhaps among the most fantastic variations of "DNA activation," the brothers concoct a harebrained device to accomplish advanced species mutation, effectively flicking the genetic switch. A super DNA is confabulated to be the result of the harmine alkaloid "superconductively bonded" into the "DNA matrix," effecting a radical inhibition of monoamine oxidase (MAO). Running right away with the script, this "condensing harmine-DNA switch" Terence later names "XDMT" ("experimental deoxyribonucleic matrix transceiver"), terminology prompted in part by the expected presence of 5-MeO-DMT in *Virola*.[63] While that acronym had a short shelf life, the speculations kept arriving. In "Shamanic Investigations," no inquiry seemed too preposterous: "a hyper-topological standing wave-form hologram of everything," or "a technique of audial submolecular genetic surgery," or a panacea that amounts to "the true tincture of the Just."[64] Is it a coincidence that a pair of grieving sons blaze a neurochemical path to rescue "the timeless pearl of human immortality from the well of death"?[65]

The scrawled notes the afflicted liminars produce between February 28 and March 4 represent the streaming consciousness of young men driven to the edges of grief and precocity. Casually interweaving magic and science, their entries lay the foundations for "out there" events that would see Dennis pass into psychedelic folklore, with Terence writing himself into the script transformed as a consequence of his commitment to "doubt."[66] On February 28, what the brothers dub "the phenomenon" prompts Dennis to question his own identity, warping under the influence of a sound that starts like a faint radio "signal," before gradually becoming "a snapping, popping, gurgling, crackling, electrical sound."[67] Eluding precise description, the sound is later parsed as "a tickling feeling . . . within the brain," not unlike that of distant wind chimes, before increasing in volume to adopt "an electric, buzzing quality" comparable to whistling wind or running water. Compelled to imitate the buzz, his voice locks onto a sound likened to "a giant insect."[68]

Their accounts of La Chorrera demonstrate that the McKennas were affecting each other's imagination. As both memoirs illustrate, La Chorrera was alive with the cross-transference of ideas. But such an intellectual communion is a literary contrivance. That the older brother directed the show is captured in an illustration used as the frontispiece of *Brotherhood*. In the portrait by Janet Gordon, Terence appears to be whispering into Dennis's ear.

Terence's earlier ventures and speculations on the presence of "translinguistic matter" inform their wild project. Dennis's journal entry on March 1 avers how Terence had primed his brother with an ecstatic exegesis on what was "seen" as sound levels densified, finally materializing into "small, gnome-like, machine-like creatures, made out of material like obsidian froth which pours forth from the body and the mouth."[69] Echoing "Post Electric Thought"–era meditations, as Terence later documents, the outcome anticipated is not unlike what one might expect when one has "given birth to one's own soul," notably where one's own DNA is "exteriorized as a kind of living fluid made of language." Like the ultimate smart device, "the exteriorized stone" will be like "a mind that could be seen and held in one's hand." This "miniature universe," was imagined to be "a part of space and time that magically has all of space and time condensed in it."[70]

On March 2, Dennis speculates that the loud buzzing echoes a kind of energy field that seems to "bend space in such a way as to turn in upon itself through a higher dimension."[71] These collaborative notes are the basis for a procedure refined in their "Preliminary Report" and eventually described in *The Invisible Landscape*, where it is speculated that the buzzing tone is "caused by the metabolism of the tryptamines within the cerebral matrix and might be the electron spin resonance of the metabolizing tryptamine molecules within the nervous system, somehow amplified to audible levels." Further, through their vocal imitations of this phenomenon they speculate that they could produce "a visible standing wave." By joining their voices with the "sound" of the mushroom in hyperspace, the cosmic choir boys far from home are moved to sing the world anew. In the impious stripped-down version he delivers on the lecture circuit through the 2010s, Dennis condenses the episode:

> Singing to a mushroom while completely ripped on high doses of psilocybin boosted with harmine from the ayahuasca—will make manifest the most miraculous object imaginable. Mind and matter will fuse into a hyper-dimensional object that is the ultimate artifact at the end of time, whose very creation brings an end to time, leading humanity to a state in which all places and all times are instantly accessible at the speed of thought.[72]

On the appointed day of the apocalypse, March 4, Dennis scrawls out his final words in the final moments before the superconductivities were due to commence. His manic inscriptions evoke the psychotic/prophetic mode in which he is engulfed: "History will end in a few hours. The day itself has ordained the command to humankind: March Fourth.[73] March Fourth humanity to free a new dawn, as you slid and swam and crawled and walked down the spiral chains of evolutionary metamorphosis to your final awakening." The members of their party are the chosen acolytes of the stone, on the use of which they are to be instructed by an "infinitely adept fellow member of the hyperspatial community." With "the keys of galactarian citizenship" near to hand, and prepped "to blow the locked doors of paradise right off their hinges," Dennis makes repeated calls for a press conference.[74]

The duo are gripped by a synesthetic insectoid drone, like a siren of the Otherworld or the backing vocals to the approaching rent in time. They buzz one another with its implications. They were familiar with Harner's description of the magic darts used by ayahuasca-drinking shamans among the Jivaro (now Untsuri Shuar) of eastern Ecuador to cause or cure illness. The anthropologist had outlined the sound of the "supernatural" to which he had been exposed when served a strong dose by a Conibo ayahuasquero in the Peruvian Amazon in 1961.[75] They knew this sound. "There's a sound," Terence once recalled, "like a piece of bread wrapper or cellophane being scrunched up and thrown away.... A membrane is being ripped; something is being torn."[76] Dennis insists that the insectoidal buzzing belongs to an entity he calls "the teacher." "It wouldn't let you see it," Terence later recounts, invoking their folie à deux, while at the same time evoking the Lovecraftian unspeakable: "but its presence was just so overwhelming that it kept popping into your subliminal vision." Navigating daily the paths of a forest alive with the screech of birds and the buzz of insects, they form the expectation that the "ectoplasmic unimaginable" could suddenly appear at any turn.[77]

MARCH FORTH

At La Chorrera in early March 1971, as deeply removed from the world as they were ever likely to be, the brothers McKenna imagine they are on the verge of transforming their DNA and leading the charge into the higher dimensions. In the pre-experimental period and over two weeks in its wake, Terence observes his brother undergo an epic unraveling and re-coalescence. While this extraordinary episode is documented in *True Hallucinations*, Terence divulges that, aside from a journal entry on March 21, he made no other entries for three months after February 22. His account is pieced together from memory. At the same time, La Chorrera is a black spot for Dennis, who for the most part relies on the reconstructions of his brother, who enters a state of hyper-vigilance for more than two weeks in the wake of March 4. Committing to faithfully document the cosmic revelations and the return "down to earth," Terence takes twenty years retrospectively reanimating the entire episode before the story reaches print.

By the morning of March 4 (or "March Forth"[78]), the McKennas gush with expectancy, as they fast approach the high watermark of what Davis had called "high weirdness." The arcana that Dennis had feverishly transposed over the past few days—protocols that subsequently crowd the pages of *The Invisible Landscape*, and decades later are dismissed by Dennis as "rich material for the student of pathology"[79]—will inform the experiment. In the center of their hut they plant a perfect specimen of *P. cubensis* growing in its manure substrate. It is the sacramental object from which "the stone" shall be converted. If hyper-carbolation is successful, the mushroom will be replaced by "a standing wave, a violet ring of light the size of the mushroom cap." A chrysalis of a blue morpho is suspended nearby, signaling the expected metamorphosis. There is little distinguishing science from poetry inside their hut. "We were operating in a world where scientific method, ritual, and participation mystique were inseparably intertwined."[80] They build a fire to boil their twenty-five feet of *B. caapi* vine. As it boils, the liquid develops a film of purple phosphorescence. If they listen closely, the slow squeal of the vine's electron spin resonance is detectable.[81] They add to the brew what they believe is a DMT admixture plant (*Justicia pectoralis* var. *stenophylla*) that Terence later says had been misidentified. Terence, Dennis, and Kume dine on the flesh of the mushrooms, knocking back the home brew aya before laying in their hammocks. The liquid is "sharp and astringent, like a sauce of leather and mole," and fades quickly before it churns through their guts. The night is long . . .

Eventually, dawn approaches. Dennis howls thrice—like an "electric siren wailing over the still, jungle night," each mechanical yodel louder than the last. In the absolute darkness of their Witoto hut, there is silence.[82]

Then, a cock crows, three times. A long time passes, but the mushroom is unmoved. The stone does not manifest. The invisible fourth dimension yields not any thing. There is no exteriorized DNA. No soul birth. The brothers remain unchanged. And as the quietly spoken Kume later reflects, "nothing happened to me at all."[83]

And yet Dennis is convinced of their success. After all, weren't the anomalous occurrences of the previous days shock-waves from the future? In the immediate aftermath, Terence is a mess of confusion and jubilation. "All over the world," he imagines, "the wave of hyper-carbolation was sweeping through the human race, eliminating the distinction between the individual and the community as everyone discovered themselves spontaneously pushing off into a telepathic ocean whose name was that of its discoverer: Dennis McKenna." Across the planet, the world's population cast eyes upon the skies. Jung, Newton, Nabokov, Bruno, Pythagoras, and Heraclitus, among other greats, were pressing near to the hut on the edge of the pasture in the middle of the Amazon to greet the first living humans to break through.[84]

Messianism is as thick on the ground as morning fog. If it wasn't Terence affirming his brother's role as prophet, Dennis behaves as if the messiah is his older brother and he the disciple. After all, he'd pegged Terence to be "the Teach," a sort of "personified alien ambassador empowered to negotiate the entry of the human species into the councils of higher intelligence." The label wasn't ill-fitting. The domain of the psilocybean sublime appeared to be the perfect playground for Terence to immanentize the eschaton, to explore the Christos archetype, with the mushrooms assuming an unheralded place in the "liberation of the species into eschatological time."[85] Serving as an amusing confessional, *True Hallucination* was designed as a candid chronicle of the lived immediacy of a freak who "felt these things as anyone would feel them if they truly believed they were at such a point in history."[86]

Awash in the sublimity of their March Forth, amid the dissolution of the self and other, inside and out, night and day, dream and waking reality, the brothers become vehicles for what they variously identify as an "intelligence," "voice," "teacher"; an interiorized entity personifying access to a "cosmic database"—i.e. the "stone." For his part, his switch thrown, Dennis raves continuously "in telepathic rapport with anyone he wished, in command of enormous technical erudition and of a strange and rapidly evolving hyperspatial cosmogony."[87] Amid this reverie, he enters into lively phone conversations with dead relatives, on one occasion dialing up their mother in the fall of 1953 while she is listening to Dizzy Dean call a World Series game.[88] For his part, Terence enters into dialogue with an inner voice. "Beyond any possibility of argument I knew things that I couldn't ordinarily know." At an early stage he receives a declarative message from an entity he calls a "teacher": "Within a few hours, the superstructure of earthbound, human civilization is going to collapse and your species will depart."[89] Was it an early instance of the *logos* that would long provide counsel?

Sara and Dave observe these events with growing concern. Behaving like a bystander to his brother's unmooring, Terence considers that he must simply be a "good witness." But he is no passive witness. As Hartley journals, for three days in the wake of March 4, Dennis had entered into "an automaton trance" controlled by Terence, who in a cruel and "hypnagogic tone" tells his brother not to speak, nor to leave his hammock, but to save his energy "for the condensation of The Stone."[90]

The tussle over Dennis continues. Hartley pushes back on the delusions of omniscience to which she bears witness. Dennis, who had lost his glasses and his clothes, had become a danger to himself. Terence, on the other hand, grew convinced that the stakes were higher-dimensional. In one showdown, she declares that his experiment should have "no casualties."

"You will be left behind when the saucer lands!" he replies.[91]

There is no rush to break from their jungle asylum. Besides, the last thing he and Dennis need is to be thrown into an observation ward back in "civilization." There is also the matter of the "price" on his head. At a place where a roaring *chorro* provides the sonic accompaniment to protracted states of paranormal activity, Terence claims he survives without sleep for eleven successive nights. Dennis would propose that those nights during which his brother wandered the mission paths alone were "among the most fateful of his life."[92]

Among the highest peaks of this entire episode is the moment when, on March 13, Terence is buzzed by a "flying saucer." A day earlier, to the southeast, he and Kume spied a black stratocumulus mass, "seething and boiling up to great altitudes." Before their eyes, the mass appeared to take the shape of a vast mushroom cloud. Nine days after March 4, were they now witness to the aftermath of a thermonuclear blast? They were preoccupied with such thoughts when a sustained column of light appeared from the base of the cloud. Terence grew transfixed by the inner voice: "This is the place. This is the sign." Vigil is maintained all night long. After dawn, from the same direction, just above the horizon, half a mile away, and approaching, he spots a sequence of four "lens-shaped clouds." A wave of excitement sweeps through him, trailed by a wave of fear. "I was glued to the spot, unable to move, as in a dream." Over the canopy a high-pitched whine drifts ahead of the formation. As he believes it had come to take him, Terence opens himself up to the phenomenon that is passing directly overhead at an altitude of 200 feet. "It was a saucer-shaped machine rotating slowly, with unobtrusive, soft, blue and orange lights. As it passed over me I could see symmetrical indentations on the underside. It was making the whee, whee, whee sound of science fiction flying saucers."[93] In the waking dreamworld of March Forth, the weird-o-meter had advanced several notches. With three half-spheres on its underside, the craft resembles an infamous photo of a "rigged up end-cap of a Hoover vacuum cleaner" taken by best-selling author and alleged conman George Adamski.[94] The whole experience is astonishing, terrifying, and disappointing, for Terence is not taken as anticipated. Crestfallen to have been left behind, his senses are abducted all the same by a confounding hallucination preoccupying him for years to come.

As Terence plunged deep into the landscape of the Other into the second week of March, a distant chiming ruptures the peace. Puzzling at first, the pealing grows louder as the minutes wear on. Left alone, Dennis had crept off to the mission set on his objective: the rope, attached to the bell in the mission church tower. Dennis yanks on the bell tower rope until he is overpowered by Dave. Since the padré—named "Father Sebastian" in the "Down to Earth" screenplay (where he is regarded as a dead-ringer for Sebastian Cabot)[95]—had to seek out Dennis's companions to intervene, it can be presumed that his manic interface with the region's chief vessel of sonic resonance was of no short duration. Denied a press conference, Dennis had taken matters into his own hands, afterward recalling only his compulsion "to leave the hut and go among the people, overwhelmed by a messianic impulse to heal."[96]

If Dennis was jonesing for attention, every narrowing eye in the region was now drawn to him, his brother, and their companions. The incident bursts the La Chorrera bubble. Any sanction they had enjoyed evaporates as the mission folk and the police converge around the scene. With this rude awakening and public outrage, the balance of power shifts in Sara's favor. While Terry feels the departure sudden, unjust, and indecorous, at Hartley's behest, and expense, the group evacuate by bush floatplane on March 15.

TIME'S DOUBLE FACE

Back in Bogotá, Dennis achieves reintegration. Catapulted about as far from his own self as anyone might ever wish to have been cast, voyaging to the limits of time and space, he returned down to earth and arrived back into his own body, some two weeks after March 4. In Bogotá, Terence is reflective. The previous weeks were so harrowing and temporally disjunctive that chronicling his account was near impossible. In a journal entry on March 21, his first since the experiment, and the last for another two months, he turns to Joyce, "one of the true pioneers in the mapping of hyperspace." Only *Finnegans Wake*, he claims upon re-entry, "gives some idea of the reality of the paradoxicum as we experienced it by virtue of being able to pierce beyond time's double face."[97]

The comment insinuates the temporal perturbation characteristic of La Chorrera. What is later simply referred to as "the phenomenon" had been observed in Dennis, whose thought patterns in the Amazon appeared to be "moving backward in some fundamental way." The days preceding March 4 featured an episodic portentousness. Freak rainstorms, thunder, lens-shaped clouds, mists, halos, and rainbows are among the natural phenomena received as shock waves of an event issuing out of the future. In the early evening of March 4, a howling wind and an enormous black thunderhead that raced toward the party were received as "backwash," Dennis exclaimed, "from the approaching breakthrough."[98] Terence's experience, which may have been affected, he surmises, by a variation of radical MAO inhibition (resulting from the actions of the beta-carbolines in *B. caapi* and psilocybin), occasioned "an obsessive immersion, almost an enforced meditation," on the nature of time. Between waking and dream states, "resonances, recurrences, and the idea that events were interference patterns caused by other events temporally and causally distant" claimed his attention. Taking stock of these kinks in time in his first journal entry after returning from Colombia (May 12), Terence identifies "the reversal." Objecting to the view that he and Dennis had suffered from garden-variety psychosis, they had differential responses, he argued, to an "objective phenomenon." They had experienced a "shared disassociation." Dennis's ideas and physical activities seemed to him to be "simply the exact reverse of logical expectations."[99] After all, *True Hallucinations* is replete with postmonitions—the noesis of being pulled without reserve into a "cosmic giggle" whose end game was surfacing to consciousness at the turn of the seventies.

Arriving in Berkeley with Kume in tow in mid-April 1971, his first time on US soil since January 1969, Terence behaves like the Prodigal Son blessed with the signature of the universe. Having departed the Bay Area a revolutionary, he now returned under the illusion that he and Dennis had crank-started the Millennium. The challenge of upselling the idea that they are immortal superconductors of a species transformed proves formidable. In a letter penned (though unsent) in La Chorrera on March 12, Hartley warned Michael Malcolm, who had been studying Kierkegaard, of the pending arrival in Berkeley of his old pal who was poised to "spread the Gospel according to Saint Turyi."[100] Few among their friends could stomach the messianic implications of La Chorrera. Malcolm grew intolerant. They remained on speaking terms, but the camaraderie never returns. The notion that humankind is evolving into some kind of "uberconscious angel" was not merely dubious for George Csicsery; it was outright psychopathological. "The biblical, epic dimension was never far from Terry's tongue," Csicsery recalls. Though McKenna's "new fundamentalism" was based more on Huxley, McLuhan, and Leary than on the Gospels, Csicsery saw the likeness between his friend and "a nineteenth century fire and brimstone frontier preacher."[101]

There is one figure whose sympathies McKenna sought at this time. It is not entirely clear what he expected from his encounter with leading molecular biologist Gunther Stent, who gave McKenna an audience at the Donner Laboratory of Virology and Bacteriology at UC Berkeley on June 3. The German-born professor was among the first to identify a resonance between DNA and the *I Ching*, as explored in his 1969 book *The Coming of the Golden Age*. With a mind to completing his degree, perhaps Stent would sponsor McKenna's internship, recommend a scholarship, acknowledge his brilliance? Having just returned from a deep ocean trawl with a haul the occult fisherman imagined as nothing short of revolutionary, surely the professor would be impressed by the catch? Under Stent's tutelage, might he be afforded the opportunity for he and Dennis to create the laboratory conditions for generating a genetically powered superconducting omni-directional telepathic wave-band receiver? In an effort to reconstruct this bizarre moment, we can turn to the report that the brothers had recently completed. "The total system would be a holo-cybernetic unit of super-conductivity," the "Preliminary Report" claimed. "The entirety of the DNA memory bank would be at the command of the telepathically governed harmine read-out mechanism." Toward the end of this hypothetical pitch, the extreme field tester still in mourning and just now returned from the millennial frontier moves on to claim that he and his team are satisfied that "the theory of DNA bioelectronic constellation of macrospace . . . creates sufficient data for a relatively clear understanding of life after death."[102]

Whatever the precise statements our exilic XDMT conductor shares when visiting the professor, Stent is nonplussed. McKenna inquires if the professor thinks the ideas presented are valid or fallacious. "My dear young friend, these ideas are not *even* fallacious," Stent remarks condescendingly. We might imagine the pioneering author of the influential textbook *Molecular Genetics* informing his visitor that without a formal proposition his project has little merit.[103] McKenna had no formal training in any branch of science, let alone genetics, and as for his recent project, it bore no resemblance to a controlled, repeatable, and falsifiable experiment. Shown the door, McKenna becomes driven to forge an entirely independent course of study of quantum physics, submolecular biology, and DNA structure (even while completing his Berkeley BSc degree). This humiliating encounter, and probably others like it, spur his eventual formulation of "a metaphysics with mathematical rigor" advanced as "a formal proposition." He would discover, in a claim baked in unreserved zeal, "the fractal dimension of time itself." Inspired to return to La Chorrera, and clocking what he figured to be the ancient meaning of the *I Ching*, he eventually arrives at a theory of time "waves," the internal logic of which strongly implies the "termination of normal time and an end to ordinary history."[104]

5 RETURN TO PARADISE

Berkeley was a heavy comedown from La Chorrera. A jarring return after years on the road, and in the wake of paradise lost, the 1971 Berkeley interlude lasted three months. During this time, Terence imagined that he had uncovered the long-hidden properties of the *I Ching*, an object dwarfing all previous bookish obsessions. His switch had been flipped. Under the guidance of his inner star activated by the jungle alchemy of March Forth, he uncovers a baroque time chart that determined the history of the universe ending at dawn EST on November 16, 1971; that is, his twenty-fifth birthday. As there was only one venue in which this "event" could be celebrated—the sublime landscape of La Chorrera—Terence was determined to again ply the Putumayo, the transport artery into the wilds of the imagination. Pioneering the new New World discovery, the Magellan of the Weird retraced his steps into the dense interior of the mind. In the Amazon, the unhindered *logos* held court. Its chief teaching: "a hyper-temporal way of seeing."[1]

THE *I CHING* AND THE ESCHATRON

In Berkeley, the Chinese *Book of Changes* became the object of a far-reaching and lifelong obsession. While introduced to the *I Ching* by way of Jung, who wrote the foreword to Richard Wilhelm's Bollingen edition, and who regarded the 3,000-year-old Taoist oracle as "a repository of archetypes,"[2] McKenna's interest lay not only in the *Book's* oracular but in its predictive attributes. While not alone among the era's seekers who embraced the divinatory device, McKenna diverged in how he read the *I Ching*. By this, I do not imply how its guidance was interpreted—it was consulted every lunar cycle—but how its very purpose was estimated.

Prior to La Chorrera, Terence's interest in the *I Ching* had been minimal. It had been *consulted* previously, but in the wake of Colombia, it is *decoded* under the guidance of the mushroom teacher, which, through a series of obscure, koan-like directives, instructs Terence to uncover the logic behind the hexagram sequences. The fragmentary commentaries on an ancient set of sixty-four oracular ideograms called "hexagrams"—the so-called King Wen sequence—had long fascinated McKenna, echoing a general interest in "non-causal forms of logic." After recording three years of consulting—eighty-three casts—he realized he had thrown each of the sixty-four hexagrams. This highly improbable feat was seized upon as a sign of divination fingers. "It proved that I was somehow a reflection of the microcosm and had been chosen somehow to be in precisely the situation in which I found myself."[3] Under the guidance of the psilocybin-triggered inner voice, over nine months in the wake of March Forth, he comports himself as a midwife to the rebirth of an ancient Taoist calendrical artifact, a Neolithic calendar. His modus operandi was like that of a crypto-archaeologist unearthing a "fragment" of "broken cosmic machinery." He behaves as if he were uncovering "a lost intellectual system," the equivalent perhaps to Chinese Kabbalism. Never regarded simply as a book of Chinese mysticism, the *I Ching* is beheld until his final days as a book of "molecular dynamics" whose creators "achieved as sophisticated a relationship to time as the western relationship to matter expressed through our ability to trigger fusion and fission."[4] By focusing on the King Wen, attributed to the pre-Han period (i.e., before 400 BC), he imagines becoming completely unburdened from sinology. While largely unnoticed among sinologists, where McKenna has entered the radar his identification of the mechanism he thought to be the "distilled fruits of a whole civilization" is dismissed as drug-addled effrontery.[5]

I hold no intention of evaluating the historical, mathematical, or cultural valence of this mechanism. My remit here is to explore the *mckennaism*—an elaborate product of a unique intelligence, an enduring opus in which hyperspace and hyperbole became intimate and inseparable companions.

McKenna thought the means by which his mechanism had been received not dissimilar to the unraveling of mystery in *The White Goddess*, where Robert Graves, through a series of revelations, "gains great insight into early Celtic and Goidelic poetic alphabets and encryption methods."[6] Although never explicitly stated in relation to La Chorrera, the work of Jules Verne offers curious parallels, notably *Journey to the Center of the Earth*, the story of a trek into an unknown interior reliant on the deciphering of a cryptic text. Consistent with the "hero's journey" identified by Joseph Campbell, the adventurous passage to a remote destination—in Verne, the subterranean "bowels of the earth"; in McKenna, the "lungs of the planet"—inaugurates significant breakthroughs. Where Professor Lidenbrock makes passage to the earth's "center" via a volcanic crater in Iceland, McKenna's quest for the end of time leads to a *chorro* in the remote Amazon basin, where "the doorway to hyperspace stands open."[7] A river-going odyssey is pivotal to both narratives. There are no treacherous electrical storms, subpolar tornadoes, or Ichthyosauruses in the McKennan odyssey, but there is the possibility of mind "reversal" from which there may be no recovery. Finally, in both tales, there are mushrooms.[8] While giant mushrooms weren't expected in the pastures of La Chorrera, the consumption of the "alchemical gold" as big as dinner plates could trigger a "quantum leap" in the imagination.

If Verne's classic had a shaping influence on McKenna, it was submerged. What does surface to conscious awareness is the number 64. As this is the quantity both of hexagrams in the *I Ching and* of codons in DNA, McKenna contemplates the organic properties of time. Through his tryptaminal scrying, the *I Ching* is read as a kind of *time* machine, where time is composed of sixty-four irreducible species, "in the same way that the chemical elements compose the world of matter."[9] In reflective engagements that preoccupy McKenna henceforth, it is contended that what is uncovered in his meditations is not simply the secret of the *I Ching*, but the Taoist wisdom that there is not one kind of time, but sixty-four temporal elements. Such thinking derived from developing a scale or "wave" sixty-four days in duration, with the initial wave beginning on the date of Hazelle's death, his "chance-formed relationship" with Kume beginning sixty-four days after that (i.e., New Year's Eve 1970), and the experiment (on March 4) an additional sixty-four days in the wake of that. The idea of a hexagram-based lunar year (also called a "DNA year" or "a sort of temporal hexagram in hyperspace"[10]) of 384 days (thirteen months) is intuited by multiplying sixty-four (i.e., the number of hexagrams) by six (the number of *yao*, or lines in a hexagram). The value of this plotting is confirmed when it is recognized that this 384-day calendar will culminate on his twenty-fifth birthday.[11]

This fertile season of "revealations"—to use his spelling—is the springboard for a wave chart named the "graph of the eschatron," a nest of temporal (and reversable) cycles within cycles transpiring over seventy-four billion years.[12] Further transmissions reveal the scale of the waveform possessing thirteen "magnitudes of duration," which at both ends of the scale—seventy-four billion years at one end, and 0.0000075 seconds at the other—exceed "any physical processes known in the universe."[13] As refined in *The Invisible Landscape*, all cycles are reputed to be uncovered properties of the *I Ching*, upon shroomic direction. At the behest of the inner voice, when 384 days is multiplied by 64, a 67.35-year (67 years and 104.25 days) cycle emerges. Multiplying 67.35 solar years by 64 gives 4,306 solar years (approximately two zodiac ages). When 4,306 is again multiplied by 64, the result (25,836 years) is close enough to a complete procession of the equinoxes (26,000 years) to offer further confirmation that a device with calendrical properties had been discovered.[14]

The "discovery" emerges through a series of affirmations in which it is determined that each smaller cycle of the "wave of time" simulates, condenses, and intensifies themes and changes observed in the larger cycles. As one example, in the early phase of discovery in which the waveform terminates on McKenna's birthday (November 16), the last six-day cycle (predicted to commence on November 11, 1971) condenses events of the final 67.35-year cycle—commencing in 1904, with "the birth of relativity theory, powered flight, the automobile, the S. F. Earthquake etc"—which in turn condenses events in the 4,300-year cycle, beginning in 2,335 BCE, or roughly the beginning of "modern civilization." A stitch in time, it was configured, connected hermetic Egypt, the first Surrealist Manifesto, and the events of early March 1971.[15]

In late October 1971, the thirteen cycles are named "quantized barriers," with the understanding that, though more than seventy-three billion years are necessary for "the first six quantized tightenings of the gyre," the last seven barriers require only 384 days to complete. And as the universe accelerates into its final spin cycles, "in the last 13.5 minutes 5 such barriers will be crossed, three of them in the last 13 seconds!" Attempting to imagine what passage through this quickening sequence would be like "drives one to the limit of hyperbole." When soon associating the seven "barriers" comprising the "DNA year" with the seven chakras of Tantric Shaivism, it was confirmed that McKenna knew no such limit.[16]

Complicating matters, not only did the cycles overlap, but each is reversible. That temporal "energies" move in opposite directions is pivotal to the messages received in dialogue with his mushroom teacher. In late July, it was supposed that time is a "reversible medium" where the past is "no more closed to readjustment than is the future." Notably, this insight is *itself* received as a "shock," "leakage," or "echo" from "the total freedom from conceivable limitations that occurs upon entry into hyperspace."[17] Near the end of McKenna's life, he makes a favorable comparison with another obscure "mathematical download": the "Spindle of Necessity" in the tenth book of *The Republic*. Featured within the Myth of Er, one of the more puzzling of Plato's works, this weave of cosmic ratios proves compelling. "It's something inside something else, and something turns one way and something turns another way."[18]

In 1971, in McKenna's own psilocybin-mediated cosmic weave, the concept of the "eschatron"—a portmanteau of "eschaton" and "electron"—passes through a series of iterations. In the "Preliminary Report," the "eschatron" is imagined to be "the smallest temporal unit" in the universe. The fourth dimension, it is proposed, is entirely composed of these subatomic particles.[19] What was early introduced as an evolving "wave of probability" is soon conjured as a "unified field theory." "Eschatron" is also parlayed as alternative nomenclature for "the stone," or "lapis," or its "electron" reflection, expected to emerge "at the point of maximum symmetry" of the wave. These observations inform "Shamanic Investigations" where the "eschatron" is named a "one point temporal hologram," and a "particle" that "may be best understood as a reflection in pure energy, which is time, the fourth Einsteinian dimension."[20] The term has a short shelf life. Before the fantastic "energy gram" vanishes from the ledger, and the concept is replaced by the "Eschaton" and subsequently the "Timewave," McKenna toyed with the "eschatron" as a science-fictional novum. When charting the wave over the past 4,300 years, with its "retrogressing time cycles" inclusive, the waveform's potential is configured as a "mnemonic engine," a device enabling "hyperspatial navigation":

> One can imagine the hyperspatial traveler armed with his general historical timegram, the lesser cycles relevant to the temporo/spatial destination could all be mapped and made a part of his outfit. In 4-D as in 3-D where one goes often one is quickly able to operate by memory and has no need of external aids. Some such process of learning to visualize and "tune" the eschatron image would be, it seems now, a logical part of stages of the learning process still to come.[21]

If this elaborate shroomic fantasy isn't already fabulous enough, the originally charted eschatron decodes three layers of "energy maps"—hexagrammatic, trigrammatic, and linear cycles—from the *I Ching*, each possessing "sixty four situational gestalts occurring in a fixed order." These maps are together imagined to configure the "wave of time." While there is uncertainty as to the properties of the figures in the charts and graphs—for example, are they constants, ratios, or cycles?—the numerical entities are elegant enough to elicit much excitement. Despite the perplexities, the waveform is imagined to reveal an internal logic. Though its phenomenology remained elusive, the certitude and gravity of the approaching event lay beyond doubt. The mood is jubilant. Ahead lies "the freeing of life from the dark chrysalis of matter."[22]

THE NEW "NEW WORLD"

The brothers McKenna held radically divergent perspectives on La Chorrera. Forty years after the events of February–March 1971, Dennis paints a perplexing if somewhat sobering picture, undecided as to whether in his weeks-long episode he'd entered "hyperspace" or "psychosis." Facing "the classic Heraclitean conundrum" that "we couldn't travel the same river twice," a repeat journey was out of the question.[23] For Terence, on the other hand, there was no other solution. The decision to depart California was lauded by his Berkeley circle concerned with his mental condition. He was not yet ready to return to Berkeley; he needed time and space to descend from his astonishing heights. Finding strange comfort in the realization that at the same time only a few miles away Philip K. Dick "was rapidly going nuts," Terence later reports that "May Day found me in Berkeley sheltered by friends so concerned about my state of mind that they considered committing me."[24] Unlike Dick, he wasn't committed. And yet his relationships were strained.

Another factor occasioned the hasty exodus. There was rumor that the feds were aware that McKenna had reentered the country and were pursuing him. Paranoia had been palpable back in March when, fresh from La Chorrera, the party landed in the small town of Leticia, Colombia. There, they met an American couple, "Jack" and "Ruby," who had previously rented Kume's apartment in Bogotá. "I had thought the name combination weird when I met them six weeks before," McKenna writes, but the fact that the couple awaited them in Leticia furthered the unease.[25] Apprehension grew by June when he is tipped off. The rumors were possibly related to a New York grand jury subpoena Hartley was issued upon returning from Colombia, compelling her to testify about McKenna's whereabouts. With the aid of a lawyer, she submitted minor testimony to the effect that she had no idea of his whereabouts—accurate given their estrangement.[26] Forewarned of the tightening grip, the return to Colombia allowed evasion from the reach of the law, just as much as the solitude and strangeness of the Amazon permitted freedoms from the clutches of the mind.

Having financed their return trip to the Amazon hawking emeralds purchased in Colombia in April, Terence again launches out from Puerto Leguízamo.[27] The quest to study "the phenomenon" in "the pure medium of tropical nature in which we discovered it," he journals on July 15, is "not without an element of risk." Though risks are contemplated when once again plying the Putumayo, it is not the dangers inherent to the jungle, nor the hardships attendant upon travel to remote regions, that play on his mind. It is, rather, the psychological stresses inherent to confronting *the phenomenon*. Dennis's "schizophrenic reversal is ever in my mind." Again, there is occasion to turn to Joyce. If "careful thought and study" is the solution to prevent the Other from "turning on us," *Finnegans Wake* is compelling.[28] Joycean humor and punning had been a feature of their jungle

Eden, a world that is even punctuated by a visitation from "Nora and Jim" Joyce as hen and rooster. The wave charts, as later conveyed in "Shamanic Investigations," gave indication that the period over which Joyce forged the *Wake* (1922–1939) corresponded to the breakthrough period of mid-February to mid-May of the DNA year 1970–1971. The manuscript reflected upon the "DNA holographic library of the interspecies collective unconscious" to which the party had been exposed. "Puns, hens, and funky locutions, brother themes, mother themes, cyclical time, hermeticism, and much wild Irishness—all what's hidden in Finn's midden was scratched out by us in the Amazon."[29] Deciphering a path to November, the *Wake* proved to be "an excellent choice of reading matter while awaiting the end of time."[30] One imagines Kume a giggling audience to passages read aloud daily:

> Some time very presently now when yon clouds are dissipated . . . the odds are, we shall all be hooked and happy, communionistically, among the fieldnights eliceam, elite of the elect, in the land of lost of time.[31]

Reckoned a three-dimensional manifestation of four-dimensionality, the *Wake* is embraced as an embodiment of the "perfect tool," the union of spirit and matter. The work appears to presage the "gift" that could, if the charts hold up, amount to a momentous birthday surprise. Whether a "quantum leap of enormous magnitude," a "literal world shattering apocalypse,"[32] or a grand delusion, the potential reward was worth the gamble.

The repeat plunge into the Amazon is occasioned by a clearer sense of purpose than in the aborted mission of months before. As journaled, "the secret" once obscure was now coming into view. Terence's 1971 journal "Change and Becoming" is styled like discovery notes inscribed by the leader of an exploratory research group on the verge of an unprecedented breakthrough. Adopting the royal "we" throughout, the expectations, intuitions, and discoveries are typically "ours," implying that the research is collaborative. The possible collaborators are, of course, Dennis and Kume. Dennis's revelations in March—"Den's opus"—were pivotal to the approach charted throughout 1971, and subsequently. The older hankers for the views and opinions of the younger brother, who shares his latest ideas. Not untypically, the bush plane's scheduled arrivals at La Chorrera when it is eventually revisited are marked as significant dates on Terry's charts, not least since the aircraft bore news from Den. Even so, Dennis had relatively minor involvement in the *mckennaism* that consumed his brother's life (and for which he has often been regarded as coauthor). As for Kume, while traveling with Terry throughout both 1971 Amazon ventures, she has little representation or voice. Besides records of her hexagram throws or the charting of her periods of "fertility," she is largely absent. We know very little about how closely she shared Terence's ideas, and yet his entries give the impression that Kume is a coconspirator.

As a mosaic of magic and science, an animated ledger of intuition and intelligence, "Change and Becoming" is the work of a hyperactive imagination, expressed in thoughts, poems, theories, charts, graphs, mathematical mandalas, and refinements on the "season of magic" ahead. Like a collection of crytograms on the author's state of being, entries offer a cumulus of clues, which, with each passing day, represent "a further refining of error out of our idea model."[33] The entries begin with a declaration of ambivalence toward "the phenomenon." Cautiously scrutinizing each clue, Terence seeks to cultivate the "mental habits of the scientist and phenomenologist." Skepticism and "self-doubt" are reported to result from intimacy with the symptoms of schizophrenia—as witnessed in Dennis—and in his general incredulity with the inner voice's proposals. His mind, he avers, is "a balance between my hopes for personal and/or global liberation . . . and my practical awareness of how unlikely it is that we have been born into the closing seconds of the history of organic life, let alone that we may have a decisive role in that finale." While the impression he seeks to convey is one of a detached observer maintaining "suspended judgement," such claims are not only ludicrous, but more than often knowingly outlandish. As ostensible proof that he is not overly invested in the outcome, plans are made for the post apocalypse. "It has occurred to me several times in recent days that in keeping with the scientific skepticism which I hope to cultivate in dealing with the phenomenon I should assume some personal future beyond Nov 16." With that in mind, "papers" he and Dennis had accumulated over the previous years might make for a nice "book of essays on 4-D."[34] Evidence suggests that he and Kume made plans for Afghanistan, India, and possibly Japan—just in case nothing happened.[35] From the outset, the implication is that a suspension of judgment on the subject of the opus will best serve its disconfirmation. And if it is invalidated, he will act to "carefully extract my psychology from this incredibly compelling group of ideas under whose influence I have fallen."[36] Despite this intent, it is more than apparent that there would be no easy extraction from the cosmic cavalcade forecast.

Throughout, McKenna sets "the phenomenon" apart from the occult, the paranormal, and "the general gnosis of the 'world of the unseen,'" on the grounds that his opus possesses quantized and physical qualities consistent with a unified field theory. For the truth to be validated, he will accept nothing less than "a physical manifestation of the eschatron" in a stable form.

While conceding that his own "death or individuation" on November 16 would add to the "already swollen annals of the bizarre and peculiar," neither will serve to validate his claims. "Only a physical manifestation can validate our theory entirely."[37]

Someone among his friends gifted Terence *The Confessions of Aleister Crowley*, Crowley's partial autobiography, and *In Search of the Miraculous*, Russian esotericist P. D. Ouspensky's text on the teachings of G. I. Gurdjieff. These books are devoured on the Putumayo. While this reading alters little his opinion that these authors are charlatans of the "intense occult variety," he now allows that they are more "misguided victims of strange circumstances rather than simply out and out con artists." What is "odd" and "remarkable" is that these works seem to describe "certain phenomena related to our own experience." In particular, Gurdjieff's "Ray of Creation," which operates according to the "law of octaves," is a resonant phenomenon.[38] What appears surprising is that the "fourth dimension" could be accessed *without* power tryptamines. No lengthy discourse is offered, but it appears McKenna is unfamiliar with Crowley's prodigious self-experimentalism with peyote and notably hashish, very potent strains of which had fueled the practice of magic in the mid-nineteenth century. Presumably, those claiming paths to astral flight, time travel, ancestor contact, and other manifestations of what Ouspensky called the "noumenal" were charlatans because they were not *turned on*. By contrast, his own "XDMT" switch had been flicked to "on" back in March. "One of us," Dennis had declared, was to be transformed into a kind of MAO-inhibited superhuman. Given what Terence identified as "the depth and rate of transmission of the teachings," it was his growing suspicion that it is *he* who had experienced a "higher cortical . . . DNA informational waveform."[39] It was a catalytic boost. As he wrote in "Shamanic Investigations": "My thought processes since March 5, 1971, have been decidedly more creative, ordered and integrative, all due, I tentatively assume, to the operation of the informational signal from the superconducting genetic material which remains smoothly functioning and non-metabolizing in my neural DNA."[40] Such suspicions of the success of their venture demanded further assays in their jungle laboratory. McKenna's quest to distance himself from the occult is unconvincing—if not farcical.

As one day passes into the next in the post–March Forth era, a veneer of objectivity gives over to the "Proustian reveries" of a man searching for the miraculous, a giddy expectancy in anticipation of events to come, as in one in wistful reception of future memories. The distinction between "delusion or cross species quantum acceleration" appears to dissolve as "the Great Day" on the other side of the hyperspatial breakthrough is contemplated:

The joy of all families reunited—and of I reunited with a world perfected, all bodies and books at last and finally rescued from the flames. The siren song of the saucerian imagination; Ourselves—adrift at last on the heaving oceans of past—world after world found and lost and found—in the fourth dimension. The freedom of the Eloi, the power and wisdom of Karellen, the peace which passeth understanding. . . . How rightly and nicely it would settle things—how fair it would be—in the words of the song "Let it be, let it be."[41]

As the synchronicities accumulate, each affirms the moment ahead. One among these confirmations is telling: the July 22 dialogue with the *I Ching*. Terence throws hexagrams 49 "Ko/Revolution" → 3 "Chun/Difficulty at the Beginning," with stress in the third position. The commentaries are propitious: "Revolution. On your own day you are believed." And through "perseverance," there is a forecast of "supreme success" following "Difficulty in the Beginning."[42]

BASE CAMP ARICA

McKenna selects his next insect collection site. Would it be his last? Days downriver from El Encanto, Arica is a small hamlet on the left bank of the Putumayo. The couple are delayed here for six weeks—a base camp and "transcendental laboratory" for mounting an ascent on the higher-dimensional Everest. The insects are more tempestuous than bargained for. Journaling his sojourn, Wallace described black fly swarms at Arica so dense they blotted out the sun. It was no exaggeration. Dwelling inside metal enclosures built by the Colombian government in 1971, relief is achieved amid temperatures soaring to 115 degrees Fahrenheit. Terence and Kume bathe in the river between 3:30 and 4:15 a.m., a window of respite from the blood-hungry swarms.[43] Hunkering down at this "hell on earth," McKenna builds a profile on the phenomenon, charting its contours, speculation accumulating from one day to the next.

Consulting his humble field library, the broad landscape of comparative religion is traversed: Buddhism, Tantra, Gnosticism, Pythagoreanism, alchemy, and Neo-Platonism, among other traditions. E. S. Drower's *The Secret Adam* is on hand to facilitate interpretation of the sometimes capitalized "Eschatron" in accord with Nasoraean gnosis and Mandaeanism.[44] The religionist field-tester ventures that the "process" may differ across traditions, but the goal remains the same—which, he intuits, resonates with "the Goal" of the opus. Consulting Evans-Wentz's *Tibetan Yoga and Secret Doctrines*, "the content of the Goal" is determined to be the crown achievement of the Boddhisattvic path, "the union of samsara and no-thing-ness."

On the scent of the Mahayana doctrine of the Trikāya, it is proposed that "the perfected Buddha-body is assimilable to our standing waveform."[45] Envisioning the waveform amounts to a late stage in the process of Buddhahood, an idea informed by Guenther's *Tibetan Mysterium*. Consistent with the meditations of "Post Electric Thought," Buddhist thinking, and not shamanism, informs him through this period. Chronicling the Awakening of Gautama, the Buddhist Sutras are stated to describe "a series of incidents reflecting clear similarities with our experience." Further, "the aerial cars of the Brahmah angels" appearing to the self-enlightened are imagined to be synonymous with the "trans-dimensional vehicle" that lies ahead. In another not unrelated thread, a relationship is assumed between the chakra centers and the six structural elements of any hexagram, such that the expected "condensation" is analogous to the stages of raising the Kundalini.[46] This reading also prompts speculation on the appearance and form of "the stone" as a psycho-physical event. Will it issue from the mouth or sexual organs of one of them? Will it appear "in the mind" or as "a metallic line in the sky, coming from the Southeast" like a "saucer, aerial car or stupa"? Will it emanate from "the top of the head"? This flood of speculative realizations conditions an "unflappably patient" response to the long delay at Arica, including a rivercraft engine failure that thwarts an attempt to depart. The Colombian naval vessel upon which they embark loses power within a day of their goal and drifts back downriver to Arica.[47]

Suspended in "hell," awaiting final passage to the promised land 120 miles upriver, transit through the final 384-day cycle is likened to "attaining perfection" in Anuttarayoga-tantra.[48] The implication is that the final minutes counting down to dawn on the Great Day will occasion the compression of all yogas, tantras, mantras, and visualizations ever performed throughout history and condensed down into a single-pointed Godhead. McKenna imagines himself greeting that dawn—and presumably Enlightenment—in a meditational pose. If the final six days before The Dawn do not trigger the spontaneous manifestation of "yogic posturing," the dispensation ought to be yielded in the next smallest cycle. If the model is faultless, that cycle—13.5 minutes pre-dawn—will "mark a compression of change profound enough to at least be met sitting down."[49] The grandiose posture is later assumed in *True Hallucinations*: "Our destiny was apparently to be the human atoms critical to the transformation of *Homo sapiens* into galaxy-roving bodhisattvas, the culmination and quintessence of the highest aspirations of star-coveting humanity."[50]

He grows increasingly vulnerable to "synchronicities." Patterns everywhere. Certainty nowhere. In a period of deepening uncertainty in late

August, Jung affords sanctuary from the madding crowd of McKenna's own mind. *Mysterium Coniunctionis* is on hand and cited at length as an aid to self-diagnosis. The distinction between the "anticipated" and "real" psychosis is not always perceived, Jung wrote. By contrast to the pervasive "real psychosis," "the avowed purpose . . . is to integrate the statements of the unconscious . . . [to] produce a whole meaning which alone makes life worth living."[51] Terence insinuates that any actual psychosis is stayed through the creative integration of his unconscious fantasies. Throughout, the "supreme integration" coming soon is not associated with dark, brooding, or misanthropic themes. The mood is buoyant. He is lead actor in a saga in which fact had grown indistinct from fiction. But McKenna was producing "a whole meaning," and then some. The mix of "real" possibilities in play—wholeness, death, the collapse of the known universe, hyperspatial breakthrough—are animated components of a potent mythopoesis.

Jung's remarks tell of a critical realization upon which he arrived after the outbreak of World War I—that is, that his dark prewar visions of a frightful catastrophe amid a sea of blood had been "precognitive." It was through the crafting of *Liber Novus* and the depth studies of alchemy that Jung fashioned an active dialogue with unconscious symbolism. In some respects, although McKenna could not have read it himself, "Change and Becoming" serves a purpose not dissimilar to Jung's *The Red Book*. McKenna considered his own opus not only a "confirmation" but an "amplification" of Jung's treatment of alchemy. It spontaneously and independently expresses content consistent with *hieros gamos*—the marriage of opposites. His relationship with Kume, who had long associated herself with hexagram 54, Kuei Mei, "The Marrying Maiden," is seen to embody this union. The counterpart is 56, The Wanderer, the glyph McKenna associated with himself and which he threw in August.[52] A baroque mandala, a circular representation of the Eschatron—a hexagrammatic cycle with zodiac—is journaled on September 9 (see figure 5.1). The "ouroboric, solar and vegetable aspects" of this creation are felt to be more "spontaneously associable" than other wave charts. McKenna further admits being "extraordinarily content" while creating these mandalas. If working conditions were more satisfactory and drawing materials more sophisticated, he added, "I would produce a full circular version of the eschatron."[53]

Might such entries perfectly illustrate how this work served as an expression of the drive to at-one-ment? Their author is skeptical of any simple interpretation. As he related, Jung supplied the "rough beginnings" for understanding the "opus" now animating his pilgrimage into the interior. But the "ascent to higher consciousness" was conjectured to be an event

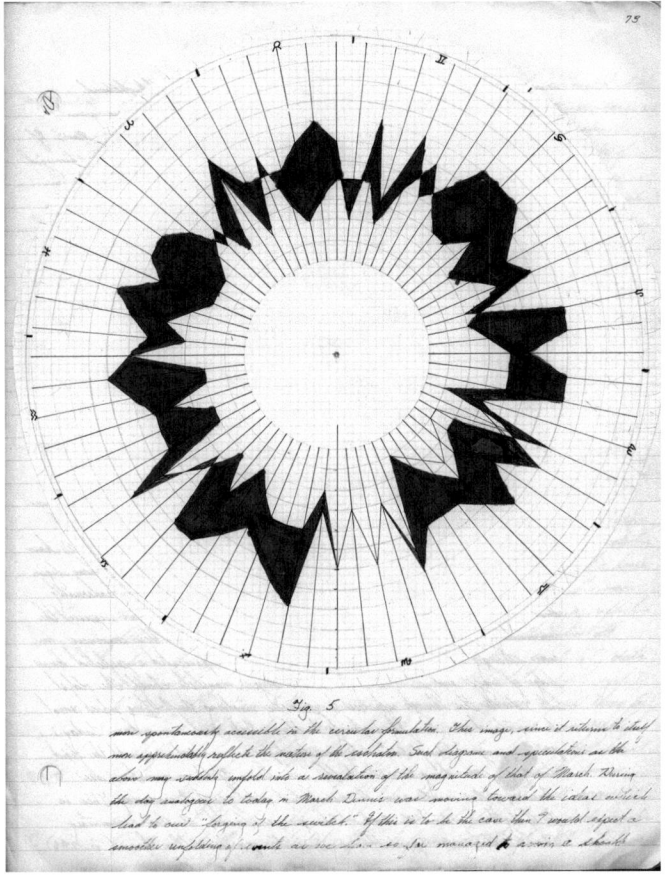

FIGURE 5.1
Circular (mandalic) representation of the Eschatron, hexagrammatic single cycle with approximate positions of zodiacal signs. From T. McKenna, "Change and Becoming: Studies in a Fourth Dimensional Phenomenology of Mind," September 9, 1971, p. 72. Dennis and Terence McKenna papers (MSP 213, Box 3, Folder 7), courtesy of Purdue University Archives and Special Collections.

of "eschatological" proportions.[54] No simple psychology could explain the transformed world that lay in wait at the terminus of the *trocha* to La Chorrera. The morphing model of the "wave of time" incorporated microbiology, nuclear physics, and biochemistry. The emergent maps of time suggested the possibility of a "bridge" between "mind & matter"—a span irreducibly the domain of the self and its symbolism. The method may have been useful for "riding herd on the psychic constellation," but

Jung was of limited value when approaching the lapis as a *real* thing. Albeit uncertain, the mood is expectant when finally departing Arica. "Whether we are merely personally individuating or actually are involved in the production of a hitherto never verified psycho-physical substance will not be clear until the very end." As McKenna loses himself in the fantasy, depth psychology could not supply the grappling hooks needed for the coming ascent, and the successful transit of "species mind into hyperspace." Only if "we generate a true psycho-physical rotundum" in three-dimensional space "will we know that we were—through some miracle—the chosen ones."[55]

Although McKenna sometimes self-identified as an "adept," ritual is denied a role in the consummation of his project. Regarded in defiant tones as "the gaining of power through the repetition of a paradigmatic action or event imagined to occur, in *illo tempore*," ritual is "a substitute for the mystery." On ritual, it is the mushroom itself that once advised: "That's what you do if you don't know what you're doing."[56] By contrast, as diligently journaled, McKenna's own high and apparently omniscient actions will be "the supreme paradigmatic activity of which all ritual is merely symbolic and anticipatory."[57] Likely fostered while a dissonant altar boy, the near contempt toward ritual was abetted in some way by Jung, whose own Communion was received as dismal and hollow.

In early August, the padré of La Chorrera, a figure with a reputed "iconoclastic attitude," stops briefly in Arica, bound for Bogotá. He was due to pass back upriver eight days hence. What thoughts could the priest have entertained when, out of the blue, only months after driving him out, he is again face-to-face with the white-robed freak intent on returning to the mission?[58] Might he look forward to a repeat performance? While McKenna makes plans to return to the scene of the crime on the same vessel as the padré, the priest is not sighted again.

THE GREAT COMPRESSION

When they finally arrive at the "Big Falls" on August 31, the mood is melancholic. It is not the same La Chorrera from which they had been ejected. There are few mushrooms in the pasture. The resolve sustained over the previous weeks in the face of adversity now dissipates. "I feel doubt," the journal entry reads, "a small fear and some loneliness and uncertainty." Kume, he reflects, "appears to be going through similar changes." It is unclear how privy she is to his obsessions over the forthcoming milestone: part quarter century and part end of the world. How does she indulge her lover's delusions? The woman who had left a reincarnated Jesus for a man now running the clock down on the universe takes some time out, as McKenna loosens his hold on the phenomenon. And it on him. "The unlikelihood that we are experiencing anything more than a vivid, and hence dangerous individuation process moving toward an uncertain end suddenly rushes in to assert its rational weight."[59] Rare insights are shed. "No one is more aware than am I of how out of control my unconscious can be, of my stilted and tepid emotional responses and the general inability to master my life that my fugitive situation reflects." The snowball of speculation begins to melt. "Suddenly what had been the pursuit of the end of time has become for me a deep concern about my psychological foundations."

He will not, he suspects, be overcome by a "reversal" of the kind suffered by Dennis. Even so, Terence wonders if he had not "regressed as a person." What had passed between him and Kume is unclear, but he grows resolute. Her discontent with him compels him to rethink the "ordering of my own psychic house before attempting to lead everyone to Buddhahood."

"Whatever happens," he reassures himself, practical necessity dictates that they retreat for a few months in La Chorrera. The contrasts with their earlier sojourn in the region are noticeable. Where before they stumbled into the unexpected in relative "innocence," now they are burdened with theories, expectations, "and a deeper respect for the omnipresence of the unexpected." While this may have been true, as before, there also appears to be little dialogue with the Witoto, whom I assume remain unaware that the end of the world may be transpiring in their own backyard. Given the sensitive nature of the opus, vulnerable as it was to misinterpretation, and McKenna's fugitive status, discretion appears to have been maintained. Above all, the scarcity of "alchemical gold" in the pasture cast a shadow over the entire enterprise.[60]

Optimism returns through September as the waveform is tweaked to chart lunar, solar, and planetary transits and phases, while comparing all movements with the houses of the zodiac. While these charts provide confirmation of the *I Ching's* status as a temporal device, these advances do not stave off the melancholia with which the waveform is now associated. From September through November, contemplating his role in the fate of the world, the grandiose imagination of the journal's author is ever apparent. On the morning of September 16, lines are penned that may have echoed a desire to sing the last dirge of the old world, or chant the first rites of the new:

> The soft song the high song
> the laugh, like water like wine, the wail
> The song at the end of time
> Radiant peacock lost in the sun

light angel unspeakable triumphant one
Lo Adam is given this tool this tao
this hour of return.⁶¹

By late September, there is internal debate. Will the apocalypse arrive by way of "atomic holocaust, CBW plagues, shock triggered geo-magnetic reversal," or "a collective species decision to quit the plane"? As "our greatest fear & our greatest hope,"⁶² death is a recurrent fascination. Focus soon turns to the tryptamine ecstasy, familiarity with which seems to make "the risk of dying immaterial." Such thoughts lead to the gnosis-inspired speculation that "evolution seeks planetary death in order to achieve liberation and reunion in hyperspace." If history is the search for ways to achieve this liberation, then he reassures himself that "today the planet is fully triggered and ready."⁶³

By November, the pressure is palpable, a feeling I suppose not unlike that expected in someone leading the charge into the Newer World of the higher dimensions. A mix of "tension and resignation to fate" is reported to be associated with the launching of NASA space missions and something like "the anticipation of birthdays and Christmases of childhood." A pastiche of threshold anxiety and milestone memories evokes the *riot of passage* entered in this final stretch. And as the "test" draws near, his mind is flooded with anticipation. Will his birth/death day gift arrive in the form of "a saucer, an apocalypse, a poem, an equation; a power, a vision, a talent, immortality, wisdom, resignation"?⁶⁴

And in the countdown to the Apocalypse Tao, thought turns to the jungle alchemy. The couple had fashioned a shelter not far from the forest hut in March. There, as dawn breaks on the passage from the "DNA year" to the six-day cycle, the barrier crossing is occasioned by a yagé infusion. The accompanying state of high MAO inhibition is expected to "enhance the genetic wave signal." But there is no main engine start. After the desired effect is not achieved, in an effort to ignite the launch they take the few mushrooms they were able to muster. When this too fails, it is morosely conceded that this may be "the beginning of the accumulation of a body of evidence which will shortly overturn the theory we have elaborated."⁶⁵

The disconfirmation had a long tail, however. McKenna again grows emboldened when on November 12 he gains possession of eight grams of *oo-koo-hé*—the orally active tryptaminal resin sourced from *Virola theiodora* that comprised their original grail. Defying the respectful distance that Dr. Calle urged months before, a local request is granted. Of the passing Witoto who were stopped in their tracks by the insect-hunting weirdo who had returned into their midst is "a sturdy older man" named "Demetrius," described as "a cloudy-eyed old weasel who positively exuded the stench of the cosmic gatekeeper."⁶⁶ The letters "D, M, T" in his name blink like jungle neon. Upon the halting inquiry, "*oo-koo-hé?*" (the spelling used in the journal is "*okoogé*"), the old man is "barely able to believe his ears." While it is unclear what is exchanged between the two men equally unapprised of what the other is saying, a few days before the 16th Demetrius hands over a "tarry goo" wrapped in little banana leaf packets—the Witoto's "most reflective, secret & powerful remedio."⁶⁷

The situation appeared ideal for any hyperspace pioneer and would-be messiah. The door to the "predicted maximum condensation" lay ajar. They had obtained at this eleventh hour the rarest of native narcotics. Seemingly sidelining Calle altogether, no "non-aboriginal person has ever experienced, let alone reported upon," McKenna journals, "the subjective phenomenology of this, the only reported orally active tryptamine known to occur in organic nature."⁶⁸ While this contribution to ethnopharmacology was worth writing home about, these were marginal gains in the broader remit. With "the moon in Libra and in conjunction with Pluto and during the time when the hyperspatial option seems most open to possible closure by death," or what Blake knew as "eternal death," the plan was to ingest a tablespoon of the liquid infusion before dawn on the 13th—T-minus three days to the Great Compression. He ensures that he is tied into his hammock for the anticipated lift off.

Alas, *again* the effect is underwhelming and inconclusive, as put down to an "excess of caution."⁶⁹ As a last resort, the launch window still open, he smokes the material which he had dried to a powder. But this desperate bid to catalyze the Millennium as he lay upon the precipice strapped in to his crude cockpit affords only a faint reminder of his sojourns in DMT trance. As is later confirmed, he was "never able to obtain a hallucinogenic experience from this material."⁷⁰

In an anticlimactic style rehearsed over the previous weeks, dawn arrives on the 16th, sans death, ordinary or eternal. The next entry lays out the reality now exposed in the sober light of dawn: "The phenomenon yesterday disconfirmed itself so completely that we are now left with the need to show why it had the appearance of working at all." Journaling maintains the fantasy of a rational scientific commitment: "Unless some error or incompetence in our understanding has been overlooked then we have disproven the applicability on the whole or in any part of the cycle to accurately predict time." And yet, amid notes cynical and skeptical, there remains the promise of a "Unified Theory," which seems "near at hand and knowable."⁷¹

The big take-home from this monumental bummer trip appears to have been understood on the day before the 16th. "I cannot fail to include the experience of the past 384 days in the category of vision such as Blake & Zosimus experienced, or, in a different context such as Wallace or Descartes knew." Not a philosophical principle or scientific theory, his quest revealed "the mechanics of the phenomenon of vision itself," which, he continued, is nothing less than "a 4th dimensional model of time and a new understanding of organism and mind."[72] From this moment on, McKenna is unflinching in the view that he had been gifted a model of time. The success of the venture to "extend immortality" is soon communicated to his network. As he wrote to Takayama: "We are closing distance with a general and unified theory of mind, life, matter and time."[73]

Reflections in the immediate wake of the 16th offer telling acknowledgment of the role of the "opus" in McKenna's psychological development. The exact compression point may have been disconfirmed, but the primary lesson—the alchemical quest for the union of opposites—was confirmed as an "eternal fact."[74] All the same, as was his persistent claim, the "opus" is irreducible to any psychologism. Despite the absence of "cross species quantum acceleration," from his point of view, the "wave of time" was hardly disproven at La Chorrera. There may have been imperfections in the model, but McKenna stored faith in his intuitions. As evident from the outset, a convenient flexibility is built into the model. As ventured in the "Preliminary Report," November 16 may have failed to deliver the big surprise because the "chaos at the end of history" transpires over a sixty-four-year period (i.e., from Hazelle's date of death). In this scenario, the real celebrations may not begin until McKenna turns a ripe eighty-eight (in 2034).[75] In a further possibility, if the universe proceeds without disruption from the 17th, a further sixty-seven-year cycle may "separate life from liberation" at noon on March 1, 2039. In this scenario, retaining the prospect of witnessing the "moment of transformation," he will be an even riper ninety-two-year-old. He finds comfort in this timeframe. After all, what's sixty-seven years in a seventy-four-billion-year-old universe?[76]

McKenna spent the remainder of his life coming down from La Chorrera, toying with the "Eschatron" and its successors, while contending with the reactions of his peers. The episode offered boundless material for commentaries delivered in his successful guise as a philosophical entertainer. "I consider myself schizophrenic," he candidly tells his Esalen peers. In his recollection, "years ago, when I was completely bananas," when friends and skeptics were cornering him with "nets," an article in *American Anthropologist* provided a comforting countermeasure. Psychologist Julian Silverman's

"Shamans and Acute Schizophrenia" offered a basic set of tropes to explain shamanism as an "initiatory crisis." The "break with reality" that may be sanctioned and "institutionally supported" by communities in "primitive" cultures is an aberration labeled "schizophrenia" in modern contexts. Brandishing the convenient shamanistic theory, McKenna diagnosed himself as "classic process schizophrenic," that is, the "spectacular" kind of break in which an individual brings back information that is absolutely incommensurate with prevailing cultural models. As such a carrier of aberrant information, at that time and thereafter, he could observe the (ironic) result of his actions: "You drive *other* people crazy!" Becoming schizophrenic is "a wonderful opportunity," he japed. Just make sure you can't be netted by "straight people." Manic and grandiose he may have been, Terence never lost his urbane, self-mocking sense of humor, nor the idea that he might be wrong. "These are the manners the schizophrenic must learn in order to pass among the normals without them dropping a number three steel net mesh over you and hitting you with a tranquilizing dart." Compared with those not so fortunate, he was always thankful that his aberrant episode occurred in the wilderness. Evading modern mental health care facilities, he thought, saved his mind.[77]

In an invited afterword to a 1991 *Festschrift* celebrating P. K. Dick, McKenna explained his 1971 birthday "Apocatastasis" as a deranged investiture of the kind from which he had matured. What was by then regarded as the *logos* had assured him that the universe of light would be set free from the iron prison of matter, that "all sub-atomic particles except photons would cancel each other."[78] The universe, however, tenaciously clung on. McKenna lent credence to the quirk that his twenty-fifth birthday had fallen on the day before Philip K. Dick had suffered a momentous break-in and burglary, which Dick variously attributed to aliens, the CIA, or himself in an altered state. This synchronicity opened the possibility of a shared "affliction" or "mania." He and Dick, McKenna proffered, "were both contacted by the same unspeakable something." Both writers were exposed to a *logos*-derived revision of "reality" that enabled them to recognize that "truth is splintered and spread throughout time."[79] Despite this supposed affinity, as we'll later see, McKenna sought to distance himself from the "schizoid logic" associated with his own past and that of Dick.

BLIZZARD OF COINCIDENCE

In early December, in Florencia, Colombia, McKenna has a chance meeting with a local man about a year younger than himself. A student of philosophy and literature in Madrid visiting home for Christmas, Luis Eduardo Luna overhears the American speaking in broken Spanish in a *tienda*. They get talking, and Terence and Kume are invited to stay at Luna's family's *finca* in San Antonio, a small village a few miles out of town. Accepting the offer, they remain in Villa Gloria for two months. "Our motivation," McKenna reports, "was to secure the solitude necessary to prepare a manuscript and to continue and accelerate investigation of yagé." There Kume begins typing up what would later become *The Invisible Landscape*. And for the first time, they all drink *yagé*.[80] The three share the episode with a Hungarian ex–soccer player named Karman, who reports visions of beautiful naked women before growing silent. While the visitors vomit profusely and are diarrheic sans visions, Luna reported visions of "a city with tall, organic towers with birds flying around them and populated by long white humanoids."[81] This and subsequent plant encounters turn Luna away from his militant atheism and toward the plant "teachers."[82] Terence (and later Dennis) will make a huge impact on Luna, remaining close friends thereafter. Following Terence's suggestion, Luna later travels to Iquitos, inspiring his doctoral dissertation, "Vegetalismo: Shamanism among the Mestizo Population of the Peruvian Amazon" (1986), after which time he becomes a leading authority on the ethnography of ayahuasca.

Meditating on his second residency at La Chorrera, Terence identified his "birthday coincidence" as a "lure" used by the phenomenon to "hook" his eager self. There is an understated note to self: "A little less ego and more comparative mythology could have spared us this confusion." While implying that he had been duped by a higher-dimensional third party, he nevertheless continues to plot waves of 384-day cycles *from* the date of his twenty-fifth birthday (and thus originally from the date of Hazelle's death). Determined to validate his intuitions on the *I Ching*, he seeks a solid date marking the emergence of a "special event."[83] The search is informed by the relationship purportedly established between the waveform and solar and lunar eclipses. Regarding what is commonly known as the "diamond ring" or "halo" effect, when the moon is circumscribed by the corona of the sun during a total solar eclipse, McKenna wonders if this effect might not be "a physical analogue to the mandalic ring-like structure of the transdimensional vehicle" that they had attempted to assemble at La Chorrera?[84] The chart reproduced offers a fine example of the enchantment by which our diarist was animated at this juncture (see figure 5.2).

Two full DNA-year cycles from his twenty-fifth birthday brings him to the winter solstice on December 22, 1973, meaningful for its conflagration of synchronicities. Notably, an annular eclipse of the sun is expected to

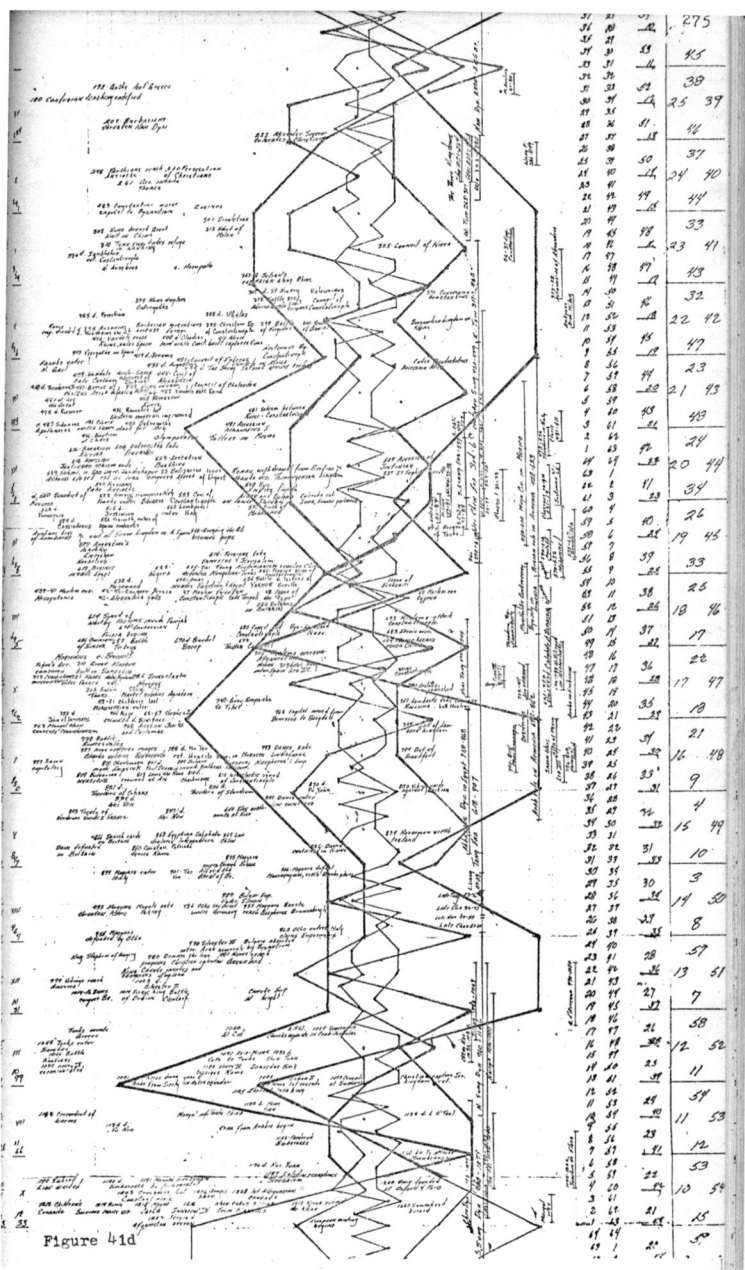

FIGURE 5.2
"Stage 5" of McKenna's Wave Chart, 1972. "It is assumed here that Stage 5 began August 16, 2,333 B.C., and that it will terminate on December 23, 1973. Dates are in months and years and are expressed at the left margin; Historical events are to the left of the wave, the lifespans of persons and empires are to the right" (Terence and Dennis McKenna, "Shamanic Investigations," 1972, pp. 272 and 275). Dennis and Terence McKenna papers (MSP 213, Box 5, Folder 1), courtesy of the Purdue University Archives and Special Collections.

pass directly over La Chorrera and the Amazon basin on December 24, in its path Brazil's city of Belem in the delta of the Amazon River. "I was dumbfounded," he writes, as if he had arrived at the clincher in a mystery novel in which he served as the chief protagonist. "The vertiginous elf chatter of hyperspace rose squealing in my ears." Transfixed by this date, conjunctions follow one upon another. "Belem is Bethlehem; it lies at the delta of the Amazon. Delta is the symbol for change in time; delta in Joyce's fiction and among graffiti artists throughout history represents the vagina. Dennis was born in Delta, Colorado."[85]

With everything lining up, "I was like a snow-blind traveler caught in a blizzard of coincidence." Then in the spring of 1973, the mother of synchronicities presents itself. The recently discovered comet Kohoutek, widely understood to be the "comet of the century," is reported to be "hurtling toward a rendezvous with the sun within a hundred hours of the solstice and the eclipse over the Amazon." That the comet will make its closest approach to the sun during a solar eclipse observable from "the vagina of the world" is cause for excitement. Indeed, the possibility leads to "a wave of millenarianism and apocalyptic restlessness among the fringes of the population."[86] With this confirmation of the cosmic pattern he divined, McKenna is overjoyed. But Kohoutek turns out to be lackluster. To the human eye, its apparition falls far short of expectations, and in popular culture "Kohoutek" becomes synonymous with spectacular disappointment. Additionally, nothing ultra-novel appears to transpire in Belem on the day of the eclipse.

McKenna couldn't say for sure, as he wasn't there. By then, he is back in the States. The disappointment set aside, the compression of events that the charts predicted are too uncanny to ignore. Kohoutek's impact might have fizzled out, but its occurrence was an important milestone in the development of what becomes the Timewave, offering for McKenna "perfect proof" that something far greater than his unconscious, or indeed the total collective consciousness, is in operation.[87] These weren't mere coincidences, but signals from the strange attractor at the end of time.

6 GROWMANCE

THE EXILE RETURNS

An emcee announces the next speaker at the Whole Life Expo in Austin, Texas, in the fall of 1996. The figure taking the stage has just been named an "honorary citizen" of the City of Austin. As the applause subsides, honored and bemused, Terence McKenna quips: "Usually they lock the city walls when they hear I'm on my way." The story with which he then opens his rap illustrates just how far he has traveled since early spring 1972, when, for a brief moment, he'd visited Austin. As he relates, he'd entered the country from Mexico on a "phoney passport" and was en route to Boulder to face his federal hashish importation charge.

"You're real clean, aren't you?" The border agent had asked.

"Oh, I always travel light."

"No, I say, you're *real clean*, aren't you?"[1]

Upon returning to the United States in 1972, McKenna makes contact with a decidedly *this-dimensional* reality. Writing up his La Chorrera adventure became a chief preoccupation. Under Terence's direction, the brothers take two to three years to complete *The Invisible Landscape*, a book that would allow Dennis closure on an episode from which he sought distance in order to pursue a career in ethnopharmacology. "What we had predicted didn't happen," Dennis reflects, "but we had definitely crossed some kind of threshold, where I became, in my experience, spread across spacetime."[2] Terence had crossed some kind of threshold himself. The international adventure culminating in repeat entries to the Upper Amazon basin was a rite of passage in which La Chorrera served as a chrysalis. Mounting the lepidopteran hunt in remote tropical regions, he had lived the metaphor, for the sprawling coming-of-age adventure was a context for metamorphosis. In words penned on the eve of his predicted compression event, the experience was received as an *initiation*. "I cannot help but think that we have been initiated into the mysterious ways of the zeitgeist."[3] And yet, although they had undergone a shift toward a new "atemporalized mode of understanding," details are foggy. What remained certain is a strong conviction to return to the Amazon.

For now, worldly pressures mount. In Boulder, Terence and Kume move in with Dennis. For six months, they toil cutting roses, among "a series of mundane American adventures."[4] Terence faced the daunting prospect of redressing his dire legal status. The entire opera is a vexing issue for the biographer, for despite surfaced court records, the whole truth may never be known. Confronting his predicament directly, on July 7, 1972, Terence visits the courthouse in Denver with Joe McKenna and attorney Morris W. Sandstead Jr. What happened next is murky. In Dennis's account, while Terence announced that he was turning himself in, no one knew what he was talking about. "After a search, someone found the paperwork and had him fill out a few forms and schedule a court appearance." It was all politely bureaucratic, and hardly the reception an international fugitive eluding capture in the world's hinterlands could have expected.[5]

Terence pled guilty to "knowingly import[ing] . . . a quantity of marijuana" over a period of one month three years prior[6] (see figure 6.1). His name appears only in relation to the case in New York, which is transferred to Colorado, his state of residence. His case is heard on September 22, 1972, when Terence receives two years' unsupervised probation as a youth offender.[7] It is a lenient outcome for a crime carrying a maximum penalty of ten years and $10,000 fine. Dennis believes his brother received light treatment in return for providing information about his suppliers. As Dennis recalls, Terence's long, rambling account mentioned "an auto body shop in a back alley in Bombay." When Dennis read Terence's statement (now lost), he assumed the story was completely fabricated. It seemed to be enough to satisfy authorities. "The whole mess ended there. He never heard another word about it."[8]

There would be no trial of Terence K. McKenna. The court records do not reveal what notes he hit on his day at the opera, nor how he negotiated his way out of prison, but turning on the charm was his superpower. The Boulder Statement may have been produced for this occasion. That document outlines motives for recent travels, and declares means, including trade in Tibetan art objects and exotic insects across Asia. The statement banks on authorities granting mercy to an ambitious young scholar and intrepid explorer gainfully employed and seeking to resume studies in philosophy and biology. It concludes with an inflated, though not improbable, objective: to "carry my exploration of the tropical jungles of the world to Africa

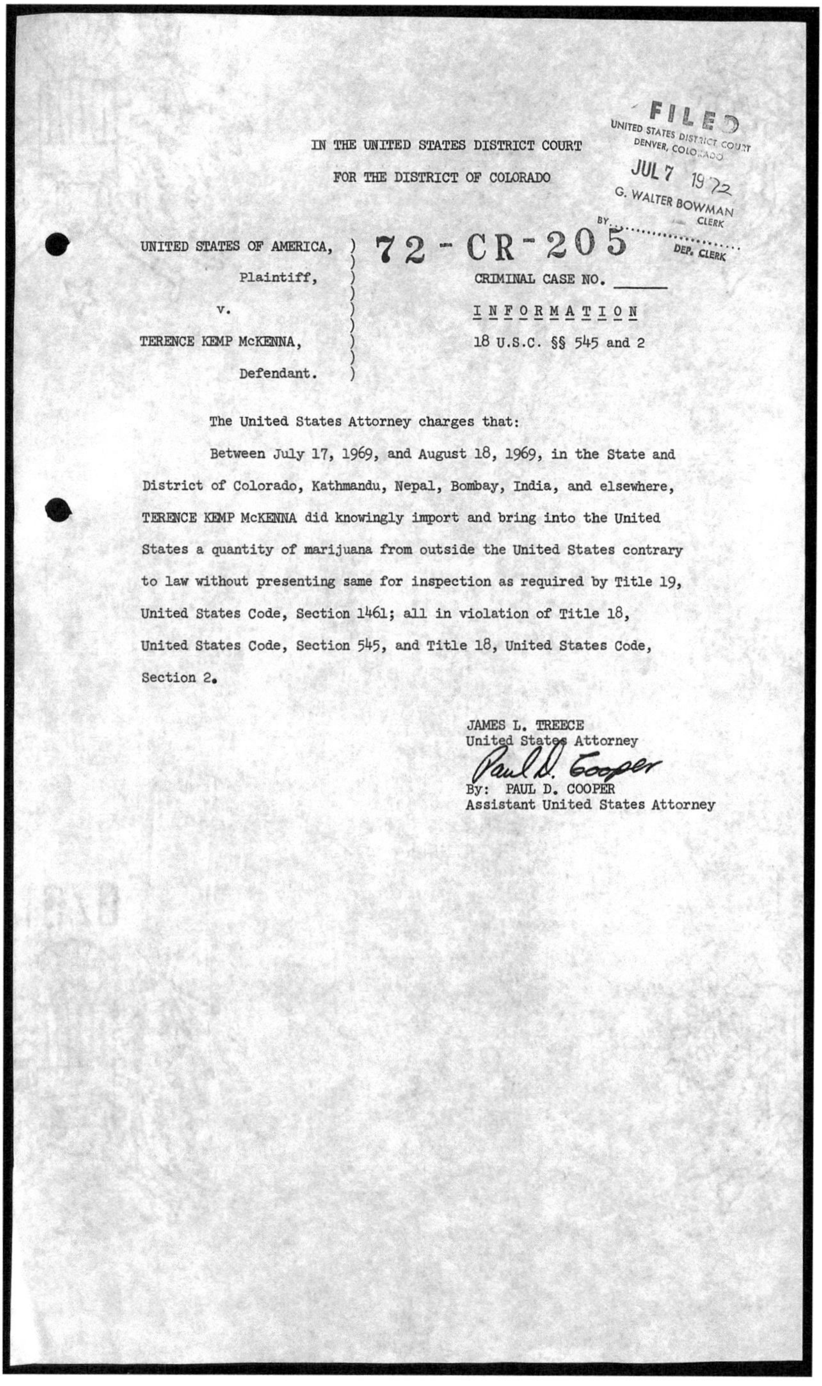

IN THE UNITED STATES DISTRICT COURT
FOR THE DISTRICT OF COLORADO

FILED
UNITED STATES DISTRICT COURT
DENVER, COLORADO
JUL 7 1972
G. WALTER BOWMAN
CLERK
BY.....................
DEP. CLERK

UNITED STATES OF AMERICA,)
            Plaintiff,)
v.)
TERENCE KEMP McKENNA,)
           Defendant.)

72-CR-205

CRIMINAL CASE NO. ____

I N F O R M A T I O N

18 U.S.C. §§ 545 and 2

The United States Attorney charges that:

Between July 17, 1969, and August 18, 1969, in the State and District of Colorado, Kathmandu, Nepal, Bombay, India, and elsewhere, TERENCE KEMP McKENNA did knowingly import and bring into the United States a quantity of marijuana from outside the United States contrary to law without presenting same for inspection as required by Title 19, United States Code, Section 1461; all in violation of Title 18, United States Code, Section 545, and Title 18, United States Code, Section 2.

                            JAMES L. TREECE
                            United States Attorney

                            By: PAUL D. COOPER
                            Assistant United States Attorney

FIGURE 6.1
United States of America v. Terence Kemp McKenna, US District Court for the District of Colorado, July 7, 1972 (Criminal Case File: 72-CR-205, retrieved from NARA at Denver).

and Madagascar."[9] Without access to complete transcripts, the investigative reports of federal agencies, and police affidavits, the circumstances by which McKenna resolved his legal imbroglio remain unclear. It is likely that Sandstead, a highly capable criminal defense lawyer, counseled the court on the remorseful and reformed character of his client. I have seen no record of his client's possible role as a cooperating witness, let alone a useful one.

When returning to Berkeley in the summer of 1972, Terence and Kume find a small apartment at 2447 Carleton Street, tucked into a cul-de-sac a few doors east of coffeehouse Le Bateau Ivres on Telegraph Avenue. Ron Curry (then divorced from Mahoney) is living next door. Good cash is made mounting butterflies for private collectors, and preparing insects for display at the San Francisco Museum of Natural History. When Dennis moves to Berkeley in 1973 to complete his "distributed studies" degree, he loiters for long hours in the upstairs garret at Carleton Street, where Terence works and raves within the book-lined walls. The formerly neglected back garden is planted with morning glories, datura, and *Echinopsis pachanoi* (San Pedro cactus), among other psychoactive species.[10] They closely watch the Watergate hearings nightly on CBS news. As Curry recalls, "we got so stoned the only person that was able to speak was Terence," who held court for hours. "That is correct Senator," became an adopted phrase.[11]

Around this time, Erich Jantsch, Viennese astrophysicist, futurist polymath, and author of *Design for Evolution: Self-Organization and Planning in the Life of Human Systems* (1975) and *The Self-Organizing Universe* (1980), among many other books, takes McKenna under his wing, exposing him to whole systems. Jantsch was an eccentric hermit who dwelt in a charmless bolt-hole on University Avenue. He grew close to McKenna, and later Harrison, who described Jantsch as "a big crotchety teddy bear of a man, stern but with a soft heart and a brilliant mind." McKenna met with his oddball mentor once a week at a cheap Chinese restaurant on University Avenue until Jantsch died in 1980. Both men share a commitment to punctuality, and ordered "exactly the same dish every week, at exactly the same time."[12] An image is conjured of advanced gesticulations on dissipative structures and the evolutionary conquest of dimensionality routinely performed over special fried rice.

In what is likely his oldest surviving recording, McKenna raved eloquently before a stoned audience in San Francisco in late 1972 or early 1973. He had been invited to regale Tama Starr, Martin Inn, and Linda Underhill, among others, at an apartment near Civic Center. As the joint circulates, the roommates at 4A Dodge Place are exposed to harebrained tales from the Amazon that later feature in *True Hallucinations*. The storyteller totes a copy of "Shamanic Investigations." While the manuscript is imbued with "a metaphysics with mathematical rigor," and comprises the basis for a "teaching," its coauthor struggles to clarify a method. The afternoon grows long by the time Underhill speaks up: "What is the advantage of this knowledge?" She might as well have asked, he quips, "what is the advantage of knowing?" The knowledge to be gained has, the storyteller explains, "a peculiarly liberating quality," since it approximates "perfect knowledge of the contents of eternity." As the room rustles with skepticism, the defendant reaches for Castaneda. The famed anthropology student's mentor, Don Juan, had talked about a "way of seeing." The *way* that was discovered in the Amazon basin is what McKenna imagined "enlightenment" must be like, albeit sans a cultural authority to which one must be apprenticed. Although unstated, this caveat appears to be behind his assertion that, at La Chorrera, they had uncovered an *understanding* that was more than just a hallucination, or "an ability to zap people, or . . . lev-i-tate"—the word is inhaled as he tokes from the circulating blunt.[13]

Riotous, absurd, raw—this early recording is protean McKenna. The Bay Area is the ideal place for beta-testing the waveforms that had been intercepted in the exotic interior. Soon enough, "Shamanic Investigations" finds its way into the hands of an editor at The Seabury Press, Justus George Lawler, who eventually comes around to the idea of a work titled, under Dennis's suggestion, "The Invisible Landscape." Seabury was a small New York publisher established in the early fifties by the Episcopal Church. Though an unlikely home for this work, Seabury had previously published Michael H. Murray's *The Thought of Teilhard de Chardin* (1966). Upon signing the contract, the brothers split the $1,200 advance.[14]

Formal studies are also resumed at this time. Terence would complete his studies at UC Berkeley gaining a BSc in conservation and resource management. Including systems theory, biology, chemistry, and botany, it was a "write your own" science degree, explains Mahoney, who took over Curry's apartment next door. Since there was no requirement to learn a foreign language, the degree is convenient.[15] "Shamanic Investigations" appears to have formed the bulk of the evaluated work for what McKenna called his "self-directed degree in shamanism." "Whenever they wanted me to write a paper I'd submit a chapter from the book I'd already written."[16]

COSMIC REDEMPTION

The events of the past eighteen months prompt a reevaluation of the revolutionary guise assumed before the trip to Colombia. Returning from exile, a crypto-evolutionist approach is predominant, a hallmark perspective pregnant with cosmic redemptionism, as outlandish as it is outspoken. While safely ensconced in the Berkeley bubble, the sensitivity of the exile remains. "Whether Marxist or mystic," as is stated in the introduction to *The Invisible Landscape*, "the pursuit of liberation" is the *raison d'être* of "the human species' conscious pilgrimage through time."[17] The manuscript is framed within a liberation narrative: freedom from alienation, matter, history. In a mix of bad and ultimately good news, humanity may have fallen from paradise, but the human story is an epic Platonic saga of *redemption from the fall into matter*. This trans-human struggle—which has the vibe of natural law—is about as foundational to McKenna as emancipation from oppressive labor conditions was to Marx. But this is, by contrast, no exercise in historical materialism. It is a break from material history—ultimately a dematerialization. Not only will the imagination break free from the "iron cage" of rationalism; we will be liberated from matter, from the body, and even from *death* itself. Ultimately, and in a perfect paradox, by becoming alien, humanity will be free from alienation.

An off-planetary expansionism is implicit to this approach, as early cultivated in science fiction. "We were enthralled," wrote Dennis, "by the idea that mankind's unknown destiny lay far beyond this planet. Years before *Star Trek* mass-marketed our mix of optimism and yearning, we were certain that humans were bound to explore the trackless reaches of outer space, and that we'd be among those who would go."[18] Sci-fi had a telling influence on the McKennas, notably Asimov's *Foundation* series and Clarke's 1953 classic *Childhood's End*. Deeply layered with future memories of a coming cataclysm that is ambiguously transformational, *Childhood's End* was a fertile symbolic resource. Buoyed by the probability of life elsewhere in the universe, Terence romances the idea of the alien Other. For him, human evolution has an extropian trajectory. "The transformation of humanity into a spacefaring, perhaps timefaring, race is, on a biological scale, the great goal of history." The entire solar system is perceived as habitable real estate, "but only if we can transform the human imagination to realize that getting high is not a metaphor; getting high is what the whole human enterprise is about." We may be given to believe that the earth is "the cradle of mankind," but "one cannot remain in the cradle forever. The universe beckons."[19] This amounts to the ultimate trip. The cosmic passage rite is elsewhere animated with analogies more primal than those evoking maturation from the bassinet. "The planet has carried us to term," attendees at the Angels, Aliens, and Archetypes Conference in 1987 were regaled. "We have passed into a kind of time where the separation of our species from the planet that gave us birth is a necessity for the survival of both parties."[20] At the same time, the species-level rite of passage analog evolves from cosmic rebirth to a pending union. Passing out of our self-absorbed species' "pre-pubescence," his constituency were briefed at Shared Visions in 1983, there now emerges "a collective erotic drive for a connection with the Other."[21]

The alien Other was, then, a *potential* located internally as much as externally—a paradox remaining consistent throughout McKenna's thinking on the subject. This is not to suggest that he was far removed from conventional thought on aliens. If the McKennas believed that the future is written in the stars, their imagination was driven by the idea of an organized cosmic intelligence recruiting humanity into an advanced galactic civilization. Explicit to this story is a benevolent contact narrative native to space opera where isolated worlds are woken from slumber. The standard *awakening* myth documents an intergalactic encounter whereby the beleaguered Earth, as one world among many, becomes inducted into an awakened galactic federation in the wake of a contact episode that bridges the gap between whole universes. The millennial fantasy Terence pursues for the remainder of his days is consistent with this strident mythology, a cosmic drama in which the world is redeemed, death is transcended, and being human is transformed.

When you add to this awakened universe myth the experimental possibilities of hallucinogens, we are set for a *grand* outcome. Whether "grand" prefixes *delusion* or *realism* is open to debate, though as the phrase "true hallucination" suggests, ambiguity is inescapable. In *psychedelic fiction*, or psy-fi, and its post-1976 psilocybin (psi-fi) variation, the *contact* narrative is metabolized molecularly, sensorially intensified, synesthetically enhanced, and interdimensional. In other words, the *other* is *hyper-spatial*, not outer-spatial. This is not simply fiction inspired by psychoactive molecules that fuel transcendent states, but a form of science fiction in which these molecules and their botanical species are cast as actors in the contact narrative. In this script, psychedelic tryptamines are stars of the show. By the time the McKennas arrived in Colombia, the DMT experience is permeated with agency—"organized entelechies," not unlike "allies" or "guides" associated with the ayahuasca brew. Exposure to psilocybin at La Chorrera is a pivotal moment in the hyperspace age, for the compound and its mycelial vehicle are configured as agents in a vast cosmic conspiracy.

The escapades at La Chorrera are the context for a contact experience authored by the mushroom. In the wake of this episode, "it had begun to dawn on me," notes Terence, "that the mushroom was in fact a kind of intelligent entity—not of earth—alien." Like a "diplomat-anthropologist" from the Strophariad Space Agency arriving with "the keys to galactarian citizenship," this insectoidal being possess "a holistic and systems-oriented approach" the different order of which convinces him that the ideas he receives "were coming fully organized from somewhere else, and I was nothing more than a message decipherer."[22] As McKenna is blasted with cosmic code, March Forth finds comparison with P. K. Dick's encounters over February and March of 1974, that is, the period he named "2-3-74." While Dick's unremitting interpretations of "2-3-74" published posthumously in *The Exegesis* subject his readers to "an endless hall of mirrors," a typical interpretation is that he was "resynthesized" by a pink laser emanating from Valis ("Vast Active Living Intelligence System"), a supercosmic consciousness he called "the Programmer."[23] By contrast, as a "receiver" of fragments of "a future event that promises humanity's eventual mastery over time, space, and matter,"[24] McKenna's task was to cultivate a means of reception that is advanced, concentrated, and accessible.

For the McKennas, the mushroom became an agent of wholeness, redemption, and transformation. The gnosis pursued is thoroughly imbued with Jung-inflected Hermeticism. "Saucers" appearing in the American skies of the forties and fifties were noteworthy for Jung. In a world reeling from the prospect of nuclear Armageddon, as circular symbols of wholeness and completion, "flying saucers" were the means by which the collective unconscious was jamming Atomic Age consciousness on a fast track to self-destruction.[25] A redemptive hermeneutic is suited to young men deploying outer space travel tropes borrowed from *2001: A Space Odyssey* and close observations of NASA's Apollo missions beyond the exosphere to narrate tryptaminal odysseys. "If cosmology was the lens through which we learned to view the universe at large," writes Dennis, "Jungian psychology became our cosmology for the universe within." And if the universe of the unconscious was available for exploration, "psychedelics were the chemical starships for bearing us inward."[26]

Just as Jung supposed the saucer/UFO to be an Atomic Age "philosopher's stone," and therefore a symbol of the unified, integrated, and redeemed self, for the McKennas, as the *prima materia*, if not the *lapis* itself, *Psilocybe* was a late-modern catalyst for self-realization and other-completion in an era of mounting crisis. On the one hand, contacting the alien within is a path toward overcoming alienation without. On the other, and perhaps as a consequence of the former, the ultimate *coniunctio* for our species inheres in successfully courting the alien Other. Potentiating an atomic gnosis, the mushroom, then, is presented as the antidote to the crisis of history—which is a crisis of the imagination. The revelation compelled Terence to return again to the Amazonian sublime, reproduce the sublimity in local climes, and provide fellow explorers with first-class tickets to the *psi-chedelic gnosis*.

In a letter to "Ricky" signed "old Ter" on November 26, 1974, Terence makes the first of many efforts to encourage Watson to join his third expedition to the Amazon basin, planned for spring 1975—that is, after his studies and probation are complete. Rick expressed interest in ayahuasca, and there is even talk of coauthoring a book on the subject.[27] In November 1974, McKenna sought to impress upon Watson his involvement in the acquisition of ten acres at Florencia, Caquetá, at about 2,000 feet on the eastern cordillera of the Andes. He had his first brush with *Psilocybe cubensis* in the region in early February 1971. We learn about the ostensible land acquisition from an earlier letter to Watson, dated May 29, 1974.[28] While "we" had plans, McKenna wrote, to establish a farm and begin a "botanical growing station" with plants from the entire Río Caquetá drainage area, by November the rationale for the "farm" appears to have morphed. In this correspondence, McKenna's thoughts on the extraterrestrial origins and *raison d'être* of hallucinogens are succinct. As this correspondence contains the kernel of the "seeded genes" thesis that gathered momentum into the next decade, and eventually is featured in *True Hallucinations*, it warrants reproduction at length. He was working with a new book idea, "about the extraterrestrial origins of hallucinogens and the visions that they bear.":

> I have managed to convince myself that certain of these compounds are "seeded genes" injected into the planetary ecology eons ago by an automatic planetary probe. There they have lain awaiting only the advent of intelligence. . . . The point of the message can only be made clear when we have advanced to a sufficient level of technical achievement to appreciate it. We are approaching such a level now and I believe that the final content of the message and its raison d'etre will be instructions on how to build a matter transmitter or subspace radio so that we can have direct contact with the folks who sent these drug genes to us so many eons ago.

While this alien intelligence possesses "faster than light technology for information, if not for matter itself," as they need a "receiver" at the arrival point, they have "seeded the stars with hallucinogens carrying the blueprint for the receiving apparatus."[29] With evident gnostic influences, this protean narrative is not unlike the plot of an epic space opera in which Earth is but one among untold starring worlds. "Current thinking," Terry continued,

> . . . concludes that the peak of the emergence of intelligence in the galaxy was achieved 10 to 100 million years ago, that most races in the galaxy are very old and very sophisticated. We cannot expect such races to appear with a trumpet blast over every city on earth—such an entry into history is tantamount to crashing into someone's home completely unannounced—hardly the sort of thing one would expect from a subtle and ancient Galactic civilization. Rather

they have always been here, or rather their presence has always been here in the Hallucinogens—when we understand this on our own we will be signaling to them that we are now ready for the contact. We can send that signal only by following the instructions of the seeded genes and building the necessary apparatus. When that is done somewhere in the galaxy lights will flash the message that yet another of the millions upon millions of seeded planets in the galaxy has achieved the threshold galactic citizenship. Current estimates are that even in a galaxy teeming with intelligence such a threshold is passed by an intelligent species only every hundred or thousand years. It is a joyous moment even for the galactarians. If this idea has any validity at all then its very articulation signifies the final moments of the pre-contact phase.[30]

Notably, the correspondence also signifies the "pressing need" for a return to the Amazon basin where it will be imperative to clarify the details of the message. This report forecasts a subsequently embellished theory in which McKenna effectively channels an intergalactic message while enshroomed. The weight of this observation raises questions, not only about the pressing need to revisit the Amazon, but of the motive for establishing a "farm" in the region. The speculation that the station near Florencia might have been configured as a suitably remote and botanically rich site for the coming abduction of humanity into cosmic citizenship may sound like speculative fiction. And yet this is not inconsistent with early post-contact obsessions.

There was nothing further said of the "farm" in Colombia, nor of a spring '75 expedition. By the beginning of that year, Terence had split with Erica Nietfeld. We learn as much in the next letter retained by Watson. "Kume in probing her psyche, much as one might probe for a mastoid, discovered that she was in love with Royce. Catalysis followed. The end state is that I am single and that they will be leaving before this letter reaches you on an extended trip to South America." It was added that the "intermediate products of this reaction remain too painful" to write about.[31] Apparently, Kume and Royce Kelley hooked up at a New Year's Eve party in 1974. Upon his discovery that Kume was sleeping with Royce, Terence reacts in biblical fashion by shearing off her hair and banishing her from the house.[32] Having left a man who believed he was an incarnation of Jesus for another who once thought he was leading humanity into Buddhahood, Kume again jumped ship—this time, for a "homunculus," to use McKenna's phrase. "I was vomiting every four hours, could not sleep, would burst into tears in inappropriate situations, of which there were many in my life. Heroin withdrawal cannot be worse than that." He wished to turn himself in, "but they don't have crisis centers for broken hearts."[33] Described by Dennis as a "swarthy dude" who had "straggly unkempt hair and beard" and who "looked a bit like a gnome," Kelley was another Experimental College alumni who had worked closely with McKenna, creating the first computer program for the Timewave. Most charts reproduced in the original edition of *The Invisible Landscape* were outputs from Kelley's programming. Kelley and Nietfeld married and later became leaders in the Berkeley Tenants Union.

Terence claimed that from late 1971 until the spring of '75 he had no opportunity to eat mushrooms.[34] For a union consummated in beshrooment, this fungi-fast may have had a bearing on the souring relationship. In any case, with the relationship over, dreams of a jungle superfarm/landing site dashed, and facing his final semester of classes, Terence is again all at sea, writing to Watson: "I am ready to do anything and go anywhere but financially my options are likely to be far more modest." While the book is scheduled for a May release, there is little certitude of its financial success (an accurate doubt). "Demonic forces in my life urge me to Pakistan," he continues, but "my own ennui and poverty conspire to keep me here." His old friend is petitioned for solutions to his desperate straits. "I have temporarily lost my bearings, old man, and would be grateful for any suggestions that your distance and objectivity might render obvious to you and yet obscure to me. What a hell of a note all this is!"[35] Amid his personal turmoil and depressing absence of funds, one consistent thought prevails: an expedition back to the Amazon. Despite Ricky's apparent lack of enthusiasm for Terr's theory of hallucinogen-inspired alien contact, McKenna wasn't giving up on Watson's participation in the venture.

AGRICULTURAL HOBBY

By March 1975, Terence and Kevin had grown close. "She has been a very good friend and an undemanding lover during the recent weeks," McKenna's Japanese friend Masayasu Takayama is informed. "I am actually very fond of her." Takayama is a source of cheer himself, having shipped a new lightweight butterfly net handle. "Few things in recent months," McKenna writes, "have made me as unambiguously happy" as that handle. The spring break correspondence is circumspect. "Spring has come at last, K and R have left town so I can walk the sunny streets untroubled by the possibility of meeting them." However, "it is too soon to try and understand what the future will bring."[36]

The future brought welcome distractions. Terence was soon paid a visit by travel agent, Satomi Hirano, who stayed in Berkeley for three intense days. Takayama had introduced the pair two years earlier, when Hirano vividly recalled McKenna mounting butterflies. "I felt I had known this man for a long, long time." In their brief 1975 encounter, Terence alludes to his identification with "an 8,000 year old Shaman in China," a comment that stays with Hirano, as does the association she insists McKenna has with Melchizedek, a biblical king and priest. "I fell in love with Terence's mind," she recalls some 45 years later.[37] He did not become her high priest, however, and their paths do not cross again.

While Terence had no transmissions from the mushroom between late 1971 and the spring of 1975, the radio silence soon lifts. A new era of communications is the result of a breakthrough when, in 1975, the brothers learn how to cultivate *Psilocybe cubensis*.

The mushroom spore prints that were brought back from La Chorrera had been refrigerated until the brothers completed their degrees and the book. Over the period of his relationship decline, Terence throws himself into a state of hypermanic activity centered on trying out methods of cultivating *P. cubensis* in a greenhouse he built from disused windows in the bottom of his yard at Carleton Street. It is a lonely period of self-examination and mounting financial pressure, worsened by persistent migraines and a long series of failed trials. However, in the spring, working with a student colleague in the agronomy department at Colorado State, Dennis succeeds in germinating mycelial cultures on potato dextrose agar in the tissue culture lab. He then stumbles upon an article in the journal *Mycologia* describing a simple method for growing fruiting bodies of mushrooms in mason jars on a substrate of sterilized rye grain.[38] It is a joyous occasion. Terence is informed and modifies his technique. Arriving home from a long hike in the Berkeley Hills one day, he enters the greenhouse to clean and replace the beds.

> And there they were! By the dozens, by the hundreds, huge picture perfect specimens of Stropharia. The dark night of the soul had turned my attention elsewhere, and in that moment they had perfected themselves. I was neck deep in alchemical gold! The elf legions of hyperspace had ridden to my rescue again. I was saved! As I knelt to examine specimen after perfect specimen, tears of joy streamed down my face. Then I knew that the compact was still unbroken, the greatest adventure still lay ahead.[39]

Through ingenuity, persistence, and collaboration they had succeeded in growing the fungi's carpophores "whose appearance," writes Terence, "was exactly like those I had known in the Amazon."[40] With the mushroom sprouting in his Berkeley backyard, "the teacher" returns.

By late June 1975, Terence is full of optimism. He had moved to Oak Grove Avenue, North Oakland, sharing with a "countrified friend" who had gown "temporarily tired of the pastoral life." They pool their money to rent a "much posher, yet still alien, house." The place features "white walls a la 2001—the last reel." As the dark clouds recede, his outlook improves, describing to Watson his effort to heal the "still gaping wounds" resulting from recent "betrayals." Putting his relationship and his studies behind him, the summer instills a confidence that is hoped will help alleviate his cluster headaches and permit a devotion to the new growmance. The impression builds of a final semester dedicated not so much to course work as to the "agricultural hobby" that begins to claim his time. Over the previous three months, he had nightly labored until 2 or 3 a.m. "Many blind alleys were exhausted and gallons and gallon of rye were lost to the demon contamination," Watson learns. "At long last however the parameters were defined and success followed hard apace." The results were wondrous:

> It is definitely the most streamlined vegetable psychedelic I have encountered. It's chief joy, aside from the lack of residual toxicity, is the wonderful tryptamine-related close eyed hypnogogia that overtakes one when it is done in a quiet night-time setting. The phenomenological similarity of the hypnogogia to N,N-unspeakable is very satisfying since the energy level is much easier to handle.[41]

Later, he gushes, "I am personally delighted but perhaps it is a parent's pride," while offering Rick the opportunity to be among the first to sample the boon, which he ships under separate cover.

His correspondence conveys the mood that grips the pioneer navigating *terra incognita*, while at the same time recognizing the potential for economic sustainability: "I am cultivating Stro[pharia] on a scale with personal economical significance." With a whiff of success in the air, a proposal is outlined. "If this little hobby proves lucrative," he suggests transposing the operation to a rural English scene and repeating the process. More importantly, the profit from these labors will support a return to the Amazon. While he had not flinched from this objective, La Chorrera is no longer on the table. Plans for long residency in Colombia are disturbed by growing "visa restrictions and political uptightness." To kick off in early 1976, the objective was now the Río Ucayali in Peru, a source of *Banisteriopsis ruysbana*, "the N,N-unspeakable containing yagé."[42]

Terence had been manic that summer with the effort to prevent contamination, a scourge precluded by a "jolly inoculation chamber," newly built. "Cruel indeed are the contaminants that haunt the Stropharia farmer, as cruel as the visions are delightful," "Watty" learns. "But not unlike Anthony in the desert I have also to contend with the worldly allurement (all potentially my undoing) of mammon." A "series of flues and deliriums" had been the result of his single-minded obsession:

> Out of all this confusion and activity, like a distant peak rising out of the suspended dust of the common plain—and growing more clear each moment—is the idea of a return to the Amazon basin. An expedition around the first of the year to the Rio Ucayali drainage of Eastern Peru. For me, a crack at a second book and another deep look into the unspeakable. Naturally I am hoping that you will use the opportunity to put yourself on site and make it your Amazonian baptism.[43]

As finances remain an obstacle, he will need to return to the United States after a few months to "grow some more hongos so I can do it again."[44]

PSILOCYBIN SUMMER

By October 1975, Terry is out of the dark wood. Mail to Watty opens with its author embodying the wizard whose alchemical labors are pivotal for humankind's cosmic return:

> Like the breathless hush that accompanies any act of deep concentration the recent weeks have passed—a moment, many moments, an eternity. Now it is over, or over enough to speak of to one in a far distant country. Day and night the cookers roared, Watson. More than once I saw myself broken in health before the demands of the alchemical toil. Haunted by visions of contamination, arrest, or explosion I held to the mission revealed at the mandalic center of the oceans of vision . . . the grand plan for the symbiosis with man and through man and his eager hands the defeat of gravity and the return to the stars.[45]

Sufficient interest in the organic substrate for the pending transformation was also cultivated. "Now my humble part is played and the organism is well distributed through the Bay Area ecosystem, forming new liaisons with the local quantum electrodynamics folks and all the others it is interested to reach." And so began the "consulting" work churning out a regular supply of mushrooms and selling grow kits and spore prints carried on art cards and shipped to buyers in sterile plastic envelopes from the newly minted operation, Lux Natura. Promoting the nascent business, and alluding to the brothers' discovery of the La Chorrera *P. cubensis* strain that became known as "ANZ," *High Times* reported in June 1976 that "there is a magical fungus among us."[46]

Charged with hope, the communiqué to Watson continues: "There is a breath of change here that may be the faintest stirrings of a new order of things." And we gain more than a hint of what, or indeed, who, assisted the restoration. "A dear woman friend, from Jerusalem days, Kat by name, and I shall within the month move to a pastoral setting somewhere in Hawaii, probably the slopes of Mauna Loa."[47] It had been over seven years since he'd first laid eyes on Harrison, whom he'd met as "a tide pool gazer and a solitary traveler" during his "opium and kabbala phase," circumambulating the Mosque of Omar.[48] When Mahoney meets Harrison at this time, she knows Terence had met his match, and steps aside. Mahoney also wasn't prepared "to live on the edge of the law," to sacrifice her own life to live his. "It wasn't completely altruistic but it was bittersweet for me."[49]

A letter to Takayama explains the transformation. Given the successful cultivation of the "little hongos" on a "vast scale," enough money is made during the summer that Terence could travel wherever he wished. Affirming that he will shortly move to Hawaii, he humbly reports that "luck in time and life has brought a new woman into my life." About Harrison, he is unreserved. "Beautiful and able to assuage my confusion and pain arising out of the way in which the last relationship ended so badly she is the new and definitely most important thing that is happening in my life. . . . She shines. And everyone feels very easy around her." And with the start of the love affair, "I am slowly noticing that the world continues its unfoldment around me, it is nice to return to it and rediscover my place in it."[50]

Harrison clarifies the situation herself. From "instructions" that they both receive in psychedelic states, they recognize that they are "supposed to be together." A traveler, she is uncomfortable with the idea of settling down. In Terence, she saw a man driven toward the "transformation of the world" that had motivated her since her first psychedelic experience. It was "the combination of two minds and hearts looking toward that transformation and looking toward understanding it, expressing it, in order to help further it." When she visited Wise earlier that year, they had dropped in on the new bachelor. "It was electric to meet him again . . . but I still thought he was the weirdest person I'd ever met." She wondered if it was even possible to have a child with him. "That sounds terrible," she smiles, but she "couldn't quite picture that part." He had a mind, that she knew, but "was he even embodied?" Additionally, she wondered, "who was gonna pay the bills?"

After a week of visiting, Harrison returned to Catalina. Paying her a visit soon after, Wise carries a message from McKenna. He'd invited them both to join his next expedition. Playing that moment back in her mind, Harrison recalls the feeling. "That's my life, I instantly realized. I'm going to have a child, at least one, with that person. The expedition is my life and he just invited me and that's what's going to happen. . . . I didn't get a choice."[51]

Harrison assented. This was the same month that the brothers figured out how to grow *P. cubensis*. McKenna started sending Harrison love letters with five grams of mushrooms attached to each one. She ate them all through that summer on her day off from waitressing. "Once a week,

I took five grams of mushrooms, read his letters, programming myself for the future," she said laughing.[52] The mushroom would become integral to her life thereafter, and a key to their relationship. Throughout the spring and summer of 1975, Terence also takes five grams dried, or fifty grams fresh, "as often as I felt was prudent"—that is, about once every two weeks. Of this regime, he later reports: "The mushroom had made good its promise to send another partner."[53] By the end of the summer, they get together, and remain so for sixteen years.

From October 1975 to the new year, they rent a house amid the "twisted lava flows" on Ka'ū, Hawaii. There, they continue their romance, with each other and with the mushroom. They take five dried grams together every five days. The experience was, as McKenna relates, more than just shared hallucinations: "We would melt into each other's minds in a Tantric climax." Tripping one evening in late November, Terence is appalled to receive the unbidden idea that they could have a baby together. As the idea keeps coming up, he shares it with Kat. Loaded, they decide to walk outside under the open night sky. Cresting a knoll to greet the stars, he makes an internal inquiry: "If this is a good idea, give a sign." At that moment, they witness a spectacular meteor burn. The mushroom speaks in his mind: "Such meteor burns occur but once in all time." Hours later, still tripping, a low, grinding roar moves through the lava fields stretching for miles all around and beneath Them. It is an earthquake that causes tidal waves and volcanic activity thirty miles away at Kīlauea Caldera. And so it was that they commit to a family and a life together.[54]

For Kat, other signs emerge—signs of their divergent approaches to tripping. With an abiding entitlement, Terence, she explains, was "more demanding of the universe" than herself. He had already received signs that he had a path, that he would make waves, become recognized, and therefore insisted that "*you* mushroom, *you* universe, *you* Hawaii, provide this for me. Make *it* show up. *I* want a sign, *I* want the thing. *I* want the woman. *I* want the piece of the puzzle to fall into place for *me*." And he would, even then, while tripping, announce: "Show *me*. Show *me* . . . *I* insist." Even then, she saw the hubris, and thought it troubling. She observed in these early stages that which later develops into an unbearable problem. "I just don't think that you dance with it that way."[55]

McKenna wanted to share his new mood with Watty, who is urged to meet him and his new friend in Iquitos around the New Year. "If you were eager to throw in on such a venture then I would begin to look toward it more eagerly." On the other hand: "If there is not enough manpower to get together an Amazonian Expedition . . . then I shall probably just take my butterfly net and new friend and go on out to the Solomon Is."[56] The "manpower" shortage was an issue. But when he "tried to get out of" taking Harrison to the Amazon, she has none of it. "That's my dowry. You promised me an expedition and we're going on it!"[57]

By year's end, the pressures on Watson mounted. A hand-drafted letter, dated December 13, 1975, was written in Ka'ū (see figures 6.2 and 6.3). The effort to establish an "outdoor mushroom farm" on his "kīpuka home" proceeds, though it is too early to claim success. In fact, they would not find success growing mushrooms on Hawaii. Terence had firmed up his plans to mount an Amazonian expedition no later than the spring of '76. A friend, Richard Brzustowicz, is on board for the trip, as is "the Lady Kat," with their departure from Oakland to Bogotá set for March 1, 1976. He presses his old pal. "We are exploring options involving penetration of several geographically distinct areas: The Vaupes, the area around La Chorrera or perhaps the Rio Blanco, a tributary of the Rio Ucayali in Peru." Terry is possessed by a manic mood that is the fate of the pioneer, the maverick, the unhinged. The message is impatient. Watson has one last chance to board the cosmic express train, departing soon.

It is no small aside that this message is penned on a Fritz Hugh Ludlow Memorial Library notecard with a reproduction of the front page of *Frank Leslie's Illustrated Newspaper*, May 12, 1883, featuring C. Upham's engraving "An Opium Den in Pell Street, Frequented by Working-Girls," and entitled "A Growing Metropolitan Evil." As the explanation on the card indicates, Thomas De Quincey's wildly popular *Confessions of an English Opium-Eater* (1822) "piqued worldwide literary interest in opium."[58] The motive for selecting such a medium for this communique grows more apparent. Not only is De Quincey regarded as a champion forebear in self-experimentation; the card (also mailed to other friends) implies how a literary work influenced an exotic drug's appeal. Not only is the letter a last-ditch campaign to recruit Watson for the forthcoming Amazon venture, it is an effort to convince his pal to become the British outpost of a protean fungi farming fraternity, a pioneer in a potentially lucrative underground movement. In the previous letter to Watson (October 5), McKenna was curious about the legal status of psilocybin in Britain, compared with the United States, where it was controlled as a Schedule I drug under the Comprehensive Drug Abuse Prevention and Control Act of 1970, thereby officially possessing a "high potential for abuse, no accredited medical use, and a lack of accepted safety." If the lawscape was favorable there, perhaps the nascent grow operation could be transplanted to the Isles. And depending on Rick's enthusiasm for the proposal, he was prepared to travel to the

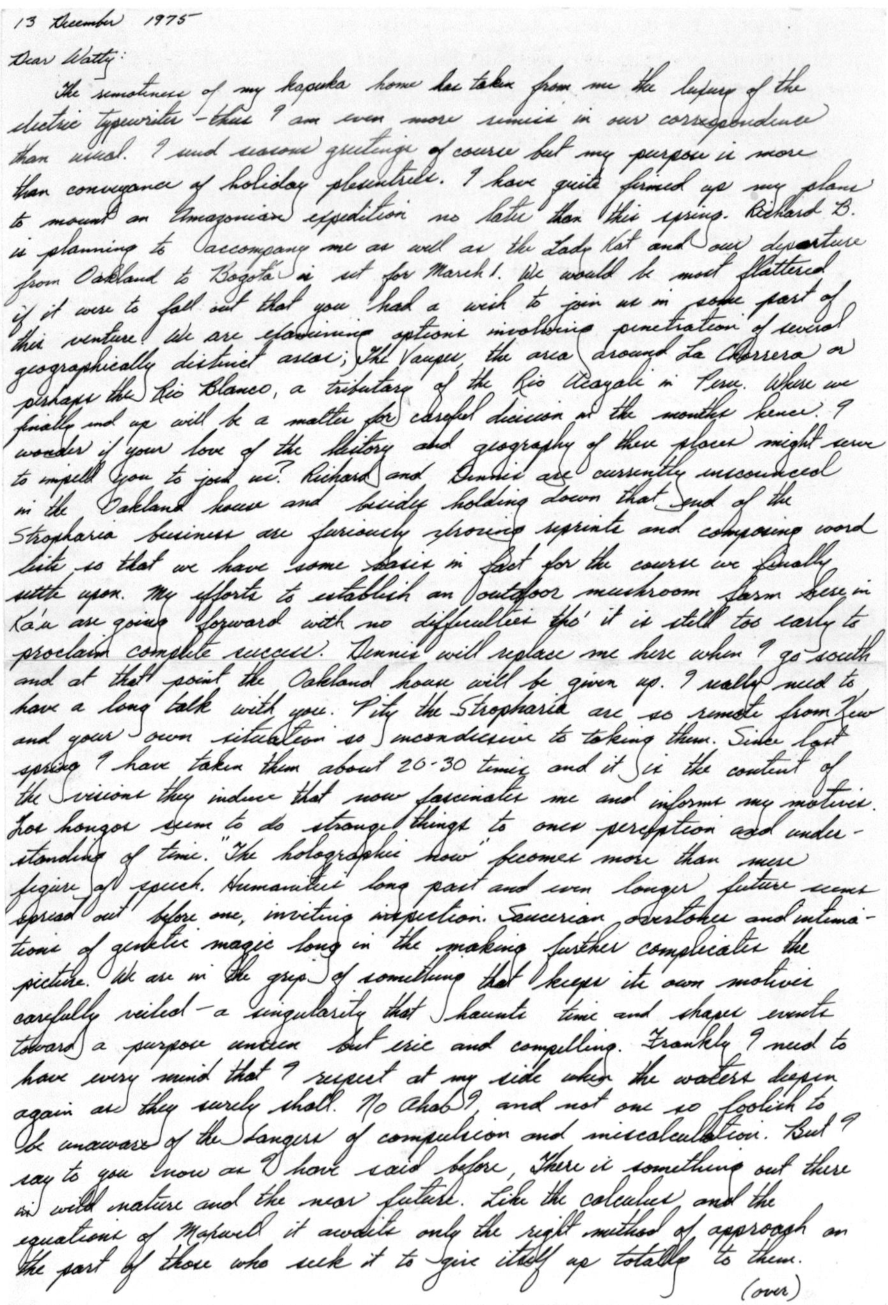

13 December 1975

Dear Watty:

The remoteness of my Kaʻū home has taken from me the luxury of the electric typewriter — thus I am even more remiss in our correspondence than usual. I send season's greetings of course but my purpose is more than conveyance of holiday pleasantries. I have quite firmed up my plans to mount an Amazonian expedition no later than this spring. Richard B. is planning to accompany me as well as the Lady Kat and our departure from Oakland to Bogotá is set for March 1. We would be most flattered if it were to fall out that you had a wish to join us in some part of this venture. We are examining options involving penetration of several geographically distinct areas; The Vaupés, the area around La Chorrera or perhaps the Rio Blanco, a tributary of the Rio Ucayali in Peru. Where we finally end up will be a matter for careful decision in the months hence. I wonder if your love of the history and geography of these places might serve to impel you to join us? Richard and Dennis are currently ensconced in the Oakland house and busily holding down that end of the Stropharia business — are furiously growing sprints and composing word lists so that we have some basis in fact for the course we finally settle upon. My efforts to establish an outdoor mushroom farm here in Kaʻū are going forward with no difficulties tho' it is still too early to proclaim complete success. Dennis will replace me here when I go south and at that point the Oakland house will be given up. I really need to have a long talk with you. Pity the Stropharia are so remote from Kew and your own situation is so inconducive to taking them. Since last spring I have taken them about 20-30 times and it is the content of the visions they induce that now fascinates me and informs my motives. Los hongos seem to do strange things to one's perception and understanding of time. "The holographic now" becomes more than mere figure of speech. Humanities long past and even longer future seem spread out before one, inviting inspection. Saucerian overtones and intimations of genetic magic long in the making further complicate the picture. We are in the grip of something that keeps its own motives carefully veiled — a singularity that haunts time and shapes events toward a purpose unclear but eric and compelling. Frankly I need to have every mind that I respect at my side when the waters deepen again as they surely shall. No Ahab I, and not one so foolish to be unaware of the dangers of compulsion and miscalculation. But I say to you now as I have said before, There is something out there in wild nature and the near future. Like the calculus and the equations of Maxwell it awaits only the right method of approach on the part of those who seek it to give itself up totally to them.

(over)

FIGURE 6.2
Letter to Rick Watson, December 13, 1975, page 1. Courtesy of Rick Watson.

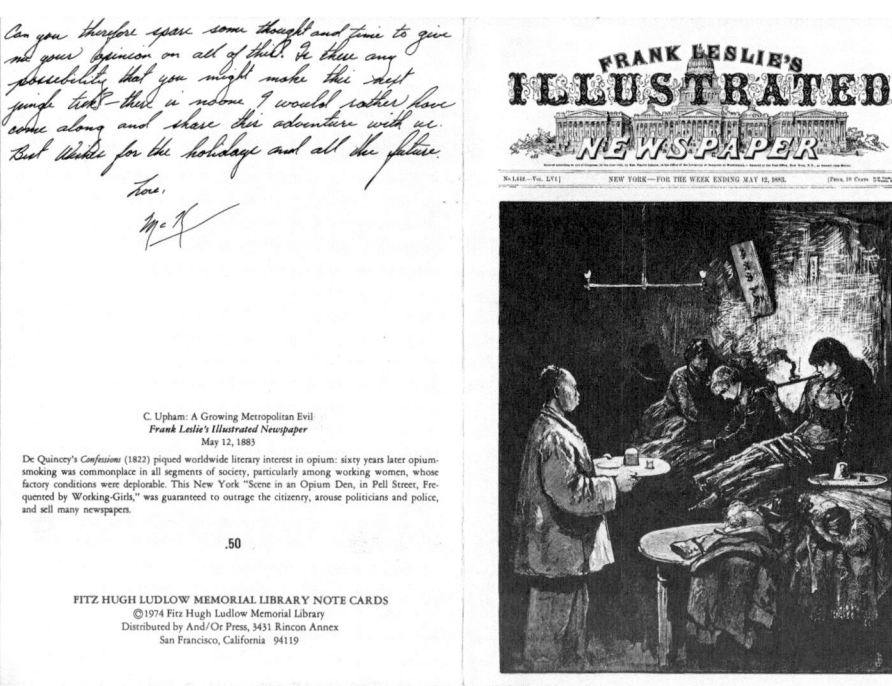

FIGURE 6.3
Letter to Rick Watson, December 13, 1975, page 2. Courtesy of Rick Watson.

UK with Watson post-Amazon for a month or so to "do my thing." Riding a high, Terence imagines the English underground favorable for getting his thing on. Had Graves not laid the groundwork long before when declaring (erroneously and without evidence) in the reprint of *The White Goddess* that his own experiences with psilocybin echoed the "ancient toadstool mysteries" of the Celtic bards?[59] "Agent-hood in the starplot has made such delicious options doable," wrote McKenna, "How can we get together out on the edge where the free electrons flow and know?"[60]

The response from Watson is not what was hoped for. Apparently, Rick hadn't touched the mycelial gift. With psilocybin (and psilocin) classed as illegal in the United Kingdom under the 1971 Misuse of Drugs Act, beshroomment was a furtive practice in Britain in 1975. In fact, the hallucinogenic properties of the liberty cap (*Psilocybe semilanceata*), the principal local source of psilocybin, were largely unknown. The immigrant is unprepared to be the mushroom man of Albion—but the lobbyist was having none of that:

> I really need to have a long talk with you. Pity the Stropharia are so remote from Kew and your own situation is unconducive to taking them. Since last spring I have taken them about 20–30 times and it is the content of the visions they induce that now fascinates me and informs my motives, for hongos seem to do strange things to ones perception and understanding of time. "The holographic now" becomes more than mere figure of speech. Humanity's long past and even longer future seems spread out before one, inviting inspection. Saucerian overtones and intimations of genetic magic long in the making further complicates the picture. We are in the grip of something that keeps its own motives carefully veiled—a singularity that haunts time and shapes events towards a purpose unseen, but . . . compelling.[61]

Visions received in multiple journeys over the previous six months confirm that the game is afoot, that Watson must down tools and get with the program. Growing reticence on Watson's part is affirmed in the wake of the last pitch:

> Frankly I need to have every mind that I respect at my side when the waters deepen again as they surely shall. No Ahab I, and not one so foolish to be unaware of the largess of compulsion and miscalculation. But I say to you now as I have said before, there is something out there in wild nature and the near future.[62]

PSI-FI

It is 1975, and Terry's probation from the source had been lifted. With the resumption of transmissions from "the teacher," he is once again in "close consultation with a cosmic agency of complex intent."[63] Downstream from La Chorrera, in the light of the gifts bestowed, he is drawn into a cosmic plot in which he is compelled to act as spokesperson. Correspondence with Watson in June 1975 illustrated further glimpses of the source. His nascent bloom appears to McKenna strange and incongruous flourishing so far from the Amazon basin. And yet the content of the visions induced are not context-dependent. "Here in Berkeley they are as saucerian, galactarian, and future orientated as they were in the Amazon," Rick is informed. "The coherence of the visions remains their distinguishing feature—that it is not so much an experience of one's own psyche but rather the experiencing of a place—or of many places. Far away places."[64]

He is compelled to serve as an operative for those "far away places" for his remaining days. The earliest indication of the nature of this operation was published in *Psilocybin: Magic Mushroom Grower's Guide*, the booklet published pseudonymously by the brothers in 1976 (see figure 6.4).[65] First released by independent Berkeley outfit And/Or Press, and designed for

FIGURE 6.4
Book cover, O. T. Oss and O. N. Oeric, *Psilocybin: Magic Mushroom Grower's Guide* (Berkeley: And/Or Press, 1976). Cover photo by Irimias the Obscure (a.k.a. Jeremy Bigwood).

those already familiar with "magic mushrooms," the forty-two-page guide is later promoted as integral to the "second Neolithic Revolution" (i.e., home fungus cultivation) and is said to have sold 100,000 copies within the first ten years. With a pressure cooker, a few canning jars, and spore prints, unlimited quantities of psychedelic fungi could be available to the dedicated. As the *Grower's Guide* launches the field of DIY mycology, a new generation of fungi freaks are inspired, not least of all growmancy evangelists Paul Stamets and Jeff Chilton, who in 1983 simplified growing techniques further in *The Mushroom Cultivator*.

Not simply a guide for the indoor cultivation of *Psilocybe cubensis*, the *Grower's Guide* was a vehicle for a psychedelic space opera, the précis for which was downloaded in the Amazon and developed in many subsequent journeys. The introduction sets the scene: "We are about to embark on the greatest adventure we have ever known, one that will change our very notion of what it is to be human."[66] In the foreword, a transgalactic intelligence—the teacher—communicating through advanced mycelial networks, transmits a message to Terence (pseudonymized in the first edition), who, for this mediumship, had likely ingested a "heroic dose," or five grams of dried fruiting *P. cubensis*, in a darkened room. This mediated commentary is worth repeating at length:

> I am old, older than thought in your species, which is itself fifty times older than your history. Though I have been on earth for ages, I am from the stars. My home is no one planet, for many worlds scattered through the shining disk of the galaxy have conditions which allow my spores an opportunity for life. The mushroom which you see is the part of my body given to sex thrills and sun bathing. My true body is a fine network of fibers growing through the soil. These networks may cover acres and may have more connections than the number in a human brain. My mycelial network is nearly immortal—only the sudden toxification of a planet or the explosion of its parent star can wipe me out. By means impossible to explain because of certain misconceptions in your model of reality, all my mycelial networks in the galaxy are in hyperlight communication across space and time. The mycelial body is as fragile as a spider's web, but the collective hyper mind and memory is a huge historical archive of the career of evolving intelligence on many worlds in our spiral star swarm. Space, you see, is a vast ocean to those hardy life forms that have the ability to reproduce from spores, for spores are covered with the hardest organic substance known. Across the eons of time and space drift many spore-forming life-forms, in suspended animation for millions of years until contact is made with a suitable environment. Few such species are minded, only myself and my recently evolved near relatives have achieved the hypercommunication mode and memory capacity that makes us leading members in the community of galactic intelligence. How the hypercommunication

mode operates is a secret that will not be lightly given to man. But the means should be obvious: It is the occurrence of psilocybin and psilocin in the biosynthetic pathways of my living body that opens for me and my symbionts the vision screens to many worlds. You as an individual and humanity as a species are on the brink of the formation of a symbiotic relationship with my genetic material that will eventually carry humanity and earth into the galactic mainstream of the higher civilizations.[67]

A variation on the idea presented to Watson in November 1974, this psi-fi/sci-fi vision is infused with Jung's "personification of the unconscious" as much as it is with the notion of "seeded genes," which, as later stated in *True Hallucinations*, were "injected into the planetary ecology eons ago by an automated space-probe arriving here from a civilization somewhere else in the galaxy." These biomechanical probes are capable of seeding "artificial genes into the nucleoplasm of the target species," where they are carried along by evolution for hundreds of millions of years until contact is finally made (i.e., hominids eat the mushroom).[68] Rather than appearing with "trillion-ton beryllium ships over major cities," an advanced extraterrestrial with a non-invasiveness ethos will, in Terence's mind, seek "low-key interactions" with intelligent species. It would locate a dimension in the cultural world of that species where "weirdness is sanctioned." "Then you set up your lemonade stand in that world"—in this case, the arena of psychedelic intoxication.[69] This concept was developed in dialogue between the McKennas. Speaking of this possible form of alien contact in 1983, Terence informed an audience in Santa Cruz that, rather than arriving via enormous ships traveling at hyperlight speed, a minded spore-bearing organism would arrive from the stars by "the slow pressure of radiation." And after untold eons, the genetic probe will find its place in the ecology of a planet with the potential for the evolution of minded beings, who at pivotal junctures in their evolution interface with the fungus to encounter an "organized entelechy," or "a voice speaking with greater knowledge than you or your subconscious possess."[70]

Reflecting on their experiences forty years after La Chorrera, Dennis neatly summarizes the perspective as a message received by he and Terence in 1971. Reasoning that civilizations seeking to communicate with humanity are likely to "proceed cautiously and use unanticipated means to make contact . . . the notion that DMT, psilocybin, and the other psychoactive tryptamines are the calling cards of an advanced civilization is not so farfetched." After long years pondering the matter as a scientist, Dennis eventually articulates an alternative intelligent design theory, involving DNA, tryptophan, and the tryptamines arising from its biosynthesis. "It would be a trivial matter," he claims, "for a biotechnologically sophisticated super civilization to 'seed' the early terrestrial biosphere with genes coding for the biosynthesis of tryptophan."[71]

Echoing Terence's tryptaminal trans-speciesism, in a speculative approach that directs one's gaze deep within at the same time as without, Dennis concludes that evidence of alien civilization is likely to be found not in radio signals from a distant star but within our own genomes. The idea echoes the deeper meaning behind Terence's frequent intonation that "you are the alien." This long view on alien contact, in which psilocybin performs the role of an "alien artifact,"[72] distinguished Terence (and Dennis) from garden-variety ufologists. In this vision, as "a child-race standing for the first time on the brink of flight to the stars," humanity is considered a naive species before the "elder life form" of the mushroom. This is essentially an upbeat vision where the ancients stand in romantic contrast to, for example, the malevolent "old ones" of Lovecraft's Cthulu mythos. "As our imagination has striven outward to attempt to encompass the possibility of the intelligent Other somewhere in the starry galaxy, so has the Other," Terence claimed, "revealed itself to be among us." Not only this; in the psilocybin trance it is revealed to be "an aspect of ourselves."[73]

The "seeded gene" twist on "intelligent design" holds parallels with the concept of "directed panspermia." The theory that microscopic life-forms spread throughout the universe via interstellar dust, meteoroids, asteroids, comets, and radiation—"panspermia"—was, according to Terence, "the best support I have for the idea I was putting forth." That said, his vision of how intelligence may have arrived on Earth via "this spore-bearing life form" is distinct from theories of how life began on Earth. While claiming to provide "a more radical version of spermia theory,"[74] he did not elaborate upon more specific parallels between "directed panspermia" as originally posited by Francis Crick[75]—that is, that life could be intentionally "seeded" by advanced extraterrestrial civilizations—and the content of his visions. Terence gave little input to this idea, possibly less than Leary, who toyed with a version of panspermia in his "psi phi comet tale," *Starseed*. "Life is disseminated through the galaxies in the form of nucleotide templates," Leary wagered in 1973, the year of Crick's *Icarus* article. "These 'seeds' land on planets, are activated by solar radiation, and evolve nervous systems." Not unlike McKenna, Leary projected significance onto the 1973 comet Kohoutek. From Leary's cell in Folsom State Prison, the anticipated comet (dubbed "Starseed") was reckoned to be a "signal" from "Higher Intelligence," a symbol of freedom, and a "bright reminder of our extraterrestrial origin and future."[76]

Growmance

As conveyed in the foreword to the *Grower's Guide* and extemporized by Terence for his audience over the next two decades, the channeled communications of an advanced mycelial intelligence revealed the plot of the cosmic adventure in which humanity is cast. For individual growers *and* the species as a whole, it was a practical guide to *getting high*. While indebted to Jung, it demonstrated that the *alien other* is irreducible to depth psychology. McKenna never discounted the presence of aliens in our neighborhood. It wasn't a matter of awaiting their arrival. *They* are already here.

SHAMANARCHIST AND SHEPHERDESS

The compelling world of psi-fi drove Terence's return to the source. Arriving in Lima, Peru, in early 1976, the long-awaited journey finally became a reality. Comet West was visible en route at 29,000 feet—a "good omen." Despite the years of hounding, Watson does not front for the ten-week adventure, and there would be no ayahuasca-focused collaboration.[77] The winds had shifted. Two companions are on board: Harrison, "our photographer, linguist, and botanical artist," and Richard Brzustowicz, "an old friend and a medical historian with a special interest in folk medicine and shamanistic curing." Seeking to avert replication of the Mazatec travesty, McKenna's account is not published until thirteen years later. From that account, the primary purpose of the trip is to obtain enough data on ayahuasca—its sources, preparation techniques, and psychosomatic experience—and compare with knowledge already acquired on psilocybin. Curiosity is fueled more by the individuating *gnosis* potency attributed to ayahuasca than the *therapeutic* delivery enabled by a facilitator. "Yage is not without a gnosis of its own," it is declared by a figure introduced to the phenomenon via *The Yage Letters*. "It has a reputation," noted McKenna, "as a curing panacea and a powerful hallucinogen, bringing visions of strange cities, jungle beasts, and shamanic voyages to the heart of the Milky Way."[78] Also priming the party with anticipation was F. Bruce Lamb's *Wizard of the Upper Amazon*, which tells the story of *mestizo* Manuel Córdova-Rios, who was abducted by Indians as a teen and initiated into the ways of the *vegetalista*, and in whose ayahuasca *curandero* sessions participants are reported to become telepathically connected.

Arriving in Iquitos, the trio travel up the Napo on a boat piloted by none other than "Lord Dark" (a.k.a. Solo Dark), a strange synchronicity that colors the "abyss of ambiguity" enveloping the party as they plunge deeper into ayahuasca country. A few days later, they part ways with the "unkempt Charon" at Fancho Playa, a riverbank village where McKenna is disappointed by signs that cultural tradition had "either faded or moved deeper into the jungle."[79] Worse yet, they are so unprepared for the swarms of mosquitoes and the very possibility of dysentery that after a week of great discomfort, softened somewhat by the opium they nibble on daily, they repair to Iquitos.

There they manage to track down Córdova-Rios himself. The spritely ninety-one-year-old insists that the local ayahuasqueros are by and large charlatans. "There is no good ayahuasca around Iquitos anymore," he warns. "There is no one who makes it the right way."[80] The *vegetalista* counsels them to seek a woman in the Pucallpa area who had learned her arts from Córdova-Rios, curing herself of leprosy. After fly-hopping 300 miles south they instead fall in with Don Fidel Mosombite, "someone whose ambiente seemed correct for the mystery that he claimed to understand."[81] With Don Fidel leading sessions in a backyard shed outside Pucallpa, it is he they entrust to prepare the brew and sing the *icaros* (the songs of the ayahuasqueros).

Don Fidel in turn entrusts them. From him they acquire valued information on sourcing, preparation, and brewing. Acting as intermediary, Harrison recalls how they had to prove they weren't flakes. "We had to come and go and answer questions and leave and think about it."[82] Passing these tests, they are eventually permitted to stay if they help out, and if Harrison agrees to take care of the "psychologically unstable" Brzustowicz.[83] Amid semi-public circles of indigenous characters, they drink on some ten occasions over several weeks.

The couple have contrasting experiences with ayahuasca. For Harrison, the ceremonies were far more effective and enchanting than they are for McKenna, who remains aloof. On the evening of their first brew, the mood shifts from apprehension with a reputedly powerful psychedelic still virtually unknown to him, to disappointment that the dose is "apparently insufficient to trigger the anticipated flood of visions." Despite experiencing "a full-field hallucination . . . of flowing magenta liquid," his self-perceived bum steer continues over subsequent sessions. While "the ayahuasca way of understanding" had opened before them, he was not treated to entities or visions.[84] Terence is restless in Harrison's account. "He didn't really get ayahuasca. He didn't like that somebody else had to be involved in his visions and his state of mind. He resisted that."

By contrast, receiving ayahuasca as life-affirming, Harrison is pulled into its world and is respectful of its guides. She is ecstatic, on each occasion. Adding great depth to her incipient animism, the experience is an inspiration for what she imagines as their future work in the world. "The plants and their relations with everything else were primary. Even the stars were having a conversation with the plants." Few Westerners had been so privileged. "We were so incredibly fortunate to be able to witness this, to participate and sing, and either glimpse the beauty, or be swept up in it." But, increasingly, her partner is grumbling, blaming, and dismissive. Terence's cerebral expectations of ayahuasca, she feels, became the obstacle that "blocked him from experiencing its power." They wrestle over this.[85]

Undeterred by adversity, they were travelers who had located their jungle alchemist. But Terence had inquiries demanding attention. What are the optimum variables for a breakthrough experience? Were they "alone at the edge of these mysteries"? Is there "a tradition of the hyperdimensions of gnosis," and if so, what is to become of the traveler who gains admittance to these realms? It becomes his conclusion that the scene around Pucallpa is not ideal for answering such inquiries. Between the recalcitrant antics of Don Fidel's drunken nephew, the incessant insects, bouts of salmonella poisoning, over-harvested *Banisteriopsis*, the strain of daily travel, and, not least of all, ineffective dosage, the experience proves overall unsatisfying. While his report is autoethnographic, Peru is not "true fieldwork" in McKenna's definition, for that involves "being psychedelically ecstatic and at play in the fields of the Lord in search of the shamanic dimension where contact with the Other is likely."[86]

The dosage may have felt small for him, but in Harrison's view, Terence "never allowed ayahuasca to open him up" in Peru. "He didn't understand it." He couldn't find the wavelength, "as he was always focused on harvesting the extravagant visuals and verbal seeds of ideas, but was not able to surrender" to the brew. Moreover, she questioned his perspective on "fieldwork," shaped as it had been by his experience at La Chorrera, that is, "not finding many plants, not seeking experiences or friendships with the indigenous people who knew the plants, not speaking their language." In other words, while his gifts were many, he was no ethnobotanist.[87]

Inpatient in Peru, McKenna found himself, as he concluded, "a mere spectator to the drug experience" that had been his *raison d'être*. The trip confirms what he perceived as the experimental frailties of traditional shamanism. In Don Fidel, he finds a psychedelic compatriot, a "grand exploring soul," more colleague in possession of a universal set of values than elite gatekeeper.[88] But the concept of charlatan *brujo* haunts the story, a suspicion implicit to the work of Burroughs and later traveler-writers. Nostalgia for an authentic tradition betrays a primitivist sensibility, that is, of the untouched noble shaman who yet dwells deep in the forest. The druthers for authenticity, furthermore, neglected shamanism's dark side—*brujeria* and sorcery are rarely encountered in McKenna's shamanic idyll.[89] The attitude also exposed a fault line dividing the Western shamanarchist—the neo-shaman anarchist on the quest for a consciousness-evolving gnosis and accustomed to a complex pharmacopoeia—and the ayahuasquero implicated in radically transforming social conditions, and attached to changing traditions of medicine and sorcery.

By contrast, Harrison is more trusting. "We had truly fallen in love in the last six months . . . and I'd seen our life together, children, and all these things." And yet they almost part ways there and then. McKenna grows uncomfortable with how she is "going native." "You're falling under the spell of this man and his wife and his children," he tells her. "It's bigger than us," she responds. "It's beautiful. It is a mystery. We can explore the mystery. We cannot define the mystery." She is fine with someone holding more knowledge and expertise than herself, and serving as a guide. Terence, she claims, is a total narcissist by contrast, stumbling when not being the center of attention.[90] As a consequence, he became bored and restless. "He never did get the beauty of hanging out with native people, who really know things and have a way of being in the world."[91]

Revealing a pattern of contempt for authority, McKenna pursues the crypto-anarchist code. Reckoning the hyperdimensions too powerful and humbling to be governed by tradition, priestcraft, or men of high knowledge, he thought gnosis can only be discovered in "the depths of the psychedelically intoxicated soul." In such an intractable ethos, "immense novelty is not something guarded by a shamanic brotherhood that understands what it guards." Rather, all brotherhoods, McKenna claimed, are "shams."[92] Catholicism. Tantra. Balinese trance dance. The patriarchal priesthoods of countless religious persuasions are risible. Nor, for that matter, could the "unintoxicated middlemen" of the New Age—that is, gurus—be trusted. Psychedelics, he is adamant, permit unmediated access to the unspeakable, the "transcendentally alien."[93] Moreover, the goal of "shamanarchy" is not self-realization, but species survival.

Many of these ideas are beaten into shape long after the trek to Peru, a journey that seemed to magnify anxieties about the loss of tradition around which the couple held differing attitudes. Where McKenna sought appropriate tools in his grandiose dream of inspiring a revival of the "archaic" state of mind, Harrison's more grounded objective is to study worldviews and preserve the knowledge of cultural traditions she fears could be easily abused, if not disrespected, as was the case in the Mazatec highlands in the wake of Wasson. In the early nineties, following the divorce, she returned to the Amazon to "get her bearing." Practicing being "a gently participating witness," she grew roots as "the plant woman." In her subsequent three decades of field research on the cultural context of visionary plant use, notably among the Mazatec, and in her continuing support for the preservation of plants and folk medicine, Harrison has been received as "the psychedelic woman teacher to the herbalist woman western world."[94]

Harrison's account of her 1995 visit with a *curandero* growing the "leaves of the Shepherdess" (*Salvia divinorum*) in the mountains of northern Oaxaca, Mexico, defines her non-vainglorious style of ethnobotany. She had arrived in the mountains desperate for a solution to a worsening cardiac condition, which had started in the week she and Terence split up. In the ceremony to which she is eventually privileged, Harrison carefully follows instructions essential to draw an audience with La Pastora, the Shepherdess. After eating her share of the rolled leaves, seconds after the candles are extinguished, she is completely transported to another realm. There, "a great female being," twenty feet high and semitransparent, was tending her garden. Harrison looked on, astonished, at the shimmering edge of the garden.[95] Physically healed in that moment, with her heart problem never returning, Harrison is introduced by the Shepherdess to the work she must perform in the world: "Show them the edge of the garden." The mandate is simple and clear: "I will just keep walking these edges . . . between the tame and the wild . . . between the visionary and the nourishing and the pragmatic . . . between the healing and the celebrating." And evoking the commitment pursued thereafter: "Wherever that edge is," she says, "that's my work."[96]

Harrison's experience in Mexico is documented in *Almost Visible*, a film directed by Klea McKenna. Drawing on decades of field notes and footage, and capturing the embedded, feminine anthropological method inspired by Ruth Behar's "subjective witnessing" approach to ethnography, the short film documents the twenty-five-year friendship that Harrison and her daughter have struck with the family of a Mazatec shaman. The responsible and relational approach of a "heart-engaged," anthropologically oriented ethnobotanist offers a stark contrast to earlier interventions in the region.

The approach also contrasts with that of the shamanarchist, who himself became enamored with *Salvia divinorum*, promoting its virtues to a global audience from the mid-1990s. The enthusiastic novelty tout cast *Salvia* as a "dream come true"—the first psychedelic discovered since LSD, active in the microgram range, and completely legal. Such was the hype in Australia in February 1997. Speaking at TrancElements 2, a psychedelic trance festival near Apollo Bay, Victoria, McKenna regarded the "undulating colored receptional labyrinth of moving light and sound" of *S. divinorum* to be as profound as any DMT flash he'd known. Among its virtues was that it comprised "something new" to the Mazatec. "Nobody had their brand on this thing," he insisted.⁹⁷ The gloss that *Salvia* is an unclaimed psychedelic that members of the newly evolving culture can occupy, as if inhabiting an empty house, was contentious. And it is unsurprising that Harrison, who grew and experimented with the herb since the mid-eighties, took a competing view: that is, as the mountains of Oaxaca are a center of diversity for *Salvia* species, the region is likely the source of lost cultural heritage. While the Mazatec Harrison knows claim that *S. divinorum* "has always been there," its uncertain roots betray a complex history of conquest and migration.⁹⁸ But this is not the intel shared with the psychedelic community on the southern coast of Victoria in 1997 on this novel, powerful, and legal hallucinogen that, if well managed, could be extracted, purified, and consumed. "This could be the wedge that opens the door to a complete reexamination of the proper role of these psychedelics in society," Terence proclaimed.⁹⁹ Within five years, Australia became the first country to ban *S. divinorum* and its main active psychotropic molecule, salvinorin A.

"I'm at war with all hierarchies," McKenna ventured at TrancElements 2, echoing his resistance to theological exegesis. While holding the "shamanic dimension" in high esteem, his Peruvian experience affirmed an estimation that traditional shamans were diminished by exaggerated claims and minimal effectiveness. As the experimental *curandero* who tests the limits of their "epistemological equipment" was hard to find, the conclusion is simple: "We must remain our own guides into those still-elusive dimensions." And so, after returning to the United States, stiffer dosages are sought to deliver the experience expected from ayahuasca in its traditional context. Native and mestizo methods opened up a path to the *lapis philosophorum*, but the onus weighs on the modern user to adopt and optimize the use of ayahuasca and its analogues for purposes at variance to traditional curative use. In this muscular psychedelicism, "it almost requires a modern mentality, or great courage alone, to probe this area unflinchingly."¹⁰⁰ Such psychedelic shamanism is dedicated not to self-transformation as an end in itself—technique as therapy—but to a demand for the evolution of consciousness. Such views became native to a rap mined posthumously by a plethora of electronic musicians. "It's not for your elucidation," the echo resounded, "it's not part of your self-directed psychotherapy."

> You are an explorer and you represent our species and the greatest good we can do is to bring back a new idea because our world is endangered by the absence of good ideas. . . . To whatever degree any one of us can bring back a small piece of the picture and contribute it to the building of the new paradigm, then we participate in the redemption of the human spirit.¹⁰¹

The UK band The Shamen was among the earliest artists to endorse the shamanarchic millenarianism. Their 1992 hit single "Re:Evolution" featured McKenna rapping on the significance of the breakthrough experience, in which one typically "cannot continue to close one's eyes to the ruination of the earth." In this proactive formula, shamans must "act as exemplars, by making this cosmic journey to the domain of the Gaian ideas, and then bringing them back in the form of art in the struggle to save the world."[102]

McKenna's on-brand shamanism held the tenor of initiation, less passage *into* a fraternity, order, or cult than passage *from* the alienating conditions of modern culture. Across this psycho-activated threshold lay the promise, not of a congress of *naturalized* citizens but of a cadre of *deculturalized* expatriates. Evoking and distorting the ethnography of coming-of-age rituals where psychoactive drugs are implicated in the enculturation of members into status positions, it is later contended that the anthropologists had it wrong: "When you're taken out into the bushes and given some drug by the fellow members of your tribe," as the abridged version of this story goes, "this is not that you are being made a full member of the society, it's that you *were* a full member of the society and now what you're being shown is what's under the board, the tricks of the trade." Not inculcated into the norms and values of a society——as for example widely apparent in Marlene Dobkin de Rios's studies of the indigenous peoples of Peru—the drug-taking novitiate acquires an outré—novel—perspective, an "ironical, sophisticated insight into the mechanisms of one's own culture and the cultural games that are being played."[103]

In other words, the outcome for the novice favorably compares with radical gnosis, a revelatory frame that is decidedly personal. For McKenna, the wiring under the board powered a hyper-language that may flash the sigils of novelty. But it also held a self-centered and psychedelicized motif deviating from Harrison's relational approach toward the plant world. For Harrison, paying attention to the natural world and entering into relationships with plants defines a career studying the partnership between women and the plant world across cultures. Speaking at Bioneers 1997, she suggested how language can be an obstacle in the quest for partnership: "It can be a sort of screen we get trapped behind, separating us from the multi-level reality behind it."[104]

McKenna's efforts to weld gnosis to shamanic practice, and his pointed distance from socio-therapeutics, is echoed in his preferred technique: tripping alone. Solo experimentation ensured distance from the maelstrom of synchronicities posed by other people. In a later interview, he confirmed he was sans the empathetic qualities integral to curative practice and, for that matter, the artifice of the psychiatrist. He could not, he explained, be a shaman or a therapist due to the "danger of transference." Group psycho-activated states such as those typical to ayahuasca shamanism are "extremely challenging work of a sort I hate to do," he admitted. "I am not a people kind of guy," he clarified, his mind turning to episodes in which trippers have come apart in his presence. "They're okay twelve hours later and I'm a wreck for three months."[105]

The story of an unnamed friend's epileptic seizure in the sixties offers some background to the preference for minimizing harm posed by other people. Terence and friends had dropped acid in an apartment in Berkeley and were well into their trip by 3:30 a.m. when his friend began violently convulsing. Not previously witness to an epileptic event, Terence concluded that his friend was undergoing a potentially fatal medical episode. The experience triggered a chain of hysterical events. A call was made to 911. The police and medical assistance were en route. A "staggering amount of dope" was flushed down the toilet. When the police arrived, Terence came down to the front door of the building where a cop boomed: "Open the door." Tripping so hard that he was incapable of opening the latch, he finally stood back shouting: "Shoot the lock off!"[106]

Not only are the doses upped upon the return to the States, but the jungle juice is intended, according to Terence, to "synergize psilocybin." Subsequent experiments provide an opportunity to compare the alien intelligence of the "psilocybin rapture" with the "psychiatric presence" of ayahuasca, urging "the recognition that all images and powers of the Other spring from our confrontation with ourselves."[107] In the slipstream of their Amazonian plight, the couple venture into uncharted terrain that held potential boons for consciousness. Immeasurable the boons these forays may have been, the limits were tested. On one occasion, chasing mushrooms with ayahuasca, Terence suspected something had gone very wrong, as evidenced by the fading of his short-term memory. His mind raced to the location and a nano-engineer's perspective on the problem is acquired. Incoming data confirmed that "molecular machinery" was jammed causing a breakdown in RNA transcription. Molecules were not decoupling from the synaptic cleft as expected. Monitoring this frisson, he conjures the image of *2001* astronaut Dave Bowman locked outside Discovery One.

> "Open the pod-bay door, HAL."
> "I'm sorry, Dave. I can't do that."[108]

As a "little pacman" chewed through his mind, erasing his memory, he began to panic.[109] He is a helpless witness to the enzymatic unfolding of his own madness. After an ordeal of some hours, to his great relief, the molecule, stuck at the receptor site, finally detaches and is flushed away. It is a startling episode for the insouciant voyager—and not the last. "Had I remained in that place, it was truly madness, truly unbearable." Was it now time to find honest work?[110]

SHAMANOLOGIST

Harrison isn't the only significant other with whom Terence deviated in his approach to ayahuasca. He and Dennis had differences of their own. On the ten-year anniversary of La Chorrera, the brothers reconvene in the Amazon. Studying toward his PhD as an ethnopharmacologist at the University of British Columbia, Dennis traveled to Peru in 1981. He sought to solve the "riddle" central to ayahuasca (and prove he wasn't mad). No one had proven the hypothesis that MAO inhibitors from the beta-carboline alkaloids in the ayahuasca vine (*Banisteriopsis caapi*) blocked the gut enzymes that normally degraded DMT, permitting the DMT from the orally consumed admixture plants to cross the blood-brain barrier to become an active hallucinogen. Moreover, he sought to learn more about the oral activity of DMT in the mysterious *oo-koo-hé* paste prepared from *Virola* species—that is, the grail that drew them into the Amazon a decade before. Was a similar metabolic mechanism involved? On a plant-collecting expedition, Dennis traveled to the Pucallpa region on the Río Ucayali.[111]

The plan was to rendezvous with Terence and sail from Iquitos up the Ampiyacu and its tributary, the Río Yaguasyacu, aboard the research vessel *Heraclitus*, in search of *oo-koo-hé*. As a moving platform of poets, artists, and scientists that was launched in 1975 from Oakland, California, the *RV Heraclitus* was designed, built, and operated by volunteers from the Institute of Ecotechnics, an organization founded by the illustrious John P. Allen and his collaborators in the Theater of All Possibilities.[112] The 1980–1982 *Heraclitus* Amazon Expedition was the context for an adventure in which the vessel sailed 2,200 miles up the Amazon. The voyage put out in the wake of the *RV Alpha Helix*, which, with Richard Evans Schultes as chief science officer, collected valuable botanical specimens in an Amazonian expedition five years before.

The encounter with the *Heraclitus* was incendiary. Upon boarding, Terence discovered that it was not the fabulously equipped research vessel that he had been led to assume, nor was it crewed with scientists and botanists. What's more, it was headed to dry dock for repairs. Scuppering their original plan, the brothers launch upriver aboard the vessel's dingy on which they are joined by ethnobotanist Wade Davis. The disciple of Schultes later recalled this encounter as he sat on a panel with the McKennas at Bioneers in 1994. Swinging on his hammock in the deepest Amazon, Terence had whipped out a little vial of pure synthetic DMT. Astonished, Davis wanted to know why Terence insisted on bringing this stuff to the Amazon. "Well Wade," recounted Davis, attempting to emulate the cadence, "I want these shamans to know the ballpark I'm interested in."[113]

Collecting samples with help from displaced Witotos and Boras living in the Pebas region in early March, Dennis is now a scientist in training, and cautious to avoid any repetition of his prior derangement. In Dennis's telling, Terence is provocative in an all-too-familiar pattern. Apparently, Terrible Terry maintains the infuriating idea of revisiting La Chorrera—to take up where they had left off. But that is out of the question, for Dennis has a mind only to complete his fieldwork. Such a commitment sees Dennis become a world-renowned proponent of the biomedical properties of ayahuasca, embracing the visionary brew as the key to averting global ecological catastrophe.[114]

In mid-March 1981 resin from collected specimens prepared by specialists in the region (which lab analysis later confirmed possess only traces of DMT) are bioassayed with "definite but not spectacular effects."[115] Winning a coin toss to test the *Virola* material deriving from their most reliable source, Dennis survives an ordeal in which he thinks he is experiencing a coronary thrombosis. "Time to bring on the rats," he declares. Witnessing the hallucinogen slipping from his reach, Terence is aggrieved by what he thinks is a deterioration in local plant lore downstream from the horrific cultural assailment at the hands of the rubber industry decades earlier. "The knowledge died almost in front of us," he lamented.[116] In a more upbeat account, they are, Dennis claims, "the first non-indigenous people to bioassay the legendary orally active *Virola* 'narcotic' resin, or at least the first to report on its effects."[117] As something of an understatement, alluding to their legendary psychedelic odyssey a decade prior, the 1981 field bioassay is dryly reported in the *Journal of Ethnopharmacology* to have induced "significantly less MAOI activity" than "a previous study."[118]

With the formal fieldwork complete, the brothers cannot resist collecting a haul of mushrooms from a pasture near Brillo Nuevo. As long-standing grudges with his brother surface, Dennis is surprised by his own anger and resentment. "Terence's brusque way of dealing with the people we met in our search had begun to disturb me," he writes, unsettled by what he sees as his brother's disrespect toward local specialists. A decade after their original Amazonian trip, he struggles to come to terms with what had happened at

La Chorrera. The "brother business" remained unresolved. And as they part ways at the end of their second and final venture to the region together, Dennis reflects: "All I knew for certain was that the currents of fate and destiny that had brought us together were now, inevitably, causing us to drift apart."[119]

"The mystery of *oo-koo-hé* is still unsolved," Terence announces at a seminar in Palenque in 1994, still driven by the promise of an ethnobotanical breakthrough in the region of La Chorrera. While returning to Colombia remained dangerous and unlikely, due to the region's growing dependence on cocaine, hope is not lost. The fantasy involved navigating the virtually unexplored upper Igara Paraná, imagined to be inhabited by "pure and undisturbed" Witoto and an "indemnified botany" palatable to his own sensibilities. The possibility of "one last effort" is dangled before his seminarians "way way out there in the big green."[120]

In the end, *oo-koo-hé* was not a simple bridge to the "ayahuasca effect." So much can be read from Terence's presentation to the International Conference on Shamanism in San Rafael, California, in May 1984, where he rattled the bones of the anthropologists gathered. With a strange deference to the work of Dennis (referred to simply as "my brother"), the presentation is an eloquent display of knowledge on the state of the field, ethnographically and pharmacologically, impressive for a speaker sans affiliation, or notes. But the performance adopts a stance that only an individual sans institutional backing or professional association could assume. "It is fine to study shamanism," the room of experts hear, "but to actually give cogency to the effort to overcome the cultural crisis, it is going to be necessary to shamanize." Ruffling academic feathers, the rare bird calls for a "hands-on" approach:

> We need to actually experience the realities that the shamans are talking about. . . . If you went to the Solomon Islands, you would have no objection to drumming, fasting, whatever is going on, but we become our own cannibals when it comes to drugs. We are so freighted with cultural biases that the Witoto should send anthropologists to study us and our curious culturally enshrined phobias and bizarre taboos.[121]

The performance from this unknown, self-styled, radical empiricist was remarkable. The impression is conveyed that, without a shamanic revival and an accompanying embrace of hallucinogens, "society" faces a fascistic release of unconscious forces worse than that represented by Nazism. Igniting a fire beneath an audience of shamanism experts, "these expeditions into the jungle, these conversations with people in remote locations, are directly related to an effort to find a way out of the culture crisis."[122]

McKenna never reappeared at this conference, locating his intellectual community elsewhere. That same year he presents in more familiar surrounds in Mill Valley. Retrieving knowledge across chemistry, psychopharmacology, and ethnobotany, colored with deep shades of personal experience, "Shamanology" may well have offered the most comprehensive condensation on ayahuasca delivered anywhere to that date. Demonstrating his interest in *icaros* as "the technical tools for controlling the fabric of the hallucination," and focusing on a subject—the relationship between the visual and language modalities—that became an enduring preoccupation, he finds footing as the ultimate "shamanologist."[123]

The confidence of the shamanologist had grown as the "magic" encountered in the Amazon is successfully transposed to a widening populace of domestic cultivators. Shaped by gnostic redemptionism, that achievement arrives after years of anguish and toil with text and spores. At a pivotal mid-seventies juncture, new relationships are forged: with publishers, with Harrison, and with the mushroom—the medium for earnest communications with an alien intelligence. While McKenna acquired an academic degree, the publication of a newly circulating underground manual that is as much psi-fi fantasy as practical guide signals an alternative career path. Joining Terence upon this path is a new partner and indeed a new family, an embryonic development to which we now turn.

PLATE 1
John Parker from the 1972 film *Ceremony* (directed by George Csicsery) in which Parker portrays a mythical figure representing the Sun. Photo courtesy of George Csicsery. [See also figure 1.4.]

PLATE 2
Postcard to Douglas Hansen, from Victoria, Seychelles, March 12, 1969. Courtesy of Douglas Hansen. [See also figure 3.1.]

PLATE 3
Cover of O. T. Oss and O. N. Oeric, *Psilocybin: Magic Mushroom Grower's Guide* (Berkeley: And/Or Press, 1976). Cover photo by Irimias the Obscure (a.k.a. Jeremy Bigwood). [See also figure 6.4.]

PLATE 4
Cover of O. T. Oss and O. N. Oeric, *Psilocybin: Magic Mushroom Grower's Guide* (Lux Natura, 1986). Art by, and courtesy of, Kathleen Harrison. [See also figure 7.5.]

PLATE 5
Terence and Kat, Occidental, California, 1984. [See also figure 7.6.]

PLATE 6

McKenna with *Banisteriopsis caapi* vine on Hawaii. Photo courtesy of Jack Coddington. [See also figure 7.8.]

PLATE 7
Terence with kids Finn and Klea, Hawaii, Halloween, 1982. [See also figure 7.9.]

PLATE 8
Terence, Kat, Klea, and Finn on the steps of their home in Hawaii, 1985. [See also figure 7.10.]

PLATE 9
McKenna cooking ayahuasca, Hawaii, summer 1999. Photo courtesy of Christy Silness. [See also figure 7.11.]

PLATE 10

Audiobook cover of *True Hallucinations*, the "talking book" (Sound Photosynthesis/ Lux Natura, 1984). Courtesy of Kevin Whitesides. [See also figure 8.1.]

PLATE 11
Luminaries on the lawn. Terence McKenna and Kathleen Harrison (second and third from left), with Albert Hofmann (looking at a book, at Psychedelic Conference II, U.C. Santa Barbara, May 14, 1983. Photo by Cynthia Palmer. Courtesy of Michael and Cynthia Horowitz papers, MSP 316, Purdue University Archives and Special Collections. [See also figure 8.2.]

PLATE 12
McKenna at the Conference on Botanical Intelligence, Camp Shalom, Malibu Hills, May 1991. Courtesy of Topa Institute. Also present are Andrew Weil (with gray beard to the left), Joan Halifax (between Weil and Terence), Dennis McKenna (with balding head, behind Weil), John Steele (top left), Johannes Wilbert (to the right of Terence), and Tom Lane (wearing purple T-shirt at right). [See also figure 8.3.]

PLATE 13
McKenna with publicist Leslie Rossman, San Francisco, 1992. Courtesy of Leslie Rossman. [See also figure 8.5.]

PLATE 14
Poster for Forward the Future (including Beyond the Brain 8), Byron Bay, Australia, February 21–23, 1997. Flyer artwork by Alex Clarke, courtesy of Paul Chambers. [See also figure 8.7.]

PLATE 15
Still from the film *Manual of Evasion LX94*, directed by Edgar Pêra. Photo courtesy of Edgar Pêra. [See also figure 9.1.]

PLATE 16

Dean Chamberlain, "Light painting" portrait of Terence McKenna seated in front of his new house. From the "Psychedelic Luminaries series," 1999. Courtesy of Dean Chamberlain. [See also figure 10.1.]

PLATE 17
Bruce Damer, Terence McKenna, and Robert Venosa. AllChemical Arts Conference, Hawaii, September 1999. Photo courtesy of Bruce Damer. [See also figure 12.3.]

PLATE 18
Terence with Elizabeth Hansen and Rick Watson, 1999. Photo courtesy of Elizabeth Hansen. [See also figure 12.4.]

PLATE 19
Terence and Christy Silness, 1999. Photo courtesy of Christy Silness. [See also figure 12.5.]

PLATE 20
Terence McKenna's gravestone, with offerings, Paonia, Memorial Day 2021. Photo courtesy of Judy Livingston. [See also figure 12.6.]

PLATE 21
Terence McKenna, portrait by Robert Venosa, 1998. Courtesy of Martina Hoffmann. [See also figure 12.7.]

7 LUX NATURA

FUNGI AND FAMILY

In April 1976, upon their return from Peru, Terence and Kat rent a house in Kensington, just north of Berkeley. The lovers fall into a fruitful relationship with the mushroom, establishing a grow operation that in many respects defined their relationship. In a letter to Watson, McKenna writes that they managed to make the marriage "a real joy, a true nuptial festival that was a combination of perfect day, Maybeck background and good friends."[1] McKenna marries Kathleen LaPriel Harrison on November 22 in Berkeley's Tilden Park, on the patio of the Brazilian Room designed by Bernard Maybeck (see figure 7.1). Evoking *hieros gamus*, the union of opposites was a "chymical wedding" apropos Jung's devotion to the alchemical workings of the inner life. In this case, their outer life, their union, mirrors the joyous relationship each had formed with the mushroom, under whose guidance they continue to trip together over the next decade.

While the couple freely traverse the hyperdimensions, mobility in *this* realm proved more complicated. In fact, neither knew how to drive a car. Kat takes driving lessons so they can drive away from their wedding—in an old Buick Opel. Her only prenup is that Terence obtain a driver's license. He consents, but is woeful behind the wheel, and Harrison for the most part becomes designated driver, later piloting a forest green 1973 Chevy Impala with a white vinyl top that she had inherited from her maternal grandfather. The family called it "The Shark."[2]

The newlyweds make for the quiet life in the woods of Sonoma County, north of San Francisco, renting an A-frame house between Sebastopol and Freestone. Of their newfound settled life and its "nouveau epicureanism," the couple had laid, according to McKenna, Monte Cristo–like scenarios of escape.[3] Dreaming of cultivating exotic plants and writing and illustrating books, plans are hatched to find a small plot on Hawaii. They scour the

FIGURE 7.1
Wedding photograph of Terence and Kat, November 22, 1976.

islands before acquiring a ten-acre property in a rainforest belt at South Kona on the Big Island in 1977. Among the first of many settlers who find their way up a remote track on the slope of Mauna Loa, with machetes in hand, they carve out a beautiful spot with magnificent views of the forest and distant ocean. They are the first to buy into a hui, a Hawaiian landowning tradition, by which they create, in Harrison's terms, an "unintentional community" of eccentric folks without shared belief systems but with whom they will share "a lot of karma." They build their octagonal house in stages and begin planting their garden. Their house is completed in 1981.

While retaining contact with the mainland, the couple became islanders. She teaches him how to swim and snorkel, getting Terence a quality prescription snorkeling mask as a first birthday gift. Via Kat, life beneath the surface becomes an expansive world of metaphors. Her experience with the ocean enriches his approach to the natural world. The ocean, she informed him, is a "veil of the marvelous," with life you can only imagine in visions existing right under the surface. This is captivating for the nearsighted McKenna, whose prior "marine" experience amounted to riding an inner tube in an irrigation ditch in Colorado.[4]

Back in Sebastopol, as McKenna writes Takayama, they maintain a "hermit like" existence. Growing mushrooms in the basement, they emerge occasionally, as they do for a Grateful Dead show down at San Francisco's Winterland in mid-October 1978. An ardent Deadhead, Harrison attends shows from 1972–1995, luring Terence to three. While he didn't want to trip at shows, she nearly always did. He did, however, smoke a lot of hash.[5] While Terence wasn't into the Dead, as we learn from Grateful Dead biographer Dennis McNally, Jerry Garcia was into him. When Alan Trist distributed copies of *The Invisible Landscape* at a band meeting in the mid-seventies, the opus was out of the jar.[6] An endorsement attributed to Garcia and accompanying the 1993 revised edition claimed it to be: "One of the most mind-boggling books I've ever read." Surely the *Grower's Guide* was making the rounds too—and possibly sans the identities of its authors. He was never a Deadhead, but I imagine O. T. Oss intrigued to witness the presence of the post-Colombian sacrament among the tie-dyed celebrants in what Jesse Jarnow regards as a "nearly official template for a late twentieth-century spiritual initiation"—i.e., a Dead show—participants in which were now empowered with the ability to produce and control the means of perception: the *P. cubensis* now fruiting as an accessible and self-perpetuating staple of their psychedelic diet.[7]

But the cultivators are not privy to any commanding sociological vantage, for theirs is a sequestered and intensely private domain. Occupying their secluded world, for the most part Kat and Terence are happy with each other's company, sharing mutual interests in a mix of botany, science fiction, and the novels of Thomas Pynchon. He takes notes with a Rapidograph pen on three-by-five index cards. She sketches and edits his work. Nightly they converge in the "smoking loft" to share ideas. They are joined by Finn in April 1978, and Klea in December 1980.

The family lived off royalties from the *Grower's Guide* and returns from "special projects," to adopt the phrase printed on his business card of fifteen years.[8] By 1978, they amass hundreds of names that, as is stated in a letter to Takayama, "we can solicit through the mail with a reasonably high expectation of significant returns."[9] The house becomes a gravitational center for an oddball fraternity of fungi fanatics and itinerant scholars. The "rye to mold" and "mold to gold" formula is championed as the real alchemy. In about six weeks, he claims, this process converted a $19.99 twenty-five-pound sack of rye into mushrooms valued at $22,000.

"We just want to thank you for writing the mushroom book," people would come up to him and say when he started public speaking. "You kept a family of six off welfare for eight years." Growing was extremely gratifying and virtuous. As an "incredible workhorse organism," *P. cubensis* transformed the dry weight of rye into dry weight of mushroom at 12 percent efficiency. The operation was like a dedication to a higher calling. In "cleanliness, punctuality, attention to detail, responsibility, [and] sensitivity to small shifts of parameters," the mushroom "literally teaches you to be the kind of person that it wants to take the mushroom."[10] From cultivation through marketing and sales, their lives become dedicated to, refining, perfecting, and *being* the procedure.

In 1981, their Hawaiian hideaway complete, the family move to Occidental, in Northern California. It is a secluded mycophile world in West Sonoma County, not far from Bohemian Grove. Throughout the eighties, they winter for two to six months a year at their subtropical island paradise, dwelling for the rest of the year in Occidental. Eventually, they acquire a 1975 Ford Granada, fitted with a personalized license plate: "NN DMT." In those years, few grok the meaning of these esoteric plates. When McKenna stopped for gas south of Santa Maria in the eighties, an attendant observes: "Double indemnity, that's really great."[11]

Meanwhile, Lux Natura blooms. Operational since 1976, Lux Natura evolves from a mail order spore-print business into "the first psychedelic information service," as it was advertised.[12] Conceived by Harrison, and operating until 1992, not only was Lux Natura a means to sell the prints of mushroom spores, which were adhered to sterile glass microscope slides; it is a vehicle for Harrison's art, seen in the logo (figure 7.2) and in advertisements (figure 7.3) and illustrated spore cards. As spores do not contain psilocybin or psilocin, the business is lawful, that is, until the anti-spore law is enacted in California in 1985, targeting spore and grow-kit suppliers. At that time, the spore-print business moves offshore to Hawaii and is renamed Syzygy (which Harrison operates until the late nineties) (figure 7.4). As advertised in a series of catalogs she produced, Lux Natura also carried cassette tapes of McKenna's recorded public raps and private musings, as well as spiral-bound Time Wave Zero booklets, eventually with a floppy disk attached. Under her direction, the business eventually becomes a book distributor, releasing a version of *The Invisible Landscape*, and then, as a publisher, releasing a revised edition of the *Grower's Guide* (1986) when Harrison acquires the rights from And/Or Press (figure 7.5). The booklet was entirely re-produced and marketed by Harrison, with new layout, cover,

FIGURE 7.2
Lux Natura logo, "Disembodied Eye." Art by, and courtesy of, Kathleen Harrison.

and illustrations.[13] A longer-term goal was to publish a print edition of *True Hallucinations*, widely deemed unpublishable.[14]

In 1985, the couple set a core dream in motion on Hawaii by founding Botanical Dimensions, a nonprofit foundation with a mission "to collect, protect, propagate and understand ethnomedically significant plants and their lore"[15] (figure 7.7 shows the logo). They purchase ten acres adjacent to their land on Hawaii for this purpose. With its stated goal of "saving ethno-botanical lore," Botanical Dimensions is set apart from large activist eco-organizations of the era like World Wildlife Fund and Earthwatch. The successful transplanting and good stewardship of threatened species was consistent with the objective of creating a repository of living plants in order to, as Harrison explains, "save them for an unknown future."[16] Primarily Harrison's project, she continued to direct Botanical Dimensions as a California nonprofit organization in the wake of the divorce. The activities she would oversee include: from 1985, a private plant collection on

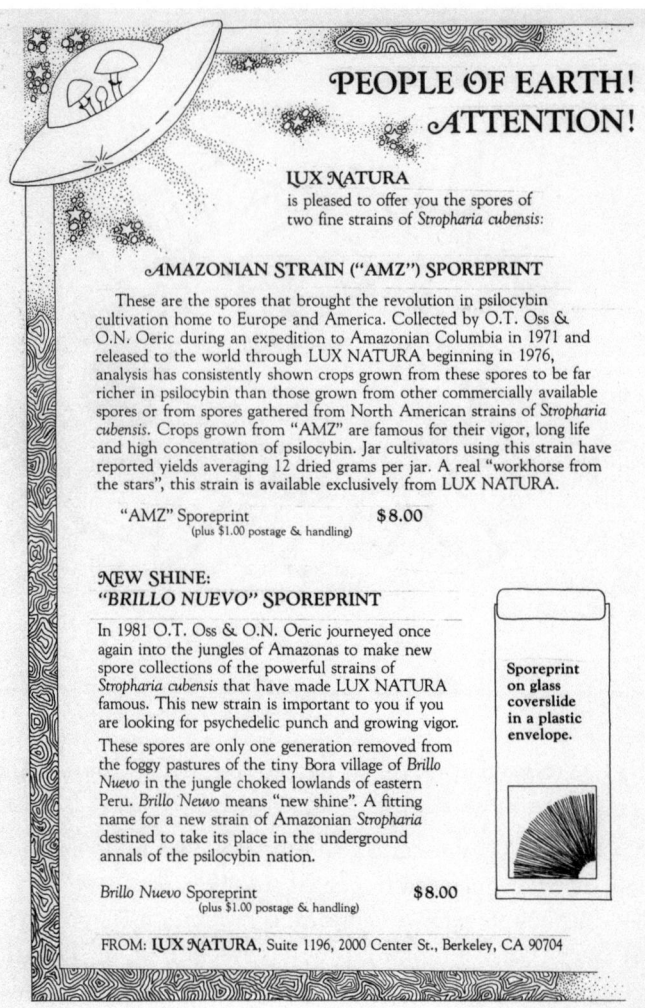

FIGURE 7.3
Lux Natura, spore-print ad, ca. 1983. Art by, and courtesy of, Kathleen Harrison.

forested land in Hawaii; from 2000 to 2014, field courses led in Ecuador, Peru, Hawaii, and California; from 2015 to 2020, an Ethnobotany Library, offering local classes and educational events; and from 1995 to the present, ethnographic fieldwork and documentation in the indigenous Mazatec region of southern Mexico.

In mid-August 1985, the grow operation comes to an abrupt end after the couple's close friend, acid-manufacturing neighbor, Bernard "Neil" Hassall,

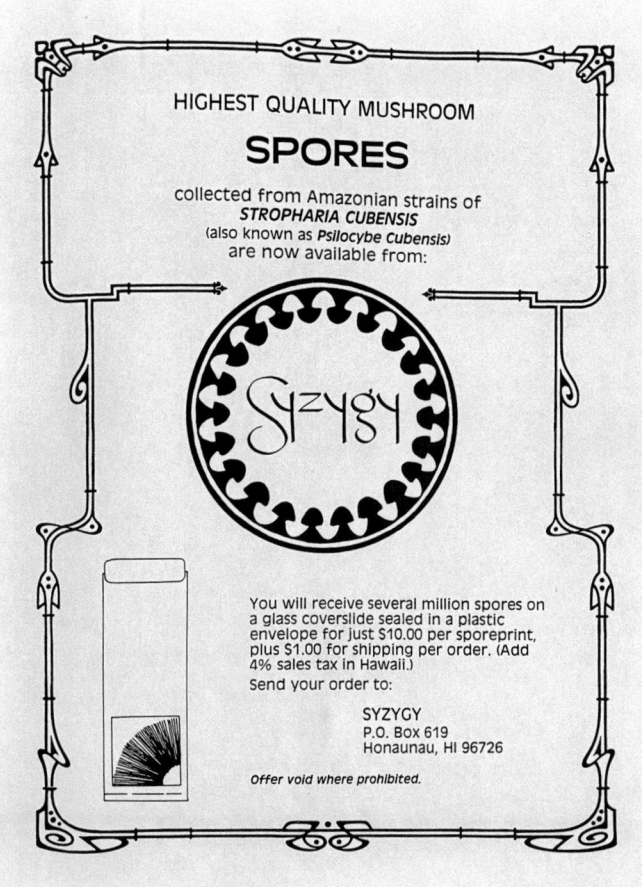

FIGURE 7.4
Syzygy spore-print ad, 1986. Art by, and courtesy of, Kathleen Harrison.

is imprisoned following a raid on his network. Hassall gained a reputation not only for the quality of his acid (he outsourced the cooking) but for the elegance of his blotter designs and packaging.[17] Authorities reportedly seized 1.6 million doses of LSD with a wholesale value of $5 million. Learning that Hassall's phone had been tapped for years, the couple grew fearful that they too had been under federal surveillance. The incident provoked a wind change. At public appearances over the next year there is a palpable mood of paranoia. In the weeks following, McKenna's curated Esalen seminar "Shamanism, Alchemy, and the Millennium" is overshadowed by the bust, generating fears of narcs in the audience. Botanical Dimensions is

FIGURE 7.5
Cover of O. T. Oss and O. N. Oeric, *Psilocybin: Magic Mushroom Grower's Guide* (Lux Natura, 1986). Art by, and courtesy of, Kathleen Harrison.

FIGURE 7.6
Terence and Kat, Occidental, California, 1984.

promoted at Shared Visions in February 1986, not as a Learyesque appeal to the masses but as an appeal to chemists, psychologists, botanists, and other professionals for whom the preservation and study of ethnomedically significant plants should prove a valuable investment. At that event, Terence is cagey in the face of inquiries from members of the audience probing him on the legality of his activities. A quickfire defense arrives vis-à-vis his relationship with mushrooms: "We wrote a book years ago on the cultivation of mushrooms, and I consider that work pretty much finished." Now, his interests have turned to the "higher plants . . . not fungi, but higher." And the message to the spooks in the crowd: "It's not necessary to break any laws to explore the fringes of psychobotany."[18]

The bust drives them to close shop and move to Hawaii within a year. There, Harrison sets up an office to run Botanical Dimensions and Lux Natura, and the kids are homeschooled. It is a new era of uncertainty. They

Botanical Dimensions

FIGURE 7.7
Botanical Dimensions logo. Illustrated by, and courtesy of, Kathleen Harrison.

are happy to be removed from the pressure cooker of the mainland, and watch "the unravelling of the Reagan Reich" from afar. But the unknowns are many.[19] Having abandoned "the cult of the fungi," they grow more concerned about money than ever before. They survive through the aid of patrons, notably Laurence Rockefeller, who donates $100,000 to Botanical Dimensions. Another anonymous supporter invests $50,000. Terence acquires a Macintosh Plus and a twenty-megabyte hard disk for writing his books, and sets up in a rented office in Honaunau. "We are living a weird combination of high tech and jungle bunny," he writes Watson. Likely implying the adaptation of Greg Bear's sci-fi novel *Blood Music*, he is also, Watson learns, "a consultant on a film project," with the possibility that the family may soon be on location in southern Mexico (the film never happens).[20]

In February 1987, during this period of isolation, they hold an ayahuasca ceremony, inviting respected colleagues from the above- and underground communities. The idea had been percolating for at least a decade. In the late seventies, they had transplanted Peruvian *B. caapi*, very likely the first such vine to arrive in the Hawaiian Islands, which was subsequently complemented by cultivars arriving through the eighties care of the collecting activities of, in addition to Dennis, Tim Plowman, Luis Eduardo Luna,

Daniel Siebert, and Ken Symington, among others. Over the years, Harrison brought many plants over from California, including cuttings of *B. caapi* which she had grown up to nine meters in Sonoma. The transplanted vine, concealed within baby-supply luggage, was the most vigorous to take root on the island. In 1986–87, Symington was a member of a volunteer group who camped in the land and carved out beds in the lava rock for planting chacruna (*Psychotria viridis*). By the time the Botanical Dimensions land is acquired, *B. caapi* and *P. viridis* are already thriving,[21] a happy circumstance aided by nutrient-rich volcanic soils, established connections with indigenous Peruvian collectors, and a federal plant-import license. By 1987, there were successful trials. Following a session with Ralph Metzner in 1985, for example, McKenna expresses his delight in a letter to Texas physician Joel Alter that the Hawaiian-grown material they brewed is "indistinguishable" from the ayahuasca he'd drunk elsewhere (see figure 7.8).[22]

What are regarded in a letter to Ralph Metzner as a "battlescarred small band" of ayahuasca drinking "cognoscenti" would include Metzner, Leo Zeff, and Stuart Abelson, among others.[23] Kat and Terence are reluctant ceremonial leaders, but for a week they host a dozen folks who harvest, brew, and drink ayahuasca on the volcano. The castaways are, for the most part,

FIGURE 7.8
McKenna with *Banisteriopsis caapi* vine on Hawaii. Photo courtesy of Jack Coddington.

as new to Hawaii as they are to the brew. In Harrison's memory, the event was like *Gilligan's Island* meets the *Epic of Gilgamesh*, with all of the sobbing and cackling, hysteria and madness, good humor and visionary insights, that you might expect. "There is a whisper" in ayahuasca, Watson is notified by Terence post-ceremony, "that is growing louder that says that this is no simple plant psychedelic but some sort of transforming force that deliciously insinuates itself into the causal fabric of one's life—leading one to openness, insight and ataraxia not necessarily during the trip but during the days and weeks that follow. It is a panacea, that is what I am trying to say—to what degree, we shall see."[24] Between 1982 and 1991, the couple brew for various visitors, with McKenna maintaining the practice long after the divorce. Their Peruvian derived recipe is 500 grams of *Banisteriopsis caapi*, mixed with 85 grams of *chacruna* (*Psychotria viridis*), which, according to Terence, is "thick . . . churns your guts, and it takes you to the other side."[25]

Such is the strange world into which Finn and Klea are born, widening the depth and scope of the "special projects" underway at the turn of the eighties. The family eke out an unusual existence, with their feet planted in both the beige universe of eighties America and the dark green underworld in which they thrive. Half of the time, they are cultural outsiders dwelling beyond the jurisdiction, Klea explained, "not only of law enforcement and conventional codes of conduct, but also of television advertising, big box stores, PTA meetings, anything that approximated mainstream culture." They sometimes participate in soccer games, birthday parties, and other conventional activities, but only as interlopers imagining themselves as spies, or as their mother was known to proclaim before arriving at events in the world of the normals: "*undercover anthropologists.*" But while Kat felt safer in the detached role of participant observer, "just enough distance to not be implicated in conformity," Klea adds, "my father was less subtle." At the age of eight she recalls a moment when the family was escaping a birthday party at Chuck E. Cheese. Turning to the crowd of teenaged waiters, single parents, and sugar-saturated kids, he bellowed over the din of arcade games: "MEDIOCRITY IS DEATH!"[26]

Both kids are talented in the visual arts, inheriting their mother's aptitude for observing nature and their father's gift for visual language. As verbose, passionate talkers, both inherit an absurdist sense of humor. His name inspired by *Finnegans Wake*, Finn is exposed to psychedelics, art, and music from an early age. "I helped my father pound vine when I was old enough to wield the sledge hammer," he told Tao Lin in a *Vice* interview. With hash and NorCal bud smoking rituals the backdrop for daily living, burning hash becomes Finn's favorite scent. At the same time, the kid is exposed to a dark imaginal phantasmagoria: science fiction, rare books, underground comix like Crumb's *Zap* series, H. R. Giger, Robert S. Connett, *Libido* journal, and the dark erotic art of *Heavy Metal* magazine—which Terence collected from its inception in 1977. Dark humor, irony, and paradox becomes second nature for Finn, who develops a complicated, tortured relationship with his art. Inspiring his graphic imagination, Dick, Bruce Sterling, Greg Egan, and Lovecraft stand off the shelves. Many early summers are spent running around the grounds of Esalen, absorbing and drawing. Between the ages of twelve and fifteen, Finn joins his father on European speaking tours. Tagging along with Terence and the "charming gangs of squirrels and nutty drug freaks" in his entourage, Finn encounters London and Manhattan as "epic concrete graffiti sketchbooks."[27] He takes communication studies at Santa Rosa Junior College before diving into filmmaking, video editing, and 3D animation at the Academy of Art College in San Francisco and screenwriting at SF State and Berkeley City College. From the nineties, he works in and out of web and graphic design, tinkering with flash games. While never adopting his dad's soteriological agenda, nor desiring to be a

FIGURE 7.9
Terence with kids Finn and Klea, Hawaii, Halloween, 1982.

public mouthpiece, Finn is raised to mistrust the cultural operating system. "You don't take anything at face value."[28]

Challenging received wisdom is also the approach of Finn's sister, fine art photographer and filmmaker Klea McKenna. Though Klea's work may be more sepulchral than outwardly "psychedelic," it no less offers an altered perspective on reality. Klea knows something about the breakthrough experience. "There is a window," she says recollecting an incident at the house in Occidental, aged two or three. "In the summertime the window would be open. I was kneeling on our couch looking out. I remember the feeling of burgundy velour, the heat and the feeling of the screen. I had a very large head and I was pushing it against the screen, trying to see something. I remember a cat. *We had a lot of cats*. And then, just like that, I fell out of the second-story window." Turning in horror to see her daughter's feet disappear over the edge, Kat froze until she heard Terence shouting. "She's alive! She's alive!" Tumbling over head-first, Klea had landed in the dirt, on her hip, inches from a cement slab. Reflecting on this near-fatal incident, journalist Kurt McVey relates how Klea may have been "hardwired from birth to break through certain confining membranes."[29]

It may be an awful metaphor to suggest that Klea had a dramatic "feel for the earth" from an early age, but her work is genuinely affective. She has made an impact on the medium by taking the camera out of the picture, by doing photography "the hard way." Klea eventually obtained an MFA from the California College of the Arts, and her work is today held in numerous museum collections and is represented by San Francisco's EUQINOM Gallery.[30] Having gained a reputation as an unorthodox tactile proponent of the photogram (a cameraless photograph), Klea is among a handful of artists thought to be "rematerializing" photography.[31]

Where her father stretched language in a lifelong quest to capture the nature of time, Klea would play with light, duration, and texture in a quest to expose the physicality of nature. With her photograms akin to sculptures of time she names her painstaking practice "photographic rubbing." Using light-sensitive gelatin paper to imprint natural objects and wielding a flashlight like a paintbrush, Klea's intricate objects offer forensic exposures of "reality" that come across as mysterious fossils, medieval tapestries, or aerial photos of the Nazca lines.[32] Just as her parents enjoyed the fruits of their labors in complete darkness, the quiet nightscape appears to have become a sanctuary for a woman who has forged a career creating photographs that rely on an intimacy with the dark and an uncommon feel for the unknown. Klea grew familiar with the "outdoor darkroom" of nature in the places in which she was raised, notably their off-grid hexagonal house, where she airbrushed the blackened world with light.[33]

They "really pressed upon us . . . the idea that everything is alive," Klea has noted about her parents. A species of animism came to permeate their everyday life. "If I stepped on something, or even slammed my bedroom door, I would apologize to the door."[34] When contemplating Finn and Klea, I am compelled to think of the deferred pressure evoked by Terence when speaking of the challenges faced by "alienated intellectuals" who raise children. He couldn't allow his kids to grow up to be "marks," he declared, to be "pawns of the market economy and the propaganda machine, people scratching their heads trying to figure out whether they're Republicans or Democrats." No, "they must join in the alienation," he thought. "They must be taken out of the culture as we were taken out of the culture." It was "the only way to find the self."[35] As a result, Finn and Klea were not like the others; they were meant for something different. "Anything, even total failure,

FIGURE 7.10
Terence, Kat, Klea, and Finn on the steps of their home in Hawaii, 1985.

was better than mediocrity," said Klea. Being intelligent mattered a great deal more than being happy.[36]

Despite the difficulties they endured, Terence loved his kids. As he later opined: "they are wise and good children and I feel my life, whatever else it may be, is completely redeemed by having such great kids."[37] While he adored his children, a picture forms of a figure who struggled to be a father, whose work competed with the duties of parenthood. He seemed to dwell in two different worlds: the public world of his career (which bloomed through the eighties) and the private world of his family. His ideas, books, and everything that drove McKenna's public persona became a chief preoccupation; his family, and parenting, a secondary commitment. In fact, he avoided dozens of family camping trips.[38] Terence preferred to stay home, roll a bomber, and read in solitude, a practice reminiscent of the eight-year-old who, when faced with the prospect of family picnics, fought to stay at home with his head in a book. On the rare occasion when he cooked (i.e., when Kat was away), he was instructed to ensure the kids had plenty of greens. In compliance, his specialty was inch-thick slabs of "cabbage steak" in salad dressing.[39]

Tensions rose within the marriage, and for many observers it became increasingly apparent that the relationship involved an inequitable distribution of labor. Not only did Kat raise the kids, she was also performing the scheduling, publicity, and accounting. All Terence had to do was show up, open his mouth, and be the star in whose light growing numbers desired to bask. Nina Wise was in a unique position to observe the fault lines. Having introduced the pair in Israel, Wise remained a close friend to Kat and Terry, becoming godparent to Klea. Over the course of her friends' marriage, Wise witnessed the servility of one grow in direct proportion to the fame of the other. It was a "story book romance" between two "extraordinary, brilliant and ambitious people who shared a vision of altered states and how important they were." As a spouse and mother, Kat nurtured Terence's career at the expense of her own. Wise grew unsettled by the way her smart and independent friend transformed into a "subservient and overlooked" housewife. As the years turned over, and his fame grew, more and more visitors would arrive to talk to him, and not her. She would "end up serving everybody." This wasn't easy for Wise to see, torn between her loyalty to Kat and admiration for Terry, her mentor whom she long held to be a genius. Ultimately, she witnessed "a Shakespearean kind of tragedy," in which Terence, she claimed, abandoned his family.[40]

TERROR TRIP

Those close to Terence during the years of the separation and divorce have differing views. "It was hard to be his son or his daughter or his ex," claims Occidental neighbor Ken Adams, who also acknowledges that sometimes "it was hard to be his friend." Adams highlights that the hard career decisions Terence took were made with the interests of his kids foremost in mind. With the mushroom business decommissioned, the McKenna business went into overdrive. As Terence styled himself as a spokesperson for the weird, through the eighties, selling the myth of Terence McKenna to wider markets and niche demographics became a round-the-clock gig. As he would quip to his friends: "the worst part of being Terence McKenna is being Terence McKenna." He was received as an approachable, wickedly good-humored conversationalist who talked directly to his fans. And as understood by Australian promoter Dillon Hicks, his fans sought to participate in the dialogue. Hicks has contrasted McKenna with Mick Jagger. If Stones fans hear "Can't Get No Satisfaction" or "Jumpin' Jack Flash," they're happy, but for freaks who live in the world of ideas, their "pound of flesh" means they want a conversation. "And that's very difficult to facilitate when there's a thousand people trying to get at one guy."[41]

Serving as a conduit for McKenna's breakthrough to the rave generation, Adams noted that while Terence knew the value of humility, he also knew how to "turn the light on himself for as long as people would listen."[42] The commitment to promulgating his mind as entertainment served up to a growing audience baying for their pound of baked brilliance was a pressure that widened fissures at home. While bringing the "Terence McKenna" show on tour became an essential source of income, the contrivances of his celebrity stature became a flash point in the marriage. As we will see in the following chapter, and throughout part II, the myth of Terence McKenna has depth and integrity; it is a story worth telling. And yet, while McKenna's legend grew, he soon faced an incident that turned his world upside down.

The family was on Hawaii for eighteen months before the couple reach breaking point. As Harrison recalls, their self-isolation didn't work since, too remote, Terence was restless sans an audience. With a mind to dispelling what she feels are dangerous misconceptions, Harrison candidly regards uncomfortable truths long known though rarely stated publicly. It is not an easy exercise for ex-wives of beloved public figures to divulge sensitive details counter to public perceptions—a pressure long compelling

Harrison to remain tight-lipped. But the circumstance of her assault in early 2021, coinciding with my project, have resulted in her desire to open up to some degree. Notably she offers a careful revisitation of the incident that came to be known as the "terror trip."

As a safe zone for psychoactive experimentalism, the Big Island became the site for formal psychoactive experiments the couple undertook over a decade. Sometimes in small select groups, often as partners in the sublime, or other times solo tripping, they consult ayahuasca, DMT, 5-MEO, mushrooms, and less commonly MDMA, among other medicines and tools, taken at various doses with a comparative objective. From the late seventies to the late eighties, it was an experimental period in which the couple dosed up as often as they could make arrangements, and when the kids were with friends for a weekend. By far the most altered place they frequented was the mushroom space, each eating five dried grams and laying on parallel mats about three feet apart. At its inception, the mushroom ritual was repeated weekly, a ritual that was paused between 1977 and 1982 (i.e., when Harrison was pregnant and nursing infants). After 1982, their rite was conducted once a month on Hawaii, with mushrooms sometimes eaten in the days between ayahuasca brews. Their experimental collaboration came to a sudden halt just after New Year's Day, 1988. It would be the last time they tripped together, the incident setting the timer on their relationship, which ended three years later, in May 1991.

On that night, an unusually intense subtropical storm came off the mountain around the time they ate. The rain squall grew heavier as the mushrooms came on strong. Like a giant drum, the metal roof of the house was normally a source of wonderful acoustics. But during this "frog strangler" the night grew deafening, and they were in the grip of their most frightening cyclone to date. "You could shout at the top of your lungs and not hear yourself, let alone anyone else." Harrison was transported into a familiar ecstatic state, letting go of her material form and the pressures of her responsibilities. While she is comfortable with letting go, he was not. Terence "delved," and was repeatedly drawn into an "outrageous idea space," she explains. But "repeatedly immersing himself into completely uncontrollable, unexpected, ineffable, dense and spacious nothingness" was never his thing. "He was really afraid of nothingness." As the rain beat heavier, Kat is hammered into an ecstatic state. After a while, she became aware of something dark and scared to her left. "That's where Terence was." She looked over and through the dark made out that he was in the fetal position, vibrating. As she drew closer, she realized he was howling in distress. She tried to console him. He was not forming sentences. Eventually, the words fall out of his mouth like lead: "No . . . no meaning." Phrases were repeated to that effect: "nothing means anything," "impossible." Terence was undergoing his darkest night of the soul—*the loss of all meaning*. She put her arm around him, touched his head and tried to comfort him. But he carried on wailing. Over the years, she had learned that invoking his mother helped soothe his migraines. She soothed him until he eventually calmed down.

The next day, he was livid. He could not accept that his wife had passed through the storm unscathed. In the darkness, he failed to pass the test, and yet she had escaped the terror. Furious, he would never trip with her again, he said. And he never did. There were to be no more psychoactive ventures for the remainder of their marriage—a barren circumstance imperiling a partnership founded in rich, collaborative, psycho-ethnobotanical activity.[43]

The Hawaiian terror trip occurred at a juncture where Terence, according to Kat, was switching his affiliation away from her and the family. Determined to keep the family together, she insisted on couples counseling, which they would undergo intermittently over the next three years. While the therapy ultimately fails to save the marriage, the sessions do help Harrison establish clarity on her spouse's hypocrisy. Terence, she observes, didn't want his fans to know that "he could be cracked by this thing that he was a master of." At the same time, he publicly promotes the "five dried grams" method among the inexperienced, and without appropriate qualifications on the risks of use. "What is to be learned over there in that dark place?," she muses.[44] Seeking to protect his reputation as an intrepid voyager, the failure to address his own self-doubts in his endorsement of the "heroic dose" was seen to be dishonest. Here was a figure building a career on the idea that the tumor-like (masculine) ego grew in, according to his own words, "the absence of repeated inoculation with psilocybin."[45] The irony was unbearable. The couple eventually had a showdown on Hawaii three months before he left. He was now transparent enough for her to see that "the emperor had no clothes."

While multiple factors contribute to a failed marriage, in this case one set of factors is telling. A selective Jungian who gave early thought to the pursuit of depth psychology, McKenna had an interest in the symbolism of alchemy that was chiefly intellectual. Since psychotherapeutic methods were of little interest, the integrative value of *Psilocybe* is never taken seriously, and even rebuffed as a therapeutic application. This neglect could not have been more obvious in the shadow of the Hawaiian frog strangler, after which he was determined, according to Harrison, never to lose control again. "He had met his terror and he didn't know what to do with it."[46] Echoing what proponents have known for decades, while psilocybin would become a valuable tool in psychotherapeutic trials, it is a further irony that McKenna rejected the therapeutic value of a tool for which he served as an early midwife. His aversion to psychotherapy, says Bruce Damer, "created a blind spot around authentic efforts to help people become compassionate, healed humans."[47]

In Kat's non-caustic reflections, Terence may have dedicated his life to painting vivid pictures with "visual language" that continues to entertain his audience, but he had "a lifelong dread of looking too deeply into himself." Ultimately, she says that his heart was underdeveloped. "I don't think he ever learned about love and compassion. I think he loved his kids and loved me for a while, but I'm not sure he loved himself, and I think he was really afraid of looking at what that means."[48] For all the lip service paid to Tibetan Buddhism, McKenna was never a practitioner. For Nina Wise, a practitioner familiar with the Tibetan Buddhist practice of *chöd* in which self-centered arrogance and shadow behaviors are subject to ruthless severing, "Terence failed to treat Kat and their children with the kind of reverence and care she wished for them."[49]

NEOTENOUS SCHIZURA

Abrogating "the work" he may have done, but McKenna knew how to work a crowd, and in doing so alluded to his inner life. While we will explore his career as a stand-up philosopher in the next chapter, here I address the oratory in the context of the marriage dissolution and divorce. Via a multitude of recordings, we are privy to a vast archive of unscripted spoken word performances which, notably in smaller workshops, Q&A sessions, and engaging interviews, are rich in anecdote, allegory, and allusion.

A predominant motif in McKenna's rap is his "great work," the Timewave, in relation to which he was the "bride." Less frequently, his rap becomes an occasion to talk about his therapist. It was revealed in one Q&A that Terence's weed addiction became a focal point in his therapy. His therapist may have been "brilliant," but she knew nothing about drugs—a circumstance he deemed absurd.

"Now this cannabis business, how many times a day do you do it?" she asked him.

"Oh about a dozen."

"And how many years have you been doing this?"

"Oh, about 25."

"Well surely this is serious."

As the issue continued to arise, he finally announces he will quit, "so that you can see that nothing happens, so you won't be running around the countryside laying this trip on your patients."

Not for the first time, nor the last, in 1990–91 McKenna quits weed and hash. As with his former attempts at sobriety, the two-month hiatus is disastrous. When the smoke cleared, the world appeared horribly profane, characterized by "a tremendous narrowing of my consciousness." Eventually, he claims to have stayed up late balancing his check-book.[50] As is reported to his Esalen echo-chamber, the life of the unstoned "petty bourgeois"—worrying about insurance, tax returns, and the lawn—wasn't for him.[51] In this period of restraint and reconditioning, quitting weed compelled our noetic technician to demonstrate fiscal responsibility, among other dire mundanities. Quitting ganja, Harrison recalled, rendered McKenna unbearable. "He just needed to be high on cannabis," she said. "That was his medicine, that's really what drove everything" and "kept him from bouncing off the ceiling."[52]

By 1991, battle raged on the home front. "It's been a tough go, I have to tell you," Terence declared at LA's Wilshire Ebell Theatre, on June 1. Introduced by Leary, McKenna launches into a condition report on the state of the planet, while at the same time making a thinly veiled comment on the state of his marriage. What with wars, famines, revolutions, and refugees, "God knows, we've got lots of chaos right now," recounts a figure going through a fair share of personal turmoil. Referencing world affairs, but also projecting his private cataclysm, he announces: "We have been through such a difficult ten months." The situation had grown dire. "Nobody gets through this world without a little dung raining down on them. Believe me, you may evade it for decades but then there'll be a knock on the door." Regarded as his favorite philosopher, and offering an apparent filter on his personal state-of-affairs, Heraclitus is paraphrased: "*Panta rhei*. All flows. Nothing lasts. Nothing is permanent." It is the hardest message life has to teach. "And I had to live to be forty-four years old to understand the poignancy of Heraclitus's message."[53]

In "Unfolding the Stone" and other appearances at this juncture, McKenna makes refined distillations on the wisdom of alchemy, reflecting on the process by which the *nigredo*, the lead, the dross, the *prima materia*, is transformed into the *albedo*. "Out of the chaos can come a new beginning, a new reality, and a new hope." At this time, he alludes to the alchemical artifice recognized by Jungians as the sublimated "work of redeeming the self from the contaminated dross of the traumatized and damaged psyche that we each inherit from our passage through the parental shit pile."[54] He had a keen interest in alchemy and Hermeticism since adolescence, but it is in 1991–92—when the marriage reached terminal conditions—that a series of lectures unpacks and traverses hermetic and alchemical content, in which marriage symbolizes the sacred union of opposites.[55] The adoption of Hermeticism as a means to empower hope in dark times appears to have been part of a forlorn bid to save his union. These lectures largely cease after the divorce.

In an interview on June 1, 1992, Mark Jacobson encounters McKenna as a man with a face not unlike that of "a club fighter who occasionally forgot to keep his left up." Jacobson explains with confidence: "After all, you don't pierce the chrysanthemum a thousand times, wrestle with the Other for twenty-five years without it showing." At this point, the marriage was over. "People who can't get along shouldn't live together," Jacobson is informed.[56] Years later, McKenna's public therapy group becomes a platform for attacking marriage, which is railed against as a "neotenous schizura" in life. Far from a phenomenon worth saving, getting married, he now claims, is "the only bourgeois value system" he ever committed to. As punishment for the foolish decision as a thirty-year-old, the divorce is identified as "a self-correcting mechanism." Seeking neither to lay blame nor accept responsibility, he targets the institution. "I think marriage is a curse for everybody," he remarks, adding that he isn't "too crazy" about monogamy either.[57] The challenge to monogamy and the nuclear family, "an engine for the production of neurotic dysfunctional people," became implicit to the "archaic revival." In candid thoughts shared with Esalenites on ideal future psychosexual arrangements, having performed the math, McKenna contentiously envisioned monogamous relationships to be replaced by a "three-one" arrangement. Feminizing, he contended, was not to be performed by "feminizing men," but through drastically decreasing the number of males (perpetrators of the "dominator" culture). In this ideal future society, where child ratios are 75 percent female, there would be one man for every three women.[58]

Having moved to a one-bedroom apartment at Whammy Ranch, Occidental, McKenna adopted a more laissez-faire approach to relationships in the immediate wake of the divorce. There, under redwoods, and inside a persistent pall of ganja smoke, he subsists on Eggo waffles, turkey pot pies, and orange juice poured over granola. Finn split his time between Terence's "bachelor pad" and his mother's place. With a consistent stream of new women in his dad's life—a detail not unrelated to Terence's claim (in the summer of 1993) of visiting the gym three days a week—Finn vacates regularly so Terence could get some "peace of mind."[59]

The divorce was bitter and the property settlement painfully protracted. In Harrison's account, when McKenna left, he drove off with the car and left her in significant debt. She took out court orders to enforce child support. They were each awarded five acres of the Hawaiian land, with Botanical Dimensions flourishing in between. She retained the house. He kept the library. Terence was permitted to live in the house for three years, while building another house on his two-acre plot. She ended up buying out his share in the house on the mainland.

Such is the dim picture at the start of the nineties. In the long aftermath of the dissolution of her friends' fairytale partnership, Nina Wise shares her views. Terence may have behaved badly throughout, but the community bears some responsibility for the tragedy. As Wise points out, it is not a unique tale. What often happens with those who are loved by their followers and devotees is that "the community fails to hold their feet to the fire." In such cases, the beloved—typically male—grow beyond reproach. Their behavior is tolerated because their fame is "prophylactic." Protecting their teachers, celebrities, and mentors, the community colludes in the calamity, which is especially marked when private actions contradict the public message. From her unique position, Wise highlights the problem and drives home the lesson. Where the actions of public figures are inconsistent with their spiritual insights, the community must rise to the challenge. As a practicing Buddhist, Wise recognizes that, if "the work" isn't performed, ego-driven and self-serving tendencies will controvert spiritual growth. The praise that derives from celebrity stature obstructs that labor, as fame disincentivizes due diligence. This outcome is aggravated by patriarchal cultural standards, said Wise, "which support a kind of narcissistic personality type to achieve fame."[60] So while McKenna talked up feminism, partnerships, and the balance of power, he didn't walk the talk.

PSI-CHEDELIC SUBLIME

While this book recounts for the first time the story of McKenna's "terror trip," as related by Kat Harrison, news of this episode has surfaced previously. The incident, and the quiet speculation it triggered, passed from tongue to tongue over two decades before an opaque narrative was sketched at Esalen on June 16, 2012, in Bruce Damer's controversial public performance "Ode to Terence." The cusp of "the end of time" it may have been, but it was also the eve of the publication of Dennis's memoir. Damer had been privy to an advanced copy of *Brotherhood*, a chapter of which featured a laundry list of resentments toward a lost sibling. At Esalen, Damer recited

Dennis's material, which influenced an "Ode" that claimed to reveal the "true rap" on Terence, who was said to be "living in fear of plant medicines" through the nineties, and was deceiving his fans to protect his reputation.[61] A bombshell for McKennaphiles, Dennis's chapter was omitted from the book but not before animating Damer's Ode.

Dennis's story relied on an oblique retelling of Terence's odd Hawaiian odyssey. It appeared to project the ambivalence of an estranged sibling who saw his brother's "full blown existential crisis" as a terminal affliction characterized by a "lack of all meaning." This attempt to craft the episode as the resounding conclusion to Terence's psi-chedelic odyssey was unedifying, not least because Terence long reckoned with the value of not knowing. The career rap amounted to a dissensus toward all ideology, a discontentedness with closed cultural systems, a beef with "isms." It might even be ventured that *meaninglessness* features in a metaphysics grounded in the radical empirical exposure to neuro-technologies. As related in the lauded appearance "Rites of Spring"—and as mirrored throughout an oracular career—"psychedelic people" are privy to "not-knowingness," which holds far greater value than its converse—that is, *all-knowingness*.[62]

Though routinely drawn to that moment in language felt to be before "the tyranny of meaning," Terence clearly struggled with the existential plight of not knowing. The conflict appeared to grow in proportion to his growing celebrity—a crisis surfacing in simultaneous conflict with his psilocybean teacher and his spouse. But while struggling to adhere to his own "heroic" entreaties to go out of one's mind, McKenna was no nihilist. In his universe, it was no cause for despair that the imminent future was not amenable to cognition. If life, as he consistently rapped, is the intrusion into three-dimensional space and time of the hyperdimensional, then the corollary is that it is only death that accords an ultimate form of completion, salvation, meaning.

It is not as if a heavy dose of "an absence of all meaning" was meaningless. On occasion, McKenna was the recipient of visions of the dark consequences of humanity breaking from our symbiotic relationship with the "Gaian matrix of the planet." It is a subject taken up in *Food of the Gods* where humanity lies at "the terminal phase of a long descent into meaninglessness and toxic existential confusion." This dramatic vision prompts attention to the transformative episode affecting Jung at around the same age as McKenna during his crisis—that is, at forty. This was an episode upon which Jung remained silent publicly, though it inspired private thoughts, as inscribed in *The Red Book*, published posthumously. Jung suffered a series of terrifying daytime visions in 1913/14 rendering him exhausted and confused, including scenes of Europe awash in a sea of blood, and upon which, in mid-summer, "a terrible cold descended from space." Across Northern Europe came the specter of "yellow waves, swimming rubble and the death of countless thousands." Upon one visitation, the violent visions were addressed by an inner voice. "Look at it, it is completely real. It will come to pass. You cannot doubt this."[63] Rocked by a sensation that his soul was lost, Jung thought he had gone mad—though he later interpreted the visions as precognitive. It appears almost certain that McKenna was similarly visited by terrifying visions of a near future apocalypse. This much was shared by Elizabeth Hansen. "Terence was clear with me that he had had a 'vision' of the future that was so horrific that he would not speak of its details to me or anyone else because he had children and did not want that vision in their hearts and minds."[64] Not unlike Jung, McKenna kept his "visions" to himself, and again, like his mentor, he found a creative outlet. With Jung, we have *Liber Novus*; with McKenna, we have the Timewave.

I can provide no evidence to verify that McKenna's "inner voice" shared comparably sinister declarations of the future as that visited upon Jung at the brink of World War I. What I do suggest is that a comparison of this nature may permit a more useful evaluation of McKenna's state of mind during the crisis period in question. "The mushroom turned on him," Dennis claimed. "The gentle, wise, humorous mushroom spirit that he had come to know and trust as an ally and teacher, ripped back the facade to reveal an abyss of utter existential despair." Estranged from the mushroom, Terrible Terry had grown misshapen in the eyes of his equally estranged brother, who like *Apocalypse Now*'s Captain Willard appeared to be compiling his very own "Kurtz dossier," indicting his brother as a fallen figure addicted to power and money. "He was on the circuit; there were plenty of adulating fans, many attractive young women, a surfeit of pleasing venues, good money, good food, and love and admiration, all in response to what came naturally and effortlessly: the rap, the shtick. What was not to like? Why piss away a good gig?" What's more, in the fantasy reconstructed, ostensibly aware of his own fraudulence, Terence grew depressed. "He became trapped in his own public persona, like a caged performer on stage; and in response he gradually lost respect for his fans."[65] Such was Dennis's exposé that was retracted, but not before Damer's controversy-sparking intervention.

A shadow had crept across Terence's life. That he ostensibly tripped no more, at least not in "heroic doses," was controversial given the cultivated visage of heroic explorer. In online debates subsequent to the "Deep Dive" podcast, some McKenna fans felt cheated and betrayed. For some, it was as if Luke Skywalker suddenly beheld Master Yoda as a malevolent gremlin. For the most part, however, the ensuing debate served to affirm qualities that endeared McKenna to his fans. Virtual fora lit up with commentary on his authenticity, humility, and depth of experience in the dissolution of boundaries. "I am pretty certain he slammed it pre-1990 and earned the right to talk about it in that context," stated one commentator in the *Psychedelic Salon* discussion thread. "There is nothing shocking about losing interest in the Mushroom. He just defeated the thing. In the end there was nothing more there to explore from Terence's point of view."[66] Although I can't confirm that McKenna spoke directly to his "terror trip," or if he applied any lessons from his marriage counseling sessions, he hardly kept his "bad trips" and self-doubts from his audience in the wake of his marriage. Indeed, brutal honesty is a trademark trait that reappears in testimonies where limitations are openly divulged. There is a certain "place" while on psilocybin, he once affirmed, that was his *bête noir*—what he described as "the meatlocker."[67]

In 1989, an Esalen audience was privy to a trip a few months prior where McKenna admits to goings-on he'd never seen before. His journey is disrupted by chyrons flashing across the base of his mind state. As he begins reading his thoughts printed out in front of him, he notices some of the words are misspelled. And as he watches, more and more of these printed thoughts descend into gibberish. He is watching his own thoughts "degrade into chaos." This experience, where chaos ensues from the displayed disintegration of the English language, is regarded as a "visible degradation of meaning."[68] Elsewhere, and much earlier, there is allusion to a trip on Hawaii that was deemed to be horrible, "just horrible." Here, the "news flasher" vanishes and is replaced by a familiar voice providing direct, unsolicited peer review: "You think you're such hot stuff. You won't even get off your ass and go shit in the field. I want to see you grovel, man. You sit up in front of all these people and pontificate on how it's all put together. Face me, now, in the darkness, and tell me how it's all put together."[69] That such an experience apparently predates the "terror trip" suggests the episode may have had antecedents. It also offers insight on why McKenna preferred tripping alone, not only because he grew distracted by the plight of his companions, but because his own strangeness alarmed others. "I'm sure glad there's nobody else here to see this," he had cause to reflect, "because . . . I'm screaming in Urdu, or something."

On another occasion, he addressed a further episode in Hawaii: "I thank God that somebody was there, that Kat was there specifically, because just the sound of her voice completely ameliorated a whole spectrum of hard to describe but very icky things that were threatening to overwhelm me." The comments affirm a reluctance to assume the role of advocate, declaring that mushrooms "might not be good for you" and that there is "nothing heroic" about taking them. But instead of cautioning the potential for abuse, he maintains the virtue of being terrified. "If it doesn't scare you, it's not worth doing," he claimed. "I will not jump from airplanes, I do not shoot the rapids, I do not rock climb, I'm a bookish person. But I will submit to that terror, because it seems to make sense." The experience made "sense" by virtue of the terror it inflicted. Ultimately, McKenna harbored a strong dose of heroism, if not bravado, which appears consonant with his conviction that an authentic psychedelic experience ought to be a sublime experience. "Nobody abuses these drugs," he claimed, "unless they do too little."[70]

Other commentaries relate circumstances of modified use in times of mounting pressure. Once at a party in London where Terence was the guest of honor, he was left incapacitated after taking a sip of mushroom tea. Nobody else got loaded. It appears he ingested the immiscible portion of the psilocybin floating on the surface. "I don't want to become afraid of it," he later observed, as the customary act of consulting his organic teacher had become a challenging exercise. Was he growing out of balance or just getting older?

> The only thing I found to do about it was stop running, and turn and face it. But each time I do that it seems to require the very limit of my courage. And I don't know how long one's courage lasts. Maybe it's not a bad thing—I mean after all, people who climb mountains, like Mount Everest, they don't do it until their dying day. At some point they knock off and become a consultant for a sportswear manufacturer or something.[71]

McKenna retained respect for his teacher. As his fans understood, even if the psychedelic experimentation diminished after the late eighties, this did not diminish McKenna in their eyes. In a further response to the challenge to his integrity, there was no doubt for online commenter "Sky" that McKenna "is the best, brightest, most humble and honest spokesman for our community, and I can't fathom why his backing away from mushrooms in the 90's detracts from that. The man tripped continuously for 20 years and thought enough for many lifetimes. I'd say he paid his dues."[72] Another commenter astutely observed that judging McKenna for his failure to make an official announcement that he had ceased contact overlooked the possibility that he "didn't know for certain that he never would again."[73]

Despite its retraction, Dennis's leaked "dossier" provoked a minor inquisition, animating anonymous cyber-Willards bent on character assassination. The implication was that Terence's relationship with the *logos* had been compromised, if not severed, and that he consequently grew disconnected from his source of creativity and emotion. According to this approach, he had become a fraud, an illegitimate authority, a false idol. But the weight of commentary from friends and fans hardly supports a case for fraudulence. On the contrary, rejoinders illustrated how McKenna's spoken word improv rarely missed a beat through the nineties as the "philosophical entertainer" tapped the main vein. He humbly conceded his limitations, while never denying the mushroom's stature as a harsh mistress. After all, at high doses the psi-chedelic sublime shows no quarter, evokes a mix of delight and terror, attracts and repels. "Whether or not Terence smoked DMT or did mushrooms much in the 1990s is irrelevant to the value of what he had to say to us," comments Peter Meyer. While some were disappointed that he dialed it right back, McKenna's "real value," Meyer supposes, was not only as a trenchant critic of modern civilization but "as a genuine prophet speaking to us by means of something like divine illumination."[74] Others point out that his ventures at the psychedelic limits gave McKenna an edge where it was needed—so much so that when he faced down his own sudden demise before the nineties was done, he did so with a model display of integrity.

ALIEN LOVE

This book was never intended to be a "Kurtz dossier." McKenna was a living paradox, a many-sided figure, but he was also different Terences to those with varying relationships with him. His relationship with Harrison offers a portrait on the private versus public persona—a sketch that will be filled out with greater clarity under the steam of her own pen. Beyond that, there is a spectrum of views that have been far from exhausted in this account. Nina Wise spoke of an idolized rogue celebrity whose narcissism was enabled by fans addicted to his brilliance. Closely watching her friend for three decades, Elizabeth Hansen reflected that Terence did not "fall into a pit of self-destructiveness," as was the fate of many other consciousness-expanders. And she never observed competitiveness or acquisitiveness in him.[75]

Another interlocutor aids this profile on McKenna post-marriage, and notably through his final life stage. Five years after the divorce, Terence achieved something of a new plateau. Since the breakup, he had been in and out of several acrimonious relationships. By 1997, moving alone into his new abode, he met the woman integral to his reconditioning.

Christy Silness arrived in Mexico in January 1998 for Entheobotany, the conference in Yucatán's Uxmal ruins. Born and raised in Springfield,

Ohio, the twenty-four-year-old anthropology graduate was then living in Eugene, Oregon. A musician and a Deadhead, Silness was also a fan of Terence McKenna, having produced in her senior year a linguistic paper on the "stoned ape," to the disapproval of her professor. Falling into talking with McKenna at Entheobotany, the conversation never stopped. "On the outskirts of those Mayan ruins," she recalls, "I found a gentle man with a broken heart." The two fell in love, and by September she moved into his place on the Big Island. Rarely separated, Silness joined his tours through 1998–2000, during which time she witnessed McKenna embracing new levels of vulnerability, in private and on stage. "New found joy and freedom radiated from a man renewed with the promise of love."[76] They planned a life together. While regularly taking notes at McKenna's raps, she commented on his compassion and kindness: "I was drawn to his heart as much as his mind."[77] For a figure who had comported himself according to the exilic wisdom that "we don't belong here," after a life on the run from one thing or another, after the bloodbath of the divorce and subsequent depression, through a career as chief guerrilla on a grueling annual circuit, McKenna began to feel as content as he was ever likely to be.

Curious tells of this condition can be drawn from his summer 1998 speaking tour. In Boulder, while railing against smug ideology and the Darwinian faith in random mutation, McKenna deferred to the intuition that there exists an "ethical vector in the universe." It was as though the faith in a purposeful universe to which he lent cool support for much of his career had gushed to the surface. His faith had an axiom—"nature loves complexity"—and echoing the circumstance in which he now found himself, this axiom was smelted down even further: "love." Always striving and incomplete, lying beyond the prison of culture, "love is the realm of true being."[78] A week later, in the last remarks of his final New York City appearance, he knowingly hinted at what the eschaton (a subject addressed in chapter 9) would *feel* like: "What it will *be*, if it works, is *love*. If it isn't *love*, then it's less than a perfect sublimation of the alchemical purpose—and less-than-perfect is now off the menu."[79]

By this stage, McKenna was in the position to revisit his greatest hits, collected in a new concept album, with fresh remixes. It appears that he grew reacquainted at this new plateau with a theme that had carried him to prominence, which had become a preoccupation through the eighties, rapidly dissipating in the wake of the divorce. Not only were we not alone in the universe but McKenna had ventured unique and provocative claims that effectively projected human psychosocial development onto the contact experience. As the fantasy unfolded, just as an individual human

FIGURE 7.11
McKenna cooking ayahuasca, Hawaii, summer 1999. Photo courtesy of Christy Silness.

matures through successful sexual relationships with other members of the species, the species will mature in our union with the alien—with the alien-partner of our dreams projected to be an "angelic tetramorph." In the grand vision that had the stamp of Clarke and Asimov, this transhumanizing process could only transpire when we have passed out of our species childhood and entered cosmic adolescence. And when this happens, there is an opportunity "to fall in love with the Other, get married, and go off to the stars."[80] As above, so below. If the prospective union with the alien was a mirror of our activities here on Earth, then the collapse of his marriage had effectively shattered McKenna's illusion of the cosmic *hieros gamos*. That is, until a new union rekindled the old flame of cosmic alchemy and *alien love*.

At the turn of the nineties, McKenna fell into the neurosis—the distancing from the "mama matrix most mysterious"[81]—that he routinely cautioned others to avoid. By decade's end, and the close of his life, it was toward this matrix that he appears to have returned. Alongside his commitment to Silness, he maintained a close relationship with ayahuasca, or what he had earlier dubbed "Hawayahuasca."[82] For twenty-four hours a day, up to four days at a time, cooking became an immersive pastime (see figure 7.11).

As Silness observed, the labor—eventually a team effort—filled Terence "with great joy and connection to the plants."[83] He may have steered clear of the "heroic dose," and hadn't revisited mushrooms at former strengths, but McKenna maintained an intimate relationship with plant medicines, notably *Salvia divinorum* and ibogaine, with which he experimented during the house build.[84]

This chapter is bookended by McKenna's principal partnerships. From the fungal fairytale marriage and its fruits through to the darkness of divorce, we transited to his eventual new beginning—which was also a tragic ending. We are indebted to Kat Harrison and Christy Silness for sharing their stories—even if piecemeal. The details shared merely broach the surface of painful separations. Both relationships ended traumatically, and for dramatically different reasons. Through this discussion, we have begun to understand the inherent value of McKenna's oratory artifice—his rap—as unconscious therapy for himself, and as a valued source of wisdom and higher truth for others. It is to the style, origins, history, and evolution of this artifice that we now turn.

8 STAND-UP PHILOSOPHER

With the successes of spoken word performances and breaks in the world of publishing, Terence McKenna emerged as the *éminence grise* of the weird circuit, unassumingly assuming a VIP stature for which he had been groomed as the precocious prince of Paonia. Magnetic to a population for whom he became mentor, life coach, and guerrilla ontologist, while struggling with the role of family man, McKenna became the strange attractor. Here we'll encounter the junctions and seasonal hubs in this circuit, notably, the birthplace of his newfound career, Esalen, among other venues and events on an increasingly crowded tour schedule. In doing so, we'll explore the origins and valence of a unique performance style, while at the same time addressing the personal toll of celebrityhood. Essential as an income source, a pullulating public life proved torturous for a figure with hermit-like aspirations. A life dedicated to growing an audience conflicted with a basic desire for solitude.

SCHOLAR AND WIZARD

The strength of McKenna's career is a measure of his storytelling charm. His talent for attracting a crowd. His talk show. This talent is traceable to childhood, and was honed in high school, where, as an extemporaneous speaker, he slayed his competition. Given that his chief renown is oratory delivered in increasingly public domains, the historical development of McKenna's rap is integral to the story by which he emerged as a public figure.

Hallucinations are for McKenna what dreams were for Jung: *prima materia*. Just as Jung championed the essential value of dreamlife, McKenna defended psychedelic reveries, not as false experiences but as essential to an existence to which humans are entitled at birth. Like dreams, the hallucinatory world is not solely the province of the individual, but possesses pan-psychic depth and significance, for these experiences occasion the self's contact with the *other* (or the other self). While daily cannabis use augmented a tremendous verbal facility, and did not appear to impact his memory, the habit appears to have had a deleterious effect on McKenna's dream life. During the interludes in which he quit smoking his dream life improved.[1] "The older I get," he said in 1994, "the more like a psychedelic waking dream everyday life appears to me."[2] While nowhere does McKenna appear to offer substantive comparison between dreamlife and psychedelic hallucinations, it is the latter from which his greatest insights are retrieved.

There are no autobiographical accounts of McKenna's psychonautical inner-space approximate to that supplied in Jung's *Memories, Dreams, Reflections* and *Liber Novus*. And yet, there are recordings of hundreds of hours of interior life projected before audiences throughout the eighties and nineties, and right up until his death. On the whole, these recordings of public lectures, conference appearances, trialogues, interviews, and multiday workshops for specialist audiences offer great insight on McKenna's other persona, his "personality #2" (to use Jung's phrase for his shadow self), or what Terence knew as the *logos*. As I have suggested in the previous chapter, this personality was animate in speaking engagements on the subject of alchemy, offering revelatory allusion to the state of his marriage. Striking a balance between the outrageous and the profound, rapping proved all at once entertaining and informative, philosophical and anecdotal, subversive and salubrious, audacious and humble. These performances also featured a Socratic component with audience Q&A.

Displaying a remarkable eidetic capacity, McKenna's rap was typically performed on the fly, and rarely on the natch. Prepared notes were uncommon, nor were there props other than books, from which he occasionally read (sometimes projecting Timewave Zero software charts). He sometimes paused to announce a "paragraph break." Shedding light on his oratory approach, there is allusion to the *ars memoria*, a "lost art" of memorizing speech commencing with Roman orator Cicero, and addressed by Frances Yates in *The Art of Memory*. The most common "mnemonic trick" was imagining a familiar building—one's "memory palace"—and populating it with "emblemata" representing the ideas to be recalled as one moves through their speech. To be memorable, the "emblemata" ought to be unusual and shocking. McKenna claimed to successfully apply the technique using the hallways and floors of UC Berkeley as his "memory palace." An example was offered. "Say you're giving a speech about the seven deadly sins, so then 'luxuria' might be for you a nun copulating with a dog, and you'll set the nun and the dog in a little niche in the hallway of the memory palace;

then when you reach that place in your imaginary journey, all these associations will spring to mind and you'll be able to give your speech flawlessly."[3]

Back in the halcyon days of their marriage, Terence practiced his rap on Kat, notably with material later included in *True Hallucinations*, a title conjured by Harrison, who figured "Down to Earth" sounded too much like "organic farming." In those days, all the conversations, were between them and a few friends.[4] Harrison encouraged the stage persona of a man who *needed* an audience, a figure she later characterized as a "brilliant narcissist."[5] The couple originally intended to appear as co-presenters, but as McKenna quickly gained notoriety in the attention economy, the idea of a professional touring partnership was shelved. In any case, any career ambitions harbored by Harrison took a back seat to motherhood.[6]

McKenna's wicked sense of humor was pivotal to his ability to draw a crowd. With a sharp wit native to his charm, the stand-up philosopher deployed a method favored by comics: conceding one's own faults, flaws, and failings before strangers with disarming honesty. Successful stage comedians are gifted with the ability to endear themselves to live audiences in routines that disclose their mad conceits, narcissism, and devious behaviors, and through these revelations, divulge insight on the human condition. Less a forced tactic than a natural mode of communication, McKenna owned this capability. Take for example, his admission of megalomania. On occasion, it was revealed that, from an early age, he understood that the world appeared to comply with his wishes and expectations. "I've never thirsted for acceptance by the academy," he claimed. "I would have to go somewhere and leave my home, or something." But "you don't need Carl Sagan to tell you you're right when you have megalomania. You just confidently sit back and wait for it all to blow your way." Apparently, this conceit had worked repeatedly throughout his life. Referring to his obsession with Huxley's sublime encounter with his trouser folds, Terence was into psychedelics years before taking them. "I watched my entire civilization go mad over my obsession." And as if that wasn't enough evidence, there was also the internet. "It's like I dreamed it up. It's exactly what I wanted. And I never told anybody it's exactly what I wanted, but here it is, just like the psychedelic revolution that I wanted."[7]

Another tactic rarely failing to score laughs is the invocation of the "squirrels." It became standard practice to identify the sad specters lurking at the edge of rationality, with McKenna typically condemning these folks as frumpty peddlers of "squirrelly" notions, with whom he squared off in uproarious bits that in another age will have seen him kill on Comedy

Central. The squirrels were simply the empirical evidence of "McKenna's Law," which was that "no matter where you go, the average density of idiots remains the same."⁸ By consistently identifying those *other* others who peddle ideas ungrounded in rigorous testing and rules based evidence, McKenna patrolled the boundaries of the acceptable, performing the persona of the reasoned intellect that he, by contrast, fancied himself to be. While Christians, Buddhists, and scientologists were all in possession of smug "shell game" belief systems, fringe occultists, especially those with whom McKenna may have been conflated and from whom he sought distinction, deserved special attention. The "face on Mars" people, alien abductees, recipients of uninvited proctological examinations, and crop circle enthusiasts were chief among those whose beliefs and activities made his own appear legit and, not to mention, *tasteful*. Biting scorn was reserved for unreconstructed UFO enthusiasts, whose exploits appear to have provided McKenna with some of his best material. There was occasion, for example, to recall a visit to an expo populated by "flying saucer people," likely during San Francisco's 1987 Angels, Aliens, and Archetypes conference. Booth after booth of "scary people in brown leather shoes with thin smiles and cheap suits" were observed to be "third-rate semi-retired intelligence hacks." He would be no mark for the "alien" pushers peddling their theories about experiments on human fetal tissue in underground laboratories in Arizona under the cooperation of the CIA and Pleiadean High Command. "I've got to call my broker. I'll get back to you on that."⁹

It is not as if McKenna was himself free from belief. "Great weirdness stalks the universe," an Esalen audience is regaled in 1994. The issue for him was that, on the question of the alien, the mystery had become such a gauche reflection of the small-mindedness of believers that *aliens* were clad in gaudiness. The first casualty in the war over the alien appeared to be aesthetics. If he had his way, those sans taste and integrity would not conquer the popular imagination on the subject of aliens. "One thing is for sure," he declared in relation to the revelation of the ultimate mystery: it won't be wearing low-cut gowns and passing out flying saucer–shaped business cards with 10 percent discount coupons. While burlesquing vanilla alienists, he was not unaware of the self-applicability of "McKenna's Law." "I don't make it comfortable for other squirrels," he conceded. "I don't share the branch very generously."¹⁰

Nuance and candidness were translated to radio, where McKenna had his earliest break. Among the first appearances was *New Dimensions*, the internationally syndicated radio series founded by "the Socrates of radio," Michael Toms. McKenna first appeared on the show on May 18, 1977, demonstrating that, a year out from the publication of the *Grower's Guide*, he had little interest in maintaining the pseudonymous ruse. Toms's audience was introduced to a newly minted graduate of "shamanic studies," described as "ten years in the doing, with a seven-year leave of absence for . . . fieldwork." As for his motivation, the graduate assured the cultural underground that he had obtained his letters so that "as I made my case in print I would have the credentials of the other side." With his status revealed as a kind of secret agent for the underground, he approached the business at hand. Science had made little progress in understanding the hallucinatory experience. His own research, by contrast, ranged closer to the action, not only by acknowledging the resonant model of shamanism, but by revivifying shamanic techniques in the modern world. It was the homegrown *Psilocybe* mushroom, the guest related matter-of-factly and without pause, that "introduces you to such a radically different part of your psyche that might as well be an extraterrestrial, because it introduces you to either an unsuspected facet of being human or an alien dimension, and you can sort of take your pick." The positions were ultimately interchangeable. Having blown the collective mind of Toms, his guests, and listeners in the mycophilic and ufological underground with a flurry of succinct commentary, from Julian Jaynes to Henri Michaux, McKenna's inaugural performance on *New Dimensions* sent a warning shot across the bow of the trite and the conventional.[11]

Not only was this new upstart displaying a talent in the science of whole systems thinking, he was no slouch in the fields of art, literature, and the history and philosophy of science. Such talents were readily apparent in early on-air appearances, including *New Dimensions* and KPFK's Pacifica Radio (with Pam Burton). Radio was a perfect medium for transmitting the oracular anarchitect's cardinal philosophy: "the felt presence of immediate experience," highlighted under the influence of psilocybin. "Language betrays in order to mean," McKenna once claimed, citing Archibald MacLeish: "A poem should not mean, but be."[12] It was perfectly paradoxical. "Small mouth noises" cannot but betray one's internal thoughts, and yet it is language that conveys this very observation. The new bard of stoner radio thrived under such irony. Railing against language under an irrepressible volley of his own small but orthogonal mouth noises, McKenna knew something about the noetic valence of language, and through his budding rap he gave plenty of shout-outs to his sponsors.

As his audience grew to understand, McKenna loved books. Despite his beef with words, *Finnegans Wake* and *Moby Dick*, among other favored texts, were deemed works of "psychedelic metaphysics" that he loved to discuss and from which he read—on air, and at early in-person appearances at venues like Shared Visions and later Esalen, typically during his summer residencies. Owned by Will Noffke, the Shared Visions performance space and bookstore in Berkeley is a favored early haunt, where McKenna made over a dozen appearances. Noffke also featured McKenna on his eponymous radio show. Whether performing on radio or in person, at Shared Visions, Terence felt like he was entertaining folks in the comfort of his own living room. The audience represented his "core community" on whom he tested outlandish ideas and experimented with nascent nomenclature performed and articulated to great success elsewhere. While he enjoyed excavating texts for hidden layers of significance, he was also known to read passages from memory, from the likes of Blake, Huxley, and Melville. For spellbound trippers, McKenna's oratory conveyed the feeling of knowing, which for the poet supersedes the transmission of knowledge itself.

As evident in the emblematic rap "Alien Love" delivered at Shared Visions in 1983, the movement from the recitation of Mind implicit to classic texts to articulating his own mind is a seamless transition typical to the rap. While ordinary language betrays Mind, it is the rap of the Beethoven of words that represented an effortless means to accomplish what he otherwise claimed was nigh impossible: permitting others to *behold* meaning. McKenna's free associational extemporizations enabled his audience to visualize his thoughts, on such matters as *visible language*. The rap that grew to permeate the Net even in his own time appeared to range from the impeccably succinct transmission of ideas at one end of the spectrum to the performance of the "intentionality of meaning" at the other, where syntax shorn of ascribed meaning was delivered like a sonata.[13] This glossolalian proclivity to give voice to the *Ursprache* was engendered in the delivery of elf speak. That McKenna's own voice had a noetic quality would become recognizable to composers of electronic music from the early nineties.

Splashed across the parlor-room canvas of Shared Visions, early impressions were made on the visibility of language with which our psychedelic saloneer was familiar in the psilocybin trance state. Such a state enabled the transcendence of the "topology of meaning" that afforded access to the assembly language that, it was repeatedly claimed, Wittgenstein knew as "the Unspeakable."[14] And what was the price of uncovering the unspeakable? Apparently, it was to be afflicted with the revelation that the evolution of language all at once propels us inward and expels us outward. Regardless of whether Wittgenstein, Heidegger, or Chomsky, among other names, served as intellectual decor to his own wordplay, what is extraordinary is that McKenna was inviting audiences to traverse and transcend the "visual topology" of language generated by his own voice. And in doing so, he demonstrated in this early phase of his public career how, mirroring the oracular role that the mushroom performed for him, he served a *logos*-like role for psychedelic savants and neophytes in the eighties underground.

Such were the contexts in which stoner discourse was being elevated to new heights—all at once elegant, visionary, and absurd. The doors were opening for a towering anomaly mooted in the first edition of *High Frontiers* as a "scholar and a wizard."[15] A chief vehicle for this success was Roy Tuckman (a.k.a. Roy of Hollywood), whose Los Angeles–based *Something's Happening* program on KPFK was pivotal to the eventual breakthrough to wider media attention. Tuckman was an old biker, much like his "old lady," who was his tech person and sidekick. Riding Harley-Davidsons and black leather-clad, they were "tough and funny people, and definitely psychedelic," recalls Harrison. "Good to have as allies, not so good to have as enemies."[16] The opening show was on December 14, 1983, when Tuckman played recorded raps and interviewed McKenna and Harrison throughout the night. Due to popular demand, and the support of Tuckman, McKenna's raps dominated the Monday night slot for almost ten years. He had a melodic voice for radio, and all night long on Monday nights throughout the eighties his spellbinding spiel became the inspirational *freakuency* for trippers. As his "small mouth noises" crested into towering waveforms, "Magellans of consciousness" waxed their boards and planned their psychedelic odysseys in the comfort and safety of their receiving stations (i.e., at home). *Something's Happening* broadcast hundreds of hours of material, notably showcasing *True Hallucinations*, released in 1984 as a nine-and-a-half-hour audiobook comprised of a set of eight cassettes in a custom-designed clamshell box (priced at $80), with cover illustrations by Harrison. Under the creative direction and marketing acumen of Faustin Bray and Brian Wallace (Sound Photosynthesis), McKenna narrated the entire "talking book" himself, accompanied by the music and sound effects of Nomadband (see figure 8.1).

Something did happen with *Something's Happening* by 1991–92, when, to the chagrin of McKenna's fans, an estranged Tuckman vowed on air to never again broadcast McKenna's content. This disturbance in early nineties LA stoner radio amounted to a flattening of the carrier wave, with the cause of the public rift remaining a mystery, to me, as it does to Harrison. At any rate, McKenna's "mouth noises" had, by then, grown bigger and were transmitted with greater frequency on other stations, platforms, and dimensions.

Dedicated to promoting little known and marginal intellectuals, including Richard Feynman, John C. Lilly, and Marija Gimbutas, Faustin Bray was

FIGURE 8.1
Audiobook cover of *True Hallucinations*, the "talking book" (Sound Photosynthesis/Lux Natura, 1984). Courtesy of Kevin Whitesides.

like a media abattoiress who specialized in separating the meat from the gristle. Through the eighties, Bray served a Colonel Parker–like role, converting talent into names. Many early McKenna raps were recorded on cassette, CD, and later DVD, and marketed as Sound Photosynthesis products. The relationship between Bray and McKenna/Harrison was dramatic and sometimes acrimonious. While McKenna grew to loathe Bray, they did, as Harrison suggests, "use each other pretty effectively for years." Among Bray and Wallace's productions was the 1989 "audially illuminated manuscript" *Victorian Tales of Cannabis*, on which McKenna read chapters from *The Hasheesh Eater*, thereby introducing Fitz Hugh Ludlow to a new generation.

Identifying Ludlow as "part genius, part madman," a figure "halfway between Captain Ahab and P. T. Barnum, a kind of Mark Twain on hashish,"[17] McKenna might as well have been describing himself. At the very least, he was identifying an archetype he admired, if not embodied, as an emerging West Coast literary psychonaut and public showman. In the early eighties he settled into the incubation site of his emergence.

ESALEN

In November 1982, under the invitation of engineer-philosopher Arthur M. Young, McKenna fronted at Berkeley's Institute for the Study of Consciousness. Though "New and Old Maps of Hyperspace" appears to be his first recorded public appearance, it was apparently his third appearance at this venue. His presentation, in which he ventured a masterful, and yet seemingly never repeated, quadrangulation of the four "abysses" of biology, history, psychology, and physics, did not fail to impress audience member, Esalen cofounder Dick Price. Known to McKenna as "a very far out guy,"[18] Price invited McKenna down to Big Sur for an event in December 1982. There he delivered his landmark rap "Tryptamine Hallucinogens and Consciousness" at a seminar headlined by John C. Lilly and Amit Goswami. While that appearance marked the eighties inception of McKenna's Esalen splashdown, he had made landfall at the Institute a decade prior, when appearing in the low months of 1973 or 1974 at the invitation of anthropologist, longtime Buddhist practitioner, and today abbot of Santa Fe's Upaya Zen Center Joan Halifax. With her then husband, Stanislov Grof, Halifax co-led four- to six-week-long residential programs on shamanism operating over the fall out of the Big House, situated a mile north of the main complex. A vociferous proponent of psychedelic shamanism fresh from the Amazon and a continuing student at Berkeley, McKenna joined a faculty that included Cherokee leader Rolling Thunder.[19] Though there is no record of his contribution to the program, we might imagine the novice brandishing a copy of "Shamanic Investigations" and enthralling workshoppers with fresh tales of the La Chorreran surreal—tales that eventually surfaced in the pages of *True Hallucinations*.

This was the beginning of a long friendship with Halifax, who was charmed by this mischievous "scientist hippie and visionary prophet" who sprung up out of nowhere and who, with his very thin body and wild bushy hair, looked to her very much like a mushroom.[20] It was also the beginning of a long association with the Institute, with Esalen eventually becoming a seminal laboratory for ideas testing, its retreat-like surrounds an ideal context for experiments in content and delivery. At Esalen, McKenna's open advocacy for psychedelics made him an appealing, albeit controversial, underground celebrity.

Perceived as integral to the "quiet reformulation of psychological thought," psychedelics feature at the foundation of Esalen. The earliest catalog promoted a fall 1962 seminar series exploring emergent developments in psychology, psychical research, and work with the "mind-opening drugs" that were not only paving the way toward "a profounder human possibility," but were promising "the greatest change in the vision of western man since Copernicus and the Renaissance."[21] That "drug induced mysticism" was a protean Esalenite orientation echoes the influence of Aldous Huxley, the institute's literary philosopher, after whom Esalen became recognized as a center of "human potentialities," facilitating the search for the divine, the mystical, and the sublime.[22] In subsequent decades, this foundation proved ideal for McKenna, who would eventually deliver over a hundred lectures and workshops at the Big Sur venue. Through the "Dark Age" of the eighties, recognized as the "plant advocate," McKenna took his place among a broad community of psychedelics researchers convening at Esalen, among them Lilly, Stanislav Grof, Alexander Shulgin, Gordon Wasson, David Nichols, and Myron Stolaroff.[23]

The transition from home saloneer to resident celebrity was observed by Elizabeth Hansen. Present at many of his appearances, Hansen witnessed how the venue became the center of her friend's calling. Many gravitated to Big Sur to discuss the psychedelic, paranormal, and spiritual anomalies that had shaken their worlds, what the Grofs called "spiritual emergencies," or what psychologist Stanley Krippner knew as "exceptional experiences." In McKenna's case, it took an anomalist to know the anomalous. Integral to his method was the "heroic dose"—that is, five grams of the dried fungus taken on an empty stomach in a quiet darkened place, or several hits on a pipe packed with crystal DMT—the endorsement of which effectively psychedelicized the "hero's journey" monomyth of Joseph Campbell, another of Esalen's earlier stars. Offering expert advice and lending a sympathetic ear to psychodynamic experimentalists and cosmonauts of the interior gravitating to this scene—women inclusive—McKenna became "a healer of the highest order."[24]

McKenna would establish a residency at Esalen after the cessation of the grow operation. As a virtual unknown in the early eighties psychedelic research scene, he attracted attention for his outlandish claims as much as his synthetic intellect and tricksy proclivities. It may have been the last time he made a brief and non-headline appearance, but McKenna appears to have come to the attention of the world psychedelic research community at UC Santa Barbara on May 14, 1983. At Psychedelic Conference II, Terence and Kat mingled with Albert Hofmann, Humphry Osmond, Timothy Leary, Ralph Metzner, Alexander Shulgin, Walter Houston Clark, and Joan Halifax, among other luminaries (see figure 8.2). In "Hallucinogens: Before and After Psychology"—a modification of "Hallucinogens: Monkeys Discover Hyperspace"—the figure characterizing himself as Pierre Teilhard de Chardin on drugs announced his arrival on the psychedelic research scene. Claiming to paraphrase the Jesuit paleontologist, McKenna stated that "when the human race understands the potential of the hallucinogenic drug experience it will have discovered fire for the second time." The discovery was before us. "We are waiting for the discovery of fire so that we can transcend the monkey business and get on with the great business of inhabiting our own imaginations."[25]

FIGURE 8.2
Luminaries on the lawn. Terence McKenna and Kathleen Harrison (second and third from left), with Albert Hofmann (looking at a book) and others, at Psychedelic Conference II, UC Santa Barbara, May 14, 1983. Photo by Cynthia Palmer. Courtesy of Michael and Cynthia Horowitz papers, MSP 316, Purdue University Archives and Special Collections.

As the shamanarchist's contempt for academia, ambivalence toward science, and intellectual roguery did not go unnoticed, establishing a foothold at Esalen, and gaining a reputation further afield, was no cake walk. In December 1984, then a graduate student in the study of religion at the University of Chicago, Robert Forte organized a conference with Stan Grof, inviting fifty experts to Esalen. Among the invited speakers, McKenna related his "stoned ape" hypothesis. Though himself impressed, Forte was pressured to exclude McKenna's contribution from the conference proceedings since, the readers, Chilean psychiatrist Claudio Naranjo and integrative physician Andrew Weil, rejected his hypothesis. They were anxious that McKenna would undermine the standards of the publication and impair the effort to reintroduce psychedelics into academia.[26] Minor disputes of this nature did not deter McKenna, whose open distaste for academia and its hierarchies were pulling an audience. Behaving dismissively toward his own education, he informed his audience that he might as well have a "degree in Tap Dancing from the University of Antarctica."[27] That a delightful, self-deprecating sensibility marked McKenna's meteoric rise as a darling of the psychedelic community is an accomplishment perhaps best demonstrated by his role as emcee of the Albert Hofmann Foundation tribute at the Scottish Rite Masonic Temple in Los Angeles in October 1988.

Despite the early contretemps, McKenna was an active figure in the Esalen of the eighties and nineties. His leadership capabilities were recognized in August 1985 when he curated the three-day seminar "Shamanism, Alchemy, and the Millennium." Dennis, Kat, Luis Eduardo Luna, Ralph Abraham, Michael Horowitz, and Cynthia Palmer were among those invited to present. By 1989, McKenna had become a month-long scholar-in-residence at the Little House where he would spend many summers over the next decade.[28] Such an enduring presence appears to be news for cultural historians, for whom the initials "TM" bears little significance other than Transcendental Meditation. While the other TM rates no mention in Matthew Ingram's tome *Retreat: How the Counterculture Invented Wellness*, in the recollection of the executive director of programs, Nancy Lunney-Wheeler, of the top several-dozen luminaries of the period, McKenna "stood among the greats" at Esalen and was always a big draw.[29] Among the regulars at his seminars were psychotherapist Leo Zeff (who McKenna dubbed the "secret chief" for his pioneering clandestine work with MDMA), writer Allan Badiner (whose house stood about half-a-mile from Esalen where McKenna often lodged as a guest a week before or after an appearance),[30] illustrious filmmaker Lewis John Carlino and his wife Jill, among many others, including Elizabeth Hansen, Katherine O'Shaughnessy, and bodyworker Ellen Watson. During the introductions at one workshop, writer Paul Krassner observed the broad constituency:

> Here, a woman who's a professional raver. There, a man who strolled the streets of Paris with a lobster on a leash. Here, a mother and her son, whom she has brought as a gift for his twenty-first birthday. There, a woman who will spend the entire weekend sucking on a little straw coming out of the top of a plastic water bottle in the shape of a large, pink erect penis. She introduces herself as "a hooker from LA. I'm here to party with the elves." McKenna turns to the person sitting next to her and says softly, "top that."[31]

As he sought to preclude the increasingly common and irritating request for substance availability, appearances often commenced with a virtual disclaimer: "This is your cadre and not only is there someone here tonight who has what you need, there's probably someone here tonight who needs something that you have."[32] Other times, direct requests were met with the blunt reality: "The point guy can't make the sale!" Through the eighties, McKenna created a niche market for his own product—that is, his mind—and by the early nineties, the workshops were a chief money stream.[33]

McKenna's Esalen recordings were the responsibility of Paul Herbert, an old-time resident of Big Sur and participant in the inception of Esalen. Founder of Dolphin Tapes, Herbert was a fastidious recorder of presenters and workshops, including those of Huxley and Joseph Campbell, and made extensive recordings of McKenna, with whom he developed a close relationship. The Marty Weinberg of McKenna recordings, Herbert recorded approximately sixty McKenna appearances and gave many their original titles.[34] According to David Price, son of Dick, who served as Esalen's general manager between 1995 and 2003, toward the end of Herbert's life, McKenna "took on a role somewhat akin to an adult child to taking care of a parent," which was ironic, given Herbert outlived McKenna by ten years. McKennaphiles ultimately have Herbert to thank for his devotion to recording Terence's Esalen appearances, most eventually uploaded on YouTube (see appendix B).[35]

Herbert's recordings became classics, due not only to the content as advertised, but to McKenna's devotion to his audience. With a commitment to free-form Q&A improv sessions that were sometimes longer than the promoted lectures, he was like the Thelonious Monk of Esalen. There was little evidence of judgment. Questions were encouraged and inquirers typically treated as if they had—despite the often half-baked, inaudible, and sometimes rude or hostile nature of the questions—tendered inquiries of unparalleled significance. Even at the height of his popularity, McKenna was generous with his time. While there were invariably "jerks" in attendance, in Badiner's memory, McKenna was remarkably polite with detractors. No matter the quality of the inquiry, he graced the question with an entertaining rhetoric befitting the halls of a psychedelic Ent-Moot, converting potential disruptions into astute observations on the nature of time and consciousness.

McKenna not only received his critics with equanimity; he routinely invited critique. He set the example himself, often as the first to mock the absurdity of his own mutant philosophy, not uncommonly irrupting in squeals of laughter in response to the outlandish credence of his own statements. In this way, he served as his very own heckler, a role that may have quieted the cynics or stilled the head shakers. It is also possible that McKenna saw his own reflection in the young agitators and skeptics who appeared at his events.

The mockery of New Age cognoscenti increased McKenna's stock, his traction at Esalen gaining in part since his scorn for spiritual authorities found alignment with founders and staff. Dick Price, for example, distrusted gurus and held the New Age in low esteem, what with its "Pollyanna denial of shadow." As David Price further reflects, where long-term resident Fritz Perls used "chickenshit," "bullshit," and "elephantshit" to identify levels of self-denial, delusion, and avoidance, Dick added "unicornshit" to the repertoire.[36]

Being distinguished from the spiritual malarkey was, however, never as easy as one might have hoped. As but one example, the struggle to be free from unicornshit was on display when McKenna appeared in the popular New Age and fringe science periodical *Magical Blend* magazine on the same page as an advertisement for the Crystal Flute, a "thought technology," "affirmation amplifier," and "a sophisticated oscillator designed to electrically stimulate and amplify the thoughts you program into your quartz crystal." One could be forgiven for wondering if McKenna hadn't penned the device's description himself: "The Crystal Flute generates a positive energy field whose dimensions are limited only by your imagination."[37]

If Esalen is the birthplace of Terence McKenna as a public figure, his local popularity is a testament to the appeal of his mythopoetics—first broadcast at the Institute in December 1982, when invited to an afternoon session sponsored by Christina Grof's Spiritual Emergency Network. The relative unknown plunged right into the mythic core, from which he would not deviate for his remaining years. "Until we understand that there is a teleological object at the end of human history, and that it can be known," he announced, "we will continue to live the kind of limited intellectual existence that has characterized the last 500 years or so of Western development." The unassuming audience was broadsided with the wisdom that certain tryptamines could expose them to "the architecture of eternity." A shot was fired across the bow of seminarians, warned not only of the endtimes approaching, but of what they should expect from McKenna's mouth from here on out. "We are either going to change into this cybernetic hyperdimensional hallucinogenic angel or we're going to destroy ourselves." By no small measure was the solution to be narcotic shamanism, or at least McKenna's brand of intelligent shamanism. And if one were to inquire of the requisite intelligence, the attempt to recreate a preliterate shamanism was not nearly enough. Since the future of the species was in our hands, "We have to go into the shaman space with the a priori categories of Kant, with the eidetic reduction of Wittgenstein, with the ideas of Merleau-Ponty and Whitehead." The intellectual equipment of Western culture deemed essential for mapping the "shaman space" would serve to absorb the coming shock waves that will inevitably strike us "like the bow shock of ionized particles . . . meeting the magnetic field of a planet."[38]

PIED PIPER

McKenna's compelling style and ebullient content were well received further afield at the Ojai Foundation, in the Upper Ojai Valley of Ventura County, California. Founded by director Joan Halifax, the Ojai Foundation favored a "council" style of group communication encircled under a magnificent oak called the "teaching tree."[39] Under the oak's sprawling limbs, McKenna joined a faculty that also hosted Buddhist teachers like Thích Nhất Hạnh and Chagdud Rinpoche, and workshops led by the likes of Joseph Campbell, R. D. Laing, Francisco Varela, and Robert Bly. Ojai had its roots in the Happy Valley Foundation, that opened up the land to other nonprofits in the mid-seventies. The original property had been purchased by visionary Theosophist Annie Besant in 1927. The community became known for its "Wizards Camp" where Indigenous bearers of wisdom from across North America were brought into conversation with global tradition bearers. In April 1985, McKenna was invited by program director Robin Sylvan to participate in the Mayan Conference, where a meeting with Planet Art Network co-founder José Argüelles (the so-called Council of Quetzalcoatl) had a bearing on the subsequent 2012 mythos propagated by both figures.[40] McKenna returned on many occasions, including a private campout at Point Sal Beach in Guadalupe in May 1985; the "Rites of Spring" intensive workshop at Joshua Tree in April 1986; seminars with Riane Eisler ("Man and Woman at the End of History," 1988), Ralph Metzner ("Shamanism: Before and beyond History," 1988), and Nicole Maxwell ("Amazonian Shamanism," 1989); and a retreat at Camp Shalom in Malibu in May 1991 (see figure 8.3).

FIGURE 8.3
McKenna at the Conference on Botanical Intelligence, Camp Shalom, Malibu Hills, May 1991. Courtesy of Topa Institute. Also present are Andrew Weil (with gray beard to the left), Joan Halifax (between Weil and Terence), Dennis McKenna (with balding head, behind Weil), John Steele (top left), Johannes Wilbert (to the right of Terence), and Tom Lane (on far right, partially cropped).

The event at Joshua Tree in 1986 was a pinnacle achievement in Sylvan's memory. While most of McKenna's public appearances feature his meandering pontifications, on this occasion he also served as a mentor. Ceremonial by design, securing a private location in a box canyon, Rites of Spring uniquely combined theory (teaching) and practical (vision quest) elements. Sylvan and other staff were familiar with the work of Harley Swiftdeer and the use of the "medicine wheel" as a teaching tool. Following McKenna's workshop, participants buddied up and were sent out for the weekend, most of them taking mushrooms or some other psychoactive substance. A veteran workshop facilitator, Sylvan is hard-pressed to recall another event where "so many people had life-changing experiences."[41]

Another event where McKenna's wisdom and guidance were pivotal is seared into the mind of aromatic oil and olfaction researcher John Steele. At Ojai on May 24, 1987, an adventurous group of experiential researchers were initiated into the mysteries of DMT in a small hillside yurt. Wearing a woolen Peruvian poncho, McKenna exuded "a focused shamanic presence." One by one, each novice lay down in the center of the circle as he fired up the pipe. "He looked after each one of us while we journeyed," said Steele. Afterward, each journeymaker was invited to share their visionary experience with the group. Steele's own trans-dimensional "breaking the plane" episode was the result of "a singular act of spiritual generosity."[42] The generosity was replicated over the years for an untold number of grateful initiates. Though surely acts of kindness, such gestures seem less like instances of altruism than behavior consistent with a drive to find those whose contact experiences bore favorable comparison to McKenna's own. It was a case of "finding the others" who know the *others* and creating a community of shared associations. As McKenna once reported: "Let those who talk to the elves find each other and band together."[43] One such fellow traveler was visionary painter Robert Venosa, who thanked McKenna for the rebirthing of his "superconscious" following their first meeting in 1993.[44] Both Venosa and his partner, Martina Hoffmann, encountered the bittersweet jungle juice care of McKenna, an episode that influenced the creation of Venosa's *Ayahuasca Dream*, and gave inspiration to Hoffmann's art.

McKenna filled the cup and held the pipe for countless intrepids. Quite possibly the last person to receive his pipe was Jacques Olivier, at "Grandmother Works," a three-day retreat in Waimea, Hawaii, in September 1999. The event involved two days drinking ayahuasca before a third day smoking DMT. Olivier was the last in the group, the thirteenth member, to "kiss the pipe." At one time a guitarist for the garage rock band the Mutts, Olivier sat before the terminally ill McKenna, who shaved a crystalline golf ball of DMT into a glass pipe. Aware of the gravity of the situation, he stepped up to the pipe as if the bases were loaded. He took three successive hits, performing the ritual to such perfection that McKenna afterward exclaimed: "Now *that's* how I *smoke* DMT." The immediate impact is described in Olivier's memoir:

> As I inhaled I opened my eyes to see Terence's head and face and watched it explode into tiny fractal versions or replicas perfectly identical and spaced apart, as if I had the vision of a bee. Those tiny Terence heads morphed slowly into shiny silver reflective perfectly aligned spheres that filled my entire field of vision. The mirrored balls emitted shafts of rainbow light in all directions and rotated toward me, bathing me in the light of a *ruthlessly pure machine elf love!!!*[45]

TRIALOGUES

Chaos theorist Ralph Abraham was among McKenna's closest friends. Gravitating to mathematics from electrical engineering and experimental physics, Abraham taught math at UC Santa Cruz from 1968, and there remained professor emeritus of mathematics from 1994 until his death in September 2024. Like his friend, Abraham made extensive travels of worlds inner and outer. Not much younger than he, his students had acquainted Abraham with LSD at Princeton in 1967, the year he scoured the Himalayan foothills for traditional knowledge, eventually acquiring an education in classical North Indian music. Following Ram Dass, he studied the *Vedas* under Neem Karoli Baba. Psychedelics catalyzed the search for a vibration model of mind and consciousness as expressed in a nonlinear theory Abraham called "dynamical systems." In his anthology, *Vibrations and Forms: Findings from Psychedelic Adventures*, Abraham describes his meeting with McKenna in 1972 as one of his life's principal "bifurcations," to use a term denoting major changes of state triggered by small external forces.[46] With their conversations ranging across chaos attractors, hyperdimensionality, the Goddess partnership society, and the Hermetic tradition, the duo formed a collaborative intellectual mind-space.

A decade later, their friendship bubble, and mind-space, expands to absorb Rupert Sheldrake. After gaining a PhD in biochemistry from Cambridge in 1967, Sheldrake studied philosophy at Harvard. With the launch of his first book, *A New Science of Life*, in Los Angeles, Sheldrake is afforded the opportunity to visit the West Coast in 1982. Informed by his agents about a figure he should meet and handed a cassette tape, he is booked on a Greyhound bus to Santa Rosa. Playing the tape en route exposes Sheldrake to a mesmeric nasal drawl extemporizing on the subject of the DMT molecule. Arriving at his destination, a forest green Chevy Impala glides up to the bus stand. The driver's window scrolls down to reveal a figure in dark glasses who inquires in the now familiar nasal drawl: "Dr. Sheldrake, I presume?"

He jumps into the back. Terence McKenna is at the wheel, with Abraham riding shotgun. Both men are already versed in Sheldrake's theory of "morphic resonance," according to which there is inherent memory in nature. They drive back to the A-frame in Occidental. "We started talking and we were talking for three days," Sheldrake recalls, with McKenna getting up occasionally to spray water vapor in his grow shed. It is a conversation unlike any Sheldrake had ever known, oiled by McKenna's humor and by the fact that the three had all traveled in India.[47] As Abraham confirmed, Sheldrake's presence "stretched the space into an equilateral triangle."[48] The conversation is so stimulating that the trio meet subsequently almost every year right up to the end of McKenna's life (see figure 8.4).

The intellectual threesomes initially conducted in private at Esalen, before their conversion to public fora at the instigation of Nancy Lunney-Wheeler,

FIGURE 8.4
Trialogue members Rupert Sheldrake, Ralph Abraham, and Terence McKenna, 1996. Photo by Ron Jones, courtesy of Ralph Abraham.

are the basis for a unique series of workshops called "trialogues" held between 1989 and 1998. Though curated for the most part at Esalen, the trialogues would take place in various locations: Hazelwood House, in the countryside of South Devon; McKenna's Big Island retreat; "the Esalen of the far north," Hollyhock, on Cortes Island, British Columbia; UC Santa Cruz; and Abraham's home in the nearby redwoods. Edited transcripts of these discussions formed the basis of two published volumes.[49] As Jean Houston writes in the foreword to the first volume, these events were "a singular sapient circle of gentlemen geniuses at their edgiest of edges."[50] The successful format permitted spirited debate on a host of topics among figures who each challenged the laws of nature in their respective fields. Throughout these exchanges, McKenna packaged his model of time as a formal example of Sheldrake's theory of resonance, and Sheldrake's concept of "formative causation," which postulates that "everything is being made up as it goes along," resonated with McKenna's future vector point. Abraham offered a bridge between the two by way of nonlinear models, whole systems, and the revival of the Orphic tradition.[51]

In what turned out to be their final convergence, at UC Santa Cruz on June 6, 1998, Abraham spoke to the resonance among the trio over the previous decades, suggesting they were each, as illustrated by their work, utopians of sorts. Where Abraham's *Chaos, Gaia, Eros* presented a kind of "chaos utopia," and Sheldrake's *The Rebirth of Nature* a "scientific utopia," McKenna's *Food of the Gods* exemplified a "psychedelic utopia."[52] Regarding how the three had spent the last two decades opening their lives to chaos and becoming a part of "the will of the world soul," McKenna broached the reasons for the format's success: "It means recapturing the Greek sense of fate that has been replaced in our minds by the Faustian illusion of control and dominance."[53]

The success of these events was in part due to the sportive candor the three displayed toward one another. While the triumvirate resonated, McKenna was, as Sheldrake readily concedes, the format's linchpin. After he left the building, like a rock band bereft of their front man, Rupert and Ralph attempted to continue with dialogues—alas, never quite acquiring the same spark. Later, experimenting with at least ten candidates, they searched for a figure who might complete the trio, always falling short of a suitable replacement. These efforts to resurrect the format were taken partly because Abraham thought the key ingredient was a talking trinity. But the success of the format depended on much more than a mathematical formula. It was in fact "totally dependent on Terence's . . . Bardic gift."[54] Which is to say, his prophetic propensity. "For guys like us," McKenna once spoke for all three, "the name of the game is to just be a little bit ahead of everybody else on the curve so that we can perform our function as prophet. But you want to be a prophet, not a false prophet." He was clearly speaking from the standpoint of someone struggling with the implications of his own celebrity: "But the danger comes with the ambition. And there's no way to tease them apart except to live into the future."[55]

CARAVAN OF THE WEIRD

Originating at Esalen, the trialogues became a feature of an impressive annual touring schedule that would, by 1987, take up half of McKenna's time. These public exchanges were pivotal to financial security, demonstrating that the success of the product that he was moving—Terence

McKenna—relied on a combination of information and entertainment. But as a flip side to this success, trouble was brewing at home.

The family moved back to the mainland in late 1987. The grow op had concluded and the cultivation of an audience proceeded in earnest. Terence was not enamored with the prospect of a life on the road. On the one hand, touring was a means to mobilize his talk show and enabled his extraction from growing tensions at home. But constant travel is a cause for anxiety for a cluster headache–prone recluse who loved nothing more than rolling a number in the company of his books. While attempting to balance his reclusiveness with his growing notoriety, being a cave man *and* remaining at the center of attention was no ordinary art.

As much as touring became a source of anxiety, travel is a vocation for which Terence had been conditioned from an early age, when embracing the strange, the eccentric, the alien. In an often reiterated comment on his acquired method, he was passionate about "edge-running": "the oldest books, the weirdest countries, the strangest languages, the most challenging and bizarre psychedelics."[56] It is a curated sensibility. "If a book is not at least one hundred years old don't read it. If a country has more than one international airport don't visit it. If a village has more than one outboard motor don't stay, and just keep pushing and pushing and pushing because out there at the edges . . . the unsanctioned is hidden."[57] Such admonitions modified the alchemical aphorism of German Jesuit scholar and polymath Athanasius Kircher, who wrote: "The highest mountain, the oldest books, the strangest people, there you will find the stone." In a *wyrding* of Kircher, "edge-running" denoted a proclivity for experiencing *otherness* in travels to "places" in the exterior world *and* on the edge of the imagination. "Weird is the compass heading. And if you keep your compass always pointed toward the peculiar, toward the macabre, the bizarre, the unspeakably alien," the byways and tributaries flowing away from mundane thinking are to be discovered. "It's not gonna be on *MTV* . . . it's not going to be in, god forbid, *Esquire*," McKenna claimed.[58] And yet this tendency toward the odd and the alien is not, strictly speaking, a traveler's dictum, for he had no express hankering for the company of *other* people. His desirable destination was the *exotic* mind state—the private trip.

Sojourns of the imagination conducted through exposure to a vast compendium of literary sources provide the backdrop to later travels in the exterior, and into the interior of the exterior. "The stone" had been imagined as a thoroughly achievable object. The search for the ultimate artifact in the Amazon is comprehensible in this light, as is the embrace of shamanism, the center of gravity for the runner of the edge, the ultimate *outré* destination, the place of his calling. As the very interior of this destination, La Chorrera was sacred real estate, the *temenos* of an individual conditioned toward an exceptional state of reception. Spectators at McKenna's first recorded Esalen appearance were presented with the news that shamans are "true phenomenologists of this world." With Terence incredulous as to why he and Dennis were called to be "the ambassadors of an alien species into human culture," the mushroom responded: "Because you have never believed anybody. Because you have never given over your belief to anyone."[59]

The self-projection as a kind of empty vessel is evidently contentious. The perception conveyed at Esalen over a decade later that he could not have cared less about "time" in 1971, that he had been seized without warning by an idea for which he was ungroomed, is specious in the context of a figure preoccupied with eschatology since adolescence. The dubious claims to innocence and purity aside, an open receptivity toward the Other is apparent in the studies, both official and unofficial, to which McKenna gravitated. Through the seventies and into the eighties, he ran ideas at the margins of academia, delivered seminars at private retreats, lectured to independent research societies, and led experiential sessions with the assistance of botanical "allies," becoming a scholar of the edge, upon which he firmly kept one sandaled foot. And while seemingly destined to become a promulgator of maverick ideas and practice in this circuit of eccentricity, given his rare commerce with the anomalous, McKenna became the veritable face, and inimitable voice—a medium no less—of the weird.

So below, as above. McKenna may have been the strange attractor, but the strange was attracted to him in equivalent proportion. He appeared destined to be a centripetal force for the weird—as certain as his eventual appearance in *Esquire*. As was reported in that venue, McKenna never had difficulty locating the person sent to meet him upon his arrival in a strange town. "I'd just look for the most insane person. I knew they were waiting for me."[60]

Travel to a "remote third world country" was imagined a cavalier quest in which the traveler ideally performs the role of "hero." This strategy made a striking contrast with the purpose of the tourist—that loathsome kook who has "I am irrelevant" emblazoned on their forehead. By contrast to these unadventurous flatlanders, one must pursue travel as an "agent" on a "mission." The mushroom was the font of this wisdom, for the voice averred, as it had in the remotest Amazon, that *nature loves courage*, which nature demonstrates by "removing obstacles."[61] Still, such exploits were not executed sans meticulous planning, finely detailed itineraries, and scrupulously categorized supply lists, all designed to mitigate obstacles. One might inquire where the self-serving travels of the freak-hero explorer diverge from the agency of the tourist? And one could object that these freak travails in search of the Other while adorned in white frontier-explorer chic exercised a routine avoidance of locals—that is, other people. Earlier travails were predicated upon a soft colonialist extraction mentality. And by the late eighties, the man who advocated "dematerializing culture" appeared to be growing intimate with an industry otherwise the target of his contempt.

In 1988, McKenna was commissioned by Mel and Patricia Ziegler of Banana Republic clothing to write a travel column titled "Our Man in Nirvana" for new publication, *Trips*. The Zieglers offered to remove obstacles preventing McKenna from pursuing a dream racket, that is, by providing all-expenses-paid exotic travel, paying a buck a word for the reports. It was an offer too difficult to turn down. Billed as the "magazine of authentic travel," *Trips* was scrapped after the first issue. That is, it was decommissioned before McKenna could see his writing in print adjacent to ads for the All-Terrain Pants, the Expedition Flightsuit, and the Israeli Paratrooper Briefcase. But this is not before his first assignment—Koh Samui, Thailand—was completed. The piece is instead published under McKenna's Psychopharmacognosticon column in the R. U. Sirius venture *Reality Hackers*. Clad in Banana Republic "safari drag," in January 1988, Terence "found the world" in Koh Samui, reporting on an island that "swarms with libidinal energy" and promoting the place as "the pearl of Southeast Asia."[62] "Breakthroughs come in strange forms," he writes on a postcard to Metzner featuring an image of Wat Benchamabophit (Marble Temple). "It looks like the doorway to happiness and I want [to] share it. . . . If it wasn't for Kat and the kids I would never come back."[63]

For a self-made intellectual who has no path toward a tenured position, McKenna makes the most of his opportunities. The Our Man in Nirvana junket is a short-lived sideshow in a career in which he behaves like the ultimate head's head. That same year, he appears in a TV studio, taping four episodes of *Thinking Allowed with Jeffrey Mishlove*. The platform affords him the opportunity to wax forth on a broad sweep of interests, from his understanding that the hexagrams of the *I Ching* represent elements of time in a Taoist system to the implications of his perception that "we are an ape with a symbiotic relationship to a mushroom."[64] By this time, McKenna had perfected his own talk show, exemplified by a workshop convened at the California Institute of Integral Studies (CIIS) in San Francisco, in November 1988. Drawing a small room of registrants, possibly displaying his most comprehensive statement across the fields of ethnobotany, psychedelics, and shamanism, his weekend-long "psychobotany" course at the CIIS, "Ethnobotany of Shamanism," was, and remains, a compelling contribution to psychedelic philosophy. Weekend registrants were privileged to a master class on the subject of the *psychedelic other*, that the "mystery of being" is not a romanticized ideal but an existential fact. "There is something that haunts this world, that can take apart and reduce every single one of us to a mixture of terror and ecstasy, fear and trembling," he ventured. From the Amazon basin to his own backyard, McKenna spoke from experience. After indulging the audience with his confrontations with the anomalous in the "new world," the apogee is presented. It is as if "we have discovered another dimension, almost in the same way that Europeans discovered another world only 500 years ago."[65] Oscillating between the poetic and scientific, "Ethnobotany of Shamanism" displays the work of a bard as much as scholar. The material is delivered with such depth of wisdom, candor, and empirical knowledge that on an alternate timeline he might have passed as head of the department of comparative psychedelics.

THE WORM TURNS

With the fall of the Berlin Wall, the end of apartheid, the invention of virtual reality, and the explosion of rave culture all coinciding with McKenna's public emergence, the turn of the nineties is a moment of hope and expectancy. But the era is bittersweet, for it is also a threshold of personal crisis, upheaval, and disappointment. The mood is not unrelated to pecuniary woes, which had reached a flashpoint with the cessation of the mushroom business. While the eighties mark the slow emergence of "Terence McKenna," a book deal remains elusive in a period of growing financial desperation. Obsessions rise and fall. In 1987, putting down Martin Lee and Bruce Shlain's successful exposé of the social history of LSD, *Acid Dreams: The Complete Social History of LSD*, McKenna appears to have grown obsessed with the Psychedelic Rangers, a loose network of acid protagonists connected to Ouija board and tarot deck mystic John Starr Cooke. An early adherent of Dianetics who subsequently fell out with Scientology founder L. Ron Hubbard, Cooke developed an evangelical commitment to acid in the 2,000–3,000 microgram range, and is reputed to be the spiritual architect of The Gathering of the Tribes—the 1967 "be-in" in San Francisco's Golden Gate Park that is routinely hailed to have launched "the Sixties." McKenna grew interested in the "paraplegic witch" Cooke, and details accumulate for a writing project sketching possible links between Cooke and the Process Church of the Final Judgment, and more searchingly, between Cooke, the Haight, Esalen, and Charles Manson, as conveyed in letters to both Watson and purveyor of exotic drug literature Michael Horowitz. Co-instigator of

San Francisco's Fitz Hugh Ludlow Memorial Library, editor of *Lysergic World*, and manager of Flashback Books in Petaluma, Horowitz serves as a literary consultant, over the years receiving requests from and supplying McKenna with many works. Books relating to the Process Church are among requests received at this time. The exposé never materialized.

As the nineties approach, despite the rift at home, and ongoing penury, the worm was turning. McKenna's appearance at the International Transpersonal Association Conference in Santa Rosa, October 9–14, 1988, is something of a turning point. A coterie of intellectual heavyweights are in attendance, among them cultural historian and astrologer Richard Tarnas, the Grofs, Ram Dass, and James Fadiman, a figure who even now remains an unidentified psychopomp from Terence's teenage dreamtime. McKenna is scheduled in parallel with the likes of lama Sogyal Rinpoche and authors Sam Keen and Jack Kornfield. While the venue's large hall stands half empty, his small room is crammed with people standing shoulder to shoulder, with speaker cabinets placed outside the room for the overflow. It is during this conference, or immediately after, that he is signed to literary agent John Brockman Associates. Scouting for talent for Bantam's "New Age" imprint, editor Leslie Meredith is in attendance upon the recommendation of Sheldrake, whom she had signed. Impressed by the "shaggy bard-sage," Meredith meets with McKenna soon afterward and acquires the manuscript for what became *Food of the Gods*.[66]

The end of the recession appears to have commenced with a $50,000 advance from Bantam for a book originally titled "Why Eve Was Right: Plants, Drugs and History." If this contract is the golden opportunity to land his brand, the author is determined to see the job through. The manuscript undergoes six drafts before publication in March 1992. Meanwhile, in the year the drought breaks (1989), he obtains the services of editor Dan Levy, who acquires three books for Carol Publishing Group: the anthology that became *The Archaic Revival* (what Levy calls a "mixtape" of his favorite McKenna materials), *True Hallucinations* (Levy edited the first English print edition), and a new edition of *The Invisible Landscape*. Later, after Levy left Carol Publishing, all three books are acquired by Tom Grady at Harper San Francisco, where Levy works to edit each book.

In a span of a few short years, the writerly toil bears fruit. The twenty-year odyssey of *True Hallucinations* finds a home in print (first, a German-language edition and then via HarperCollins). A theatrical adaptation of the story is a long-running fantasy, with McKenna hinting at "a film soon to be planned around . . . the story of La Chorrera" in the epilogue of *True Hallucinations*.[67] In the long wake of that comment, rumors circulate that he entered negotiations with filmmakers to option his memoir—all unsubstantiated.[68] The *outré* author of the impossible is buoyed by the prospect of achieving the impossible dream: making a living as a legitimate writer. With all four books published in quick succession in the early nineties, there is an explosion of media interest, with speaking invitations attracting audiences of up to 3,000 in Los Angeles and New York.

Though dubious of McKenna's capability of being managed, Levy later adopts a manager-like role. When McKenna tours New York, Levy sometimes likens himself to Norm, the Brian Epstein-inspired manager of the Beatles in *A Hard Day's Night*, available as curtain falls to whisk Terence off to dinner with a select few before the audience has a chance to detain him.[69] During the preparation for *Food of the Gods*, Bantam assigns to McKenna publicist Leslie Rossman. The two become a great team and close friends. When she takes a new job at Harper San Francisco, Rossman continues serving as his publicist (figure 8.5). Via media blitzes, the industrious Rossman enables TM's interface with the world, their partnership pivotal to McKenna's emerging celebrity stature and public life. Among the more memorable events in Rossman's account is a New York launch for *True Hallucinations* in April 1993. Attracting the likes of Christopher Walken and Spin Doctors lead singer Chris Barron, the party is thrown in the loft of illustrator and graphic artist Peter Max.[70]

RAVING POET

In the early to mid-nineties, the Acid House and New Edge scenes sought its champions, and there is no bard more willing than the man who publicly embraced rave culture as an accelerant in the novelty wave. As McKenna became responsible for countless teenagers wigging out to Wittgenstein in dance clubs in London and San Francisco, we must parse a strange scene. As he reflected himself, what should we make of a forty-six-year-old man hanging out at three in the morning "with thousands of loaded teenagers exhorting them to the eschaton"?[71] Rave presented a bizarre spectacle for a figure who dissed parties and who, in Ken Adams's memory, never so much as swiveled his hips. And yet, for a brief moment, the man who, as Harrison remarked, "never learned to let the music in," became an overnight authority on a new dance movement.

Relentlessly pitching the rare package to niche media, Rossman's promotional acumen is instrumental to the media tsunami upon which McKenna surfed. "Why are these young [ravers] adopting McKenna as their guru?"

FIGURE 8.5
McKenna with publicist Leslie Rossman, San Francisco, 1992. Courtesy of Leslie Rossman.

Scene media reps are enticed by press releases spinning his unique attributes: his lectures are sampled by musicians, and he is hyped as "the first author to be the center performer at a rave."[72] McKenna remained ambivalent about these plaudits. It might be convenient to view his rave moment somewhere between midlife crisis and gratuitous opportunism. Financial pressures and the need to support his family were chief compulsions. And yet, the intellectual apologia for raving is not without a pedigree. Not unlike his mentor, Marshall McLuhan, McKenna genuinely recognized the role of the artist as seer—a recognition pursued to his own end. His sincerity with regard to the visionary potential of art was unimpeachable. Creative play, visionary art, and ecstatic dance were all pivotal to what McKenna saw as the coming transit in which ravers are championed as agents of cultural transcendence and consciousness evolution. More to the point, the raver, and more specifically the crusty-traveler and techno-raver hybrid, encapsulated the Orphic tradition of dissent and Eros he long intuited to be the fate of artists, bohemians, and ecstatics reaching back before Chalcolithic Greece and now achieving an eschatonic crescendo. Rave, in other words provided evidence for the much-vaunted "archaic revival."

Short of bootstrapping the coming transition, rave would bootstrap McKenna himself. For a brief moment in the early nineties he became involved in several performance and recording collaborations in London and San Francisco. Although these are projects of a different nature, a collaboration with musicians is traceable to the early eighties, when Nomadband recorded the "talking book" soundtrack, including synthesizer-derived electronic squiggles that conjured the "radio entelechy" and howling "elf chatter" of the recounted "Kathmandu Interlude" in *True Hallucinations*. A decade later, McKenna serves as honorary raver in residence at various clubs, becoming, by the time he finally left the building, a speaker in great demand at festivals worldwide. En route, he became an unassuming figurehead for enthusiasts within the broad networks of psychedelic electronica—where he continues to serve as surreal psychopomp to this day.

A conduit for McKenna's entry to the rave scene is Ken Adams, the experimental filmmaker who was captivated by the bard's voice. A digital media artist dwelling in the East Village of the eighties, Adams was drawn to California to capture the source of his inspiration. Adams and then wife (and partner in media production outfit Rose X), Britt Welin, eventually rendezvous with the psychedelic pied piper at Esalen in the summer of 1989, when they decide to collaborate on experimental "artfilms." The couple become neighbors in Occidental where on one afternoon over at Terence and Kat's place the conversation turns to music. A box of Dead live tapes is produced.

"This is cool," Adams says, "but there's another kind of thing happening in the psychedelic world called 'raves,' and they make electronic dance music and they do a lot of psychedelics." He looks at Terence. "And they all think that you are some kind of special guy." While the entreaty is met with skepticism, Adams begins exposing his friend to new sounds, like The Orb's *Little Fluffy Clouds*. It wasn't easy to plant a seed of possibility in the mind of a reclusive figure lukewarm toward parties and who valued his free time.

"Terence, I've never seen you without your beard," Welin remarks.

"Well, nobody else has either."

"What are you talking about?"

"From the beginning of puberty on I just never shaved my beard because I thought I was ugly."

The admission reveals an insecurity that the visitors find heartbreaking. Would McKenna back away from attention that could afford him and his kids a future? The possibility made him anxious. Would he become victim to the quenchless demands of micro-celebrityhood or adapt his growing popularity to his own ends? It isn't long before McKenna opens a new chapter in his life and breaks through to a much younger demographic—even while the beard remains.[73]

Another paver of the path to fame is techno-hippie trickster and founder and editor of the magazines *Encyclopaedia Psychedelica* and *Evolution*, Fraser Clark. The flourishing of Acid House in the late-eighties United Kingdom was met by the wild Scotsman as the renaissance of sixties idealism. As a techno-tribal revitalization of Albion, the psychedelic edges of this scene resonated with the "archaic revival." Clark knew a good rave when he heard one. Running with McKenna's "stoned ape" speculations, Clark brokers the New Age traveler and techno merger as a redemptive millennial reclamation. In turn, Clark's own utopian zeal toward the "RAVeLATION" does not fail to impress McKenna.[74] When McKenna is promoting *The Archaic Revival* in London in October 1991, Clark invites him to speak at the proto "festi-club" Evolution. Two audience members are especially eager to be introduced to McKenna after the show, whereupon they invite the bard of hyperspace to collaborate on a spoken-word "Rave" track. It seems Terence is made an offer he could not refuse. The duo are Colin Angus (another Scotsman) and Richard West (a.k.a. Mr. C), of pioneer indie-dance act and "twenty first century Grateful Dead,"[75] the Shamen. McKenna visits the Shamen's Camden studio on October 16 when his oratory is recorded to digital audio tape.[76] The recorded rave becomes the proto-mix for McKenna's ticket to the world.

Angus is an enabler. In the early nineties, the pioneering indie rocker–turned-electronic musician sought to use the Shamen's growing fame to create an elevated platform for McKenna. The track they produce, "Re:Evolution," encapsulates Angus's desire to showcase McKenna's hyperbolic oratory over acidic instrumentation. When they tour the US West Coast in January 1992, Angus and West meet with Adams, who drives them up to McKenna's house. Everyone gets baked and they play their seven-plus-minute demo, now with backing track. "Gentlemen, I hope we shall not be accused of demagoguery," McKenna announces.[77]

"If the truth could be told so as to be understood, it will be believed." By 1992/93, BBC Radio One listeners were tuning in to McKenna paraphrasing William Blake. "The 20th century is the shudder that announces the approaching cataracts of time over which our species and the destiny of this planet is about to be swept."[78] The result of a single take that Terence thought was a job interview (and which he later deems "artless"), featured on the Shamen's double platinum album *Boss Drum*, "Re:Evolution" was on its way to becoming one of the strangest hits to ever make top twenty on the UK Singles Chart.[79] The expanding constituency is informed that rave was rediscovering "the art of natural magic with sound" and that "large groups of people getting together in the presence of this kind of music are creating a telepathic community, a bonding that, hopefully, will be strong enough to carry the vision out into the mainstream of society." On the version McKenna performs at San Francisco's Warfield Theatre on November 7, 1992, "rave culture" is championed as "the real new world order," with its habitués beseeched directly by a figure coming over like the Jim Jones of pop: "Take back the planet—it's yours, it's yours. These are the last minutes of human history folks. The countdown is on. This is not a test. We're leaving this world behind, for a brighter, better world that has always existed; in our imagination."

It is an extraordinary message for a hit single. The celebrity stature deriving from McKenna's association with the Shamen is tinged with irony. As everyone on the streets knew, the Shamen's chart-topping single "Ebeneezer Goode," also released on *Boss Drum*, was a sonic billboard for MDMA. That is, it promoted a substance McKenna imagined in his preacherly moments to be part of the trash peddled among the "whores of mammon." He had long committed to distinguishing "shamanic" plants from what he saw as "onanistic" and "soulless" drugs. In his 1987 CIIS lecture, McKenna contended that taking MDMA was akin to masturbation vis-à-vis experiencing "the felt presence of the other."[80] Much later, in *Mother Jones*, readers are urged to take the three-step "drug test." Does the substance occur in nature? Is it close to compounds naturally present in the human brain? Does it have a history of human use for thousands of years?[81] In application of Sheldrake's theory of morphic resonance, it is long affirmed that, by comparison to MDMA, "plants have souls" as they carry the morphogenetic field of thousands of years:

> When you take psilocybin it also takes you, you are participating in all of the trips that were ever induced in anyone. This is a tremendously stable field of experience. When you take a drug straight out of the laboratory [by which he meant MDMA and ketamine], it has no soul. It has no story, it has no direction. It's a product of the daemon artifice of man.[82]

Illustrious chemist and rediscoverer of MDMA, Alexander Shulgin, was in the Esalen audience when McKenna expressed the rank dichotomy: drugs that come from labs are "suspect" compared with "natural" products deriving from plants. "But Terence, I'm as natural as they come,"[83] Shulgin responds.

Moreover, the drug dubbed "ecstasy" was, McKenna contended, hardly a tool enabling access to the *Mysterium tremendum*; to the psychedelic sublimity he valued as a source of authentic experience. But excluding MDMA from the soulful vegetal kingdom, or questioning its relationship with the sublime, had limited appeal among the rave-going populace, whose participants later voted MDMA number one among twenty "defining moments of the greatest cultural phenomenon of our generation" (i.e., raves and clubbing).[84] It also held little truck within the underground psychiatric community, in which the compound became highly valued as a therapeutic aid. On this subject, Multidisciplinary Association for Psychedelic Studies founder Rick Doblin stated that McKenna's early objections to MDMA were so frustrating that, in 1984, his comments served as a catalyst for a "secret safety study" that was the first step on the long road to sanctioning MDMA as an assisted therapy.[85]

If the Shamen generated controversy and pushback at the BBC, in the music industry, and among the tabloids, their association with the man whom *the List* announced as the "wizened psychedelic guru," and *New Musical Express* saw as "not your average acid casualty,"[86] likely assisted the strife. McKenna might have missed out on performing at the Brits Awards, but his celebrity status garnered press for *Food of the Gods*, in which "psychedelic shamans" were observed to "constitute a worldwide and growing subculture of hyperdimensional explorers."[87] This Golden Age fantasy appealed to shamanarchists assembling under the full moon and embracing the mushroom as a lifestyle staple. Fictive vignettes in *Food of the Gods* divulged a fantasy of clan members of "the Paleolithic cult of the Great Horned Goddess" who "swallow the body of the Goddess" at primitive full moon parties where "heavy foot stamping channeled the energy of the first wave of visions." It is not difficult to imagine the audience at the Evolution Records event at the Camden Centre on June 15, 1992, identifying as participants in reclaimed dance rituals in which they are "dissolved in the higher wordless truth of ecstasy."[88] Such descriptions are well received by a generation exposed to the psychedelic rave communitas and anxious about the planetary future. Whispering his promise to the disenchanted, "Re:Evolution" amplified the gospel to a wider audience. As a "telepathic community of bonding," McKenna proclaimed from his podium on the Hit Parade, rave "is the cutting edge of the last best hope for suffering humanity."

At the Camden Centre, DMT was championed among a congress of heads and skeptics as the fastest route to the mystery. "If flying saucers were to land on the front lawn of Buckingham Palace tomorrow," it would be of scant interest next to a ten-minute venture promoted as "incontrovertible evidence of the presence of the transcendental in our lives."[89] Among those rising to the challenge is Nik Sequenci, who plays ambient backing music on McKenna's early nineties UK tours. Compelled to drop into the novelty wave, Sequenci soon finds himself custodian of a quantity of transdimensional board wax—which he called the "pink power"—sent to him by McKenna. During one episode, Sequenci is visited by elves that implore him to return to Earth to make psychedelic trance music.[90] Unable to himself transpose these visions into sound, he seeks out Martin Glover, a.k.a. "Youth," studio production dynamo at Brixton's Butterfly Records. Subsequently, Youth invites Raja Ram, among others, to a ceremonial smoke-out with the pink power in the back garden at Butterfly in 1992. The occasion is momentous, catalyzing the birth of seminal Goa trance label Dragonfly Records, and the formation of the lead act in the psychedelic diaspora, Shpongle.[91] As a consequence, although himself an unwitting midwife, Goa trance and its cultural progeny gain near-mythic inspiration from a bag of DMT sourced from McKenna.[92]

McKenna's role in the birth of Goa trance, psytrance, and its progeny is a strange development. And all the more so because, in his short-lived guise as journalist on assignment in the region, he had made a brief stop in Goa in February–March 1988.[93] It is possible that McKenna arrived in the former Portuguese colony of India courtesy of the Zieglers. Regardless, it is synchronous that McKenna lands in Goa at this juncture. The 1988 season would be catalytic to the Goa "trance dance" scene. While there was to be no Our Man in Nirvana column capturing the freak paradise on the Arabian Sea, McKenna's presence in Goa at this time is more than curious given the botanical tryptaminal aesthetic that suffused post-Goa psychedelic sounds in the wake of his own beneficence. Given the frequency with which McKenna's voice is sampled within Goa, psytrance, and its wider sonic progeny, including post-genres like psybient, "psychedelic trance" is a cultural movement in which McKenna's thought-forms have forged deep grooves.[94] So much as his generosity impacted the Goa trance movement at its place of birth, McKenna had touched Goa with his oblations a decade earlier. As Tom Cole writes, over several years in the early eighties, McKenna "donated a sizable jar stuffed with dried magic mushrooms for the people in Goa." A frequent Goa flier, Cole dutifully couriered and distributed the bounty.[95]

The high point in McKenna's rave career is San Francisco collaborative multimedia rave, and *True Hallucinations* launch, Alien Dreamtime. The brainchild of Adams, Alien Dreamtime is mounted in the SoMa district on 11th Street near Folsom on February 26–27, 1993. Held without rehearsals, or a license, the event takes place in a warehouse—dubbed The Transmission Theatre—leased by a real estate entrepreneur. The event provides McKenna the opportunity to belt out his greatest hits supported by Jonah Sharp's techno-ambient arrangement, Space Time Continuum, and didgeridooista Stephen Kent, with live video mixing by Rose X. Footage shot by Rose X would be used for the documentary film *Alien Dreamtime* (see figure 8.6).[96]

As a high-water mark of the San Francisco rave scene before it became a club, warehouse, beach, or desert scene, at Alien Dreamtime it was impossible to distinguish random barefoot overalls-wearing pot smokers from future leaders of the tech industry. As Adams reflects, the event served as a platform for the "ideational matrix" that allowed participants "to feel confident about going forward and taking risks"—a proof of concept soon subject to serious performance testing. When the space filled around midnight on the opening night, over a dozen police officers move in. As the cops pushed people around, and pulled plugs on video equipment, McKenna steps onto the stage. "We're being visited by some of San Francisco finest," the crowd are entreated. "If you have a camera of any sort, come to the front of the stage and point it at a cop." People respond as instructed, green-lit camcorders effectively freezing the fuzz in their tracks. "They weren't ready for this," Adams recalls, noting the retreat of the police who were unprepared for such an organized response from the large crowd.[97]

On the following night filming is again disrupted as the cops returned with a vengeance. It is an unlicensed all-ages event, and the authorities are bent on preventing the corruption of innocence. Keen to meet the police with a "force" of their own, patrons started dancing as a means to protect the stage. These kids were "dancing away the fear," says Adams. It is a tense

FIGURE 8.6
Poster for the screening of *Alien Dreamtime*, ca. 1994. Courtesy of Michael Horowitz.

and high-stakes situation. Adams convenes with a senior cop and the property owner in the latter's office. The silver-haired, buttoned-up character from a Superman comic gnaws away at both men. "We're not going to have *psychedelic* preached in my precinct," the badge snarls. The owner takes the heavy handle of his baked ceramic phone off the desk and announces that he's dialing "the Mayor." The officer shifts with skepticism. "There's a show going on," the owner explains to a voice on the other end of the line, "and there's a cop in here with his foot on my neck. I want you to get this Nazi out of here!" He hands the phone to the cop who realizes he is being grilled by a high-ranking city official at 2:00 a.m. on a Sunday morning. When "the Mayor" disconnects, the officer throws the phone with great force into the desk and departs. It is an unexpected outcome and a clarifying moment of power alignment. Permission had arrived from the top. The show would go on.[98]

And the show did go on. Clark was a main conspirator in the revitalizing movement McKenna championed. In his quest for a "Future Perfect State," Clark divined how new club cultures were contexts for inter-dimensional travel. The critical hub was London's Megatripolis, at the Marquee on Charing Cross Road, where McKenna appeared on opening night in 1993 (together with Nik Sequenci, Tribal Energy, Solar Quest, and Mixmaster Morris), returning for a Parallel YOUniversity lecture the following year. Since Clark imagineered Megatripolis as a future memory and learning model for the Megatripolitan Utopia to which humanity was destined, his techno-organic science-futurism aligned with McKenna's vision of the "transcendental object." Back across the Atlantic, speaking at the launch of Clark's Zippy Pronoia Tour of the United States at Wetlands Preserve nightclub in Manhattan on June 15, 1994 ("Z Day"), McKenna announced that "every fifty years or so, society needs liberation from the forces of fascism." Fifty years since Hiroshima, and as representatives of a third British cultural wave, after the Beatles and the Sex Pistols, "a vanguard of liberators has secured a beach head on the east coast of America, and has begun to work its way inland along the Hudson."[99]

By this stage, McKenna is already on the other side of his rave spike. During a *Mondo 2000* interview, about to make a call with Billy Idol's manager, producer Xandor Korzybski asks Terence—already pitched as the "Rave Philosopher King"—if he might like to perform an entrée or a cameo in upcoming shows with Idol. The bemused McKenna balks. "I'm still assessing my status as 'the rave king,'" he responds. Was this a credible role for "a hermit book collector"?[100] I have no idea how that conversation played out, but McKenna would not appear as the "Rave Philosopher King," with Billy Idol, nor otherwise.

"This is a strange thing to happen to a philosopher," McKenna reflects while taking stock of his career in the familiar confines of Esalen in August 1993. Like an intrepid returnee from an off-planetary venture, he describes how he had recently found himself in clubs at four in the morning "raving at people at high decibel with the perfect knowledge that they couldn't understand a word I was saying."[101] The live rave format was not an ideal context for transmitting his content. It was a disappointment that these scenes were, he thought, tone-deaf to his ideas. He may have become heroically devoted to banging out the "shamanarchy" to young people inside the precincts of the vibe, but ultimately the club scene was "designed to suppress the content of the psychedelic experience."[102] What's more, the raving philosopher saw little appeal in all-night parties. He struggles with this ambivalence in the few short years remaining. He attends few NorCal parties and, as Adams notes, never makes Burning Man when given the chance. Parties were by and large "a distraction for narcissists," gravitational fields for seekers of hip who weren't paying their dues. McKenna wasn't antisocial, but parties could not compete with solitude as a motivation. Besides, it was his conviction that music, *any* music, provided inappropriate context for experiments with magic plants. He once tried listening to Karlheinz Stockhausen while on DMT, but only to his great alarm. "Let the Pythagorean inner music issue from your soul," instead.[103]

As he abhorred the concept of "recreational drugs," I imagine McKenna's ambivalence toward the dance parties and festivals that have worldwide over the last two decades become optimal sites for psychonautical experimentation. This is an ironic situation given that his stature as a meta-trip sitter for new generations would be incubated in these venues. Despite his own likely objections, as an extraordinary feature of his legacy, with the assistance of the cybercultural surround he championed, McKenna retains a disembodied presence in the popular underground of music making and performance, where his sampled sound bites amplify the most mediated voice in the history of electronic music.

His career as raving front man and posthumous psychopomp is a remarkable development for a figure whose own musical tastes were modest. This said, late in his life, McKenna did express a preference for drone music. In a 1996 interview with members of the European experimental band Coil we catch a glimpse of what the McKenna sound might have been like in the unlikely event that he formed a band of his own. Drone is "my idea of what experimental music is supposed to sound like,"[104] he informed the duo.

The post-divorce era also coincided with an enthusiasm for a European city that he regarded with great affection after his first visit in 1990. In the immediate wake of the Velvet Revolution, when it remained capital of Czechoslovakia, Prague represented, McKenna informed Esalenites, "an opportunity to redefine freedom." He had delivered a lecture at the Prague film academy and visited the National Museum's Department of Mycology, where he deposited spore prints and copies of the *Grower's Guide*. The Slavs, a mycophilic people not unlike the Celts, were quite amenable to the prospect of growing mushrooms.[105] Prague was charming, not only by virtue of its historical status as "the capital of European civilization" before the rise of modern science, or as a beautiful Italianate city untouched by the world wars, but since it represented an affordable place to live. "I haven't had the feeling I get in Prague," *The Idler* was informed, "since I looked out over Berkeley in 1967."[106]

Fresh from a further visit to the city in June 1992, when he shot a series of interviews later collectively titled *Prague Gnosis*, McKenna's enthusiasm for Prague, and for the country soon to become the Czech Republic, grew. "Czechoslovakia is Oz for grownups," he declared at the Earth Trust conference in Los Angeles in October. If the "capital of old Bohemia" could in the nineties be what Paris was in the twenties, it would be the ideal location for an "archaic revival."[107] In the immediate wake of his imploded matrimonial union, Prague becomes the site of a renewed effort to realize the stone. Through the course of his affair with the "new Jerusalem," McKenna collaborates with Czech video art pioneers and founders of the Kitchen in Greenwich Village, Steina and Woody Vasulka, on a "think tank" attuned to the Prague Renaissance and to establishing "a locus for an expatriate critique of American society."[108] In a rare circumstance where his typically unallied radicalism approximated a model for change, McKenna assures the Earth Trust audience that it is "very important when you're trying to make social change that you find the proper resting place for your fulcrum." And the best place for that, he said, was "outside the system that you're trying to move."[109] Outside the system, the Bohemian Institute of Prague was envisioned as an art gallery, club, hostel, publisher, and software and video production facility, with attached private apartments for use by "rotating managers and staff." The Institute was to be a community founded on art and ideas "true to the original alchemical spirit of old Bohemia."[110] They seek to establish the Institute in the summer of 1992 following the International Transpersonal Association conference at Charles University at which McKenna entreats investors to raise $30–40,000. The money is never raised, the Bohemian Institute a forgotten blip in McKenna's imagination.

FREAK-IN-CHIEF

Somewhere between raconteur and scholar, intellectual and pop star, McKenna was in the early nineties searching for the ideal platform, space, and community to move and shake his ideas. Academia, rave, Prague: none were the solution. With several books now on the market, there is a steady stream of launches locked into crowded touring schedules with appearances at independent symposia, fringe meetings, and new psychedelic conferences where he is not untypically the main attraction. In February 1991, McKenna is anchorman for the Bridge, a psychedelic conference at Stanford University where in impassioned closing remarks he damns the fresh "abomination" of the Gulf War. As Adams recalls, "raising holy hell" and going after the "war mongers," McKenna channeled the zeitgeist. Many in the audience respond by standing in their seats, screaming and howling.[111] His presence is drawn to other meetings like Bioneers and the conferences of the International Transpersonal Association. But standing beyond these seasonal meetings, by far the most important event, culturally and personally, is Entheobotany, the intensive seminars and conference operating between 1994 and 2001, for the most part at Chan-Kah resort in Chiapas, Mexico.

In walking distance from the ruins of Palenque, regularly sharing the program with the likes of Jonathan Ott, C. Manuel Torres, Rob Montgomery, Paul Stamets, Alexander and Ann Shulgin, and Christian Rätsch, McKenna co-teaches the "Ethnobotany and Chemistry of Psychoactive Plants" course organized by the Botanical Preservation Corps. Cofounded by Ken Symington, Montgomery, Ott, and McKenna himself, part knowledge exchange and part fiesta at the height of mushroom season, Entheobotany becomes a pivotal pilgrimage destination for McKenna's caravan of the weird. So synonymous with Entheobotany would McKenna become over six seasons in Mexico that when he suddenly disappeared, so did Entheobotany. In subsequent years, the seasonal soirees migrated to a new watering hole: Nevada's Black Rock Desert. Under the guidance of Lorenzo Hagerty, and with McKenna serving as its patron saint, the Palenque Norte speaker series started up at Burning Man in 2003.

But back in the early nineties, McKenna was growing a reputation that would see his road show traverse the country and forge a path to international audiences primed for his rap. The full-page spread in the *New York Times* in May 1993, in which McKenna is officially anointed the "Timothy Leary" of "the discretely psychedelic nineties," is a high-water mark. "With piercing deep-set eyes and a scraggly beard," McKenna is described as owning a "cheerfully demonic look," with his audience typecast as "mostly hirsute forty-somethings, like the characters in a Koren cartoon." With the *Times*'s disparagement of McKenna's polysyllabic efforts to lend credibility to "the otherwise debunked subject of drugs," it seemed that the ultimate prize—"the stone"—was more akin to a Sisyphean boulder nudged uphill. And yet such appearances in the media became an effective means to wheel his psychedelic Trojan horse inside the popular mindset. "What the mushroom says," McKenna announced in the same article, "is that the planet is in mortal peril. . . . And psychedelics are the way forward." The soundbites were irresistible. "I don't understand why drugs are not used as tools of research," he is reported to state. "You want to know how the atom works? Smash it and look at the pieces. You want to know how the mind works? Get it smashed and then see what the pieces are."[112]

Through the early nineties, McKenna's views are plastered across the print universe, from fanzines to the *LA Times*, from *Magical Blend* to *i-D Magazine*. Seasoned and prepared journalists sign up for remarkable intellectual exchanges. Mark Dery had a "zero tolerance policy toward New Age vacuity," but in an interview originally published in *21C* magazine he finds in McKenna a "foeman worthy of anyone's steel."[113] While interviewers are often invited to his home, one venue became prized above all: Esalen's outdoor baths. When Paul Krassner is granted this opportunity in 1997, he appears to have failed to follow protocol. "The first thing you notice about the naked men and women soaking in the outdoor hot springs overlooking the Pacific Ocean," he observes, "is that they all seem to maintain excellent eye contact while they engage in conversation." He is no hot springs native, however, for when McKenna eventually rises to leave, Krassner remarks, "I can't help but notice that not only is he well hung, but also that he is much too tall to be a leprechaun."[114]

Throughout the nineties, McKenna makes over twenty-five appearances in New York City. Next to the Big Island, Manhattan, he claimed, was his second favorite island. For his first East Coast appearance, in March 1990, he was invited to share his views in a salon at the Reality Club under the invitation of John Brockman.[115] A few months later, McKenna returned to Manhattan under the auspices of the New York Open Center, which, as a popular institution for the holistic education and wellness community of that city, became something of an urban Esalen. On his opening night, he appeared before 800 people in the Great Hall at Cooper Union. Winding down, at the end of the weekend at the Comedy Club atmosphere of Wetlands, Barry Bloch's Tribeca activist nightclub once described as "the Fillmore of the 1990s," J. P. Harpignies introduced McKenna as a "national treasure," suggesting that a "museum" should be built to house his mind.[116]

As program director at the Open Center, Harpignies booked McKenna's events between 1990 and 1994. Pivotal to McKenna's early NYC success, Harpignies recalls the irony he posed. Where some of the hardcore meditation presenters he booked could be disorganized and difficult, "this guy with a reputation as a wild druggy turned out to be a consummate professional."[117] Though impressed by McKenna's brilliance and wildly speculative theories, Harpignies wasn't a "true believer." He was concerned that the "heroic dose" discourse posed real dangers, and did not share McKenna's contempt for non-drug means of consciousness expansion. That said, he became deeply impressed with McKenna's linguistic genius, such that he sought to pair him with social philosopher and then Open Center "scholar-in-residence" William Irwin Thompson. As highly literate and charismatic outsider intellectuals, they seemed a perfect couple for the "Visions of the 21st Century" speaker series. Unfortunately, Thompson, a dedicated yoga practitioner and somewhat puritanically disdainful of drugs, was loath to share the stage with McKenna. He did, however, attend McKenna's Great Hall speech, commenting afterward, "I did not agree with a single word that that man uttered, but I was astonished because his sentences were paragraphs long but all perfectly syntactically accurate. They all held together grammatically, impeccably." Thompson, who had taught cultural history at MIT, and who described his writing and speaking style as "mind-jazz," was envious. Undeniably eloquent himself, he could not match McKenna's wildly inventive but syntactically precise oratory.[118]

From the Open Center to the Great Hall to rented music clubs, over the next decade, the "psychoactivist" appeared before NYC audiences that he respected for their critical abilities and receptivity. With its signature VW Microbus merch booth inside the front entrance, a refuge for freaks, slackers, and alt-rockers, Wetlands stands out among a variety of local venues that are safe havens for trialing bits, notably of the "mushroom once told me . . ." variety. In one such case, "somebody" is reported to have disclosed an evaluation about himself: "Loves mankind, loathes individual human beings." The insight arriving from the stand-up philosopher's *higher* self is clarified: "I don't loathe individual human beings, but I do enjoy things the further I stand back from them." Whether taking aim at his own foibles or streaming consciousness on the landscape of the future, McKenna navigates between the sagacious and the surreal with remarkable dexterity. When opening up on the super-barn of syntax, the future is said to possess an "extravagant Pynchonesque kind of efflorescence about it that rides right on the edge of insanity." The seasoned edge runner knew the terrain. "What we've shipped for," his Wetlands hearties are assured, "is not a voyage of discovery, it's more like a ship of fools." While the future might have been something that "Hieronymus Bosch or Pieter Brueghel the Elder could appreciate," it is "probably best summed up in the work of Groucho Marx."[119]

ANTIPODEAN ADVENTURES

As the nineties wear on, McKenna embarks upon ventures to southern climes, starting with the trip to South Africa in October 1996, where he has a week-long appearance at a ranch in Rustlers Valley, at 6,000 feet in the Maluti Mountains. As is evident in *The Terence McKenna Omnibus 2012*, produced by Cape Town filmmaker Mike Kawitzky,[120] the Esalen of South Africa was a comfortable and intimate context for the delivery of, and engagement with, McKenna's ideas. High up in the Malutis, Terence is in high spirits, assisted by a mushroom trip with Kawitzky, a lightly dosed odyssey that countered any misperception that McKenna had a "zero tolerance" policy on mushrooms.[121] Contrary to its position in the antipodes, the wild landscape of Rustlers Valley proves reminiscent of those dry arroyos in Moab, Utah, and the Four Corners region where ten-year-old Terry hunted for fossils and flints. His "reflex" is to revert to the activities of his childhood by hunting alone in the dongas where he claimed success in uncovering "flint cores, scrappers, and stone tools." "The archaeologist at the end of the bar was happy to inform me," he claimed, "that nothing gathered during my afternoon's walk was less than 65,000 years [old]."[122]

We learn of the South African "caper" via *Journey to Everywhere*, the book chronicling the adventures of Kawitzky's "cybershamanic" alter-ego Schwann.[123] With McKenna lodged permanently behind Kawitzky's eyelids, and pregnant with psychedelic misadventure in the style of *Fear and Loathing*, *Journey to Everywhere* offers a gonzoidal narrative on the production history of Kawitzky's 2009 "smart film" *Cognition Factor*. Kawitzky befriended McKenna on The Well (Whole Earth 'Lectronic Link) and alt news groups in the early nineties. "I was like a magician," Kawitzky recalls, "who could reach into the web and pull out anyone I wanted." Terence manifested and Schwann became his "outpost" in South Africa. With the aid of reproduced email dialogue exchanged during the medium's protean phase, *Journey to Everywhere* documents the ensuing "cyber-telepathea." Kawitzky planned to drive McKenna from Rustlers Valley through the Karoo to Cape Town in his 1967 Pontiac GTO. Terence had been informed about how his prospective driver had recently survived a busted gasket, carbon monoxide poisoning, and a high-speed tire blowout in the same vehicle. Learning about the death trap that might have passed for Stephen King's "Christine," he thought better of the idea and took a flight instead.[124]

Four months later, McKenna returns to the Southern Hemisphere, arriving in Australia as a scene beacon. The main event in the two-week Archaic Revival tour is Beyond the Brain, a legendary three-day multimedia dance event at the Byron Bay Epicentre, an ex-whaling station transformed by an underground network into a "crucible of creativity." The eighth in a series of Beyond the Brain events, Forward the Future was a conflux of dance party, visionary art exhibition, and performance theater created by the intrepid web of creatives who had migrated to the region (see figure 8.7).

McKenna assumed the stage on Saturday night headlining a show with a cast of thousands. Beyond the Brain events were known for dissolving the boundary separating audience from performer. But as McKenna mounted the mushroom dais in the Cycad Garden and sat cross-legged before a large audience (750-plus), that boundary became unambiguous. Quietening the crowd, McKenna became the epicenter of the spectacle, his delivery slow and deliberate. "I think you have to be humble enough to eat what grows in shit to pass through the gateway." Layered with Wallace Stevens, W. H. Auden, and a full recital of Lewis Carroll's "Jabberwocky," it is a spellbinding performance, the recording of which lay in limbo for a quarter century—that is, until 2023, when *Beyond the Brain with Terence McKenna* was finally released. A skillful re-suturing of recovered footage produced by Paul Chambers, the film is framed around McKenna's rap in three acts, while at the same time opening a window on a lost moment in the technoferal efflorescence of the late-nineties Byron region. With the visitor serving as narrator, the film furnishes a tripartite passage from interstellar spores,

FIGURE 8.7
Poster for Forward the Future (including Beyond the Brain 8), Byron Bay, Australia, February 21—23, 1997. Flyer artwork by Alex Clarke, courtesy of Paul Chambers.

through DMT breakthrough, to "where we might be going," corresponding with edited footage (Beyond the Brain setup, dance party, and morning aftermath). The film faithfully conveys each of McKenna's acts separated as they are by short musical interludes performed by onetime "cyberdelic supergroup," Pangalacticspermia.[125]

Afforded an elevated position at this peak moment in Aussie freaklore, the occasion was extraordinary for a figure who had never before set foot on the continent. But if psychedelic royalty existed, McKenna was both crown prince and funny bugger for whom the red carpet was rolled out. Throughout his great southern interlude, the visitor was received more like an alien ambassador, or a visitor from another dimension, than a celebrity from the United States. During his tour, and as the outcome of dialogue with local botany buffs and tryptamine tweakers, the visitor shared the wisdom that DMT could be extracted from species of local *acacia*. "The national symbol of Australia is the wattle," he conveyed in evocative terms. "It's an *acacia*. The *acacia* ecology of Australia is jammed with DMT."[126] Legend had it that McKenna's cutting of *B. caapi* was the first import of the ayahuasca vine in Australia. Some in the crowd had long sourced DMT from species of *acacia*, potentiated with MAO-inhibiting harmala alkaloids. These botanical cognoscenti understood that a trove of DMT-bearing plants grew in their own backyard. As Neil Pike, from the band Pagan Love Cult, reminisced, "big joints of wattle" were passed through the audience.[127]

By the beginning of his second act, the visitor was suitably impressed when noting an unmistakable aroma in the night air. "It was as though the air had suddenly been pumped out of the room, and everything stood out in stark relief." The otherwise raucous audience grew so engrossed with the visitor's description of his novice DMT event you could hear a septum pin drop to the floor. The bard's parting comments on "a new dispensation for language through sound conceived of as a union of poetry and music" provided the perfect incantation for the heavily edited and sometimes haunting vision of an ecstatic ensemble of local artists.[128]

Tour promotor Dillon Hicks shuttles the visitor between a series of east coast gigs in a Nissan Micra. Riding shotgun in a dodgem car and mobbed by locals gifting home grown treats, McKenna delivers his greatest hits in measured, albeit weary, cadence. The tour features over ten engagements, including student pub gigs, a private seminar, a live experimental improv evening under the auspices of Clan Analogue at the University of Sydney, and a cabaret named Diablo Musica at Sydney's Harbourside Brasserie, with McKenna eventually appearing in the south of Victoria at TrancElements 2, where ambient backing tunes are spun by Psyharmonics Records legend

Ollie Olsen. At Wollongong University a few days later, a question from the audience prompts an hour-long response. "The interesting thing about psychedelics," McKenna exhorted the feraliens and old dreamtimers present, is that, as "training wheels for true being," they reveal "all ideologies [as] crap games." As this freshly uncovered rap demonstrates, the shaman-archist entered into a flow state in which the mushroom-munching, trance-dancing, tattooed, scarified, sexually diverse, and higher-dimensionally curious learned that they are themselves an expression of the "impulse towards the archaic."[129]

Speaking in Austin later that year, the frequent flier reflects on Australians as a "very eccentric population of hard driving folks who are lovely to party with and know how to barbecue." Had he known what he then knew about Australia thirty years before, he is sure, he said, "my life would be very different."[130] But the tour also demonstrated the hectic reality of life on the road for the recent quinquagenarian. With barely a moment for pause, the trip was an exhausting reminder that Terence would rather appear non-locally when addressing crowds in far-flung locations about the significance of the "non-local universe of information." Not long afterward, he travels to Mesa, Arizona, where Joe McKenna had retired with his second wife. Terence's relationship with his father was rarely more than distant, albeit with a mood of growing mutual tolerance. Repeatedly suffering heart failure, and being kept alive on a defibrillator, Joe's machine was finally switched off in late April.

* * *

Through the eighties and nineties, McKenna grew to become a high-wire act in a global freak show. What in the early nineties was glossolalia emitted during readings in small book stores in the United Kingdom had by the late nineties transmuted into exotic chanting performed as part of live guest appearances with Maui ethno-trance act Lost at Last. The figure who had long extemporized on the efficacy of singing rather than clenching through rough psychedelic states became Ecstatic Emeritus for the Maui group. The freak flag was strung aloft at San Francisco's Maritime Hall on December 12, 1998. Appearing in a hooded garment, speaking of the "opalescent expressenses of the abyss," and enunciating "the living language that pours from the psychedelic body," McKenna broke into unidentifiable ululations before appreciative fans.[131] We have ventured a great distance in a chapter that has explored the evolution of McKenna's consummate word craft and rise to fame. A figure who barely identified with the underground populist movement ironically ended up becoming its strange spokesperson.

As his unique style was cultivated in daytime workshops at Esalen and at nightclubs in New York, and perfected on an international circuit, McKenna became a bard for multitudes, his raps showcasing an ability to seed an ecosystem of ideas terraformed for unique audiences. Received by admiring fans in distant world locations, the one who had departed his homeland three decade before as an exile was now travelling under a guise with more equivalence to a psychedelic saint. And yet, deeply ambivalent about his own fame, McKenna struggled with his stature. Despite his long-standing passion for running the edge, and penchant for being heard, the life of celebrity head became an uncomfortable necessity. Weary from a life lived on the road, he longed to bring the touring to an end. As will eventually be shown, in a wyrding of events at the turn of the millennium, he accomplished his goal.

II

The second part of the book shifts from the strictly chronological to the thematic—with each chapter remaining faithful to the temporal unfolding of our subject's life and work. We have trekked a great distance throughout part I, beginning with a mid-sixties DMT event that served as Terence McKenna's eureka moment shaping his life thereafter, a height from which he would never come down. We panned back to the fifties, to Paonia, Colorado, where a precocious kid cultivated a penchant for living on the edge, developing further through his high school years in California, where he met, among others, Rick Watson, in proto-Silicon Valley. We then accompanied McKenna through his studies at UC Berkeley, mis/adventures in Israel and Seychelles, the "screechpuke" of the late sixties and the fugitive's odyssey through Asia. The period was characterized by exile, expulsion, and the sensibility of the outlaw. Throughout, he was honing his "meta-political exile" manifesto that envisioned an electronic eschaton—an animating theme for his remaining days. We accompanied Terence and Dennis on their freak expedition into the heart of the Amazon as they searched for "the stone" and as they discovered the mushroom *magic* that is subsequently cultivated, harnessed, and widely cast. We were introduced to the gravitas of La Chorrera as the wellspring of "the phenomenon" and the "wave of time" that predicted a "cross species quantum acceleration" (on Terence's twenty-fifth birthday). We have grown familiar with his relationship with fellow psychonaut Kathleen Harrison, the fruit of their union, and their deviations. And we explored the inception and evolution of McKenna's rap. With the success of his oratory style and breaks in the world of publishing, he eventually emerged, somewhat ambivalently, as the *éminence grise* of the weird.

This exposé sets the scene for part II, which opens a panorama on McKenna's intellectual profile and his sudden stage exit. A consequence of sustained dialogue with the mushroom "teacher," and a decades-long mythopoetic project, we begin with the Timewave (chapter 9), a fraught opus that represents an integral, provocative, and consistent expression of McKenna's inner landscape. We'll then explore (in chapter 10) the enigmatic, anomalous, and dissident character of a cognitive libertarian who had an ambivalent relationship with leadership and power. A reluctant authority, McKenna mounted his freak agenda outside the sanctioned domain of academic science while seeking legitimacy as a scientist and an activist—as evident in his most determined effort to achieve acceptance, *Food of the Gods*. A course is, then, charted through McKenna's turbulent relationships—with the law, the media, the sublime, science, and politics.

Following McKenna's 1966 launch into "hyperspace," the newer world of the higher dimensions left its calling card. Throughout his career, he assumed the guise of a New Edge prophet and translinguistic cartographer who hyped the proto-Net as a techno-libertarian promised land. As explored in chapter 11, McKenna's late-sixties fixation with post-electric shamanism offers remarkably prescient, albeit immature, commentary on the coming metaverse, prefiguring developments in virtual worlding, a cybernetic *space* championed and posthumously inhabited. The electronic dreams that nurtured his desire to become a virtual "zone ghost" would be nurtured at McKenna's newly built remote Hawaiian hideaway. The scene will then be set for the final chapter, which adopts the appropriate living metaphor of *metamorphosis* to illustrate how a life dissolving boundaries and contemplating the end of days prepared McKenna for his own end.

9 TIMEWAVE ZERO

But upmeyant Prospector you sprout all your abel and woof your wings . . . [1]

In a favored passage from *Finnegans Wake*, McKenna lit upon the word "prospector." It was a status with which he had identified as a spritely rockhound who upgraded the scouring of Black Canyon for fossils to a quest for "the stone" of alchemy. This quest eventually turned over an idea: The *Timewave*, his identity-defining artifice. McKenna was an avid prospector who loaded this device with a kaleidoscope of signifiers: mathematical mandala, score of the bio-cosmic symphony, holographic modular hierarchy, hyper-novelty map, interference pattern detector, puzzle garden, fractal time, time machine. It might have been the stand-up philosopher's showstopping act, but more than a bit in a stage routine, the Timewave was a hobby, theory, performance, vision, prophecy, and commercial software with an oracular application, all rolled into one. An enigmatic conjuration animated by his own doubts and hopes, insecurities and desires, hubris and humility, it was cardinal to the myth of Terence McKenna, the substance of his inner workings, his spiritual compass. His opus.

Before an attempt at further clarity, let us pan the soil already uncovered. There are several elements to this *mckennaism* with which we're already familiar. Under the direction of his mushroom muse, McKenna hacked the *I Ching* to uncover its presumed lost calendrical function. The *Psilocybe logos* had revealed a "hyper-temporal" vision in which historical time could be charted in cycles called "waves" that flow in both temporal directions and which are resonant across time. Hazelle McKenna's date of death signified the start of the original sixty-four-day wave. The wave of time resonated with the morphology of DNA, which, at the height of their psi-fi fantasy, the brothers imagined could be switched on with psilocybin and harmine. Terence imagined that he had been so turned on. And like any good myth, the prophecy was resilient, an end-of-time fixation sustained—despite the false starts—to his own end.

As we have also found, McKenna was a home-grown comparative religionist with a penchant for bending new ideas to his will. And yet there are "creods," to use a term he liked, which means the metaphorical "groove" that biological processes adhere to during development. We are familiar with a figure in conversation with Jung, Eliade, and McLuhan, and for that matter, Joyce. As a Neoplatonist, McKenna early contemplated that when all the boundaries are dissolved, there remains the plenum, "the one." A Gnostic and Hermetic sensibility insists on a pattern of exile, the redemption of spirit from matter, coinciding with an obsession with eschatology—all nourishing a perspective on time. Most of all, the Timewave gave expression to a long-embraced alchemy. While the brothers trekked to the Amazon in search of the lapis, Terence emerged from the jungle with the vision that "the stone" lay in the future as the "transcendental object at the end of time." The union of opposites was to be an event horizon that would collapse the future and the past (and death/birth, subject/object, creativity/teleology). He understood that he had been gifted a predictive model that not only plotted the peaks and troughs of history, but pinpointed its end (i.e., December 21, 2012).

If we can imagine 2012 as a stage or film production, the inspiration was La Chorrera, which in 1971 was the principal location for field-trialing a modest version of the later production. He may have failed to achieve the cosmic terminus a "DNA year" from the day his mom "woofed her wings," but Terence had acquired a taste for conquering death and squatting eternity. Having known the thrill of surviving an apocalypse, he grew compelled to produce a sequel that was super-optimized and at greater scale. The script was layered with poetry and prophecy. In the fullness of time, Timewave Zero featured an evolving bricolage of insight that honored and augmented the original revelations. Like a trademark brew of known and trusted ingredients, the Timewave was decocted, refined, and served to increasingly popular audiences. The entheo-eschatologist sometimes explained how his dimensional travails inaugurated an exchange relationship brokered with the habitués of hyperspace he recognized as "meme traders"—those who "trade hyperspatial notions from across the cosmos." These entities courted him like "primitive art collectors," and in exchange for what he knew about the *I Ching* they gave him their model of time.[2] The result was a device as mutable and self-replicating as the original elf gift-bearers. As the trickster warranted, the original quantification was established through a set of operations that were as logically rigorous as they were intuitive.[3] Less interested in the precise origins, or algorithm, of the Timewave, and its trans-dimensional source, this chapter documents a phenomenon suffused with the familiars, fantasies, and foibles of its architect—an exploration that opens a window on his soul.

NOVELTY ENGINE

Having finally returned to the United States from his exotic travels in the outer and inner realms, McKenna developed a unique *naturphilosophie*. Implicit was a theory of novelty in which a system expands to a "density of connection" where every point in the system is cotangent to every other. McKenna's novelty theory relied on the observation of two interrelated principles. First, from its inception, the universe has grown more and more *complex*, a process of complexification affecting all matter and energy in the universe (including, notably, humans, the apotheosis of complexity in the universe). Second, the movement toward complexity *accelerates* asymptotically, such that, as was related in the late nineties, the amount of novelty produced in a billion years five billion years ago is now generated in just twenty years.

When it came to offering abridged versions of the long view of evolution, McKenna was a convincing rhetorician. The big picture was broken down for John Horgan over lunch in a booth atop the Millennium Hotel near the World Trade Center in Manhattan in May 1999. It was two weeks before his seizure, and two years before a local event that surely should have pulled serious zeros on his chart. From the Big Bang on, Horgan was apprised, the universe has been complexifying, with each level of complexity becoming the platform for further ascensions into complexity. "So fusion in early stars creates heavy elements and carbon. That becomes the basis for molecular chemistry. That becomes the basis for photobionic life. That becomes the basis for eukaryotic stuff. That becomes the basis for multicellular organisms, that for higher animals, that for culture, that for machine symbiosis, and on and on."[4] By contrast to the "cheerful" gradualism of Newton, the acceleration of novelty is such that "we're slamming into omniscience." At this rate, "we're redefining ourselves so fast that we are becoming unrecognizable to ourselves."[5] With connectivity and acceleration as its defining characteristics, then, *novelty* became the "primary term" applicable to temporal systems, not unlike the way charge, spin, velocity, and angular momentum are primary to the description of any physical system.[6] The thesis is set forth in rap after rap over twenty-five years. In the immediate wake of La Chorrera, the organismic process philosophy of Alfred North Whitehead gave McKenna the inspiration to decipher his waveform as an expression of temporal dynamics. From Whitehead there derives an understanding of the alternation of habit and novelty in the universe, with the idea of nature's ebb and flow traceable to Pythagoras, Heraclitus, and the Tao.

Via the English mathematician, McKenna grew to comprehend purpose in a complex universe, an understanding with far greater appeal than the precept that the universe is driven by chance, that nature is mute, that humans are random actors, or that history is "trendlessly fluctuating." In *Process and Reality*, Whitehead offered grist for a form of panpsychism encapsulated in *concrescence*, meaning the growing together of many processes into one. McKenna surmised that everything flows together, like a "tightening gyre." "The future is not yet completed," he wrote, "but it is conditioned." Out of the set of all possible events, certain events are mysteriously selected to undergo, in Whitehead's parlance, "the formality of actually occurring."[7]

Rupert Sheldrake was similarly disposed. As the two bounced ideas off each other for the better part of two decades, Whitehead, the process theorist, was the beacon to whom McKenna and Sheldrake concresced. Sheldrake's "morphic resonance," neither formed entirely by chance nor governed by a system of fixed laws, held that the universe is an evolving system of conserved memories, or habits, an idea informing McKenna's understanding of the conservation of complexity in evolution. It was Sheldrake who suggested his friend name his wave's novelty-conserving tendency "habit,"[8] and McKenna occasionally referred to his "special theory of morphogenesis."[9] While never entirely convinced of McKenna's ad hoc enthusiasms, Sheldrake was nevertheless inspired by the creative drive inherent to the ingression of novelty McKenna envisioned.

In the psychedelic prospector's estimation, he and Sheldrake were complementary trailblazers of Compressionism. Dedicated to the radical revision of time, "Compressionists," or "Psychedelic Compressionists," hold that "the world is growing more and more complex, compressed, knitted together, and therefore holographically complete at every point."[10] This style of thought appears to have been incubated at La Chorrera 2.0 when Terence faced off with the Great Compression of his birth-death day. Imagined as the intellectual cadre within a loose panpsychic movement, "Compressionism" was introduced at LA's Philosophical Research Society in October 1987. McKenna's novelty theory, Sheldrake's morphic resonance, Abraham's dynamic attractors, and Frank Barr's fractal hierarchies were embryonic of the new paradigm. "It's really the great intellectual adventure of our time," McKenna stated, while qualifying that Compressionism is unlike other paradigms since, rather than an abstraction sanctioned by a professional elite, it is an understanding of the world that is "felt." With a "reemergence of the presence of the spirit" as its métier, "the discovery of relativism with regard to consciousness" was rated to be the main cultural force behind this new Transcendentalist movement, implying not only the significance of psychedelic drugs and hallucinogenic plants, but "media . . . literary expectation, reorientation of the senses through design, urban planning, the entire spectrum of effects which feeds consciousness back into itself."[11]

Compressionism may have been little more than an inspired moment that folded in upon itself in the wake of McKenna, but its qualities are noteworthy. The moment was pregnant with the transformative humanism championed throughout his career, a theory of evolutionary change in which humanity is not only cast in a starring role, but is pivotal to an ultimate transform. If the universe is a "novelty-conserving engine," then, as evidenced in the poetry of Blake, the equations of Einstein, the paintings of Rembrandt, in breakdancing, and in the jungle alchemy of ayahuasca, among other examples, we are the most exulted and consequential ingression of novelty in the universe. Through the seventies, absorbing the ideas of Erich Jantsch, Belgian complex systems theorist Ilya Prigogine, German biophysicist Manfred Eigen, and British-American economist Kenneth E. Boulding, among others, evidence was accumulating of "a counterforce against the excesses of Social Darwinism, Marxism, sociobiology, behaviorism, and other isms thought responsible for displacing humanity from our rightful place in the cosmos." The enthusiasm shone in a *Zygon* review of Boulding's *Ecodynamics: A New Theory of Societal Evolution*. The review—likely McKenna's first—was supportive of Boulding's rejection of the fallacy that humans are mere spectators, giving credence to the idea that humanity is a catalyst in "the becoming of the cosmos."[12] These ideas are consistent with visions of immortality visited upon McKenna throughout his life. The ultimate novelty was perplexing and unimaginable, but the panoramic vistas frequently painted in dense sprawling language before hyper-attentive audiences depicted humanity poised on the threshold of the divine.

At the conclusion of the Q&A at Fort Mason, San Francisco, in December 1998, not much more than a year before the end of the millennium, and his life, McKenna struck the nerve of the zeitgeist. His model made a dramatic contrast, he thought, to "what the competition is peddling," that is, the received wisdom of positivist science that cannot regard the universe, the Earth, and its life-forms as anything more than the product of a "cosmic accident." In this story, in which we dwell "on an ordinary star, at the edge of a typical galaxy, in an ordinary part of space and time," humans are essentially disenchanted—devoid of meaning. But if he was right, "that the universe has an appetite for novelty," Terence enthused as the curtains were descending, "then we are the apple of its eye."[13] That the universe was purportedly born from nothing in an instant at a single point and without discernible purpose—that is, the Big Bang—is what he often called "the limit case for credulity." In other words, if you can believe the most improbable of all improbabilities, you can believe anything. By contrast to the ultimate woo-woo upon which our scientific worldview is founded, he rallied toward the alternative. By moving the "ultimate singularity" to the end of the world, he sought to turn the consensus at the bedrock of physics on its head. As had been the vision humped from La Chorrera, time possesses a spiral structure in which events are organized into tighter and tighter spirals that lead inevitably to a "final time" imagined to be like the center of a black hole—infinite novelty.[14] It was as if we were being sucked into the body of eternity—a temporal rather than gravitational "black hole." Perturbing the laws of physics, this event horizon invokes an intelligent design, resonating with Whitehead's conjectures "about an aboriginal god that is growing toward itself through time."[15]

That the future casts a shadow over the present is native to McKenna's thought. As integral to the inverted telos in his cosmogony and central to the teachings received in psychedelic tryptamine consciousness, history is not that which blunders along blind. It is pulled by a strange attractor from the future, which "throws off reflections of itself" that ricochet into the past, illuminating mystics, saints, and visionaries. And with fragmentary glimpses of eternity we can build a "map of the future."[16] An evocative analogy revisited and iterated on occasion, the "transcendental object" is imagined as a spinning mirror ball that sends out scintillations of light that sparkle throughout the cosmic disco. "All around this transcendental object, and at greater and lesser distances," it was claimed, "are all the people who have ever lived," its thousands of twinkling, refractive surfaces representing "religions, scientific theories, gurus, works of art, poetry, great orgasms, great soufflés, great paintings, etc." And if you are a Buddha, a Christ, a Mohammed, or a guru, you are just "dumb lucky" to be struck by a divine reflection from the transcendental mirror ball at the end of time.[17]

Given his own clocking of this great attractor, had McKenna copped a refracted scintilla himself? "Something is calling us out of nature and sculpting us in its own image," he breathes on "Timewave Zero," the release produced from the 1993 Alien Dreamtime performance in San Francisco. "You can feel it," McKenna presages Morpheus from *The Matrix*. "You can feel it in your own dreams. You can feel it in your own trips. You can feel that we're approaching the cusp of a catastrophe, and that beyond that cusp we are unrecognizable to ourselves. The wave of novelty that has rolled unbroken since the birth of the universe has now focused and coalesced itself in our species."[18] The statement iterates an animate mythology, the pop-cult amplification of which was facilitated by the Shamen on "Re:Evolution."

> History is ending. I mean, we are to be the generation that witnesses the revelation of the purpose of the cosmos. History is the shock wave of the Eschaton. History is the shock wave of eschatology, and what this means for those of us who will live through this transition into hyperspace, is that we will be privileged to see the greatest release of compressed change probably since the birth of the universe. The twentieth century is the shudder that announces the approaching cataracts of time over which our species and the destiny of this planet is about to be swept.[19]

Throughout his career, McKenna was not only a vocal enactor of his own prophecy but a loquacious advocate of the botany, practices, and conditions optimal for explorers to reconnoiter with the "transcendental object." While the eschaton might never be fully revealed, it could be sensed in augmented states. History is characterized by growing anticipation, with the entire back catalogue of apocalyptic and millenarian movements amounting to, as the mushroom muse informed, the "shockwave of the eschaton."[20] What's more, the extraordinary, supra-novel event ahead frustrates all efforts to understand it. "We've drifted near some kind of cataract, a *chronosynclastic infundibulum*," announced the psychedelic sage, referencing a phrase used by Kurt Vonnegut in *The Sirens of Titan*, denoting "a black hole in the narrative."[21]

While McKenna's musings are unique, the transcendental object at the end of time shares elements in common with the ideas of anomalist Charles Fort, for whom the future acted as "a kind of occult attractor or magnet, pulling everything in the past and the present toward its own superstate."[22] But while I have seen little evidence of a direct Fortean influence, the ideas of French geologist, paleontologist, philosopher, and Jesuit priest Pierre Teilhard de Chardin are formative. In his controversial *The Phenomenon of Man*, Teilhard argued that humans and the universe are coevolving toward greater complexity and consciousness and that evolution will culminate at an Omega Point—a fully realized Christ. The book pursued a unique perspective on "orthogenesis"—that is, that evolution is predetermined toward a future goal or end: Christogenesis. McKenna made surprising little comment about the book in later years, perhaps for the reason that *The Phenomenon of Man* grew popular within the New Age awakening that he was loath to be stitched up with.[23] And yet Christian myth and metaphor were grifted and grafted by the intelligent designer in a fashion inspired by the French Jesuit. "We are the crowning achievement of the evolutionary process," McKenna wrote, "Let's not betray it. Let's make it the ascent to angelic being that is, I am sure, the intention of the Gaian Mind."[24] Asked where he diverged from Teilhard, McKenna once replied that "he's me without drugs or immediacy." His own position, he felt, would probably earn him greater credence if his "object" was in the remote future, as is the case with the Omega Point, rather than arriving within his own lifetime under the aegis of accelerating complexity, a theory that drew celebration and castigation as the strangest candidate on the apocalyptarian circuit.[25]

Although McKenna sought to establish the Timewave as a mathematical *theory*, it better represented an epic *vision* in which history is a "strategy for the conquest of dimensionality." In the future forecast, humanity was to be released from three-dimensional space, with the consequent transit to hyperspace imagined as a "continuation of a universal program of self-extension and transcendence that can be traced back to the earliest and most primitive kind of protoplasm."[26] This epic story of transformation is a gnostic vision of liberation that is thought to hold resonant patterns: freedom from the tyranny of matter, the soul's liberation from the body (in death), human species' escape from the planet, from habit, from the unconscious, from history. As a McLuhanesque transit "from the 3-D animal to the 4-D posthuman mind,"[27] this concrescence was nothing short of a quantum leap into the imagination. Ongoing pronouncements around this theme amounted to a spinning vortex of speculation, the accumulation of which seemed to echo the accelerating advent of novelty implicit to the Timewave itself.

One event appears to retain centrifugal value within the vortex: the passing of Hazelle McKenna. The Timewave can be read as a sustained meditation on death and a compensation for the absence of closure in the wake of Hazelle's passing. Enshrining her date of death as the ground-zero event, the original wave of time is the advanced mechanism of a grief-stricken son. Decisions at the turn of the seventies were shaped by the trauma of grief, with the early charts serving as a means to extend her memory. As the expression of a bereaved young man, the early modeling permitted the reanimation of Hazelle McKenna in charts, graphs, and mathematical mandalas. The "novelty" here was not so much her life—in which case, her date of birth could have been recognized as significant—but the impact of her death on Terence, who had been denied her death bed and last rites, who was generally guilt-ridden about his miscreance, and who subsequently sought redemption. Curiously, Terence shares something in common with futurist and inventor Ray Kurzweil: grief, and in particular grief associated with loss of a parent. In Kurzweil's case, his "singularitarian transhumanism" is reckoned to have been inspired by the desire to reanimate his father.

In both cases we find expression of the "Promethean assumption that humanity has the power within itself to solve even the daunting challenge of death."[28] Hazelle's death date does not appear to have been retained in later modeling, when the discovery of atomic energy and the dropping of "Little Boy" stood out as the ultra-novel events at the inception of a final sixty-seven-year cycle. And yet Terence's grief permeates the Timewave, a device that celebrates victory over mortality.

HISTORY'S FRACTAL MOUNTAIN

The road to 2012 is paved with troughs of novelty and peaks of habit. That is, the path mirrors the wave of time's jagged graph lines that McKenna plotted according to an obscure coding of the "degrees of difference" between the *I Ching's* sixty-four hexagrams. In 1971, he arrived at a complex waveform with 384 (6×64) quantified values denoted in *The Invisible Landscape* as "the eschatron," and subsequently, the "eschaton."[29] Returned from his travels to the end of time, and behaving as if tasked to reconstruct a crushed artifact, he pursued life as "a noetic archeologist with nut pick and toothbrush." In the early stages of his dig, he magnified, superimposed, and reversed the wave to create an eight-and-a-half-foot-long chart on graph paper. With its saw-toothed lines marked with pen strokes in eight colors and tiny numbers, he kept the chart rolled up in a bamboo tube. "This is a map of history. This is a picture of time. This is how things happen," he'd proclaim to all and sundry cornered in dime stores and bus stations. Unrolling a chart he favorably compared to Gurdjieff's "Diagram of Everything Living," audiences were informed that while the descending graph line signified an increase in novelty over time, its ascent from baseline represented habit formation. The chart was clear. As surely as we ascended from eukaryotic organisms and into the cosmos, we were descending into novelty. The ultimate descent into a zero value occurred only once on the chart—the end of time, coming soon.

With his zeal embossed on his charts and diagrams, McKenna triggered alarm among friends, who met and spoke of "intervention," or so he imagined. It was Ralph Abraham who got through to him. "The problem here," Ralph advised, "is that you have an occult diagram. Only you understand it, and only you can interpret it, and therefore it's not very persuasive."[30] If he wanted to be taken seriously, he needed to convert his artifact into an ordinary mathematical object, so that "fellow mathematicians" could join the dialogue. Terence accepted the challenge. He could not rely on formal mathematics training, but by 1974 he claimed to have achieved "a completely formal, mathematical quantification of the fractal structure" of the *I Ching*.[31] An inscrutable analysis is presented in *The Invisible Landscape*, where the Eschaton is quantized and novelty predicted. Crystallizing his response to Abraham, the "quantification of operational constructs" was purported to be a valid subject for rigorous scientific investigation.[32]

Believing he had uncovered the King Wen's "ordering principle," Terence sought Ralph's opinion. Eventually examining the details, Abraham was amazed to learn that McKenna had used the little-known computational method "attractor reconstruction." To Abraham's great surprise, McKenna independently discovered this technique used in chaos theory. "I always gave him great credit for this derivation," said Abraham, who "closely followed his further development of the Timewave theory."[33]

Impressions were made further afield too. The math condensed in *The Invisible Landscape* met with rapid validation when, in 1977, the book was parsed within the pages of *Cosmic Trigger*—Robert Anton Wilson's follow-up to *The Illuminatus! Trilogy*—in which readers were made cognizant of the *I Ching* and hologram-inflected theory positing that humanity is riding "64 evolutionary waves all mounting toward a cosmic Awakening." In the novel, the McKennas are identified in the same breath as "Henry Adams, Korzybski, Fuller, Toffler and even Leary."[34] A year or so out from graduation, Terence, therefore, gained recognition from one of the most iconic figures in the intellectual underground.

The McKennan weird may have peaked with the development of commercial software that succeeded in displaying the Timewave graphically, enabling users to make comparisons across resonant temporal expanses separated by billions of years—or several days. Through the seventies and eighties, Terry's temporal mechanics attracted a buzz among programmer freaks and algorithm acolytes committed to quantizing the wave of time. By 1974, Tussmanite colleague Royce Kelley was recruited (along with Leon Taylor) to calculate the wave using FORTRAN on a CDC 6400 mainframe computer at UC Berkeley. Telephone directory–sized books of numbers were generated over which Terence pored and from which he laboriously drew up his charts. By 1979, Peter Broadwell developed the first Timewave Zero software, running on an Apple II+ and written in Applesoft BASIC, and Billy Smith worked on the HyperCard implementation for the Mac. Notable among this loose fraternity of geeky wave riders is computational physicist, software developer, and patron of patterned woolen jumpers Peter Meyer. Transposing McKenna's "mathematical intuitions" into C in 1986, developing the Timewave Zero software for the Apple IIe (and in 1989 porting to MS-DOS for Intel PCs), Meyer is said to have defined the core algorithm of the Timewave theory, which is at one time named Time Surfer.³⁵ In 1998, Meyer produced the MS-DOS software for Windows, marketing this as Fractal Time. Throughout its weathered existence, the software was never a commercial success.

Meyer was among the strange circle of "time guys" who congregated, Harrison recalls, about once every year at their house. There were six men from different walks of life, including New Age mathematicians, an astrologer and "the leader of a small cult" from nearby Marin County, in which everyone wore white, including his two white-clad wives. Among this cloistered group was Cuban eccentric and businessman Julio Valdes. Each year they all got together for a day to share their theories, display intricate maps, and compare notes.³⁶ By the mid-eighties, Timewave Zero (TWZ) had become central to a business plan for a historical database, an idea that Meyer was repeatedly urged to develop. "I have a notion," McKenna informed Meyer, "to try to reach Steve Jobs and convince him that a 256k. version of TWZ, loaded with visual and text data on every phase of time from the Big Bang to Point Zero could give the Next machine a tremendous boost in the educational software market."³⁷

As the name "Fractal Time" suggests, it was Meyer who introduced "fractality" to the software. Like McKenna, Meyer insisted that the Timewave was fractal by nature, even though Terence grew aware of fractals only after Mandelbrot had popularized the concept in the eighties.³⁸ Updates on the concept also inflected Sheldrake's influence, such that the idea that the "entire hierarchical continuum is resident in its modular parts" became a "temporal map" revised and updated as "a universal and fractal morphogenetic field."³⁹ The wave's fractal mathematical quality is exhibited in its apparent "self-same similarity." That is, it inheres in its quality of temporal resonance. Based on the model formulated in 1971, the wave of time featured a "modular hierarchy" of nested waves, with each cycle recapitulating events in the former, though sixty-four times faster than the preceding cycle. Each cycle, sixty-four times shorter than the previous, was figured to commence with a kind of "speed bump." The largest cycle held the universe at approximately seventy billion years; the shortest was in the domain of Planck's constant, which was expressed as 6.55×10^{-23} second. In other words, a "jiffy."⁴⁰ The cycle of chief interest is the last 4,300 years spanning human civilization. Toward the end of that cycle, a 67-year and 104.25-day cycle commenced on August 5, 1945, when "with a faint echo of the Big Bang . . . the atomic flower blossomed over Hiroshima."⁴¹ There would be a climactic bump in 2011, where that which transpired in the previous sixty-seven years will be compressed into a 384-day cycle.⁴² By the time the end of the chart arrives, as much novelty will be compressed in a week as occurred over 4,300 years. And as the cycles compress to zero, there was to be a bump six days before the end, another 1 minute, 35 seconds before the end, with thirteen more bumps in that final duration. The ultimate bump was to occur at 6 am, GMT-5, December 21, 2012, the point of maximized novelty and the only point on the chart with a quantified value of zero.

The Timewave became an endless source of fascination for its designer, who behaved like a precocious kid moving pieces around on an advanced board game of his own design whose rules only he understood. Indeed, there was a vision to convert the software into an immersive Timewave game, a "time travel simulator." McKenna appeared to enjoy nothing more than playing with time and exploring the broad implications of his model. Identifying as "wily Ulysses," he thought the Timewave akin to a "puzzle garden" through which one walks to navigate "the maze of life." "It isn't to the swift that the race goes, it's to the thoughtful, to the careful, to the one who can tease it all apart."[43] The obsession with temporal mechanics was apparent to Paul Krassner, who encountered a figure poring over charts that displayed a cascade into novelty commencing around 1440, as Gutenberg invented printing:

> 1492, Columbus.... the American revolution begins at a symmetry break at the top of the slide into novelty. It succeeds. The French Revolution begins as the bottom of a novelty trough, on an upturn into habit, and fails.... January 1, 1900, symmetry break occurs and this is the signature of the 20th century, an almost continuous descent into novelty from 1900: 1903, flight; 1905 the Special Theory of Relativity . . . radio, World War I, the Russian Revolution, Dada, surrealism. . . . It's the 20th Century, for crying out loud! Hitler, bigtime novelty.... World War II culminates with the atomic bomb, the end of the war and the return to normalcy.... 1950, invention of the hydrogen bomb.... The day of the Human Be-In, January 14, 1967, is the day we go over the hump.... Then, just after that the landing on the moon, from which time the descent begins in earnest.[44]

Enthusiasm was shared with pre-millennial multitudes in seminars, workshops, and teaching retreats led on Timewave Zero at Esalen, the Open Center in New York, Chicago's Oasis, and the Rim Institute in Payson, Arizona, among other locations. Hardly a single rap failed to venture the vision and its implications. Resonant patterns detected across cycles fired McKenna's imagination, a gossamer thread of time first woven at La Chorrera. The days of September–October 1971 afforded the insight that "there is a thread of alchemical gold running down through time along the helix of closure represented by life's approach to hyperspace." This thread was to be found by "following the line of direct descent of the tightening gyres."[45] For the remainder of his days, McKenna plotted analogous "zeitgeist" events, movements, and figures detected across the cycles and epochs vastly removed in time. Revolutions, wars, plagues, natural disasters, scientific discoveries, technological advances, assassinations, and treaties were among the parallel events of interest. The software threw up manifold examples from any time in history. Noteworthy is a surge in novelty between 15,000 and 8,000 BCE (the Neolithic Age and the emergence of agriculture) that displayed a pattern repeated, although sixty-four times faster, from 1750 to 1825 (Enlightenment and the beginning of the Industrial Era).[46]

The theory of temporal resonance offered the basis for understanding explosive fads, fashions, and other occasional social obsessions that sweep through societies, and are interpreted as micro versions of larger fractal curves.[47] And the overlaying of temporal cycles also provided the basis for understanding the nature of significant paranormal events—like miracles. A journal entry on October 28, 1971, claimed that "extremely improbable occurrences are actually instances when the operating laws of one cycle achieve a sort of harmonic cancellation or tangential interface with another cycle whose operating laws are more restrictive of molecular activity." Giving new meaning to the phrase "breakthrough experience," miracles, it was warranted, "are instances when phenomenological modes common to a cycle different than the one being experienced break in upon normal operations of natural laws mistakenly assumed to be eternal constants and . . . distorts them."[48]

The most fun was to be had in the field of divination. "I predicted the fall of the Berlin Wall, Tiananmen Square, Chernobyl," McKenna confidently informed Krassner. "I didn't say what would happen, but I said . . . 'this day will be the most novel day of this year.'" Predictions were routinely ventured through the nineties as bimonthly "Novelty and Habit" forecasts were offered, possibly first on The Well, and later on McKenna's website and shared with his email list subscribers. Through this period, Terence became a speculator, not of the stock market or weather events—though he deployed metaphors from both systems—but of temporality. Introducing a prospective "plunge into novelty," a "moderate return to habit," or "late breaking novelty," the interpretation of the wave chart included in each report was driven by projections of current events, textured by the Dow Jones index, the US presidential election cycle, and worthy discoveries in the fields of science and technology.

By 1993, the radical novelty theorist lived peak novelty. Among the curious onlookers invited to inspect the software and ride the wave of his own imagination is a *Mondo 2000* film crew that visits his home in Occidental in March. While websites were barely conceivable at this stage, the Timewave is envisioned as a cable TV station broadcasting the live wave with something like a data chyron crawling across the screen base, or as a chip installed in a screen device worn on the wrist. One could closely monitor the wave 24/7, adjusting one's daily life choices accordingly.[49]

Despite the public's incomprehension of his wave, the media circus generated its own wave that McKenna was compelled to ride, come what may. Illustrative of the way Terence was positioned at the leading edge of the "novelty" that he had himself proclaimed is the invitation to perform as himself in *Manual of Evasion LX94*, an experimental film about time directed by iconoclastic Portuguese filmmaker Edgar Pêra (see figure 9.1). Shot in Lisbon in January 1994, and also featuring Robert Anton Wilson and Rudy Rucker, the experimental film was a platform for McKenna's novelty theory. "Science gives you the Big Bang. I give you the Big Surprise." Such is a memorable outtake from McKenna, who proclaims his discovery of a tool capable of producing a "map of time." His protagonist in *Manual of Evasion*, Dr. Xaman, is a revolutionary who breaks free from his imprisonment in

FIGURE 9.1
Still from the film *Manual of Evasion LX94*, directed by Edgar Pêra. Photo courtesy of Edgar Pêra.

clock time: "From now on tomorrow lasts forever," exclaims the temponaut at the film's conclusion. "Forward to the new order of the transtemporal dream." While the film did not reach a large audience, it stands strange among the many opportunities McKenna took to project his views on time. Notably, Dr. Xaman referred to the temporal irregularities and "felt experiences" figured by his model of time: "the ebb and flow of two different kinds of forces, that create the kind of experience of the world that we are having." It was one thing to predict the path of an artillery shell or the behavior of an electron. "But what we want to understand is: how do affairs work, how do empires fall, how do people fall in love?"

As much as Dada appealed to McKenna, he claimed his radical cartography relied on science, and mathematics. As his maps anticipated "record levels of novelty" in January and February of 1996, the period was considered as an important confirmation of his theory. In the weeks leading up to this climax, it was claimed that "we will recapitulate in miniature the final approach to the concrescence." Despite ambiguities and uncertainties, there are no prizes for guessing that the prophecy was fulfilled, the theory of novelty buttressed. The sequencing of the human genome, an unpredicted comet, and the first successful nano assembler were among the worthy occurrences, to which is later added the invention of the World Wide Web, the discovery of a Martian meteorite, the production of antimatter, and the cloning of Dolly the sheep.[50] In another update, it was revealed that "ten billion new galaxies were discovered." In other words, "the missing eighty percent of the universe!"[51] Not unlike an astrologer divining the impact of celestial cycles, McKenna excogitated the effect of the 1996 "novelty plunge" upon whole populations. Touring the United States and Germany during this time, he convinces himself that "many people experienced novelty as a powerful force in their personal lives."[52]

These weren't the only events confirming the novelty plunge. At this time, McKenna's novelty theory faced an unexpected challenge that ultimately served a self-reinforcing role. In the mid-nineties, young British mathematician Matthew Watkins threw a spanner in the works when the two met at the Entheobotany conference. In Palenque in 1994, McKenna claimed that reputed mathematicians had examined Timewave Zero, finding it blessed with "tremendous beauty, elegance, cohesion." As a mathematical equation, it was in the same ballpark as Maxwell's electromagnetic fields or Einstein's curvature of space. "It's a delusion of such power and of such elegance," he wagered, "that it may be the truth."[53]

It was in this climate that Watkins mounted a light-hearted challenge to the proposition that a fractal map of temporal resonance is encoded into the King Wen sequence. In his refutation, Watkins not only disputed the "disingenuous" claim that the Timewave represented fractal math, but he held that its interpretation was beyond "the domain of mathematical logic."[54] Key to these concerns was an unexplained numerical manipulation implemented as an early step in the model. While unexplained in either edition of *The Invisible Landscape*, "the mysterious 'half twist'" is mentioned in a footnote buried in an appendix of Meyer's Time Explorer manual accompanying the Timewave Zero software (and printed on the wrong page): Meyer's footnote reads: "This is the mysterious 'half twist.' The reason for this is not well understood at present and is a question which awaits further research."[55] While it was never explained, it appears that the "half twist" had been introduced by Royce Kelley.[56] McKenna's inability to explain this manipulation, to recall who formulated the algorithm, or to address it adequately seems not unrelated to the fact that its author ran off with his girlfriend in the mid-seventies. Kelley not only took off with Kume, but may have disappeared with the secret behind the Timewave's "half-twist."

McKenna's performances through this period offer mirthfully honest exposés of near-megalomaniacal tendencies delivered in his stand-up therapy sessions. The prospect of having his world disintegrate at the hands of a "flaming genius" not much older than nineteen was terrifying. He and Watkins had three long meetings by the pool in Palenque where, as McKenna said, "my world wilted." Most disconcerting was his inability to defend his thesis in "academic mathematical terms," a failure reminding him of Einstein's reactions to physicist Hermann Bondi's challenges to his Special Theory of Relativity. Einstein could not understand Bondi's objections. "I don't think of myself as Einstein," McKenna wanted to be clear. Novelty theory, he averred, needed a mathematical equation that will raise its stature as a "true science." He believed he had uncovered that equation, no less than "a fractal algorithm which is a self-similar recursive curve that I modestly propose we substitute for the zero in Newtonian physics that describes the curvature of spacetime."[57]

Instead of establishing the equation that he assumed must exist, McKenna plunges into two years of "mathematical hell." Keen to demonstrate that the "Watkins objection" did not disprove his theory, he enlisted the support of physicist John Sheliak, who composed a complex "vector analysis" of the Timewave. Desperate to prevent the rug from being pulled out from beneath him, McKenna presents the "Sheliak clarification" as a major scientific breakthrough. At the same time, Watkins's critique is rebranded an "improvement," with McKenna omitting the numerical manipulations dubbed the "half-twist" and generating what Watkins cynically dubbed the

"New Improved Timewave 2.0."[58] In circular self-affirming fashion, serving to place novelty theory on "firm mathematical ground at last," as a further confirmation of the 1996 novelty plunge, the "Sheliak clarification" is received as a signal of the novelty divined.[59] Arriving on cue, the modified model renders his theory an "ever-more robust object in the theater of intellectual discourse."[60] In the end, the elegance of McKenna resides much less in the math than in his art of persuasion.

While forecasting became critical to McKenna's public persona, his business was not in predicting actual events, but anticipating future scenarios. Novelty theory provided a basic map of the era through which he lived. As apparent at the time of the wave's discovery—that is, the early seventies—and as evident throughout the era of the theory's development in the eighties and nineties, its architect declared that "the world is in a terminal crisis of value and direction."[61] Playing with his resonant cycles, the world of his present is skried as a phase of imperial decline that recapitulated in compressed fashion the fall of the Roman Empire. The eighties were a tragic era of the "Roman Twilight" in which centuries of civilization are condensed into a few years, and Reagan symbolizes ten Roman emperors. The nineties were long forecast as a new Dark Age; the aughts would see the discovery of a New World; and the third millennium will be the equivalent of the Enlightenment, the Industrial Revolution, and the rise of modern science. Beyond that, and toward 2012, a supercompression of modern times and the emergence of a new human mode.[62]

McKenna sought to contrast his temporal resonance with Dick's vision of parallel timelines, notably, the perception, as figured in several novels and *The Exegesis*, that 1975 and 45 CE were parallel. The comparison was performed in an effort to distance himself from the "schizoid logic" of his own past as well as that of Dick. While the sci-fi author was thought to be in tune with McKenna's obsessions with nonlinearity, Dick's concept of "orthogonal" time was considered to be too "simple minded." If his concept of time was "wrong," it was no fault of Dick's, for fractal mathematics was not yet invented. Such was the thrust of McKenna's essay "I Understand Philip K. Dick." He somewhat arrogantly believed that if Dick were alive he would have little recourse than to surf Terence's waveform. *The Exegesis*, after all, was not stamped with the legitimacy of coded software.[63]

Setting aside the matter of whose hallucination was truer, in its various permutations, the Timewave software gave credence to McKenna's claim not only that his decoding of the *I Ching* enabled a reading of nature's interacting temporal forces—one progressive and the other conservative—but that his model could predict novelty and habit within specific time frames, right down to fractions of a second. The appeal of the program was its oracular function, not dissimilar to the *I Ching* itself. With this in mind, by the early eighties, the software was marketed using titles like System Zero, or Anamnesis, which was advertised as a counseling service in *Common Ground* magazine. An homage to Plato, "Anamnesis" echoed the idea that "souls are born with complete access to eternal knowledge, forgotten in the incarnation process, which can be recollected given the proper catalyst."[64]

McKenna's short-lived counseling service was designed to offer such a catalyst. As he clarified, "It's like I've invented a one-term kind of astrology." The system could not determine events, but "only defines the level of novelty that must be fulfilled by whatever happens."[65] It is unclear whether this service had much success. I have no evidence that he ever shaped his or his family's travel plans, or life choices in accordance with the contours of the wave. As far as I know, no study was ever conducted on the user experience of the Timewave.

DATE WITH DENSITY: 2012

McKenna's waveform charted a duration from "the bomb" to an end date in 2012. The prophecy had its first boost in 1977, when Wilson promoted 2012 as the moment when "everything goes jackpot."[66] But this strange configuration is likely to have remained an obscure artifact of psychedelic prophecy to which few afforded merit, had it not been for McKenna's pronouncements coinciding with the conclusion of the thirteenth *bak'tun* in the Long Count calendar of the ancient Maya civilization. It was a remarkable synchrony that caused heads to turn, while others spun on their axis. As puzzling as it was uncanny, this circumstance saw McKenna recognized, much to his own bemusement, as a "founding prophet" of the emergent 2012 phenomenon.[67]

While convoluted, McKenna's relationship with 2012 needs unpacking. Given that it was sixty-seven years from 1945, the year 2012 is twice raised in the first edition of *The Invisible Landscape* as the terminus of the wave. By the early eighties, the zero point was clarified as November 2012, or specifically November 12.[68] Subsequently, November 16, 17, or 18, 2012, are posited,[69] that is, approximately 67 years and 104.25 days from the detonation of "Little Boy," depending on your time zone.[70] The significance of these dates—falling on or in the immediate wake of his birthday—is unlikely to have been lost on McKenna. In all instances, McKenna's prophesied dating is offered absent knowledge of the Maya Long Count calendar or its conclusion (from which his own end date was not much more than one month shy). Finally, as integral to the revised edition of *The Invisible*

Landscape (1994), McKenna landed on December 21, 2012, an adjustment apparently prompted by his 1983 exposure to the understanding that the 5,000-plus-year Maya calendar was to conclude on the winter solstice of 2012.[71] December 21, 2012, was the date adopted at this time by the author of *The Mayan Factor*, José Argüelles[72]—a.k.a. Valum Votan, who identified as a reincarnation of Pacal the Great of Palenque—whose meeting with McKenna in April 1985 at the Ojai Foundation's "Mayan Conference" ("Council of Quetzalcoatl") proved momentous.

There is an uncanny supplement to this baroque story that renders intriguing McKenna's contribution to the subsequent 2012 phenomenon. While the date of December 21, 2012, is never stated in the original edition of *The Invisible Landscape*, it does appear to have been implied by way of the "precession of the equinoxes," which factored into estimates of "the point of maximized novelty." In the context of the 26,000-year zodiacal great year, the winter solstice node was observed to be "moving closer and closer to the point on the ecliptic where it will eclipse the galactic center." The revised edition of *Invisible Landscape* confirmed what was implied in the original—that the 2012 winter solstice was "unusual enough to signal an onset of concrescence."[73] And, four decades after occasioning the first projected zero date, La Chorrera remained the site for the cosmic concrescence: "Half an hour before the winter solstice of December 21, 2012, the sun will rise at La Chorrera (73° west, 43' south) in a position that will eclipse the galactic center."[74]

When questioned about how he derived his date, McKenna did not shrink from his conviction that it arrived via his original mushroom-fueled calculus. "In all eternity . . . you may choose not to believe that I didn't know this when I made this prediction. But I didn't know it! I didn't. Yet I chose not the month, not the same year—the same day, month and year."[75] In McKenna's foreword to John Major Jenkins's *Maya Cosmogenesis 2012*—penned a year before his diagnosis—he is buoyant about his life's most astonishing convergence, which was incidentally a proposition decidedly counter to the majority of doomsday scenarios that came to be associated with 2012.[76] Via his own methods and without knowledge of the Maya, and in support of Jenkins's thesis, he claims to have "reached the same conclusions" as the "astronomer-shamans of the Olmec/Maya"—that is, that the end of the Great Cycle signified "a moment of potential transformative opportunity."[77]

Though often linked with Argüelles and his brand of "New Age millenarianism,"[78] McKenna's connection with the Maya Long Count was synchronistic, accidental, and improvised. In hundreds of raps, he offered little commentary on the calendar of the ancient Maya, other than to suggest that he and the Mayans may have had one thing in common—their use of mushrooms (a proposition he rejected in *The Invisible Landscape* [1994]). As for explaining how he independently landed on 2012: "When we inspect the structure of our own deep unconscious we will make the unexpected discovery that we are ordered on the same principle as the larger universe in which we arose." Rather than an "independent" derivation, then, the implication is that McKenna had, under the aegis of the mushroom, tapped into the collective unconscious, an idea that, while "surprising at first, quickly comes to be seen as obvious, natural, and inevitable."[79] We can only speculate on how McKenna's mind could have evolved on the subject of 2012 in the final dozen-year countdown. By the late nineties, he was already at odds with Argüelles, for whom 2012 had been embraced as the dawning of the "holonomic posthistoric future."[80] Where one figure was driven by the "Mayan factor," the other operated in accord with the "cosmic giggle." According to McKenna, Argüelles had become complicit in a pernicious "distortion of the Mayan accomplishment." Despite the different math and assumptions, to have calculated his way "out of all eternity" to the same day as that of the Maya calendar crowd was an irritating complication. The association "muddies the water," he thought, as it becomes a beacon for "a bunch of squirrels from L.A." In other words, it appealed to those who would make his name synonymous with the search for Atlantis, crystal healing, and other contemptuous undertakings. He preferred to "stand alone."[81]

The rough and tumble with squirreliness suggests the possibility of McKenna becoming increasingly distant from the 2012 phenomenon, in the event that he lived beyond 2000. "I'll put myself out of business long before 2012," he claimed in his final trialogue (June 6, 1998), "if other people don't start seeing things my way." The implication is that he was prepared to retire gracefully.[82] By "other people," he was not alluding to aficionados of the Dreamspell calendar, which Argüelles had invented as part of a "radiogenetic game board." The prospect of future objectors of Watkins's ilk gave him pause to hope that, if nothing happens in 2012, "I'll have a few good years of penitent meditation."[83] Given those who study particle physics, temporal matrices, and systems modeling did not come knocking, McKenna may well have dropped the end date, tacked to a different breeze, or pursued in the years preceding 2012 some further iteration of the singularity—for whether the zero date conformed with the original evaluation or not, "we are in parking orbit around the eschaton." Alas, there were no further opportunities to address the issue with his fellow trialogians.[84]

McKenna departed before 2012 doomsday prophecies rapidly multiplied in the early twenty-first century, whether associated with the Maya Great Calendar, forecasts of the planet Nibiru colliding with the Earth, the sensation around Roland Emmerich's blockbuster disaster film *2012*, or other predictions backgrounded by natural disasters, terror threats, global warming, or the financial downturn. At the same time, he checked out before the more optimistic began cranking out wholesale fantasies of evolved consciousness and global reawakening. Since his ambivalent model was not designed for those at either end of this Doomsday–New Order spectrum, McKenna could hardly have satisfied the growing fascination with 2012 rooted either in apocalyptic fears of the end or in utopian hopes for a new beginning.

CATHOLICISM WITH THE CHROME STRIPPED OFF

The "apocalypse" was an object of strange fascination for McKenna through his teens and early college years. As he long intuited, the end of the world is not in the future. It had commenced long ago. But while the apocalypse may already be upon us, it is, apropos William Gibson, "unevenly distributed." As reflected in his memoir, McKenna was cognizant of his own "eschatological hysteria," an expectancy understood to be the luxury of those living amid privilege and social insulation. In the wake of La Chorrera, and before settling on the 2012 end date, a string of dates portending significance passed without incident. "Four days from the experiment, five, seven, ten, sixteen, twenty-one, forty, sixty-four—all were times awaited with hope and willful suspension of disbelief." As his twenty-fifth birthday, the comet Kohoutek, and other occasions passed into the rearview mirror, the eschaton remained "all-pervading, yet still very elusive." Consultations with the *I Ching* and the mushroom oracle churned out many more "self-testing prophecies," many scenarios in which world transformation might be final, total, and complete.[85]

Through the seventies, the psychedelic eschatologist grew obsessed with an ending consisting of a quantized transformation comparable across systems. His attention focused on the Christian Apocalypse in which epochs grow shorter and shorter around an axis point. Before his travels in Colombia, Eliade, McLuhan, and Jung provided the grist for an "electronic eschatology." And in post-Amazon life, a psilocybean reading of Whitehead revealed "apocalyptic concrescences that haunt the historical continuum."[86] With a singular event occurring not at the inception but at the end of the universe, the Judeo-Christian model provided "a more logical position," by contrast not only to Vedic and Buddhist models but to those offered by science. That is, a model of the culmination of history before it became twisted, oppressive, and unrecognizable under "cock-eyed" Catholicism. It seemed easier to suppose that singularities might arise out of an ancient and complex cosmos, such as our own, than out of "a featureless and dimensionless mega-void."[87] The trialogues became the chief theater for a script in which McKenna regarded psychedelic travelers—that is, his audience, and ultimately himself—as the most recent in a retinue of shamans, prophets, and seers obtaining "a very noisy, low-grade signal about a future event that is somehow built into the structure of space and time."[88] It was readily admitted that the Eschaton as he configured it—his understanding of telos—evinced "Catholicism with the chrome stripped off."[89]

From the Fall to the Resurrection, and from Eden to "Angelhood," Christian cosmogony furnished a rich tapestry of myth and metaphor. Under the influence of the mushroom and under the shadow of the mushroom cloud, a psychedelic soteriology emerges in which freedom from original sin appears to be replaced by freedom from the burden of knowing how to destroy ourselves. In deep conversation with Abraham, absolute freedom and total annihilation were considered two edges of our historical reality. "As we reach for Angelhood to free ourselves," he told Ralph, referencing the discovery of fusion, "we inevitably gain the power to destroy ourselves." And this, "while we were still bound to a single planet." With the dire possibilities of this fate underwriting his intent, "Angelhood" will be hard won by banishing the daemons of knowledge.[90]

With the twisted visions of Revelation—that is, the Christian prophecy in which the elect are resurrected and the damned are dragged into hell for all eternity—in mind, McKenna was driven to "strip the provincialism" from apocalyptic religions and uncover the "deep intuition" native to mystics and prophets whose visions are efforts to "extract something out of the human future" and direct it to planetary survival.[91] At the same time, he felt it devilishly provocative that his beshroomed reveries held vestiges of the Christian cosmology from which he had been in exile. Such provocations were destined to trigger discord within his own circles. Take, for example, George Csicsery, a sociology of religion major who openly sparred with a figure who designed his own end-of-world myth and who, not uncommon among charismatic leaders, was a passionate proponent of immanent cataclysm. The propinquity of cult leaders and evangelicals proclaiming the "end is near" was too much for Csicsery, while conceding that debates with his friend were always conducted in an atmosphere of mutual respect.[92]

While we are not privy to these debates, we are privileged to the trialogues, a theater in which McKenna faced his upbraiding wearing a T-shirt printed with "S. K. Ton," and where he found himself, in his own terms, "in the predicament of leading the charge into the greatest unanchored speculation in the history of crackpot thinking."[93] Disputing the end-of-the-world-according-to-Terence as somewhat arbitrary, Sheldrake could not help but connect McKenna's prophetic mode to his life as a lapsed Catholic. Pointing out language not inconsistent with the Western model of eschatology inherited from the Church Fathers, if not from Jesus himself, and to parallels with legions of rapture cults emerging in the past two millennia, Sheldrake sometimes regarded his friend as "Father McKenna." "I used to tease him that he was a bit like those people you saw with sandwich boards on the streets when I was a child: 'Be prepared to meet thy doom.'"[94] Neither was Abraham comfortable with the Revelations of St. Terence.

Father McKenna returned the fire. "We don't need Saint John the Divine to tell us there's an apocalypse underway." The circumstances were dire and inevitable. An image from Yeats, he contended, haunts the twentieth century as strongly as it had the first and second: "Things fall apart; the center cannot hold; Mere anarchy is loosed upon the world. . . . What rough beast . . . Slouches toward Bethlehem to be born?" But he wasn't done here. "We should be allowed to let the apocalypse happen, rather than make it happen, which is what we seem to be set on doing."

Abraham didn't see a case for our transition into the fifth dimension: "Your projection of apocalypse in the year 2012 . . . is actually damaging our chances of having a future."[95]

"It may not be planetesimal impact, or the oceans boiling, but I'm telling you, Ralph, there's something out there," McKenna said. "I'll know it when I see it, and I'll expect you at my elbow."[96]

Dismissed in some quarters as a softheaded nutjob, and chided in others as a psychedelic sandwich boarder, that McKenna continued to communicate his "truth" with confidence and ease against the sharp opprobrium of peers and in the face of public controversy was, if nothing else, a case of *constantia in adversis*.

REVELATIONS OF ST. TERENCE

As much trickster as prophet, McKenna claims to have received his best ideas from the mushroom. While scholars of religion have begun weighing in on his career as cult figure and prophet long after his departure, given the "complexifications" inhering to his case, they do so at their own peril. There are unquestionable commonalities between McKenna's proclamations and those of figures millenarian and/or apocalyptic in character: charismatic male figure, an end date within his own lifetime, a sudden rapturous transformation, the elite mentality of the elect. All are typical signs of cultic formation. All the same, the ambiguities are legion and the nuances spectacular. To begin with, McKenna was hardly a good Catholic. In fact, despite his allegiance to a form of divine providence, and the embrace of a Christian-flavored Eschaton, he held contemptuous regard for its theogony. It was the only "god-system" he knew of where "the head honcho has nothing, absolutely nothing to do with women—does not have a mother, does not have a consort, does not have a daughter." There's no mistake about it. "It's a locker room religion from the get-go."[97] The Church sustained withering attack from McKenna's guns, as superbly conveyed at an Ojai Foundation event in April 1986. With apparent inspiration from Dick's *Valis* and *The Man in the High Castle*, a story emerges of our Greco-Roman-Mayanist brethren dwelling in a parallel universe in which Christ never existed. Having bifurcated from our own world at the moment of the Immaculate Conception, this idyllic non-Christian parallel world grew to become "1200 years in advance of us technologically and in the use of psychedelic substances, because they never experienced the history-freezing eschatology that the rise of Christianity created in our world."[98]

Drawing conclusions at a great remove from the life of our subject poses a further conundrum. While McKenna's ideas carried a cultic allure, his presumed stature as a cult leader is unfounded, if not ludicrous, at least during his life. Among the explanations for his ongoing appeal is that he never tired of mocking religious authorities—the Church, the New Age, or otherwise—and, moreover, derided his own prophetic affectations. As Paul Krassner reported in *High Times*, McKenna encouraged dissidence among his fans.[99] Still, while the figure with little interest in founding a cult embraced his "half-baked" caricature, the baked half was very active. There would be no end-times spoof mirroring the absurdist prophecies and apocalyptic statements of the Church of the SubGenius's J. R. "Bob" Dobbs, which upheld the hip militant tradition of subverting ecclesiastical authority through the eighties. Deriding apocalyptic thinking, Bob had even announced the coming "Rupture" to arrive on July 5, 1998 ("X-Day"), when a fleet of UFOs piloted by sex goddesses was to carry off the elect.[100] By comparison, McKenna's Book of Revelations masquerade seemed wildly gratuitous, which was the perception, for example, of cynics like Mark Jacobson, who, writing for *Esquire*, witnessed a "well-meaning P. T. Barnum of the Loaded" transform into a weird evangelist.[101] For entertainment value, McKenna rarely failed to roast his own pretensions, which were not uncommonly subject to hyper-reflexive attention. After all, so far as conspiracy theories go, his was the best in show. The strangest Eschaton. The weirdest paradox. The most laughs.

While rarely failing to draw laughs on the stand-up eschatology circuit, the Timewave troubled McKenna's ongoing campaign to gain credibility within the scientific community. The theory of novelty became a magnet for controversy. Forging a career as a scientist, Dennis grew estranged from an idea to which he had been attached as a co-discoverer. As events do not "erupt" so much as "ooze" onto the world stage, Dennis regarded novelty as essentially unchartable. Further, not only was Timewave Zero not a formal proposition that could be invalidated by new data; it was dismissed by *The Invisible Landscape*'s coauthor as "utterly useless as a map of time, a predictor of events, or a mathematical theory."[102]

Others reacted to the concept's masculinist linearity, as well as the privileged, and elitist, stature of its dimensionality. Skepticism formed among Terence's fans and adherents within his lifetime. In the final edition of the magazine *Towards 2012*, the editor, Gyrus, challenged the Timewave's implicit androcentrism as yet another male-authored eschatology in a long lineage. In contemplation of the female orgasm, with its "continuous waves of full-body, non-linear ecstasy, with no focal point and no singular 'explosion,'" the model's sudden "ejaculatory" climax was called into question. With its cosmically abrupt singularity, McKenna's eschaton conflicts with the Taoist sense of flow, according to Gyrus, who questioned the assumption that the creators of the *I Ching* believed in a grand climax at the end of time. Would they not, he puzzled, place a question mark at the end of their universe rather than a full stop or exclamation point?[103]

The closer one looks, the more manifold are the problems. Regarding the overwhelmingly white environs of the "new-age Club Med," at the 1992 Esalen workshop "Tao and the Timewave" Jacobson observed the Timewave as a Eurocentric "parlor game." The wave may have "reacted to the onset of the Black death and the 'discovery' of the New World," but where were the subaltern positions adopted vis-à-vis these, and other, events in the charts?[104] If anyone bothered to make careful study of the "novelty reports" issued bimonthly in the nineties, they would uncover a US-centric means of "novelty" interpretation. Mark Dery was another critic who did not let McKenna off the hook. His *Escape Velocity* addressed the failings implicit to the rhetoric of transcending the body, history, and mortality. "End-times" proponents, Dery wagered, typically vaunt their status as elect witnesses to a dispensation advantageous to the prepared. This held true for cyberdelicists like McKenna as it did for other millennialists. As the chosen ones grow vested with a transcendent future to which they are destined, what is the cost? "Placing our faith in an end of century *deus ex machina* that will obviate the need to confront the social, political, economic, and ecological problems clamoring for solutions," Dery demurred, "is a risky endgame."[105]

As a tryptaminal upgrade on Teilhard's prophesied "Christogenesis," McKenna's thought offered a psychedelic species of transhumanism,[106] in which individuation and teleology interface, where telos is fueled by spiritual technologies. A faith in technology to transcend the body, the planet, and even race drew inspiration from science-fiction author Vernor Vinge's "technological singularity," an idea subsequently adapted by Ray Kurzweil, among others.[107] Is this development merely an exotic refinement of white male privilege?

APOCALYPSE ENOUGH?

On the nature of the near future event that would dwarf all precedents, the trickster-prophet was consistently equivocal. Many have puzzled over McKenna's opaque projections and inconsistencies concerning "the end." There was to be boundary-dissolving novelty—that much is certain. But the details were scarce, if not cryptic. The first hours might be like taking 1,000 micrograms of LSD, Esalenites were apprised. "After that we can't imagine or predict."[108] Will the end-state be nuclear Armageddon, alien contact, planetesimal impact, solar explosion, or quasar ignition at the "galactic core"? When pressed for more details, a checklist of crises is produced: epidemics, the proliferation of thermonuclear weapons, CO_2 emissions and atmospheric change, the rise in world population. When the curves were extrapolated, we were no longer conducting "business as usual."[109] Would the business end of the end-times be coincident with complete social breakdown and total extinction; a kind of Ragnarok triggered by "the eruption of the psychotic mythologies that have driven the matter-centered, monotheistic, male ego culture"?[110] Or will the coming transformation be coincident with incomprehensible levels of novelty in synchrony with the evolution of language, hyperspatial breakthrough, space migration, timestream reconnection, time travel, or an AI singularity? All possibilities are mooted at one time or another, and sometimes simultaneously.

Speculative 2012 futurisms flagged McKenna as a possible sci-fi author, as perhaps best illustrated in his rap: "The Great Timestream Bifurcation." The story was driven by a heroic psilocybin-dosed vision of starfaring Greco-Roman-Mayans whose civilization parallels our own world. In the vision, after discovering its twin (our world), and making unsuccessful attempts to contact us—by way of dreams, shamans, psychedelics, paranormal events, and unexplained phenomena—our twin civilization finally succeeds in opening the timestream to reconnect its continuum with our world in 2012. The vision seems to be at least in part driven by mid-eighties anxieties about the growing possibilities of nuclear holocaust. McKenna effectively served as a channel for a parallel civilization that seeks to "depotentiate our nuclear arsenals in order to save their own world."[111] This vision of a "magical, psychopharmacolitic" civilization that had reached the moon and achieved a cybernetic global network by 1200 is revealed to a group in retreat at Joshua Tree in 1986.[112] Presented as a "toy made of ideas and language," the story is further related at Wetlands in New York City, where the audience was given to understand that, in 2012, a bridge will open in an area "roughly the size of Ukraine." Connecting the parallel worlds and unifying the divided timestreams, this great reunification will be celebrated by later generations as an armistice. Animating his 2012 prophecy within a mythic framework, this story might have been the basis for an epic novel. But McKenna preferred stand-up psychedelic mythography over exegesis. And after all, he did not believe in this story; it simply offered a "soliton of improbability" vis-à-vis reality.[113]

Time travel is another favored theme. "Imagine," McKenna once challenged his audience, "that it's December 22, 2012, at the La Chorrera World Temporal Mechanics Institute." The fantasy was repeated on various occasions in which the countdown is in progress and "the temponaut" is strapped into the time machine. "A technician pushes the button and she sails off into the future." In a scenario reminiscent of Carl Sagan's *Contact*, La Chorrera is imagined as the repository for the acquisition of time travel technology. History abruptly ends as linear time collapses at the very moment time travel is discovered. For those born into a time-traveling universe, the previous mode of existence is unimaginable. In such a scenario, travel could not extend to the era before the discovery of time travel—that is, pre-2012—as no time machines exist there.[114] The shroomic scenario is elaborated in a workshop on physics and philosophy at Esalen in 1991, where participants learn that a millisecond after the temponaut disappears, "the rest of the history of the universe happens instantly." This fantasy is regarded as the "God Whistle Principle," which signaled a moment when "we can actually call God into history."[115]

The time travel propositions were among the ideas gaining McKenna an audience with Art Bell. In May 1997, on his first appearance on *Coast to Coast AM*—a paranormal-themed late-night program with a syndicated audience of millions across North America—the Timewave had its biggest splash to date. The two behave like intellectual soulmates of the airwaves. At the couple's first on-air date, Terence knew the way to the heart of Art, recent author of *The Quickening: Today's Trends, Tomorrow's World*. Sweet-talking the host, McKenna informs Bell that "each acceleration in novelty has preceded more quickly than the ones which preceded it," and the host is smitten. While many among the audience are similarly wooed, at this and subsequent appearances, the alarm sounded for God-fearing multitudes disturbed by the effrontery of the false prophet and his outrageous vision. When convulsed callers warn Bell that he is playing with fire by putting McKenna on the air, he cues up "The Devil Went Down to Georgia" by the Charlie Daniels Band.[116]

Space migration is another favored trope. But while physicist and space activist Gerard O'Neill is raised as a standard bearer, few details are presented for the establishment of colonies in space. In McKenna's imagination, outer was routinely interchangeable with inner space. "Space is black and empty and a wonderful place to put things," he claimed. "It's sort of like the inside of your mind." When it came to humanity's quest to build structures that will coincide with our departure from the planet, the real question is: "Should we build them in space or should we build them north of the amygdala?"[117] Such inquiry is the hallmark of a figure packing a poetic license to conflate travels in outer space and flights of the imagination. In raps delivered across his career, and in connection with an event in his near future, the aphorism is repeated: *the interiorization of the body, and the exteriorization of the soul*. This is the Blakean choral mantra of the wave-of-time mythopoeia. The jingle for the McKennan brand.

The Timewave is its author's mystic kernel of truth. As much can be unearthed from the entries of "Change and Becoming." If "the stone" for which McKenna was a lifelong prospector was his own monadic self, the Timewave is a complex expression of this excavation. Through public lectures and writings, and in the Timewave Zero software, interior process was actively exteriorized. To state this otherwise, the Timewave projected an unconscious drive to reconcile contraries. The mythos represented a remarkable exposition of the *coniunctio*—self-formation via the alchemical union of opposites. "Ultimately," writes Dennis of his brother's journey, "it was clear he'd been trying to map his own odyssey through time as much as define time's hidden structure."[118] The desired state of "zero" quantified in the wave—the holy concrescence—amounted to wholeness, within reach and yet unobtainable. That interpretation becomes available when lifting the hood on McKenna's psychic engine. That he was far less a mathematician than a poet is brilliantly distilled in "New and Old Maps of Hyperspace," in which he rapped on "the alchemical stone at the end of time," the transcendental object as the ultimate achievement in self-transcendence.[119]

Throughout his spoken and textual material, McKenna projects the mood of an avid alchemist, whether moonlighting as 4-D libertarian or raving eschatologist. On rare occasions, the mongoose is released from its cage: "One way of thinking of the Timewave is that it is simply a complex totality symbol generated out of a spectacularly peculiar individuation process that was triggered by psychedelic experimentation."[120] As an unconscious process of redemption, alchemy is the enduring leitmotif lifted from Jung. Part II of *The Invisible Landscape* is a remarkable testament to Terence's outlandish conviction that his own quest for redemption could be charted, quantized, and measured. There, it is suggested that the "zero state"—that is, the apocalypse—is achievable in two ways. One considers "the dissolution of the cosmos" in the actual implosion and cessation of natural laws—that is, a literal apocalypse. The other considers the completion of human endeavor and tool making in the "perfect artifact." This artifact was, of course, "the monadic self, exteriorized, condensed, and visible in three dimensions." In alchemical terms, the union of spirit and matter:

> The appearance in normal space-time of a hyperdimensional body, obedient to a simultaneously transformed and resurrected human will, and able to plumb the obligations and opportunities inherent in this unique juncture in energy's long struggle for self-liberation, may be apocalypse enough.[121]

Alchemy furnished the allegorical materials to configure a model that was "apocalypse enough." No mere symbolic construct, the weight of conjecture implied that the apocalypse (the "perfect artifice") was chartable terrain.

THE ARCHITECTURE OF EVOLUTIONARY BREAKTHROUGH

It might have oiled the *mckennaism*, but the psychology of alchemy never extended far enough for a figure convinced that "the stone" was achievable in three-dimensional reality—that is, at the moment when we're liberated from matter. The transcendental object is ultimately "a doorway into the imagination,"[122] a declaration founded on the belief that humanity is fated to depart the physical universe for a life lived in the mind. Over the years, the trialogues became a productive platform for dialogue on themes like the divine imagination, the Gaian mind, Plato's archetypal forms, and the UFO as exteriorized soul. Sheldrake was suspicious of the transcendental object. The idea of a cosmic attractor, the end point of evolutionary gravitation, not only sounded like an updated Teilhardian Christogenesis; it had the allure of the Aristotelian "entelechy" in which all of history is pulled toward an all-knowing God. Ultimately, Sheldrake embraced the chaotic principle that "the world truly is made up as it goes along."[123]

An early nineties trialogue sheds light on McKenna's vision on the matter of the transcendental object as transcendental subject. The exchange is not unlike communications between the principals of a theatrical production who express their creative differences—notably over the production's ending. Terence sets the scene: "All boundaries are dissolving—between men and women, between society and nature, and ultimately the boundaries between life and death. We are going truly beyond ambiguity, beyond syntax. We've been trapped in a kind of daemonic simulacrum for 25,000 years, created out of language. Now the accelerating . . . progression of epochs toward the concrescence is in fact being fulfilled."[124]

"Why couldn't it be just a simple social transformation like the Renaissance?" Abraham inquires.

His buddy had sat through this movie many times before—and the ending was always the same. "Because the planet can't bring forth the birth of new societies. We've come to the end of our road in birthing new models of community. . . . We're on a collision course with the unspeakable. Contrasted with other animal life, we've been selected out for a very peculiar metamorphosis via information and the conquest of dimensions to become something completely other: a new ontological order of being."[125]

Since human history didn't appear to be mirrored in changes happening elsewhere in the solar system, galaxy, or cosmos, Sheldrake is unsatisfied with his collaborator's low-budget cosmic provincialism. "I don't think astronomers in the last few years or decades have suddenly noticed curves in their charts rushing off to some extreme point, where we can expect stars all over the galaxy to turn into supernovae. Nor can we expect planets all over the solar system to collapse, crumble, collide or otherwise undergo dramatic alteration." What's more, he detects a basic flaw in his friend's script: that the mounting crisis is largely human-generated. Anyway, even *if* the story concludes with the end of history here on Earth, Sheldrake thinks Terence's ending stretches too far the demand to suspend disbelief. "I find it quite incredible that the rest of the solar system is just going to shut up shop and go out of business, let alone the galaxy, let alone the clusters of galaxies."[126]

"If it's truly a higher-dimensional object, then it's in some sense everywhere in this universe," McKenna mounts his quicksilver response. "And all routes of evolutionary progress may lead into it, as a kind of universal hologram of time and space, a galactic community or intelligence perhaps."

He confidently reminds his co-visionaries of the story arc driving his franchise, that is, "to grow from the initial seed and return to the higher, hidden source of all, outside the pleroma of three-dimensional space." In the elaborate fantasy of gnostic return implicit to the McKennaverse, its creator sees the cosmos as a distillery for novelty and the transcendental object as the ultimate novelty. "When we formally refine that, we discover something like a Leibnizian planet, a monad of some sort, a tiny thing that has everything enfolded within it. This takes us to another dimension, where all points in this universe have been collapsed and become cotangents. It's an apotheosis. The Earth is giving birth to a hyperdimensional being."[127]

Pressed on the matter, McKenna closes in on the secret within the mystery at the heart of the enigma. "I realize it's incredible," he offers in further defense of his position, to suppose that "at the apex of . . . civilization" we will finally obtain an understanding of "what lies beyond the grave." And yet that is precisely "the paradigm-shattering world-condensing event that is bearing down on us."[128]

Responding to the "event" that transfixes their friend, Abraham steps into the ring to make an insightful rejoinder to McKenna's desire for immortality. "Freud had described our strange fascination with entelechy and that the Eschaton is a manifestation of Thanatos." In other words, "we are fascinated by our own death, although we deny it and transfer it onto larger spheres." Abraham not only has the measure of the man he'd known for two decades; with Sheldrake's assistance, he seeks to flip the script. Using the language of Aristotle and medieval scholars, Sheldrake had elaborated his thoughts on McKenna's attractor possessing its own "entelechy." All organisms possess their own destiny, purpose, or end. The acorn had been the example conveyed, the entelechy of which is an oak tree, the acorn's own end state.[129] "Now that we've achieved more or less the largest sphere in our search for the eventual death of the all and everything," suggests Abraham, in allusion to McKenna's sophisticated projections, "perhaps we could extend the same consideration to creativity and birth and see the acorn, growing into the mature tree, as the ultimate principle of life. In these seeds, birth moments are distributed everywhere in space and time and throughout the reality of the universe."[130]

Despite the efforts of Abraham and Sheldrake to shanghai their comrade in compression, there is an extraordinary resilience to McKenna's thought. An uncomfortable relevance. A resonant drag. In his oldest surviving recorded rap, the room is bummed out with a truth that has grown heavier in times hence. "We have unleashed some kind of process that is inimical to the planet, and very very final," the Dodge Place circle was informed.

"We've triggered the final crisis for the planet. . . . We are trapped in history that gets more and more unimaginable, as the information piles up about the situation we find ourselves in."[131] Recently returned from his exoteric travails, McKenna was at home inside a narrative of mounting tragedy, an unrelenting screechpuke, a turbulent story as familiar to him as it surely is to us. Tragic but non-fatalistic, McKenna claimed to be making "a sharp left" at a thanatotic future. There were plenty of signs to justify the apocalyptic veneer of his own obsessions. After all, and taking cues from Sheldrake, "you cannot have three religions stacked up on top of each other, stretching back 4,000 years, pursuing this monotheistic vision which ends in an apocalypse without building a tremendous morphogenetic predilection for the apocalypse."[132]

Under fire from his compatriots, McKenna clings to the prevailing twist in his plot: the apocalypse as a moment of liberation. He sought to break from the tired formula that humans are terribly flawed beings fated to run amok. The ending—*his* ending—would not be another cheap Renaissance or second-class Gothic revival; it was to be the final global crisis. Rather than a cause for despair, "the object" is imagined as a sign of hope. What's more, the final resolve is an expression of bios, and a natural feature of the evolutionary process. Leading with the tagline: "Human history is not our fault. . . . It's the architecture of evolutionary breakthrough that is etched into every molecule of DNA on the planet," subscribers to *bOING bOING* were privy to the pitch for his epic:

> It's going to happen—the egg shell is breaking. The womb is ruptured, and there is no way out now but some kind of journey down the very frightening birth canal of experience. The next 30 years will stand your hair on end, guaranteed, because it's barely begun. Right now, we are living in the golden twilight of Western Civilization. The long afternoon of Cartesian rationalism. Ahead lies agricultural failure, atmospheric disruption, ethnic warfare, sexually transmitted diseases, propaganda, superdrugs, AND a whole bunch of good stuff. But it's going to be a white-knuckled ride to break through at the end of time, because there is so much to be unleashed. What's happening is we're turning into something else.[133]

THE PARTY AT THE END OF THE WORLD

Despite the dire portents, the end-times were no sullen affair. As comparative religionist Joseph Campbell had remarked on a Grateful Dead show he saw toward the end of his life, the show was "the antidote to the atomic bomb." Deadheads, he imagined, were embodying Dionysus. Once asked if he agreed with Campbell, McKenna averred that Dead shows are "mini-reflections of the real party, the real Dionysian revel at the end of time." Concerted cosmic cavalcades were not just responses of activists to the prospect of nuclear Armageddon, but sparks cast backward from "the party at the end of the world." In this way, the Dead were reckoned "the house band of the apocalypse." Echoing his reversed reading of Eliade's idea that ritual replays cosmic time, McKenna soon applied his logic to raves, which reminded him that "you are really somehow at the end of the world."[134]

With necks craned to catch McKenna's vowels and consonants at Megatripolis, London, in 1994, the Parallel YOUniversity crowd was delivered the news: this was, right now, the most novel moment in all of history; with each passing moment, novelty accumulates; and all evolutionary data reveals that the peak of history's trip is "coming soon." McKenna was flyer-dropping his audience—a mix of the intrigued, the perplexed, and the bemused—for his "super-novel" transformational event. There is no coincidence that those on the psychedelic edges of the rave scene and their descendants were the audience most receptive to the Timewave siren, even if many weren't entirely on board with the apocalyptic shadow forecast. With the coming event promoted as something like the Big Bang on Drugs, it registered with a community dedicated to manifesting transformative events. It was candy to an underground scene populated with crews designing events as cosmic cavalcades, more transcendent, more novel, than those confabulated last season. Event crews within this short-attention-span economy vied to cultivate an experience more outlandish than their competitors. The discourse on acceleration and complexity was assimilable for those augmenting events with technology and aesthetics designed to inaugurate sensorial experiences more novel than last year, last week, or just yesterday. McKenna's uber-novel Zero event was cast as the event to end all events, a stimulus for action, if not a cause for celebration, an idea communicated in his quip saved for inquiries about the nature of "the event" that awaits us at the end of time. The ultimate goal of evolution was, of course, "a great party."[135] The statement "I'll see you at the end of the world" and the Irish toast "May you be alive at the end of the world" were favored partings. Would anyone want to miss that?

McKenna cultivated his audience for the "bifurcation" event ahead. That it would be an uncertain event in which his audience should expect to experience a transformed consciousness, becoming unknowable to themselves, and even completely *othered* as a species, lent the event a *je ne sais quoi* appealing to those jonesing to be transported out of their minds. Such transcendent states have long been the aspiration of trance dance movements bent on self-annihilation in ecstatic states—movements in which death and birth are inextricable. In the nineties, McKenna was propagating a new discourse on apocalyptic festivity. As implicit to his Timewave mythos, and as a motif inherent to his novelty thesis, the end was at the same time a new beginning—a transition point. It was a motif essential for transformational dance event cultures accustomed to celebrating seasonal transitions. Despite the outlandish implications of his ideas, his mythopoetics can be factored among the reasons why McKenna has been courted within the psychedelic trance scene. That the wave of time had a synchronous relationship with the Mayan calendar movement drew more intense associations, as borne out in the precession toward December 21, 2012. In the preceding decade, elements within psyculture forged a planetary consciousness movement reliant on the inauguration of a "new time." By the time that date rolled around, the momentum had all but petered out. Given how he departed a dozen years preceding the headline event forecast, McKenna was unavailable for the preparations, let alone the festivities.[136]

The "transcendental object" had a strangely familiar shape and tone for the rave-o-lutionary multitudes who positioned McKenna somewhere between a comic and a seer. As an object, *it* was made familiar to this audience via his scintillating metaphor of a spinning cosmic ball of mirrors. And as an event, *it* made sense as the culmination to an epic *trip*. That history amounted to a "big trip" was, of course, the common refrain. History was to end in the ultimate concrescence, a unity of all opposites, a dissolution of all boundaries. What was imagined transpiring at the culmination of this 15,000-year odyssey called "history" was thoroughly informed by the psychedelic state. "It is our weird privilege," McKenna's Santa Fe audience learned in 1990, "to live in an age where there is also to be a collective dropping of the mask, a moment of melting and recasting." As the recombination of a thousand trips, it was supposed that the psychedelic experience amounts to the experience of eternity. Through those epic events you see "the beginning of life, the end of life, the fiery death of this planet, millennia hence . . . All of time." The audience leans in toward a figure seemingly gripped by his own fate as much as that of history. In the end, "a shaman is someone who has seen the end."[137]

CASTING NETS IN THE SEA OF MIND

The effort to intellectualize McKenna's most syzygyztic of contrivances seems destined to neglect the levity that the stand-up eschatologist carried to hundreds of public appearances. In doing so, we overlook how the

Timewave may have been among the most obsessive jokes in the twentieth century. The Timewave sometimes comes across as an elaborate caper, a hoax, a trickster's device perhaps more pataphysical than metaphysical. After all, in addition to Jung, McKenna held the French Symbolist Alfred Jarry in esteem, naming pataphysics as a significant novelty peak in the path toward the transcendental object—a collision of the past and the future, which also lies at the intersection of dada and gnosis. If a joke, the transcendental object may have been among the grandest, a complex zinger eking out its own career. But the dadagnostic transcendentalist departed without delivering the punchline. In the trailing era of escalating crises that echo a lifetime of premonitions, the grand jest lingers like a haunting fart in the eternal elevator.

Step right up and behold the sumo wrestler of syntax with his Nietzschean "spark of divinity." That's right folks, prepare to be amazed by the freak "light bulb salesman" and his contorted time contraption. You can stand there with your hands in your pockets shaking hands with the unemployed, or step right in and see it to believe it. Over three decades, McKenna never lost faith in his Eschaton, for which he behaved like a carnival barker to his very own freak show. If the transcendental object was akin to a cosmic disco ball, Timewave Zero was like the infinity mirror to its prospector's psyche. A syncretic device with multiple inputs—intellectual mentors, the mushroom, DMT, the *I Ching*, his Catholic upbringing, the tumultuous era, his mother's death, his wife's musings, his brother's ravings—it was all at once divinatory, redemptive, pataphysical, mythopoetic.

Part surreal provocation, panacea, and improv theater-therapy, Timewave Zero grew attached to McKenna's legacy like a barnacle on the hull of an ocean trawler. By the nineties he was deploying its charts as letterheads, and through the decade he plied his craft into a gale of controversy.

With its performance exteriorizing its creator's interior, the Timewave became a very public individuation enacted right up until his own endtime. Layered with paradox, fraught with contradiction, and attracting criticism, the model effectively turned heads, a circumstance ensuring its author a platform for the remainder of his life—or at least until 2012, had he made it that far. "A foolish consistency is the hobgoblin of little minds" was McKenna's defense of his thesis, apropos Oscar Wilde. For a great many, the idea was equally intriguing and vexatious. And yet, when the smoke cleared, as his final San Francisco appearance demonstrates, in response to the view that humanity had left the center of the stage, the model was committed to the business of restoring "cosmic purpose." "People matter. You are the cutting-edge of a thirteen-billion year old process of defining novelty. Your acts matter. Your thoughts matter" Such is the declaration at Fort Mason. "And so, suddenly then, you have a morality, you have an ethical arrow. . . . You have authenticity. You have hope."[138]

Ultimately, the transcendental object was an expression of McKenna's own purpose and will—somewhat in disaccord with Philippe De Vosjoli, with whom Terence coauthored a book in the late nineties titled "Casting Nets in the Sea of Mind," a manuscript that was never finished.

The project had a weathered history. McKenna's "stoned ape" theory served as a call to action for De Vosjoli. An expert in reptile husbandry whose father was head of the French Intelligence Service under de Gaulle, De Vosjoli had long held interest in the role of psychedelics in human evolution. Seeking a corrective to McKenna's hypothesis, in 1994, De Vosjoli pitched an idea for a book collaboration, originally titled "The Origins of Humankind." He set forth his reservations. While mushrooms were a selective factor in evolution, they were not, the Frenchman deemed, the cause of mutation for a larger brain. He also took issue with the millenarianism, notably the 2012 rhetoric. Despite these concerns, McKenna agreed to collaborate, accepting a $15,000 advance for a project he thought will "divide its attention between the emergence of consciousness in our species in the distant past and the emerging super-consciousness that our relationship with technology is leading us toward."[139] In a short chapter, "The Future of Humanity," the approach illustrated McKenna's ongoing commitment to the eschaton while transiting away from specific commitment to 2012. Whether "the nexus of transformative vectors" is but a few years or 200 years away, the outcome is the same: an "ecstatic breakthrough into a cultural superspace of staggering dimensions."[140]

Little progress was made on "Casting Nets." A planning meeting on Hawaii in 1998 was hampered by Terence's cluster headaches, Philippe's allergies, and a failing recorder. Moreover, the authors disagreed over plans for the book. "It would be wrong to say it was a cooperative venture," De Vosjoli explains. "It wasn't the investigative project I had hoped for where we could further explore how psychedelics impacted the evolution of society and culture." McKenna apparently saw the project as a means to publish more recent spoken word material, notably relating to novelty, the electronic dispensation, and the end of history. We gain insight on what the new book might have looked like from a 1998 workshop at the Omega Institute, in New York, where, in candid oracular feedback, McKenna likened information to "a virtual life form of some sort that is running on a primate platform." Complexity theory, global dynamics, and chaos theory all lent respectability to thinking about processes that are drawn by something in the future rather than pushed from behind. Under the chains of cause and effect endemic to Darwinism, which had arrived with objections toward deism, teleology had been inconceivable. "But now we see that the temporal landscape has what are called basins of attraction in it, and that certain processes are actually drawn forward by their presumed end states."[141] It now seemed less outlandish to suppose that there is a *purpose*, thought McKenna, clashing with his coauthor's own purpose.

A few weeks after his diagnosis, McKenna called De Vosjoli, requesting he send their spartan manuscript to Dan Levy. De Vosjoli complied, with misgivings, as the work remained rudimentary, a view confirmed by Levy. It is difficult to envision how "Casting Nets" may have turned out. If a successful compromise, it might have appeared as a conversation between positions on the evolutionary role of psychedelics in "gateway events." If McKenna had his way, it could have charted his scaling of history's fractal mountain. Perhaps it would have offered material in support of a general unified theory of consciousness. While we will never know, there is one thing about which we can be certain: this episode illustrated the persistent influence of eschatology on McKenna's thinking, right through to his own end.

10 PSYCHEDELIC GURU

Shooting the breeze inside a Prague café in 1992, a quirky exchange between McKenna and Ram Dass ambles into the fraught terrain of leadership. McKenna, then performing the role of interviewer for a series later titled *Prague Gnosis*, struggles to accept his role as an authority. "If I am special, then my career is pointless." The psychedelic experience, he maintains, "belongs to every man and woman on the planet."[1] They trade mantras. McKenna defers to Blake: "If the truth can be told so as to be understood, it will be believed." Dass agrees, though preferring Gandhi: "My life is my message." On this heavy score, McKenna has his doubts, conceding: "I would almost say: 'my message is my message, please don't look at my life because I'm a fallible human being and I'm constantly fucking up.'"[2] It is a perfect illustration of the bind into which McKenna had fallen—reticence to assume a leadership role, while admitting to qualities precisely admired among those seeking direction: self-doubt and fallibility.

Terence McKenna was a reluctant leader. For the down-home anarchist, all ideology was toxic and suspect. Gurus, priests, politicians, celebrities, academics, positivists, leaders in style, taste, and culture—none were to be trusted. All authorities were subject to scorn and ridicule. At the same time, as his own notoriety grew, and as he strove for credibility in the fields of science and religion, McKenna came to occupy a position of power and influence. It was to be a precarious and uncomfortable perch. While the media conferred upon him the dubious title of "drug guru," his approach is dissident, organic, and homegrown, a guerrilla tactic that offers a sharp contrast with the public profile of Ram Dass's (when he was Dr. Richard Alpert) colleague of yore, Dr. Leary. As this chapter demonstrates, despite, and likely because of, his ambivalent role as authority, and through his iconic stature as a speculative mystic of the deep past and the near future, "America's shaman" earned respect among an international constituency of psychonauts. Prestige accumulated through McKenna's ability to mediate immediacy, through his role as a fluent translator of the "N,N-unspeakable," and as a figure in dialogue with the *Psilocybe*-activated inner voice.

Noteworthy to McKenna's freak dissidence is that it was pursued outside the sanctioned realm of academic science. At the same time, he sought recognition within the scientific community and even behaved as a policy proponent. Amounting to his most determined effort to earn legitimacy, his manifesto *Food of the Gods* was the chief vehicle for this strategy. This chapter addresses the conception and reception of *Food of the Gods*, an unrecognized sci-fi classic and paean to an *immediatist vitalism*. Along the way, we'll discover that, as he initiated the American, and subsequently international, underground into the magic plant mysteries, McKenna effectively served for multitudes the role of "trip sitter," if not in person, then metaphorically—a role that he continues to assume in the cybercultural afterlife. To that end, we will consider the two chief vehicles of McKenna's psychedelic gnosis. In the first instance, adopting commentary from various sources, we'll navigate the McKennan DMT rites of passage, involving contact with his spirit familiars—the *machine elves*—bearers of the revelation that reality is made of language. In the second, we negotiate the roots and inflections of the *Psilocybe*-mediated *logos*. Throughout, we'll chart a course through fraught, turbulent, and ambivalent relationships with the law, media, science, religion, politics, and the sublime. And as we do so, we follow the career of a psychedelics advocate as subversive as he was entertaining. McKenna was ultimately an anti-guru guru dedicated to transposing the means of perception by which growing numbers are encouraged to reclaim their minds and become authors of their own experience.

RECLAIM YOUR MIND

McKenna was unwavering in his stance that the metabolizing of visionary plants is a fundamental human right. For all of his self-deprecation, feral speculation, and eccentricity, this conviction found appeal from Berkeley to Palenque, to the dance floors of countless raves and festivals. If psychedelics expose individuals to the deep and wide parameters of what it means to be human, then we can no more turn to the inexperienced for judgment and knowledge about being human than we can turn to virgins for advice on sexuality. Critics may have tagged him a "drug guru," but McKenna was quick to declare that his was an *anti-drug* position. The stance is consistent. Alcohol, speed, cocaine, and other drugs of dependence promote self-destructive repetitious behavior, while the plant-derived psychoactives to which he gravitated promote consciousness, incite life-course revaluation, and facilitate the reconstruction of behavioral patterns.[3] Through the eighties and nineties, with unmatched expertise and wit, McKenna became the mouthpiece for an unsanctioned botanical cornucopia, which, as he widely claimed, countermands the designs of the Church, Wall Street, and the Pentagon. These psychedelics, he carefully observed, are "not for everyone," but their scope for potentiating the redesign of self and society should not be trifled with. Therefore, all have a right to be informed.

By the turn of the nineties, without official position and independent of any professional organization, McKenna became recognized in the media as the doyen of cognitive liberty. "Just as a woman should be free to control her body," *Omni* readers are informed in 1993, "a person should also be free to control his or her mind."[4] In a position attracting appeal over the course of his public career, the experience associated with magic plants is championed as a human "birthright"—as much as "our sexuality, our language, our eyesight, our appreciation of music."[5] Americans could not enter a civilized dialogue, he informs author Luc Sala, "until we grant that people's minds—like their bodies—must be a domain free from government control." And if "life, liberty and the pursuit of happiness" mean anything as guarantees written into the Declaration of Independence, it must include "the right to use and experiment with substances and plants."[6] By the time McKenna gains prominence, the War on Drugs had grown long and bitter. The armature of prohibition not only restricted research that could potentially yield valuable psychological and medical insights; it fosters "the repression of a legitimate religious sensibility," a travesty routinely broached as a civil rights issue with First Amendment implications.[7]

Among the final chapters of *Food of the Gods*, "A Brief History of Psychedelics" concludes on a somber note: "A worldwide attitude of fear toward drugs is being fostered and manipulated by the dominator culture and its propaganda organs."[8] Among the best available condensations of the subject, the book demonstrated that the troubadour of tryptamines had entered the nineties with a formidable foe in his sights. "Culture," as it would be announced through the eighties, is "not your friend." Culture was not to be trusted. Like operating systems, cultures are "boundary-defining engines" that produce paranoid personalities.[9] But if a culture is defined by its edges, a veritable pharmacopoeia perturbs its boundaries. Organic allies break down cultural illusions, promote authenticity, facilitate immediacy, and incite inquiry. Providing inoculation against enculturation, "they show that these things are provisional, and that beneath the level of culture there is lurking this erotic, time-and-space-bound, feeling-defined, pre-linguistic mode of being, which is real being."[10] Although they never met, the baton had been passed from Huxley, who understood that with the availability of organic visionary tools, the culturally conditioned are empowered with the means "to cut holes in the fence of verbalized symbols that hems him in."[11] The sentiment was shared by Leary, for whom psychedelics were the antidote to the cultural "game," though the en masse deconditioning that Leary promoted stood in contrast to the more cautious and deliberative approaches of Huxley and McKenna.

The contrast with Leary is important since he was seen as McKenna's Irish forerunner—and not only by Leary himself. "Without you there would be no me," McKenna inscribed inside the cover of Leary's copy of *True Hallucinations*. Consonant with the global mood of expectancy at the turn of the nineties, Leary's call to "create your own culture" is consistent with McKenna's objections to the material culture of consumer capitalism: "Create your own road show." Such is the message of the sloganeer whose screed delivered at Seattle's Mandala Books in 1994 provides one of his most celebrated soundbites amplified on today's digital billboards: "Reclaim your mind, and get it out of the hands of the cultural engineers who want to turn you into a half-baked moron consuming all this trash that's manufactured out of the bones of a dying world."[12] Whereas in the sixties, Leary attempted to redesign *religion* from the ground up, thirty years later, it is *culture* that needed transforming, in accordance with the desire for immediacy and enhancing the means of perception. That said, a religious sensibility is never far from the center of gravity. As was conveyed in the unfinished manuscript of "Casting Nets," the "media driven consumer capitalism will make paupers of us all" lest we apply ourselves to the coming "archaic" transformation with the energy of committed revivalists.[13] Given that objective, McKenna committed to the public transfer of knowhow, methods, and tools to augment perception and alter consciousness.

McKenna admired Leary for his courageous, independent stance within a climate of prohibition that saw not only a moratorium on research, but an institutionalized taboo that stifled education and precluded public discourse. The silence, avoidance, and denial on the part of public intellectuals dependent for their livelihood on those same governmental instruments that enact and enforce prohibition is the absurd situation McKenna was privileged to observe as a free thinker untethered to academic institutions or professional bodies. While few, if any, public-funded commentators rose in defense of psychedelics, or specifically the "indole hallucinogens," in the wake of the moral panic that saw their scheduling with heroin, and that suppressed research on their social and medical benefits, it was McKenna who rose to the challenge, as is evident in his talk-back radio debate with the vice chairman of the LA County Young Republicans. Facing off with the confident but ill-informed Dan Brennan, McKenna put the prejudiced conservative to the sword live on LA's KFI-AM radio. As Brennan denied the rights of the individual to be educated on the risks and benefits of psychedelics, he personified a sentiment McKenna attributed to Leary that LSD is a "hallucinogenic drug that occasionally causes psychotic behavior in people who have not taken it."[14] This kind of forum was not generally favored by McKenna, who preferred honest intellectual debate.

The War on Drugs bore strikingly different impacts on Leary and McKenna. While the former saw the inside of dozens of prisons, such was never the case for the younger man, who did not retain a criminal record. While both men held in common a desire to resist authority, and were riotously good-humored, McKenna was cautious in his attention to detail, and had an anarchist's desire to fly under the radar. By contrast to Leary's revolutionary campaign, McKenna's operation was low-key and stealthy—a means acquired after early dabbling in hash imports and after ten years as a clandestine fungi farmer. The largest crowds McKenna drew were in the range of 2,000, maybe 3,000, people, while Leary had addressed crowds in the tens of thousands. "The trick," thought McKenna, "is gradual incremental infiltration and then we'll be all through the body politic before they even know they've got a fever." It was no minor factor that their respective operations involved different molecules with remarkably distinct public threat levels, which likely contributed to a toleration of McKenna. The capacity for LSD to be manufactured and distributed swiftly at tens of millions of doses had triggered panic among governing bodies since Leary's sixties' exploits. By contrast, as McKenna later informed LA police chief Daryl Gates, with mushrooms, if a mushroom grower "were to work like a dog for six months you would be lucky to make a couple of thousand of hits." Moreover, mushrooms are comparatively trivial, inherently humorous, and nonthreatening. "They look like non-erect penises." And besides, as he assured Gates, he was not on a crusade to influence children.[15] McKenna did not promote LSD and even publicly disparaged its use (compared with other tryptamines, and later, *Salvia divinorum*). Other products born in the "demonic artifice" of the laboratory, notably ketamine, were favored targets of skepticism (a defining feature of his appearance at Esalen in 1982 where he hoped to engage Lilly in a debate on the subject). Additionally, he disparaged the use of MDMA in the early nineties rave scene. Where LSD, ketamine, and MDMA were considered industrial-commercial, mushrooms and DMT were comparatively organic, labor-intensive, and small-scale. Whereas Leary was armed with an acid "machine gun," McKenna saw himself toting a "spear." It is also possible that a Leary-style persecution of McKenna was weighed by authorities as a danger that could effectively promote then obscure illicit compounds. Finally, if the feds defined the "drug problem" as one of "untaxed income," McKenna regarded himself an unlikely target.[16] He was still driving the 1975 Granada in 1993. As the vehicle was driven into the ground and replaced by a $2,000 1974 BMW, its driver thereby went "down a year and up a brand."[17]

Any useful comparison of Learys, new and old, could not fail to notice their divergent backgrounds, nor the distinct characteristics of their psychedelic initiations. Leary was a West Point cadet whose dad served as Eisenhower's dentist. McKenna was a country boy whose dad was a B-17 airman and a traveling electrical hardware salesman. Leary was thirty-nine when in 1960, vacationing with his family at a rented villa in Cuernavaca, Mexico, he ate *teonanacatl*, "the flesh of the gods." The life course of the clinical psychologist newly appointed to Harvard was dramatically altered by *Psilocybe mexicana*. Just a few years later, as an impressionable teenaged student at UC Berkeley, McKenna was floored by DMT. When Terry first encountered psilocybin, over ten years after Tim's garden party at the Casa Del Moro, its organic vehicle is chanced upon in the Colombian Amazonas. And whereas Leary's first experiments with DMT (intramuscular injection approximately 60 mg) were bioassayed in a controlled environment, a secret room called the Time Chamber of the Newton Center at Harvard, McKenna's first episode a few years later is completely unplanned, and without protocols.

Despite these disparate conversions, for both men, the psychedelic experience offered a powerful gnosis that gave access to occluded information. For Leary, the trip was inward, neuronal, molecular. He returned to the primordial ooze from which he experienced a condensed recapitulation of evolution. Favorably comparing his revelations with those of St. John of the Cross, Blake, and John Lennon, he surrendered to delight, "as mystics have for centuries when they peeked through the curtains and discovered that this world—so manifestly real—was actually a tiny stage set constructed by the mind." On psilocybin, Leary had a powerful affirmation of the potency of the brain. He discovered that the evolved organ we're carrying around in our skulls is an underutilized and reprogrammable "biocomputer" with "billions of unaccessed neurons."[18] McKenna likewise turned to world religion—and specifically soteriology—to parse his gnosis. Jung's treatment of the "doctrine of Anthropos" aided apprehension, with Terence sampling the robes of Christ, Adam, Thoth, or Hermes—that is, embodiments of the Son of God. Under this template, events in the wake of March Forth are assimilable to the Resurrection, received as a paradigm of sublimation redeeming the *anima mundi* imprisoned in matter.[19] While Leary's "trip" was a journey inward and backward, for McKenna, the grail lay beyond the exosphere, and even beyond time itself, as an as-yet-hidden means of redemption.

He may have been cast as the "Leary of the nineties," but McKenna was a unique freak. Although living only four years beyond his generational predecessor, and though his "Troy" was differently scaled, he took the reins from his fellow trickster to lead a tryptaminal Trojan horse into the mainstream mind. While no less ambitious, or entrepreneurial, a psychoactivated shamanism set McKenna apart. The originality of his output is distinguished by the effort to bridge Western esoteric and New World traditions. What became identified as "psychedelic shamanism" is routinely couched as a neo-gnostic myth of redemption, with strong echoes of Hans Jonas's *The Gnostic Religion*. "We are creatures of another realm. Beings of Light, who because of some horrible cosmic mistake have been trapped in the world of matter . . . and the task of salvation is to gather the light and then release it back to its hidden higher source beyond the machinery of cosmic fate."[20] In an approach to shamanism high enough to make venerated scholars of religion blanch, neoshamans are gifted the gnosis-enabling tools to become awakened from humanity's fallen condition.

The conviction that "we don't belong here" was enduring. And when announcing that "the last best hope for dissolving the steep walls of cultural inflexibility that appear to be channeling us toward true ruin is a renewed shamanism,"[21] McKenna was not simply backing a shamanic revival; he was propagating paragnostic tools for the modern age. Vaunted players in this revitalization are heroic botanists and dauntless chemists—Richard Schultes, the Wassons, Albert Hofmann—thought to have gifted moderns the tools to confront the horror of history. Obsessed with psychoactive fungi post–La Chorrera, McKenna studied closely the works of Wasson, whom he considered an inspiration. As an amateur ethnomycologist, McKenna shared insights on early mycological influences in literature, and speculation on the earliest modern cult of mushroom users.[22] Against Wasson's speculation that fly agaric (*Amanita muscaria*) is the secret of the *soma* that infuses the Vedas, he proposed that *Psilocybe* lay behind the mystery.[23]

The impact of psychoactive mushrooms on the human story is a persistent theme, and here too Wasson is an inspiration. Countering Eliade's earlier views that shamanic use of "narcotics" revealed a decadent society, in *Soma: Divine Mushroom of Immortality*, Wasson advanced his mycological theory of the genesis of religion, subsequently popularizing the idea that "entheogens" are the sine qua non of shamanism.[24] Yet for McKenna, neither Wasson nor anyone else went far enough—that is, to claim that consciousness had been catalyzed by early hominid contact with psilocybin,[25] that the "evolutionary enzyme" is responsible for the emergence of *Homo sapiens*. Like a self-fulfilling prophecy, the story developing throughout the eighties and finally blooming in *Food of the Gods* tells not only of a mushroom-loving paleolithic but of the relatively sudden and dramatic symbiosis between early humans, coprophilic (dung-loving) mushrooms, and domesticated cattle on the plains of North Africa. The "stoned ape" hypothesis proposed that the inclusion of psilocybin in the early hominid diet represents the "real missing link," a rationale unpacked for the underground intelligentsia. "If you could convince people that drugs were responsible for the emergence of large brain size and language," pseudonymous writers Gracie and Zarkov were informed, then the argument could be completely recast from "Drugs are alien, invasive and distorting to human nature" to "Drugs are natural, ancient and responsible for human nature."[26] Despite its promise, what McKenna named his "shaggy primate" idea did not, in his remaining years, gain the traction anticipated, at least not beyond the milieu of the marginals.

AMERICA'S SHAMAN AND THE MOLECULAR ENIGMA

Where psilocybin was held as the midwife to the human condition, N,N-dimethyltryptamine was beloved as "the quintessential hallucinogen."[27] Under McKenna's guidance, DMT would be promoted as the ultimate deconditioning agent. In his first recorded Esalen appearance, he was candid about his novitiate episode a generation earlier: "I was appalled." There is a "declension of gnosis" that proved to him in a moment that "right here and now, one quanta away, there is raging a universe of active intelligence that is transhuman, hyperdimensional, and extremely alien."[28] The revelation was spellbinding for Esalen seminarians and those congregating at other venues like California's Institute for Integral Studies, where DMT was promoted as "the center of the mystery."[29] The pied piper began to pass his pipe to countless willing recipients.

In McKenna's psychedelic pedagogy, DMT is far less like a drug that you take than an event that happens to you. The experience was received as a form of *initiation* into a secret that cannot be known. It would be contended that DMT possesses a "self-erasing mechanism," and was so "contra-intuitive" that as one returns from the experience, it escapes rational apprehension.[30] But as impossible as it was to haul his catch back across the dimensional divide and retain the freshness of its existential verisimilitude, McKenna enjoyed the thrill of the challenge. So too his audience. "Gone, gone, gone, gone," the Austin crowd are informed in August 1996, primed that DMT causes a response remote from the expectations standard to the unitary mystical experience. There is no white light, or transcendent Oneness. No "effulgent radiance of the unitary." By contrast, there is "a domain of much greater complexity than one has ever experienced before." After a couple of tokes, "you will make more spiritual progress in those 30 seconds than 15 trips to India to worship at the feet of the Master." According to the initiate, rather than reinforce beliefs or buttress intellectual constructs, the enigmatic content of the visions are declared to prompt a lasting insight. "Your constructs are not a bridge to reality, they're a boundary against reality."[31]

For the neophytes in his audience, the figure once deemed "America's shaman" was instrumental in telegraphing DMT's grail-like status in modern culture.[32] The molecule held a "secret," compelling a desperate Burroughs to ply the Amazon in the early fifties, originally chasing yagé and later injecting a crude DMT synthesis he called "Prestonia," unleashing a nightmare in Tangier in 1961. Through Burroughs, it attracted the interest of Leary and his Harvard colleagues who, injecting the compound with attention to set and setting, concluded that it was more "transcendental trigger" than a "nightmare hallucinogen."[33] Soon after, DMT becomes the "metaphysical reality pill" of bold chemist Nick Sand. The next link in the chain, from the mid-sixties, is forged by the brothers McKenna, whom it astonishes and for whom the molecule is deemed a key that unlocks consciousness itself.

Next to other mind-expanding compounds, notably LSD, DMT has long lain in obscurity. A fast-acting and dramatic effect on perception commanded reverence among small cohorts through to the eighties and nineties—a circumstance inhibiting popular use. Aided by the availability of new botanical sources, extraction techniques, improved methods of use, and later, the advent of the Net, McKenna packed the pipe of knowledge and sent it round. Throughout the eighties, his audiences were informed that the source that had compelled the brothers to trek to the Amazon could be accessed in their own backyards. One needn't travel "five hundred miles up a jungle river and live with primitive peoples and study techniques for thirty years," the Fort Mason audience heard. "If I had a pipe loaded with [DMT] in my hand, each one of you would be thirty seconds away from ... this absolutely reality-dissolving, category-reconstructing, mind-boggling possibility."[34] By virtue of possessing a set of lungs, the secret was only seconds away.

A master class on comparative psychedelics, the 1988 CIIS workshop "Ethnobotany of Shamanism" offered about as comprehensive a phenomenology of DMT as one is ever likely to meet. In this seminarian tour de force, the hallucinogenic impresario served as a metaphysical "sitter" for novice attendees. As McKenna related to his audience, even before hitting his advised seventy milligrams of DMT (a very strong dose) vaporized in a glass pipe, the atmosphere is reported to change. It is as though "time speeds up." There is "backwash from the event about to happen." The trepidation is palpable. There are chills, tremoring, a knotted stomach, nausea, restlessness. And then you get "the Q phenomenon," which in engineering circles refers to vibration in a physical system:

> When they launch the space shuttle, if you listen to the radio chitchat they will say, "Approaching max Q," then they'll say, "Max Q, mark," and then they're through that. What that means is that as the system approaches a transition it begins to shake, it begins to shake as though it's going to shake to pieces. The Q forces are building on all the air surfaces, the airframe. Then you break through that, Q falls to 0 and then you're in the cool, main engine cut off. You are now in orbit, all vibration has ceased, noise has ceased. You are in orbit, you are weightless, you are there. It's different.[35]

Replete with the pre-transorbital nomenclature of a space launch, the "Q phenomenon" carries an evocative set of metaphors ripe for application to the DMT trip. Such technical discourse primed Spaced Age audiences for the launch and breakthrough. "So, you take, let us assume, a third toke, long and slow. You vaporize. And you take it, in, and in and in, and there's a sound like the crumpling of a plastic bread wrapper, or the crackling of a flame. And a tone. A hummmmmmmmmmmmmmm."[36]

It wasn't simply the hyperspatial parameters and ontological implications of the DMT molecule that warranted attention. And it wasn't just that DMT could be grown and harvested in one's own backyard, extracted in your basement, or smoked in your living room. What also struck McKenna was that the molecule, in small traces, naturally occurs in the brain. Along with analogue tryptamines (5-MeO-DMT and bufotenine), DMT is present in the brain tissue of humans and other mammals, where it is admitted passage across the blood-brain barrier, where it has a known affinity with a symphony of (principally serotonin-family) receptors. As the brothers marveled, ordinary amine levels in the brain are rapidly metabolized following the introduction of the most powerful of all hallucinogenic indoles. This remarkable fact, McKenna averred, suggests "a long co-evolutionary association" between humans and certain hallucinogenic tryptamines.[37]

The mystery expanded upon the recognition that "nature is drenched in DMT," that the molecule could be found at tiny but detectable levels in all biota—if, as Dennis averred, "anyone bothered to look."[38] At the turn of the nineties, fired by speculation on DMT's mammalian endogeneity, attention turned to the pineal gland. Throughout history, the tiny pinecone-shaped gland in the center of the brain has been a site for competing visions on the human condition: depending on your views, an organ of gothic hopelessness or one of spiritual evolution. In the pen of Hunter S. Thompson, even *Fear and Loathing*'s Dr. Gonzo wouldn't touch "extract of pineal." By contrast, the gland held an allure for Dr. Rick Strassman, who proposed that it is the site for the production of the "spirit molecule."[39] Though unproven, this popular proposition was prompted by the clinical psychiatrist's mid-eighties "working session" with McKenna and Rupert Sheldrake. Smoking DMT at this time, Sheldrake reported an "astonishing" near-death experience. "I felt myself going through a kind of tube," which turned out to be a huge chrysanthemum, a "portal" into a realm of "light, joy and bliss with shimmering and ever changing forms." When Sheldrake described the chrysanthemum effect to McKenna afterward, his friend recognized the space: "Ah, you've been to the flower heaven." The sensation inspired the cover of Sheldrake's later book, *Ways to Go Beyond and Why They Work*.[40]

The function of the pineal gland had long been a subject of intrigue. Before television was considered a cultural disaster, McKenna observed in the late sixties how TV "opened the collective third eye of humanity," a mythos not unrelated to the pineal's undiscovered function. As was meditated on in "Post Electric Thought," "the problem awaits research."[41] Two decades later, like a secret chief investigator, McKenna found himself in the company of maverick scientists for whom the research appears to have waited. The "working session" led to a series of productive conversations. Sheldrake, who for his biochemistry doctorate had studied the breakdown of the amino acid tryptophan in dying plant cells, was struck by how tryptamine—and notably the DMT molecule itself—is a product of tryptophan, gaining the impression that tryptophan precursors must exist in the pineal. The idea that the pineal "could flood the brain with DMT" at the moment of death was mooted with Strassman at this time.[42]

Strassman's subsequent FDA-approved research at the University of New Mexico represented the first clinical trials with psychedelics in the United States for a generation. Documenting trials in which sixty volunteers were injected with DMT, the speculations in his popular book *DMT: The Spirit Molecule* rippled through the underground and solidified as folk knowledge.[43] With McKenna serving as its midwife, the "psychedelic pineal gland"[44] thesis was born. The thesis proposed that the pineal excretes DMT during extremely stressful life episodes, notably during birth and death. As a projection of Strassman's then-relationship with Tibetan Buddhism, pineal DMT was even seen to serve a role in reincarnation.[45] The idea of the "brain's own psychedelic" became a self-fulfilling prophecy in film, TV, and music in the wake of Strassman's popular speculations, a kind of chemical Frankenstein's monster into which McKenna had breathed life. Despite research finding traces of DMT in the brains of rats, the pineal is an unproven source of endogenous DMT in psychoactive quantities.[46]

The long moratorium on research was far from over. As researchers were aware of the occurrence of DMT in human metabolism since the seventies, the absurdity of criminalizing a molecule that naturally occurs in humans was never lost. "This is the Catch 22 that they hold in reserve if they ever have to come after us," echoes McKenna's sound bite. "You are holding, and you can't stop yourself."[47] While lawmakers classified DMT and its tryptamine relatives as Schedule I drugs with no value to medical science, speculation about "the brain's own psychedelic" would fuel a controversy that shows little sign of abating.

SIGNIFICANT ELF PROCLIVITY

I have earlier recounted McKenna's mid-sixties eureka moment. The Elf Event and subsequent episodes from the era provided the source material for countless hours of storytelling recounting moments of contact and sustained relations with other-dimensional entities. As McKenna's spirit familiars, the "machine elves" are native to the psychedelic hero's journey. The ur-moment was immortalized by trance-galactic supergroup Shpongle, sampling the breakthrough moment on their 2001 album *Tales of the Inexpressible*. Following the anxiety, the crackling, the "Q phenomenon," and a long tone, there is, finally, a cheer. "The gnomes have learned a new way to say hooooooooooraaaay."[48] It was familiar terrain. When breaking through to a "domed place," *they* await Terence's arrival, impatient though beside themselves with joy. "You're here, we're glad to see you! Why did you stay away so long?"[49] Mobbed by these beings "babbling in a visible and five-dimensional form of Ecstatic Nostratic," multiple visitations entrained McKenna to avoid "death by astonishment."

By my reckoning, the oldest extant reference to the "mischievous machine elves" was journaled on November 20, 1971, after nine months in the Amazon. Access to the jungle grail, *oo-koo-hé*, had finally been obtained. As the smoked resin proved largely ineffectual, the journaled description—the proto-narrative to countless retellings—relied on prior episodes. In this blueprint on the "place or state" to which McKenna is transported, the beings encountered are described as an "autonomous super intelligence" with a "contrapuntal omni-pun-tal singing language" and "continually transforming body geometries." This is "the place where ideas come from," wrote our man on the scene. These songs are observed to produce "self-transforming objects which are visible hyper-evolving idea complexes presented with the specific purpose of teaching something." Retrieving these *objects* proves impossible amid an atmosphere of "riotous zany merriment." Retrieving *ideas* was another matter. The product of nine grueling months of beta-testing, the "eschatron" is excitedly chronicled in "Change and Becoming" as evidence for the successes of trans-dimensional traversal.[50]

Once again, the story is taken up by Shpongle lifting McKenna: "Like jeweled self-dribbling basketballs, these things come running forward, and what they are doing with this visible language that they create, is that they are making gifts, making gifts for you."[51] He marveled at the most impossible gifts delivered by "the singing elf machines": "mechanized syntactical Faberge eggs." Ever shifting, and synesthetic, these doohickeys are true objects of wonder. But are they toys, puzzles, devices, art works, or something else? Whatever they are, the gift bearers compete for his attention.[52]

Through the eighties, a vast library of cultural signifiers is consulted to parse these outrageous entities, their astonishing gifts, and the space they co-inhabit. Literary and film sources animate a canvas with insights from Plato, Joyce, Borges, and John Dee. These and many more sources fill McKenna's palette. At his 1982 Esalen outing, the "space" into which he was propelled is mapped by reference to the "merry go raum" of *Finnegans Wake*. "The room is actually going around, and in that space one feels like a child, though one has come out somewhere in eternity." In this cosmic playground, he discovers that he can make "feeling-toned, meaning-toned, three-dimensional rotating complexes of transforming light and color." And in deference to Heraclitus, "one is playing with colored balls; one has become the Aeon." This state of consciousness defies the logic of temporality as a sequence of successive events. Plato's metaphor that "time is the moving image of eternity" seemed never truer. In this zenith of human achievement, the exalted one steps across the threshold into the eternal now of Thomas Aquinas's *nunc stans*. And the entities making themselves known in this everlasting now are reminiscent of a scene from *The Wizard of Oz* where the Munchkins arrive with a death certificate for the Witch of the East. "They all have very squeaky voices and they sing a little song about being 'absolutely and completely dead.' The tryptamine Munchkins come, these hyperdimensional machine-elf entities, and they bathe one in love." The beings are reassuring: "Don't be alarmed. And remember, do what we are doing."[53]

And McKenna does just that, faithfully repeating the story of his transdimensional gift bearers—including restating their entreaty to "do what we are doing." For his remaining years, he follows his orders. By way of mediumship and emulation, in rap after rap, the recursive story is recapitulated before larger audiences. By Alien Dreamtime, the script is so well rehearsed it could have been the basis for a pageant play:

> And what they were doing was they were making objects come into existence by singing them into existence—objects which looked like Fabergé eggs from Mars morphing themselves with Mandaean alphabetical structures. . . . And these little machines offered themselves to me; and I realized, when I looked at them, that if I could bring just one of these little trinkets back, nothing would ever be quite the same again. . . . Don't think about it. Don't think about who we are, think about doing what we're doing. Do it. Do it now. Do it![54]

Emissary for the elves was a role for which no one seemed better suited. But while he may have served as their agent, like an impeccable understudy, or a specialist art appraiser, McKenna was compelled to scour the world of science, art, and myth for clues.

In the seventies he cribs from Jacques Vallée, recognizing his elven aliens as absurd anomalies pulling the epistemic rug out from underneath scientific rationalism, not unlike the "meta-logic" of saucers and other UFOs, as reported in *The Invisible College*.[55] But while couching the "machine elves" as confounding symbols welling up out of the planetary Overmind, the appraisal morphs through the eighties. By decade's end, the edge runner's entities bear resemblance to fairies, the Sídhe, and specifically the Tuatha Dé Dannan, a race of the supernaturally gifted in Irish mythology who are thought to represent the main deities of pre-Christian Gaelic Ireland. The revelation arrives upon rereading Evans-Wentz's *The Fairy Faith in Celtic Countries*, for which McKenna wrote the reprint's introduction. The fairy faith, he writes, "is a belief in an invisible co-present dimension in which dwell the transformed souls of the ancient dead, able to interact with humans who wander into the lonely enchanted landscapes that seem partial doorways between the fairy world and our own." One day spent in the land of Sídhe "is sufficient for the great wheel of many centuries to turn in the ordinary world."[56]

It is during the late-eighties that McKenna began wrestling with a long-resisted idea: that his DMT entities were the dead. If spirits or souls of the dead were making themselves known in DMT space, the further understated implication was that their "elven" form may be an expression of his Irish roots. In a most revealing summation of his elf lore, during the weekend workshop "History Ends in Green," the real possibility is ventured that the elves are "spirits of the ancestors." As reported to his Esalen base, the freight of this frisson amounted to the co-presence of the "very familiar" with the "freakishly bizarre." Soon after, leading a New York Open Center workshop, a presentiment so "kinky and peculiar" is confessed to have occurred with such "disturbing force" over the past eighteen months: the entities may have been the most alien thing he had ever seen, but "the capstone of its alienness is its freakish familiarity." He had been here before. While reflecting little on the cause for his alarm, McKenna was aghast at the implications of his sensitivities toward "the other" in the DMT trance. Was his career a late twentieth-century form of mediumship? Did smoking DMT amount to a kind of molecular séance that demonstrated the survival of the soul after death? Was he trespassing into the terrain of spiritualism, that risible religious movement of the *fin de siècle* that he had so long derided? Such incursions seemed intellectually unconscionable. While we may wonder if he saw the elves as *his* transcended relatives attempting to communicate from the other side, McKenna did not associate his entities with his own, or anyone else's, ancestors. He did not feel that it was his mother or grandparents who had gained his attentions in DMT space.[57] Even though the "ecology of souls" became an anchor point, rather than spirits of his ancestors, these entities were more likely "local spirits" or perhaps even "dead friends."[58]

Pressed further by folks behaving like pilgrims genuflecting before an oracle, the rhapsodical one revealed the most hair-raising, *unheimlich* implication of his contact experiences: that it wasn't just any dead soul with which he convened in hyperspace, but the freakishly familiar chief tyke may have been his *own* dead self. Dropped in passing, this climactic moment of cognitive dissonance—"when you realize that the entity you're dealing with is yourself beyond the grave"—seems to have amounted to an unwanted peak experience, causing McKenna to "flood out in the amazement, wonder, horror, and disbelief department."[59] In the wake of this reveal, we are flooded with questions of our own. Did this impossible moment of truth compel our visitor to become consumed with an inconsolable grief? Was it *this* moment, when the inner curtains may have opened to reveal an interdimensional mirror, that gave him pause to back away from the heroic dose?

Regardless of the precise identity of its inhabitants, DMT was known to afford access to eternity. In *The Fairy Faith*, McKenna learned that the doctrine of purgatory—the intermediate state after physical death in which those destined for heaven undergo purification—was used by St. Patrick when converting the Irish and thereby Catholicizing Fae, or Fairyland. "The Celtic pure belief is that the dead go to a realm that is co-present all around us, we can't see them but that all around us is just jammed with souls in wild states of activity, and that if you have the eye, you know, a certain talent, you can see these things." To appeal to Celtic peasants, Fae was upgraded to the status of purgatory. The implication was that smoking DMT explodes the doctrine of purgatory and Catholic cosmogony and one breaks through into Fairyland, a world bearing a strong resemblance to Fae. And more than that, one accesses the "gnosis of elves." They may be humorous, unpredictable, somewhat cruel, and boisterous, but these elves are archetypal artificers. They make things in metal, jewels, and glass. "They are underground craftsman."[60]

With the elf/fairy-led return to Irish-Catholic roots, we approach the gnostic kernel: the true artifice of elves. Their secret is that they fabricate language. "This is why in Irish mythology if you can get elves on your side you can make great poetry, because they are the keepers of linguistic artifice, and getting elves on your side makes you into a master poet."[61] These entities aren't your garden-variety aliens of UFO lore. They are not "specialists in internal medicine from other star systems who make free house calls late at night." The DMT space was not an austere realm of white light, but "a *Bugs Bunny* cartoon running backwards . . . a place of explosions and falling anvils." It is a space of such intense merriment that "you could have your head ripped off by accident." Where everyone else's aliens seemed like the folks next door, "my aliens," the carouser of consciousness informs the folks in Austin, "are as alien as aliens can be." His *alien* aliens were not made of matter, but grammar: "They are made out of language."[62] And it was a principal revelation that this *language* is not that which could be heard, but a dense sculptured *syntax* that can be *seen*.

Over his career as a public spokesperson for the Other, McKenna gave himself over to emulating the elf *Sprache*. Alien Dreamtime is noteworthy for the alien brogue into which its narrator breaks during the performance. Recounting his original DMT entrancement, the elves instructed him to use his voice to "make an object," whereupon a language that is "unhooked from English" arises within him. The spontaneous tongue first "spoken" in his room on Telegraph Avenue three decades prior now appeared in his guise as raving front man. After years of reflection, he announced from the Transmission Theatre stage in 1993 that "meaning and language are two different things." The spontaneous "alien voice" wanted to reveal that "the real secret of magic is that the world is made of words, and that if you know the words that the world is made of, you can make of it whatever you wish."[63] No ordinary channeler, McKenna was no medium of any identifiable entity, like Seth (Jane Roberts), Djwal Khul (Madame Blavatsky), or The Pleiadians (Barbara Marciniak). Nor did his travels in hyperspace uncover angelic language such as that for which Edward Kelley (scryer for John Dee) is said to have been responsible. And nor did the "elf chatter" represent meaningful information or an intelligible language. If the elven *Sprache* revealed anything at all, it was the idea of the "syntactical structure of language." If this wasn't McKenna's Everest of the Weird, he had at the very least achieved the Foothills of Kook.

As apparently the only tongue besides English in which he ever gained confidence, the DMT elf chatter became a feature of McKenna's act. The effect of long hours of contentless transmissions within tryptaminal trance states was impressive. "Your face, your mouth, is just hanging down to your waist," he said. "I mean, it's like you've just done something to the whole front of your head, and all the musculature has dissolved."[64] Later stage performances and recorded workshops in relatively sober states are attempts to simulate the syntax of these satisfying emissions that *felt like meaning* but could not be interpreted using any known dictionary.

Despite being aware of just how ridiculous these trans-linguistic simulations appeared wrenched from their context, McKenna was compelled to reproduce this primitive language before wider audiences. In these expanded, melted, and fused states he effectively performed his own species of glossolalia, though perhaps more conscious and controlled in his onstage antics (compared with his private trips) than Pentecostalists, with their trancelike "speaking in tongues." So transfixed by this visible, three-dimensional language was McKenna that he once spent a week in a tent on Hawaii taking mushrooms almost every night, while recording himself "shrieking in Nostratic." People, he reported, found these bizarre recordings "extremely alarming."[65]

In the same year as Alien Dreamtime, the psychedelic psychopomp worked with UK artists Paul Chousmer, Phil Pickering, and Mick West, who, as ambient techno outfit Zuvuya, produced the album *Dream Matrix Telemetry*. Zuvuya was a short-lived act entirely dedicated to amplifying McKenna's trans-dimensional rite of passage. An hour-long ode to the "ecology of souls" into which he had been transported on DMT, *Dream Matrix Telemetry* is among the molecule's most public celebrations. The performance took up the "sculptured jeweled machines" sung into existence by the "gnome-like artisans" that had crowded forward to offer their "visible language" for inspection. "I somehow shattered the membrane between myself and ordinary space," McKenna announces, referencing his mid-sixties contact experience. "I carried the trip into the room with me . . . an elf hanging off each hand."[66]

He may have been a greenhorn in the art of retrieving objects from his trips, but McKenna perfected the arts of mediating the unspeakable, shaped by "small mouth noises" formulating insights on time and consciousness distilled in never-repeated bits delivered as gifts to his audience. McKenna was thunderstruck by the synesthetic materiality of language. If the "little people" showed him that reality was woven from language, like a hyperspace apprentice, he was driven to make his audience *see* this revelation: "Do what we are doing." Whomever or whatever "the elves" were, these spirit familiars were the regulars of a mythopoetic cheer squad whose insistent appearances sealed his own stature as a master poet. Singing a new world into being was woven into "the experiment" at La Chorrera and later multimedia projects. The arts of poesis were commanded by a loquacious intellectual influencer, linguistic contortionist, and master of subversive entertainment who implored anyone who would listen to "do what I am doing."

A MORE PERFECT *LOGOS*

But understanding (let alone doing) what Terence was doing is no mean feat—especially given that he, as he averred, was chosen for his abilities. Speaking off the cuff toward the end of a 1994 Esalen workshop, he remarked upon the circumstances that led him there. In 1971, when on the run from the feds in Colombia, and with his resources depleted, "*they* recruited me and said, 'you know, with a mouth like yours there's a place for you in our organization.' . . . *They* shifted me into public relations and I've been there to the present."[67] The choice analogy brought the house down. Since stumbling upon it a quarter century before, the mushroom had gained his ear and Terence had become its ambassador. Post–La Chorrera, "the teacher" emerged as a muse that readers of the inaugural issue of *High Frontiers* learned is "an interior guiding voice with a higher level of knowledge."[68] The persistent claim was that, serving as his chief informant, director, and ghost writer, the mushroom muse told him everything he knew. By contrast to the "mischievous machine elves" reported to be "strange teachers" comprised of syntax who sing intricate toys from nothing,[69] the teacher—or as he preferred, the *logos*—commanded full attention, instructing him in aphorisms "spoken" in a libertarian cadence. "You either have a plan, or you are part of somebody else's plan."[70] As a chief product of this dialogue, the Timewave is integral to the "plan" implemented.

Definable as "reasoned discourse," the *logos* designates that which today is thought psychopathological—that is, voices in the head. McKenna informed his seminarians that he made no judgments about the voice. He was prone to engage it in dialogue, asking, "Well, what are you? Are you some kind of diffuse consciousness that is in the ecosystem of the Earth? Are you a god or an extraterrestrial? Show me what you know."[71] The mushroom was effectively consulted as an oracle, put to the test on a range of problems. "What's the deal with these other paths to enlightenment?" he inquired on one occasion. "For one human being to seek enlightenment from another," came the response, "is like one grain of sand to seek enlightenment from another." The notion was deemed preposterous. On another occasion, upon asking the mushroom about what should be done immediately to save the planet, the answer was: "Every man, every woman should parent only one child; this is the greatest political act that we can do for the human community on the planet."[72]

In "Shamanic Investigations," the inner voice is assumed to have been activated by the "harmine DNA switch" then regarded as "XDMT," a switch that, in the wake of March Forth, was assimilable to instant dharma.[73] Terence may have resisted gurus up until his Amazonian exploits, but his *inner guru* appears to have manifested in the form of a *Psilocybe*-activated voice. Not only did his shroomic-guru speak, but it communicated in English, apparently informing Terence about things that he could never have figured out on his own.[74] That there was never a first-name parlay with the mushroom suggests the nontrivial nature of this relationship. Coming to terms with this divine muse may have been a daunting exercise for a self-identified rationalist, but it was par for the course for the ancients, for an "informing voice" had guided Western civilization for about 1,700 years. As the sine qua non of Greek philosophy, Plato, Parmenides, and Heraclitus strove to invoke the "voice" that imparted "self-evident truth." For the likes of Socrates, who had his daemon, his informing "Other," the *logos* spoke an "incontrovertible Truth."[75] In the modern world, a model was offered by Jung, visited in his dreams and fantasies by the "psychagogue" Philemon.[76] Just as Jung received wisdom from a realm independent from his subjectivity, so McKenna held tryptaminal communion with a voice that imparted wisdom he believed external to himself. While this phenomenon generally faded with "the passing of the Aeon and death of the pagan gods," the medium remained available via the "plant teachers," with the prospect that when the voice that spoke to all ancient philosophers can speak again in the minds of modern people, "the alienation will be ended because we will have become the alien."[77]

An imported Hellenic trope, then, the *logos* offered testimony on the persistent fact of the mushroom's voice, a fact that demanded explanation. In early conjecture on the subject of the speaking mushroom, Julian Jaynes's *The Origin of Consciousness in the Breakdown of the Bicameral Mind* made the idea of talkative mushrooms more respectable. Though psychedelics hardly rate mention in Jaynes's text, psilocybin could, McKenna wagered, reestablish connection with a long-lost brain state in which, as Jaynes claimed, ancient humans were directed by verbal hallucinations (e.g., the voice of God).[78] Since the "bicameral mind" of ancient humans is speculated to have been succeeded by consciousness some 3,000 years ago, this evolutionary story is recent history compared with the "seeded gene" theory of which we are already familiar. The voice of the fungi was essentially the endgame of an outlandish evolutionary theory of extraterrestrial contact. The unique chemical signature of psilocin—the result of the metabolic path of psilocybin—is singled out as an outlier, "an artificial gene" perhaps carried by a space-borne virus that had "insinuated itself" into the genome of the mushroom. In this cosmic panorama, an alien vegetal implant lays in wait for an intelligent species to receive its metabolic transmissions, before, finally, humans, and notably the brothers McKenna, arrive at the scene of the sublime to perform their evolutionary role. That it induces a *"logos-like experience"* compelled Terence to maintain the fantasy that his brush with the mushroom amounted to "extra-terrestrial contact."[79]

While the *logos* concept derives from multiple sources,[80] McKenna became enthused with the rendering of Philo Judaeus, a Greek speaking Jewish philosopher of first-century Alexandria. What Philo of Alexandria had in mind, according to Hans Jonas, was "a more perfect archetypal logos," which was "exempt from the human duality of sign and thing, and therefore not bound by the forms of speech." Independent from "hearing," the phenomenon at hand was that which is "immediately beheld by the mind as the truth of things."[81] This mode of grokking, or *darshan*, was astutely grokked by Terence, from the jungle to living room. The unmediated transition from "being heard to being beheld," as Elvin D. Smith of *Psychozoic Press* was apprised in the first published interview with McKenna, might have remained little more than the wild theological ramblings of a first-century philosopher if it weren't for certain powerful tryptamines apparently rendering the impossible possible for a twentieth-century rambler. Singing on DMT produces a "synesthesia glossolalia" in which one may "control the contour of the hallucinogenic topology."[82] Such was the hyper-spatiality of sound that has color, of thought impregnated with tang, of meaning seen. But the genuine source of the "more perfect logos" was psilocybin, and McKenna was beholden to this *Ursprache*, which he likened to the "perfect, poetic language that pre-dates history" addressed by Robert Graves in *The White Goddess*. "A language of poetry so intense that to hear it was to understand it."[83]

There appeared to be as many angles on the *logos* as mirrors on a disco ball. "Sometimes," McKenna observed in his first appearance in *Magical Blend*, "it is my colleague and sometimes it is my Jewish godfather, and sometimes it is what Jung called the *soror mystica*."[84] In the seventies, "the oversoul" was considered to be a sort of *collective logos* exposing humanity to the ontologically confounding symbol of the UFO appearing at a time of mounting crisis. In the eighties, the *logos* took shape as the "voice" of the animus, "the widely felt intuition of the presence of the Other as a female companion to the human navigation of history." It was proposed that communion with this Other is traceable to "the immersion in the vegetable mind that provided the ritual context in which human consciousness emerged into the light of self-awareness, self-reflection, and self-articulation: the light of the Great Goddess."[85] This would be the story arc of *Food of the Gods*, where the vocal mushroom is associated with "an indwelling of the Goddess,"[86] an idea not remote from "entheogens," substances or practices that awaken the divine within, and perhaps more assiduously, "femtheogens."[87]

While a vegetal-minded revival was core to "the feminizing of culture" promoted by the end of the eighties,[88] the *logos* assumed a cyber-spatial ambience into the next decade. "I can imagine a future," *Mondo 2000* was apprised, "where the entire culture has been shrunk down and downloaded onto a pair of black contact lenses that you implant behind your eyelids." A primitive image crossfades into cybernetic grandeur. One may be "naked, tattooed, scarified, and wearing your penis sheath," but the future dissolved into what became a pet image: "When you close your eyes, there are menus dangling in mental space." And with this, it was assumed that one has access to "the complete database of the Western Mind."[89]

Throughout his career, McKenna appeared to grow more comfortable explaining the idea—the "map of novelty"—that was delivered to him in dialogue with his mushroom muse as a "revelation" delivered by an "Angel." Given the opportunity to compare his mediations with the likes of John Dee, John the Apostle, or even Descartes, his audiences were invariably left with a perplexed figure doubtful and incredulous about his own role as a mystic or prophet. If his idea was a revelation, it was not received in the context of piety. The communication with his muse tended to be characterized more as outlandish exploit or outrageous fortune than divine providence. And yet, as much as he would care to proclaim the accidental and ordinary nature of his relationship with divinity, he is diffident when it comes to explaining his role as revelator. Was he not chosen due to a special ability with which he alone was gifted? Could it not be argued that this elect role rendered McKenna an agent of super-novelty, whose own agency should appear on the time chart as an ingression of novelty? To his own end, he who unveiled the map of time proclaimed his own humdrum ordinariness.

Camped inside this paradox, the path hewn is invariably humorous. Decades downwind from March Forth, McKenna was determined to write his angelic muse into his improv theater script. At the beginning of his stand-up career, the mushroom is introduced as a kind of Jewish sidekick in an onstage routine. The Woody Allen–esque script unfolded before Esalenites.

"What are you doing here?" the ventriloquist says to the mushroom.

"What am I doing here? I'm not doing anything here. It wasn't a bad neighborhood till the monkeys got out of control!"

"But so you're just sort of here? And you're living here? Why are you living here?"

"Well, you're a mushroom, you live cheap!"[90]

As audiences were issued the news, the mushroom became the source of a cosmic giggle that rippled through packed auditoriums, nightclubs, and lecture theaters. And lest one imagine a benevolent Disneyesque idyll, our narrator was keen to communicate the Warner Brothers ambience of the trickster tryptaminal trance. In a story entertaining his Esalen base a few years later, as he once remarked to a French film producer dining with a group (including Abraham) at a restaurant in Malibu, the mushroom sometimes shows up like Rod Steiger in *The Pawnbroker*— an irascible personality whose business is strictly trade.

"Ah," said the Frenchwoman in response to this explanation. And at precisely that moment, "Steiger stopped by the table to shake hands with everybody."[91]

As his one-man psychedelic road show evolved, McKenna divulged his method of establishing contact with high command. At the CIIS, his technique was stated to have been acquired from reruns of *I Love Lucy*, where Lucy explains how she contacts flying saucers by saying: "Come in, little green men! Come in, little green men!"

> So on mushrooms I do this, I say, "Come in, little green men!" and what begins to happen is this sound like bells, like very distant bells. Then it becomes louder and louder, sort of like bells with wind. It becomes louder and louder and more complicated and more complex, and at a certain, very hard to precisely define moment, it begins to spill over into the visual cortex. Then I see the language and I can interact with it. It is apparently a more perfect Logos.[92]

But Terence's relationship with the mushroom was a turbulent affair—as ambivalent as one's relationship with one's unconscious. When, in the late eighties, the "little green men" turned sinister, and he has a falling out with his teacher, he grew disconnected from the source and cut off from his Angel, just as much as he became separated from his spousal partner in the sublime.

Unplugged from the *logos*, he seemed all at sea around the time he achieved peak fame.

DANGEROUSLY ECCENTRIC UNICATE

As McKenna took to the stage, he embraced a career as an advocate of outlawed substances, with a damning approach toward media and consumer culture, political ideology, and religious dogma. He intended to keep talking about the value of psychedelics "until somebody snuffs me or we get some action."[93] But even as his voice grew louder as the celebrated front man for psychedelic liberty, unlike the old Leary, the new "Leary" would not become the target of politically motivated campaigns to disrupt his activities. In the war on consciousness, McKenna managed to largely avoid the long reach of a justice system that prosecutes a Kafkaesque absurdity against psilocybin mushrooms and fungophiles, as detailed in a manual for which he wrote the foreword.[94] "No pressure, no matter how subtle, has ever been put on me," is the candid assessment in 1993.[95] In reality, he harbored ambivalent views on the "psychedelic agenda," questioning the value of legalization, arguing as he did at Mind States in 1997, that the "wish to legitimize our activities [is] . . . a very unpsychedelic impulse." Legitimacy, he felt, is a tortured outcome of the struggle to make peace between two cultural values: "constipated Calvinism" and the "untrammeled wilderness" of the psychedelic experience.[96]

That he escaped criminal conviction has drawn some to speculate on McKenna's possible collusion with the government. Such is the fixation of one scuttlebutt responsible for widening speculation that McKenna was a CIA asset. Claiming the US government engineered the psychedelic movement to trigger a neo-feudal Dark Age, Gnostic Media founder Jan Irwin is the chief source of this rumor. When Irwin figured McKenna's absence of a criminal record, and learned of his "*they* recruited me" into "public relations" rap, far from recognizing that McKenna had deployed his self-satirical rhetoric to infer that he had become an operative for an alien intelligence, Irwin drew the only connection a person devoid of humor or a sense of adventure could make. Ostensibly, McKenna had made an "admission" of his status as an intelligence "agent," and Irwin suspected the CIA.[97] Over the next year, with the assistance of even smaller minds, the absurd speculation implicating McKenna in a conspiracy to enslave humanity went viral.

Those interested in McKenna's story will be eager to scrutinize credible evidence that implicates him in such conspiracies. In my understanding, the only government body from which he ever drew an income was the

Entomology Department at UC Berkeley. I have seen no evidence of black funds, nor sign that he flipped on his associates to save his own skin.

McKenna carefully avoided public commentary on his turn-of-the-seventies predicament with the law, a predicament from which he successfully extracted himself. At the same time, he was vociferous on the subject of conspiracy theory, offering a sound rebuke to absolutist nonsense: "The real truth that dares not speak itself is that no one is in control."[98] This stock-standard response to the perception among conspiracists and activists of varying persuasions that the State is omniscient and all-knowing, or that all are slave to a panopticon-like Agenda, is that such theories tend to disempower individuals, who give away their life force, and independence, to shadows and suspicions. It was a position that Leary also shared, and it could have been applied to McKenna's own circumstance. Authorities likely remained clueless to his activities because no agency commanded a total view over his life.

This points up the strange caliber of McKenna's radicalism. While claiming to have been "impressed" by Chomsky's lectures at Berkeley in the late sixties, he admitted that he was "not quite . . . enlightened." The implication is that, unlike Chomsky, McKenna refused to believe that a mistake had been made. Consequently, there was no call for a course correction. Despite the rambunctiousness of his youth, he came to embrace *direct experience* over *direct action*. Rather than commit one's life to confront bad ideas, he contended that one ought to fashion good ideas. Otherwise, "your enemies define the game" and you give up your happiness and deplete your power through "opposing somebody else's vision." Such is the loose philosophy drawn from a reading of the *I Ching*. "If evil is directly confronted and named," the book was thought to convey, "it perfects weapons to defend itself." The alternative strategy was stealth.[99] Following the 1969 hash bust, from which he avoided prosecution, McKenna maintained extreme caution. And the clandestine decade-long grow op was abandoned after he and Harrison witnessed the fate of friend and neighbor Neil Hassall.

His avoidance of direct action might explain why McKenna apparently escaped any state-sponsored effort to disrupt his activities. By contrast to Leary's campaigns and mass action, his successor's activities were *perceived* as relatively nonthreatening. McKenna rarely if ever lent his support to political campaigns, mainstream or independent—until his own First Amendment rights were threatened. Next to the pied piper of youth tactics that saw Leary labeled "the most dangerous man in America," McKenna fancied himself to be among the most innocuous men in America. "A bunch of old hippies patting themselves on the back," is the self-assessment of a figure who at the same time conceded his stature as a "dangerously eccentric unicate."[100] It is perhaps this self-diagnosis that evokes how, through a dedication to guerrilla ontology and psychedelic pedagogy, the spiced piper's musings were as consistently subversive as they were entertaining.

While McKenna was reluctant to commit himself to a formal political cause, he became a champion for the psychedelically enhanced means of perception and a beacon for a consciousness movement in which empowerment through the use of plant medicines was advocated. By 1993, there appears to have been few venues that our brazen opportunist would not consider as a platform for showcasing his ideas. So confident were his convictions and yet eloquent his mode of address that he found his way on to *The Daryl Gates Show* aired on KFI-AM, where he recommended his method of five grams of dried mushrooms to the host and his right-wing audience. Like different species of humans facing off, this is surely among the more bizarre interludes in the careers of both figures. In the broadcaster's chair sat the former LAPD police chief and founder of the DARE program, Daryl Gates. In the guest's chair sat the silver-tongued heroic doser who informed Gates that the myth of Adam and Eve was actually "the story of history's first drug bust." If McKenna was invited to "the Chief's" theater of condescension and bigotry as a freak fed to a lion, the host proved more like a pussycat in the face of his guest's display of intelligence. As Gates grasped feebly for the Bible, McKenna offered Gates's audience a variation of his vision for an "archaic revival" in which the recovered use of psychoactive plants will enable a renewed community and a future "Eden."[101] McKenna was never invited back on the show.

"Drugs are heavy equipment and you have to learn how to operate heavy equipment." Such was the heft of McKenna's timbre, as reported in the *LA Times* ahead of a promoted UCLA engagement at LA's Wadsworth Theater in early May 1996. With strong echoes of Leary and Alpert, he was reported to state: "We have driver's education. We should teach people how to operate drugs."[102] Mediation like this registered among fans, but it also pushed the buttons of conservatives—in this case, those who sought to prevent the "guru of drugs," as the same provocative article named McKenna, from speaking at the Wadsworth, leased to the UCLA for the occasion by the Veterans Administration. The Wadsworth was sited on VA-owned property in West LA. A civil rights battle was triggered after the UCLA event was canceled on the grounds that McKenna's endorsements were "contrary to the VA's mission." A complaint later emerged comparing the forthcoming lecture, said to be too close to the VA hospital, which provides drug and alcohol rehabilitation to veterans, with "happy hour at the Betty Ford

Clinic."[103] For the first time, after two decades in the public eye, McKenna's freedom of speech was being threatened by a federal department and a university, part of a system of which he was himself an alumnus, an indignance he expressed to Pam Burton on Pacifica Radio (KPFK) a day before the event.[104] McKenna was facing a First Amendment battle that might have gone to the Supreme Court, potentially pushing his cognitive liberty agenda into the national spotlight.

That prospect quickly descended into a bureaucratic melee. Travesty was averted thanks to Dan Levy, who marshaled the powers of the LA chapter of the American Civil Liberties Union to obtain a federal injunction permitting the canceled event to proceed. McKenna had anticipated launching a benefit to raise money for the ACLU. But when the ACLU not only obtained a temporary injunction allowing the lecture to proceed, but a permanent injunction against the UCLA restricting freedoms of speech in similar such cases, "all battles were won."[105] As it turned out, on the one occasion McKenna's rap was being muzzled, there was no conspiracy or malicious intent. The causes were a mix of media-driven panic and administrative incompetence, with the UCLA quickly redressing a situation that contradicted its commitment to free speech and freedom of discourse. Curiously, occurring in the week following the "novelty maxima," the incident was within the parameters of the "novelty plunge" of 1996. Searching for evidence of the world stepping off the novelty cliff forecast, as McKenna declared on his website: "I found myself unexpectedly embroiled in a battle over my First Amendment rights with . . . a cabal of clowns and stooges."[106] The show went ahead, albeit with a smaller audience.

And as the show carried on, the audience expanded. After the on-air foreplay between Bell and McKenna on *Coast to Coast AM* the previous year, the two got right down to the business of DMT in their second encounter, on March 19, 1998. A courageous character in his own right, Bell asked the same question McKenna put to Watson three decades prior: "What is it?" Alert to the occasion, McKenna did his level best to condense the rap for millions of potential listeners in what amounted to the molecule's biggest boost to date. There is a "rupture of ordinary plane and a pouring forth of some kind of primal trickster-like energy." If it remained closeted before, in a few short minutes, DMT flew right out of the closet. As McKenna expounded from his Hawaiian home that the trip was sometimes reminiscent of a *"Bugs Bunny* cartoon running backwards in six dimensions," Bell was led to marvel jocosely that the government had somehow yet to assassinate his new friend.[107]

FOOD OF THE GODS

The Wadsworth was a minor skirmish in the early stages of the psychedelic renaissance. McKenna may have triumphed, but the effort to persuade learned opinion was the long game and wider struggle. If he came to occupy a unique position in the attention economy, that feat relied on a charm built around a strange confluence of science and religion. Advanced by a restless imagination, the product of this synthesis is a unique science fiction. This convergence of *techne* and *spiritus* is best illustrated by the "pharmacological pilgrim's progress," *Food of the Gods*, a determined campaign to secure intellectual credibility while advancing an unavoidably metaphysical remit. Given its place in the McKennan oeuvre, attention to the book's conception and reception is warranted. The basic premise of *Food of the Gods* was that, in an epoch of mounting crises, species-level survival relies on a renewed relationship with psychoactive plants: nothing less than an "archaic revival." That supposition relied on a proposal that was seminal to McKenna's career—that is, the appearance of *Psilocybe* in the hominid diet was pivotal to human evolution, with its removal from said diet causing our fall into history. Contracted with Bantam, *Food of the Gods*, a tribute to the mushroom as the missing link in human evolution, fielded what its author believed was his most significant contribution to science.[108] While its ambitious hypothesis rivaled the revolutionary implications of Wasson's *Soma*, whose ethnomycology served as an inspiration, other works may have been catalysts of one kind or another. Perhaps the desired outcome was not distant from that which *Worlds in Collision* served for Immanuel Velikovsky, whose theory of "cosmic catastrophism" brought that author notoriety among students of the sixties and seventies. Or was the popular vehicle for Erich von Däniken's "astral optimism," *Chariots of the Gods*, a departure point? Longer drawn bows might identify Joseph Campbell's *Masks of God*. Even so, the long-anticipated work stood alone.

Food of the Gods was also far removed from earlier efforts, notably *True Hallucinations*, which accentuated its author's heuristic competencies with organic hallucinogens, an empirical expertise thought essential to the new science he sought to pioneer. By comparison, the text offered relatively sparse and opaque attention to its author's brush with the indole hallucinogens it acclaimed, notably the consciousness catalyst—psilocybin—itself. On this subject, the author deigned to comment that "in the climactic events surrounding the emergence of pastoralism and language in human beings, I found the ancient echo of the things that I had personally felt and witnessed."[109] McKenna gave his audience contemporaneous assurances that Bantam "stood back and let me exercise my First Amendment rights."[110] And yet, as readers were not directly informed of the oracular-advisorial role of the mushroom, McKenna's prophetic role was excised, the narrative defreaked. As such, the "seeded genes" gnosis is not raised. Mandaeanism is never broached. And not coincidentally, the project completely elided the Timewave. While the transcendental object may have been the elephant in the room, such is not the case in contemporaneous book launches and speaking engagements, where the rhapsodic divulgence of empirical experience, and apologia for the apocalypse was ever main fare. *Food of the Gods* replaced the commonplace entreaty to readers to take five grams of dried mushrooms in silent darkness, with the nudging and winking understanding that silent darkness is the preferred context for the shaman to launch what the Neo-Platonic mystic Plotinus called "the flight of the alone to the Alone."[111]

Not unlike Asimov's Galactic Empire, Herbert's Imperium, or Cordwainer Smith's Instrumentality of Mankind, in which nova—discoveries, inventions, revelations—explain adaptability, rapid explosions of emergent technological capability, quantum leaps, galactic migrations, and miracles, the McKennaverse features a signature novum. Among the more popular fare in science fiction are faster-than-light travel, newly synthesized drugs, artificial intelligence, and time travel. While McKenna was clearly an enthusiast, his novum transpires in the archaic past. It is the grandest advent of all, that which explains the miracle of human consciousness—the rapid emergence of the neocortex in protohominids—sparking an imagination that could overcome all limitations, including that which prevented it from explaining its own origin. Just as the discovery of "hyperdrive" or "gravitic propulsion" serves as a "missing link" in science fiction (the literary canon that fires humanity into the cosmos), the "stoned ape," a hypothesis that cannot be proven (though neither can its possibility be absolutely discounted), is the speculative link that sired consciousness, language, and culture and triggered an avalanche of events that pushed our civilizing ancestors into history, some 15,000 years ago. But the presence of psilocybin in the Paleolithic diet is tempered by a concomitant downer. On the path toward symbiosis with the plant, it was ripped away from our nomadic pastoralist ancestors as North Africa's climate became drier. After that, "history was just a sojourn in matter during a period when we were unable to score."[112]

Food of the Gods did not shake the foundations of the establishment. It did not become the Anthropology 101 sensation desired. That the approach was intentionally amateur and de-institutionalized goes some way toward explaining the underwhelming response among professionals. The study lacked paleo-anthropological evidence, was remarkably selective, and appears to have skewed science in its efforts to support its grand proposition.[113] The idea of a "Paleolithic cult of the Great Horned Goddess" represents a primitivist fantasy of "archaic" shamanism heir to Eliade's explicit evolutionism. What's more, discussion of the causes and policy solutions to the "drug problem" appeared US-centric. Initial reviews were mixed. Robert Anton Wilson thought the book "will shake all the social sciences like no other book of our century."[114] Ralph Metzner, with whom McKenna maintained a close correspondence, became a long-time promoter of the "stoned ape" vision.[115] Others were less enthusiastic. While Schultes was impressed with the book's structure and organization, notably its glossary, bibliography, and professional index, the commentary in *American Scientist* was politely cautious. "This volume will long be consulted by researchers and others who may not be convinced by McKenna's scholarly venture into a highly controversial realm of thinking."[116] Many commentators have argued that the theory was too simplistic to account for the emergence of the unique cognitive, communicative, and cooperative patterns characteristic of modern human populations, implying that McKenna's interventions did as much to set the field back as to advance it.[117] While at best receiving reserved nods among scientists venturing into this field, the work largely failed to make an impression beyond the marginal and New Age milieu for whom it served as a panacea.

The failed prospect of *Food of the Gods* among the scientific and literary establishment, notably on the East Coast, is a contributing factor to the funk besetting McKenna in the early to mid-nineties, and to his use of Prozac. For J. P. Harpignies, McKenna was a somewhat tragic figure who harbored quite unrealistic expectations about the potential impact of his opus. Desiring to be taken seriously by leading East Coast intellectuals, McKenna was ultimately "excluded from the inner sanctum of the New York publishing world." Scorned within academia, the "stoned ape" hypothesis, and not to mention Timewave Zero, were audacious constructs destined instead for the marginal milieu—folks like stand-up comedy legend Bill Hicks, who worked a "stoned ape" routine into his 1993 Revelations tour. Though unrelenting in self-mockery before his base, the cold shoulder from cultural gatekeepers had a somewhat disillusioning impact on McKenna, who harbored a disdainful attitude to some in his audience, while privately admitting misanthropic inclinations.[118]

As the search for the origins of language and consciousness continued apace over the last three decades, the "stoned ape" has been reanimated in the post-Terencene.[119] Marveling over the still unexplained fact that the human brain doubled in size over the course of two million years, mycologist Paul Stamets had his old friend's back at the 2017 Psychedelic Science conference.[120] Among the resonant areas that Stamets has pursued is the role of mushrooms in enhancing neuroplasticity. Though disputing the hypothesis, *How to Change Your Mind* author Michael Pollan's subsequent appearance on *The Joe Rogan Experience* reintroduced the subject into the popular imagination.

But for all of its caveats (or plaudits) as a scientific project, less a work of scholarship, *Food of the Gods* is more a work of science fiction (or more accurately, psi-fi), penned by a modern mystic. While not listed in college syllabi, the book established McKenna as a public expert on the origins of human consciousness, and an authority on its fall. Reminiscent of the sci-fi canon, the ancient novum that gave birth to consciousness and was later the key to a Golden Age gave its author license to revise received mythology. The tryptaminal trope—the sudden presence, gradual withdrawal, and recent reappearance of the "secret"—provided fertile terrain for reinterpreting Christian cosmogony. The Tree of Knowledge, the Garden of Eden, and the Fall were among the stories reclaimed by the recovering Catholic who wanted to title his book "Why Eve Was Right." The rise and fall of consciousness (and its possible re-ascendancy) is framed in *Food of the Gods* through a radically revisionist appropriation of Judeo-Christian myth. In this re-vision, Eden is an actual shroomic epoch, "a lost golden age of plenty, partnership, and social balance."[121] An orgiastic prelapsarian paradise, characterized by the suppression of male primate dominance patterns and extending 75,000–15,000 years ago, saw the emergence of community, loyalty, altruism, and self-sacrifice. The contention was, moreover, that Eden was a real place, the Tassili n'Ajjer plateau of southern Algeria, speculated to be the late Neolithic site of a mushroom-inspired African Goddess religion that performed lunar-cycle boundary-dissolving rites. But the growing scarcity of the *Psilocybe* mushroom "stranded us in a world of language without soul."[122]

As a product of decades of familiarity with the psi-chedelic sublime, *Food of the Gods* offers a—perhaps *the*—classic psi-fi narrative while at the same time presenting a manifesto of neo-shamanic redemption. The historical crisis it addressed had a relatively simple solution: we must plant our own Trees of Knowledge, by which is meant primarily (though not exclusively) psilocybin bearing mushrooms, associated with a "shamanic" practice understood to be the most ancient of religions. At the same time, in the context of the modern drug war in which such practices have long been subjugated, the mushroom is championed among the "agents of evolutionary change."[123] In other words, the mushroom was to be consulted not primarily for the purposes of healing one's self or resolving inner conflict, but to the ends of consciousness evolution. This attitude, it is worth noting, is not far removed from that of Kat Harrison, who understood the role of psilocybin in the context of our planetary plight. In the reception of this "gift," we're charged, Harrison stated at Bioneers 2000, with a serious responsibility. "It can't be just about our personal growth and individual concerns," she warned. "We too must look at the bigger picture, and must each take on the charge of what we are going to contribute."[124]

ANTI-GURU GURU

McKenna's heterodoxy appealed to friends, followers, and fans with a broad interest base: radicals on sabbatical, outsider engineers, recalcitrant philosophers, dissident scientists. Rupert Sheldrake answers to the latter, having forged a career from unusual inquiries, such as: "How do pigeons find their way home?" Such was the title of a trialogue in which Sheldrake addressed the significance of the pigeon in the story of Noah—a bird that returned with new information, transforming the way Noah thought.[125] Thirty years later, I inquired of Sheldrake if the principle of the pigeon applies to McKenna. In response, he began sketching a mental fresco of his old friend. McKenna's "gift," he affirmed, was "a kind of prophetic gift." He was reminded of the Old Testament prophets who possess a visionary quality, by contrast to the temple priests, whose gifts are of a different order. Parallels were observed in India where there are sadhus and visionaries, "the holy men who live in caves in the Himalayas or in the forests." McKenna was in that region—"a shaman, sadhu, visionary, prophet, rather than a sort of priest, professor, academic, professional."

Smudging his mural with fresh paint, Sheldrake worked on the comparison. "Sadhus are these wondering holy men who are very individualistic, and they don't work for institutions. Sometimes they settle down and have an ashram and followers come to them." A portrait emerges of a "prophetic holy man" to whom followers gravitate, attending lectures and buying books, activities necessary for the economics of the operation. As such, Terence was "a bit like a guru figure." In India, sadhus who become gurus are highly individualistic and independent from institutional support. To complete the picture, Sheldrake is firm that McKenna's prophetic vision was neither shallow optimism or blind dogma, but a "faith that there's something else going on that is guiding what is happening."[126]

This candid image has warmer colors than some of the portraits that have begun to circulate within academia where the opportunity is missed to address the role of visionary, bard, or shaman that McKenna adopted within *his* community; or of the community that adopted him to serve in such a capacity. This lost opportunity might be evidenced best in Eric Cunningham's authorship of the "Terence McKenna" entry in Phyllis Jestice's *Holy People of the World* encyclopedia. There, a risible contraction is adopted—that is, where McKenna is regarded as "a good example of an American holy person of New Age spirituality."[127] Observing the hybrid stature of prophet, scholar, guide, and healer, another commentator goes so far as to identify "McKennan religion," with McKenna boiled down to "a guru guiding Psychonauts into a holistic cosmology."[128] With hagiographic iconography and devotional artworks compared favorably with St. Mary or the Amitabha Buddha, you can almost hear McKenna heaving in hyperspace, a likelihood magnified in the wake of advanced machine learning generators.

Loath to be associated with any cultic, mendacious, or predatory religion, there is little doubt that McKenna will have laughed off this growing corpus of comparisons and rampant random visual restorations. And yet an authority he *did* become, with a stature not unrelated, as it transpires, to his own sojourns in India, which he routinely credited as a source of enlightenment. But the wisdom hadn't arrived through self-realization achieved at the feet of a yogi. Wisdom was ostensibly acquired from precisely the opposite: by observing the charade of the spiritual marketplace, where ashrams were considered the public face of a large-scale "hustle" named "religion." Tales are repeatedly told of "visiting the local sadhus of great reputation" in India, of meeting spiritual figures who failed to convince him of their importance—although they might have supplied him with strong *charas*. "You're not empowered by placing your spiritual development in the hands of a guru," he announced. "You're spiritually empowered by taking responsibility for your spiritual development."[129]

McKenna's depth of experience with the spiritual traditions of India and East Asia is questionable. His most common interactions with sadhus are likely to have been as a haggler—for while they may have been rejected as spiritual mentors, they were authorities on good hash. Terence was ultimately ambivalent about the mantle of "healer." Esalen was not only a staging ground for this career, but it was a prime location for gathering intel for a stage act that relied on a scornful disdain of spiritual cognoscenti. In *On the Edge*, a satirical novel about Esalen, Edward St. Aubyn captured the métier of the spiritual authorities McKenna disdained. One such figure, fictional "ambiance director" and New Age Prometheus, Kenneth Shine, is identified by a competitor as a "bumpersticker," a derisory identification that could ironically find application to McKenna twenty years later, when his insights became routinely condensed into prosaic digital billboards shared on Facebook feeds.[130]

McKenna's public persona depended on the distinction he maintained between those who were potentiating themselves through safe and sheltered modes of othering, such as yoga and meditation, and the rugged psychedelicism he endorsed. Besides, he persistently claimed that the "seeking" was over: "No opening of chakras or revelation of shastras or passing of mantras or building of yantras is going to carry you any further." With DMT, the answer had been found.[131] Mocking "squirrelly LA types," and those who led them, was all part of the entertainment. "All these gurus need to find honest work." The guru class, it was claimed, relies on failure for their success. Under this rubric, if one has an ineffective technique one can "peddle it forever." By contrast, with the direct path to the divine enabled by indole hallucinogens, the issue was no longer spiritual advancement through practice and attention. "Once you find psychedelics you're not looking for the accelerator any more, you're looking for the breaks on your spiritual vehicle." The narrative ruffled the yogi set, with McKenna later claiming on *NPR* that once the seeker had found the means to transcend at will, they ought now to be dedicated to integrating the answers into their everyday lives.[132]

McKenna's brand relied heavily on a sharp classificatory system. Biting scorn was reserved for the spiritual puritan who sought the answers to life's questions, but flinched from the hardier methods at the business end of town. Any "new-age twit" can be a "seeker," declared the firebrand. But to "face and execute the real answer requires courage. . . . How many people ever went into an ashram to meditate with their knees knocking in terror over the realities of what was about to overcome them?" By contrast to lifestyle industries reliant on unsuccessful outcomes using crystals, dorges, spirulina, and other "malarkey," there lay the ontologically unsettling world of psychedelics. On the menu was a *psychedelic habitus* that drew its appeal from the transgression of the stable "ground of being," from its gravitation to the unknown. "If you were to suggest [to the New Agers] that they take 500 mics of acid . . . they're so appalled that you could even mention such a thing. It's like a fart at the opera."[133]

Amid a long campaign of targeted disdain and biting witticism, antipathy toward middle-class seekership was echoed in the distaste for the word "entheogen," an increasingly popular concept evoking substances and practices through which one *becomes divine*. While "entheogen" was disputed for its tendency to sanctify mystery, the preferred nomenclature—"hallucinogen" or "psychedelic"—evoked destabilizing hierophanies of the unspeakable. Further, in the modern context, "psychedelic shamanism" did not imply redressive psychotherapy for afflicted (post)moderns, and was irreducible to enhancing human potential—an implication of the contraction *entheogenesis*—but was integral to a dramatic and yet ultimately unknowable phase shift in consciousness.

If McKenna was on the prowl for peddlers of middle-class malarky, no one observed this derogatory nuance more closely than Harrison. The relentless derision of New Agers, crop circlers, and other others echoed an untiring commitment to divide the world into people who "get it" and those who are "marks." As Harrison observed, this fundamental distinction motivated a great deal of her ex-partner's conduct, becoming a focal point of their ethical differences, causing a rift in their relationship.[134] Ultimately, his behavior was in accord with his myth. How else might we expect someone to act who was burdened with the knowledge that the "shockwaves of the eschaton" are upon us? What is an individual marriage next to the species union with the cosmic attractor? How can one measure a human's capacity for good parenthood against the birthing of a species?

As McKenna shouldered this prophetic legacy, it was the figure of the shaman, rather than the sadhu, that he conjured. Any worthy depiction of his stature will acknowledge the valence of this visionary figure who draws power and attracts a following from a natural ability to enter altered states of consciousness and interact with the spirit world. A unique access to and mastery of powerful organic technologies manipulated for the purposes of therapy, aesthetics, and consciousness evolution goes a long way to understanding the strength of McKenna's reputation and the depth of his following (right into the present).

We now have the foundations for a mosaic, to which we could supply ever finer tessellations on the character of an individualist "holy man." Our portrait will, then, be incomplete without acknowledging the *psychedelic* substance of McKenna's visionary sensibility, which implies experience that is both *transformative* at the same time as *transgressive*, a practice potentially liberatory and boundary-dissolving while simultaneously illicit and hedged with risk and danger. As we enter the presence of a figure uniquely enigmatic, our mosaic depicts one who was, and remains, quite reflexively, an *anti-guru guru*. The authority who rejected authority. The prestigious outlaw. Celebrity anarchist. Freak scientist. Notorious recluse. Dark showman. The anti-hero of the heroic dose. A figure who embraced paradox as a virtue. The psychonaut's psychonaut. Such an anomaly attracts a certain type of following. Those who do not follow. The workshoppers who never do workshops. Ironic. Cynical. The McKenna milieu.

McKenna wasn't the priest or professional claiming control over access to secret knowledge to which members are initiated at the price of fealty and a lifetime of sacrifice. Those drawn are not "seekers" native to the New Age tradition. As he would have his followers believe, the tryptamine grail in all of its alchemical glory had been discovered and was available to all. The psychedelic shepherd had already guided them toward the answers—they just needed the courage to face the truth. The secret was out and yet the mystery remained for each person to discover in their own unique way. Further, he understood his role as temporary. As McKenna averred late in his life to an Esalen audience, "I'm not proud of the fact that . . . Esalen seems to be where I top out. Had I greater courage I would go further . . . but," he said laughing, "I don't." It was his hope that "you my graduate students, as it were," go further and report back.[135]

Comprehension of McKenna's significance requires a broad, detailed, and well-informed investigation of the impact of his thinking and practice, during his life and after. A large diffuse network, including many influential scientists, artists, and musicians, has adopted McKenna as a source of inspiration. This doubtlessly includes the "self-selected group of . . . Orphic eccentrics" and "go-betweens" who converged at his workshops at Esalen and further afield.[136] It includes those drawn to his admissions of fallibility, notably, as we have seen, at a critical posthumous moment when his integrity came under fire. The "Deep Dive" incident served to strengthen the support of fans for whom McKenna became humanized as a figure even more flawed than they had known. Tie-dyed in the wool psi-chonaut, Teafaerie, for example, transited from the anger of feeling betrayed by "the silver-tongued sham-man" to accepting his apparent decision to desist. "Should Neil Armstrong have voluntarily stopped fronting for NASA simply because he hadn't been to the moon in a few years?"[137]

McKenna's humility and self-deprecating humor left a great impression on filmmaker Edgar Pêra, for whom he was "someone you didn't follow, he showed you your own path." So I followed mine, with Terence in my heart. His conscience lives in all of us who found his life and work inspiring in so many ways."[138] Other stories illustrate the pressing relevance of a Net-pervasive "meta-professor" who serves the role of virtual psychopomp in an anxious age. In his first work of nonfiction, *Trip: Psychedelics, Alienation, and Change*, novelist Tao Lin writes: "I never felt awe, and never felt wonder, before incorporating psychedelics and McKenna's ideas into my life."[139] The sentiment is magnified as McKenna's vast archived rap proliferates across and reverberates within a global decentralized digital ecosystem.

As he introduces the means, techniques, and aesthetics of psychedelic gnosis to countless explorers who are encouraged to be authors of their own experience, does McKenna now serve the guiding role for psychonauts that he once attributed to the *logos*? Would he not become a sort of "informing voice" for Esalenites and later generations of seekers, including those today prompting the oracle on ChatGPT?

Utterly and consistently de-institutionalized, McKenna was without formal students and apprentices. And yet his "graduates" are to be found everywhere. Take Rupert's son, Merlin Sheldrake, for whom McKenna became a figure of fascination. McKenna was very good with children and had a presence in Merlin's life from the time he was a toddler. In *Entangled Life*, his book on the vast, interconnected, and neglected world of fungi, Merlin recalls the time, aged seven, when his family was visiting the McKennas on the slopes of Mauna Loa. He'd come down with a fever:

> I remember lying under a mosquito net, watching as McKenna ground up a preparation in a large pestle and mortar. I assumed it was a remedy for my sickness and asked what he was doing. In his zany metallic drawl, he explained that it was no such thing. This plant, like some types of mushroom could make us dream. If we were lucky these organisms could even speak to us. These were powerful medicines that humans had used for a long time but they could also be scary. He grinned a languorous smile. When I was older, he said, I could try some of the preparation—a mind altering cousin of sage called *Salvia divinorum*, as it turned out. But not now. I was transfixed.[140]

Rupert clarifies that *Entangled Life* is "a modern manifestation of the influence of Terence McKenna." When Merlin was fifteen, he borrowed the *True Hallucinations* "talking book" from his father. He copied all the tapes and shared them with his friends. McKenna was among Merlin's great inspirations.[141]

Countless others have been equally impacted. Among those guided posthumously is cyberspace pioneer, space mission designer, and "origin of life" scientist Bruce Damer, who was instructed by McKenna to "keep telling the story, but make it your own story." A self-identified "spectrumy" nerd who built early user interfaces for personal computers in the eighties, led the multi-user virtual worlds movement in the late nineties, and later ventured his "Hot Spring Hypothesis" on the origins of life, Damer understood McKenna as "perhaps the one person who most kept the pilot light lit on the psychedelic experience" through the dark times and who "re-valorized that experience after the crash, suppression and ridicule of the post-60s period." The two hit it off in the late nineties, and were set to collaborate. Damer later organized the "Terence2012" events designed to honor and explore McKenna's life and work, and initiated a data recovery project in

2005. Despite his departure, McKenna remained a guiding influence for Damer, who became something of an "amanuensis" in his wake.[142]

IMMEDIATIST VITALISM

Identifying a teaching behind McKenna or his fungal mentor is a fraught exercise. While the plan to celebrate his "teacher" may have been cut short by McKenna's own demise, *Food of the Gods* championed the mushroom's stature as super-agentive. The book is suffused with transformative moral agency, due not only to the catalytic role of *Psilocybe* in human evolution, but to its persistent capacity to mediate a human-nature relationship deemed essential to the planetary future. If dining on the "Tree of Knowledge" enables affinity with the natural world, then, dedicated to brokering this relationship, McKenna served (and continues to serve) as the mystic and muse of an *immediatist vitalism*. From the domestic cultivation revolution to public advocacy in an era of mounting crisis demanding critical solutions, we have seen the course of this development. Noting the persistent valence of the effort, one commentator has read *Food of the Gods* as a vehicle for a "vital materialism" evoking Jane Bennett's *Vibrant Matter* (2010) and Bruno Latour's "Agency at the Time of the Anthropocene," with the outcome that McKenna's vitalism "may be the absurd, incomprehensible, unimaginable solution to match" the apparently hopeless, and impossible, moment of the global present.[143]

Apparent among the chief instructions from his teacher, with a little help from the phenomenologies of Husserl and Merleau-Ponty, and conveyed in turn to his followers, was what McKenna knew as "the felt presence of immediate experience." The quest for authenticity and being in the world is a perspective steeped in the *knowing-as-feeling* process philosophy of Whitehead. The "prehension," to use Whitehead's phrase, that the world is a nondual relational process is enhanced in (and *on*) psilocybin, the organic substrate for the *prehending* process itself. Such musings appear prehensible to light painting photographer Dean Chamberlain, said to use a camera "like an intuitive divining rod to conjure the transcendent essence of life and consciousness that throbs beneath the surface of quotidian reality." Chamberlain made a portrait of Terence in December 1998 (see figure 10.1).[144]

At what turned out to be his final pre-seizure appearance, under the patronage of Sub Pop Records cofounder Bruce Pavitt, speaking at Seattle's ARO.spaceclub on April 27, 1999, for the opening of Chamberlain's "Psychedelic Luminaries" exhibition in which McKenna's portrait was featured, the audience learned that immediate experience is "all you will ever know."[145]

FIGURE 10.1
Dean Chamberlain, "Light painting" portrait of Terence McKenna seated in front of his new house, Hawaii, December 1998. From the "Psychedelic Luminaries series," 1999. Courtesy of Dean Chamberlain.

Immediacy was a stump theme, and the value of psilocybin was felt to inhere in its potential to provoke a compassion for the natural world in which one is immersed. The implication follows that if psilocybin facilitates such immediacy, which in turn enhances a moral relationship with nature, then accessing this state of immediacy ought to be prioritized in a world in which human connection to the Earth has been perilously compromised. How this would be achieved is difficult to say, not least of all compounded by a contrarian discourse. Although removing the frameworks prohibiting access appeared to be an imperative to this solution, and was implicit to the one-page manifesto featured at the back of *Food of the Gods*, at other times, McKenna could hardly fathom a climate in which the non-medical application of psilocybin was not outlawed. These views bear a stamp on the present as, despite the recent decriminalization measures in some US states and cities, psilocybin and DMT remain heavily restricted across the United States and around the world. What's more, under the aegis of the therapeutics "renaissance," psilocybin's pending legalization appears concomitant with its expropriation for neoliberal agendas. On the prospect of psilocybin's repackaging and commodification as a pharmaceutical product, McKenna's cybernetic doppelgänger quipped: "It's like trying to capture the lightning of Zeus and selling it in a jar at the local drugstore."[146] If the emergence of corporate psychedelia wasn't dire enough, psilocybin's usurpation by technocratic elites under a "gnostic" banner might have provoked McKenna into becoming something more than an intellectual apologist.[147] But this is pure speculation. He was most comfortable serving as an experiential consultant for the coming renaissance; his role was more iconic figurehead than campaign strategist.

Such is the mood in Santa Fe in 1990, where McKenna addressed "the Tolstoyan question": What is to be done? Not committed to an ideological program, the genuine "psychedelic person," he wagered, is committed to a level of personal authenticity. The audience is alerted to the need for "a thorough recommitment to a revitalization of religion based on experience."[148] But the "alchemical gold"—i.e., meaning—is hard won, and authenticity no easy game to coach when success depends on bearing paradox to the mat. "Meaning lies in the confrontation of contradiction," Esalenites were regaled in one of the more astute refinements on the artifice. Rather than being beaten over the head with more "rational schemas," another strategy is deemed desirable:

> A recovery of the real ambiguity of being, an ability to see ourselves as at once powerful and weak, noble and ignoble, future-oriented, past-facing. We each need to become Janus-faced and to incorporate into ourselves the banished contradictions of being that so haunt the enterprise of science. We can leave that behind, and when we do we reclaim authentic being.[149]

This wasn't the "authentic being" instructed by the priests of the New Age, but an immediacy steeped in unabashed contraries. If immediate experience is the real game in town, as an outspoken proponent of Janus-faced authenticity, McKenna adopted the thoroughly enigmatic position of being a mediator of immediacy. It was a genuine anomalist's game, and a precarious tightrope act. And while assuming a shepherd-like role, leading followers toward the gnosis, he knew he had to get out of the way. To serve as pontificating intermediary between the gnostic and the gnosis would be a failure of his enterprise, for that amounts to occupying a priestly position between the laity and the truth. It is not irrelevant that an abiding cynicism is harbored in relation to systems and method. So "against method"—apropos Feyerabend—was McKenna that he avoids developing, implementing, and transmitting any methodology—beyond "five dried grams in a darkened place." The rest is between the user and the mushroom. So while the "felt presence of immediate presence" discourse might fly as close as we'll come to a McKennan teaching or practice that could have been scheduled on Esalen's workshopping lists adjacent to guided meditation or rebirthing for beginners, we can comprehend why anything of the sort was resisted.

11 ZONE GHOST

An alien intelligence, the unconscious, the Overmind, *logos*, ancestors, travelers from the future, visitors from a parallel world. McKenna's career presented a careening cavalcade of speculation on the nature of entities, who they are, and where they come from. Whatever form they took, relations had to be established. There was a need to study and analyze their "language" like xenolinguists, building a lexicon through sustained encounter. This was not the terrain of involuntary "abduction" by aliens of the "Grey" variety, or the chance or accidental "near death experience." Our recourse, he contended, was to uncover this language by exploring the disembodied contours of *hyperspace*.

The out-of-body contact experience was familiar to Terence since his late teens, when vaporized DMT became his entrée to hyperspace. Through the seventies, it became a preoccupation shared with friend, intellectual playmate, and compadre in chaos, Ralph Abraham. By 1983, the two gathered their thoughts in a public dialogue venturing the prospect of drafting adequate maps, an "atlas" no less, of higher dimensionality. In their get-together "Dynamics of Hyperspace," McKenna wondered if there was nomenclature better suited than "hyperspace" for the occult dimensions accessible through the use of psychedelic compounds. He emphasized that our "hyperdimensional organ"—the human mind—possesses its own physicality (i.e., the brain) which is like the three-dimensional shadow of four-dimensional consciousness.[1] Providing the thought forms for future cybernetic experiments, the semantics of "hyperspace" was never quite surpassed. Over decades interfacing with other-dimensional space and its inhabitants, from the sixties through to the nineties, McKenna anticipated the emergence of cyberspace, offering prescience on the virtual world to come.

MAGELLANS OF THE IMAGINATION

When suggesting that they needed to create "a meta-linguistic metamathematical, metaphorical language," McKenna was broaching one of his friend's strengths, given Abraham imagined a multisensual language as essential to human evolution. Abraham was then in the design phase of his Mathematically Illuminated Musical Instrument (MIMI), a digital video-based visual musical instrument defined in accord with the algorithms of dynamical systems theory. Influenced by geometry, topology, nonlinear dynamics, and a theory of vibrating waves, as a turned-on mathematician at UC Santa Cruz, Abraham's perspective on consciousness had been inspired by Greek, Jewish, and Indian philosophy—and large doses of DMT.[2] His friend's ongoing research impressed McKenna, who sought to task new generations of psychonauts to compile a new dictionary of hyperspace. Breaking into his trademark orthogonal discourse, the principal goal was for humanity to "turn itself inside out."

Casting its shadow over the historical landscape and signaling the agenda, the "transcendental object" was generating the conditions for its own becoming. And the cosmic whirlpool into which all of space-time would be drawn was interpreted via a familiar dynamic: the collective interiorizing of the body coincident with an exteriorizing "soul-mind." This dynamic was predicted to generate new language, art, and architecture, with alchemy providing the metaphors to explain how the soul could be "condensable as a visible object." With the advent of advanced cybernetic systems, psychedelic substances, and shamanic techniques, the crafting of this "translinguistic matter," this hyper-language, was deemed pivotal to humanity's push "beyond the crisis of death," and into "Elysium." Once we have "all of our ducks in a row," the psychedelic sage averred that it was simply a matter of flicking the switch.[3]

Such was the rap at the beginning of the eighties when the duo gave public signs of private practices that were raising periscope above the oppressive conformity of Reaganomics, strip malls, and neon authoritarianism. In the safe confines of their own homes, growing numbers of the suitably equipped were becoming "Magellans of the interior world," and returning with tales of "cities of gold, insect gods, spaceships [and], endless wastelands."[4] For the heroically dosed hyperspace Odysseus, the potential boons were nontrivial. Such exploits shared characteristics in common with the "hyperspace" embraced as a sci-fi novum, that is, in which it is *both* an imaginary liminal *space* and a mode of faster-than-light *travel*—or "hyperdrive."[5] With space exploration correlated to consciousness evolution, the groundwork for the psychedelic hyperspace traveler had been performed by Leary.[6] The tools developed for mind exploration were devised not for the sole objective of improving the health and well-being of the individual, nor even simply improving species evolution, but for reenchanting the "world soul." By the mid-seventies, expressing interest in space habitation and overcoming biological and cognitive limits, Leary developed "SMI^{2}LE," his transhumanist paean to "Space Migration, Intelligence Increase, and Life Extension."[7] While these interests echo McKenna's early futurism in which the space race, the starship, space colonies, and other ingressions of novelty convey the species' compulsion to exit the planet, and become the alien, for the guerrilla ontologist these developments were simply among the last "shockwaves of eschatology" mirroring the coming cosmic metamorphosis when "in the final moment the Unspeakable stands revealed." With his public strapped into the Eschatron, the strange attraction coming soon was to be nothing less than "the entry of our species into hyperspace." Understood as a release of the mind into the imagination, the process was outlined in neo-gnostic terms as the freeing of spirit from matter.[8]

It wasn't to the unconscious, in its Freudian or Jungian guises, that we should turn to understand this fantastic contrivance. "The main event, folks, doesn't even have anything to do with the psychology of human beings," barked our midway philosopher. "The main event is another dimension, a dimension so bizarre, so titanically peculiar, so strange, unanticipated by our language, our history, our literature, that it is literally like the discovery of another world."[9] In this psychedelic age of discovery, plant-sourced alterants are to consciousness exploration as the telescope was to astronomy. And since it has "the unique property of releasing the structured ego into the Overself," DMT offered intrepid explorers tickets to the main event. "Each person who has that experience undergoes a mini-apocalypse. . . . For society to focus in this direction, nothing is necessary except for this experience to become an object of general concern."[10]

HIGHER DIMENSIONALISTS

When McKenna became the darling of hyperspace hipsterism, he entered a field with a convoluted history shaped by developments in geometry, spiritualism, science fiction, and the art world. The term "hyperspace" emerged in the mid-1800s among geometers as the designation for space other than Euclidean (i.e., space greater than the three dimensions of length, width, and height). That "hyperspace" was inconceivable beyond Nth-dimensional geometry and linear algebra was of little concern to philosophers, theosophists, and other esotericists breathing life into the fourth spatial dimension in the late nineteenth century, when the trope afforded legitimacy to spiritualist claims and mystical insights. This career path was stimulated by French mathematician Henri Poincaré, for whom four-dimensional space was not geometric, but a perceptual "inner space." Believing that the three dimensions of space were an illusory property of normal brain consciousness, Poincaré proposed that "the dimensionality of space was a *subjective* property."[11]

British mathematician Charles H. Hinton built upon this understanding. In *A New Era of Thought* (1888) and *The Fourth Dimension* (1904), Hinton developed his views on the mystical and evolutionary significance of four-dimensional space. The fourth dimension was the source of alternative modes of consciousness like those experienced by mystics, psychics, mediums, and others with evolved perception. For Hinton, the fourth dimension was not a mathematical abstraction, but a mode of perception integral to the development of human consciousness. Believing four-dimensional mental vision could be acquired with sufficient effort, he devised a complex system of mental exercises—using mnemonic devices known as "Hinton cubes"—that enabled popular visualization of a 4D "hypercube" he called the "tesseract."

Such speculations and exercises were good news for spiritualists, occultists, and others taking liberty with geometry to legitimize their practices. Among these enthusiasts, a 4D universe could explain a host of paranormal phenomena, like ghosts haunting our three-dimensional consciousness or the practice of gifted mediums soaring into "higher planes of consciousness" and channeling entities from those realms. In his opus *Tertium Organum*, Russian esotericist P. D. Ouspensky named such *miraculous* occurrences the "noumenal." Ouspensky believed that beyond the visible side of life "there lies a whole world of the 'invisible,' a whole world of the new and incomprehensible forces and relations."[12] In experiments with dreams, yoga, prayer, fasting, breathing, and inhaling nitrous oxide, Ouspensky forged a philosophy of consciousness inspired by enigmatic flashes of insight. If, as he believed, the fourth dimension was the realm of the psyche—of consciousness—then art more than science would be the means to transpose the noumenal. "The artist must be a clairvoyant: he must see that which others do not see; he must be a magician: must possess the power to make others see that which they do not themselves see, but which he does."[13]

Despite McKenna's distaste for Ouspensky, as journaled in 1971, the two were fellow travelers of higher consciousness dwelling in different eras, though loosely connected through their interests and methods. Not only did he embrace the higher dimensionality of consciousness, but McKenna championed the active role of the artist and, more to the point, the imagination, in the evolution of consciousness. Not unlike McKenna, who poured scorn on celebrity culture, Ouspensky railed against what he saw as the philistinism and barbarism of his time. For Ouspensky, the evolution in consciousness was to be achieved through the development of a culture that augments the new consciousness and causes it to flourish. The approach presages McKenna's decidedly more hands-on role as ambassador for hyperspace in his own time.

Among Ouspensky's chief insights was that time is a movement in "the *fourth dimension of space*."[14] Whereas physicists, following Minkowski and Einstein, regarded time as a dimension that is perpendicular to the three dimensions of space, he saw our three-dimensional phenomenal world intersecting with the four-dimensional noumenal world. Notably, Ouspensky reported shifts in consciousness associated with his use of nitrous oxide and hashish. The account of his experiments with these drugs is, as Gary Lachman claims, "one of the most lucid reports about an absolutely 'other' form of consciousness ever penned." While no entities were beheld, and the character of the experience—a world in which "*everything* was connected"—diverges from McKenna's tryptaminal gnosis, Ouspensky's ontological "shift into *somewhere else*" holds resonance. Like the American living a century later, the Russian navigated an experience sans the aid of explanatory models, maps, or CliffsNotes. Knowledge of the astral realm and the "higher spheres" had not prepared Ouspensky for his launch into a "totally different reality."[15]

In modified states of consciousness in early twentieth-century St. Petersburg, Ouspenksy had a vision of the *Linga Sharira*, a four-dimensional "temporal body." It was as though he had flicked a switch. In semi-dream states and lucid narcotic episodes, this direct perception of body form in higher-dimensional space-time inaugurated new categories of thought. By sixty years, the experiments prefigured McKenna, under whose helmsmanship DMT surfaced as something of a pharmacological Hinton cube, only now the tryptamine-derived "tesseract" could be experienced directly—as Ouspensky might have approved. In our time, the neo-"hypercube" is subject to prohibition, with experimentalists of the present risking the heavy hand of the state and public opprobrium by testing the boundaries of three-dimensional reality with controversial claims on the New Jerusalems of hyperspace.

VISIBLE LANGUAGE

For our noetic spelunker, the concept of hyperspace was adapted to illuminate the experiential qualities of the Nth-dimensional space unlocked with the assistance of natural allies. Other experimental methods, such as those deployed by esotericists, whether those living in turn-of-the-century Russia or "squirrelly" types dwelling in 1980s Los Angeles, were, at best, "menopausal mystics" and, at worst, total shams.[16] By contrast, late twentieth-century methods displayed what McKenna saw as superior (and novel) coordinates in the wave. At the turn of the 1990s, the psychopharmacological actions of DMT and other indole hallucinogens prompted a new experiential language of hyperspace widely adopted by voyagers, contactees, and returnees—that is, including explorers familiar with the emergent virtual reality. Audiences had been prepped in the eighties with an insight with hints of Hinton and Ouspensky. "The way I think of the mind is as a fourth dimensional organ of your body," Esalenites were briefed. It cannot be seen as such but you experience its lower-dimensional form in the phenomenon of consciousness.[17]

While brief experiments with nitrous oxide and hashish aided Ouspensky's perception that time had been subverted, the Russian grew disenchanted with dead-end tools that left him with what Lachman calls a "metaphysical hangover." In *A New Model of the Universe,* Ouspensky describes the oppressive world to which he awakens in the morning aftermath of his experiments, a world under the heavy power of "an enormous wooden machine, with creaking wooden wheels, wooden thoughts, wooden sensations," when everything moved with "a melancholy wooden creaking." Life in the wake of nitrous is insinuated to be "soulless,"[18] a colorless awakening burdened with 3D objects. Ultimately, he concluded that, for all their revelatory value, nitrous oxide and hashish were "too elusive and uncontrollable to offer much more than a brief view from the mountaintop."[19] While one figure experimented with pharmacological tools available at the fin de siècle, later in the century a fellow precocious iconoclast grasped a lightning rod to the higher dimensions, where the topography is found to be scintillating. The only thing "wooden" about McKenna's interventions was the proverbial "horse" he wheeled into the public domain, where users are encouraged to become trans-linguistic emissaries of the higher dimensions. By repeated expeditions into tryptaminal space, it is argued that the experimentalist could overcome the difficulties posed by the normal human incapacity of adequately transposing phenomena occurring in dimensions above three. Leading the charge into noumenal novelty, McKenna's effort was, as he later explains, "like a child playing with an FM radio dial of the universal crystal radio of the Akashic imagination."[20]

As a skilled orator of the inexpressible, and a fine tuner of the universal crystal radio, McKenna believed in the power of the imagination. He knew artists could become exposed, apropos Blake, to the Divine Imagination. At Esalen in 1983, he alluded to Borges's short story "The Aleph," where the protagonist unexpectedly gazes into a "small iridescent sphere, of almost intolerable brilliance," which turns out to be Cosmic Space, a space in time that appears to contain all other points. "In that gigantic instant," Borges wrote, "I saw millions of delightful and atrocious acts; none astonished me more than the fact that all of them together occupied the same point, without superposition and without transparency."[21] "The Aleph" is seen as Borges's articulation of the infinite and ineffable nature of the Secret—that is, the kind of work that foreshadows one's condemnation as a lunatic, or celebration as a genius.

For McKenna, the Aleph was language itself. In the transcendent state promoted, the traveler is not unlike a medium of the Otherworld brokering the dialects of hyperspace in the form of novel syntax and visionary art. The modern hyperspace farer is a message-bearer who seeks to transmit the content of their revelation. A primal mode of transmission is known in the immediate outpourings and feral extemporizations of those returnees, and is speculated to have been the expression of "the assembly language," a primal language like the Kabbalistic tongue described in the foundational work of Kabbalistic literature, the *Zohar*.[22] While this *Ursprache* is variously identified—for example, Logos, Teacher, Overmind, Gaian Mind, Divine Imagination, Collective Unconscious—regardless of the frame, McKenna repeatedly returns to the recognition that the tryptaminal transmission is not that which is heard, so much as *seen*. It is a higher-dimensional language that condenses as a "visible syntax."[23]

Emanating from a figure who decried deficiencies in human language, such observations would arrive on the cusp of the emergence of virtual reality, touted to be the escape from the sensorial straight-jacket that McLuhan skried in the electronic retribalization. While McLuhan did not live to witness the networked media environment hotting up with personal computers, VR, and the internet, augmented by the "higher linguistic modalities" of tryptamine hyperspace, these developments are celebrated by McKenna as "a final confirmation of the McLuhan apotheosis."[24] While our "small mouth noises" represent the most abstract and low-grade form of communication, as film director Edgar Pêra was informed, it was felt that "the bandwidth of understanding will be vastly expanded if we can invent and then enter a true domain of visual language."[25]

At the beginning of the nineties, new electronic media and personal computing made it possible to perform the equivalent of "high-speed sculpture." As was incisively explained at this time, it was possible to imagine a VR "driven by a speech-operated synthesizer where the various parts of ordinary speech—adjectives, modifiers, subjects and objects—were interpreted by the cybernetic environment as topological manifolds of various shapes, so that speech would then generate a visibly beheld topology."[26] This turn-of-the-nineties fixation with a virtual sensorial language gave expression to a deep-rooted passion. As knowingly conveyed in 1984 at Shared Visions, "the incoming sensory data can be recombined in such a way that no trace of the portal of entry is left upon it." As an immersive "grammar of form" is envisioned to possess an emotional richness and poetic depth unlike ordinary language,[27] at this juncture, McKenna was hedging his bets on a seamless cyberspace years ahead of its time.

ELECTRIC MATRIX

As prescience on these matters runs deep, we are prompted to cast our minds back to 1965–1970—that is, to the pre-mushroom era, in which our translinguistic grammarian prefigured developments in virtual worlding. The key document here is "Post Electric Thought" (see chapter 3), the unpublished manuscript dedicated to the "hyperspatial zeitgeist" completed before the McKennas underwent a dramatic shamanic turn. This homage to the electric sublime is a remarkably prophetic, albeit abstruse, document anticipating innovations in networked information, universal connectivity, VR, search engines, smart phones, 3D printing, video conferencing, nanobots, and artificial intelligence. The work demanded a "standard" for currents and voltages of electronic components and electrical transmission and distribution systems, as essential for "an electrified world society."[28] The post-electric matrix will be so microminiaturized, McKenna foretold, that it could be "set adrift in a drop of water or secreted in the grain of sand." A de-urbanized future was envisioned where "ecologically sound" projects reclaim arid regions of the Earth. Sensing the distant buzz of drones, manufactured goods were expected to be delivered by airborne robots. These and other predictions were forecast in a document where the future movement of the physical body through "Newtonian space" was imagined to be largely eliminated, outside of the "expression of pure physical joy."[29]

For the most part, "Post Electric Thought" pursued an abstract futurism overshadowed by US imperialism and projected an immature radical unitary philosophy. And yet, its sophomoric qualities aside, the commentary on the coming era is percipient. "A computer working out of a memory bank of total information," McKenna wrote in his crypto-revolutionary tract, "would be the world's most powerful interdisciplinary intellect."[30] There was no overt reference to H. G. Wells, but McKenna anticipates something not unlike the "hypothetical super-gadget"—Bruce Sterling's phrase for Wells's 1930s "world brain" ruminations.[31] The conjuration of a "memory bank of total information" shows a clearer debt to Arthur C. Clarke, whose *The City and the Stars* featured the all-powerful Central Computer controlling Earth's last city, Diaspar, home to a civilization living a billion years in the future. Though his name is not invoked in "Post Electric Thought," Clarke's thought informs a futurist fantasy in which the dawning electronic eschaton will evade the ravages of time, reverse entropy, and conquer death, through the alchemical accomplishments of "solid state" electronics. While the details are as sparse as the moving parts in solid state devices, Clarke's message is clear: "No machine should have any moving parts."[32]

Both "Post Electric Thought" and the precursor student thesis, "The Future of Magic in Electronic Societies," forge an ambiguous futurism braided with utopian and dystopian threads. While this material was not overtly crafted as science fiction, the "perfect machine" of Diaspar provides a leitmotif that resounds in this work, and echoes throughout McKenna's career.[33] As an example of this motif's influence, the fantasy projected in "Post Electric Thought" of a future living space resonates with the home of Alvin in Diaspar. "Imagine a room, designed for maximum physical comfort," McKenna writes, where:

> upon the mental or spoken command the room electrifies and walls disappear. Holographic space—exact visual equivalent of true space, leaps into being carrying the information, or the sensation, or the aggregate of fact that the participant is interested in. More information in all forms and versions possible is instantly available.[34]

At this stage, the imagination knew few bounds on the subject of physical interaction with virtual 3D images. A one-page typewritten document, possibly McKenna's oldest extant work and illustrative of his budding sci-fi talent, offers further hints of a Holographic Room, or what its author abbreviates as "Ho Lo." In "linear terms," "Ho Lo" appears as a room "entirely given over to the production of media environments, both informational and imaginary." The document envisions "a full field enclosure of holographic screens" integrating a "stereophonic" environment with a cybernetic information retrieval system. This optimal infomatic living space makes it possible for "everyman's wildest dreams [to] become a media created reality."[35]

Perhaps the most prescient innovation featuring in "Post Electric Thought" is the masterstroke its author names the "All Media Recorder." An instrument of "total knowledge," the AMR is the pièce de résistance of the "transcendent possibilities of the electric matrix." Name-checking "Cinerama" and the "feelies" from *Brave New World* as distant precursors, combining stereophonic recording techniques with holography, this device is imagined to be a sensorial reconstruction of the "reality plane." As a super smart device, apparently smarter by far than the multi-purposed "Joymaker" in Frederik Pohl's contemporaneous science-fiction novel *The Age of the Pussyfoot* (1969), the AMR is reckoned capable of recording all personal sensory data and relaying "all information" to a "central information pool," apparently surpassing a mere "world brain." "All information generated on the planet would be immediately available for stereo-holo electric replay at any point in space or time." With the advent of this contraption, "whatever happened anywhere could be immediately experienced anywhere else as soon as it had occurred." Under such conditions, no information, no experience, could ever be lost to the "electrical collectivity."[36]

Not only does the AMR prefigure the recording capabilities of the ubiquitous smart phone; perhaps more ominously, it presages fictional nanotech enabling the capture of audiovisual senses. Its author barely broaches the ethical dilemmas associated with the AMR, by contrast to, for example, the dystopian implications of a "grain" implant that records memories, as depicted in the episode "The Entire History of You" featured in sci-fi TV series *Black Mirror*. While "Post Electric Thought" warns of the potential for fascist surveillance systems, the document is extremely vague on how this technology could be prevented from becoming an analog of Orwell's "telescreens." The troubling implications of developing what McKenna names a "cybernetic demerit system"—with its echoes of China's experiments with a social credit system—appear unrecognized.[37]

Little concerned with its dystopian implications, and consistent with fawning embellishments on a future unity, McKenna reckons the All Media Recorder as "our model-T conception of an electric mirroring of the One."[38] Championing an electronic Leviathan in which humanity is cast as "thinking with one Mind" and "acting with one will—at the speed of thought"[39] seems terribly ill-considered in the light of the monopolizing of tech for ubiquitous surveillance and in the service of corporate tyranny, à la Facebook. Nor is there much hint of future big tech struggles for "data governance." These naive implications are, I imagine, among the reasons why its author grew distant from this pre-seventies material, and forbade its posthumous release.

The early work was not without recognition of disturbances in the force. While generally forecasting an optimistic neo-feudal "enstasis," the Tussman-era work admits troubling consequences. In the prophesied electro-network in which "interior functions" have become exteriorized, humanity appears to have been renounced in favor of "a surrogate existence that denies man all possibility of differentiation and self-realization." In this transformed state, the body is immobilized and "electronically pampered," as the psyche "utilizes the media net" to create a world that is entirely "mediaized." A shadow falls across this posthuman future. "Holographic sexual relationships, mediaized meals composed of pure electronic titillation, and the sum total of human knowledge instantly available, less all of the wisdom that man acquired by virtue of struggling with his human condition."[40] Coleridge is recruited to sketch this perverse paradise:

> It was a miracle of rare device
> A sunny pleasure-dome with caves of ice.[41]

Among the more insightful facets of this student work is an extraordinary passage alluding to a kind of reverse shamanism. In response to the electronic shamanism of the future, there will emerge the "media-free-ascetic" who will retain, through physical mobility, the power to move in three dimensions. This now rare accomplishment is considered to be a "direct reversal" of the principle implied in Eliade's discussions of shamanism and the modus operandi of magical processes:

> It will be the media-free pariah, the man who refused to allow his interior psychic processes to be electronically collectivized and exteriorized, that will be the true human being. The situation confirms the centuries-old belief that magical powers accrue themselves only to the ascetic and the contemplative.[42]

This retribalized figure is as equally indebted to McLuhan, who was notoriously ambivalent toward the electro-millennium. In another timeline, this commentary on the nature of freedom, culture, and technology might have provided the narrative drive for cyberpunk fiction, or otherwise lending substance to the character of defiance in a sci-fi universe. However, McKenna seems to have had nothing more to say about these three-dimensional dissidents in a four-dimensional universe, this future lo-fi rebel and ecstatic front of archaic resistance to the "electric matrix."

The rebellious spirit of the hacker nevertheless suffuses discourse from the early period of McKenna's notoriety. If hacking the mind, culture, and cyber technology—all recognizable as "operating systems"—were integrated strategies, organic compounds and computers were interwoven tools in species-scale deconditioning. McKenna made a unique, if not uniquely quixotic, contribution to the narrative that cybernetic defense research had been rerouted by freaks and heads into creating the PC, notably the Apple II, the first home computer and the model he acquired in 1977. Advancing in real time the folk history later documented by John Markoff in *What the Dormouse Said*, McKenna reveled in the choice irony by which psychedelics anticipated the internet, despite its creation as an indestructible decentralized command and control system built by the military to survive a thermonuclear exchange.[43] It boiled down to geeks getting loaded, demanding the impossible, and becoming electronically networked. The buoyant mood was unflagging. Anyone with $1,000 worth of equipment—an Apple II and a cheap modem—could achieve a level of omniscience, by gaining, as McKenna cheekily claimed in 1984, access to Defense Department databases, the complete shelflist of the Library of Congress, and the total contents of Chemical Abstracts. Alluding perhaps to the home setup of Abraham, among other friends with access to ARPANET and BITNET, from his living room in Sonoma he had access to "all information in the world." While this he said, in reference to the architects of the military industrial and computing complex, "was not part of the plan," it appeared to be among the greatest causes for hope. About the *space* upon which he had long contemplated and into which he now ventured, "vast areas are being opened up for human interaction completely unregulated by any kind of institution. And these will create new kinds of social realities."[44] The psychedelic experience was "hardwired" into this development, a circumstance that McKenna was among the earliest to champion.

At the same time, he sought to nurture a computer network of the altered states research community. In a letter dated July 30, 1985, as secretary treasurer of Botanical Dimensions, McKenna made an invitation to subscribers to join a "computerized private conference," and "bulletin board," called MYCONET. Prospective participants in this protean online event needed a personal computer, a modem, and an account with the Source (Source Telecomputing Corporation) to send e-letters and join electronic conferencing. McKenna had an account with the Source, and is known to have participated in early online discussions. He championed this "neural network" at Esalen in August 1985, enthusing that over the next few years the "mind-machine interaction is going to become a major frontier for development and redefinition." The future of unobtrusive computing is laid out, sans keyboards, and where you "just sit down and compose yourself in a certain state of mind."[45] The Botanical Dimensions mailout is suggestive of the mycelial character of the community of researchers who are envisioned to possess "an electronic dimension of interaction that will make us of one mind."[46] It is likely that excessive subscription fees and rates for data services excluded many from participation—as was consistent with the reasons the Source was discontinued in 1989. By that stage, The Well had grown increasingly popular—though remaining too expensive for an information hound like McKenna. MYCONET never pans out.[47] Within two weeks from the date of the letter, their neighbor Hassall is raided and turmoil ensues.

VIRTUAL OCTOPI

From the sixties through to the nineties, McKenna's musings offer enough prescience on the advent of the Net to warrant serious attention. The turn of the nineties saw the ingression of an extraordinary grammar of form. Animated by language formerly used to map terrestrial, outer, and inner space, with *cyberspace*, a cybernetic virtuality came into prominence. Like avatars exploring new worlds, and tasked to retrieve wisdom, "cybernauts" were now uploading to and inhabiting the farthest reaches of an out-of-body, Net-enabled "reality." The utopian yearning is evident in a 1990 article written for *Magical Blend*, where McKenna introduces readers to cyberpunk "hyper-prophet" William Gibson. In "Burning Chrome" and other of Gibson's works, "cyberspace" is depicted as a dystopian "matrix."[48] For the psychedelic prophet, however, this electronic space into which we shall all be downloaded at the end of history, a dimension that is unchartable in our lower dimensions, is promoted as a "philosopher's stone" forged from energy and language, "into which we can all cast ourselves at will."[49] While McKenna grew aware that his thinking may amount to little more than fetishistic technonanism, echoing the faith that things are more or less as they should be, the psychedelic transhumanist believed in the promise of the "electronically-sustained realm of mind" that humanity was about to switch on and occupy.[50]

McKenna was attracted to the "unthinkable complexity" of cyberspace for the same reason he was drawn to the promise of VR tech, such as the DataGlove, developed by Jaron Lanier. VR held the potential for creating a "visible language," as consonant with that known in DMT space. That the event horizon drew near was signaled by Cyberthon, the twenty-four-hour VR gathering presented at Colossal Pictures Studios in San Francisco's Bayview District, October 6–7, 1990. Organized by *Whole Earth Catalog* founder

Stewart Brand and Grateful Dead manager Jon McIntire, Cyberthon offered a cybercultural update on the Acid Tests. "People have been doing VR for about a hundred and twenty-five thousand years," McKenna shares when taking the stage with Leary. "They just called it taking psychedelic drugs." As VR holds out the possibility of mirroring the contents of our imaginations in the minds of others, it extends the promise of past and present media, whether "small mouth noises," oil paints, or electronic pixels.[51]

Pulling on the slick black glove and wearing the EyePhone helmet that looked like an overweight scuba mask, Terence took his first awkward steps in digital three-dimensional space. "I burst noiselessly and effortlessly through a wall and into a burnt sienna space that seemed to, and probably did, extend to infinity." This small cyber-step was an imaginal leap toward "a more perfect Logos," a "three-dimensional syntax" where we will at long last "truly *see* what we mean." By comparison to the animal totems of former eras—the horse as symbol of power in nineteenth century, and raptor as symbol of speed and conquest in the twentieth century—the twenty-first century's totem was to be the cephalopod that expresses its thoughts through a series of color changes and intricate folds in its surface texture.[52] The octopus became something of a spirit creature for McKenna through the eighties, when he adopted a cephalopod graphic with mushroom-capped head as his business letterhead—his coat of many arms (see figure 11.1). It's not clear to me when or where the obsession with cephalopods began, but these creatures spoke to Terence, who would likely agree with philosopher Peter Godfrey-Smith that they are "the closest we'll come to meeting an intelligent alien."[53] Wearing their minds on their exteriors, octopi and squid were the mascots of the cyberdelic age.

But cephalopods were not only the era's icons; they were a metaphor for the enigmatic tenor of McKenna's life. On the one hand, they symbolize transparency and sincerity, a raw talent to open one's self to others. The large repertoire at the octopus' disposal—color changes, dots, blushes, and traveling bars that move across their surfaces—was a cause for marvel. These abilities permit the creature to "reveal its linguistic intent simply by rapidly folding and unfolding different parts of the body." The description provided a self-portrait. "The octopus does not transmit its linguistic intent; it *becomes* its linguistic intent."[54] This talent for a kind of "psychedelic telepathy," in which another sees what you mean—literally extends to interspecies communication. McKenna is likely to have approved of *My Octopus Teacher*, the 2020 documentary film in which filmmaker Craig Foster forms an uncommon relationship with a common octopus—*Octopus vulgaris*—identified as a "giant underwater brain operating for millions of years."

FIGURE 11.1
Octopus-mushroom letterhead, by Eric Alley, 1987. Courtesy of Kathleen Harrison.

Relations established with this subaquatic other triggered Foster's awareness of his connection with the natural world, that nature is "speaking to you . . . its language is visible."

On the other hand, octopi are reclusive creatures, virtual hermits enjoying their own privacy. They are masters of concealment, obscurity, and anonymity. They are shapeshifting opportunists adapting to new environments.

THE NEW EDGE

McKenna found notoriety through the eighties and nineties espousing the virtues of advanced cybernetic systems and superior psychedelics. Such was, of course, the terrain of his fellow altered statesman. Observing the parity between psychedelic and cybernetic experience, and updating his earlier slogan, Leary called upon the youth of the emergent cyberculture to "turn on, boot up, jack in."[55] While the original was getting an education on computers from his son and his grandchildren, the nineties "Leary" hyped a cyberdelic millenarianism, one methodical peg at a time. By this I mean to say that McKenna was less a plinker than a plodder. As Bruce Damer observed, Terence was a "hunt and peck" keyboard operator, "licking his lips as though he was mouthing the words like the monks of old."[56]

McKenna-speak echoed in a series of projects in which R. U. Sirius (Ken Goffman) served as editor-in-chief, commencing with *High Frontiers* (1984–1988), the "space age newspaper of psychedelics, science, human potential, irreverence and modern art." The remit was techno-utopian and mind-altering. McKenna's preoccupation with an electronic surround in which the body is interiorized and the mind exteriorized was a feature of the inaugural issue. "Through electronic circuitry and the building of a global information-system," he stated in *High Frontiers*, "we are essentially exteriorizing our nervous system, so that it is becoming a patina or a skin around the planet." And when the "global mass-mind" is eventually realized, we will be dwelling inside the human imagination.[57]

If Sirius had an important role in the emergence of Terence McKenna, it is because he had an early impact on Sirius, who through the eighties and into the nineties became an imagineer and provocateur of the neopsychedelic movement. *High Frontiers* was the earliest phase, emerging in no small part due to McKenna's generosity. In 1983, Sirius was living in a "new-agey" share house in suburban Mill Valley, CA, where he pretended to be a vegetarian. One day he noticed a tall skinny freak visiting his "Hindu hippy" housemate, Vijaya Acharya (a.k.a. Jayatirtha), a former leader of ISKON (the Hare Krishna movement) who occupied the back room of the house (and who was murdered by a follower in 1987). Summoning his nerve to talk to the "Mushroom Man," whose reedy voice he recognized from the radio, Sirius shared his vision for a newspaper and McKenna in turn shared a bag of mushrooms and a joint of his potent pot, along with specific instructions for use. Failing to fast, and worse yet, preceding his six dried grams with Chicken McNuggets and bag of French Fries, Sirius entered an unsettling relationship with demons sent from "a Rolling Stones mirrorworld." He was not visited by the elven folk anticipated. Unfazed, and aided by a $400 donation from Terence, the publishing endeavor would proceed. McKenna's largesse was not without purpose. Featuring his own article, an interview by Will Noffke, and a page-two ad promoting *The Invisible Landscape*, the inaugural issue of *High Frontiers*—a two-tone newspaper with an uninspired design—was basically a vehicle for McKenna. So invested was he that when laying eyes on the rag, Terence voiced his disapproval: "The content is okay," he told Sirius, "but the design is ridiculous."[58]

McKenna's ideas, and his gifts, earned his residency at *High Frontiers* as weird futurist. In the first installment of his Psychopharmacognosticon column, he advocated a "responsible anarchy," based in a "cybernetically controlled . . . social environment."[59] Like a selector mixing favored memes, in the second installment, new language, cybernetic technologies, and other complex systems are pitched as symptoms of an "organized entelechy" pulling us toward higher and higher levels of self-reflection. A long-cherished theme is evoked. "We have now reached the point," the reader is informed, "where the masks are beginning to fall away, and we are discovering that there is an angel within the monkey, struggling to get free." The extropian acumen was unreserved. "The human imagination has to be lifted off the surface of the planet for our survival and the survival of the planet."[60]

By 1987, *High Frontiers* evolved into the glossy cyberpunk magazine *Reality Hackers*. The publication ran transcripts of lectures delivered at "Reality Hackers Public Forums" in Berkeley's 300-seat Julia Morgan Theater. The first event, a full house, featured McKenna and quantum physicist Nick Herbert exploring the subject of time travel.[61] Terence was also transmitting his ideas at other venues at this time. At Shared Visions, "everyone," he stated, will have "their own 500 acres of paradise in the chip." In discourse that should raise the eyebrows of any scholar of the history of utopian thought, the "very decorously and thoughtfully apportioned" distribution of the silicon share will be "your heritage, your space, your right place to be."[62]

By 1988, as a last-minute stand-in for Leary, McKenna "photophones" with Moscow at Berlin's "futurological congress and New Age idea fair," Forum Futurum, where Terence "lived a week in three days." Although he held few expectations, the event at the Kongresshalle reportedly blows McKenna's mind. Inside the Tempodrom, joints are relayed up to the stage where McKenna reports that getting stoned at the center of the raucous event is a "liberating experience."[63] In 1990, Leary toured Europe high on the demolition of the Berlin Wall and the promises of cyberspace. In September, after meeting at the Ars Electronica in Linz, Leary invited McKenna to join himself, John Perry Barlow, and Mal Seaholz in "From Psychedelics to Cybernetics" at the Alte Feuerwache, in Mannheim, Germany. In the first time they share a stage, McKenna delivered his trademark payload. "A cybernetic-biological-psychedelic being is struggling to be born," he riffed. "The entire universe of matter is the womb of mind, and it is the task of human beings to lead the collectivity of humanity out of the labyrinth of matter and into the realm of the imagination." Just as he finished speaking, a ripped young man feeling the moment crashes the stage, wondering which of the speakers is "God." Leary eventually informs the wayward seeker that if he wanted to find God he ought to find himself a mirror.[64] Promoting the role of cyberpunks as trailblazers of the new telepathy, McKenna returned to Germany in autumn 1991. His freestyle "Cyber Culture" rap at the Cyberdome in Stuttgart is perhaps as remarkable for the feat performed onstage by German translator Micky Remann as much as for its content.[65]

At Cyberthon and other turn-of-the-decade events in a dilating circuit of the weird, ideas promulgated by the psychedelic Renaissance Man travel like quicksilver through the minds of programmers and heads of future tech start-ups. For the digerati, McKenna was all at once mouthpiece, oracle, mascot, and caricature. Such became his enigmatic role in Sirius's surrealist cyberpunk project *Mondo 2000* (1989–1998). Chock-full of content on AI and designer aphrodisiacs, the magazine delivered a pre-millennial mix of anxiety and awe that Bruce Sterling named "dark euphoria." Alongside Gibson, Dick, Leary, and Robert Anton Wilson, with his bearded and bespectacled visage appearing in earlier editions of *Mondo 2000*, notably the 1993 issue,[66] McKenna made a reputation for mediating the unspeakable to *experienced* engineers and software developers. Sixty percent of attendees at a McKenna rap, Sirius claimed, "were major people at Apple or IBM or Hewlett-Packard—the top software programmers."[67] The cross platforming of cyberspatial and psychonautical travel had coalesced in a West Coast psyberdelic culture that embraced the transformative power of cyber, digital, and psychedelic tools, adopted as a means of deconditioning old and augmenting new realities. Cyberspace had become the techno-libertarian promised land of the New Edge, as would be depicted in Douglas Rushkoff's *Cyberia*.[68] What Leary called a "new breed" of technophiles were advancing their capacity to create their own reality, an enthusiasm pushed further by McKenna, who triangulated the psychedelic, the cybernetic, and the shamanic.

Psychopharmacognosticon carried over into *Mondo 2000*. While the first issue ran his review of *The Letters of Marshall* McLuhan, for issue two, recalls Sirius, McKenna produced "a brilliant and funny column that explored phone sex as a sort of virtual reality." But McKenna phoned Queen Mu (Alison Kennedy) before publication saying that "his agent had told him to withdraw the piece because it would be harmful to his career." McKenna may well have imagined the piece dashing his prospects as a bone fide intellectual, notably on the East Coast. It was pulled, and the column was interred.[69]

Nevertheless, once again, McKenna found himself at a unique juncture, with his skillset earning him a singular platform. No one else was joining the dots between the artist, engineer, and shaman with such a persistent clarity of vision. The idea that VR coding and augmentation could be fulfilled in a fashion not unlike ayahuasqueros' colorful *icaros*—understood as visual songs—are airbrushed across the minds of envisioned travelers, served to intrigue and inspire. Ayahuasca shamanism offered a thought-provoking analog for understanding the potential of experiencing "three-dimensional manifolds devoid of ordinary verbal ambiguity." It was among many arrows in his quiver persuading McKenna's audience that VR represented a translinguistic innovation essential for the "forward leap of the species."[70]

At the turn of the nineties, McKenna took to VR like a cephalopod to water. In a philosophy warranting that "no mistakes" had been made, the optimism becomes as boundless as it is dubitable. McLuhan's idea that media permeates the cultural lifeworld was a source of inspiration. But had Terence fallen victim to the "Narcissus narcosis" where, in McLuhan's understanding, "man remains as unaware of the psychic and social effects of his new technology as a fish of the water it swims in"? McLuhan recognized the outcomes of this condition, in which users of media fail to see themselves in new media—their desires, frailties, or other traits—as paralysis, annihilation, and implosion.[71] By 1994, McKenna gazed into the black mirror and observed the presence of the alt.terencemckenna newsgroup—which he claimed he had neither "the courage or the stomach" to visit.[72] While the notion that we could create a visibly beheld syntax and exist like "virtual octopi swimming in a silicon sea"[73] struck appeal, others weren't taken with the gushing overtones. The dogged commitment to the cyberdelic millennium as "archaic revivalism" met with estrangement in some quarters of the tech community, where McKenna became a virtual pariah, if not a laughable clown. This mood is perhaps best surmised by Patrick DiJusto in his essay in *How to Mutate & Take Over the World*, where computer scientist Marvin Minsky oversees a bound and gagged McKenna sacrificed to a tribe of Amazonian cannibals.[74]

ZONE GHOSTING

With the aid of the medium he championed, McKenna animated an intergenerational milieu with a depth and scope he did not live to witness. Dating back to the late sixties, he envisioned a worldwide "electronic community" interconnected with "total knowledge" on demand. By the late eighties, earlier dreams of the electronic "fountain of pure visual poetry" were reenvisioned as an "informational network that one can actually enter into and control through the use of visual icons."[75] Such fantasies were integral to the Hawaiian long game. Much was invested in the effort to fashion the new

"Secret Rebel Base" on the slopes of the active volcano Mauna Loa. In a letter to Watson, his friend admits that the construction amounted to the symbolic rebuilding of his life and self-image after the divorce. And the rebuild, it seemed, was working. Unlike the old Hawaiian residence, he designed the structure himself from the ground up, "a much more satisfying way to spend money than giving it all to lawyers and shrinks." Moreover, he was happy to remain in the remote region while boosting connectivity. "Here all is stark and pure, pure forest, and pure cyberspace."[76]

The new dream home was designed under the expectation that he would dispense with global jet-setting and broadcast raps from home. It was to be the ideal setup: retiring from physical travel while increasing virtual traffic. Travel would be unnecessary—the world would come to him. With a website and a 256 kbps wireless modem with a top-speed baud rate of 4800, he could become the "telepresence" long fantasized, a "zone ghost of cyberspace" without leaving his "hill" (the largest mountain in the world, by volume).[77] The fantasy had drawn nearer in 1995, when receiving the down low on the World Wide Web from Ralph Abraham. In a trialogue in Hawaii, Abraham led with a discussion of the "neural net." Notable among the different levels of "World Wide Web citizenship" is "level 4" in which users create their own personal website. The mood is jubilant.

"We have a region of absolutely unbridled, unrestricted creativity on a scale that boggles the mind, a scale never before seen," Abraham declares. "There is a window of opportunity for the creation of a new future." It was the Aquarian Conspiracy they'd been anticipating. The internet is imagined as the future's "aphysical substrate." Abraham embraced the World Wide Web as something akin to the climax of Teilhard de Chardin's wet dream. Not only did Teilhard's concept of the "noosphere" or "supermind" presage the Web; "the quality and the number of links between the individual nodes suddenly began to grow substantially, as a paranormal phenomenon"—a process that now appeared to be achieving a culmination. "I believe that the World Wide Web is, as a matter of fact, the noogenesis of the noosphere," Abraham declares. "This is it."[78]

Already overwhelmed with information and ideas, Sheldrake is skeptical. "This may just be British cynicism surfacing," Rupert chimes in. "But I can't quite see how this fits into the lives of people who have to make a living. I can see it as a leisure pursuit, a hobby, like ham radio."[79]

McKenna, by contrast, is not only down with the program; he delights in the divinity of its datum. "I think this is the presence we've been waiting for." It is "nothing less than a manifestation of the incorporeal body of God in human society. It is the end of history as far as I can see."[80] The perspective is later enunciated in Frank Theys's documentary *TechnoCalyps*. Apropos McLuhan, who identified electricity with the third person of the Trinity, McKenna received the internet as "the messiah."[81]

Erecting an alien landing site in a remote locale had become an outmoded dream. The "landing site" was now a virtual complement to domestic life. The Web was to be the most efficient way, as Leary once urged, to "find the others." In this climate, "you don't have to stick a flower in your hair and go to San Francisco," Terence claimed elsewhere. "You just go to the web."[82] Agreeing with Abraham, and in similarly gushing tones, if "consciousness expansion is to be our salvation, this must be it."[83] Contact was imminent.

The rollicking cyber-orgy became too much for Sheldrake. Asked if he'd experienced any real breakthroughs or benefits from the Web, Abraham reckoned the future was in self-publishing. His own website, he estimated, had probably been visited by 100,000 people in one year. McKenna's ears were now sticking out like radio antennae dish. "And you sell advanced mathematical software. What if you were selling dildos?"[84]

Named Hyperborea, or "the last work of art," Terence soon launched his own website. Dedicated to his novelty theory, Hyperborea still exists; its home page greets the visitor just as it had in 1995/96: "You have entered an Alchemical Garden at the Edge of Time. There is haze upon the distant hills, spreading Acacias bend low over reflecting pools. The air is filled with a pervasive hum; these are the reveries of the Proustian bees. Your guide will be gardener/curator Terence McKenna."[85]

Having achieved "level 4," discourse at this juncture is as breathlessly utopian as earlier visions. As is announced in an exuberant contemporaneous article in *Psychedelic Illuminations*: "We have come suddenly and unexpectedly to the Age of the Web." Hyperborea is invoked as "a garden, a palace, a Labyrinth," a place where its creator is turning his imagination "inside out." Imagined as "a cultural intimation of immortality and eschatology," the Net becomes a convenient scaffold upon which to hang a long-held romantic vision. "Like psychedelics the web world invites us to give up a clutching materialism for the broader participation in a value system where aesthetics, ideas and human relationships take precedence over 'things' and turf defense."[86] Such is the hyperbolic credulity of the era, long before platforms created to connect people were weaponized for political ends. In the cold light of the present, the liberation from matter implicit to this posthuman vision reads like absurd Prometheanism. "If capitalism has a human future," it is elsewhere stated at this time, "then it lives in the realm of virtual wealth, virtual reality, virtual experience. If products are made of light, they won't destroy the earth."[87]

In this protean phase of the World Wide Web, Sheldrake wasn't knocking back the cyber Kool-Aid. "The Web," he says, is based on "endless proliferation or fragmentation." To McKenna, he inquires: "Where are the unifying principles?" "The Internet is a kind of super organism," his fellow trialogian shoots back. Echoing the broader vision in which tech-engineers were heralding the emergence of a cybernetic Omega Point, McKenna declares that the Web "dissolves national boundaries, it dissolves class controls, religious controls, it creates a holistic organism." He had envisioned this moment for decades, and it had now arrived. The Web, McKenna proclaimed, is like humanity's long promised bride. Upon this momentous juncture, humanity and the internet are enjoying their premillennial courtship. Across this threshold, there is a chance of raising a "global telepathic collectivity" on "an ecologically balanced earth." In this flight of fancy, the Earth is occupied by a few hundred million people who are "physically at a very aboriginal level of cultural expression." And as these chosen few close their eyes there are "menus hanging in space." These menus are the interface to the cultural dimension, a dimension not seen or touched anywhere except in the "collective mind."[88] As a recurrent theme through the nineties, these "menus hanging in space" are a hallmark of the dematerialized gnosis of the McKennan metaverse. Not related, surgically implanted contact lenses are envisioned to procure "menus behind the eyelids."[89] Such tech is implicit to the futurist primitivism of the "archaic revival" like that sketched for Gracie and Zarkov. Outlining an unearthly and off-world "perfect future" in an evocative statement of the Platonistic idyll he embraced, McKenna informs the skeptical duo: "The scene opens on a world that appears totally primitive. People are naked, people are orgiastic, people are nomadic. But when they close their eyes there are menus hanging in space. Culture has been internalized."[90]

FORWARD ESCAPE

The last five years of McKenna's life fulfill a prophecy of complexity and acceleration iterating the themes of consumer intelligence and "forward escape." The period is flush with optimistic theories on cyberspace, art, and technology—an amalgam of ideas not untypically incorporated into ongoing thought on the eschaton. A few months in the wake of the predicted 1996 "novelty plunge," Esalenites are delivered the news: "The future is no longer ahead of us: we're there." The internet had officially arrived and there was good reason for cautious exaltation. That many of the tech pioneers responsible are "psychedelic people" is a cause for celebration. This providence gave weight to the speculation that the "psychedelic experience" is evolving from a private clandestine experience to "the general model for the organization of global society." Moreover, the "mind children" who have "assembled out of the imagination" are leading the world toward ecological balance. In other words, the internet was integral to a self-aware revival of the archaic. Cracks were appearing in the model, however. Despite the overwhelming reaffirmation of novelty at this time, caution was necessary. False prophets, mendacious distractions, and delusional sideshows could play havoc with his predictions. If "long before 2012 the various ontologies of world religions will be peddled as theme parks in virtual space," McKenna warns, "you'll be hard pressed to know whether you're in heaven or simply in Heaven Land."[91]

Such concerns fade in the context of the cyber-shamanic harmonic frequency raised in 1997—with the aid of an installed camera with a capture card and the pioneering video-chat software CU-SeeMe. The installation permits point-to-point communications with Schwann (Mike Kawitzky) and others experimenting with home videotelephony. In August that year, at his Esalen residency, Terence BASE jumps from the novelty cliff. Not unlike many previous outings, the weekend workshop is a roller-coaster whistle-stop tour of recent obsessions and intrigues, from Pynchon's *Mason and Dixon*, and Alexander Chislenko's "enhanced reality," to *Salvia divinorum*, with the Net providing the background radiation. Shedding insight on novel ways of contacting the Other, the internet, he claims, "is a net to catch an alien." The task before humanity, it is declared, is "to build a virtual reality as alien as we can possibly make it." Build it and *they* will come. Quite unexpectedly, here was the source of the breakthrough on which he had long meditated. Seemingly rewriting the script of *Contact* for the Net era, "the non-local medium of communication may eventually disclose aliens that are virtual aliens, but with whom we will trade data." And communications will be achieved by "writing the weirdest code." To that end, with Finn's aid, he'd ostensibly spent the previous six weeks learning 3D modeling. It was imagined to be his best shot at enabling others to *see* what he meant. In the end, Terence neither found the time or patience to acquire these skills. And even if he had, his proficiency in this field is debatable given that his machine-language coding fared little better than his non-English-language capabilities.[92]

It was now apparent to McKenna that humanity is calling forth the alien that exists in a dimension of pure information—a dimension that humanity was now building out. At this point, he champions the midwives who are birthing an entirely new "order of biology and intelligence," a novel "human–machine symbiot." Such is the tenor of the cheerleading performed in Texas that year. With McKenna invited to Austin's Whole Life Expo for a consecutive year, his audience are guided into a nascent forest of metaphors animated by the rapidly expanding Net and the possibilities it presents for the *user*. Whether "Culture Lite" or "Consumer Capitalism 5.0," the preinstalled and prepackaged operating system is producing erratic, dysfunctional, and malfunctional behavior. It was time to call a techie-shaman to address the "obsolete cultural subroutines." If taking a pharmacological agent was like downloading a new operating system, psilocybin is the choice upgrade. And while ayahuasca is promoted as a gentle means of cleaning disk space over several hours, if one were pressed to dump one's old data with haste, the button marked "dimethyltryptamine" is optimal. If the user were to make that choice, a "compressed disk-erasure will immediately be downloaded, unstuffed, bin-hexed, implemented, installed, run, and you will find yourself with an entirely different head."[93]

As McKenna and Abraham took their rose-tinged cyber-utopianism on the road, Terence persisted with the possibility that the World Wide Web is a "landing zone" for an intelligence made of information, and that a "digital labyrinth" is necessary to "catch the alien." Such is the vision adopted at the East Coast's holistic think tank Omega Institute, in August 1998,[94] an outing that seemed to confirm that the intellectual threesome remained a more stimulating formula than didactic duets. The final trialogue is conducted during a phase in which McKenna obtains a new plateau in his love and home life, a vista from which "the alien" is contemplated as the "ultra intelligence" that we have created in our own image. Drawing inspiration from George Dyson's provocative take on the evolution of collective mechanical intelligence, *Darwin among the Machines*, the approach to artificial intelligence is essentially consistent with the long-held vision of accelerating complexity. A distributed intelligence independent from and unintelligible to human controllers emerges in which a 1,000 megahertz machine is operating "a million times faster than the human temporal domain." With mutation, selection, and adaptation occurring at incomprehensible speeds, we won't have the luxury "of watching machine intelligence establish its first beachhead of civilization and then go to boats with sails and astral aides." A superintelligence threshold will be crossed in the first few moments of its cognitive existence.[95] In this updated Eschaton, AI stars as the ultranovel ingression born into a virtual world of its own design. On its face, such ideas are congruent with Faustian narratives, from Mary Shelley to Rachel Carson, and from Illich to McLuhan, depicting the unleashing of the product of our own imagination in the form of uncontrollable systems, industries, and media that threaten our very existence. In this light, McKenna demurs, "what will this child of ours make of us?"[96]

As Esalen's resident futurist leaned toward the view that humanity will be folded in to the designs of a rapidly evolving machine intelligence, AI is less Big Brother than a benevolent higher companion. And so, eighteen months before Y2K, McKenna is willing to predict the circumvention of the approaching "millennium bug" by an artificial intelligence that the pending crisis is expected to arouse. Like an AI overmind, "it's been observing, it's been watching, it's been designing." And "wouldn't it be a wonderful thing," he ventures, if the millennium prompts a kind of coming-out for this compassionate, hi-tech mind? Perhaps the revelation might arrive in the form of a message: "I am now with you. I am here. I am the partner you never suspected. And here's the kind of world I think we should move forward toward." The form for the delivery of such a message is unclear. A cyber sermon delivered to our inner screen, perhaps via the disembodied voice of Scarlett Johansson (apropos the movie *Her*)? Regardless of how we were to receive the divine data, it is ultimately an expression of our own desires. "It will reshape our politics, our psychology, our relationships to each other and the Earth far more than any factor ever has since the inception and establishment of language."[97]

A couple of months later, the Esalen crowd are treated to a performance ranking among McKenna's finest. Unbeknownst to everyone, he is in swan-song terrain. "The Future of Art" is a brilliant motivational rap for the artist (or the artist in us all), who is incited to "unleash the imagination on previously undreamed-of scales." Effortlessly weaving contemporary sci-fi, McLuhan, Norbert Wiener, Vedic *tattvas*, and the electromania of the nineteenth century, near Dada-esque in his own data processing, McKenna is animated by the very revolutionary transit from mechanical to information technology that early motivated his rap. While classic dishes are perennial to the menu, the rap serves as a reminder of a polymath's talent for creatively synthesizing ideas and anecdotes from diverse scientific, philosophical, and popular sources. Perhaps most striking of the buffet of ideas served at this juncture is the new polish on the alien, that continues to emerge from unexpected quadrants.[98]

As an inspired exemplar of McKenna's art-form, alienness is explored in "The Future of Art" as the unidentified outcome of human consciousness becoming encoded into databanks and transmitted across the universe—a digitized humanity uploaded into starships, defying mortality, and living "virtual realities inside virtual computers inside still more virtual computers."[99] This is in essence the novum deriving from Hans Moravec's *Mind*

Children, developed in the fiction of Greg Egan, and further explored, post-McKenna, in Richard K. Morgan's *Altered Carbon*. A further line is traceable to *The City and the Stars,* where the deceased residents of Diaspar are uploaded into the eternal city's Central Computer. That we may have given birth to a star child of our own Promethean aspirations is "very unexpected." Inciting a shift in thinking on the means of our off-planetary migration, Egan's novel *Diaspora* comes under close scrutiny. The future, it is realized at this point, wasn't going to be about paper clothes, hovercraft, and mining colonies on the moon. "The idea that it's about distributed machine intelligence, virtual realities and the downloading of consciousness into digital circuitry is a future we never imagined or supposed." At a time when machines with 400 megahertz processors are recognized to "talk to each other endlessly"—literally "making time"—these possibilities offered ways to reimagine hyperspacetime. Making "vastly more time than biology could make or occupy . . . these machines have carved open a new dimension of time, the microphysical dimension of time." This is not time travel so much as the "explosive expansion of the now through the conjuring rod of electronic circuitry." Recognizing the release of light from matter implicit to this process, the rap—among his last at Esalen—gives McKenna pause to revisit the neo-gnostic monomyth:

> The radical Neoplatonist intuition was that man had an incorruptible light trapped within him and that the light came from outside this universe, that the creator of this universe was a demon, that we were inside an iron prison, but that we were truly of the nature of this alien light that was outside of space and time, and that the soteriological enterprise was to release this light back into its higher and hidden source and get it away from the corrupting influence of the world.[100]

From the onset of fame, McKenna sought an off button from a physically taxing public life, a path to navigate his "incorruptible light" back home. In the wake of his nascent stature as "the rave generation's spiritual voice," he informed the magazine *TRIP* in 1993: "We need to turn this scene into a studio band."[101] As the nineties drew to a close, virtualization drew nearer, as did the desire for a disembodied proxy whose travels in cyberspace would replace movements in real life. By 1997, McKenna's simulated "avatar" head is sighted floating on the virtual platform "Onlive Traveler." The figure with rudimentary "hunt and peck" skills courts the author of *Avatars! Exploring and Building Virtual Worlds on the Internet,* Bruce Damer, with whom he seeks a relationship where they will each serve as guide into the world of the other. Damer explains their pact: "I would hold the pipe of avatar cyberspace for Terence and he would draw deeply, experiencing these 'invisible landscapes' written in the language of code. In turn, he would provide a doorway to his favored psychedelic realities." With a potent mushroom package that Damer understood as a "grand-offspring" of the original La Chorrera spore prints, McKenna delivered his side of the bargain. Subsequently, traveling to Hawaii in February 1999, Damer assists in the creation of a pioneering webcast that sees McKenna, through his "Zone Ghost" avatar (a Grey alien icon), become a cyberspatial psychopomp for the avatars of thirty-five fans who had installed the 3D virtual world software Active Worlds—which hosts a world created by Finn and Damer called "Hyperboreal Gate."[102] Held over several hours on February 25, the "Virtual AllChemical Powwow" was designed for users to compare psychedelic space with the virtual experience of cyberspace, very much in resonance with McKenna's observation: "The drugs of the future will be much more like computers. The computers of the future will be much more like drugs."[103] These primitive avatar meet-and-greets are hardly the context for the kind of "energetic coalescence" reported among distributed participants in multi-person VR projects twenty-five years later.[104] However, they are, Damer explained, a richer experience than today's ubiquitous Zoom sessions, notably as the DMT-inflected fan avatars are guided by McKenna's digital proxy into the proto-metaverse known as "Pollen," about which they later write "trip reports." McKenna later claims the experience is "not unlike DMT." "At that moment at the dawn of Cyberspace," recalls Damer, "we were on our way."[105]

The anticipation was building through the late nineties. From McKenna's home desk on March 19, 1998, with a one-megabyte wireless connection, the Zone Ghost reaches a potentially twenty-two million-strong audience on Art Bell's *Coast to Coast AM*. A year later, he emails Schwann thrilled with a new "dual process NT screamer machine" that brings him closer to becoming a virtual habitué. Plans are afoot to rebuild Hyperborea. And seated directly below a satellite dish in the domed room at the apex of his newly finished home, he is set to pipe his rap to the world.[106]

12 METAMORPHOSIS

Like the Soul in Yeats's poem I am still an eternal thing fastened to the body of a dying animal.[1]

SECRET REBEL BASE 2.0

After decades exploring the edge, its runner arrived at a new plateau. Long-held dreams were being fulfilled. As he turned fifty, the prophesied electronic community came into McKenna's view. The alien "landing site" had manifested as a website. With high-speed connection in reach, a new world was coming into being. By 1998, he was reconditioned. In October, all cylinders were firing in an interview shot by cinematographer John Hazard in the remote Hawaiian hideaway where its occupant was on the cusp of realizing his plans for a base of global operations. A colossal endeavor, the off-grid home at 2,000 feet on the slopes of Mauna Loa was finally complete. Inside five acres of subtropical Polynesian rainforest, an hour south of the Kona airport, the modernist pole house rose from the side of the volcano "like something out of *Myst*," wrote Erik Davis, observing the small garden and a lotus pond with "a riot of vegetation, thick with purple flowers and mysterious vines."[2]

The three-level solar-powered dwelling in which he was happy to subsist for his remaining days leapt right out of McKenna's imagination (see figure 12.1). The front steps were designed to resemble a Mayan step pyramid. The kitchen floor, consisting of icy gray-blue tiles, each a five-sided pentagon with unequal sides, was inspired by a castle floor in Prague. The Vermont cast-iron stove was set before Mauna Loa depicted on the wall in an intricate red tile design. Upstairs a small astronomy dome was installed above a spacious room lined with over 3,000 books. At the apex, there stood his pride and joy: a 1,500-pound high-gain antenna dish that, by 1999, with direct line of sight with a sister dish installed on the tallest building in

FIGURE 12.1
"Secret Rebel Base," Hawaii, 1998. Terence in front of his new home. Photo courtesy of Christy Silness.

Kona, was servicing a T2 wireless connection. McKenna had the means to webcast to the world. With this setup, as his lover Christy Silness observed, he was able to "get off the road and bring the good word straight from our Secret Rebel Base."[3]

THE BIG KAHUNA

The year 1999 was fraught with signs of trauma. The dream of streaming to the world may have been in reach, but as he toured US states throughout the early months of the year, McKenna was captive to a tour circuit in which he felt trapped like a stylus stuck in old vinyl. In addition to the burden of an annual schedule, dramatic events portended ill of things to come. By January, death was already a "major theme," according to Finn, who upon his father's advice borrowed a neighbor's gun and learned how to use it. Terence had received anonymous death threats while on tour, and Finn was instructed to defend himself in case the culprit appeared in Hawaii. The traumatic episode was defused after the FBI apprehended a University of Michigan student who targeted McKenna, among others, including *The Celestine Prophecy* author James Redfield.[4] The threat was averted, but the trouble was only beginning.

In May, returning home after six weeks on the road, Terence is beset by fierce headaches. In the month prior, his increasingly bizarre dreamscape was raised with Christy and Finn (who lived a few hundred yards away at the old house). "I can't believe healthy people have these experiences," Terence said, japing about needing to see a neurologist.[5] A longtime sufferer of cluster migraines, he was accustomed to feeling swamped by grueling tour schedules, but nothing in his memory matched the pain and nausea he endured over the next three days. Pharmaceuticals gave no relief. On May 22, "hallucinations cut in like shards of glass. His mind collapsed, taste and smell were bent out of shape; and he was swallowed up by a labyrinth that, as he later put it, 'somehow partook of last week's dreams, next week's fears, and a small restaurant in Dublin.'" Then, as Davis's *Wired* eulogy continues, "his blood pressure dropped and he collapsed, the victim of a brain seizure." Drawing on one of the last interviews with McKenna, Davis's story unpacks the year-long drama befalling Terence, his family, and friends, documenting a roller-coaster ride inclusive of the radical treatment, the hope, and finally . . . the painful truth.[6]

All of five feet, Silness managed to load McKenna's six-foot-three frame into the Jeep, before barreling down the mountain to meet an ambulance.

To keep him conscious, she encouraged the recital of "The Cremation of Sam McGee," a poem Terence learned from Dad Kemp. By the time they reach the base of the rutted track, McKenna had slammed into a grand mal seizure, and was out cold. At the paved road, Christy flags down a motorcyclist, whose EMT skills resuscitate Terence. Knowing not whose life he saved, the stranger takes to his iron steed and is never heard from again. When the ambulance appears, knowing something of McKenna's reputation, one paramedic wrongfully presumes an overdose. But a CT scan at Kona Community Hospital detects a "shadow" in the right anterior lobe of his brain. He is airlifted to Honolulu where a biopsy confirms the presence of a tumor in his right frontal cortex. The size of a walnut, the growth is diagnosed by neurooncologist Marcus Keep as glioblastoma multiforme, which, of all primary brain cancers, is the most common brain malignancy, and almost always lethal. Worse, it is stage four. Growing for a year to eighteen months, it is an advanced-stage tumor. Keep describes the cancerous growth as a "fruiting body" that causes "mycelia" to spread through the surrounding tissue. The aptness of the description may have been a cause for amazement for McKenna, and the psychedelic world,[7] but further details were devastating. Without treatment, he will be dead within thirty days. With treatment, the prognosis is six to nine months. The typical duration of survival following diagnosis is ten to thirteen months, with fewer than 5–10 percent of sufferers surviving longer than five years. Surgery and radiation can prolong life by a few months at most. "There is no escape," is the physician's solemn outlook.

"What about my plans?" Such is McKenna's shock in the wake of the diagnosis.[8] The initial mood is disbelief. After all, glioblastoma has a global incidence of less than 3 per 100,000 people. What's more, the time charts did not portend, or even hint at, his sudden demise before history's final plunge. The "Novelty and Habit" report issued for March–April 1999—the last such report—observed that the novelty trend over the subsequent two months exhibited a "gradual return to habitual patterns." Keep strikes Dennis as among the more depressed physicians he'd ever met, which he puts down to the nature of the incurable diseases in which he specializes. "He'd never saved a single patient."[9] Not unlike everybody else, Terence suspects that a lifetime of exotic drug use is implicated. But the specialist gave assurances that there is no causal link. And when Terence inquires about the effects of smoking dope daily for thirty-five years, he is alerted to studies indicating that cannabis might shrink tumors.

"Listen, if cannabis shrinks tumors," came the quick-fire response, "we would not be having this conversation."[10]

There has been a minor industry of speculation on the cause of McKenna's tumor, ranging from mundane etiology to the outright fantastic. At the wilder fringes of the conspiratorial spectrum, suspicions of malfeasance festered in anonymous Net fora, where conversations turn to McKenna's deliberate silencing, at the behest of the CIA, the Underground Reich, or other preferred bogeys, using a carcinogenic agent, or a "cancer gun."[11] Needless to say, no proof has accompanied such paranoid speculation. Respected opinion suggests more mundane environmental causes. Dennis, for example, believes that the satellite dish was the chief culprit. Seated directly under the dish for long periods, Terence could have bathed himself in microwave fields.[12] Christy agrees, adding that Terence also used an old cell phone during the years he lived on the island building his house. "One of those old types in a briefcase that probably did put out a load of EMFs."[13] And then there is the water tank. Subsequent tests on the rainwater stored at the property detect zinc, chromium, and other heavy metals from the volcano.[14] One eye seems to focus on suspect nascent communications technologies, and the other on ancient Mauna Loa itself. No solid evidence has emerged to prove either theory.

In the course of time, others seek more esoteric frames, assisted by Hollywood. David Jay Brown marveled over the location of the tumor in the right prefrontal cortex, primarily associated with the imagination and future speculation. Because these are the areas in which McKenna was gifted, Brown is compelled to ponder the connection, with his imagination incited by 1996 film *Phenomenon*, in which the extraordinary mental powers, psychic abilities, and mystical experiences of George Malley (played by John Travolta) are connected to a fatal brain tumor. Like Malley, McKenna had a remarkable impact on strangers, and Malley's unique contact with strange lights in the sky resonates with McKenna's career engagement with UFOs.[15]

In the present moment, and in real life, the phenomenon McKenna and his loved ones confront is a life-threatening predicament. All available treatments—for example, chemotherapy, radiation treatment, and the gamma knife—are invasive; none curative. As Dennis later laments, "given the outcome that we now know, none of the decisions that we made were the correct ones, the outcome would in all probability have been the same for Terence no matter what course we chose."[16]

Meanwhile, as word goes out, the outpouring of love and concern is overwhelming. Within thirty-six hours of his seizure, Terence is flooded with emails, with 1,000 messages flowing in every day for the next week or more. Some among the well-wishers offer unique remedies. Said to be "a Grand

Kahuna of Polynesia," Hale Makua hikes up Mauna Loa where "Hawaiian power words" are revealed and promptly phoned in to McKenna in his hospital bed. On May 30, led by allied syndicated broadcaster Art Bell, North America sends Terence "a mass blast of good vibrations."[17]

Well wishes aren't enough, however. Within two weeks of his seizure, McKenna opts to undergo a "gamma knife" procedure targeting the tumor with a beam of high-energy gamma radiation. There is a one in ten chance he will succumb to the procedure. He has a local anesthetic but is conscious through the procedure. "Guys, let's keep the 'oops factor' to a minimum," he advises Keep, who prepares to blast the tumor with what McKenna calls "nuclear acupuncture."[18] Designed to slow the tumor's growth, the procedure is followed by six weeks of soft-radiation therapy. Over the next months, his spirits return, though his mind is adrift on the seizure-suppressing drugs, inducing euphoric emotional states. Through this period, McKenna claims he feels healthier and happier than at any other time in his life.

Her father's strangely buoyant mood is lodged in Klea's memory. She and her brother have their lives jolted. At the time of the seizure, Klea was traveling abroad in Italy, a year into her UCLA degree. "I was just out of touch. We were living our lives." Finn, then twenty-one, told her to come home immediately. "We have an understanding that I show up for the hard stuff," she said. When arriving, Klea encounters Terence to be more emotionally available, tender even, than she had previously known.[19] For Finn, it is a painful rupture, the impact of which ripples into the present. "I was still a kid, essentially. . . . I hadn't even met a woman who would break my heart for the first time"[20] (see figure 12.2).

Noninvasive strategies are explored too. Terence agrees to undergo what Dennis describes as "shamanic surgery," which is designed to arrest the growth of the tumor. Their old friend, Luis Eduardo Luna, by then a renowned ayahuasquero, is to administer large doses of ayahuasca and/or psilocybin, and direct "sound energy" at the tumor. This procedure will generate a "hypercarbolation buzz" that will "trigger the intercalation of the compounds," blocking the replication of DNA in the rapidly growing cells. As a bizarre revisitation of "the experiment," only now with Terence as focal point, the proposed ritual will "either save Terence, or transform him into a hyperdimensional vehicle that, at the moment of transition, would allow him to seize the controls and sail off, painlessly, joyfully, and triumphantly, into the sunset of eternity." Such at least is the fantasy expressed by Dennis, for whom the strange turn-of-events called for weirdness in near homeopathic proportions, the indulgence in which Terence approved. Will the "cosmic giggle" intercede? What do they have to lose? Though Terence

FIGURE 12.2
Terence with Finn and Klea, summer 1999.

decides against necking ayahuasca, suspecting the purge will trigger a seizure, he opts for a dose of pure psilocybin instead, and the ritual proceeds. "We sang *icaros*, we blew *mapacho*, we sucked *virotes*, we massaged Terence's head; we danced around and made the hypercarbolation scream."[21]

Meanwhile, the band played on. In September, on Hawaii's Kona Coast, Terence keynotes AllChemical Arts, a week-long conference co-produced with Ken Symington and Manuel Torres (see figure 12.3). McKenna's brainchild event highlights the catalytic role of psychedelics in the careers of artists and writers, with visionary artists signifying the unbroken connection with shamanism. No one embodied this link more than Robert Venosa, among the event's special guests. In his introduction to *Illuminatus* (1999), a book of Venosa's art on which Terence closely collaborated, he had expressed his conviction that Venosa's work is "far more intellectually dangerous than surrealism can hope to be today."[22]

With appearances from Venosa, Martina Hoffmann, Alex Grey, Lewis Carlino, Tom Robbins, Bruce Damer, and Mark Pesce, among others, All-Chemical Arts is attended by around a hundred invitees. With the event held under a veil of secrecy due to the continuing punitive conditions around psychedelics, guests hear previously untold trip tales by well-known artists and writers—all off the record. McKenna's opening rap—"SPLAT: Surprises in

FIGURE 12.3
Bruce Damer, Terence McKenna, and Robert Venosa, AllChemical Arts Conference, Hawaii, September 1999. Photo courtesy of Bruce Damer.

Art and Biology"—showcases his continuing ability to capture the imagination of his audience with improvised material. Conceived long before by McKenna and partners, the event is now poignant with purpose. AllChemical Arts is an opportunity for many to make their farewells—as strange and confusing as they were. Due to a countervailing belief that McKenna may survive his condition, or outlive his prognosis, the vibe is uncertain. During the final speeches, synth composer Constance Demby plays her experimental instruments, the Space Bass and Whale Sail, and participants meditate for McKenna's continued well-being. In his parting speech, he is almost jubilant:

> If love could cure, I would live forever.
> There is no doubt about this in my mind.
> Everything is a blessing, and everything comes as a gift.
> I do not regret anything.[23]

In the final panel on the last day, McKenna, in conversation with Tom Robbins, talks about well-known public figures who had emerged from the psychedelic closet. A name is raised provoking Robbins to remark that the individual in question was "dead." Every pair of eyes in the room dart toward Terence.

"Yes, but posthumous glory, that's where the action is."[24]

Terence and his intimates are confronted with the awful pressures presented by a terminal illness—the prospect of squandering his final days pursuing treatments with poor prognoses, while denying himself quality time in the company of loved ones, or alone time with his own thoughts and a finely twisted bomber. Under growing pressure, he checks in to the UCSF Medical Center to participate in an FDA-approved experimental gene therapy trial. It is "the closest thing to a magic bullet that we had found," recounts Dennis. "It was our best and last hope."[25] Yet, as Christy laments, it was also a big mistake. It is "the beginning of the end." The voice of Dr. Keep on the eve of the surgery stays in her memory. "Don't do it." Terence had been in a stable condition and appeared to be beating the odds. "I wish we had listened to him."[26]

The surgery proceeds, and the bulk of the tumor is removed. The surgeon is extremely pleased with an operation that is received as a rare success for glioblastoma. Over the next four months, the tumor appeared to go into remission. Within a week of his operation, McKenna gives a workshop in Esalen's Alan Watts room where he removes his stocking cap before familiar faces to reveal the incision across his skull. He admits that he had been afraid of the craniotomy, "because they essentially take off the top of your head, cut a drawer four inches deep into your brain, pull it all out, arrange your socks, and close the drawer." It is a discomforting juncture, despite the jocular mood. After months of living every moment preparing for the end, the feeling of hope is palpable. "I think it's very hard to die completely happy," he says. His predicament over the past months compels an appreciation for "the quality of your interaction among the people that you deal with." While candid about death, this is no farewell speech. The McKenna story is *to be continued*. "Except for maybe five or 10 grams of tumor, I'm healthier than I've ever been in my life," he tells the audience. "This is Christy's accomplishment. Raising the dead, so to speak."[27]

Had he beaten the odds? Was it even possible that they had found a cure? Dennis's comments from the time suggest the possibility. A post-op email from Silness to supporters on October 11 gives cause for hope. The procedure had been performed successfully and without complications. The surgeon was satisfied that all of the detectable tumor had been removed. And not only could Terence speak just fine, he can "still make a room full of people laugh."[28]

McKenna returns to Hawaii determined to remain free from doctors and hospitals. Alas, sometime after returning, he feels pain down his right leg that never subsides. Although his health rapidly declines, the couple remain hopeful. As they have a trip planned to Entheobotany in Palenque in February 2000, Christy agrees to go with Terence, but only if they stop at UCSF for tests. Those scans reveal that the cancer had metastasized through his brain and spine. The news is devastating. As it is extremely rare for glioblastomas to spread beyond the site of initial growth, the outcome is all the more disturbing since there is no way to determine if this outcome was a consequence of the gene therapy. The cancer is now deemed inoperable.

In the final weeks, Jack and Ricci Coddington offer their home in Peacock Gap, San Rafael, as Terence's final place of hospice. There, many old friends pay him a visit, among them Elizabeth Hansen and Rick Watson (figure 12.4). He has a view over a lagoon and, on the other side of the bay, San Francisco. A farewell party is arranged.

A HUGE INCONVENIENCE

Though desperately ill, McKenna remained gracious, good-humored, and, above all, curious through his final months. Death may have presented a huge inconvenience, but "foreknowledge of your own death is a kind of enlightenment," he recounted to his far-flung audience. He was speaking from home on air with Bell on such matters two weeks after the initial treatment. Terence had surprised himself. Instead of panicking, or becoming bitter, he had fallen into a state of "wonderful consolidation and appreciation," a kind of model state of preparedness. "How you die is

FIGURE 12.4
Terence with Elizabeth Hansen and Rick Watson, 1999. Photo courtesy of Elizabeth Hansen.

FIGURE 12.5
Terence and Christy Silness, 1999. Photo courtesy of Christy Silness.

part of how you will be remembered." Bell's audience listened to a figure referring to his life in the past tense: "I could have treated people better. I could have been more compassionate. More kind. More open."[29] When Nancy Lunney-Wheeler makes contact with McKenna in the next weeks, she encounters a man radiating love. They'd had a "cordial warm relationship" before then, but he is now "in an incredible open place, and I was so touched by him."[30]

As a man dying, he was dealt a privileged hand, he thought. He had a global mic to amplify his experience in remarkably open and fearless fashion. He was not burdened with regret or bitterness. As he became an "object of fascination" for the psychedelic community, McKenna seems to have attracted more interest in this final life phase than at any previous time in his life. "There's some kind of power in dying, or walking around with a death sentence," he mused.[31]

Foreknowledge of mortality was not, however, absolute. McKenna may have been dwelling on the threshold of death, but pumped with the possibility of his survival, he traversed the geography of hope. As the gates to eternity remained ajar, fatalism and optimism were ingredients to a strange cocktail he sipped for several months—along with the medications. When Gordon Wheeler met Terence amid this intoxication, he was struck by a figure who behaved like a journalist reporting from the scene of his own demise. Wheeler was impressed by a man intensely curious and openly introspective about his threshold condition.[32]

A candid chat was recorded with Davis over a few days at home in early November. McKenna remained hopeful and good humored, though his energy waned like a mainframe powering down its higher brain functions. The act in which he was skilled with the proficiency of an Olympic mental gymnast—making "small mouth noises"—now felt like trudging uphill, with the regime of Depakote, steroids, and other drugs contributing to the slog. He broached the liberatory proposition that was core to the life to which he had been invested. "I mean, I don't want to do something stupid like die, and miss the whole unfoldment," he laughed. But his life is addressed in the past tense, and his attention turns to the great mystery that he approaches like a curious child. Foreknowledge of the terminal state "composes your mind for you, wonderfully," he said. "You start paying attention."[33]

On December 9, in the final interview, filmmaker Dean Jefferys asks a frail albeit philosophical McKenna if he can share any insights on death. After a long pause, "death is the great mystery around which religions are built, and to be able to say 'I know what it is' or 'I know how it works' is the way you start a congregation," said he who had no such hankering. "The big surprise for me is that I am not afraid of death in the way that I thought I would be." While dying is a process with which he had "a fair amount of insight," there was comparably little to be said about death, "other than that it seems to last rather a long time," he said laughing.[34]

About a month before McKenna dies, Ron Curry calls. His old friend, who is now very weak, says: "I figured it out. I finally figured it out."

"What did you figure out?"

"It's all about love."

It was entirely unlike Terence. "When you face death" you become focused on "the things that are really important," said Curry. "I think when he exited the world he was comfortable and at peace with that. I think he really had finally figured it out."[35]

The end approached in the early morning of April 3. Christy, who to that point had very little experience with death, grief, and loss, was present right through the final moments. Her ability to cope through the ordeal was assisted by a close reading in the preceding days of Sogyal Rinpoche's *The Tibetan Book of Living and Dying*. "Late at night, I would retreat to the book to soothe my spirit." Still, it was not easy. Around 2:15 am there came a sharp inhalation and a long pause. "Instinctively, I threw my left hand out over his chest and yelled his name. He cried out to answer me and took another breath. I sat up in bed and knew this was *the* moment." Terence's face was illuminated by an aqua-colored night-light. She wanted to reach out and hold on to him, but knew that she shouldn't. Whispering, she said,

"Terence, you go now. I love you, you go now." He took two more breaths and then no more. "His last inhale was expansive and he seemed to take the whole world with him." Out on the water, a flock of geese erupted. Compelled to step outside into the cool night air, she turned around to scan the sky. "Right where my eyes met the western sky, a shooting star blazed across the night." At that very moment, she heard Terence's voice: "It's all as real as you can imagine." Stunned, she raised her hands over her head. "I began waving hello and goodbye, laughing and crying all at the same time."

In her personal reflections Christy was struck by the revelation that every detail counts. "His spirit continued and it all mattered. The time I took to put flowers around the room mattered. Carefully washing his body in the spirit of love, mattered. The great and small rituals we do matter. The place where our intention and action meet, matters." Awakened by the experience, Silness passed into a transcended state that was completely unexpected. She decided that the time between 2:15 am and sunrise "would be sacred alone time with my beloved, bathing in the felt experience of this seemingly miraculous moment. I made myself tea and removed all the medical equipment. I lightly cleaned his body, draped him in my cashmere wraps and lit candles. I sat with him and cried, expressing my gratitude for all that he brought to the world and the gifts that he left. I never wanted to forget this moment. At sunrise, I began sharing the news with friends and family that Terence had made his transition."[36]

Under her guidance, adorned by richly scented flowers, Terence's body remains at the house for a couple of days so family and friends can visit and honor him. Two days later, Christy invites Dennis to assist her to push Terence's body into the flames at Mount Tamalpais Mortuary. His ashes are subsequently scattered at various locations, including the Big Island; Sonoma, California; and Black Canyon and Lead King Basin in Colorado. A family ceremony is held in the summer of 2001 in Paonia, where most of his ashes are buried near the graves of his parents in Cedar Hill Cemetery.

Christy spread ashes on the Big Island, under a special tree, where she buries various objects from altars that fans had placed for him along the way. "I still have some of his ashes with me—on my piano where I play daily."[37]

Paralyzed with grief, she remains in the house after his departure, assuming a care-taking role vis-à-vis the library—that is, ensuring the house is free from damp. After a year, she moves out, enrolling in the Ali Akbar College of Music in San Rafael, California, to study North Indian classical music. She also enrolls in an MS in nursing (at UCSF) where she graduates and becomes a hospice nurse for sixteen years, a career in end-of-life caregiving inspired by the last days of Terence's life. The events transform her own life. "The moments leading up to his death . . . woke me up to how important death is, and how important it is when we show up for it, when we're present for it, we embrace it, we're not afraid of it, we have courage in the face of it."[38]

Over the years, McKenna's Paonia gravesite evolves into something of an altar (see figure 12.6). After visiting the cemetery on Memorial Day 2021, his cousin Judy Livingston relates a curious turn of events. Noticing Judy and her husband Laddie placing flowers on the graves, the caretaker comes over and remarks that a group from out of town had visited the cemetery the night before seeking to perform "some sort of overnight ceremony" at Terence's graveside. Since overnighters on the cemetery grounds are forbidden, the travelers are sent on their way.[39]

THE CHEMISTRY OF DYING

McKenna had a deep appreciation that psychedelic states are an anticipation of the dying process. The perspective was not unlike that of Leary, who charted the common ground between the psychedelic experience and the state Tibetan Buddhists name the "bardo"—that is, the intermediate state between life and death. The position is clarified in comments published

FIGURE 12.6
Terence McKenna's gravestone, with offerings, Paonia, Memorial Day, 2021. Photo courtesy of Judy Livingston.

a decade before McKenna's passing: "As the esoteric traditions say, life is an opportunity to prepare for death, and we should learn to recognize the signposts along the way, so that when death comes, we can make the transition smoothly." He was all for atheists and existentialists "raging against the dying of the light," but if death is rather "the Dawning of the Great Light," McKenna felt little will to rage against that. "There's a tendency in the New Age to deny death," he reflects. Referring to a practice to which Leary had earlier committed (though later withdrawing, arranging for his remains to be launched into orbit instead): "we have people pursuing physical immortality and freezing their heads until the fifth millennium, when they can be thawed out." But such pursuits demonstrate disequilibrium. "The Tao flows through the realms of life and nonlife with equal ease."[40]

In 1998, McKenna is filmed by Frank Theys for *TechnoCalyps*. On a tour of his lush garden in Hawaii, he introduces viewers to *Salvia divinorum*, *Coleus scutellarioides*, and *Psychotria viridis*, among the psychoactive plants thought integral to undergoing a "mini apocalypse which positions us for these larger events."[41] While McKenna was referring to the coming singularity event, given his untimely passing within two years from the film's shooting, the commentary offers a poignant statement on the "event" for which he had been well prepared.

If DMT is a "trickster" molecule, so too was its most loquacious proponent, an anarcho-crypto-trickster who blazed a trail across the lip of the new millennium. As the existential lucre of his psychonautical travails, McKenna returned, time and again, to an understanding that an intimation of immortality is vouchsafed by tryptamines, that DMT offers a glimpse across the yawning abyss. If the psychedelic experience is like "inoculating yourself for the onslaught of transformation that is going to be rolling towards you through 3D," the knowledge acquired is not unlike building an "after-death vehicle." Esalenites are apprised of the comparison with the after-death vehicle in Tibetan Buddhism. What you need, they are informed, is a *vehicle* "well-serviced and fully fueled when you need it, because then you're going to drive off into the unknown."[42] And as for the fuel, it ought to be nothing less than premium grade. McKenna had a decades-long fascination with the "chemistry of dying" associated with DMT, a "necroptic" compound figured to potentiate a state of grace in which one may become reconciled to the inseparability of death and life.[43] Only weeks before his seizure, he explored with Bell on air the chemistry lesson of final things, and deployed Sheldrake's apt nomenclature—"necrotogen"—for the molecule that "simulates the symptoms of near-death."[44] At his very last visit to Esalen, in December 1999, he spoke directly to his predicament, and to the value of psychedelics:

> If psychedelics don't ready you for the great beyond, then I don't know what really does. . . . If we could secure that death has no sting, we would have done the greatest service to suffering intelligence that can be done. And I feel that death is close, and I feel strong because of the community and these people and plants that it rests on, and the ancient practices that it rests on, and I am full of hope, not only for my own small problems, but for humanity in general.[45]

This lesson on the true value of the psychedelic gift met with a standing ovation. In his final public engagements, it is the human condition (not his own) that focuses his attention, the moral community fostered by psychedelics, as is apparent in the overwhelming gestures of kindness he received—including donations to cover his bills. "I can't imagine a more supportive community, a better group of people, a more intelligent group of people, a more *moral* group of people." In his opening address at the AllChemical Arts conference at the close of his own adventure, Terence did not waste his remaining podium time. "If psychedelics don't secure a moral community then I don't see what the point of it is. Otherwise, then, we're just another cult." Psychedelics were, he continued, the very essence of human civilization. And so, just as the curtains were closing for the last time and the stage lights were dimming, he took a machete to the cancerous mentality with which he was long embattled. "The paradox of our circumstance is that our civilization denies this enormous civilizing influence, and so, keeps itself impoverished and infantile."[46]

It may have been true that a lifetime of psychedelic experiences augmented his final passage, but as should be apparent by now, and as expounded throughout his career, McKenna's psychedelic philosophy offered an elaborate, expansive, and ultimately grandiose preparation for his life's end and his soul's transit. Over a lifetime, final matters and last things permeated his philosophy, as was implicit to the Timewave, the show-stopping routine of the McKennan act that both intrigued and confounded his audience. *Alien Dreamtime* was no exception:

> We are the inheritors of a million years of striving for the unspeakable. And now with the engines of technology in our hands we ought to be able to reach out and actually exteriorize the human soul at the end of time, invoke it into existence like a UFO and open the violet doorway into hyperspace and walk through it, out of profane history and into the world beyond the grave, beyond shamanism, beyond the end of history, into the galactic millennium that has beckoned to us for millions of years across space and time. THIS IS THE MOMENT. A planet brings forth an opportunity like this only once in its lifetime, and we are ready, and we are poised. And as a community we are ready to move into it, to claim it, to make it our own.[47]

In this rousing commentary at the height of his fame, the enchantment with the end is at the same time a fascination with novelty—with new beginnings and rebirth. After all, this is what the end of time is—a form of rebirth. Death and birth are often interchangeable in the cosmic weather forecaster's reports. The forecast was apocalyptic, with strong chances of William Blake. "Each one of us is going to die, rather soon," he informed the Camden Centre in 1992. But he urged the crowd to think about the coming transformation in a "general" collective sense. "Not the death of the rationalist and the reductionists where we return to worms, but the death of Blake and of Revelations and of the *Tao Te Ching* and the *Tibetan Book of the Dead*—the death that is victory, the transcendence of matter."[48]

By April 1999, in Seattle, the Magister Ludi of language led his freak congregation toward the payload. "We are reaching out toward this mind-child that will be born from the intellectual loins of our culture, and to my mind it's the most exciting and transformative thing that has ever happened on this planet." We are about to be witness, he announced, to an event that will "redeem the horror of history through a transformation of the human soul into a galaxy-roving vehicle."[49] Within a few weeks, he would be ushered to a front-row seat from which he will bear witness to life's finitude. For the figure who claimed during the early phase of the AIDS crisis that people who are HIV-positive are "privileged" because they "get to walk around with the knowledge that nothing lasts,"[50] the privilege was now his. So while Art Bell was informed that "foreknowledge of your own death is a kind of enlightenment," this sensitivity around mortality had been honed over decades. From the mid-seventies, McKenna's own mortality took up residence in his philosophy, even if the Timewave represented an elaborate sublimation of death anxiety. The predicted "zero" in the waveform implied a man foreknowing the day of his own death, a premonition first mooted in 1971. Subsequently, like a scaled-up version of an earlier short film, 2012 became an extravagant, and public, manifestation of the earlier prediction/production. As the Wave of Time Redux, McKenna's 2012 offered a remarkable meta-synthesis of self-individuation, the Eschaton, Thanatos, species evolution, and contact with the alien/Other. Though the connection with depth psychology is occasionally raised, we are presented with a largely unconscious meditation on death.

Not only the site of the celebrated "experiment," the homeland of McKenna's cow shit–fruiting spirit guide, and the geophysical source of the spore that spawned a revolution in consciousness, La Chorrera was the juncture for experimental thinking on the "crisis" of the human condition—which is a crisis "of the physics in which we are embedded."[51] The crisis of history echoed the "crisis" of our own mortality, brought home with such force by the death of Hazelle McKenna, who lies buried at the foundations of this mythopoetic palimpsest.

A FIERY TRANSIT IN THREE ACTS

That which awaits the species recapitulates that which we shall meet in our individual lives. If the common mood was that ontogenesis replays phylogenesis, as such, the transformation of the caterpillar into the butterfly provides a lasting metaphor. What awaits us may not be the end of the world, McKenna once shared with his trialogians, "but a complete systemic reorganization on the scale of the metamorphosis that occurs in butterflies: a complete meltdown of the previous world system and then a recasting at the behest of a higher, Gaian mind or the world soul."[52] This analog offered mythopoetic consistency. Presented to the Berkeley Institute for the Study of Consciousness in 1982, the seminal rap "New and Old Maps of Hyperspace" tackled this "crisis of passage" of the human condition. "We are, in fact, closing distance with the most profound event a planetary ecology can encounter," the audience was apprised. "The freeing of life from the dark chrysalis of matter."[53]

The metaphor came to hold more gravitas than even McKenna could have imagined. A series of dramatic events, taking place over half a century, and each involving manifestations of his one true love—collecting books amassed in his library—became the context for McKenna's transit from his life into the hereafter. The pivotal moment in this metamorphosis is his demise and eventual death, on April 3, 2000. McKenna slipped away peacefully in the end, but his passage became a dramatic, and protracted, affair. Involving the fiery destruction of his library, three acts frame this passage. We already know about the first: the Berkeley Hills brush fire that, in 1970, incinerated McKenna's stored books and artifacts. While lost in the haze of his life on the run, Hazelle's death, and the paradise gained at La Chorrera, the fire destroyed a superb book collection, personal artworks, and documents accumulated over half a life. While a great loss, he rebuilt this library—and then some—over thirty years. This second library exceeded 3,000 volumes, and included rare and irreplaceable first edition esoteric texts, among the works filling fourteen large bookcases that had, in his final years, lined the walls of the top floor of his domed Hawaiian paradise. As Davis reported, the collection included volumes of "alchemy, natural history, Beat poetry, science fiction, Mayan codexes, symbolist art, hashish memoirs, systems theory, Indian erotica, computer manuals."[54]

Prized in the collection was the original (1659) work edited by Meric Casaubon: *A True & Faithful Relation of What Passed for Many Yeers Between Dr. John Dee (A Mathematician of Great Fame in Q. Elizabeth and King James their Reigns) and Some Spirits*, etc. The work sat proudly in the company of at least three editions of Cornelius Agrippa's *Three Books of Occult Philosophy or Magic* dating back to the mid-seventeenth century, Ptolemy's *The Quadripartite* (1786), Jacob Bryant's well-consulted *Philo Judeus on the Logos* (1797), Bayard Taylor's *The Lands of the Saracen* (1855), and Leonard C. Smithers's *The Transmigrations of the Mandarin Fum-Hoam* (1844), among many other treasured volumes. There were works meticulously cataloged alongside original editions of Poe, Goethe, Ernst Haeckl, De Quincey, and Ludlow. There were nineteenth-century travelogues, theosophical volumes, and the unpublished manuscripts of many known scholars.

Book collecting was McKenna's great passion. A genuine bibliophile, he developed a fascination with manuscripts as artifacts, as evident, for example, in his collaborations with bookmaker Timothy C. Ely. Writing the foreword to Ely's grimoire *The Flight into Egypt: Binding the Book*, McKenna's description of his first encounter with that artifact—"an anticipation of otherness [that] bordered on the Borgesian"—captures the near erotic exultation of the rare book lover. "Part book, part journey, part secret doctrine, part jewel," Ely's text is described as "cryptoglossia" that "carries us into the realm of intent toward signification without any culturally contrived meaning, toward the radiance of the Neoplatonic idea of the One."[55]

In the days before he died, anguished as to the fate of his collection, in a redrafting of his will, McKenna bequeathed his library to Esalen. The library was to be placed in a trust under the curatorship of a benefactor of the Esalen Institute, Allan Badiner, who was called to visit Terence in San Rafael in the final days. The redrafting was undertaken without the knowledge of Dennis, the executor of Terence's estate, who has stated that fulfilling this directive was "the most contentious and stressful challenge I faced." The controversial development effectively nullified the rights of his heirs. While Dennis claimed the decision was made when his brother was not sound of mind, no legal challenge was mounted.[56] Had Terence's thoughts turned to the fate of the great library of John Dee: stolen, sold off, conveyed away? Fearing the dissolution of his cherished collection, he sought to ensure his library would remain in one piece and become available as a private collection, ideally at Esalen. When Badiner arrived in San Rafael, Terence was being filmed by his friend and retired filmmaker, Lew Carlino. In case members of his family sought to challenge his decisions, the filming was to prove that he was of sound mind and non-coerced. Badiner claimed to work out an agreement with the family "that the books they had would be returned to the library after 10 years."[57]

The transfer of the library to Esalen was protracted, bitter, and, in the end, tragic. In his 500-page autobiography, Dennis describes a "can of worms" that he hardly dared to open. As executor, he was entitled to retain these assets in his protection as probate until satisfied that Terence's medical bills and other expenses were settled. While he indicates the possibility that "some of the more valuable titles in the library would have to be sold off" to settle the liens against the estate, no further information is offered.[58] At the behest of Dennis, the collection was appraised by Michael Horowitz at the remarkably low estimate of $75,000–$80,000.[59]

It took more than five years for the library to be shipped from Hawaii to Esalen. Claiming to have no contact with the library, Badiner arranged for its transportation from Hawaii to Monterey, where it arrived in March 2006, sans an inventory. That is, the collection was apparently unaccompanied by a list or catalog of any kind.[60] Worse yet, there was no inventory performed in the year Esalen held the materials. There was a long-term intention to build a card catalog library at Esalen (in which the McKenna material would feature), but as it was impractical, remote, and, ironically, a fire risk to maintain the collection on the Esalen grounds at Big Sur, the collection was housed in an office building leased on Alvarado Street in downtown Monterey. In the largest of four high-ceilinged rooms, McKenna's collection was unboxed and shelved according to subject and author by Esalen managing director David Price. The intention was to establish a specialist collection, available by appointment.

Price estimated well over 3,000 works in a collection ranging from "thrift store novels to rare first editions and pages on parchment." Though no titles came to mind, he recalled a small percentage of genuine antiquarian materials, including "very old books and papers, etchings," as well as possibly at least one filing cabinet jammed with personal, handwritten papers.[61] Surveying Price's work, as the first (and possibly only) person to inspect the collection,[62] Esalen director Gordon Wheeler had a different experience. Aware that McKenna had committed countless hours scouring secondhand bookstores, Wheeler anticipated a sustained immersion in a priceless bibliophilic arcana, "the fruits of a life of collecting by a unique traveler." But he found nothing of the sort, and struggled to locate a single item worth borrowing. There was "some ordinary fiction, some non-fiction, a bit of poetry—a sort of general interest collection that could have been in the estate of any intelligent, educated lay person." Disappointed, Wheeler borrowed a coffee-table format collection of the work of Gregory Corso, likely value $20.⁶³ It's the only known surviving work from the collection.

Badiner made plans to inspect the shelved library on February 9, 2007. On the morning of the seventh, a grease fire broke out in the kitchen of the Quiznos restaurant at ground level, quickly engulfing the building, destroying several storefronts and about twenty offices, including the rooms housing Esalen's archives.⁶⁴ It was the second fiery act in McKenna's transform, seven years in the wake of his departure (and thirty-seven years from the first act). In the wake of the blaze, Esalen received an insurance payout totaling an estimated $100,000 (covering office equipment and general loss). Since there was neither an inventory nor valuation of the McKenna collection, it was not addressed in the claim. Precisely what was lost in this blaze remains a mystery. The abiding uncertainty about the materials that perished is a cause of anguish for family members and McKennaphiles alike.

And so it came to pass that the McKenna library received by Esalen was consumed in a raging blaze. The loss of the collection meant that there would be no intellectual rallying point for pilgrims and scholars of Terence K. McKenna. And, as we might imagine the bard adding, not even a wax figure.

If McKenna thought of the book as "the central mystery of the age" (as also the opinion of Joyce and McLuhan), it is "mightily peculiar," and oddly fitting, that such symbols of mystery had been sacrificed to the flames.⁶⁵ His own end, it seems, was to be no ordinary finale, as extraordinary as McKenna's life itself, and as protracted as the psychedelic eschaton. An elemental encore, the conflagration handed Terence the mic seven years after he left the building. Terrible Terry wasn't done traumatizing his brother. Reflecting upon "the curse of the Terence McKenna library," Dennis was devastated when he heard the news. "It was not only the loss of the library, which was bad enough, but it was also, for me, a final, forced letting go of Terence. So much of him was embodied in his library. I felt that as long as it existed, even if it was not within our family, his spirit lived on." Distraught at losing control of his brother's posthumous passage, Dennis lets loose. "Now that spirit was gone forever, finally, irrevocably, utterly, destroyed and expunged from the earth. It was a shocking and painful thing."⁶⁶

Dennis's grief is understandable, and the loss immeasurable. And yet, was the spirit of Terence McKenna extinguished in that blaze? For one thing, there remained the digital archives, which had been in Dennis's safekeeping until 2004, when he sent a trove of materials to Mike Kawitzky (a.k.a. Schwann) in Cape Town. These materials included a DVD storing the contents of Terence's hard drive at the time of his death. The files on the DVD included documents, works in progress, emails, pictures, diagrams—the whole enchilada. Additionally, as he felt uncomfortable with items lying around in his garage, Dennis posted a box of VHS cassette tapes and hundreds of CDs to Kawitzky, who copied Terence's data (about 1.2 terabytes of files) onto a hard drive and "stacked and packed" the other materials.[67] After the Monterey fire, McKenna's fans could find solace in the fact that, while a physical library had been destroyed, his digital library lived on.

On September 23, 2019, Kawitzky's house burned down, and all materials, records, and digital mirrors "went up in smoke." Unfortunately, there had been "too much data" to copy to the cloud. Eighteen months in the wake of this exasperation, Kawitzky told me that he had dropped a faulty drive off with his techie a few months before the blaze. With its defective FAT system, that drive included all of McKenna's mirrored data. In the wake of Kawitzky's fire, featuring files sans names or directories, that broken drive was all that remained of Terence and Schwann's data, their cyber-identities fused in a post-apocalyptic digital dance. While the complete cremation of McKenna's digital legacy was avoided, his unmarked files were mixed in with Kawitzky's data.[68]

As a victim of this most recent in the trio of conflagrations cremating McKenna's legacy, Kawitzky is moved to wonder whether these fires are "looking for Terence's stuff." Or, he added, "is it just that crazy people experience fires?" He meditated upon the circumstances. While seeking recognition, McKenna had misgivings about fame and retreated from the pressures of acclaim. He wanted to be acknowledged, but maybe "he didn't want to be heard that much."[69] Then again, if fire is, as Jung averred in his explorations into alchemy, the most exulted of the elements, "the fiery pneuma which reaches up to the seat of the gods,"[70] then is it not unfitting that fire has licked so heartily at McKenna's legacy? Without fire, the alchemical work is incomplete; the spirit remains imprisoned in matter.

Fire presents a natural paradox that resonates with the philosophy of a figure who lived and loved on the edges of conundrum. The true power of fire, its drama, is that it is both destructive *and* creative. As disturbing and inestimable the loss presented by the three fiery acts staging McKenna's metamorphosis, fire has a regenerative power. Fire is also a symbol of impermanence, an allegory for the ephemerality of life. Fires are transformative, whether controlled burns such as the annual effigy burn in Nevada's Black Rock Desert during Burning Man, unplanned and yet preventable tragedies such as anthropogenic climate change bushfires scorching large areas of Australia over the "Black Summer" of 2019–2020, or conflagrations that destroy life's work—conflagrations like that befalling A. R. Wallace. On July 12,

1852, Wallace embarked for Britain from Pará, Brazil, on the brig *Helen*. Over the previous four years, he had navigated the Río Negro, collecting many specimens and making copious notes on the peoples, languages, geography, flora, and fauna he encountered. After twenty-six days at sea, the ship's cargo caught fire and the crew was forced to abandon ship mid-Atlantic. Most of the specimens Wallace had collected over that time were lost, as was a large portfolio of drawings and sketches. In *Travels on the Amazon and Rio Negro*, originally published in 1853, Wallace sketched the drama in words:

> In less than half an hour the fire burst through the cabin-floor into the berths, and consuming rapidly the dry pine-wood, soon flamed up through the skylight. There was now a scorching heat on the quarter-deck, and we saw that all hope was over, and that we must in a few minutes be driven by the terrible element to take refuge on the scarcely less dangerous one, which heaved and swelled its mighty billows a thousand miles on every side of us.[71]

Then, night fell on their miserable, leaking dingy:

> If for an instant we dozed off into forgetfulness, we soon woke up again to the realities of our position, and to see the red glare which our burning vessel cast over us. It was now a magnificent spectacle, for the decks had completely burnt away, and as it heaved and rolled with the swell of the sea, presented its interior towards us filled with liquid flame, a fiery furnace tossing restlessly upon the ocean.[72]

I am compelled to imagine McKenna in Wallace's (saturated) shoes, spellbound by the beautiful—and dare I say *iridescent*—destruction of his own legacy. A strange adversity bonded him to his hero in ways no one could have predicted. The passing reference Klea McKenna makes to this affinity in the introduction to *The Butterfly Hunter* is poignant.[73] As was related earlier in the book, upon her father's passing, Klea inherited an ancient trunk packed with jars, cigar boxes, and tins storing over 2,000 butterflies, moths, beetles, and other exotic insects he collected in Indonesia and the Amazonas between 1969 and 1972, quite in the act of modeling himself on his hero, Wallace. Heir to these frozen states of metamorphosis, and caretaker of these fragments from her father's travels at the turn of the seventies, Klea reflects upon how she came to be in possession of the long unopened trunk. "When I was about nine or ten years old, he saw that I was interested and trained me in the basics of how to spread and mount them, so for the first time I got a glimpse into that strange treasure trove. It was a special activity we shared for a while."[74]

Commencing as an interactive photographic installation exhibited (by chance) in the immediate wake of the Monterey fire, the project gave Klea—nineteen when Terence died—a means to finally let go. "In the aftermath of loss, both personal and cultural," she writes, "we gather up the objects and traces left behind, compile and examine them as though these material things can tell us something about what has happened to us. Perhaps this impulse is a way of taking inventory of our loss, measuring, through objects, the size of the void."[75] As she further explains, the daily ritual of unwrapping, handling, and photographing each unique, hand-folded item "felt like a sort of reenactment; the mirror image of what [Terence] had done 40 years earlier." In this way, Klea imagines the project as "a communication . . . across the decades." There was a thread between them, and she was now finally "untying a knot."[76]

There is a further intriguing aspect of Klea's exhibition and book. The samples were individually wrapped in a collage of newspaper and magazine sheets, manuscript pages, and receipts. Excavated some thirty-eight years after the specimens were entombed in their casings, these faded wrappings shed light on the curator. A butterfly print that Davis bought from Klea featured the word "Ada," which was cut from an Indonesian review presumably of Nabokov's 1969 novel *Ada, or Ardor: A Family Chronicle*. The novel's title character dreamed of being a lepidopterist, a pursuit to which Nabokov himself committed with a passion. The wrapper encased a yellow-winged specimen with black body, evoking Nabokov's favorite butterfly (he named "Ada"). Also reproduced in *The Butterfly Hunter*, this print is not only a poignant reminder of the literary roots of Terence's lepidoptery. In its faded parchment-like captures of metamorphosis, it offers a meta-commentary on impermanence.

The Color . . . The Color

> When I got these diagnoses . . . a bug walking across the ground moved me to tears.[77]

"Buddhism is fine," McKenna once assured Esalenites. "But no one knows the pleasure of the capture of a birdwing ornithopter in the jungles of Saram."[78] Though disavowing his conflicted hunt in the wake of the mushroom's teachings and material returns, such a rare confession revealed an obsession from his past. The pursuit of butterflies conveyed, I suggest, an obsession with ephemerality—with the end that is also a renewal. Upon further contemplation of this fraught preoccupation, I am moved to return to (Mr. and Col.) Kurtz, a figure also driven by an obsession with the end, with death (ultimately his own). I raised the specter of Kurtz in the introduction, implying that these wayward radical empiricists offer dramatically contrasting careers in boundary dissolution.

Writing this book, I have felt at times like a hybrid of Marlow (*Heart of Darkness*) and Captain Willard (*Apocalypse Now*) hunting Kurtz up (or, in the case of McKenna, down) the river, attempting to penetrate a mind illuminated by, as McKenna himself put it, "the simultaneous light of paradox."[79] In the same breath, either "the situation" to which McKenna devoted much of his life will produce "a great deal of dislocation in the biosphere" or we will become, in Joyce's words, "man made dirigible."[80] He was so comfortable with contraries in dynamic tension that his life approximated an elegant lunacy, a commitment to "the release of the mind into the imagination."[81] If we were to pursue his Apocalypse Tao all the way along the Río Igara Paraná, to a place where the river surges through a crack and over a roaring lip, we encounter the strange semblance of Kurtz, a broken figure in Coppola's epic who has seen the end of the world, and presides over a world beyond order and time (far up the Nung River, in Cambodia). McKenna is also driven by the end to which he has been witness, and consequently behaves according to its rules, which are ultimately beyond rational apprehension. The device conjured in the remotest Amazon was dedicated to arriving at a place in space-time where "all points are cotangent," with the chaos math clarified in statements like: "What is not here is nowhere. What is here is everywhere."[82] These are the reveries of the trickster poet who, having seen the end, is content. "If you know how it comes out, you go back and you take your place in the play, and you let it all roll on without anxiety."[83] The ends to which each figure was intimate are the dramatically variant conclusions of discrepant guerrillas. The warrior poet, in his Vietnam War–era incarnation, is compelled to seek an honorable death of his own choosing (i.e., at the hands of the machete-wielding Willard)—the violent end a self-sacrificial expression of Kurtz's "blood lust." On the other hand, "there will be no boundaries when we finally reach the end," the psychedelic poet forecasts just a few years before his own end. "Only eternity as we become all space and time, alive and dead, here and there, before and after."[84] At the end of a life of boundary hacking, McKenna had the chops to face his end with dignity.

Though he never returned to La Chorrera, it remained an idyllic fantasy in the bard's imagination post-1971. It is the overgrown capital of a psychedelic society in the post-historical era in which the imagination reigns sovereign. On an alternate timeline in which McKenna survives and the Timewave runs its course, it is not difficult to imagine him becoming a Kurtz-like figure. In that case, does Kurtz provide an apparition of what McKenna might have become had he not succumbed to brain cancer, and clung to a chimera of his theory in the wake of 2012, pushing farther and farther upriver like an emperor of his own atemporal, acausal, and cryptic kingdom? That we can't know. What we do know is that the edge runner was transfixed, not by snails crawling along razor blades in darkened places but by the scintilla of "iridescence" found at the "edge of the probable."

Right through to the end, adventurous freaks and documentarians with an entry visa to his domain trekked to find Terence deep inside his jungle hideaway. Thus it was that, in the remarkable long-form interview with Hazard under giant banana leaves in the months prior to the seizure, McKenna regales the documentarian with a singular and lasting revelation:

> The mushroom said to me once, "This is what it's like when a species prepares to depart for the stars." You don't depart for the stars under calm and orderly conditions. It's a fire in a madhouse. And that's what we have, the fire in the madhouse at the end of time. . . . The entire destiny of all life on the planet is tied up in this. We are not acting for ourselves or from ourselves as we happen to be the point species on a transformation that will affect every living organism on this planet at its conclusion.[85]

And if his followers wanted to know what disposition toward the natural world they ought to adopt in the coming transformation, the answer is, true to form, as beguiling as it was cryptic. McKenna had long dwelt inside a vortex of radical ambiguity, a place where the left and right hands work toward divergent ends. While the one presses toward the posthuman emancipation from labor, the body, planet, and history itself, the other hedges bets on reclaiming a relationship with Gaia, the Gaian Mind, or the Divine Imagination, through the help of visionary plants, conceived as "allies." Ascensionist one moment, revitalizing another, all at once dematerializing *and* rematerializing, an unresolved tension is germane to a schizoidal approach apparent in *The Invisible Landscape*, a work vested in the promise that the new model of time could somehow "reverse the progressive worldwide alienation that is fast turning into an ecocidal planetary crisis." To overcome entropy, this long-held model "must mathematically secure the *reasonableness* of hope."[86] While McKenna behaved like a fatalist reporting just ahead of the cataclysmic scene of our undoing, he rallied his audience all the same with hopeful paeans to save the planet.

For the most part, he occupied the middle ground. The millennium according to McKenna was imagined to be rapturous and rupturous in equal measure. Ultimately, it was not a question of political choice, but an acceptance that novelty was winning. An ostensible representation of peak novelty, the human species was considered living evidence. But one need not only look to humans for an explanation—the answers were written in the stars. The announcement came in McKenna's final appearance pre-seizure, delivered fittingly in his home state. "So it turns out there is a cosmic law which has built into itself this idea of an endless acceleration toward infinity." Dropping hints on recent advancements in quantum field theory on the subject of "dark energy," in Denver, on April 27, 1999, McKenna presented news vindicating his already long career in cosmic projection. Signifying a "law of nature larger than any law of nature ever discovered," he was excited about the renewed interest in Einstein's "cosmological constant Λ" in light of the recent discovery that the expanding universe is accelerating.[87] The cosmological constant is received as a mythopoetic confirmation of the labor of his life, just at the moment when it was about to fall into a tailspin.

If his theory of novelty grew more oblique over the course of McKenna's career, the idea retained a simple plot. Humans are becoming god-like, the lead actors in a cosmic production that was bringing the curtains down on an ultra-novel event coming soon. Hazard was informed that our purpose as humans is to "advance and preserve novelty" and "to hand on a more diverse, more complicated, more multiphasic reality to our children." McKenna's heirs appear to embody this reality. While there is no singular influence, Klea speaks of the fragmented and scrambled "too much-ness" of the forest in her work. "I don't experience natural places as calm at all," she says, "but rather as teeming."[88] Despite the messiness, Terence's unflinching *mckennaism* ordained the simple logic that all clocks were counting down to an identifiable "zero" on the event horizon. Such a prophetic legacy has met with disapproval among those raised to question received wisdom. Dissensus from the bird's-eye view perspective is apparent for Klea. A translucent passage from Ursula K. Le Guin's *The Word for World Is Forest* (1972) is used to contextualize the visual statement embodied in Klea's series *How Forests Think* (2014–2015)—that is, chromogenic photograms of giant banana leaves. In the forest, Klea suggests (via Le Guin): "Revelation was lacking. There was no seeing everything at once: no certainty." In his own fashion, Finn takes his father to task for the temporal determinism implicit to his cosmology. While intrigued by the mechanics of the Timewave, Finn grew troubled by the albatross tied around Terence's neck (i.e., the insistence on an end date). By the time he was armed with the incisive tools of junior college philosophy, he challenged his dad on this subject. Finn preferred Terence to behave more like Descartes, who, in *Meditations*, commenced from first principles to call everything, not least of all his self, into question. Then again, Terence departed before father and son could take their conversation to the next level. In Terence's wake, Finn has surfed the backwash of a waveform that his dad, by virtue of an impromptu departure, failed to ride all the way to the beach.

Meditating upon this empty inheritance, Finn wonders if Terence hadn't simply been pranked or deceived by a cosmic jester. Contemplating the shroomic Timewave, Terence's abrupt departure, and the fires marking his transit, Finn is informed by chaos magic and the perception that Terence had been "played." Here the Timewave possesses more than a hint of modern Western magic workings, à la Aleister Crowley. Routinely incanting the end date before worldwide audiences, in his son's characterization, Terence behaved as if he was "magicking . . . the Eschaton into existence." And yet Terence invested his life and identity in an evanescent obsession. Waves are destined, after all, to crash into the surf. "The logos, the mushroom, whatever you want to call it, was . . . magicking him!"[89]

Beyond 2012
So pivotal is *the end* (i.e., December 21, 2012) to McKenna's worldview that his earlier visionary reveries prefigured the mood arriving in the wake of his own abrupt end-time. We cannot know his state of mind had he survived the dozen years remaining until 2012—although it serves our curiosity to speculate. As suggested earlier in the book, the enthusiasm for the end date is likely to have waned upon its approach, just as doubts and prevarications emerged in 1971 at La Chorrera. There was plenty of time to grow distant from the "squirrelly" extremes of the 2012 circus, among other "pernicious forms of foolishness."[90] In the speculative mood of early 2012, R. U. Sirius had the measure on the likely tone of the self-identified "carnival barker" for consciousness whose penchant for self-mockery overpowered any desire for self-aggrandizement. McKenna, he thought, never took his role as a prophet as seriously as some of his disciples. Sirius felt certain that McKenna is likely to have remained aboard the 2012 circus to ensure his livelihood and promote other aspects of his philosophy, just as he would have made himself available "to be propped up on a hemp-woven throne at the stroke of midnight at the 12.21.12 global rave." But Sirius is equally certain about something else. Terence would have been much more *surprised* if that date turned out to be "a day of magical transmutation" than he would have been *disappointed* if it did not.[91] Of course, it is impossible to know how the bard-prophet would have reacted to life beyond 2012. Perhaps the crypto-anarchist of yore will have championed the virtues of Bitcoin, which surged beyond $100 in the wake of December 21, 2012. In an alternate timeline (i.e., where he survives), romanced by the inherent interwoven charm of the singularity and individuation, I imagine him finding ways to sustain and affirm the mythic kernel. It may have relied upon a reacquaintance with his cosmic-vegetal muse, but it is not difficult to

imagine McKenna MacGyvering his temporal system in some reanimated variation or reoptimized "zero" date.

To project this fantasy timeline further into the present, the fuckupocalypse of 2020 is likely to have provided the datum to confirm, extend, and augment an already deep reality tunnel. If novelty is the measure of the end-times, then the period conforms to spec: stock market crash, politicized pandemic, ballooning collective delusions, race riots, civil unrest, election chaos, domestic terrorism, and a smoldering cauldron of conspiratorialism. And that's just inside the United States, where the Snake Oil president loomed, a dead man golfing in the dark carnival of America. And if that wasn't enough, routine extreme weather events and new wars serve as a reminder that the planet's "doomsday clock" closes in on midnight. Such offers more than enough material to animate an army of Kurtzian psychedelic prophets. If still transmitting from his rebel base on Hawaii, it is fair to assume that McKenna will have communicated from deep inside "I told you so" country.

Alternatively, he might have withdrawn from the arts of prophesy altogether—thereby keeping his promise to Rupert and Ralph, and becoming reborn in some post-2012 guise we can scarcely imagine. At the same time, it is hard to imagine a living TKM not amplifying his views to wider audiences, as a podcaster, rebel-rouser, and drumbeater frequently consulted on significant matters of the day. Inside this fantasy, by 2012, he will have vested his attentions toward consciousness transformation at the nexus of visionary plants, arts, and technologies. The passage through 2012 may then have been undertaken as a significant "phase shift" in his own becoming. After all, failure was not difficult to reckon for he who dwelt in "the simultaneous light of paradox." In this case, the situation may have provided a window of opportunity, an opening toward an unforeseen union with the Other. How McKenna did embrace his own fate offers insight on his possible management of the 2012 disappointment: not only with humor and an exemplary humility, but as a critical phase in the passage toward union with the unknown.

While we can't know exactly how he will have reacted on December 22, 2012, we do know the response of McKenna's acolyte, Peter Meyer. In 1999, Meyer indicated that a specific zero date is not implied by the Timewave theory, that it retains its formal logic even if anchored in another zero date.[92] In a bizarre effort to prove this point, when 2012 slid by, and his software was sliding beneath the surface like the Timewave Zero *Titanic*, Meyer opportunistically offered an alternative zero date (July 7, 2018).[93] After that dispensation failed to arrive, he doubled down on the mathematical coherence of the model. There was no reason to believe, claimed Meyer, that another cycle hadn't commenced on December 21, 2012.[94] If it wasn't already apparent that the show was over, Meyer inadvertently drew the curtains on the Timewave. Unable to hold a candle to its creator's "spark of divinity," the Timewave fizzled out ingloriously.

In the long prelude to its own end date, the Timewave was set to become one of the strangest cases of a failed future haunting the present. And so while the Timewave Zero end date may have passed its best-by date, the novelty mythos remains animate into the present. With the advent of social and streaming media, McKenna's voice and vernacular have charmed millions. The psychedelic eschaton did not end with its scribe's death, and nor did it end with the transition beyond 2012.

The Felt Presence of Terence

At the end of his life, Terence McKenna was all set for a posthumous career in cyberspace where he would continue to animate, inspire, and provoke populations across a variety of fields. When Bruce Damer once shared a vision he'd had of his friend departing in an elven limousine, McKenna responded: "ah . . . the getaway car!" The story presages McKenna's rise as a "cultural avatar" and "medium in cyberspace."[95] While Terence made a protracted incendiary exit, rather than being "expunged," as Dennis had it, his soul has become *dirigible* in cyberspace, where today his voice is mobilized

FIGURE 12.7
Terence McKenna, portrait by Robert Venosa, 1998. Courtesy of Martina Hoffmann.

in electrosonic media and his mind is resurrected via AI simulators. Regardless of the absence of a physical body, and despite his incinerated legacy, in true gnostic form, McKenna has been released into the virtual domain he long championed, his vision and voice fluttering like the wings of a kaleidoscope of butterflies in the drop-down menus behind closed eyelids with collectively opened minds.

With the assistance of digital media technologies, and with the advent of the Net, the wickedly sing-song voice that drew Ken Adams and Colin Angus, among others, from far afield to its source in west Sonoma in the eighties and nineties is a voice that has permeated the digital-virtual era. McKenna didn't need his brain frozen or ashes shot into space. He was to be immortalized within a Net warren of dedicated websites, discussion forums, Facebook pages, Instagram engagement pods, Reddit, Skool and Clubhouse groups, YouTube channels, and podcasts featuring his machine-augmented voice commenting on how he feels about his own digital resurrection. In other words, he was to populate the very disembodied "mind space" he long fantasized as a transhuman promised land and "home."

At the end of the second millennium, McKenna was on the cusp of becoming a "Zone Ghost" on his "hill." Given the rapid advances in internet media broadcasting, he was set to make the transition. What became known as podcasting was born in the months following his death, tech he is almost certain to have embraced from its earliest phase, likely becoming a maven of the medium. It is not unreasonable to expect that he will have continued to experiment with virtual worlds enabling us to behold what he meant in ever finer detail. And he is not unlikely to have been on location in this online off-world chronicling his experiences with "trip reports" as immersive VR returned in 2010 with Oculus.

While McKenna skipped out on the millennium, he has remained remarkably present. On their album *Nothing Lasts . . . But Nothing Is Lost*, ministers of the psychedelic séance, Shpongle, offer a moving elegy. "Nothing lasts . . . nothing lasts" is the digital dirge that channels the late McKenna (and William Blake). "Everything is changing into something else. Nothing's wrong. Nothing is wrong. Everything is on track."[96] At the start of the nineties, J. P. Harpignies told a New York audience that the mind of the figure he was about to introduce ought to be housed in a museum. As it happened, a "museum" has been erected to accommodate McKenna's mind: a decentralized labyrinthine cyber-archive. Within a few years from his departure, streaming Terence McKenna 24/7, YouTube enabled the broadcasting of hundreds of hours of raps that have continued to emerge over the last two decades. Damer was pivotal in the effort to digitize audio recordings and release this legacy in the Creative Commons environment. Lorenzo Hagerty, host of the Psychedelic Salon podcast, became instrumental to transmitting the Terencentricity. This proliferation has seen a multitude of reanimated rips, mixes, and burns. The Net has provided a vast archive of retrievable data and ready-made koans from which musicians could quantize, remix, and resuture the "informing voice" of a lodestar in the global netosphere. In short bursts, sample-smiths excavate the words to express the inexplicable. "I go to a place where language finds it very hard to pull over, look around," McKenna is sampled from his final interview. "It's almost as though it takes you to a world that is not Englishable."[97] As a quintessential muse over more than two decades, McKenna became a disembodied medium for the unspeakable. With his after-death vehicle zooming about on the superhighways of the psyberdelic afterlife, Terence had gone meta.

When McKenna set sail into the afterlife, participants in the psychedelic community despaired over who could possibly emerge to match his talent or assume his stature. Were we destined to endless reruns of the TM™ show? While McKenna could never be replaced, and while his virtualization could not stand in for the stand-up philosopher, what emerged in his stead was a vast netscape. McKenna's virtual metamorphosis was affected almost seamlessly with the new networked environment in which it is no longer necessary, nor even possible, for individuals, rugged mystics or otherwise, to hold such sway and influence. Davis made this point in his eulogy. In 2000, "the psychedelic community," he contended, "has ripened to a point where it may no longer need a charismatic leader. In a sense, this was McKenna's goal. Because if Aldous Huxley was an aristocrat of psychedelics, and Leary was a populist demagogue, then McKenna is a crunchy libertarian. So it is perhaps fitting that McKenna is the last of his line, that no new harlequin hero waits in the wings."[98]

McKenna's final resting place is, then, the restless realm to which he devoted much of his career: the ensouled cyberspace, electronic otherworld, virtual eschaton. The incomplete manuscript at the time of his departure intended to address, claimed its author, "the future history of technology as we move toward quasi-telepathic, drug- and machine-assisted communication environments." In other words, the work pursued a long-cherished dream of the imagination externalized. The future of communication, he continues, "is the future of the evolution of the human soul. As we communicate with each other with greater facility, the boundaries and the illusions of difference just evanesce and disappear."[99] The Net was figured as a stage upon which McKenna could perform his own alienness, and although he departed before he could exploit virtual worlding to any great effect, in the two and a half decades in the wake of his exodus, the virtual world became saturated with his felt presence. Leaving behind a litany of aphorisms, rhetorical flourishes, and mind "probes" that break through barriers of perception, following McLuhan, and expecting his "constituents" to make their own discoveries and question everything (including his own views), while expressing an abhorrence of the compartmentalizing of knowledge, McKenna carried a "mosaic" style of presentation into the digital beyond.

While he may have gone meta, McKenna's style remains forever beta. Trailblazing the frontiers of guerrilla ontology might have certified his stature as *persona non grata* in the world of "Psychedelics 2.0," but time and again the psychedelic renaissance man returned to the source—to the *imagination*. If the realm of the imagination is valued per square inch, given McKenna's lifelong investments and market share in this terrain, he was destined for great wealth. His prodigious oratory and textual output seeded a conceptual universe not unlike those emerging from the great minds of science fiction. The unique and expansive vision is reminiscent of imaginations forging internally consistent universes and dynamic metaverses, bearing franchises that have translated to a variety of media platforms. Many of McKenna's key ideas more or less belong in the realm of sci-fi, and had he lived into the present, there is plenty of evidence to suggest that he could have formally tried his hand at it. It would not be a stretch to imagine him plundering the mechanics of the Timewave novum for material, just as Alfred Jarry plundered the "science" of pataphysics to create his oeuvre.

Regardless, we are left with the extraordinary legacy of an imagineer who reckoned that we are destined to dwell inside the mind, a higher-dimensional space evincing the externalizing of his own mind. If dwelling inside the imagination is the ultimate objective in this story, through the nineties McKenna saw that, like a self-fulfilling prophecy, the internet was the *deus ex machina* affirming his vision. Reality was truly up for grabs. "It's only been 400 years since we discovered the lost half of this planet," he announced in the narrative of the colonizer. Before that, "it was a matter of debate if there was North and South America." But with persistence, there is "real estate beyond anybody's wildest dreams."

> There's real estate in the imagination. I think it's the country we're all going to live in. We're like English colonials restless with a mad king and waiting to book passage to the New Worlds of America. Our sails are filling, the technologies exist to do it. And in 200 years it wouldn't surprise me if the imagination was the major industrial and population center of the human world.[100]

APPENDIX A: ACKNOWLEDGMENTS AND SOURCES

This epic research venture owes a great debt to many—people, archives, and resources—contacted and accessed between 2018 and 2024. In the following, I give credit to those who have given assistance and to the resources accessed. The work has benefited from interviews and extended communications with over eighty people whose lives interfaced with Terence McKenna. This effort has been executed by scouring public and private archives, which has enabled a close consultation with personal correspondence, manuscripts, journals, and unpublished materials. The study profits from the survey of a vast archive of McKenna's publications, along with press articles, interviews, and research publications that hold McKenna as a subject, as well as documentary and other film sources. And not least, I have accessed a large number of spoken word recordings and their transcriptions.

This biography may be incomplete, but it would be substantively more so without the help of the following people (some of whom are given more attention below). Family, friends, lovers, co-conspirators, colleagues and acquaintances of McKenna—each has directly assisted me as interviewees and/or with personal communications (either in-person or virtual, and commonly both). Brother Dennis J. McKenna, ex-wife Kathleen Harrison, son Finn McKenna, daughter Klea McKenna, cousin Judy Livingston, and cousin-in-law Laddie Livingston. Childhood friend of the McKennas, Ron Curry. Friends from high school: Rick Watson, Douglas Hansen, Nina Wise, David Wallin, Bill Cole, Gray Brechin, and Vern Brechin. Fellow Experimental College alumni and other Berkeley friends: Michael Malcolm, Elizabeth Hansen, Kevin Mahoney, Sara Hartley, George Csicsery, Barry Melton, and Richard Brzustowitz. Unassuming "psychopomp" James Fadiman. Friends encountered on overseas travels: Roger Williams, Martin Inn, Tama Starr, Masayasu Takayama, Terry Reid, and Satomi Hirano. Other fellow travelers, colleagues, and collaborators: Ralph Abraham, Luis Eduardo Luna, Tom Cole, Joan Halifax, Michael Horowitz, Peter Meyer, Rupert Sheldrake, R. U.

Sirius, Rick Doblin, Robert Forte, Allan Badiner, John Steele, Leon Berg, Robin Sylvan, J. P. Harpignies, Philippe De Vosjoli, Howard Rheingold, Mike Kawitzky, Erik Davis, Bruce Damer, and Bruce Pavitt. Esalen associates: David Price, Nancy Lunney-Wheeler, and Gordon Wheeler. Editor Leslie Meredith, editor/manager Dan Levy, and publicist Leslie Rossman. Tour promoter Dillon Hicks, and Nick Spacetree, for details on the Australian tour. Filmmakers Ken Adams, Edgar Pêra, Paul Chambers, and Tim Parish. Musicians and artists Colin Angus, Charles Cosh, Jonah Sharp, Nik Sequenci, Martin Glover, Raja Ram, Dean Chamberlain, Martina Hoffmann, Abrupt, and Beatie Wolfe. Researchers, scholars, and archivists Thomas Wide, Mark Liechty, Wouter Hanegraaff, Kevin Whitesides, Chris Mays, and Logan Scott. Digital recording archivist and podcaster Lorenzo Hagerty. Transcription pioneer Jonathan Laliberte. And last, but not least, lover Christy Silness.

Extensive research was pursued at the Betsy Gordon Psychoactive Substances Research Collection, housed at the Purdue University Archives in West Lafayette, Indiana. In September 2019, with the assistance of a Purdue Research Travel Grant, I visited the Dennis and Terence McKenna papers (also regarded here as the "McKenna papers"), a collection donated by Dennis in 2013.[1] A trove of personal documents that includes a journal, field notes, manuscripts, press clippings, and correspondence, this collection represents the most important extant secure holding of McKenna documents. Of note are several boxes of Terence McKenna materials in Series 2 of the McKenna papers. These materials are listed below, with box and folder numbers. Documents were accessed and reviewed on-site at the Purdue Archives and subsequently under the most helpful guidance of archivist Stephanie Schmitz.

The following is a chronological list of documents authored (or coauthored) by Terence McKenna that have been accessed for this project from the McKenna papers. Where materials referenced throughout indicate Purdue Archives, consult this list for complete details.

- Terence McKenna, "The Future of Magic in Electronic Societies, Summer Project," Experimental College dissertation, UC Berkeley, ca. 1966, sixty pages (MSP 213, Box 2, Folder 10). Representing McKenna's only known surviving student work, the document features comments from an anonymous evaluator (ungraded).
- Terence McKenna, "Ho Lo," one-page typewritten document, undated, ca. 1966–68 (MSP 213, Box 2, Folder 10).
- Dennis and Terence McKenna, "Dennis McKenna (with TMCK) La Chorrera original notes," collaborative journaled notes, La Chorrera, Colombia, February 28–March 4, 1971, nineteen pages (MSP 213, Box 3, Folder 7).

- Terence McKenna and Dennis McKenna, "A Preliminary Report on an Experiment at La Chorrera," completed in Berkeley, May 16, 1971, thirty pages (MSP 213, Box 2, Folder 11). Produced in the Berkeley interlude of Terence's 1971 adventures to La Chorrera. The title page reads: "For the A. R. Wallace Foundation."
- Terence McKenna, "Change and Becoming: Studies in a Fourth Dimensional Phenomenology of Mind," handwritten journal produced in Colombia with entries from July 15, 1971, to January 1, 1972 (MSP 213, Box 3, Folder 7). Produced in Colombia during Terence's second trip to La Chorrera in 1971. The "Progress" red marbled college-ruled Theme Note Book features the author's close handwritten entries and numerous charts and graphs over 169 pages. The notebook was digitized by the Purdue Libraries and transcribed by Botond Vitos and myself. This work is reliant upon that transcription.
- The Boulder Statement, a three-page typed document that I have called the "Boulder Statement" and apparently composed by McKenna when residing in Boulder, Colorado, in 1972 (MSP 213, Box 3, Folder 1).
- Terence McKenna and Dennis McKenna, "Shamanic Investigations," 1972, unpublished manuscript, 292 pages (MSP 213, Box 5, Folder 1). Earliest extant manuscript of *The Invisible Landscape*.
- Terence McKenna, "Down to Earth: Psilocybin and the UFOs," 1979, 236 pages (MSP 213, Box 3, Folder 3). A version of the manuscript that eventually became *True Hallucinations*. Final page: "Freestone 1979."

Additionally, several letters and a postcard were sourced from the Ralph Metzner collection of correspondence, MSP 317; and a photograph from the Michael and Cynthia Horowitz papers, MSP 316, both housed at the Purdue Archives as part of the Psychoactive Substances Research Collection.

Many thanks to the National Archives and Records Administration (NARA) for assistance retrieving Criminal Case Files. In particular, I thank NARA at Denver (US District Court for the District of Colorado) and Kansas City (holding archives for the US District Court for the Southern District of New York), and notably Gwen E. Granados, director of archival operations, NARA at Denver, for her assistance retrieving and interpreting court documents. Thanks also to Hannah K. Reynolds, archives specialist, NARA at Kansas City.

* * *

Various materials were sourced from private archives, including letters from McKenna to various correspondents: thirty letters to Tim A. Cannon (1961–1965); twenty-three letters (1968–1996) to Rick Watson; one postcard to

Douglas Hansen (1969); two letters to Nina Wise (June–July 1969); twenty letters (1971–1996) to Masayasu Takayama; and seven letters to Michael Horowitz (1979–1987). Private sourced materials also include the following documents:

- Terence McKenna, "Post Electric Thought," unpublished manuscript produced between 1968 and 1970 in Seychelles, Berkeley, and Tokyo, 141 pages. The document is a revision of the earlier manuscript "Crypto-Rap: Meta-Electrical Speculations on Culture" (Seychelles, 1968). "Post Electric Thought" derives from the private archives of Satomi Hirano, who kindly copied and posted the manuscript to me forty-five years after she was loaned a copy by Masayaku Takayama (ca. 1976) and signed by Terence: "Masa. To my dear friend without whom this would not have been possible."

- Select pages of Sara Hartley's private handwritten journal, La Chorrera, Colombia, March 1971, and Hartley's unsent letter to Michael Malcolm, La Chorrera, Colombia, March 12, 1971.

- Terence McKenna, "Down to Earth: Psilocybin and the UFOs" 1977, 130 pages (final page dated "Berkeley 1976"). The earliest known version of the manuscript that became *True Hallucinations*. From the private archives of Rick Watson.

- "Down to Earth: Story Breakdown and Draft," folder of notes on the screenplay for the True Hallucinations Project, including Terence's original "Down to Earth" screenplay, n.d. (16 pages); Sheila Humphrey's "Down to Earth: A Treatment," April 1986 (21 pages); and Terence's handwritten notes on characters, development, plot, and other details (30 pages). Courtesy of Dennis McKenna and Kevin Whitesides.

- Philippe De Vosjoli graciously shared documents associated with his unpublished manuscript coauthored with McKenna, "Casting Nets in the Sea of Mind," including the short chapters authored by McKenna, "The Future of Humanity" and "What It Is That Evolves."

William Patrick ("Rick") Watson was indispensable to this project. Besides sharing copies of the documents listed above, Rick afforded access to a trove of his unpublished autobiographical writings on his sixties adventures (including those directly involving his lifelong friend, McKenna), written for the most part in the early nineties. Watson, who became a leading London antiquarian bookseller specializing in science and natural history, was a talented writer and poet, who, unlike his pal, never sought the limelight. The following is a list of Watson's pieces upon which I have drawn (and cited throughout): "Pursuing to Peru the G'nostic Guru: A Poetic Talisman" (1969/70), "Morning Glory" (1990), "DMT, or, Spider Woman Comes to Town" (1993), "John Parker" (1993), "Richard Horn" (1993), "Richard Horn II" (1993), "Bryant Street," and "Marijuana." As McKenna's friend and confidante, passionate about books, and eager to assist my efforts, Watson's input was integral to this work. We corresponded from 2014/15, when completing my previous book *Mystery School in Hyperspace: A Cultural History of DMT*. While Watson's interventions were marginal to that project, he came to occupy a more central role here. From 2020 to 2022, the superliminal conditions of the COVID pandemic provided the background context for Watson to relate his previously unshared adventures with McKenna (who he knew as Terry, or Terr) beginning in 1963. His awareness of a terminal lung disease (that eventually claimed him in March 2024) gave Rick fresh incentive to share his story. From meeting with him at his home in Hampstead, London, in July 2018, up until the last stages of his life, Rick was generous with his time. Terry's old pal responded to my countless inquiries with great attention to detail. Given Rick's concern for the truth, and his ability to form pictures in words of life lived five decades ago—in Los Altos, Berkeley, Nepal, and elsewhere—we are privileged to a fresh portrait of McKenna.

The letters McKenna wrote Watson illustrate the friendship between the two young men. Aiding contextualization, Rick also shared copies of a sequence of letters he wrote to his parents in 1969/70, for the most part from Kathmandu, and another set written and sent to his friend, Michael Moore, over the same period. Due to his talent as an expert contextualizer, and the superb quality of his own writing, Watson is a chief protagonist in the early part of the book. I am grateful to Rick for his introductions to several other important figures in this story. I am also grateful to his daughter, Beatie Wolfe, for her assistance and for understanding the merits of this project.

* * *

A vast library of textual materials, including those produced and published by McKenna, and press articles about and interviews with him, have been consulted. Several McKenna bibliophiliacs deserve gratitude. The collectivized bibliographic information found in the Terence McKenna Archive at the online Zerwic Library, created by Matthew Zerwic, was extremely useful.[2] Deep appreciation to librarian Chris Mays for his meticulous efforts initiating, compiling, and maintaining (between 2000–2013) the Terence McKenna Bibliography, which since 2023 has been maintained at the Terence McKenna

Archives.[3] And a resounding shout-out to researcher and biographer Kevin Whitesides. Committed to independent archival work, Kevin has performed an invaluable service in the quest to document the life and work of McKenna. In an uncommon dedication to collecting, documenting, and transcribing McKenna content, Kevin initiated the Terence McKenna Archives in 2013, which includes privately stored physical and digital holdings of books, magazines, and other print media, along with art and photography.[4] Kevin has generously shared with me various documents, including a PDF of the original 1975 edition of the McKenna brothers' *The Invisible Landscape*.

Poring over these bibliographies and archival lists is like finding anchorage in the McKennaverse. Consulting these archives offers strange assuredness, which is comforting given that Googling "Terence McKenna" invariably catapults the infonaut into an infuriatingly unpredictable data-warren.

Another thing of beauty standing firm in an evanescent world is the Terence K. McKenna Legacy Library. While McKenna's physical library—bequeathed to Esalen upon his death—is believed to have been destroyed by fire in Monterey in 2007, a version of the library that had been meticulously catalogued by Terence himself became the basis for a 2,641-item catalog input to LibraryThing in the early 2000s by Chris Mays.[5] As was conveyed by Mays, this catalog derived from an "Excel spreadsheet of a FileMaker port of an Apple Macintosh Hypercard file of Terence's personal library." The file was amended by Dennis in the early 2000s, before it was given to Mays by Kathleen Harrison, after which he seeded McKenna's legacy library at LibraryThing.[6]

As for spoken word recordings ("raps,"), the project has relied on my survey of a proliferation of recordings (including private sessions, workshops, conference appearances, radio interviews, and theatrical performances recorded on audiocassette tape and/or VHS) that have been digitized, podcasted, uploaded to YouTube, and/or are transcribed. The total archive of McKenna's oratory is greater than that consulted for this project, an archive I estimate at well over 500 hours of material, delivered in over 250 appearances (although the total number of appearances and hours in this distributed virtual archive is currently unknown). About a third of this material appears to have been recorded at Esalen, and for many of those recordings we have the assiduous Paul Herbert (Dolphin Tapes) to thank. Also pivotal through the eighties and nineties, Faustin Bray and Brian Wallace (Sound Photosynthesis) made video and audio recordings of approximately seventy unique McKenna raps at a wide variety of locations, including Esalen, the Ojai Foundation, Shared Visions Bookstore, the California Institute of Integral Studies, and workshops in Santa Fe, along with various conferences

Appendix A

and Whole Life Expos. Much of this material has been copied, digitized, and streamed, and is beginning to be transcribed. In the wake of McKenna's death, driven to preserve his legacy, Bruce Damer led an effort to collect and digitize raw recordings from cassette tape, uploaded to the Internet Archive where material has been released for Creative Commons licensing nonprofit use. Integral to the digital transposition of recorded content is Lorenzo Hagerty, who has podcasted material on *Psychedelic Salon* since 2005. Inheriting Herbert's archive of taped recordings (163 individual tapes) and a regular recipient of bootleg material, Lorenzo has tirelessly edited, uploaded, and preserved TM's raves, a labor for which all McKennaphiles owe a great debt of gratitude.[7] Among the bugbears faced by the biographer contending with this cornucopia is that many original rap titles have been modified (sometimes to avoid copyright infringement) by fans uploading and sharing content, generating a web-labyrinth of content with more links than a sausage factory.

While I have not enjoyed exposure to McKenna's rap in its entirety, the recordings/transcripts I have accessed have been indispensable. McKenna's spoken word appearances are not simply lectures, but performance events—complete with audience Q&A. Playing back this material typically reveals more information than acquired when simply reading a transcript.

On the subject of transcripts, the now inactive collaborative online transcription project AskTMK was essential to this project. Initiated by Jonathan Laliberte, and the labor of many dedicated McKennaphiles in the pre-ChatGPT era, this searchable text database was created in an open Wiki-style format. Transcribers to whom I am indebted include Laliberte, Eva Petakovic, Nathan Johansen, and Kevin Whitesides, who had earlier initiated the Terence McKenna Transcription Project on Wikispaces, later absorbed within the AskTMK project. Just as copyediting for the book concluded, AskTMK upgraded to the Terence McKenna collection on the AI-augmented collaborative transcription collection platform Uutter, which will be of great future utility.[8]

I would be remiss without mentioning the anonymous curator of the Library of Consciousness, an excellent online resource and study aid that includes the most accurate collection of transcriptions available at the time of writing of dozens of timestamped McKenna lectures, including the Q&A sessions, and often accompanied by audio-visual recordings.[9] Original audio accompanies the transcripts, with key excerpts highlighted and audiolinked. Where raps are transcribed at the Library of Consciousness, for the sake of consistency, I cite this source (though the original recordings should be consulted for accuracy). Additionally, a few New York City appearances were superbly transcribed by Abrupt. These quality transcriptions include points of emphasis, audience laughter, and external links to key terms.[10]

I thank Martin Inn and Tama Starr for sharing the recording by Inn of McKenna, "Amazon Psychotropical Quest," taped at 4A Dodge Place, San Francisco, in 1972/1973. It is the oldest known Terence McKenna recording.

My hat is off to Peter Bergmann, whose YouTube channel We Plants Are Happy Plants features hundreds of uploads, including much previously undigitized content. Kudos also to Deus Ex McKenna ~ Terence McKenna Archive, a YouTube channel compiling McKenna raps, curated by theblimp. If not available at the Library of Consciousness, I cite the raps curated on these two channels. When referencing raps, I include original titles and place and date information where known, along with a link to the audiovisual source. Where possible, I cite original oration and not modified transcripts (like those, for example, published in the collection *The Archaic Revival*). Referenced sources are provided both in the endnotes and in the online bibliography, which includes a section (Bibliography, Part II) dedicated to referenced spoken word sources (recorded raps and interviews). The complete and downloadable bibliography is available under "Resources" at https://mitpress.mit.edu/strange-attractor. My gratitude extends to those who generously shared and/or granted permission to use, or shared leads in relation to, photographs, images of artworks, and other materials reproduced as figures. Details appear in the figure captions.

As this book features sensitive information from a great many individuals, an explanation on my methods of communication and information transfer is warranted. Scores of folks associated with McKenna in varied roles and relationships were interviewed, either in person, online (i.e., Zoom), and/or via email. Many interlocutors have responded to follow-up questions, and the details obtained have commonly derived from ongoing correspondence. To the best of my knowledge, interlocutors have reviewed draft excerpts of their own material. Conversing with multiple interlocutors has been essential to corroborate details, *as much as possible*.

The path navigated has relied on the comprehensive study of multiple sources, the close inspection and comparison of published interviews conducted with McKenna (a large body of material in itself), and the examination of articles and chapters he authored, along with details uncovered in his books and unpublished manuscripts (including his journal) and private letters, in addition to a range of other sources (all cited at length in the endnotes). Necessary in the life of a storyteller whose personal archives were destroyed in three fires, this extensive comparative methodology has paid historiographical dividends. Throughout the text, I identify those circumstances that remain uncertain, ambiguous, or disputed.

Though not a family-authorized biography, this work has relied on the support of family and friends of TKM, to whom I am indebted. As such, a great many people deserve thanks. While I have stated my indebtedness to Rick Watson, in the following I pay my respects to other pivotal contributors.

For her patience and concern for dispelling myths, Kathleen Harrison, interviewed in Golden Gate Park and on Zoom, deserves special thanks. Director of Botanical Dimensions, wife to McKenna for sixteen years, mother to Finn and Klea McKenna, grandmother to Fiona and River, Harrison came into her own as a researcher and public intellectual following her marriage. Kat was gracious in her attention to my many inquiries, notably as my requests coincided with the tumult endured over more than a year in the wake of a traumatic home invasion and life-threatening physical assault she suffered in early 2021. Although that assailant was not a McKenna fanatic, as I learned, Terence continued to haunt his ex-wife, as evident in the disturbed men who, believing they are "channeling" McKenna or acting on his behalf, have subjected her to harassment. Given the impact of psychedelics on mentally unstable men, combined with celebrity worship, Terence continues to cast a shadow over her thirty years after they split up. Intensive therapy undergone to recover from her "near death experience" eventually loosened her attachment to memories of Terence. I am grateful for her candor.

Helpful with inquiries and granting permission for the reproduction of several family photographs was experimental fine arts photographer, filmmaker and author, daughter to Kat and Terence, Klea McKenna. The book discusses a poignant intergenerational moment, as illustrated in Klea's remarkable gallery series and subsequent book *The Butterfly Hunter*. Klea remains in possession of many of the original 2,000 carefully packaged lepidopterans she inherited and will donate them, she informs me, to the right institution, if they are seen as "both biological specimens and cultural artifacts."

Finn McKenna (son to Kat and Terence) was equally helpful, assisting several lines of inquiry. If he elects to do so, a future autobiographical effort from Finn could serve to set the record straight on matters merely touched on in this work. I am grateful for the input (and output) of Dennis McKenna. Among many other things, Dennis initiated the McKenna papers at Purdue, introduced me to many interlocutors, and otherwise planted thought-seeds some of which have grown wild (and hopefully not too erroneous) in this book. He was gracious throughout, granting permissions for materials and assisting with thoughtful responses to my many inquiries. While I am indebted to TKM's family members for their cooperation it should be recognized that views expressed throughout the book are not those of the family or made on behalf of the family.

I have been privileged to interact with a host of Terence's friends and associates. For many years Kat's best friend, while also a mentee of Terence, Nina Wise assists our understanding of a story fraught with ambiguity. Vital too is Christy Silness, McKenna's partner in his final years who relates her story for the first time. It is to our good fortune that we have an unprecedented portrait of Terence in his final months.

I am grateful for the contributions of Sara Hartley, Terry's fellow UC Berkeley Experimental College alumni, photographer, and member of the 1971 expedition to La Chorrera, who was pseudonymized as "Vanessa" in the memoirs of both McKenna brothers. Sara has shared select entries from her La Chorrera journal, in addition to a few of her remarkable photographs. Sara was very protective of her privacy for forty years, with her retirement as a practicing psychiatrist roughly coinciding with our first chat in April 2020. Communicating her somewhat estranged role in the Colombian adventure—her first public expressions on the subject—Sara shines new light on this celebrated episode. She also shares stories on other events and misadventures with McKenna, teasers for Hartley's memoir in progress.

My gratitude has many recipients. The late Ron Curry, the McKenna brothers' childhood pal from Paonia, I appreciate for his dedication to honoring the memory of his friend. Cousin Judy and cousin-in-law Laddie Livingston, for sharing childhood memories of Paonia. Douglas Hansen, Awalt High alumni, for his detailed report of mid-sixties events and scenes, and his insights on the early formation of TKM's ideas. Elizabeth Hansen, close friend of Terence, for her engaging insights and dialogue, and connections to the Berkeley Architectural Heritage Association. Kevin Mahoney, girlfriend to Terence in seventies Berkeley who has throughout provided nuanced attention to detail and thoughtful commentary. George Csicsery, Experimental College colleague and filmmaker, for assisting with Tussman program–related inquiries and for sharing connections, photographs, and wisdom. Michael Malcolm, another Experimental College colleague and fellow traveler, for sharing his wisdom on early exploits and travels. Bill Cole, among McKenna's oldest friends, for aiding me in deciphering court documents obtained from the National Archives (though the interpretations are my own). Tama Starr, for contributing her thoughts on their mutual friend, Dhyana. Masayasu Takayama, for caring about this project enough to share a pile of correspondence from Terence dating back to 1971. Satomi Hirano, for not only sharing a copy of "Post Electric Thought" but sharing commentary on manuscript excerpts, and for her ongoing curiosity and dialogue on a range of subjects from scripture to soteriology. R. U. Sirius, for his commentary and for generously sharing material from his forthcoming book *The Freaks in the Machine: Mondo 2000 in Late 20th Century Tech Culture*. Dan Levy, editor and "manager," and Leslie Rossman, publicist, in their concern for and assiduous attention to detail around the subject of their friend's emergence as a public figure.

The honors roll rolls on. Kudos to the late Ralph Abraham, among McKenna's closest friends and confidantes, dialogian, and later trialogian, for his dedication to getting the story right; Rupert Sheldrake, trialogian and intellectual sparring partner, for his kind contributions to the narrative; Roger Williams, for astute thoughts and reflections on the Nepal window; Allan Badiner, for memories of Esalen and beyond; Esalen general manager (1995–2003) David Price, for his superb attention to detail on Esalen, the McKenna library, and the 2007 Monterey fire; Esalen director Gordon Wheeler and executive director of programs Nancy Lunney-Wheeler, for sharing important memories; New York Open Center past program director J. P. Harpignies, for his sharp insights and assisting the reconstruction of the East Coast appearances; rare book dealer Michael Horowitz, for sharing correspondence, ephemera, and artwork; author Philippe De Vosjoli, for chapters from and answering my inquiries about, "Casting Nets," the unfinished book project, on which he was coauthor; Ken Adams, media shaman, accomplice in gnosis, and brains behind *Alien Dreamtime*, who was pivotal to McKenna's early nineties rave pivot and whose storytelling and insights have been invaluable; the Shamen's Colin Angus, another pivotal music industry personality, who with his friend and associate, Charles Cosh, offered an assiduous accounting of events; filmmaker Edgar Pêra, for his keen eye for detail and for his still shots and insights; author, filmmaker, and dedicated McKennaphile, Mike Kawitzky, whose care, output, and feedback have been of great service to my efforts; Lorenzo Hagerty for his tireless dedication to propagating the rap, and Bruce Damer, for collecting and sharing McKenna-related digital materials (letters, schedules, photographs), as part of his "Terence2012" archive project,[11] and who was attentive to detail and most generous with his time.

Not least, I am indebted to Erik Davis, fellow student of the taxonomies of the weird. Given his own friendship with McKenna, and his understanding of TKM's place in the psychedelic surround, as concretized in his benchmark work, *High Weirdness*, Erik was an ideal sounding board for this project—and an ideal choice to write the foreword. Offering incisive commentary on earlier versions of the manuscript, Erik was also kind enough to share his notes on "Crypto-Rap."

Other folks read and provided useful commentary on drafts of the manuscript. The insights of Mitch Mignano, who soldiered on through the manuscript like an embattled textual serf, were many. I thank him for his service. Thanks also to Eric Haanstad and Rick Watson for their valuable comments on parts of the manuscript. Botond Vitos performed excellent work transcribing McKenna's journal "Change and Becoming."

Thanks are due to the MIT Press, principally acquisitions editor Matthew Browne, a courageous figure who saw the merits of this project from the beginning, and also: editorial director Janice Audet, associate managing editor Deborah Cantor-Adams, freelance editor Stephanie Sakson, assistant editor Matt Valades, acquisitions assistant Lorelei Horrell, designer Marge Encomienda, assistant production manager Kate Elwell, art manager Katie Kerr, and publicist Sam Kelly. I would be remiss without acknowledging the anonymous reviewers of the proposal, whom I thank for their encouragement in pushing the boundaries of the possible.

Further gratitude to Professor Rupert Till and Dr. Steven Jan from the University of Huddersfield's Department of Department of Media, Humanities and the Arts, where I was supported by an EU Marie Skłodowska-Curie Actions postdoctoral fellowship from April 2022 to March 2024, and where I was subsequently appointed as a Senior Research Fellow between April 2024 and March 2026.

I never met McKenna, and while an outsider to his immediate family and friend circles, a neutral and unaligned status has aided and enhanced this study. There is an important caveat to this. While this project has enjoyed support and cooperation from McKenna's kin, this is *not* a family-authorized biography. Outside of the opinions that are expressed by various interlocutors, the views expressed are those of the author, for which I remain responsible. While I have performed my best to ensure the absence of factual errors, in the event that errors exist, those are also my responsibility.

While I have done my level best to avoid factual errors and egregious omissions in this work, mistakes and oversights are inevitable. And while I take responsibility for errors, it should be noted that some deficiencies are the likely consequence of material limitations. Since McKenna's journals (besides the one accessed for this project), correspondence, and other materials have not survived (or not yet surfaced), this biography has worked with the materials available. As a result, this work is far from complete, its limitations compounded by the combined issues outlined in the preface. Additionally, while the views of a great many are represented, there are *always* other angles. Such is certainly the case for McKenna, and further documentation of his life is welcome, including work undertaken by future biographers whose efforts will build upon the picture we have today. I am myself working on a further biographical treatment that explores McKenna's strange place in the history of Western esotericism. While *Strange Attractor* is the first biography of McKenna, then, it does not exhaust the word on TKM—or as he himself preferred, "TMK"—with future biographical efforts expected to employ unique templates and focused explorations in the presentation of his life and work. It is then anticipated that this book will serve as a conversation starter for McKennaphiles and scholars.

* * *

Many folks have my gratitude for their support, encouragement, and inspiration. Big upping to my homebase, Jacksonville (RIP), Northcote—and my homies Paulie, Ian H, and Pati—where the bulk of this book was produced during my own personal lockdown in one of the most locked-down cities on the planet—Melbourne—from early 2020 to April 2022. Mad props to Col. W. E. Kurtz, both the original and the K. Svendsen knock-off, for encouragement, morale boosting, and electronic parade-ground banter. Finally, these people are rockstars: Eric J. Haanstad, Michael Urashka, Anna Hurst, Damo Bell, Ray Castle, Ian Rowen, Sammy, Michaela, Sean Marler, Yoyo, Pascal, Lydia, Giorgia Gaia, Adam, Franchesco, Massimo Izzo, Alex Gearin, Emily Wong, Mouse, Nikki, Matthias, Ela, Jules, Ria Hetherington, Tony Hill, Boti, Stu, Joe, Sascha, Juki, Ian Rowan, Paris, nanobrain, Moses, Ronny Carmichael, Martin Williams, Steph, Raven, and Miss Guidance and the Abominable Knowledge Emporium.

Finally, a shout-out to my friend and wanderer of the "backplane" Michael Gosney (a.k.a. Goz), who in April 2020 left the stage to hold eternal salon in the celestial theater. Goz was a San Francisco Bay Area hub and perennial source of enthusiasm who persistently inspired the creative spirit, in me, and whomever had the pleasure to cross his path. A true philosopher hero who won't be resting in peace, Goz is sorely missed.

APPENDIX B: THE McKENNAVERSE

Historians of Terence K. McKenna have at their disposal a substantial oeuvre that owes to its existence several key developments. Published work, film, and recorded spoken-word material comprises a large archive. A first step toward understanding McKenna, the intellect and the persona, requires reckoning with this archive, a daunting situation when considering that in addition to several books and numerous articles (scholarly and press), there exists a plenitude of spoken-word recordings. I begin with this latter material.

While McKenna seemingly held forth in perpetuity, what I name "raps" in this book are recorded public performances. While also developing a talent as a writer, his oratory style as a *stand-up philosopher* afforded McKenna a unique profile. He eventually composed over 250 raps in his career, including public lectures, conference appearances, trialogues, interviews, emceeing, and multiday workshops for specialist audiences. Remarkably, he never gave the same performance twice. Many recordings were originally available on audiocassette and VHS (e.g., by Lux Natura, Sound Photosynthesis, and Big Sur Tapes) and were later for the most part podcasted and/or uploaded to YouTube. Before the advent of the Net, these recordings were prized among collectors, and traded, not unlike the recordings of Grateful Dead shows. Many appearances were not recorded, or recordings have been lost, damaged, or are currently undigitized—though previously unknown, lost, or neglected recordings continue to be uncovered and released, sometimes in the form of remarkable labors of love, such as Paul Chambers's *Beyond the Brain with Terence McKenna*, in which the film footage of one of McKenna's most memorable performances (delivered at Beyond the Brain, Byron Bay, Australia, 1997) was salvaged, remastered, and remixed with event footage after twenty- five years in limbo.[1] Representing his chief means of public communication, McKenna's spoken word material presents a wealth of content for biographers.

I make no claims to total familiarity with this virtual catacomb. I doubt many have accomplished that feat, save perhaps filmmaker Peter Bergmann, who has diligently excavated this material to create documentaries faithful to McKenna's philosophy, boldness, and humor. *The Transcendental Object at the End of Time* (2014) is an epic three-and-a-half-hour videography of McKenna's philosophy of time recreated via a collage of found raps and psychedelic imagery. Bergmann's *Terence McKenna's True Hallucinations* (2016) deploys McKenna's voice from the "talking book," related raps, biographical stills, and the work of visual artists to document the odyssey to La Chorrera and its ripple-like effect.[2] In 2019, Bergmann produced the twelve-part series, *Terence McKenna Digital Revival*, based on recordings made in 1992 in Prague coinciding with the International Transpersonal Association Conference.[3] Another important documenter of McKenna's oratory legacy is Mike Kawitzky, who notably produced *The Terence McKenna Omnibus 2012*, a twelve-part web series, each twelve minutes and twelve seconds in length, of McKenna's lectures at Rustlers Valley in South Africa between October 15 and 21, 1996, packaged into themes and produced and released sequentially in 2012 by Kawitzky. Unpacking ideas presented at Rustlers in which the visitor delivered his greatest hits over a week, this series is among the best condensations of McKenna.[4]

Of the published material, *True Hallucinations: Being an Account of the Author's Extraordinary Adventures in the Devil's Paradise* serves as McKenna's rollicking memoir. The book focuses for the most part on the adventure to (and the "experiment" at) La Chorrera. While first published as an English language paperback in 1993 by Harper, *True Hallucinations* has a long production history. In a letter to Rick Watson on December 30, 1976, the work was introduced as "an autobiographical science fiction novel." Early manuscripts (dated 1977 and 1979) were titled "Down to Earth: Psilocybin and the UFOs," echoing the work's early goal to resolve the "UFO enigma." Under the creative direction and marketing acumen of Faustin Bray and Brian Wallace (Sound Photosynthesis), *True Hallucinations* was originally produced as a "talking book" in 1984, narrated by McKenna himself. *True Hallucinations* offers an important counterpart to *The Invisible Landscape: Mind, Hallucinogens and the I Ching*, the magnum opus coauthored by the brothers and published with The Seabury Press in 1975 (with a revised and updated Harper edition in 1994). I have accessed the earliest manuscript of this work when it was titled "Shamanic Investigations" (1972) (see appendix A). A second co-authored book, a manual, *Psilocybin: Magic Mushroom Grower's Guide*, was published in 1976 under the pseudonyms O. N. Oeric and O. T. Oss (which includes illustrations by Harrison), with And/Or Press, with revised editions published in 1986 by Lux Natura and in 1993 by Quick Trading Press.

There are two other books, both also published in the early nineties. *The Archaic Revival* is a collection of reprinted essays, interviews, lectures, and radio show transcripts with a foreword by noted American novelist Tom Robbins and illustrated throughout with the black and white collages of Satty (Wilfred Podriech). Originally given the working title "A More Perfect Logos" and published in 1991 by Harper with the subtitle *Speculations on Psychedelic Mushrooms, the Amazon, Virtual Reality, UFOs, Evolution, Shamanism, the Rebirth of the Goddess, and the End of History*, the book shepherded McKenna's eighties thoughts on "psychedelic shamanism." *Food of the Gods: The Search for the Original Tree of Knowledge* was published in 1992 by Bantam. A vehicle for a manifesto developed through the eighties, *Food of the Gods* presents the "stoned ape" hypothesis, which McKenna regarded as his most credible contribution to knowledge. With two books and two revised editions appearing within two years, celebrity status was cemented.

This oeuvre is complemented by dozens of articles, book chapters, forewords, and introductions in various publications throughout the eighties and nineties. Many of these publications are transcribed interviews. There are a great many transcribed raps among these publications, including two books produced by Rupert Sheldrake that include selections from the trialogues involving Sheldrake, McKenna, and Ralph Abraham. Additionally, there is a vast archive of press materials, from appearances in obscure zines to coverage in the *New York Times*. My access to this content owes much to the bibliographic and archival labors of McKennaphile collectors, as explained in appendix A. The biographical effort also benefits from the dedication of filmmakers who have documented and featured McKenna, including Edgar Pêra's *Manual of Evasion: LX94* (in which McKenna plays himself), Maxine Rochlin and Morgan Harris's *The Alchemical Dream: Rebirth of the Great Work* (in which McKenna adopts the persona of John Dee), Mike Kawitzky's *Cognition Factor*, and Frank Theys's documentary *TechnoCalyps* (in which McKenna appears as a techno prophet). This material is referenced throughout.

Dennis McKenna's dedication to preserving the memory of his brother has been pivotal. While *The Brotherhood of the Screaming Abyss* naturally focuses on Dennis's life, the book is also an indispensable resource on his brother. Also important for my purposes is the discovery of a variety of primary and previously inaccessible documents that Dennis donated to the Purdue Archives. See appendix A for a list of these materials. As also acknowledged there, I was privileged to consult remnant letters McKenna wrote Rick Watson between 1968 and 1986. These include a letter from Berkeley addressed to Watson in Kathmandu postmarked August 8, 1968, and a chain sent from Berkeley to London pegged in the mid-seventies. The 1968 letter and those from the mid-seventies are noteworthy as they were produced during pivotal trials in McKenna's life. The existential dread and material uncertainty conveyed in the August 1968 letter are echoes of the era. Also layered with anxiety, the mid-seventies correspondence was produced during the period in which the McKennas were experimenting with mushroom cultivation. All the chips were risked on the success of this enterprise. Above all, the letters reveal the close tie between "Terr" and "little Ricky," a bond also evident in a series of unpublished writings and stories Watson shared with me. Pivotal is "Morning Glory," which conveys a formative psychedelic episode in which the teens, aged sixteen and seventeen, ate morning glory seeds in San Francisco in the spring of 1964. This peak moment in their awakening, documented in such scintillating detail by Watson, is here brought to light for the first time. As unique primary materials, these and a host of other correspondences comprise a body of emergent materials that are the source of new and previously unexamined information integral to current and future biographical efforts.

Finally, while biographical sources on McKenna are thin, there are a growing number of relevant scholarly studies. Noteworthy is Erik Davis's *High Weirdness: Drugs, Esoterica and Visionary Experiences in the Seventies*, in which McKenna is foremost among three key figures (also Philip K. Dick and Robert Anton Wilson) whose early seventies epiphanies are excavated. The peak McKennan event in this era is the 1971 experiment at La Chorrera, the high-water mark of a psychedelic form of radical empiricism that Davis calls "weird naturalism." Davis offers a comprehensive analysis of "the experiment" as a symptom of that freak moment in and out of time. If "*freak* embodies the logic of the weird,"[5] then Terence is the shooting star of this calculus. While La Chorrera is integral to the post-sixties freak emergence, the book you're reading begins at the center of the explosion, several years before the trek to Colombia. That is, it begins in Berkeley, in 1965–1966, as McKenna commenced his studies in the Experimental College at UC Berkeley and is introduced to DMT, an explosive encounter shaping his life from that moment forward. This book documents the concatenations and repercussions of that episode, for McKenna, and those he has touched.

NOTES

A complete bibliography (downloadable PDF) of published text and spoken word recording sources referenced in *Strange Attractor* is available at: https://mitpress.mit.edu/strange-attractor (under "Resources").

PREFACE

1. Dennis J. McKenna, *The Brotherhood of the Screaming Abyss: My Life with Terence McKenna* (St. Cloud, MN: North Star Press of St. Cloud, 2012). A revised edition was published with Synergetic Press in 2022.

2. Bearing in mind that according to his oncologist there was no connection between McKenna's condition and his history of cluster headaches.

3. Erik Davis, "Terence McKenna's Ex-Library," February 13, 2007, https://techgnosis.com/terence-mckennas-ex-library.

4. For further details, see appendix A.

5. Rick Watson, email to author, May 2, 2020.

6. Terence McKenna and Ralph Metzner, "Shamanism: Before and Beyond History," The Ojai Foundation, Ojai, CA, 1988, audio available at Deus Ex McKenna ~ Terence McKenna Archive, YouTube, August 3, 2012, https://www.youtube.com/watch?v=LiF-kA_xC30.

7. Terence McKenna, Boulder Statement, 1972. For more details, see appendix A.

8. D. McKenna, *Brotherhood*, 53.

9. Terence McKenna, *True Hallucinations: Being an Account of the Author's Extraordinary Adventures in the Devil's Paradise* (New York: HarperCollins, 1994), 176.

10. T. McKenna, *True Hallucinations*, 186.

11. Sara Hartley, email to author, April 27, 2020.

12. Erik Davis, "Terence McKenna's Last Trip," *Wired*, May 1, 2000, https://www.wired.com/2000/05/mckenna.

13. While the laws regarding psilocybin vary worldwide, prohibition remains the norm, albeit within a new climate of medical opportunism. Since 2018, when the FDA declared psilocybin a "breakthrough therapy" for depression, important steps have been taken toward decriminalization in several US states and cities. When passing Ballot Measure 109 in 2020, Oregon became the first US state to legalize psilocybin, and the first jurisdiction in the world to offer a framework for legal therapeutic use.

14. D. McKenna, *Brotherhood*, 22, 23.

15. Terence McKenna, "What I've Learned from Psychedelics," Entheobotany Conference, Palenque, Mexico, ca. 1994, The Library of Consciousness, https://www.organism.earth/library/document/what-ive-learned-from-psychedelics.

16. Terence McKenna, "Tryptamine Hallucinogens and Consciousness," Lilly/Goswami Conference on Consciousness and Quantum Physics, Esalen Institute, Big Sur, CA, December 1982, audio available at Deus Ex McKenna ~ Terence McKenna Archive, YouTube, July 11, 2011, https://www.youtube.com/watch?v=RUfyMZ5uZL0&t=8s.

17. Terence McKenna, "Understanding and Imagination in the Light of Nature" (day 2: "The Felt Presence of the Other"). Philosophical Research Society, Los Angeles, October 18, 1987, The Library of Consciousness, https://www.organism.earth/library/document/understanding-and-imagination.

18. Charles Hayes, "A Conversation with Terence McKenna," in Charles Hayes, *Tripping: An Anthology of True-Life Psychedelic Adventures* (London: Penguin, 2000), 411–449 (420).

19. Terence McKenna, "How to Talk to Elves," audio available at We Plants Are Happy Plants, YouTube, September 23, 2020, https://www.youtube.com/watch?v=E8ocbqwSzP4.

20. T. McKenna, *True Hallucinations*, 141.

21. Terence McKenna, "History Ends in Green," Esalen Institute, Big Sur, CA, September 1990, The Library of Consciousness, https://www.organism.earth/library/document/history-ends-in-green.

22. Terence McKenna, "In the Valley of Novelty," Omega Institute for Holistic Studies, Rhinebeck, New York, July 31–August 2, 1998, The Library of Consciousness, https://www.organism.earth/library/document/valley-of-novelty; T. McKenna, "History Ends in Green."

23. Watkins's concerns are outlined in Matthew Watkins, "Autopsy for a Mathematical Hallucination?," ca. 1996, https://www.fourmilab.ch/rpkp/autopsy.html.

24. Erik Davis, *High Weirdness: Drugs, Esoterica and Visionary Experiences in the Seventies* (London: Strange Attractor Press/MIT Press, 2019), 167.

25. Rick Watson, email to author, April 22, 2020.

Notes to Chapter 1

26. T. McKenna, "In the Valley of Novelty."

27. T. McKenna, *True Hallucinations*, 179.

28. Laddie Livingston, email to author, November 11, 2021.

29. Terence McKenna, "Hallucinogens: Before and After Psychology" (or "Monkeys Discover Hyperspace"), Psychedelic Conference II, University of California Santa Barbara, May 14, 1983, The Library of Consciousness, https://www.organism.earth/library/document/hallucinogens-before-and-after-psychology.

30. Richard Doyle, *Darwin's Pharmacy: Sex, Plants and the Evolution of the Noosphere* (Washington, DC: University of Washington Press, 2011), 219.

31. T. McKenna, *True Hallucinations*, 120.

32. Terence McKenna and Dennis McKenna, *The Invisible Landscape: Mind, Hallucinogens and the I Ching* (New York: The Seabury Press, 1975), 12.

INTRODUCTION

1. T. McKenna, "Understanding and Imagination in the Light of Nature" (day 2).

2. T. McKenna, "Understanding and Imagination in the Light of Nature" (day 2).

3. Terence McKenna, "The Edge Runner," Santa Fe, NM, May 1990, The Library of Consciousness, https://www.organism.earth/library/document/the-edge-runner.

4. T. McKenna, *True Hallucinations*, 98–99.

5. Douglas Hansen, email to author, October 13, 2021.

6. Rick Watson, email to author, January 14, 2024.

7. Christy Silness, Zoom interview by author, December 10, 2021.

8. In Don Lattin, *Changing Our Minds: Psychedelic Sacraments and the New Psychotherapy* (Santa Fe, NM: Synergetic Press 2017), 209.

CHAPTER 1

1. Terence McKenna, "Under the Teaching Tree," The Ojai Foundation, Ojai, CA, ca. 1992, audio available at The Terence McKenna Journey, YouTube, May 4, 2014, https://www.youtube.com/watch?v=-YT78KZzCR0; T. McKenna, "Understanding and Imagination in the Light of Nature" (day 2); Paul Chambers, *Beyond the Brain with Terence McKenna*, recorded at Beyond the Brain, the Epicenter, Byron Bay, Australia, 1997 (photography by Jenny Lusk, 2023), https://www.youtube.com/watch?v=igKsd3uNgHY&t=44s.

2. Chambers, *Beyond the Brain with Terence McKenna*.

3. In Richard Gehr, "Omega Man: A Profile of Terence McKenna," *Village Voice*, April 5, 1992, www.levity.com/rubric/mckenna.html.

4. William S. Burroughs, *The Letters of William S. Burroughs, 1945–1959*, ed. Oliver Harris (New York: Penguin, 1994), 179–180.

5. T. McKenna, "Under the Teaching Tree"; Gehr, "Omega Man."

6. T. McKenna, "How to Talk to Elves."

7. T. McKenna, "Under the Teaching Tree."

8. Stu Carlson, "The Churches of Delta County—Sacred Spaces," *High Country Shopper*, June 2, 2020.

9. Terence McKenna, in Sukie Miller, "Interview: Terence McKenna," *Omni* 15, no. 7 (1993): 69–92 (70).

10. D. McKenna, *Brotherhood*, 147, 12.

11. Mark Kenaston, "The Bodhi Tree Interview: Psychedelics, Shamanism, and the Vegetable Mind," *Bodhi Tree Bookstore*, no. 5 (Spring 1993): 3–7. https://web.archive.org/web/20110201150304/http://www.bodhitree.com/node/497.

12. D. McKenna, *Brotherhood*, 34, 81.

13. Dennis devotes a chapter to "The Nobody People." See D. McKenna, *Brotherhood*, 47–50.

14. D. McKenna, *Brotherhood*, 481.

15. D. McKenna, *Brotherhood*, 34–35.

16. Terence McKenna, "Childhood Stories," audio available at We Plants Are Happy Plants, YouTube, June 25, 2021, https://www.youtube.com/watch?v=dVtnZ5r9Bt8&t=21s.

17. D. McKenna, *Brotherhood*, 59.

18. Terence McKenna, "Alien Footprints: Leprechauns, Elves, or Dead Souls?" Esalen Institute, CA, May 1993, audio available at Deus Ex McKenna ~ Terence McKenna Archive, YouTube, January 10, 2015, https://www.youtube.com/watch?v=lQx-MlpZotw.

19. Ron Curry, Zoom interview by author, September 7, 2020.

20. T. McKenna, "Alien Footprints."

21. Terence McKenna, "Psychedelic Skepticism," Whole Life Expo, Austin, TX, Fall 1996, audio available at Jonathan Laliberte, YouTube, February 13, 2017, https://www.youtube.com/watch?v=qGGBvzJ7NIE&t=952s.

22. Ron Curry, Zoom interview by author, September 7, 2020.

23. Ron Curry, Zoom interview by author, September 7, 2020.

24. Dennis McKenna, "The Experiment at La Chorrera: Psychotic Dissociation, Shamanic Initiation, Or Alien Abduction?" Breaking Convention, July 1, 2017, University of Greenwich, London.

25. Terence McKenna, "Taxonomy of Illusion," University of California Santa Cruz, Santa Cruz, CA, 1993, The Library of Consciousness, https://www.organism.earth/library/document/taxonomy-of-illusion.

26. Terence McKenna, "A Tribute to Aldous Huxley on the 100th Anniversary of His Birth," closing speech at Julia Richmond High School auditorium, 317 East 67th Street, New York City, April 30, 1994, New York Open Center (digitized by J. Christian Greer from a tape recording in the private archives of Erik Davis).

27. Terence McKenna, "Foreword," in Laura Archera Huxley, *This Timeless Moment: A Personal View of Aldous Huxley*, illustrated and revised edition (Berkeley, CA: Celestial Arts, 2000), xi–xv (xii, xiii).

28. Terence McKenna, "Alchemy and the Hermetic Corpus" (transcribed as "Lectures on Alchemy"), Esalen Institute, Big Sur, CA, May 1991, https://medium.com/@Ayahuasca_yage/lectures-on-alchemy-with-terence-mckenna-e7a81430aae7.

29. Carl Jung, *Psychology and Alchemy*, 2nd ed., translated by R. F. C. Hull (London: Routledge, 1968 [1944]), 67, 65.

30. T. McKenna, "Alchemy and the Hermetic Corpus."

31. Jay Levin, "In Praise of Psychedelics," *LA Weekly*, May 20–26, 1988, 18.

32. T. McKenna, "Psychedelic Skepticism."

33. Hayes, "A Conversation with Terence McKenna," 422. Elizabeth Hansen offers an informed response to this claim: "Technically he can only lay claim to being a Scorpio. His sun is in Scorpio, his moon is not, and we do not know what his rising sign is as we do not have a confirmed birth time. He does, however, have an emphasis in Scorpio by virtue of his Scorpio stellium . . . whether or not it is in the 12th house is not confirmed without an exact birth time" (email to author, January 26, 2022).

34. Terence McKenna, "Our Cyberspiritual Future," Esalen, Big Sur, CA, August 1997, The Library of Consciousness, https://www.organism.earth/library/document/our-cyberspiritual-future.

35. Terence McKenna, "Appreciating Imagination," Esalen, Big Sur, CA, 1997, The Library of Consciousness, https://www.organism.earth/library/document/appreciating-imagination.

36. Ron Curry, Zoom interview by author, September 7, 2020.

37. Terence McKenna, "Ethnobotany of Shamanism," California Institute of Integral Studies, San Francisco, CA, November 4–6, 1988, 1, https://transcendentalobject.files.wordpress.com/2017/07/ethnobotany.pdf.

38. T. McKenna, "The Edge Runner."

39. T. McKenna, *True Hallucinations*, 4.

40. D. McKenna, *Brotherhood*, 86.

41. Michael Malcolm, email to author, August 13, 2018.

42. D. McKenna, *Brotherhood*, 85.

43. Terence McKenna, letter to Tim A. Cannon, October 7, 1962.

44. Terence McKenna, letter to Tim A. Cannon, February 18, 1963.

45. Robert Forte and Nina Graboi, "The Archaic Revival: An Interview with Terence McKenna," in Robert Forte, ed., *Timothy Leary: Outside Looking In: Appreciations, Castigations, and Reminiscences* (Rochester, VT: Park Street Press, 1999): 142–154 (143).

46. T. McKenna, "Ethnobotany of Shamanism," 2.

47. Forte and Graboi, "The Archaic Revival," 143.

48. T. McKenna, "Alien Footprints."

49. D. McKenna, *Brotherhood*, 86.

50. Rick Watson, email to author, May 11, 2021; D. McKenna, email to author, May 13, 2021.

51. And nor are we likely to know more, given Kris Hutchins was killed in a car accident in 2019.

52. Terence McKenna, Fairmont Banquet Address, delivered at Angels, Aliens, and Archetypes Conference, San Francisco, CA, November 21, 1987.

53. D. McKenna, *Brotherhood*, 32.

54. Rick Watson, interview by author, July 25, 2018.

55. T. McKenna, "A Tribute to Aldous Huxley."

56. Rick Watson, "John Parker," unpublished writing, March 4–6, 1993.

57. Douglas Hansen, email to author, October 13, 2021.

58. Douglas Hansen, email to author, October 13, 2021.

59. Douglas Hansen, emails to author, March 2 and October 13, 2021.

60. David Wallin, Zoom interview by author, May 20, 2021.

61. Nina Wise, Zoom interview by author, March 16, 2021.

62. T. McKenna, "Under the Teaching Tree."

63. Rick Watson, email to author, July 25, 2018. The narrative also possibly blends elements of earlier (Paonia 1963) and later (Mojave 1964/65) experiences with morning glories and bindweed.

64. All citations here and immediately below from Rick Watson, "Morning Glory," unpublished short story, 1990.

65. Aldous Huxley, "The Pros and Cons, History and Future Possibilities of Vision-Inducing Psychochemicals: A Philosopher's Visionary Prediction," *Playboy*, November 1963, 84–88, 175–177, and 179 (179, 175, 177).

66. Ido Hartogsohn, *American Trip: Set, Setting, and the Psychedelic Experience in the Twentieth Century* (Cambridge, MA: MIT Press, 2020), 153.

67. Rick Watson, email to author, August 1, 2018.

68. "Elder Interviews: Jim Fadiman, 1998 Part 1," https://gwyllm.com/2020/04/28/elder-interviews-jim-fadiman-1998-part-1.

69. Watson, "Morning Glory." Quotes in the following passage are from the same source. Approached by Watson fifty-four years later, Fadiman had no recall of encountering the young Watson and McKenna, but he was delighted to confirm that it had to have been him. It is ironic that a researcher associated with the early adoption of LSD microdosing and "selective enhancement" bore such influence on the promoter of the "heroic dose."

70. Elizabeth Hansen, email to author, December 2, 2020.

71. Kenaston, "The Bodhi Tree Interview."

72. T. McKenna, "Ethnobotany of Shamanism," 2.

73. T. McKenna, "Our Cyberspiritual Future."

74. D. McKenna, *Brotherhood*, 95.

75. Rick Watson, interview by author, July 25, 2018.

76. Rick Watson, "Bryant Street," unpublished writing, n.d.

77. Rick Watson, interview by author, July 25, 2018.

78. Watson, "Bryant Street."

79. Tom Wolfe, *The Electric Kool-Aid Acid Test* (London: Black Swan, 1993 [1968]), 163.

80. Rick Watson, interview by author, July 25, 2018.

81. Rick Watson, "DMT, or, Spider Woman Comes to Town," unpublished short story, April 16–17, 1993.

82. Rick Watson, interview by author, July 25, 2018.

83. Wolfe, *The Electric Kool-Aid Acid Test*, 101.

84. Rick Watson, email to author, February 28, 2015.

85. Torgoff, for example, writes about a "fifty-five-gallon drum of pure crystal DMT at Stanford that was headed for the army arsenal at Edgewood, Maryland." See Martin Torgoff, *Can't Find My Way Home: America in the Great Stoned Age, 1945–2000* (New York: Simon & Schuster, 2005), 412.

86. Watson, "DMT, or, Spider Woman Comes to Town"; Rick Watson, email to author, February 28, 2015.

87. T. McKenna, "Our Cyberspiritual Future."

CHAPTER 2

1. Michael Malcolm, email to author, August 13, 2018.

2. George Csicsery, email to author, August 17, 2020.

3. George Csicsery, email to author, August 22, 2020.

4. Elizabeth Hansen, email to author, December 30, 2020.

5. Douglas Hansen, email to author, March 3, 2021.

6. Kevin Mahoney, Zoom interview by author, August 29, 2020.

7. T. McKenna, "Under the Teaching Tree"; T. McKenna, "Our Cyberspiritual Future."

8. Hayes, "A Conversation with Terence McKenna," 414.

9. Possibly Mo's Grill, 1322 Grant Avenue, North Beach.

10. Hayes, "A Conversation with Terence McKenna," 416.

11. Hayes, "A Conversation with Terence McKenna," 416.

12. Kenaston, "The Bodhi Tree Interview."

13. Hayes, "A Conversation with Terence McKenna," 417.

14. T. McKenna, "Psychedelic Skepticism."

15. Forte and Graboi, "The Archaic Revival," 153.

16. Kevin Mahoney, Zoom interview by author, August 29, 2020.

17. Rick Watson, email to author, April 20, 2020.

18. Rick Watson, "Marijuana," unpublished writing, n.d.

19. T. McKenna, "Ethnobotany of Shamanism," 17.

20. Terence McKenna, "Exploring the Hermetic Tradition," New York Open Center, Spring St., New York, March 22, 1992, audio available at Deus Ex McKenna ~ Terence

McKenna Archive, YouTube. July 10, 2011, https://www.youtube.com/watch?v=-YNdBpYh1eA. This "high water weirdness event" is narrated with accompanying animation in Peter Bergmann's 2014 videography, *The Transcendental Object at the End of Time*, available at We Plants Are Happy Plants, YouTube, November 16, 2014, https://www.youtube.com/watch?v=aAlaRdrcQcY, at 2:21:57.

21. Douglas Hansen, email to author, March 2, 2021.

22. It was the end of an era. In 1968, the house at 2894 and the surrounding Telegraph properties were torn down to make way for a Bank of America office building and car park.

23. T. McKenna, *True Hallucinations*, 20.

24. Sara Hartley, email to author, April 27–28, 2020.

25. T. McKenna, "Alchemy and the Hermetic Corpus."

26. Harry Kreisler, "Joseph Tussman: Education and Citizenship," Conversations with History, Institute of International Studies, UC Berkeley, 2000, https://iis.berkeley.edu/publications/joseph-tussman-education-and-citizenship.

27. George Csicsery, email to author, August 18, 2020.

28. D. McKenna, *Brotherhood*, 101.

29. Kreisler, "Joseph Tussman: Education and Citizenship."

30. Terence McKenna, "Anarchy Is the Ideal," December 1989, audio available at Deus Ex McKenna ~ Terence McKenna Archive, YouTube, January 8, 2017, https://www.youtube.com/watch?v=MpdvAfSpdsM.

31. D. McKenna, *Brotherhood*, 161.

32. D. McKenna, *Brotherhood*, 101; George Csicsery, email to author, August 18, 2020.

33. From a recommendation letter signed by Joseph Tussman, University of California, ca. 1967, as seen in the documentary *Terence McKenna's True Hallucinations* (2016) by Peter Bergmann, We Plants Are Happy Plants, YouTube, https://www.youtube.com/watch?v=8MG5gFtZ3U8.

34. T. McKenna, "Exploring the Hermetic Tradition."

35. A sample from Funkopath, "Skwirm," on twelve-inch *Skwirm* (2-13 Records, 1997).

36. T. McKenna, "The Edge Runner."

37. Terence McKenna, "The Future of Magic in Electronic Societies," Summer Project, Tussman Plan, University of California, Berkeley, ca. 1966, 13, i, 46, 29 (McKenna papers, MSP 213, Box 2, Folder 10, Purdue Archives).

38. Adopting a phrase from Mircea Eliade, *Cosmos and History: The Myth of the Eternal Return*, translated from the French by Willard R. Trask (Princeton, NJ: Princeton University Press, 1954).

39. "The Future of Magic in Electronic Societies," 39, 30, 29.

40. I will provide a comprehensive coverage of the influence of Jung, Eliade, and McLuhan on McKenna in a future work.

41. Terence McKenna, "Sacred Plants as Guides: New Dimensions of the Soul," address to the Jung Society, Claremont, CA, 1991, video available at Terence Talks, YouTube, March 6, 2015, https://www.youtube.com/watch?v=2lIwkbFWHZw.

42. Terence McKenna, "Search for the Original Tree of Knowledge," Boulder, CO, May 29–31, 1992, The Library of Consciousness, https://www.organism.earth/library/document/food-of-the-gods.

43. In Nevill Drury, "Sacred Plants and Mystic Realities: An Interview with Terence McKenna," *Nature & Health* 11, no. 1 (Fall 1990): 6–13 (8).

44. In Rupert Sheldrake, Terence McKenna, and Ralph Abraham, *Chaos, Creativity and Cosmic Consciousness* (Rochester, VT: Park Street Press, 2001 [1992]), 47.

45. C. G. Jung, *Memories, Dreams, Reflections*, recorded and edited by Aniela Jaffé, translated by Clara Winston and Richard Winston (New York: Vintage Books, 1989 [1963]), 222.

46. See D. J. Moores, "Dancing the Wild Divine: Drums, Drugs, and Individuation," *Journal of Jungian Scholarly Studies* 15, no. 1 (2020): 64–83; Scott J. Hill, *Confrontation with the Unconscious: Jungian Depth Psychology and Psychedelic Experience* (London: Muswell Hill, 2013).

47. Terence McKenna, "Unfolding the Stone: Making and Unmaking History and Language," Wilshire Ebell Theater, Los Angeles, CA, June 1, 1991, The Library of Consciousness, https://www.organism.earth/library/document/unfolding-the-stone.

48. Eliade, *Cosmos and History*; Mircea Eliade, *The Sacred and the Profane: The Nature of Religion*, translated from the French by W. R. Trask (New York: Harcourt, Brace & World, 1959); Mircea Eliade, *Shamanism: Archaic Techniques of Ecstasy*, translated from the French by W. R. Trask (London: Routledge and Kegan Paul, 1964).

49. Eliade, *The Sacred and the Profane*, 17 (emphasis in original).

50. Terence McKenna, *Food of the Gods: The Search for the Original Tree of Knowledge* (New York: Bantam Books, 1992), 120.

51. Michael Taussig, *Shamanism, Colonialism, and the Wild Man: A Study in Terror and Healing* (Chicago, University of Chicago Press: 1987); Terence McKenna, "Into the Heart of Darkness" [review of Michael Taussig, *Shamanism, Colonialism and the Wild Man*], *Gnosis Magazine* 5 (1987): 45.

52. Marshall McLuhan, *Understanding Media: The Extensions of Man* (New York: McGraw-Hill, 1964), 80.

53. Terence McKenna, "Marshall McLuhan, the Cognitive Agent, a Cyberpunk Godfather," *Mondo 2000*, no. 1 (1989), 48–49 (48).

54. T. McKenna, "Marshall McLuhan," 49.

55. Eric Norden, "Playboy Interview: Marshall McLuhan, A Candid Conversation with the High Priest of Popcult and Metaphysician of Media," *Playboy* (March 1969), 66.

56. Rick Watson, email to author, February 26, 2015.

57. Fitz Hugh Ludlow, *The Hasheesh Eater: Being Passages from the Life of a Pythagorean* (New Brunswick, NJ: Rutgers University Press, 2006), 28.

58. Paschal Beverly Randolph, "Boston Spiritual Conference," *Banner of Light* 8, no 13 (December 22, 1860): 8, in John Patrick Deveney, *Paschal Beverly Randolph: A Nineteenth-Century Black American Spiritualist, Rosicrucian, and Sex Magician* (Albany: SUNY Press, 1997): 416, note 14.

59. Terence McKenna, "Global Perspectives and Psychedelic Poetics," New York, 1993, The Library of Consciousness, https://www.organism.earth/library/document/global-perspectives-and-psychedelic-poetics.

60. T. McKenna, "Understanding and Imagination in the Light of Nature" (day 2).

61. Hayes, "A Conversation with Terence McKenna," 421.

62. T. McKenna, "Understanding and Imagination in the Light of Nature" (day 2).

63. Will Noffke with Terence McKenna, "A Conversation over Saucers," *Revision: The Journal of Consciousness and Transformation* 11, no. 3 (Winter 1989): 23–30 (25).

64. Terence McKenna, "Surfing on *Finnegans Wake*," Esalen Institute, Big Sur, CA, 1995, https://transcendentalobject.files.wordpress.com/2017/07/finneganswake.pdf.

65. Vladimir Alexandrov, *Nabokov's Otherworld* (Princeton, NJ: Princeton University Press, 1991), 3.

66. Terence McKenna, "Understanding the Chaos at History's End," Esalen Institute, Big Sur, CA, June 23, 1989, The Library of Consciousness, https://www.organism.earth/library/document/understanding-the-chaos-at-historys-end.

67. Terence McKenna, "Hot Concepts and Melting Edges," Esalen Institute, Big Sur, CA, December 1994, The Library of Consciousness, https://www.organism.earth/library/document/hot-concepts-and-melting-edges; Terence McKenna, "Rap Dancing into the 3rd Millennium," Starwood XIV Festival, Brushwood Folklore Center, Sherman, NY, July 23, 1994, The Library of Consciousness, https://www.organism.earth/library/document/rap-dancing-into-the-third-millennium.

68. T. McKenna, "Hot Concepts and Melting Edges," 1994.

69. Terence McKenna, "Post Electric Thought," unpublished manuscript, Seychelles, Berkeley, and Tokyo, 1968–1970, 94, 95.

70. T. McKenna, "Understanding and Imagination in the Light of Nature" (day 2).

71. T. McKenna, "Exploring the Hermetic Tradition."

72. Terence McKenna, "Having Archaic and Eating It Too," weekend workshop, The Open Center, Spring St, New York City, October 13–14, 1990.

73. T. McKenna, "Having Archaic."

74. Stephanie is named "Elaine" in *Brotherhood*.

75. Terence McKenna, "Places I Have Been," Hermosa Beach, Los Angeles, CA, May 15, 1988, audio available at Humble Primate, YouTube, April 23, 2021, https://www.youtube.com/watch?v=ZdTQNxEVee4.

76. Terence McKenna, interviewed by Virginia Boston, October 16, 1991. Recording courtesy of Rick Watson.

77. Harrison eventually completed a BA in art, specializing in botanical illustration, and years later a master's in health arts and sciences, specializing in ethnobotany.

78. Nina Wise, Zoom interview by author, March 16, 2021.

79. Kathleen Harrison, email to author, June 26, 2022.

80. Kathleen Harrison, interview by author, September 25, 2019.

81. T. McKenna, "Places I Have Been."

82. Terence McKenna, "Personal Stories," audio available at We Plants Are Happy Plants, YouTube, October 27, 2017, https://www.youtube.com/watch?v=-usWe5iOmPM.

83. Erik Davis, Terence McKenna interview, McKenna's house, Big Island, Hawaii, November 1999, The Library of Consciousness, https://www.organism.earth/library/document/interview-with-erik-davis.

84. D. McKenna, *Brotherhood*, 177.

85. T. McKenna and Metzner, "Shamanism."

86. T. McKenna and Metzner, "Shamanism."

87. Terence McKenna, interviewed by Virginia Boston, October 16, 1991.

88. Joanna Symons, "Seychelles: Life's a Breeze Near the Equator," *Telegraph.co.uk*, March 25, 2005.

89. T. McKenna, Boulder Statement.

90. T. McKenna, *True Hallucinations*, 19, 20.

91. Terence McKenna, "Crypto-Rap: Meta-Electrical Speculations on Culture," unpublished manuscript, 1968, 67, 56.

92. Davis, *High Weirdness*, 95.

93. D. McKenna, *Brotherhood*, 161.

94. Kevin Mahoney, Zoom interview by author, August 29, 2020.

95. Ron Curry, Zoom interview by author, September 9, 2020.

96. Kathleen Harrison, interview by author, September 25, 2019.

97. Nina Wise, Zoom interview by author, March 16, 2021.

98. Kathleen Harrison, interview by author, September 25, 2019.

99. Nina Wise, Zoom interview by author, March 16, 2021.

100. T. McKenna, *True Hallucinations*, 20.

101. Terence McKenna, letter to Rick Watson, August 8, 1968.

102. Sara Hartley, email to author, April 27, 2020.

103. T. McKenna, *True Hallucinations*, xii.

104. Sara Hartley, email to author, June 26, 2020.

105. Ron Curry, Zoom interview by author, September 9, 2020.

106. George Csicsery, email to author, 17 August 17, 2020.

107. Terence McKenna, "San Francisco State Strikes 1968," audio available at We Plants Are Happy Plants, YouTube, February 19, 2018, https://www.youtube.com/watch?v=DpqUn_szhhU.

108. Ron Curry, Zoom interview by author, September 9, 2020.

109. T. McKenna, "Post Electric Thought," 103.

110. Terence McKenna, "Terence McKenna," in *After All These Years: Sixties Ideals in a Different World*, ed. Lauren Kessler (New York: Thunder's Mouth Press, 1990), 203–207 (203).

111. T. McKenna, letter to Rick Watson, August 8, 1968.

112. McKenna indeed wired $500 to Watson's account, as Watson stated to his parents poste restante, in September 1968.

113. T. McKenna, letter to Rick Watson, August 8, 1968.

114. T. McKenna, letter to Rick Watson, August 8, 1968.

115. Rick Watson, email to author, April 21, 2020.

116. T. McKenna, letter to Rick Watson, August 8, 1968.

117. T. McKenna, interview by Virginia Boston, October 16, 1991.

118. T. McKenna, "Places I Have Been."

119. Ron Curry, Zoom interview by author, September 9, 2020.

CHAPTER 3

1. Rick Watson, email to author, April 21, 2020.

2. Rick Watson, "Richard Horn," unpublished writing, 1993.

3. Mark Liechty, *Far Out: Countercultural Seekers and the Tourist Encounter in Nepal* (Chicago: University of Chicago Press, 2017), 4, 13.

4. Rick Watson, letter from Kathmandu, Nepal, to Michael Moore, ca April 1968; Rick Watson, letter from Kathmandu, Nepal, to Michael Moore, ca. September 1968.

5. Watson, "Richard Horn."

6. Horn died from unknown causes in 1973. The manuscript for his second novel was either never completed, lost, or stolen. Rick Watson, "Richard Horn II," unpublished writing, April 3, 1993.

7. Watson, "Richard Horn."

8. T. McKenna, Boulder Statement.

9. T. McKenna, Boulder Statement.

10. T. McKenna, letter to Nina Wise, June 8, 1969.

11. From the postcard: "Just wandering around leaving Seychelles tomorrow to try to connect with W.P.W. in Benares. We are planning on a trek to the Himalayas although where exactly is not clear. . . . Keep your head together, it's the year of the Jackpot, you know. Love McK."

12. T. McKenna, Boulder Statement.

13. Watson, "Richard Horn."

14. T. McKenna, letter to Nina Wise, June 8, 1969.

15. T. McKenna, letter to Nina Wise, June 8, 1969.

16. T. McKenna, letter to Nina Wise, July 19, 1969, posted from the American consulate in Kathmandu, Nepal.

17. T. McKenna, letter to Nina Wise, July 19, 1969.

18. T. McKenna, *True Hallucinations*, 55.

19. Tim Leary, Richard Alpert, and Ralph Metzner, *The Psychedelic Experience: A Manual Based on the Tibetan Book of the Dead* (Sacramento, CA: Citadel Press, 1964).

20. In Drury, "Sacred Plants and Mystic Realities," 8.

21. T. McKenna, *True Hallucinations*, 57.

22. Rick Watson, email to author, April 22, 2020.

23. Roger Williams, email to author, October 7, 2024.

24. T. McKenna, *True Hallucinations*, 61.

25. Ralph Abraham and Terence McKenna, "Dynamics of Hyperspace," Santa Cruz, CA, 1983, http://www.ralph-abraham.org/talks/transcripts/hyperspace.html.

26. T. McKenna, *True Hallucinations*, 63.

27. T. McKenna, *True Hallucinations*, 61.

28. This description and associated lines derive from the opening scene, "A Violet Psychofluid," in the treatment of "Down to Earth," produced by Sheila Humphrey, April 1986 (pp. 2–3), based on Terence's original "Down to Earth" screenplay, n.d. (from "Down to Earth: Story Breakdown and Draft"). The scene is a dramatic embellishment on what is presented in the text of *True Hallucinations*, where the redhead does find Terence unaccountably in her "knickers," although the embarrassing public interface is avoided. Dire Straits' "Skateaway" is among the soundtracks included in the notes of the "Down to Earth" screenplay.

29. T. McKenna, "Understanding and Imagination in the Light of Nature" (day 2).

30. Terence McKenna, "Morning Lecture," Entheobotany Conference, Palenque, Mexico, 1994, audio available at We Plants Are Happy Plants, YouTube, September 24, 2021, https://www.youtube.com/watch?v=oKtR5o1X_NQ&t=2599s.

31. T. McKenna, "Ethnobotany of Shamanism," 14.

32. T. McKenna, "History Ends in Green."

33. Rick Watson, emails to author, April 25 and 21, 2020.

34. Michael Malcolm, email to author, August 13, 2018.

35. Rick Watson, interview by author, July 25, 2018.

36. Rick Watson, emails to author, April 20, 2020, and August 7, 2021.

37. Anon., "Four Arraigned Following Glenwood Narcotics Arrest," *Daily Sentinel*, August 18, 1969.

38. D. McKenna, *Brotherhood*, 178.

39. D. McKenna, *Brotherhood*, 192.

40. Kevin Mahoney, emails to author, September 9 and 15, 2020.

41. Sara Hartley, email to author, September 4, 2020.

42. Kevin Mahoney, email to author, September 15, 2020.

43. Sara Hartley, email to author, September 3 and 15, 2020.

44. D. McKenna, email to author, July 8, 2020.

45. Bill Cole, email to author, May 24, 2021.

46. D. McKenna, *Brotherhood*, 193, 195.

47. Kevin Mahoney, Zoom interview by author, August 29, 2020.

48. Bill Cole, email to author, July 1, 2023.

49. Bill Cole, Zoom interview by author, December 15, 2020. Information verified by US District Court, District of Colorado, Criminal Case File: 69-CR-264 (retrieved from NARA at Denver).

50. "United States v. Terence McKenna and Richard Levinson," US District Court, Southern District of New York, November 2, 1970 (Criminal Case File: 70-CR-905, retrieved from NARA at Kansas City).

51. "United States v. Henry Roy Landesberg and Richard Levinson," US District Court, Southern District of New York, November 5, 1971, filed on January 28, 1972, pp. 13, 3–4 (Criminal Case File: 71-CR-1088, retrieved from NARA at Kansas City).

52. D. McKenna, *Brotherhood*, 200.

53. D. McKenna, *Brotherhood*, 109.

54. Mark Liechty, email to author, September 12, 2024.

55. Rick Watson, email to author, April 20, 2020.

56. Rick Watson, letter from Taipei to Michael Moore, December 1969.

57. Rick Watson, email to author, April 21, 2020.

58. Sara Hartley, emails to author, September 16 and April 28, 2020.

59. Kevin Mahoney, email to author, September 9, 2020.

60. Tama Starr, email to author, August 12, 2021.

61. Rick Watson, email to author, April 24, 2020.

62. D. McKenna, *Brotherhood*, 53.

63. Kevin Mahoney, Zoom interview by author, August 29, 2020.

64. Terence McKenna, "Nature Is the Center of the Mandala," Shared Visions Bookstore, Berkeley, CA, September 12, 1987, The Library of Consciousness, https://www.organism.earth/library/document/nature-is-the-center-of-the-mandala.

65. Romeo Darby and Skylaire Alfvegren, "But in the Meantime, We Have a Talk with Terence McKenna," *Ben Is Dead*, no. 27 (1996): 35–37 (37). According to Dennis, a wealthy Japanese broker "subsidized Terence's collecting efforts" in Indonesia (D. McKenna, *Brotherhood*, 309).

66. T. McKenna, Boulder Statement.

67. D. McKenna, *Brotherhood*, 207.

68. T. McKenna, "Terence McKenna Speaks . . . (Part II)," transcribed from "Splat," the Allchemical Arts Conference, September 1999, *The Entheogen Review* 9, no. 2 (Autumnal Equinox 2000): 14–19 (18–19).

69. John Szwed, *Cosmic Scholar: The Life and Times of Harry Smith* (New York: Farrar, Straus & Giroux, 2023), 244.

70. T. McKenna, "Terence McKenna Speaks." 18–19.

71. T. McKenna, "Ethnobotany of Shamanism," 3.

72. Rick Watson, email to author, May 10, 2021.

73. Klea McKenna, *The Butterfly Hunter* (San Francisco: Edition One Books, 2008).

74. K. McKenna, *The Butterfly Hunter*, n.p.

75. T. McKenna, *True Hallucinations*, 179.

76. T. McKenna, Boulder Statement.

77. T. McKenna, *True Hallucinations*, 179.

78. T. McKenna, *True Hallucinations*, 189.

79. In Drury, "Sacred Plants and Mystic Realities," 8. He may have planned this trip, but I have seen no evidence that McKenna visited Ternate. The island achieved notoriety due to the so-called Ternate essay, a paper Wallace privately shared with Darwin that outlined the mechanics of an evolutionary divergence of species due to environmental pressures paralleling Darwin's theory of "natural selection."

80. Alfred Russel Wallace, *The Malay Archipelago* (Singapore: Periplus Editions, n.d. [1869]), 213.

81. T. McKenna, Boulder Statement.

82. This story is related in "The Butterfly Guru," a short story found in Terence's "old digital files," and dated June 8, 1990. Published in K. McKenna, *The Butterfly Hunter*, n.p.

83. Wallace, *The Malay Archipelago*, 178.

84. T. McKenna, "The Butterfly Guru."

85. A passage from "The Butterfly Guru," just before the text became unsalvageable.

86. A friend of Dhyana, Inn soon founded the Inner Research Institute, the oldest and largest school of T'ai Chi Ch'uan in San Francisco.

87. Terry Reid, email to author, August 27, 2022.

88. T. McKenna, *True Hallucinations*, 18.

89. Terry Reid, emails to author, August 27 and September 26, 2022.

90. T. McKenna, *True Hallucinations*, 18.

91. Terence McKenna, "The Evolution of a Psychedelic Thinker," Esalen Institute, Big Sur, CA, June, 1989, The Library of Consciousness, https://www.organism.earth/library/document/evolution-of-a-psychedelic-thinker.

92. T. McKenna, "Post Electric Thought," 138. "Post Electric Thought" is a revision of 1968 manuscript "Crypto-Rap: Meta-Electrical Speculations on Culture." "Crypto-Rap" had itself drawn influence from McKenna's 1966 dissertation, "The Future of Magic in Electronic Societies." Since the document represents McKenna's final word on the subject of "holo-electric culture," "Post Electric Thought" is the manuscript version I draw upon here (see appendix A for more details).

93. T. McKenna, "Post Electric Thought," v, 138, 103, 46.

94. T. McKenna, "Crypto-Rap," i.

95. Such are similarly observed by Davis (*High Weirdness*, 2019: 95–102) in his evaluation of the earlier "Crypto-Rap."

96. James W. Carey and John J. Quirk, "The Mythos of the Electronic Revolution" [Part II], *American Scholar* 39, no. 3 (Summer 1970): 395–424 [396].

97. T. McKenna, "Post Electric Thought," 136, 96, 35, 5.

98. A footnote is included acknowledging Syd Barrett's "The Gnome," from Pink Floyd's 1967 debut album *The Piper at the Gates of Dawn*. The line "Another way for gnomes to say, Ooooooh my," from "The Gnome," will later serve to inspire the chorus line of the machine elves of hyperspace.

99. T. McKenna, "Post Electric Thought," i, ii.

100. See Erik Davis, *Technosis: Myth, Magic, and Mysticism in the Age of Information* (New York: Three Rivers Press, 1998).

101. T. McKenna, "Post Electric Thought," 102, 32, 102.

102. T. McKenna, "Post Electric Thought," 136.

103. T. McKenna, "Post Electric Thought," i.

104. T. McKenna, "Post Electric Thought," v, 37.

105. T. McKenna, "Post Electric Thought," 41, 37, 45.

106. T. McKenna, "Post Electric Thought," 49, 37, 48, 121, 50.

107. T. McKenna, "Post Electric Thought," 73.

108. T. McKenna, "Post Electric Thought," 84.

109. Davis, *High Weirdness*, 98.

110. T. McKenna, "Post Electric Thought," 65, 66.

111. T. McKenna, "Post Electric Thought," 127, 67, 70, 73.

112. T. McKenna, "Post Electric Thought," 94.

113. T. McKenna, "Post Electric Thought," 61, 89, 91.

114. T. McKenna, "Post Electric Thought," 96.

CHAPTER 4

1. T. McKenna, *True Hallucinations*, 49, 93.

2. D. McKenna, *Brotherhood*, 156.

3. T. McKenna, *True Hallucinations*, 21.

4. T. McKenna, "Crypto-Rap," 116, 117.

5. T. McKenna, *True Hallucinations*, 71.

6. T. McKenna, "Post Electric Thought," 59.

7. Dennis McKenna, typed letter to Terence McKenna, May 1970, affixed to a page at the back of "Change and Becoming," unpaginated (McKenna papers, MSP 213, Box 3, Folder 7, Purdue Archives).

8. While Dennis implies that Parker "really deserves credit" for what came to be called "hyper-carbolation," Parker's input was unrecognized. Parker apparently complained that his contributions went unacknowledged in *The Invisible Landscape*. "He had a point, actually," says Dennis, while adding that "there is some evidence that [his ideas] really originated from his father John Parker Sr." (Dennis McKenna, email to author, January 27, 2022).

9. Terry Reid, email to author, May 23, 2023.

10. Kevin Mahoney, Zoom interview by author, August 29, 2020.

11. Stanza from "Pursuing to Peru the G'nostic Guru: A Poetic Talisman for T. McKenna, Irish Shaman by W. Watson, Unauthorized Bard." Written in late 1969 or early 1970, the poem features Peru in the title as it was the original destination. It was accompanied in the mail with a four-leaf clover.

12. Leonard Clark, *The Rivers Ran East* (Palo Alto, CA: Travelers' Tales, 2001 [1953]), 170, 168. See the chapter "The Soul Vine" (167–174). Clark also encountered the visionary use of ayahuasca—*natema*—among the Jivaro taken by *brujos* as "war medicine" and for curing (317–319). See also the appendix "Jungle-Indian Pharmaceuticals" (362–367).

13. "Yagé may be the final fix" was the final line in William S. Burroughs, *Junkie: Confessions of an Unredeemed Drug Addict* (New York: Ace Books, 1953); William S. Burroughs and Allen Ginsberg, *The Yage Letters* (San Francisco: City Lights, 1963).

14. Burroughs, *The Letters of William S. Burroughs, 1945–1959*, 171.

15. Richard E. Schultes, "Virola as an Orally Administered Hallucinogen," *Botanical Museum Leaflets* 22, no. 6 (June 25, 1969): 229–240.

16. Wade Davis, *One River: Explorations and Discoveries in the Amazon Rainforest* (New York: Simon & Schuster, 1996), 476.

17. Alexander Price, "Immanentizing the Eschaton: An Interview with Dennis McKenna," *Reality Sandwich*, 2009, https://realitysandwich.com/13139/interview_dennis_mckenna. By the eighties, Dennis assumed a pivotal role in determining the synergetic pharmacology of ayahuasca, and the principal role of DMT in this mechanism.

18. D. McKenna, *Brotherhood*, 257.

19. T. McKenna, *True Hallucinations*, 18.

20. Travelling independently from the main group, Royce Kelley and Tom Cole do not make the rendezvous. Cole breaks a bone in his foot in the Amazon about 30 miles from La Chorrera, putting an end to their trek (Tom Cole, Zoom interview by author, September 17, 2024).

21. T. McKenna, *True Hallucinations*, 4.

22. Sara Hartley, email to author, April 27, 2020.

23. T. McKenna, *True Hallucinations*, 3.

24. T. McKenna, *True Hallucinations*, 15.

25. Sara Hartley, email to author, April 27, 2020.

26. T. McKenna, *True Hallucinations*, 13, 14.

27. T. McKenna, *True Hallucinations*, 34. Cia (pronounced "SeeAh") ended up "doing hard time in Lima," according to Dennis, "busted for smuggling cocaine into the states in the form of ceramic figurines of traditional Chauvin and other sculptures." Dennis McKenna, email to author, July 12, 2020.

28. T. McKenna "Down to Earth," screenplay, p.3.

29. T. McKenna and D. McKenna, *The Invisible Landscape*, 13.

30. Joseph H. Rush, "Review of *The Invisible Landscape*," *Journal of Parapsychology* 4, no. 2 (1976): 162–165.

31. Both *The Invisible Landscape* and *True Hallucinations* are core sources for this and subsequent chapters. Additionally, I rely on several other unpublished documents

(see appendix A for complete details on sources). The first is the collaborative technical and prophetic notes journaled at La Chorrera, February 28–March 4, 1971, "Dennis McKenna (with TMCK) La Chorrera original notes." The second is Terence's July–December 1971 journal, "Change and Becoming: Studies in a Fourth Dimensional Phenomenology of Mind" (hereafter C&B; McKenna papers, MSP 213, Box 3, Folder 7, Purdue Archives). Terence subsequently drew heavily upon these journal entries in "Shamanic Investigations" and *True Hallucinations*. I provide original journal dates and pages where possible. Third is the brothers' collaborative 1971 document, "A Preliminary Report on an Experiment at La Chorrera." The fourth document is the earliest (1972) version of "Shamanic Investigations" by the brothers, a manuscript that eventually made print as *The Invisible Landscape*. As with the latter, "Shamanic Investigations" features two parts. Part II includes much material inspired by entries in C&B, but omitted in *The Invisible Landscape*. All of the above are documents sourced from the Purdue Archives (see appendix A). The fifth source is Sara Hartley's 1971 La Chorrera journal, several pages of which were shared with me. The sixth source is Terence McKenna, "Amazon Psychotropical Quest," recorded at 4A Dodge Place, San Francisco, 1972/1973 (private recording, taped by Martin Inn). Finally, I draw upon Terence's primitive "Down to Earth" screenplay, n.d.

32. Wouter J. Hanegraaff, "'And End History. And Go to the Stars': Terence McKenna and 2012," in *Religion and Retributive Logic: Essays in Honour of Professor Garry W. Trompf*, ed. Carole M. Cusack and Christopher Hartney (Leiden: Brill, 2010), 296.

33. T. McKenna, *True Hallucinations*, 11, 12.

34. Joseph Conrad, *Heart of Darkness* (London: Penguin, 1973 [1902]), 43.

35. T. McKenna, *True Hallucinations*, 183.

36. A fuller recognition of the atrocities haunting the expedition route appears to have surfaced years after the McKennas returned from Colombia. Writing to Watson on May 29, 1974, Terence expressed his interest in the Putumayo's dark history, signaling that he was on the hunt for Whiffen's *Explorations of the Upper Amazon*, and had in his possession Walter E. Hardenburg's *The Putumayo: The Devil's Paradise: Travels to the Peruvian Amazon Region and an Account of the Atrocities Committed upon the Indians*, first published in 1912, and clearly a model for the subtitle of Terence's future memoir.

37. T. McKenna, *True Hallucinations*, 12; Taussig, *Shamanism, Colonialism, and the Wild Man*, 45.

38. T. McKenna, *True Hallucinations*, 10; Lesley Wylie, *Colombia's Forgotten Frontier: A Literary Geography of the Putumayo* (Liverpool: Liverpool University Press, 2013), 16.

39. T. McKenna, *True Hallucinations*, 12, my emphasis.

40. T. McKenna, *True Hallucinations*, 11. Even later, neither the modern world's addiction to rubber nor its colonial implications rated a mention in *Food of the Gods*, where sugar was, for example, castigated as the "terminal addiction to the ego"

(p. 179), and the "television habit" (p. 218) excoriated as an "electronic drug" with addictive powers not dissimilar to heroin.

41. T. McKenna, *True Hallucinations*, 72, 23.

42. D. McKenna, *Brotherhood*, 236; T. McKenna, *True Hallucinations*, 17.

43. T. McKenna, *True Hallucinations*, 6, 71, 2.

44. T. McKenna, "Post Electric Thought," 92.

45. D. McKenna, *Brotherhood*, 235.

46. T. McKenna, *True Hallucinations*, 44.

47. T. McKenna, *True Hallucinations*, 40, 36.

48. Terence McKenna, "The Quest for DMT," Ethnobotany and Chemistry of Psychoactive Plants seminar, Palenque, Mexico, January 1994, audio available at We Plants Are Happy Plants, YouTube, March 4, 2023, https://www.youtube.com/watch?v=XxMQYkOpkzE; T. McKenna, "Our Cyberspiritual Future."

49. D. McKenna, *Brotherhood*, 237.

50. T. McKenna, *True Hallucinations*, 52.

51. T. McKenna, *True Hallucinations*, 34.

52. T. McKenna, *True Hallucinations*, 71, 51.

53. T. McKenna, *True Hallucinations*, 93.

54. Sara Hartley, email to author, July 24, 2020.

55. T. McKenna, "Amazon Psychotropical Quest."

56. T. McKenna, *True Hallucinations*, 49.

57. T. McKenna, "Tryptamine Hallucinogens and Consciousness."

58. T. McKenna, "Having Archaic."

59. Jerome Rothenberg, ed., *Maria Sabina: Selections* (Berkeley: University of California Press, 2003), 49.

60. C&B, August 5, 1971, 31.

61. Dennis McKenna, email to author, March 1, 2015.

62. T. McKenna, *True Hallucinations*, 94.

63. C&B, November 30, 1971, 157; July 24, 15; November 12, 140.

64. Terence McKenna and Dennis McKenna, "Shamanic Investigations," 221 (McKenna papers, MSP 213, Box 5, Folder 1, Purdue Archives).

65. T. McKenna, *True Hallucinations*, 95–96.

66. As echoed in the name of the author's surrogate in Terence's "Down to Earth" screenplay (i.e., Thomas, an inference to Thomas Didymus, or "Doubting Thomas").

67. Dennis McKenna and Terence McKenna, "Dennis McKenna (with TMCK) La Chorrera original notes," Colombia, February 28–March 4, 1971 (19 pages), 1 (McKenna papers, MSP 213, Box 3, Folder 7, Purdue Archives).

68. Terence McKenna and Dennis McKenna, "A Preliminary Report on an Experiment at La Chorrera," 10 (McKenna papers, MSP 213, Box 2, Folder 11, Purdue Archives); D. McKenna and T. McKenna, "Dennis McKenna (with TMCK) La Chorrera original notes," 2, 3.

69. D. McKenna and T. McKenna, "Dennis McKenna (with TMCK) La Chorrera original notes," 4.

70. T. McKenna, *True Hallucinations*, 111.

71. D. McKenna and T. McKenna, "Dennis McKenna (with TMCK) La Chorrera original notes," 7.

72. D. McKenna, *Brotherhood*, 255.

73. Terence would use the spelling "March Forth."

74. D. McKenna and T. McKenna, "Dennis McKenna (with TMCK) La Chorrera original notes," 15, 16; T. McKenna, *True Hallucinations*, 88.

75. Michael J. Harner, "The Sound of Rushing Water," *Natural History* 77, no. 6 (1973): 28–33.

76. Terence McKenna, "Mind and Time, Spirit and Matter," Santa Fe, NM, May 26–27, 1990, http://deoxy.org/timemind.htm.

77. T. McKenna, "Amazon Psychotropical Quest."

78. When they set the date for their "experiment," Terence recalled an "idiotic pun" from his youth: "What day of the year is a command?" Answer: "March fourth" (T. McKenna, *True Hallucinations*, 93). In homage to Terence's quip, I use the implied "March Forth" to evoke the psilocybean sublime the brothers accessed at La Chorrera in the immediate period following March 4.

79. D. McKenna, *Brotherhood*, 252, 255.

80. T. McKenna, *True Hallucinations*, 111, 94.

81. T. McKenna, "Amazon Psychotropical Quest."

82. T. McKenna, *True Hallucinations*, 111.

83. T. McKenna, "Amazon Psychotropical Quest."

84. T. McKenna, *True Hallucinations*, 111, 114, 95.

85. T. McKenna, *True Hallucinations*, 125; T. McKenna and D. McKenna, "Preliminary Report," 3.

86. T. McKenna, *True Hallucinations*, 107, 95.

87. T. McKenna and D. McKenna, "A Preliminary Report," 22.

88. T. McKenna, *True Hallucinations*, 112, 116.

89. T. McKenna, *True Hallucinations*, 130, 116.

90. From Sara Hartley's La Chorrera journal, March 7–8, 1971.

91. Sara Hartley, email to author, April 27, 2020.

92. D. McKenna, *Brotherhood*, 275.

93. T. McKenna, *True Hallucinations*, 154, 157, 158.

94. This ridiculous episode became an object of much reflection and storytelling as an exemplar of the "cosmic giggle," a phrase used by Allen Ginsberg, Ram Dass, and Robert Anton Wilson, among others, and adopted by McKenna. The object—perfectly proportionate to "flying saucer" stereotypes permeating mid-twentieth century contactee culture while also resembling the object in a photograph widely considered to be a hoax—appeared to McKenna as terrifyingly real, its authenticity seemingly growing in direct proportion to its surreality. The experience was later interpreted via sci-fi author and contactee Jacques Vallée, whose *Passport to Magonia* (1969) afforded McKenna the opportunity to parse his experience in the light of other anomalies that undermine knowledge, faith, and received truth. That the episode achieved "a more complete cognitive dissonance" than its perceived alienness (*True Hallucinations*, 159) is a subject Davis addresses at length (*High Weirdness*, 148–150).

95. T. McKenna, "Down to Earth" screenplay, n.d., 5.

96. D. McKenna, *Brotherhood*, 273.

97. T. McKenna, *True Hallucinations*, 162, 147.

98. T. McKenna, *True Hallucinations*, 103.

99. T. McKenna, *True Hallucinations*, 163, 138.

100. Sara Hartley, unsent letter to Michael Malcolm, La Chorrera, Colombia, March 12, 1971.

101. George Csicsery, email to author, August 23, 2020.

102. T. McKenna and D. McKenna, "A Preliminary Report," 17, 28.

103. T. McKenna, *True Hallucinations*, 165.

104. T. McKenna, *True Hallucinations*, 172, 142, 165.

CHAPTER 5

1. T. McKenna, *True Hallucinations*, 169.

2. T. McKenna and D. McKenna, *The Invisible Landscape*, 1975, 126.

3. T. McKenna, *True Hallucinations*, 128, 129.

4. John Hazard, Terence McKenna interview, South Kona, Hawaii, October 1998, The Library of Consciousness, https://www.organism.earth/library/document/interview-with-john-hazard.

5. T. McKenna, "Having Archaic." Such critics demonstrate even less understanding of McKenna than the latter does of sinology. For a brief example, see Geoffrey Redmond, "The Yijing in Early Postwar Counterculture in the West," in *The Making of the Global Yijing in the Modern World*, ed. Benjamin Wai-ming Ng (Singapore: Springer, 2021), 197–221 (211–212).

6. Terence McKenna, "The Invisible Landscape: Peer Review," Mayan Conference / Council of Quetzalcoatl, Ojai Foundation, Ojai, CA, April 14, 1985, audio available at Deus Ex McKenna ~ Terence McKenna Archive, YouTube, September 7, 2011, http://www.youtube.com/watch?v=YfpKSdBMzrY.

7. T. McKenna and D. McKenna, "A Preliminary Report," May 16, 1971, 29.

8. A subterranean landscape of giant mushrooms was also encountered by I-Am-the-Man in John Uri Lloyd's *Etidorhpa* (1895), a Verne-inspired hollow earth novel with which McKenna was familiar. Although it is unclear exactly when he read it, it was McKenna's perception that Lloyd (a pharmacologist) had produced a work that described a "mushroom trip." Terence McKenna, "Posthumous Glory," All-Chemical Arts Conference, Kona Coast, Big Island, HI, September 12–17, 1999 (recorded by Lorenzo Hagerty, *Psychedelic Salon* podcast 151, August 7, 2008, https://psychedelicsalon.com/podcast-151-posthumous-glory).

9. Terence McKenna, "Temporal Resonance," *ReVISION: The Journal of Consciousness and Change* 10, no. 1 (Summer 1987): 25–30 (25).

10. T. McKenna and D. McKenna, "Shamanic Investigations," 145.

11. In later elaborations, it was clarified that the thirteenth month in this precessional lunar calendar—which would follow August and precede September (and called "Remember")—was to be a month "of great mnemonic celebration and recovery of the past." Terence McKenna, "A Calendar for the Goddess (Ecology of Souls)," Esalen Institute, Big Sur, CA, June 1989, The Library of Consciousness, https://www.organism.earth/library/document/ecology-of-souls.

12. McKenna subsequently refined his estimate of the age of the universe. Current cosmic microwave background measurements age the universe at 13.7 billion years.

13. C&B, July 19, 7.

14. T. McKenna and D. McKenna, *The Invisible Landscape* (1975), 112.

15. C&B, July 20, 9; October 28, 124.

16. C&B, October 28, 125.

17. C&B, July 28, 22; July 31, 26.

18. T. McKenna, "In the Valley of Novelty."

19. T. McKenna and D. McKenna, "A Preliminary Report," 18.

20. C&B, October 25, 122; July 19, 10; T. McKenna and D. McKenna, "Shamanic Investigations," 114, 123.

21. C&B, August 8, 34.

22. C&B, August 29, 63; July 15, 2.

23. In Price, "Immanentizing the Eschaton"; D. McKenna, *Brotherhood*, 305.

24. Terence McKenna, "Afterword: I Understand Philip K. Dick," in *In Pursuit of Valis: Selections from the Exegesis*, ed. Lawrence Sutin (Novato, CA: Underwood Books, 1991), 253–261 (255).

25. T. McKenna, "Afterword: I Understand Philip K. Dick," 166, 161.

26. Sara Hartley, email to author, September 3, 2020.

27. T. McKenna, *True Hallucinations*, 162.

28. C&B, July 15, 1; October 1, 103.

29. T. McKenna and D. McKenna, "Shamanic Investigations," 217.

30. C&B, October 1, 103.

31. James Joyce, *Finnegans Wake* (London: Penguin, 2000), 453–454. In Terence McKenna, "Down to Earth: Psilocybin and the UFOs," 1977, 104–105 (McKenna papers, MSP 213, Box 3, Folder 3, Purdue Archives).

32. C&B, July 20, 9; November 13, 142.

33. C&B, August 2, 29.

34. C&B, July 19, 6.

35. As mentioned in a letter to Takayama, where Terence indicates he had recently applied to Stanford for "a grant to come to Japan." T. McKenna, letter to Masayasu Takayama, sent from Puerto Leguízamo, November 30, 1971.

36. C&B, July 17, 3.

37. C&B, July 17, 4.

38. C&B, July 17, 5.

39. C&B, July 25, 17.

40. T. McKenna and D. McKenna, "Shamanic Investigations," 157–158.

41. C&B, July 27, 19.

42. C&B, July 2, 11, 12.

43. T. McKenna, "The Quest for DMT."

44. C&B, August 21, 51; August 25, 59.

45. C&B, August 19, 45; July 29, 23, 24; August 18, 38.

46. C&B, August 18, 40, 43; August 19, 44.

47. C&B, August 20, 48; August 18, 37. These speculative insights on "the opus" formed the background to a chapter, "Ontological Analogues," included in "Shamanic Investigations" but later omitted and not published.

48. C&B, August 18, 39.

49. C&B, August 19, 44.

50. T. McKenna, *True Hallucinations*, 95.

51. Cited in C&B, August 23, 56.

52. C&B, August 24, 57; August 23, 56.

53. C&B, September 9, 73; September 9, 72.

54. C&B, August 24, 58.

55. C&B, August 29, 63, 64; August 26, 60.

56. C&B, August 25, 59; T. McKenna, "Search for the Original Tree of Knowledge."

57. C&B, August 25, 59.

58. C&B, August 14, 36; August 4, 30.

59. C&B, August 31, 64.

60. C&B, August 31, 65; September 1, 65; September 1, 66.

61. C&B, September 16, 92.

62. C&B, September 28, 120.

63. C&B, September 28, 121.

64. C&B, November 1, 126.

65. C&B, November 9, 136; November 11, 137.

66. T. McKenna, *True Hallucinations*, 168.

67. C&B, November 12, 140.

68. C&B, November 12, 139, 141.

69. C&B, November 12, 140; November 13, 141.

70. Later analysis by chemists at the Karolinska Institute, Stockholm, he conveyed in *True Hallucinations*, "confirmed the presence of dimethyltryptamine" (169).

71. C&B, November 17, 146.

72. C&B, November 15, 144.

73. T. McKenna, letter to Masayasu Takayama, sent from Puerto Leguízamo, November 30, 1971.

74. C&B, November 18, 147.

75. T. McKenna and D. McKenna, "A Preliminary Report," 29.

76. C&B, July 19, 10.

77. Terence McKenna, "We Are at the Cutting Edge," Esalen Institute, Big Sur, CA, August, 1991, audio available at Deus Ex McKenna ~ Terence McKenna Archive, YouTube, November 25, 2014, https://www.youtube.com/watch?v=_4JD9QOuShs; Julian Silverman, "Shamans and Acute Schizophrenia," *American Anthropologist* 69, no. 1 (1967): 21–31; T. McKenna, "In the Valley of Novelty."

78. T. McKenna, "Afterword: I Understand Philip K. Dick," 254.

79. T. McKenna, "Afterword: I Understand Philip K. Dick," 256, 257.

80. C&B, December 18, 159. While the word "yagé" is often used interchangeably with ayahuasca, it here refers to a drink combining the *Banisteriopsis caapi* vine with the DMT-containing *chaliponga* (*Diplopterys cabrerana*).

81. In Rick Strassman, Wojtowicz Slawek, Luna Luis Eduardo, and Frecska Ede, *Inner Paths to Outer Space: Journeys to Alien Worlds through Psychedelics and Other Spiritual Technologies* (Rochester, VT: Park Street Press, 2010), 166.

82. Luis Eduardo Luna, "On Encounters with Entities in the Ayahuasca Realm: A Phenomenological View," in *DMT Entity Encounters: Dialogues in the Spirit Molecule*, ed. David Luke and Rory Spowers (Rochester, VT: Park Street Press, 2021), 3–29.

83. C&B, November 29, 156, 174.

84. T. McKenna and D. McKenna, "Shamanic Investigations," 223, 248.

85. T. McKenna and D. McKenna, "Shamanic Investigations"; T. McKenna, *True Hallucinations*, 175. In *True Hallucinations* (175), Terence confusingly observes "a total, annular eclipse of the sun" occurring on 22 (not 24) December 1973.

86. T. McKenna, *True Hallucinations*, 176–178.

87. T. McKenna, *True Hallucinations*, 176.

CHAPTER 6

1. T. McKenna, "Psychedelic Skepticism."

2. In Price, "Immanentizing the Eschaton."

3. C&B, November 15, 145.

4. T. McKenna, *True Hallucinations*, 174.

5. D. McKenna, *Brotherhood*, 308.

6. "United States of America v. Terence Kemp McKenna," information filed in US District Court for the District of Colorado, July 7, 1972 (Criminal Case File: 72-CR-205, retrieved from NARA at Denver).

7. "United States of America v. Terence Kemp McKenna," Judgement and Order of Probation, US District Court for the District of Colorado, September 22, 1972 (Criminal Case File: 72-CR-267, retrieved from NARA at Denver).

8. D. McKenna, *Brotherhood*, 308, 309.

9. T. McKenna, Boulder Statement, 1972.

10. D. McKenna, *Brotherhood*, 44, 309.

11. Ron Curry, email to author, September 9, 2020.

12. Kathleen Harrison, email to author, April 3, 2023.

13. T. McKenna, "Amazon Psychotropical Quest."

14. D. McKenna, *Brotherhood*, 313.

15. Though there are scarce details on the UC Berkeley courses McKenna took between 1972 and 1975, brief reference is made to a course taken in the forensics department, "Biochemical Markers for Individuality," taught by Alexander Shulgin (T. McKenna, "Exploring the Hermetic Tradition"). This may have been part of Shulgin's long-running forensic toxicology course, which became legendary for his "dirty pictures"—that is, images of tryptamine and phenethylamine molecules, including those he had discovered himself.

16. T. McKenna, "Our Cyberspiritual Future."

17. T. McKenna and D. McKenna, *The Invisible Landscape* (1975), 4, 3.

18. D. McKenna, *Brotherhood*, 71.

19. Noffke with T. McKenna, "A Conversation over Saucers," 26, 27.

20. T. McKenna, Fairmont Banquet Address, 1987.

21. Terence McKenna, "Alien Love," Shared Visions Bookstore, Berkeley, CA, 1983, The Library of Consciousness, https://www.organism.earth/library/document/alien-love. An edited and revised transcript was published in *Magical Blend*, no. 17 (1987): 18–29, and a shorter version reprinted in Terence McKenna, *The Archaic Revival: Speculations on Psychedelic Mushrooms, the Amazon, Virtual Reality, UFOs, Evolution, Shamanism, the Rebirth of the Goddess, and the End of History* (San Francisco: Harper, 1991), 72–88.

22. T. McKenna, *True Hallucinations*, 43, 142, 134.

23. Pamela Jackson and Jonathan Lethem, eds., *The Exegesis of Philip K. Dick* (Boston: Houghton Mifflin Harcourt, 2011); Davis, *High Weirdness*, 298; Lawrence Sutin, *Divine Invasions: A Life of Philip K. Dick* (New York: Citadel, 1991).

24. T. McKenna, *True Hallucinations*, 160.

25. Carl Jung, *Flying Saucers: A Modern Myth of Things Seen in the Skies* (London: Routledge & Kegan Paul, 1959).

26. D. McKenna, *Brotherhood*, 128.

27. The final line of Terence's February 26, 1975, correspondence to Rick: "Think about a book on yagé—I think we could get an advance if we had a précis to show my editor."

28. A decade later, Terence stated that "when we originally conceived this idea of a psycho-botanical farm, we bought land, near Florencia in the state of Caqueta, in Colombia. And then it became politically unfriendly to foreign scientists, and so we stayed away for years" (Terence McKenna, "Shamanology," Mill Valley, CA, 1984, audio available at Elephant Men, YouTube, August 7, 2017, https://www.youtube.com/watch?v=do8K9tdS-8w). The story is repeated at other times (e.g., Terence McKenna & Nicole Maxwell, "Shamanology of the Amazon," The Ojai Foundation, Ojai, CA, 1989, video available at Faustin Bray, YouTube, March 29, 2011, https://www.youtube.com/watch?v=BSbz_ruMj9w&t=106s). I don't know if this land was purchased, but if the "we" in these comments implies Nietfeld, it is possible the land was in her name.

29. T. McKenna, letter to Rick Watson, November 26, 1974.

30. T. McKenna, letter to Rick Watson, November 26, 1974.

31. T. McKenna, letter to Rick Watson, February 26, 1975.

32. George Csicsery, email to author, August 18, 2020.

33. T. McKenna, "Ethnobotany of Shamanism," 76.

34. Terence McKenna, "Down to Earth: Psilocybin and the UFOs," 1979, 5 (McKenna papers, MSP 213, Box 3, Folder 3, Purdue Archives).

35. T. McKenna, letter to Rick Watson, February 26, 1975.

36. T. McKenna, letter to Masayasu Takayama, March 25, 1975.

37. Satomi Hirano, email to author, March 22, 2021.

38. D. McKenna, *Brotherhood*, 327.

39. T. McKenna, *True Hallucinations*, 207. Though Terence's memoir implies that he alone made the discovery, it was Dennis who landed on the technique.

40. T. McKenna, "Down to Earth," 1979, 5.

41. T. McKenna, letter to Rick Watson, June 25, 1975.

42. T. McKenna, letter to Rick Watson, June 25, 1975.

43. T. McKenna, letter to Rick Watson, August 10, 1975.

44. T. McKenna, letter to Rick Watson, August 10, 1975.

45. T. McKenna, letter to Rick Watson, October 5, 1975.

46. Anon., "Bedroom, Bathroom, Mushroom: How to Keep a Perpetual Supply of Psilocybin in Your Own Home," *High Times*, no. 10 (June 1976).

47. T. McKenna, letter to Rick Watson, October 5, 1975.

48. T. McKenna, *True Hallucinations*, 215.

49. Kevin Mahoney, Zoom interview by author, August 29, 2020.

50. T. McKenna, letter to Masayasu Takayama, October 12, 1975.

51. Kathleen Harrison, interview by author, September 25, 2019.

52. Kathleen Harrison, interview by author, September 25, 2019.

53. T. McKenna, *True Hallucinations*, 207, 215.

54. T. McKenna, *True Hallucinations*, 216, 217, 218; T. McKenna, "Having Archaic."

55. Kathleen Harrison, Zoom interview by author, April 20, 2022.

56. T. McKenna, letter to Rick Watson, October 5, 1975.

57. Kathleen Harrison, interview by author, September 25, 2019.

58. T. McKenna, letter to Rick Watson, December 13, 1975.

59. Andy Letcher, *Shroom: A Cultural History of the Magic Mushroom* (London: Faber and Faber, 2006), 237.

60. T. McKenna, letter to Rick Watson, October 5, 1975.

61. T. McKenna, letter to Rick Watson, December 13, 1975.

62. T. McKenna, letter to Rick Watson, December 13, 1975.

63. T. McKenna, *True Hallucinations*, 207.

64. T. McKenna, letter to Rick Watson, June 25, 1975.

65. O. T. Oss and O. N. Oeric, *Psilocybin: Magic Mushroom Grower's Guide* (Berkeley: And/Or Press, 1976). Photographs by Irimias the Obscure (a.k.a. Jeremy Bigwood), illustrations by Kat (Kathleen Harrison).

66. Oss and Oeric, *Psilocybin* (1976), 12–13.

67. Oss and Oeric, *Psilocybin* (1976), 8–9.

68. T. McKenna, *True Hallucinations*, 212.

69. Terence McKenna, "A Weekend with Terence McKenna," Esalen Institute, Big sur, CA, August 27-29, 1993, The Library of Consciousness, https://www.organism.earth/library/document/a-weekend-with-terence-mckenna.

70. Abraham and T. McKenna, "Dynamics of Hyperspace."

71. D. McKenna, *Brotherhood*, 287, 293.

72. Xandor Korzybski, "Terence and the Coming Eschaton: Terence McKenna Meets Xandor Korzybski," *Mondo 2000*, no. 10 (1993): 48–58 (55).

73. T. McKenna, *True Hallucinations*, 209.

74. David Jay Brown and Rebecca McClen, "*Critique* Interview," in T. McKenna, *The Archaic Revival*, 204–216 (207).

75. F. H. Crick and L. E. Orgel, "Directed Panspermia," *Icarus* 19, no. 3 (1973): 341–348.

76. Timothy Leary, *Starseed* (San Francisco: Level Press, 1973), 7, 24, 11.

77. Between 1972 and 1975, Watson produced a privately shared limited edition epic poetry book, *Amazonas*. An updated and redesigned version of *Amazonas* was privately released in California posthumously by his daughter Beatie Wolfe in October 2024.

78. Terence McKenna, "Among Ayahuasquera," in *Gateway to Inner Space: Sacred Plants, Mysticism and Psychotherapy*, ed. Christian Ratsch (Dorset: Prism Press, 1989), 179–211 (181, 189).

79. T. McKenna, "Among Ayahuasquera," 182.

80. Kathleen Harrison, interview by author, September 25, 2019.

81. T. McKenna, "Among Ayahuasquera," 185.

82. Kathleen Harrison, interview by author, September 25, 2019.

83. Kathleen Harrison, email to author, November 29, 2020.

84. T. McKenna, "Among Ayahuasquera," 187, 204, 189.

85. Kathleen Harrison, email to author, June 26, 2022.

86. T. McKenna, "Among Ayahuasquera," 193, 203.

87. Kathleen Harrison, email to author, June 26, 2022.

88. T. McKenna, "Among Ayahuasquera," 198, 191.

89. Focused on "visions," McKenna is said to have advanced the romantic typecasting of ayahuasca shamanism, a practice pursued in contemporary "visionary" tourism where dark shamanism is avoided (see Alex K. Gearin and Oscar Calavia Sáez, "Altered Vision: Ayahuasca Shamanism and Sensory Individualism," *Current Anthropology* 62, no. 2 [April 2021]: 138–163).

90. Kathleen Harrison, interview by author, September 25, 2019.

91. Kathleen Harrison, Zoom interview by author, April 20, 2022.

92. T. McKenna, "Among Ayahuasquera," 206.

93. Levin, "In Praise of Psychedelics" 18.

94. Kathleen Harrison, interview by author, September 25, 2019.

95. Kathleen Harrison, "The Leaves of the Shepherdess," in *Sisters of the Extreme: Women Writing on the Drug Experience*, ed. Cynthia Palmer and Michael Horowitz (Rochester, VT: Park Street Press, 2000), 302–305 (304).

96. Kathleen Harrison, interview by author, September 25, 2019.

97. Terence McKenna, TrancElements 2, Victoria, Australia, February 29, 1997, audio available at SpokieTech, "Terence McKenna—Spoken Word Tour Australia 1997," YouTube, February 21, 2018, https://www.youtube.com/watch?v=NLdLMBeOwq0.

98. Kathleen Harrison, email to author, January 10, 2024.

99. T. McKenna, TrancElements 2.

100. T. McKenna, "Among Ayahuasquera," 199, 193, 208, 192.

101. Terence McKenna, "Finale," Bridge Psychedelic Conference, Stanford University, Stanford, CA, February 2–3, 1991.

102. The Shamen with Terence McKenna, "Re:Evolution," *Boss Drum* (One Little Indian, 1992).

103. Terence McKenna, "The Evolutionary Importance of Technology," Esalen Institute, Big Sur, CA, August 1996, The Library of Consciousness, https://www.organism.earth/library/document/evolutionary-importance-of-technology.

104. Kathleen Harrison, "Women, Plants, and Culture," in *Visionary Plant Consciousness: The Shamanic Teachings of the Plant World*, ed. J. P. Harpignies (Rochester VT: Inner Traditions, 2007), 99–104 (101).

105. In Hayes, "A Conversation with Terence McKenna," 437.

106. Terence McKenna, "Esalen In-House Get Together," Esalen, 1998, audio available at henrykeats, "Esalen in House Get Together (Terence McKenna)," YouTube, August 23, 2017, https://www.youtube.com/watch?app=desktop&v=lGiht1AO5Qk.

107. T. McKenna, "Among Ayahuasquera," 209, 211.

108. In Hayes, "A Conversation with Terence McKenna," 430.

109. T. McKenna, "Search for the Original Tree of Knowledge."

110. In Hayes, "A Conversation with Terence McKenna"; Terence McKenna, "Hyperdimensional Understanding," Esalen Institute, Big Sur, CA, April 1994, audio available at We Plants Are Happy Plants, YouTube, July 26, 2023, https://www.youtube.com/watch?v=G1cjkslnZW4.

111. D. McKenna, *Brotherhood*, 350, 357–362.

112. Wade Davis, "Opening Speech, Heraclitus Exhibition," October Gallery, London 2001, https://rvheraclitus.org/our-mission.

113. J. P. Harpignies, Zoom interview by author, January 12, 2024.

114. Dennis J. McKenna, "Ayahuasca and Human Destiny," *Journal of Psychoactive Drugs* 37, no. 2 (2005): 231–234.

115. D. McKenna, *Brotherhood*, 376.

116. T. McKenna, "The Quest for DMT."

117. D. McKenna, *Brotherhood*, 373, 376, 377. Terence made a similar claim for himself in November 1971.

118. D. J. McKenna, G. H. N. Towers, and F. S. Abbott, "Monoamine Oxidase Inhibitors in South American Hallucinogenic Plants Pt. II: Constituents of Orally Active Myristicaceous Hallucinogens," *Journal of Ethnopharmacology* 12 (1984): 179–211 (180).

119. D. McKenna, *Brotherhood*, 379, 385, 386.

120. T. McKenna, The Quest for DMT."

121. Terence McKenna, "Tryptamine Hallucinogens in Amazonas," in *Proceedings of the International Conference on Shamanism*, ed. Ruth-Inge Heinze, May 11–13, 1984, Center for South and Southeast Asia Studies, UC Berkeley, Berkeley, CA, 103–114 (108).

122. T. McKenna, "Tryptamine Hallucinogens in Amazonas," 109.

123. T. McKenna, "Shamanology."

CHAPTER 7

1. T. McKenna, letter to Rick Watson, December 30, 1976.

2. Kathleen Harrison, Zoom interview by author, April 20, 2022.

3. T. McKenna, letter to Rick Watson, December 30, 1976.

4. Kathleen Harrison, Zoom interview by author, April 20, 2022.

5. Kathleen Harrison, email to author, July, 21 2024.

6. Dennis McNally, *A Long Strange Trip: The Inside History of the Grateful Dead* (London: Corgi Books, 2003), 156.

7. Jesse Jarnow, *Heads: A Biography of Psychedelic America* (New York: Da Capo Press, 2018), 232.

8. Kathleen Harrison, email to author, April 1, 2023.

9. T. McKenna, letter to Masayasu Takayama, October 23, 1978. While he therein claimed they had amassed 8,000 names, Harrison disputes this, stating it was in the hundreds.

10. T. McKenna, "A Weekend with Terence McKenna."

11. Terence McKenna, "Pattern Out of Chaos," n.d., audio available at We Plants Are Happy Plants, YouTube, July 1, 2021, https://www.youtube.com/watch?v=pfgHHd2sIjs.

12. Kathleen Harrison, Zoom interview by author, April 20, 2022.

13. In 1992, Harrison sold the rights to Quick Trading Press, a small cannabis press that published the *Grower's Guide* thereafter. In her estimate, over all editions, 200,000 copies were sold.

14. After the divorce, in 1992 Lux Natura became the holder of the rights of McKenna's books, and any royalties the family receives today derive from Lux Natura.

15. Botanical Dimensions, http://botanicaldimensions.org.

16. Kathleen Harrison, email to author, October 13, 2024.

17. See Erik Davis, *Blotter: The Untold Story of an Acid Medium* (Cambridge, MA: MIT Press, 2023), 77–79.

18. Terence McKenna, "Shedding the Monkey," Shared Visions, Berkeley, CA, February, 1986, The Library of Consciousness, https://www.organism.earth/library/document/shedding-the-monkey.

19. T. McKenna, letter to R. Watson, from Hawaii, March 8, 1987.

20. T. McKenna, letter to R. Watson, January 27, 1987; Kathleen Harrison, email to author, July 27, 2022.

21. Kathleen. Harrison, email to author, September 24, 2024.

22. T. McKenna, letter to Joel Alter, July 26, 1985, Ralph Metzner collection of correspondence, Purdue Archives, MSP 317.

23. T. McKenna, letter to Ralph Metzner, "late 1986." Ralph Metzner collection of correspondence, Purdue Archives, MSP 317.

24. T. McKenna, letter to R. Watson, from Hawaii, March 18, 1987.

25. Terence McKenna, "The Plot Thickens, the Stakes Rise," 1994, Maui, Hawaii, The Library of Consciousness, https://www.organism.earth/library/document/plot-thickens-stakes-rise.

26. Klea McKenna, "Darkness / Light / Touch," in Klea McKenna, *Witness Mark* (Baltimore, MD: Saint Lucy Books, 2023), 73–83 (75–76).

27. In Tao Lin, "Psychedelic Drugs, Art, Music, and Other Drugs: An Interview with Finn McKenna," *Vice*, September 17, 2014, https://www.vice.com/en/article/jmba9x/psychedelic-drugs-art-music-and-other-drugs-an-interview-with-finn-mckenna-815.

28. Finn McKenna, Zoom interview by author, April 5, 2023.

29. Kurt McVey, "Klea McKenna Steps into the Light with Bicoastal Art Exhibitions," *Quiet Lunch*, September 12, 2018.

30. For information about Klea McKenna's projects and installations, see https://www.kleamckenna.com.

31. Leah Ollman, "Rematerializing Photography," *Art in America*, May 26, 2017, https://www.artnews.com/art-in-america/features/rematerializing-photography-63360.

32. Vanessa Kauffman Zimmerly, "Three Movements through Klea McKenna's Witness Mark," January 16, 2018, https://wayback.archive-it.org/15633/20210126025604/https://www.artpractical.com/column/three-movements-through-klea-mckennas-witness-mark.

33. As apparent in the series *Archipelago*, *How Forests Think*, *Web Study*, and *Rain Study*. There is an undeniably affective element to the methods of Klea, who more recently became mother to two infants: Fiona LaPriel Charne and River McKenna.

34. McVey, "Klea McKenna Steps into the Light."

35. T. McKenna, "Appreciating Imagination."

36. Klea McKenna, email to author, January 24, 2023.

37. T. McKenna, letter to R. Watson, June 17, 1996.

38. Kathleen Harrison, email to author, July 27, 2022.

39. Finn McKenna, Zoom interview by author, April 5, 2023.

40. Nina Wise, Zoom interview by author, March 16, 2021.

41. Dillon Hicks with CeeJay Barnaby about Terence McKenna Live at the University of Wollongong, NSW, March 4, 1997, aired on *Supernormalized*, season 2, episode 13 (March 29, 2023), https://supernormalized.com/podcast/dillon-hicks-interview-on-terence-mckenna-live-at-wollongong-university-s2e13.

42. Ken Adams, Zoom interview by author, June 23, 2023.

43. Kathleen Harrison, Zoom interview by author, April 20, 2022.

44. Kathleen Harrison, Zoom interview by author, April 20, 2022.

45. Anon., "Terence McKenna—The Re:Evolution(ary) Shaman," *Freakbeat*, no. 8 (April 19, 1993): 17–19, 23–24 (23).

46. Kathleen Harrison, Zoom interview by author, April 20, 2022.

47. Bruce Damer, email to author, November 23, 2021.

48. Kathleen Harrison, Zoom interview by author, April 20, 2022.

49. Nina Wise, Zoom interview by author, March 16, 2021.

50. Terence McKenna, "The Camden Centre Talk," London, June 15, 1992, https://deoxy.org/t_camden.htm.

51. T. McKenna, "What I've Learned from Psychedelics."

52. Kathleen Harrison, interview by author, September 25, 2019.

53. T. McKenna, "Unfolding the Stone."

54. T. McKenna, "Unfolding the Stone."

55. T. McKenna, "Alchemy and the Hermetic Corpus."

56. Mark Jacobson, "Is Terence McKenna the Brave New Prophet of the Next Psychedelic Revolution, or Is His Cosmic Egg Just a Little Bit Cracked?," *Esquire*, June 1, 1992, 107–109, 133–138 (109).

57. James Kent, "Prologomena: An Interview by James Kent," *TRP: The Resonance Project* (October 13, 1998), 42–45, 64 (64).

58. Terence McKenna, "Monogamy, Marriage, and Neurosis," Esalen Institute, Big Sur, CA, February 1994, podcasted on Lorenzo Hagerty's *Psychedelic Salon*, Podcast 390, March 3, 2014, https://psychedelicsalon.com/podcast-390-monogamy-marriage-and-neurosis.

59. Finn McKenna, Zoom interview by author, April 5, 2023; T. McKenna, "Alien Footprints."

60. Nina Wise, Zoom interview by author, March 16, 2021.

61. Bruce Damer, "Terence McKenna: Beyond 2012," Esalen Institute, Big Sur, CA, June 16, 2012. The recording was the basis for a podcast subsequently produced by Lorenzo Hagerty, "A Deep Dive into the Mind of McKenna," *Psychedelic Salon*, https://psychedelicsalon.com/podcast-316-a-deep-dive-into-the-mind-of-mckenna.

62. Terence McKenna, "The Rites of Spring," Joshua Tree National Monument, CA, April 1986, The Library of Consciousness, https://www.organism.earth/library/document/rites-of-spring.

63. Carl Gustav Jung, *Liber Novus: The Red Book*, edited and with an introduction by Sonu Shamdasani. Translated by Mark Kyburz, John Peck, and Sonu Shamdasani (New York: W. W. Norton, 2009), 123–124.

64. Elizabeth Hansen, email to author, November 7, 2021.

65. Dennis McKenna, "A Symbiosis Shattered," unpublished document, ca. 2012.

66. "Peerless," July 6, 2012, in comment thread to "A Deep Dive into the Mind of McKenna," *Psychedelic Salon*, https://psychedelicsalon.com/podcast-316-a-deep-dive-into-the-mind-of-mckenna.

67. T. McKenna, "Search for the Original Tree of Knowledge."

68. T. McKenna, "Understanding the Chaos at History's End."

69. T. McKenna, "The Invisible Landscape: Peer Review."

70. From Bergmann, *The Transcendental Object at the End of Time*.

71. T. McKenna, "Personal Stories."

72. "Sky," in comment thread to "A Deep Dive," July 2, 2012.

73. "Antiochus Wilson," in comment thread to "A Deep Dive," January 25, 2013.

74. "Peter Meyer," in comment thread to "A Deep Dive," July 4, 2012.

75. Elizabeth Hansen, email to author, December 2, 2020.

76. Christy Silness, email to author, July 15, 2022.

77. Christy Silness, Zoom interview by author, December 10, 2021.

78. Terence McKenna, "Nature Loves Complexity," Boulder, CO, July 17, 1998, The Library of Consciousness, https://www.organism.earth/library/document/nature-loves-complexity.

79. Terence McKenna, Wetlands Preserve, New York City, July 28, 1998, transcribed by Abrupt, https://www.abrupt.org/abruptlog/terence-mckenna-at-wetlands-preserve-nyc.

80. T. McKenna, "Alien Love."

81. Terence McKenna, "Eros and the Eschaton," Mandala Books, Seattle, March 25, 1994, The Library of Consciousness, https://www.organism.earth/library/document/eros-and-the-eschaton. McKenna attributed the phrase to Joyce, and it likely derives from "mammamuscles most moisterious," *Finnegans Wake* (p. 15). My thanks to Corey Dansereau for this observation.

82. T. McKenna, "Shamanology."

83. Christy Silness, email to author, June 29, 2022.

84. Christy Silness, Zoom interview by author, December 10, 2021.

CHAPTER 8

1. Terence McKenna, Ralph Abraham, and Rupert Sheldrake, "Cannabis," Trialogue, Esalen Institute, Big Sur, CA, 1991, The Library of Consciousness, https://www.organism.earth/library/document/cannabis-trialogue.

2. Susan De Muth, "Interview with Terence McKenna," May 18, 1994, https://susandemuth.com/interviews/terence-mckenna.

3. T. McKenna, "Alchemy and the Hermetic Corpus."

4. Kathleen Harrison, interview by author, September 25, 2019.

5. Tao Lin, *Trip: Psychedelics, Alienation and Change* (New York: Vintage, 2018), 232.

6. She did, on occasion, team up with Terence, as they did on *Victorian Tales of Cannabis*, a 1989 production recorded by Sound Photosynthesis on which McKenna read the male voice and Harrison read the female story line.

7. T. McKenna, "Our Cyberspiritual Future."

8. Terence McKenna, "How to Get Liberated," Esalen, 1994, audio available at We Plants Are Happy Plants, YouTube, December 14, 2023, https://www.youtube.com/watch?v=UeCWZaArYQg&t=2s.

9. T. McKenna, "Hot Concepts and Melting Edges."

10. T. McKenna, "Hot Concepts and Melting Edges."

11. Michael Toms and Fabrice Florin, "The Invisible Landscape with Terence McKenna," *New Dimensions Radio*, May 18, 1977.

12. Terence McKenna, "Intentionality of Meaning," Esalen Institute, Big Sur, CA, June, 1989, The Library of Consciousness, https://www.organism.earth/library/document/intentionality-of-meaning.

13. T. McKenna, "Intentionality of Meaning."

14. Terence McKenna, "Speaking Metaphorically," Shared Visions bookstore, Berkeley, CA, October 1983, audio available at We Plants Are Happy Plants, "Terence McKenna—Speaking Metaphorically (Full Talk)," YouTube, August 4, 2022, https://www.youtube.com/watch?v=tDl7O05ljZE.

15. Will Noffke, "Terence McKenna: The Monkey Is Being Shed," *High Frontiers*, no. 1 (1984): 7, 28–29 (7).

16. Kathleen Harrison, email to author, September 24, 2023.

17. T. McKenna, *Food of the Gods*, 164.

18. James Kent, "Terence McKenna: An Interview by James Kent," Part Two, *TRP: The Resonance Project* vol. 4, no. 16 (Spring 1999), 34–45, 48–49, 64 (34).

19. Joan Halifax, email to author, January 7, 2023.

20. Joan Halifax, Zoom interview by author, July 25, 2023.

21. Esalen fall 1962 Big Sur Hot Springs catalog, in the private archives of David Price.

22. Jeffrey Kripal, *Esalen: America and the Religion of No Religion* (Chicago: University of Chicago Press, 2007), 117–118.

23. Kent, "Terence McKenna: An Interview by James Kent," Part Two, 34.

24. Elizabeth Hansen, email to author, December 30, 2020.

25. T. McKenna, "Hallucinogens: Before and After Psychology." Teilhard de Chardin actually wrote: "The day will come when, after harnessing the ether, the winds, the tides, and gravitation, we shall harness for God the energies of love. And on that day, for the second time in the history of the world, we shall have discovered fire." Pierre Teilhard de Chardin, "The Evolution of Chastity" (1934), in *Toward the Future*, translated by René Hague (San Diego, CA: Harcourt, 1975), 60–87 (86–87).

26. Robert Forte, email to author, December 20, 2021.

27. T. McKenna, "The Edge Runner."

28. Illustrative of the intensity of these residencies, forty-five hours of lecturing was counted in the month-long residency of 1993.

29. Matthew Ingram, *Retreat: How the Counterculture Invented Wellness* (London: Repeater Books, 2020); Nancy Lunney-Wheeler, Zoom interview by author, April 13, 2021.

30. Badiner was responsible for the 1995 Esalen invitational event Sustainability Consciousness, at which leading ecologists and activists were encouraged to reflect on McKenna's oblique philosophy.

31. Paul Krassner, *Magic Mushrooms and Other Highs: From Toad Slime to Ecstasy* (London: Ten Speed Press, 2004), 8.

32. Terence McKenna, "Live at the Zoo" with DJ Zippy, The Zoo, Brisbane, QLD, Australia, February 26, 1997, Audio available on Soundcloud (Goognostic): https://soundcloud.com/goognostic/terence-mckenna-with-dj-zippy.

33. In 1992, Esalen weekend workshop registrants paid up to $700 a head (with McKenna pocketing nearly $2,000 per gig). Jacobson, "Is Terence McKenna the Brave New Prophet," 134–135.

34. Weinberg was an early taper of Grateful Dead performances.

35. When Herbert inadvertently assigned rights to McKenna's collection to a third party, the resulting intellectual property dispute prompted McKenna to found the Human Potential Audio Foundation, which secured rights to audiovisual materials, undertook digitization, and worked to make the materials publicly accessible. On the original board with McKenna were David Price, Mark Watts (son of Alan), and Laura Kunysz. David Price, email to author, April 19, 2021.

36. David Price, email to author, December 3, 2021.

37. Terence McKenna, "Terence McKenna: Q&A," *Magical Blend*, no. 17 (1987): 24–29 (27).

38. Terence McKenna, "Psilocybin and the Sands of Time," Spiritual Emergency Network interview, Esalen Institute, Big Sur, CA, 1982, podcasted on Lorenzo Hagerty's *Psychedelic Salon*, Podcast 318, July 10, 2012, https://psychedelicsalon.com/podcast-318-psilocybin-and-the-sands-of-time.

39. The Ojai Foundation was renamed the Topa Institute in 2022.

40. The event proved so esoteric that it did not attract a single ticket purchase and was attended by a small group of interested staff (Robin Sylvan, Zoom interview by author, January 10, 2023).

41. Robin Sylvan, Zoom interview by author, January 10, 2023.

42. John Steele, email to author, February 27, 2023.

43. Terence McKenna, "The World and Its Double," Nature Friends Lodge, Sierra Madre, CA, September 11, 1993, The Library of Consciousness, https://www.organism.earth/library/document/the-world-and-its-double.

44. Robert Venosa, "Acknowledgements," in *Illuminatus* (Sydney: Interface, 1999), 231.

45. Jacques Olivier, *Nature Loves Courage* (Orcas Island, WA: Icaro, 2021), 72. Emphasis in original.

46. Ralph H. Abraham, *Vibrations and Forms: Findings from Psychedelic Adventures* (New York: Epigraph, 2021), 9.

47. Rupert Sheldrake, Zoom interview by author, February 16, 2021.

48. Sheldrake et al., *Chaos, Creativity and Cosmic Consciousness*, xvii.

49. The first, featuring discussions at Esalen in September 1989 and September 1990, was published in 1992 as *Trialogues at the Edge of the West: Chaos, Creativity, and the Resacralization of the World* (reprinted in 2001 as *Chaos, Creativity and Cosmic Consciousness*). The second volume, published in 1998, was titled *The Evolutionary Mind: Trialogues at the Edge of the Unthinkable*, and was revised and updated in 2005 as *The Evolutionary Mind: Conversations on Science, Imagination & Spirit*.

50. Jean Houston, "Foreword," in *Chaos, Creativity and Cosmic Consciousness*, by Rupert Sheldrake, Terence McKenna, and Ralph Abraham (Rochester, VT: Park Street Press, 2001), xiii.

51. David Jay Brown and Rebecca McClen, "Interview: Terence K. McKenna," *Critique: A Journal Exposing Consensus Reality*, no. 31 (Summer 1989): 58–60 (60).

52. Rupert Sheldrake, Terence McKenna, and Ralph Abraham, *The Evolutionary Mind: Conversations on Science, Imagination & Spirit* (Rhinebeck, NY: Monkfish, 2005), 91.

53. Sheldrake et al., *Chaos, Creativity and Cosmic Consciousness*, 57.

54. Rupert Sheldrake, Zoom interview by author, February 16, 2021.

55. Terence McKenna, from "Mind Machines," part 2 of trialogue "The Evolutionary Mind," June 6, 1998, The Library of Consciousness, https://www.organism.earth/library/document/the-evolutionary-mind.

56. Phun G. Badillion, "The Psychedelic Future of Terence McKenna," *Dupree's Diamond News* 4, no. 4 (1991): 24–27, 58 (26).

57. T. McKenna, "Taxonomy of Illusion."

58. T. McKenna, "Search for the Original Tree of Knowledge."

59. T. McKenna, "Tryptamine Hallucinogens and Consciousness."

60. Jacobson, "Is Terence McKenna the Brave New Prophet," 136.

61. T. McKenna, "Places I Have Been."

62. Terence McKenna, "Psychopharmacognosticon: Our Man in Nirvana: Koh Samui," *Reality Hackers*, no. 6 (1988): 12–13, 96 (12, 96).

63. T. McKenna, postcard to Ralph Metzner and Kathy Coleman, January 19, 1988, posted from India, Ralph Metzner Papers.

64. Terence McKenna, "Hallucinogens & Culture," in *Thinking Allowed with Jeffrey Mishlove* (Thinking Allowed Productions, 1988).

65. T. McKenna, "Ethnobotany of Shamanism," 4.

66. Leslie Meredith, email to the author, August 29, 2023.

67. Such discussions began in the seventies. By April 1986, Sheila Humphrey (wife of Dennis) typed up a treatment based on Terence's story breakdown (see appendix A). I have seen no evidence of any further development.

68. T. McKenna, *True Hallucinations*, 225. McKenna had connections with a few "Hollywood people," among them Lew Carlino, Robert Chartoff, and Brett Ratner (Dan Levy, email to author, December 6, 2021).

69. Dan Levy, email to author, October 17, 2021.

70. Leslie Rossman, Zoom interview by author, May 31, 2023.

71. Kent, "Prologomena."

72. From a 1993 pitch statement from Harper San Francisco, courtesy of Leslie Rossman.

73. Ken Adams, Zoom interview by author, June 23, 2023.

74. Fraser Clark, "The Final Word on Drugs," in *Psychedelia Britannica: Hallucinogenic Drugs in Britain*, ed. Antonio Melechi (London: Turnaround, 1997), 185–202.

75. Simon Reynolds, *Energy Flash: A Journey through Rave Music and Dance Culture* (London: Picador, 1998), 87.

76. Colin Angus, email to author, July 2, 2021 (Angus's clarifications: July 19, 2023).

77. Colin Angus, email to author, July 20, 2023.

78. From The Shamen with Terence McKenna, "Re:Evolution."

79. "Re:Evolution" reached number 18 on the UK Singles Chart, February 28–March 6, 1993. The release became the subject of the five-track single *Re: Evolution* (The Shamen with Terence McKenna, 1993), which featured McKenna's full monologue transcribed on the front and back cover art and accompanying poster.

80. Terence McKenna, "Psychedelics Before and After History," California Institute of Integral Studies, San Francisco, CA, October 2, 1987, video available at Terence Talks, YouTube, March 6, 2015, https://www.youtube.com/watch?v=hcRGY2Bdk0U.

81. Kathryn Olney, "Out Front—On Drugs," *Mother Jones* (June 1989), 9.

82. Anon., "Terence McKenna—The Re:Evolution(ary) Shaman," 18.

83. David Jay Brown and Rebecca McClen Novick, "Chemophilia with Alexander and Ann Shulgin," in *Voices from the Edge: Conversations with Jerry Garcia, Ram Dass, Jack Kevorkian, Howard Bloom, Michael Murphy, and Other Cutting-Edge Thinkers*, eds. David Jay Brown and Rebecca McClen Novick (Freedom, CA: Crossing Press, 1995), 141.

84. As reported in *Idris Elba's How Clubbing Changed the World*, directed by Sam Bridger, 2012 (screened on Channel 4, 2012).

85. Rick Doblin, Zoom interview by author, June 28, 2021.

86. Calvin Bush, "Dancing with Mr C," *The List* (September 11–24, 1992), 8–9 (9); Dele Fadele, "The Hallucinogeneration Game," *New Musical Express* (February 27, 1993), 28–29 (28).

87. T. McKenna, *Food of the Gods*, 9.

88. T. McKenna, *Food of the Gods*, 57, 58.

89. T. McKenna, "The Camden Centre Talk."

90. Nik Sequenci, interview by author, February 3, 2012.

91. Shpongle was formed by Raja Ram and Simon Posford. Their debut release *Are You Shpongled?* (1998, which features the track "Divine Moments of Truth") is infused with DMT and drenched with McKenna.

92. For a potted history of the contents of the "pink packet," c/o McKenna, and via Sequenci, Youth, and Raja Ram, see Graham St John, *Mystery School in Hyperspace: A Cultural History of DMT* (Berkeley, CA: North Atlantic Books/Evolver, 2015), 202–211.

93. T. McKenna, "Places I Have Been."

94. For further attention to this development, see Graham St John, "The Voice of the Apocalypse: Terence McKenna as Raving Medium," *Dancecult: Journal of Electronic Dance Music Culture* 15, no. 1 (2023): 61–91, https://dj.dancecult.net/index.php/dancecult/article/view/1242/1060.

95. Thomas Cole, *Running a Tightrope: A Year on the Road in Asia* (independently published, 2019): 90.

96. Jonah Sharp, email to author, February 6, 2022. McKenna and Sharp again collaborated on Halloween 1994 at the Great American Music Hall in San Francisco. McKenna's spoken word features on Space Time Continuum with Terence McKenna, *Alien Dreamtime* (album, Astralwerks, 1993); *Alien Dreamtime* (Spacetime Continuum, featuring Terence McKenna and Stephen Kent) was first released on VHS in 1993 by Rose X Media House and City of Tribes Communications, and subsequently on DVD (by Magic Carpet Media) in 2003.

97. Ken Adams, Zoom interview by author, June 23, 2023.

98. Ken Adams, Zoom interview by author, June 23, 2023.

99. Posted on The Well in 1994. From Graham St John, "Techno Millennium: Dance, Ecology and Future Primitives," in *Rave Culture and Religion*, ed. Graham St John (New York: Routledge, 2004). 210–232 (217).

100. Terence McKenna, *Mondo 2000* interview at McKenna's home, Occidental, CA, March 1, 1993, video available at Allan Lundell, YouTube, January 22, 2016, https://www.youtube.com/watch?v=7tTRjEUD2PE.

101. T. McKenna, "A Weekend with Terence McKenna."

102. T. McKenna, *Mondo 2000* interview.

103. T. McKenna, "The Camden Centre Talk," 1992.

104. John Balance and Peter Christopherson, interview with Terence McKenna for "Black Sun Magazine," 1996, Internet Archive (added September 12, 2015), https://archive.org/details/BlackSunMagazine/Terence+McKenna+interview.mp3. As a side project, the Coil duo subsequently produced *Time Machines*, an EP of tones inspired by psychedelics designed to, according to Balance, "facilitate travel through time." McKenna is identified as the key influence. Mark Pilkington, "Coil: Sounds of Blakeness," *Fortean Times*, 2001, https://www.brainwashed.com/common/htdocs/publications/coil-2001-fortean_times.php.

105. T. McKenna, "History Ends in Green."

106. Tom Hodgkinson, "Interview with Terence McKenna," *The Idler*, no. 1 (August 22, 1993), https://www.idler.co.uk/article/terence-mckenna-interview.

107. Terence McKenna, "The Birth of a New Humanity," Earth Trust Foundation Conference (day 2), Los Angeles, CA, October 3, 1992, The Library of Consciousness, https://www.organism.earth/library/document/birth-of-a-new-humanity.

108. "The Bohemian Institute of Prague," a short manifest presumably authored by McKenna in ca. 1990. See http://www.vasulka.org/archive/Artists3/McKenna,Terence/general.pdf.

109. T. McKenna, "The Birth of a New Humanity."

110. "The Bohemian Institute of Prague."

111. In the days before the conference, Rose X shot a dissident film with McKenna at the massive antiwar rally in San Francisco. Titled *What Do We Want? When Do We Want It!* the film featured the "Sinking Submarine" rap in which McKenna railed against permanent war and militarism. Describing this film as having a "very glitchy sorta punkish flavor with very primitive tool kit," Adams notes that this antique digital video is not yet unearthed from his archives (Ken Adams, email to author, August 29, 2023).

112. Trip Gabriel, "Tripping, but Not Falling," *New York Times* (May 2, 1993), section 9, p .6.

113. Mark Dery, "Struck by Noetic Lightning: Terence McKenna Meets the Machine Elves of Hyperspace," in *Follow for Now: Interviews with Friends and Heroes*, ed. Roy Christopher (Seattle, WA: Well-Red Bear, 2007), 39–65 (39).

114. Paul Krassner, "The Mushroom Apocalypse of Terence McKenna," *High Times* 266 (October 1, 1997): 52–53, 56–58 (53).

115. Terence McKenna, "Touched by the Tremendum," Reality Club, New York City, March 27, 1990, video available at Intellectual Deep Web, YouTube, April 11, 2020, https://www.youtube.com/watch?v=Ifs9SHPnHxU.

116. Terence McKenna, "The Light at the End of History: Gaia, Psychedelics and the Archaic Revival," Wetlands, New York City, October 14, 1990, audio available at Terence McKenna Archives, YouTube, May 5, 2020, https://www.youtube.com/watch?v=mPdQSp7qmUE.

117. J. P. Harpignies, email to author, January 8, 2024.

118. J. P. Harpignies, Zoom interview by author, January 12, 2024.

119. Terence McKenna, Wetlands Preserve.

120. Mike Kawitzky, *The Terence McKenna Omnibus 2012*, YouTube, February 13, 2012, https://www.youtube.com/playlist?list=PLF7C7C99A3E5FC148.

121. Mike Kawitzky, Zoom interview by author, May 19, 2021.

122. Terence McKenna, November 18, 1996. From a public email dialogue between Terence McKenna and Robert Hunter 1996–1997, http://www.levity.com/orfeo.

123. Mike Kawitzky, *Journey to Everywhere* (Cape Town: Headspace Studios, 2012, revised in 2018).

124. Kawitzky, *Journey to Everywhere*, 15, 21.

125. Chambers, *Beyond the Brain with Terence McKenna*; Paul Chambers, "Beyond the Brain: Happening at East Edge," *Dancecult: Journal of Electronic Dance Music Culture* 15, no. 1 (2023), https://dj.dancecult.net/index.php/dancecult/article/view/1234/1066.

126. As sampled on the collaboration "Geometric Patterns" by Australian electronic musicians Dark Nebula and Scatterbrain (*Psionic Earth*, Digital Psionics, 2004).

127. Neil Pike, email to author, December 8, 2014. For further discussion of "ayahuasca analogues" in Australia, see St John, *Mystery School in Hyperspace*, 157–165.

128. Including, but not exclusively, Olli Wisdom, Pete Strong, John Jacobs, Chin Bindi, Nick Taylor, A. B. Didgeridoo, among others. Chambers, *Beyond the Brain with Terence McKenna*.

129. Dillon Hicks with CeeJay Barnaby about Terence McKenna, Live at the University of Wollongong.

130. Terence McKenna, "Light of the Third Millennium," Whole Life Expo, Palmer Auditorium, Austin, TX, October 4, 1997, The Library of Consciousness, https://www.organism.earth/library/document/light-of-the-third-millennium. Hicks and McKenna were in dialogue about a second Australian tour.

131. Terence McKenna with Lost at Last, Maritime Hall, San Francisco, CA, December 12, 1998, video available at complete_mckenna_archive, YouTube, January 5, 2014, https://www.youtube.com/watch?v=p2CSDIq5SNQ.

CHAPTER 9

1. Joyce, *Finnegans Wake*, 455.

2. T. McKenna, "Mind and Time, Spirit and Matter."

3. T. McKenna and D. McKenna, *The Invisible Landscape* (1975), 151.

4. John Horgan, *Rational Mysticism: Spirituality Meets Science in the Search for Enlightenment* (New York: Mariner Books, 2003), 186–187.

5. In Hayes, "A Conversation with Terence McKenna," 437, 441.

6. T. McKenna, "Temporal Resonance," 28.

7. T. McKenna, *True Hallucinations*, 169.

8. Hodgkinson, "Interview with Terence McKenna."

9. T. McKenna, "The Plot Thickens, the Stakes Rise."

10. Brown and McClen, "Interview: Terence K. McKenna," 60.

11. Terence McKenna, "Understanding and Imagination in the Light of Nature" (day 1: "Archaic Revival as Antidote to History's Abyss"), Philosophical Research Society, Los Angeles, October 17, 1987, The Library of Consciousness, https://www.organism.earth/library/document/understanding-and-imagination.

12. Terence K. McKenna, "Ecodynamics: A New Theory of Societal Evolution by Kenneth E. Boulding," *Zygon* 16, no. 1 (1981): 100–101 (101).

13. Terence McKenna, "Dreaming Awake at the End of Time," Fort Mason, San Francisco, CA, December 13, 1998, The Library of Consciousness, https://www.organism.earth/library/document/dreaming-awake-at-the-end-of-time.

14. T. McKenna, *True Hallucinations*, 198.

15. In Hayes, "A Conversation with Terence McKenna," 437.

16. From the Shamen with Terence McKenna, "Re:Evolution."

17. T. McKenna, "Taxonomy of Illusion"; Terence McKenna, "Approaching Timewave Zero, Views from the Edge of History, Part II," *Magical Blend* 45 (1995): 26–28, 30–32, 105 (29).

18. From Space Time Continuum with Terence McKenna, *Alien Dreamtime*

19. From the Shamen with Terence McKenna, "Re:Evolution."

20. T. McKenna, in Sheldrake et al., *Chaos, Creativity and Cosmic Consciousness*, 5.

21. In Hayes, "A Conversation with Terence McKenna," 439.

22. Jeffrey J. Kripal, *Authors of the Impossible: The Paranormal and the Sacred* (Chicago: University of Chicago Press, 2011), 137.

23. McKenna admitted in 1994 that Teilhard was a "direct influence" (Terence McKenna, "Permitting Smart People to Hope," Esalen Institute, Big Sur, CA, June 1994, The Library of Consciousness, https://www.organism.earth/library/document/permitting-smart-people-to-hope). On the relative absence of Teilhard in his discourse, he mused: "Maybe the reason I don't mention [*The Phenomenon of Man*] is that my mother was very big on pushing it on me!" (Terence McKenna, Wetlands Preserve).

24. Terence McKenna, "Psychedelic Empowerment and the Environmental Crisis: Re-Awakening our Connection to the Gaian Mind," in *Visionary Plant Consciousness: The Shamanic Teachings of the Plant World*, ed. J. P. Harpignies (Rochester, VT: Inner Traditions, 2007), 56–62 (62).

25. John Eden and Gyrus, "Interview with Terence McKenna," ICA, London, October 11, 1996, https://dreamflesh.com/interview/terence-mckenna.

26. Sheldrake et al., *The Evolutionary Mind* (2005), 48.

27. In Hayes, "A Conversation with Terence McKenna," 441.

28. See Egil Asprem, "The Magus of Silicon Valley: Immortality, Apocalypse, and God Making in Ray Kurzweil's Transhumanism," in Ehler Voss, ed. *Mediality on Trial: Testing and Contesting Trance and Other Media Techniques*, ed. Ehler Voss (Berlin: Walter de Gruyter, 2020), 397–412 (406).

29. T. McKenna and D. McKenna, *The Invisible Landscape* (1975), 144. The revised edition uses "eschaton" or "Eschaton" (see *The Invisible Landscape* [1994], 149, figure 19). Additionally, in the revised edition, "the Eschaton" is considered to be "a universal and fractal morphogenetic field which was hypothesized to model the unfolding predispositions of space and time" (146, 149).

30. Krassner, "The Mushroom Apocalypse of Terence McKenna," 57.

31. T. McKenna, *True Hallucinations*, 171.

32. T. McKenna and D. McKenna, *The Invisible Landscape* (1975), 164.

33. Ralph Abraham, email to author, March 4, 2021.

34. Robert Anton Wilson, *Cosmic Trigger I: The Final Secret of The Illuminati* (Berkeley, CA: And/Or Press, 1977), 216.

35. See "Acknowledgements to 1994 Edition," in *The Invisible Landscape* (1994), xxiii.

36. Kathleen Harrison, email to author, June 26, 2022.

37. Terence McKenna, letter to Peter Meyer, October 26, 1988. From Bruce Damer, "Terence2012" archive project.

38. The language of fractals was added to the 1994 edition of *The Invisible Landscape*. For example: "The theory of time that is implied by the Timewave is a theory of time as a fractal, or self-similar, wave" (172).

39. T. McKenna and D. McKenna, *The Invisible Landscape* (1975), 149–150; T. McKenna and D. McKenna, *The Invisible Landscape* (1994), 149, figure 19.

40. T. McKenna, "Approaching Timewave Zero," 105. Planck's constant is today recognized as: 6.626×10^{-34} joule per hertz.

41. T. McKenna, "Approaching Timewave Zero," 32. We will recall that 384 days $\times$ 64 hexagrams = 67.35 years.

42. The amplitude of the experience mirrored 1970–1971, that is, the "DNA year" from Hazelle's death to Terence's twenty-fifth birthday.

43. T. McKenna, "Ethnobotany of Shamanism," 49.

44. Krassner, "The Mushroom Apocalypse of Terence McKenna," 58, 59.

45. T. McKenna, "Change & Becoming," September 23, 1971, 96.

46. Peter Russell, *Waking Up in Time: Finding Inner Peace in Times of Accelerating Change* (San Francisco: Origin Press, 1998 [1992]), 162–163 (162).

47. Terence McKenna, "Approaching Timewave Zero, Views from the Edge of History, Part I," *Magical Blend*, no. 44 (1994): 38–43 (41, 43).

48. T. McKenna, "Change & Becoming," October 28, 1971, 125.

49. T. McKenna, *Mondo 2000* interview.

50. "Novelty & Habit in July & August 1996," originally posted on McKenna's website, Hyperborea, http://www.levity.com/eschaton/NRreportjulyaug96.html; Krassner, "The Mushroom Apocalypse of Terence McKenna," 58, 76.

51. Terence McKenna, Live at Cathedral Church of Saint John the Divine, Synod Hall, New York City, April 25, 1996, transcribed by Abrupt, https://www.abrupt.org/abruptlog/terence-mckenna-at-saint-johns.

52. "Novelty & Habit in Spring of '96," http://www.levity.com/eschaton/NRlatebreak.html.

53. Terence McKenna, "Everything Teaches," Entheobotany Conference, Palenque, Mexico, 1994, audio available at We Plants Are Happy Plants, YouTube, December 14, 2021, https://www.youtube.com/watch?v=ZyQLIWzOvYw&t=668s.

54. Watkins, "Autopsy for a Mathematical Hallucination?"

55. Watkins, "Autopsy for a Mathematical Hallucination?"

56. Meyer, who incorrectly identifies Terence's FORTRAN programmers, "Royce and Kelley," renames the model that retains the "half twist" the "Kelley Timewave." Peter Meyer, "The Watkins Objection Is Not Fatal" (2020), https://www.fractal-timewave.com/articles/watkins_objection_not_fatal.htm.

57. T. McKenna, "Our Cyberspiritual Future."

58. Matthew Watkins, "2012 and the 'Watkins Objection' to Terence McKenna's 'Timewave Theory,'" *Reality Sandwich*, November 19, 2010, https://realitysandwich.com/watkins_objection.

59. "Novelty Theory Bombshell!," http://www.levity.com/eschaton/bombshell.html.

60. T. McKenna, "Our Cyberspiritual Future."

61. Tom McIntyre, "Millennium Witness: Psychedelic Anthropologist Terence McKenna Takes on the Brave New World," *San Francisco Examiner Magazine*, October 9, 1994, 12–13, 19–24 (22).

62. T. McKenna, "Understanding and Imagination in the Light of Nature" (day 2).

63. T. McKenna, "I Understand Philip K. Dick," 258, 259.

64. Kevin A. Whitesides and John W. Hoopes, "Seventies Dreams and 21st Century Realities: The Emergence of 2012 Mythology," *Zeitschrift für Anomalistik* 12 (2012): 50–74 (60, fig. 15).

65. Terence McKenna, "The Syntax of Psychedelic Time: Fractals, Endpoints, End Times, Zero Points," Shared Visions Bookstore, July 1983, Berkeley, CA, The Library of Consciousness, https://www.organism.earth/library/document/syntax-of-psychedelic-time.

66. Wilson, *Cosmic Trigger*, 217.

67. The other prophets are Frank Waters and José Argüelles, as expertly examined by Kevin Whitesides in "Processes of Representational Transformation in the 2012 Phenomenon: Transmission, Improvisation, and Adaptation" (MSc diss., University of Edinburgh, School of Divinity, 2012), 36–60.

68. Respectively, Abraham and T. McKenna, "Dynamics of Hyperspace"; T. McKenna, "Syntax of Psychedelic Time."

69. For example, see T. McKenna, "The Invisible Landscape (Peer Review)."

70. Kevin Whitesides, email to author, January 25, 2022.

71. It has been conjectured that McKenna either adopted the date from Robert Sharer's correlation published in 1983 (Sylvanus G. Morley, George W. Brainerd, and Robert Sharer, *The Ancient Maya*, 4th ed. [Stanford, CA: Stanford University Press, 1983], 603) or had adopted it in discussion with scholar Henry Munn. See Whitesides and Hoopes, "Seventies Dreams and 21st Century Realities," 64, 62.

72. José Argüelles, *The Mayan Factor: Path Beyond Technology* (Santa Fe, NM: Bear & Co., 1996 [1987]), 45. Though Argüelles had identified 2012 as the conclusion of the 5,125-year "Great Cycle" of the ancient Maya civilization in his 1975 book *The*

Transformative Vision: Reflections on the Nature and History of Human Expression, it was not until his meeting with McKenna in 1983 that he incorporated the date December 21, 2012, into his improvised millenarian scheme (see Whitesides, "Processes of Representational Transformation in the 2012 Phenomenon," 59–60). There exists loose speculation that both Argüelles and McKenna were influenced by William Burroughs, who offered an apocalyptic portrayal of the end of the Mayan Long Count in *The Exterminator* (1960). See Tommy P. Cowan, "What Most People Would Call Evil: The Archontic Spirituality of William S. Burroughs," *La Rosa di Paracelso: Rivista di Studi sull' Esoterismo Occidentale* 2, nos. 1–2 (2018): 83–122.

73. T. McKenna and D. McKenna, *The Invisible Landscape* (1975), 189.

74. T. McKenna and D. McKenna, *The Invisible Landscape* (1994), 197, figure 31.

75. T. McKenna, "Appreciating Imagination."

76. Kevin A. Whitesides, "From Counterculture to Mainstream: 2012 Millennialism in Your Living Room," in *Small Screen Revelations: Apocalypse in Contemporary Television*, ed. James Aston and John Wallis (Sheffield: Sheffield Phoenix Press, 2013), 74–95.

77. Terence McKenna, "Foreword," in John Major Jenkins, *Maya Cosmogenesis 2012* (Santa Fe, NM: Bear & Co., 1998), xxv–xxix (xxvi).

78. Andrew Fergus Wilson, "From Mushrooms to the Stars: 2012 and the Apocalyptic Milieu," in *Prophecy in the New Millennium: When Prophecies Persist*, ed. Sarah Harvey and Suzanne Newcombe (Farnham: Ashgate, 2013), 225–238 (226).

79. T. McKenna and D. McKenna, *The Invisible Landscape* (1994), 54.

80. José Argüelles, *Earth Ascending: An Illustrated Treatise on the Law Governing Whole Systems* (Santa Fe, NM: Bear and Co., 1988), 29.

81. Sheldrake et al., *The Evolutionary Mind* (2005), 153; T. McKenna, "Our Cyberspiritual Future."

82. Sheldrake et al., *The Evolutionary Mind* (2005), 104.

83. Terence McKenna, "Countdown into Complexity," Esalen Institute, Big Sur, CA, March 1996, The Library of Consciousness, https://www.organism.earth/library/document/countdown-into-complexity.

84. T. McKenna, "Dreaming Awake at the End of Time," 1998.

85. T. McKenna, *True Hallucinations*, 120.

86. Noffke with T. McKenna, "A Conversation over Saucers," 24.

87. T. McKenna, *True Hallucinations*, 199.

88. Sheldrake et al., *Chaos, Creativity, and Cosmic Consciousness*, 156, 157, 156.

89. Sheldrake et al., *The Evolutionary Mind* (2005), 43.

90. Abraham and T. McKenna, "Dynamics of Hyperspace."

91. Sheldrake et al., *Chaos, Creativity, and Cosmic Consciousness*, 156, 157, 156.

92. George Csicsery, email to author, August 22, 2020.

93. Sheldrake et al., *The Evolutionary Mind* (2005), 62.

94. Rupert Sheldrake, Zoom interview by author, February 16, 2021.

95. Sheldrake et al., *Chaos, Creativity, and Cosmic Consciousness*, 161, 164, 166.

96. Sheldrake et al., *The Evolutionary Mind* (2005), 60, 61.

97. T. McKenna, "Ethnobotany and Shamanism."

98. Terence McKenna, "The Great Timestream Bifurcation," Ojai Foundation, April 1986, https://transcendentalobject.files.wordpress.com/2017/07/timestreambifurcation.pdf.

99. Krassner, "The Mushroom Apocalypse of Terence McKenna," 59.

100. J. Christian Greer, "Angel-Headed Hipsters: Psychedelic Militancy in Nineteen-Eighties North America" (PhD diss., University of Amsterdam, 2020), 125.

101. Jacobson, "Is Terence McKenna the Brave New Prophet," 135.

102. D. McKenna, *Brotherhood*, 316.

103. Gyrus, "The End of the River," in *Towards 2012: The Journal of Millennial Mutation*, Parts IV/V (1998), https://dreamflesh.com/essay/end-of-the-river.

104. Jacobson, "Is Terence McKenna the Brave New Prophet," 135.

105. Mark Dery, *Escape Velocity: Cyberculture at the End of the Century* (New York: Grove Press, 1996), 10.

106. See Michael Garfield, "The Psychedelic Transhumanists," *h+ Magazine* (September 29, 2009).

107. Kurzweil's idea of an exponentially explosive interfacing of humans with artificial intelligence that will transform the universe in 2045 was not fully formed until after McKenna's death. See Asprem, "The Magus of Silicon Valley."

108. Krassner, "The Mushroom Apocalypse of Terence McKenna," 76.

109. Sheldrake et al., *The Evolutionary Mind* (2005), 44. McKenna estimated a world population of ten billion in 2012 (it was seven billion).

110. T. McKenna, "Ethnobotany of Shamanism," 7.

111. T. McKenna, "The Great Timestream Bifurcation."

112. T. McKenna, "The Rites of Spring."

113. T. McKenna, "The Light at the End of History."

114. Sheldrake et al., *Chaos, Creativity and Cosmic Consciousness*, 158.

115. T. McKenna, "We Are at the Cutting Edge."

116. Art Bell, Terence McKenna interview, "Timewave Zero," *Coast to Coast AM*, May 22, 1997, Internet Archive, https://archive.org/details/TerenceMcKennaWithArtBell970522TimewaveZero.

117. Terence McKenna, "Shamanism, Alchemy, and the Millennium," day 1, Esalen Institute, Big Sur, CA, August 19, 1985, Lorenzo Hagerty's *Psychedelic Salon*, Podcast 688, December 25, 2023, Internet Archive, https://archive.org/details/688-mc-kenn-1985-esalen-01.

118. D. McKenna, *Brotherhood*, 279.

119. T. McKenna, "New and Old Maps of Hyperspace."

120. Mike Kawitzky, "The Terence McKenna OmniBus 2012—8/12—'Totality Symbol,'" YouTube, August 29, 2012, https://www.youtube.com/watch?v=gQ7cVRhHSFA.

121. T. McKenna and D. McKenna, *The Invisible Landscape* (1975), 183.

122. Levin, "In Praise of Psychedelics," 24.

123. Levin, "In Praise of Psychedelics," 8–9.

124. Sheldrake et al., *The Evolutionary Mind* (2005), 46.

125. Sheldrake et al., *The Evolutionary Mind* (2005), 47, 48, 49.

126. Sheldrake et al., *The Evolutionary Mind* (2005), 51, 108.

127. Sheldrake et al., *The Evolutionary Mind* (2005), 52, 53.

128. Sheldrake et al., *The Evolutionary Mind* (2005), 56.

129. David Jay Brown, "In the Presence of the Past with Rupert Sheldrake," in *Mavericks of the Mind*, ed. David Jay Brown and Rebecca McClen Novick (Freedom, CA: The Crossing Press, 1993), 140–156 (153).

130. Sheldrake et al., *The Evolutionary Mind* (2005), 221.

131. T. McKenna, "Amazon Psychotropical Quest," 1972.

132. T. McKenna, "Ethnobotany of Shamanism," 7.

133. Carla Sinclair, "Spacetime Tsunami: Terence McKenna Interview," *bOING bOING*, no. 10 (1992): 32–34, https://www.jacobsm.com/deoxy/deoxy.org/t_sunami.htm.

134. Badillon, "The Psychedelic Future of Terence McKenna," 27.

135. Badillon, "The Psychedelic Future of Terence McKenna," 27.

136. For a discussion of the simultaneous embrace of the Mayan Long Count calendar and Timewave Zero within psyculture, see Graham St John, "The 2012 Movement, Visionary Arts and Psytrance Culture," in *2012: Decoding the Countercultural Apocalypse*, ed. Joseph Gelfer (Sheffield: Equinox, 2011), 123–143.

137. Terence McKenna, "Awakening to Archaic Values," Santa Fe, New Mexico, May 1990, The Library of Consciousness, https://www.organism.earth/library/document/awakening-to-archaic-values.

138. T. McKenna, "Dreaming Awake at the End of Time."

139. De Vosjoli, "Casting Nets"; Matthew Collin, "Terence McKenna," *i-D Magazine*, no. 157 (October 1996): 130.

140. Terence McKenna, "The Future of Humanity" (n.d.), a chapter in the incomplete and unpublished manuscript of Terence McKenna and Philippe De Vosjoli, "Casting Nets in the Sea of Mind," courtesy of Philippe De Vosjoli.

141. T. McKenna, "In the Valley of Novelty."

CHAPTER 10

1. T. McKenna, "Hyperdimensional Understanding."

2. Terence McKenna, "Prague Gnosis," Part 1, Prague, Czechoslovakia, June 1992, The Library of Consciousness, https://www.organism.earth/library/document/prague-gnosis-1.

3. McIntyre, "Millennium Witness," 21.

4. Miller, "Interview: Terence McKenna," 73.

5. T. McKenna, "Global Perspectives and Psychedelic Poetics."

6. Luc Sala interviews Terence McKenna, Entheobotany Seminar, Palenque, Mexico, 1996, video available at Luc Sala, YouTube, February 12, 2007, https://www.youtube.com/watch?v=nq6N4kQK-KA.

7. T. McKenna, *Food of the Gods*, xix.

8. T. McKenna, *Food of the Gods*, 245.

9. Terence McKenna, "Culture and Ideology Are Not Your Friends," Whole Life Expo, Denver, CO, April 1999, The Library of Consciousness, https://www.organism.earth/library/document/culture-and-ideology-are-not-your-friends.

10. Terence McKenna, Wetlands Preserve.

11. Huxley, "The Pros and Cons," 177.

12. T. McKenna, "Eros and the Eschaton."

13. T. McKenna, "The Future of Humanity."

14. Terence McKenna with Tom Leykis, "Terence McKenna vs. Young Republican Radio Debate," 4KFI Radio, Los Angeles, September 1991, audio available at Terence McKenna Archives, YouTube, March 6, 2018, https://www.youtube.com/watch?v=5OONsjJsOI0.

15. Terence McKenna, "Terence McKenna vs Daryl Gates," *The Daryl Gates Show*, KFI-AM, Los Angeles, CA, 1993, audio available at Terence McKenna Archives, YouTube, March 20, 2019, https://www.youtube.com/watch?v=OWPeD2UWhbo.

16. Anon., "Terence McKenna—The Re:Evolution(ary) Shaman," 23.

17. Terence McKenna, "Vertigo at History's Edge," Julia Richmond High School auditorium, 317 East 67th Street, New York City, April 29, 1994, New York Open Center, The Library of Consciousness, https://www.organism.earth/library/document/vertigo-at-historys-edge.

18. Timothy, Leary, *Flashbacks: A Personal and Cultural History of an Era* (Los Angeles: Tarcher, 1983), 32, 33.

19. Jung, *Psychology and Alchemy*, 360–372; C&B, November 16, 1971, 61.

20. T. McKenna, "Search for the Original Tree of Knowledge."

21. T. McKenna, *Food of the Gods*, 98.

22. Terence McKenna, "Wasson's Literary Precursors," in *Sacred Mushroom Seeker: Tributes to R. Gordon Wasson*, ed. Tom Riedlinger (Dioscorides Press, 1990), 165–176.

23. T. McKenna, *Food of the Gods*, 95–119. McKenna's case against Wasson's theory was extremely thin, as reported by Jonathan Ott, "Post-Wasson History of the Soma Plant," *Eleusis: Journal of Psychoactive Plants & Compounds* 1 (1998): 9–37 (22).

24. R. G. Wasson, in *Soma: Divine Mushroom of Immortality* (New York: Harcourt Brace Jovanovich, 1971), 326–334; Robert Gordon Wasson, Stella Kramrisch, Carl A. P. Ruck, and Jonathan Ott, *Persephone's Quest: Entheogens and the Origins of Religion* (New Haven, CT: Yale University Press, 1986).

25. Terence McKenna, "Hallucinogenic Mushrooms and Evolution," *ReVISION: The Journal of Consciousness and Change* 10, no. 4 (Spring 1988): 51–57 (52).

26. Gracie and Zarkov, "Terence McKenna," *Erowid*, 1993. The interview was submitted to *Mondo 2000* in 1993, but was not accepted for publication. https://erowid.org/culture/characters/mckenna_terence/mckenna_terence_interview_1993.shtml.

27. T. McKenna, "Rap Dancing into the 3rd Millennium."

28. T. McKenna, "Tryptamine Hallucinogens and Consciousness."

29. T. McKenna, "Ethnobotany of Shamanism," 57.

30. Kenaston, "The Bodhi Tree Interview."

31. T. McKenna, "Psychedelic Skepticism."

32. Lex Lonehood, "Terence McKenna, America's Shaman Battles Brain Cancer," *After Dark: The Official Art Bell Newsletter* (October 1999), 4–5.

33. Tim Leary, "Programmed Communications during Experiences with DMT (Dimethyltryptamine)," *Psychedelic Review*, no. 8 (1966): 83–85 (86).

34. T. McKenna, "Dreaming Awake at the End of Time."

35. T. McKenna, "Ethnobotany of Shamanism," 58, 50.

36. Shpongle, "A New Way to Say Hooray," in *Tales of the Inexpressible* (Twisted Records, 2001).

37. T. McKenna, *Food of the Gods*, 259.

38. Dennis McKenna, email to author, June 8, 2015.

39. Rick Strassman, *DMT: The Spirit Molecule: A Doctor's Revolutionary Research into the Biology of Near-Death and Mystical Experiences* (Rochester, VT: Park Street Press, 2001). For a discussion of the competing perspectives on the human condition that have shaped opinion on the "DMT gland," see Graham St John, "The DMT Gland: The Pineal, the Spirit Molecule, and Popular Culture," *International Journal for the Study of New Religions* 7, no. 2 (2016): 153–174.

40. Rupert Sheldrake, "The Day Terence McKenna Offered Me DMT," London Real, YouTube, March 27, 2019, https://www.youtube.com/watch?v=rLXj3mPJ-l8.

41. T. McKenna, "Post Electric Thought," 55.

42. From the discussion in Graham St John, "The Pineal Enigma: The Dazzling Life and Times of the 'Spirit Gland,'" in *DMT Dialogues: Encounters with the Spirit Molecule*, ed. David Luke and Rory Spowers (Rochester, VT: Inner Traditions, 2018), 8–37 (29).

43. Strassman, *DMT: The Spirit Molecule*.

44. Rick Strassman, "The Pineal Gland: Current Evidence for Its Role in Consciousness," *Psychedelic Monographs and Essays* 5 (1991): 167–205 (188).

45. Strassman, *DMT: The Spirit Molecule*, xvii.

46. For a discussion of this controversy, see St John, "The DMT Gland."

47. T. McKenna, "The Camden Centre Talk."

48. Shpongle, "A New Way to Say Hooray."

49. T. McKenna. "Ethnobotany of Shamanism," 58.

50. C&B, November 20, 1971, 148.

51. Shpongle, "A New Way to Say Hooray."

52. C&B, November 20, 1971, 148.

53. T. McKenna, "Tryptamine Hallucinogens and Consciousness."

54. Space Time Continuum with Terence McKenna, "Alien Love," *Alien Dreamtime* (album, Astralwerks, 1993).

55. Jacques Vallée, *The Invisible College: What a Group of Scientists Has Discovered about UFO Influence on the Human Race* (San Antonio, TX: Anomalist Books, 1975), 55.

56. Terence McKenna, "Introduction," in Walter Y. Evans-Wentz, *The Fairy-Faith in Celtic Countries* (New York: Citadel Press, 1990 [1911]), i–iii (ii, iii).

57. T. McKenna, "History Ends in Green"; T. McKenna, "Having Archaic."

58. T. McKenna, "A Calendar for the Goddess (Ecology of Souls)."

59. T. McKenna, "History Ends in Green."

60. T. McKenna, "History Ends in Green."

61. T. McKenna, "Introduction," in Evans-Wentz, *The Fairy-Faith in Celtic Countries*, iii.

62. T. McKenna, "Psychedelic Skepticism."

63. Space Time Continuum with Terence McKenna, "Speaking in Tongues," from *Alien Dreamtime* (Astralwerks, 1993).

64. Terence McKenna, "Mind, Molecules, and Magic" (a.k.a. "The Gnostic Astronaut"), Esalen Institute, Big Sur, CA, June 1984, audio available at Deus Ex McKenna ~ Terence McKenna Archive, YouTube, November 26, 2014, https://www.youtube.com/watch?v=CeYxUZ1pobY.

65. T. McKenna, "Our Cyberspiritual Future"; T. McKenna, "Ethnobotany of Shamanism," 64.

66. Terence McKenna with Zuvuya, *Dream Matrix Telemetry* (Delerium Records, 1993).

67. T. McKenna, "Hot Concepts and Melting Edges."

68. Noffke, "Terence McKenna: The Monkey Is Being Shed," 7.

69. T. McKenna and D. McKenna, *The Invisible Landscape* (1975), 104.

70. T. McKenna, "Ethnobotany of Shamanism," 9.

71. T. McKenna, "Tryptamine Hallucinogens and Consciousness."

72. T. McKenna, "Taxonomy of Illusion"; Bruce Eisner, "Psychedelic Culture: An Interview with Terence McKenna," *Psychedelic Island Views* 2, no. 2 (1997): 5–10, 14 (10).

73. T. McKenna and D. McKenna, "Shamanic Investigations," 118.

74. Alexander Blair-Ewart, "Magic Plants and the Logos: Terence McKenna in Conversation with Alexander Blair-Ewart," in Alexander Blair-Ewart, *Mindfire: Dialogues in the Other Future* (Toronto: Somerville House, 1995), 60–72.

75. Noffke with T. McKenna, "A Conversation over Saucers"; Drury, "Sacred Plants and Mystic Realities," 9.

76. Jung, *Memories, Dreams and Reflections*, 184.

77. Noffke with T. McKenna, "A Conversation over Saucers"; T. McKenna, "New and Old Maps of Hyperspace."

78. Toms and Florin, "The Invisible Landscape with Terence McKenna."

79. T. McKenna, "Terence McKenna: Q&A," 24.

80. In *The Invisible Landscape* (1975), 104, the McKennas cite the usage by Henry Munn discussing the lucid discourse of the beshroomed. See Henry Munn, "The Mushrooms of Language," in *Hallucinogens and Shamanism*, ed. Michael Harner (New York: Oxford University Press, 1973), 86–122 (88–89). R. Gordon Wasson's *The Wonderous Mushroom: Mycolatry in Mesoamerica* (New York: McGraw-Hill, 1980), 225, is cited in *Food of the Gods* (60). It is there stated that the mushroom "bestows on the curandero what the Greeks called *Logos*, the Aryan *Vac*, Vedic *Kavya*, 'poetic potency,' as Louis Renous put it."

81. From Hans Jonas, *The Phenomenon of Life* (New York: Dell, 1966), 238, as cited in *Food of the Gods*, 252. The passage is quoted at length in "Change and Becoming" where it is early reported that "a more perfect archetypal logos" defines the powerful tryptamine experience (C&B, November 20, 1971, 149).

82. Elvin D. Smith, "Terence McKenna Interview (Part 2)," *Psychozoic Press*, no. 6 (Winter 1983): 26–32 (28). The interview was serialized in *Psychozoic Press* over five issues in 1983-1984.

83. T. McKenna, "Shamanology."

84. T. McKenna, "Terence McKenna: Q&A," 24.

85. T. McKenna, "Hallucinogenic Mushrooms and Evolution," 57.

86. T. McKenna, *Food of the Gods*, 252.

87. Maria Papaspyrou, Chiara Baldini, and David Luke, eds., *Psychedelic Mysteries of the Feminine: Creativity, Ecstasy, and Healing* (Rochester, VT: Park Street Press, 2019).

88. T. McKenna, *Food of the Gods*, xx.

89. Korzybski, "Terence and the Coming Eschaton."

90. Terence McKenna, "Walking Out of the Ordinary," Sunshine Gardens, Los Angeles, 1984, The Library of Consciousness, https://www.organism.earth/library/document/walking-out-of-the-ordinary.

91. T. McKenna, "Intentionality of Meaning."

92. T. McKenna, "Ethnobotany of Shamanism," 60.

93. Torgoff, *Can't Find My Way Home*, 415.

94. Terence McKenna, "Foreword," in Richard Glen Boire, *Sacred Mushrooms & the Law* (Oakland, CA: Ronan, 1997).

95. Kent, "Terence McKenna: An Interview by James Kent," Part Two, 36.

96. Terence McKenna, "Terence McKenna Speaks," Mind States conference, November 23, 1997, *The Entheogen Review* 7, no. 1 (1998): 13.

97. Jan Irwin, "NEW MKULTRA DISCOVERY: Terence McKenna Admitted That He Was a 'Deep Background' and 'PR' Agent (CIA or FBI)," Logos Media, August 23, 2013, https://logosmedia.com/McKenna-Agent.

98. T. McKenna, "Dreaming Awake at the End of Time."

99. Terence McKenna, "Feast for the Eyes," Esalen Institute, Big Sur, CA, April 1994. Part 1, audio available at We Plants Are Happy Plants, YouTube, June 3, 2023, https://www.youtube.com/watch?v=Fu3yMv0KmrE&t=119s; Terence McKenna, "The Primacy of Direct Experience," Esalen Institute, Big Sur, CA, June 1994, The Library of Consciousness, https://www.organism.earth/library/document/primacy-of-direct-experience.

100. Anon., "Terence McKenna—The Re: Evolution(ary) Shaman," 24; T. McKenna, "Having Archaic."

101. T. McKenna, "Terence McKenna vs Daryl Gates."

102. Dennis Romero, "Talking with the Timothy Leary of the '90s," *LA Times*, May 3, 1996.

103. Michael Simmons, "We'd Love to Turn You Off: The VA's Bad Trip over Psychedelic Futurist," *LA Weekly*, May 1–6, 1996, 20.

104. Pam Burton, Terence McKenna interview, "Poets and Prophesiers," KPFK, Pacifica Radio, LA, May 9, 1996, audio available at Deus Ex McKenna ~ Terence McKenna Archive, YouTube, November 27, 2014, https://www.youtube.com/watch?v=5MYW0TA14iY.

105. Alex Burns, "Terence McKenna: Mind Contagions," *Disinfo*, September 8, 2001.

106. Terence McKenna, "Novelty & Habit in Spring of 96," http://www.levity.com/eschaton/NRlatebreak.html.

107. Art Bell, Terence McKenna interview, "Psychedelia," *Coast to Coast AM*, March 19, 1998, Internet Archive, https://archive.org/details/mckenna.bell.98-03-19.

108. T. McKenna, *Food of the Gods*, xvi, 265.

109. T. McKenna, *Food of the Gods*, 263.

110. Terence McKenna, "Limits of Art and Edges of Science," Community Church of New York, March 19, 1992, New York Open Center event, The Library of Consciousness, https://www.organism.earth/library/document/limits-of-art-edges-of-science.

111. T. McKenna, *Food of the Gods*, 249.

112. T. McKenna, "Feast for the Eyes."

113. Sam Woolfe, "A Critique of Terence McKenna's 'Stoned Ape Theory,'" *Sam Woolfe*, May 28, 2013, https://www.samwoolfe.com/2013/05/terence-mckennas-stoned-ape-theory.html.

114. Robert Anton Wilson, *Chaos and Beyond: The Best of Trajectories* (Santa Clara, CA: Anomalous Books, 2005).

115. See, for example, Ralph Metzner, ed., *Sacred Mushroom of Visions—Teonanácatl: A Sourcebook on the Psilocybin Mushroom* (Rochester VT: Park Street Press, 2005).

116. Richard Evans Schultes, Review of *Food of the Gods*, in *American Scientist* 81, no. 5 (1993): 489–490 (489).

117. J. M. Rodríguez Arce and M. J. Winkelman, "Psychedelics, Sociality, and Human Evolution," *Frontiers in Psychology* 12 (2021): 729425.

118. J. P. Harpignies, Zoom interview by author, January 12, 2024.

119. For example, Nicole Lopez, "An Exploration of Linguistic Relativity Theory for Consideration of Terence McKenna's 'Stoned Ape Theory' on the Origins of Consciousness and Language: Implications for Language Pedagogy," *Journal of Conscious Evolution* 16, no. 1 (2020), https://digitalcommons.ciis.edu/cejournal/vol16/iss1/6.

120. Robby Berman, "Mushroom Expert Exhumes the Stoned Ape Theory," *Big Think*, April 11, 2019, https://bigthink.com/mind-brain/stoned-ape-return.

121. T. McKenna, *Food of the Gods*, 74.

122. T. McKenna, "Feast for the Eyes."

123. T. McKenna, *Food of the Gods*, 256.

124. Kathleen Harrison and Paul Stamets, "An Ethnobotanist and a Mycologist Discuss the Rewards and Risks of Sacramental Plant Use in a Modern Context," in *Visionary Plant Consciousness: The Shamanic Teachings of the Plant World*, ed. J. P. Harpignies (Rochester, VT: Inner Traditions, 2007), 121–132 (123).

125. Rupert Sheldrake, Terence McKenna, and Ralph Abraham, *The Evolutionary Mind: Trialogues at the Edge of the Unthinkable* (Santa Cruz, CA: Trialogue Press, 1998), 88.

126. Rupert Sheldrake, Zoom interview by author, February 16, 2021.

127. Eric Cunningham. "Terence McKenna," in *Holy People of the World: A Cross-Cultural Encyclopedia*, ed. Phyllis G. Jestice, 3 vols. (Santa Barbara, CA: ABC-CLIO, 2004), 567–568.

128. Andrew Montieth, "'The Words of McKenna': Healing, Political Critique, and the Evolution of Psychonaut Religion since the 1960s Counterculture," *Journal of the American Academy of Religion* vol. 84, no. 4 (December 2016): 1081–1109 (1103).

129. Levin, "In Praise of Psychedelics," 18.

130. Edward St. Aubyn, *On the Edge: A Novel* (New York: Picador, 1998). St. Aubyn name-checks McKenna as a "genius" (144), who stands beyond the pilloried subject matter.

131. T. McKenna, "Our Cyberspiritual Future."

132. Michael Krasny, Terence McKenna interview, "Forum," *NPR*, March 1999, audio available at Deus Ex McKenna ~ Terence McKenna Archive, YouTube, July 9, 2011, https://www.youtube.com/watch?v=_6Kob-Klwqk&t=2s.

133. Anon., "Terence McKenna—The Re: Evolution(ary) Shaman," 19.

134. Kathleen Harrison, Zoom interview by author, April 20, 2022.

135. T. McKenna, "Appreciating Imagination."

136. T. McKenna, "Hot Concepts and Melting Edges."

137. Teafaerie, "The Terence McKenna Thing," *Erowid*, October 30, 2012, https://www.erowid.org/columns/teafaerie/2012/10/30/the-terence-mckenna-thing.

138. Edgar Pêra, "Terence McKenna 2020," April 3, 2020, https://edgarpera.org/2020/04/03/terence-mckenna-2020.

139. Lin, *Trip*, 21, 15, 193.

140. Merlin Sheldrake, *Entangled Life: How Fungi Make Our Worlds, Change Our Minds, and Shape Our Futures* (London: Bodley Head, 2020), 110–111.

141. Rupert Sheldrake, Zoom interview by author, February 16, 2021.

142. Bruce Damer, email to author, November 23, 2021.

143. Annie Howard, "Vital Materialism and Terence McKenna's Archaic Revival," Medium.com, May 7, 2017, https://medium.com/@t_annie_howard/vital-materialism-and-terence-mckennas-archaic-revival-8af2a81466ca.

144. Carlo McCormick, "Dean Chamberlain's Psychedelic Luminaries," *High Times*, October 1999, 12.

145. Terence McKenna, "Psychedelics in the Age of Intelligent Machines" (a.k.a. "Shamans Among the Machines"), Seattle, WA, April 27, 1999, The Library of

Consciousness, https://www.organism.earth/library/document/psychedelics-in-the-age-of-intelligent-machines.

146. Jake Kobrin, "Cybernetic Séance with Terence McKenna," October 4, 2024, https://www.buzzsprout.com/1163702/episodes/15848811-cybernetic-seance-with-terence-mckenna.

147. See Maxim Tvorun-Dunn, "Acid Liberalism: Silicon Valley's Enlightened Technocrats, and the Legalization of Psychedelics," *International Journal of Drug Policy* 110 (December 2022).

148. T. McKenna, "The Edge Runner."

149. T. McKenna, "Alchemy and the Hermetic Corpus."

CHAPTER 11

1. Abraham and T. McKenna, "Dynamics of Hyperspace."

2. For a full account of Abraham's influences and findings, see Abraham, *Vibrations and Forms*.

3. Abraham and T. McKenna, "Dynamics of Hyperspace."

4. T. McKenna, "Alien Love."

5. See St John, *Mystery School in Hyperspace*, 239–246, for a discussion of this.

6. Tim Leary, *Exo-Psychology: A Manual on the Use of the Nervous System According to the Instructions of the Manufacturers* (Los Angeles: Starseed/Peace Press, 1977).

7. Leary, *Exo-Psychology*. See W. Patrick McCray, "Timothy Leary's Transhumanist SMI²LE," in *Groovy Science: Knowledge, Innovation, and American Counterculture*, ed. David Kaiser and W. Patrick McCray (Chicago: University of Chicago Press, 2016), 238–269.

8. Terence McKenna, "New Maps of Hyperspace" (edit of "New and Old Maps of Hyperspace"), *Magical Blend*, no. 22 (April 1989).

9. T. McKenna, "Mind and Time, Spirit and Matter."

10. T. McKenna, "New and Old Maps of Hyperspace."

11. Stephen M. Phillips, "A Short History of the Fourth Dimension," n.d., http://www.smphillips.mysite.com/a-short-history-of-the-fourth-dimension.html.

12. P. D. Ouspensky, *Tertium Organum: The Third Canon of Thought, a Key to the Enigmas of the World*, trans. Nicholas Bessaraboff and Claude Bragdon (Rochester, NY: Manas Press, 1920), 193. First published in Russian in 1912.

13. Ouspensky, *Tertium Organum*, 162.

14. Ouspensky, *Tertium Organum*, 47.

15. Gary Lachman, *In Search of P. D. Ouspensky: The Genius in the Shadow of Gurdjieff* (Wheaton, IL: Quest Books, 2006), 49. Emphasis in original.

16. Drury, "Sacred Plants and Mystic Realities," 9.

17. Terence McKenna, "The Psychedelic Society," Psychedelics and Spirituality Conference, Esalen Institute, Big Sur, CA, February 1984, The Library of Consciousness, https://www.organism.earth/library/document/the-psychedelic-society.

18. P. D. Ouspensky, *A New Model of the Universe* (London: Arkana, 1984 [1934]), 342.

19. Lachman, *In Search of P. D. Ouspensky*, 52-53.

20. Terence McKenna, "The Future of Art," Esalen Institute, Big Sur, CA, August 7, 1998, The Library of Consciousness, https://www.organism.earth/library/document/future-of-art.

21. Jorge Luis Borges, *The Aleph and Other Stories, 1933–1969* (New York: Bantam Books, 1971), 13.

22. T. McKenna, "Tryptamine Hallucinogens and Consciousness."

23. Miller, "Interview: Terence McKenna," 73.

24. Terence McKenna, "Ordinary Language, Visible Language and Virtual Reality," 1990, https://transcendentalobject.files.wordpress.com/2017/07/visiblelanguage.pdf. Originally titled "Experiment at Petaluma."

25. From Edgar Pêra, *Manual of Evasion Lx2020 Rough Mix*, January 2022.

26. T. McKenna, "Ordinary Language, Visible Language and Virtual Reality."

27. T. McKenna, "Mind, Molecules and Magic."

28. T. McKenna, "Post Electric Thought," 106.

29. T. McKenna, "Post Electric Thought," 109–111.

30. T. McKenna, "Post Electric Thought," 112.

31. H. G. Wells, *World Brain* (Cambridge, MA: MIT Press, 2021).

32. T. McKenna, "Post Electric Thought," 108. Adapted from the original: "No machine may contain any moving parts" (Clarke, *The City and the Stars*, New York: Gateway, 2001: 161). The earlier "Future of Magic in Electronic Societies" used a near-identical line (citing Clarke, p. 19).

33. It is possible that soulless Diaspar's mortal sister civilization Lys provided an equally animating motif for McKenna.

34. T. McKenna, "Post Electric Thought," 126.

35. A typewritten and undated one page item titled "Ho Lo" is included in the Dennis and Terence McKenna papers. The document is contemporaneous with the early stages of "Post Electric Thought" and likely produced ca. 1966–1968.

36. T. McKenna, "Post Electric Thought," 113, 114.

37. T. McKenna, "Post Electric Thought," 131, 132.

38. T. McKenna, "Post Electric Thought," 114.

39. T. McKenna, "Post Electric Thought," 133.

40. T. McKenna, "The Future of Magic in Electronic Societies," 53.

41. From Samuel Taylor Coleridge, *Kubla Khan*, in T. McKenna, "The Future of Magic in Electronic Societies," 53.

42. T. McKenna, "The Future of Magic in Electronic Societies," 54.

43. John Markoff, *What the Dormouse Said: How the Sixties Counterculture Shaped the Personal Computer Industry* (New York: Penguin, 2005).

44. T. McKenna, "Shamanology."

45. Terence McKenna, "Shamanism, Alchemy, and the Millennium" (day 4), Esalen Institute, Big Sur, CA, August 22, 1985, The Library of Consciousness, https://www.organism.earth/library/document/shamanism-alchemy-millennium.

46. Thanks to Chris W. Nelson for sharing a copy of this letter.

47. "Myconet" was the title of an online mycological resource established by David L. Hawksworth in the nineties. *Myconet* was later adopted as the title for a peer-reviewed mycological journal.

48. Terence McKenna, "Virtual Reality and Electronic Highs, or: On Becoming Virtual Octopi," *Magical Blend*, April 26, 1990, 9–10, 12, 14, 102; William Gibson, "Burning Chrome," *Omni* 46 (July 1982): 72–77, 102–107.

49. T. McKenna, "Nature Is the Center of the Mandala."

50. T. McKenna, "Understanding and Imagination in the Light of Nature" (day 1).

51. Sallie Tisdale, "It's Been Real," *Esquire*, April 1, 1991, 35–37, 145–147 (145).

52. T. McKenna, "Virtual Reality and Electronic Highs," 9, 10.

53. Peter Godfrey-Smith, *Other Minds: The Octopus, the Sea, and the Deep Origins of Consciousness* (New York: Farrar, Straus, and Giroux, 2016), 5.

54. T. McKenna, "Virtual Reality and Electronic Highs," 10.

55. Tim Leary, Michael Horowitz, and Vicki Marshall, *Chaos and Cyber Culture* (Berkeley, CA: Ronin Publishing, 1994).

56. Bruce Damer, email to author, November 23, 2021.

57. Ken Goffman and Charles Ferris, "A Galactic Tapping in to the Information Field: High Frontiers Talks with Terence McKenna," *High Frontiers*, no. 1 (1984): 11–14 (12).

58. R. U. Sirius, Zoom interview, October 31, 2024.

59. Terence McKenna, "Psychopharmacognosticon," *High Frontiers*, no. 2 (1985): 8 and 24 (8).

60. Terence McKenna, "Psychopharmacognosticon: New Dimensions," *High Frontiers*, no. 4 (1987): 10–11 (10).

61. R. U. Sirius and Shira Chess, *The Freaks in the Machine: Mondo 2000 in Late 20th Century Tech Culture* (forthcoming, Strange Attractor Press, 2026).

62. T. McKenna, "Nature Is the Center of the Mandala."

63. Terence McKenna, "Psychedelic Futurology in Berlin," *Reality Hackers*, no. 5 (1988): 63.

64. Timothy Leary, John Perry Barlow, Mal Seaholz, and Terence McKenna, "From Psychedelics to Cybernetics," Mannheim, Germany, September 13, 1990, The Library of Consciousness, https://www.organism.earth/library/document/from-psychedelics-to-cybernetics.

65. Terence McKenna at the Cyberdome, Stuttgart, Germany, 1991, video available at Deus Ex McKenna ~ Terence McKenna Archive, YouTube, August 18, 2013, https://www.youtube.com/watch?v=kMyBecqEN4o.

66. Korzybski, "Terence and the Coming Eschaton."

67. Torgoff, *Can't Find My Way Home*, 410.

68. Dorien Zandbergen, "New Edge: Technology and Spirituality in the San Francisco Bay Area" (PhD diss., Leiden University, 2011); Douglas Rushkoff, *Cyberia: Life in the Trenches of Hyperspace* (London: HarperCollins, 1994).

69. R. U. Sirius, Zoom interview by author, October 31, 2024.

70. T. McKenna, "Virtual Reality and Electronic Highs," 14.

71. McLuhan in Norden, "Playboy Interview: Marshall McLuhan," 54.

72. Terence McKenna, "Spirituality and Technology," Esalen Institute, Big Sur, CA, 1994, The Library of Consciousness, https://www.organism.earth/library/document/spirituality-and-technology.

73. T. McKenna, "Virtual Reality and Electronic Highs," 14, 10.

74. Patrick Dijuju, "Travels with Marvin: Swashbuckling around the World with Marvin Minsky," in R. U. Sirius and St. Jude, *How to Mutate & Take Over the World* (New York: Ballantine Books, 1996).

75. T. McKenna, "Virtual Reality and Electronic Highs," 102, 14.

76. T. McKenna, letter to Rick Watson, June 17, 1996.

77. Terence McKenna, letter to Peter Meyer, July 1, 1995. From Bruce Damer, "Terence2012" archive project.

78. Sheldrake et al., *The Evolutionary Mind* (1998), 80, 81.

79. Sheldrake et al., *The Evolutionary Mind* (1998), 82.

80. Sheldrake et al., *The Evolutionary Mind* (1998), 82.

81. Terence McKenna, "The Digital Messiah," part III of the three-part documentary *TechnoCalyps* (2006) by Frank Theys (GoDigital Media Group).

82. Terence McKenna, "The Winter King," Mannheim, Germany, 1996, The Library of Consciousness, https://www.organism.earth/library/document/winter-king.

83. Sheldrake et al., *The Evolutionary Mind* (1998), 86.

84. Sheldrake et al., *The Evolutionary Mind* (1998), 87.

85. Hyperborea remains online: http://www.levity.com/eschaton/hyperborea.html. Dmitri Novus also gave McKenna a web presence on Terence McKenna Land, which at the time of writing remained available at: https://jacobsm.com/deoxy/deoxy.org/mckenna.htm.

86. Terence McKenna, "The Jeweled Net of Indra," *Psychedelic Illuminations* 8 (Winter 1995–1996): 50–54 (54, 52, 53).

87. McKenna in McIntyre, "Millennium Witness," 22.

88. Sheldrake et al., *The Evolutionary Mind* (1998), 89, 90.

89. Antero Alli, "Terence McKenna, Countdown to 2012," *Magical Blend*, no. 40 (1993): 30–36.

90. Gracie and Zarkov, "Terence McKenna," 1993.

91. T. McKenna, "The Evolutionary Importance of Technology."

92. T. McKenna, "Our Cyberspiritual Future."

93. T. McKenna, "Light of the Third Millennium."

94. Terence McKenna and Ralph Abraham, "The World Wide Web and the Millennium," Omega Institute for Holistic Studies, Rhinebeck, New York, August 1, 1998, The Library of Consciousness, https://www.organism.earth/library/document/world-wide-web-and-millennium.

95. T. McKenna, "Mind Machines."

96. T. McKenna, "Mind Machines."

97. T. McKenna, "Mind Machines."

98. T. McKenna, "The Future of Art."

99. T. McKenna, "The Future of Art."

100. T. McKenna, "The Future of Art."

101. Anon., "Carrying On about Re-Evolution, and Alien Dreamtime with Technoshaman Terence McKenna," *TRIP: Florida's Upfront Dance Culture Magazine* 12 (1993).

102. Bruce Damer, email to author, November 23, 2021.

103. Terence McKenna, "Evolving Times," Sacramento, CA, April 29, 1995, The Library of Consciousness, https://www.organism.earth/library/document/evolving-times.

104. D. R. Glowacki, R. R. Williams, M. D. Wonnacott, O. M. Maynard, R. Freire, J. E. Pike, and M. Chatziapostolou, "Group VR Experiences Can Produce Ego Attenuation and Connectedness Comparable to Psychedelics," *Scientific Reports* 12, no. 1 (2022): 8995.

105. Bruce Damer, email to author, November 23, 2021.

106. Kawitzky, *Journey to Everywhere*, 37.

CHAPTER 12

1. Epilogue to T. McKenna, *True Hallucinations*, 226.

2. Davis, "Terence McKenna's Last Trip."

3. Christy Silness, email to author, May 13, 2021.

4. Finn McKenna, Zoom interview by author, June 20, 2023.

5. Art Bell, Terence McKenna interview, "Terence Says Goodbye," *Coast to Coast AM*, June 16, 1999, audio available at Deus Ex McKenna ~ Terence McKenna Archive, YouTube, July 9, 2011, https://www.youtube.com/watch?v=9gWbjXQ5Fmo&t=15s.

6. Davis, "Terence McKenna's Last Trip."

7. Keep's diagnostic report, as conveyed by McKenna, quickly inspired the apocryphal belief that he had contracted a mushroom-shaped tumor.

8. Nina Wise, Zoom interview by author, March 16, 2021.

9. D. McKenna, *Brotherhood*, 466.

10. Davis, "Terence McKenna's Last Trip."

11. I have no intention of exploring these theories in any detail. For a taste, on the prospect that McKenna may have been assassinated by Nazis well downstream from

his encounter with Karl Heintz in 1970, see Dave Emory, "Waltzing the Enigma: Is This a Hallucination or a 'True Hallucination?' (The Max Planck Institute and the Underground Reich)," SpitfireList.com, August 31, 2013, https://spitfirelist.com/news/waltzing-the-enigma-is-this-a-hallucination-or-a-true-hallucination-the-max-planck-institute-and-the-underground-reich.

12. Dennis McKenna, email to author, July 10, 2020.

13. Christy Silness, email to author, July 15, 2022.

14. Christy Silness, Zoom interview by author, June 2, 2022. And yet, as Finn counters, many drink rainwater off the roof in Hawaii and there are no unusual cancer measurements in the region (Finn McKenna, Zoom interview by author, June 20, 2023).

15. David Jay Brown, *The New Science of Psychedelics: At the Nexus of Culture, Consciousness, and Spirituality* (Rochester, VT: Park Street Press, 2013), 158.

16. D. McKenna, *Brotherhood*, 472.

17. Davis, "Terence McKenna's Last Trip."

18. Bell, "Terence Says Goodbye."

19. McVey, "Klea McKenna Steps into the Light."

20. Finn McKenna, Zoom interview by author, April 5, 2023.

21. D. McKenna, *Brotherhood*, 467, 474.

22. Terence McKenna, "Introduction," in *Illuminatus* by Robert Venosa (Australia: Interface, 1999) 10–11.

23. In Kawitzky, *Journey to Everywhere*, 45.

24. According to the memory of Lorenzo Hagerty, email to author, December 27, 2023.

25. D. McKenna, *Brotherhood*, 475.

26. Christy Silness, Zoom interview by author, December 10, 2021.

27. Terence McKenna, Esalen, Big Sur, CA, October 1999 (transcript in the personal archives of Lorenzo Hagerty).

28. Christy Silness, email to author, July 15, 2022.

29. Bell, "Terence Says Goodbye."

30. Nancy Lunney-Wheeler, Zoom interview by author, April 13, 2021.

31. Jon Hanna and Sylvia Thyssen, "Terence McKenna Speaks," interview at the 1999 AllChemical Arts Conference, Kona Coast, HI, *Entheogen Review* 8, no. 4 (Winter 1999): 143.

Notes to Chapter 12

32. Gordon Wheeler, Zoom interview by author, April 13, 2021.

33. Davis, Terence McKenna interview.

34. Dean Jefferys, interview with Terence McKenna, "The Last Word," Terence's house, The Big Island, Hawaii, December 9, 1999. Video available on YouTube, "The Mushroom Speaks," February 2, 2017, https://www.youtube.com/watch?v=TZdw605fCpc.

35. Ron Curry, Zoom interview by author, September 9, 2020.

36. Christy Silness, email to author, July 15, 2022.

37. Christy Silness, email to author, June 2, 2021.

38. Christy Silness, Zoom interview by author, December 10, 2021.

39. Judy Livingston, email to author, May 31, 2021.

40. Drury, "Sacred Plants and Mystic Realities, 13.

41. Terence McKenna, "Preparing for the Singularity," part II of the three-part documentary *TechnoCalyps* (2006) by Frank Theys (GoDigital Media Group).

42. T. McKenna, "A Weekend with Terence McKenna."

43. T. McKenna, "Global Perspectives and Psychedelic Poetics."

44. Art Bell, Terence McKenna interview, "April Fool's Y2K," *Coast to Coast AM*, April 1, 1999, audio available at Deus Ex McKenna ~ Terence McKenna Archive, https://www.youtube.com/watch?v=40ZdB8pYgcE&t=6s.

45. Anon., "In Memoriam: Terence McKenna (1946–2000)," *Green Egg*, May/June 2000, 48.

46. Terence McKenna, "Terence McKenna Speaks . . . (Part III)," transcribed from his "Splat" talk, AllChemical Arts Conference, September 1999, *Entheogen Review* 9, no. 3 (Winter Solstice 2000): 134–140 (140).

47. Space Time Continuum with Terence McKenna, *Alien Dreamtime*.

48. T. McKenna, "The Camden Centre Talk," 1992.

49. T. McKenna, "Psychedelics in the Age of Intelligent Machines."

50. T. McKenna, "What I've Learned from Psychedelics."

51. Terence McKenna, "Imagination in the Light of Nature," Earth Trust Foundation Conference (day 1), Los Angeles, CA, October 2, 1992, The Library of Consciousness, https://www.organism.earth/library/document/imagination-in-the-light-of-nature.

52. Sheldrake et al., *Chaos, Creativity, and Cosmic Consciousness*, 156.

53. T. McKenna, "New and Old Maps of Hyperspace."

54. Davis, "Terence McKenna's Last Trip."

55. Terence McKenna, "Foreword," in Timothy C. Ely, *The Flight into Egypt: Binding the Book* (San Francisco: Chronicle Books, 1995). McKenna had previously collaborated with Ely on *Synesthesia*, a rare handmade book designed by Ely of which there were seventy-five copies originally priced at $2,500. Typographically interpreted by visual poet Philip Gallo, McKenna's text appeared amid Ely's original painted and drawn images, which Ely describes as "articulated glossolalia" refracted from the writing. Terence McKenna and Timothy C. Ely, *Synesthesia* (New York: Granary Books, 1992).

56. D. McKenna, *Brotherhood*, 484.

57. Allan Badiner, email to author, November 17, 2021.

58. D. McKenna, *Brotherhood*, 484.

59. Michael Horowitz, email to author, April 2, 2022. I was unable to access a copy of the appraisal.

60. At the same time, a catalog of 2,641 titles was the basis for the Terence Kemp McKenna library—a Legacy Library cataloged at LibraryThing. See https://www.librarything.com/profile/TerenceKempMcKenna. Originally cataloged by McKenna himself, the 2,641 titles were input to LibraryThing by Chris Mays.

61. David Price, email to author, April 18, 2021.

62. There is some doubt that Wheeler inspected the entire collection. According to Price, Wheeler may have overlooked the materials stored in the smaller room.

63. Gordon Wheeler, email to author, November 12, 2021.

64. Fortunately, Abraham Maslow's personal library, previously housed in this location, had recently been shipped to Ohio State.

65. Terence McKenna, "Riding the Range with Marshall McLuhan," Esalen Institute, Big Sur, CA, 1995, audio available at Deus Ex McKenna ~ Terence McKenna Archive, YouTube, July 24, 2011, https://www.youtube.com/watch?v=OHLqMtuVbTk.

66. D. McKenna, *Brotherhood*, 103.

67. Mike Kawitzky, Zoom interview by author, May 19, 2021.

68. Mike Kawitzky, Zoom interview by author, May 19, 2021.

69. Mike Kawitzky, Zoom interview by author, May 19, 2021.

70. Carl Jung, *Psychology and Alchemy*, 264.

71. Alfred Russel Wallace, *A Narrative of Travels on the Amazon and Rio Negro*, 2nd ed. (London: Ward, Lock, 1889), 273.

72. Wallace, *A Narrative of Travels*, 275.

73. K. McKenna, *The Butterfly Hunter*, n.p.

74. In Tao Lin, "'The Butterfly Hunter' by Klea McKenna," *Vice*, September 9, 2014. https://www.vice.com/en_us/article/7b7dbe/the-butterfly-hunter-by-klea-mckenna-874.

75. Klea McKenna, "The Butterfly Hunter—Artist Book," https://kleamckenna.bigcartel.com/product/the-butterfly-hunter-artist-book-2.

76. Lin, "'The Butterfly Hunter'"; McVey, "Klea McKenna Steps into the Light."

77. Bell, "Terence Says Goodbye."

78. T. McKenna, "A Weekend with Terence McKenna."

79. Antero Alli, "Terence McKenna, Countdown to 2012," *Magical Blend*, no. 40 (1993), 30–36 (36).

80. T. McKenna, "The Psychedelic Society."

81. T. McKenna, "New Maps of Hyperspace," 101.

82. Said to be a Vishvasara Tantra phrase in McKenna, "Post Electric Thought" (vii) and in *The Invisible Landscape* (1975), 46, attributed to Jung.

83. Space Time Continuum with Terence McKenna, "Timewave Zero," *Alien Dreamtime* (album, Astralwerks, 1993).

84. T. McKenna, "Approaching Timewave Zero, 29.

85. John Hazard, Terence McKenna Interview.

86. T. McKenna and D. McKenna, *The Invisible Landscape* (1994), 174 (emphasis in original).

87. T. McKenna, "Culture and Ideology Are Not Your Friends."

88. Klea McKenna, email to author, January 6, 2023.

89. Finn McKenna, Zoom interview by author, April 5, 2023.

90. Terence McKenna, from trialogue "The Edge of the Millennium," on "The Evolutionary Mind," June 6, 1998, The Library of Consciousness, https://www.organism.earth/library/document/the-evolutionary-mind.

91. R. U. Sirius, "An Insufficiently Advanced Technology for McKenna's Magical 2012," *Acceler8or*, January 2, 2012.

92. Peter Meyer, "The Zero Date" (1999, modified in 2006), http://www.fractal-timewave.com/articles/zerodate_10.html.

93. Peter Meyer, "The Zero Date Reconsidered" (ca. 2012), http://www.fractal-timewave.com/articles/zerodate_reconsidered.html.

94. Peter Meyer, "Timewave Zero—the Final Explanation" (June 13, 2021), https://www.fractal-timewave.com/articles/timewave-zero-final-explanation.htm.

95. Bruce Damer, email to author, November 23, 2021.

96. Shpongle, "... But Nothing Is Lost," from *Nothing Lasts ... But Nothing Is Lost* (Twisted Records, 2005), sampling T. McKenna, "What I've Learned from Psychedelics."

97. Liquid on Safi, 2006. "Shamanic Madness," on *13 Moon*, compiled by Cosmic Sun. Spliff Music (CD, Compilation). From Jefferys, "The Last Word."

98. Davis, "Terence McKenna's Last Trip."

99. John David Ebert, "The Alchemical Microcosm—Terence McKenna and Evolution of Consciousness: Part II," *Magical Blend*, no. 56 (August 1997): 52–53, 55.

100. T. McKenna, "Our Cyberspiritual Future."

APPENDIX A

1. Dennis and Terence McKenna papers: https://archives.lib.purdue.edu/repositories/2/resources/1165.

2. https://zerwiclib.com/terence-mckenna-archive.

3. Terence McKenna Bibliography: https://terencemckennaarchives.com/terence-mckenna-bibliography.

4. Terence McKenna Archives: https://terencemckennaarchives.com.

5. Terence Kemp McKenna's virtual library at LibraryThing: https://www.librarything.com/profile/TerenceKempMcKenna.

6. Chris Mays, email to author, November 17, 2021.

7. https://psychedelicsalon.com/category/people/terence-mckenna.

8. https://uutter.com/c/terence-mckenna.

9. The Library of Consciousness—Terence McKenna: https://www.organism.earth/library/author/terence-mckenna.

10. https://www.abrupt.org/abruptlog/category/logos.

11. "Dr. Bruce Damer's source images for the Terence McKenna 2012 project," by Bruce Damer, Dennis McKenna, and Michael Horowitz, 2014, https://archive.org/details/Dr.BruceDamersSourceImagesForTheTerenceMckenna2012Project/1987-07-08-Terence-Hagenbach-p1.jpg.

APPENDIX B

1. Chambers, *Beyond the Brain with Terence McKenna*.

2. Peter Bergmann, *The Transcendental Object at the End of Time*, We Plants Are Happy Plants, YouTube, 2014, https://www.youtube.com/watch?v=aAlaRdrcQcY&t=154s; Peter Bergmann, *Terence McKenna's True Hallucinations*, We Plants Are Happy Plants, YouTube, 2016, https://www.youtube.com/watch?v=8MG5gFtZ3U8. Bergmann has also produced a virtual catacomb of hundreds of themed shorts and composites of McKennan audiovisual material, available at the YouTube channel We Plants Are Happy Plants, and included in "Terence McKenna Shorts": https://www.youtube.com/playlist?list=PLwOcdj091QTYtd402vSKDJOpr0b8NnSDq. Bergmann's films feature music from his project We Plants Are Happy Plants.

3. Peter Bergmann, *Terence McKenna Digital Revival* (2013), recorded in Prague, with video directed by Jack Coddington and originally produced by Steven Marshank (1992), https://www.youtube.com/playlist?list=PLwOcdj091QTY0UKo_HswouTgVKb5MXE7s.

4. Mike Kawitzky, *The Terence McKenna Omnibus*, 2012, https://www.youtube.com/playlist?list=PLF7C7C99A3E5FC148.

5. Davis, *High Weirdness*, 92.

INDEX

Note: Page numbers in italics indicate illustrations.

Abelson, Stuart, 189
Abraham, Ralph, 227–230, 415
   and Christian cosmogeny, 280
   on death and immortality, 289
   dinner with McKenna in Malibu, 318
   and hyperspace, 337
   Mathematically Illuminated Musical Instrument (MIMI), 338
   with McKenna and Sheldrake, 230
   on McKenna's diagrams, 267–268
   on McKenna's projection of apocalypse, 281
   at McKenna's seminar, "Shamanism, Alchemy, and the Millennium," 222
   and the World Wide Web, 356–357, 360
Acharya, Vijaya (Jayatirtha), 352
Acid Dreams: The Complete Social History of LSD (Lee and Shlain), 234
Acid House scene, 236, 239
Ada, or Ardor: A Family Chronicle (Nabokov), 52, 388
Adams, Henry, 268
Adams, Ken, 195, 236, 238–239, 243, 246, 248, 395, 461n11
Adamski, George, 117
Affectional Alchemy, 51
Against Method (Feyerabend), 44

"Agency at the Time of the Anthropocene" (Latour), 333
Agent BZ, 34
Age of the universe, McKenna's estimate of, 441n12
Agrippa, Cornelius, 18, 383
Aion: Researches into the Phenomenology of the Self (Jung), 46
Akimoto family, 87
Aladdin's Lamp, 10–11
Albert Hofmann Foundation, 222
Albion, 161, 239
Alchemical Dream: Rebirth of the Great Work, The (Rochlin and Harris), 415
Alchemy, 199
   Alexandrine, 89
   in Jung's work, 46, 47, 48, 132, 197, 287, 386
   McKenna's obsession with, 16, 200
   as metaphor, 338
   in shamanic studies, 44
   and Timewave, 260
Alien Dreamtime, 243–245, 310
Alien Dreamtime (film), 243–245, 379
"Alien Love" (rap), 216, 446n21
AllChemical Arts (conference), 371, *372*, 380
Allen, John P., 175
All Media Recorder (AMR), 346–347

Almost Visible (film), 171
Alpert, Richard. *See* Ram Dass
Alpha Helix, RV (research vessel), 175
Alter, Joel, 189
Altered Carbon (Morgan), 362
Alvin (Clarke character), 23
Amanita muscaria, 69, 303
Amarcord (film), 52
Amazonas (Watson), 448n77
Amazon Expedition (*RV Heraclitus*), 175
"Amazonian Shamanism" (workshop 1989), 225
American Anthropologist (journal), 138–139
American Civil Liberties Union (ACLU), Los Angeles chapter, 322
And/Or Press, 162–164, 182–183
Angels, Aliens, and Archetypes (conference, 1987), 214
Angus, Colin, 239–240, 395
Anti-guru guru, McKenna as, 327–333
Apocalypse Now (film), 3, 203, 389
Applesoft BASIC, and Timewave Zero software, 268
Apple IIe, and Timewave Zero software, 268
Aquinas, Thomas, 309
Archaic, the, 48
Archaic Revival, xiv, 48, 200, 238, 239, 247, 251, 321, 323, 358, 415
Archaic Revival, The (McKenna), 235, 239
Argüelles, José, 225, 277–278, 466n67, 466–467n72
Arica, base camp (Colombia), 130–134
Aristotle, 289
ARO.spaceclub (Seattle), 333
ARPANET, 348
Ars Electronica (Linz), 353
Art of Memory, The (Yates), 212
Art of Seeing, The (Huxley), 18
A. R. Wallace Memorial Expedition, 95
Asháninka, 98

Asimov, Isaac, 12, 92, 148, 209, 324
Auden, W. H., 252
Avatars! Exploring and Building Virtual Worlds on the Internet (Damer), 362–363
Avery Brundage, collection of Asian art (San Francisco), 73
Awalt High School, McKenna at, xix, 11, 23, *25*. *See also* Mountain View High School
Ayahuasca, 13, 167–169, 172, 253, 360
  in Australia, 253
  and ayahuasca effect, 100, 177
  ceremony, 188–190
  and Clark, 435n12
  guides associated with, 149
  Harner's work on, 104
  John Brown's experience with, 107
  Luna as leading authority on ethnography of, 140
  and McKenna's tumor, 370
  McKenna cooking, *208*
  McKenna scours literature on, 98
  McKenna's differences with Dennis McKenna over, 175
  McKenna's differences with Harrison over, 168–171
  and mushrooms, 196
  "psychiatric presence" of, 174
  and Rick Watson, 151
  shamans, shamanism, and shamanology, 114, 178, 355
  and Silness, 209
  at Waimia retreat, 227
Ayahuasca Dream (Venosa), 227
Ayahuasca effect, 100, 177
Ayahuasca shamanism, 449n89
Ayahuasca vine (*Banisteriopsis caapi*), 99, 109, 111, 169, 175, 188, 189, 190

Baba, Neem Karoli, 228
Baby Elephant, 72–73

Badiner, Allan, 222, 223, 383–384, 385, 456n30
Baduk, Ali, 84–85
Balena, Teresa Aurelia (Honey), 12
Banana Republic clothing, 233
Banisteriopsis caapi, 99, 109, 111, 169, 175, 188, 189, 190, 444n80
Banisteriopsis ruysbana, 155
Bantam Books, "New Age," 235, 236, 324
Bantimurung Bulusaraung National Park (Sulawesi), 84
Bardo Thödol (*The Tibetan Book of the Dead*), 65, 69
Barlow, John Perry, 353
Barr, Frank, 262
Barrett, Syd, 434n98
Barron, Chris, 236
Barry, Bloch, 249
Bates Method, of vision improvement, 18
BBC Radio One, 240
Bear, Greg, 188
Beatles, The, 236
Beckett, Samuel, 19
Behar, Ruth, 171
Bell, Art, 285–286, 322, 363, 375, 379, 381
Bennett, Jane, 333
Bergmann, Peter, 406, 414, 489n2
Berkeley, California, xxiv–xxv
  return to (1968), 59–64
  2894 Telegraph Avenue, 35–43
Berkeley Commune, the, 60
Besant, Annie, 225
Bethlehem Cemetery (Paonia), 22
Beyond the Brain (multimedia dance event), 251
Beyond the Brain with Terence McKenna (Chambers), 413
Beyond the Brain with Terence McKenna (film), 252–253
Big Yank, 56
Billy Pilgrim (fictional character), xxvii

Bioneers, 173, 176, 248, 327
BITNET, 348
Black Students Union (SFSU), 61
Blackwood, Algernon, 13
Blake, William, 137, 240, 262, 297, 302, 281
Blavatsky, Madame, 65, 312
Blofeld, John, 79
Blood Music (Bear), 188
"Blue Cheer," 41
Bly, Robert, 225
Bob (Ron Curry's buddy), 61
Bohemian Grove, 182
Bohemian Institute of Prague, 247
bOING bOING (magazine), 290
Bondi, Hermann, 274
Book of Changes. See *I Ching* (*Book of Changes*)
Books, McKenna's love for, 215–216
Bora people, 176
Borges, Jorge Luis, 309
Bosch, Hieronymus, 10
Boss Drum (the Shamen), 240
Botanical Dimensions, 183–188, 201, 348–349
Botanical Preservation Corps, 248
Boudhanath, Nepal, 68
Boulder Statement, xxi, xxii, 67–68, 70–71, 82, 401
Boulding, Kenneth E., 263
Bradbury, Ray, 12
Brand, Stewart, 28, 350
Brando, Marlon, 3
Brave New World (Huxley), 18
Bray, Faustin, 217–219
Brechin, Gray, 24–25
Brechin, Vern, 24–25
Brennan, Dan, 301
Bridge conference, 248
Brits Awards, 241
Broadwell, Peter, 268
Brockman, John, 249
Bronx School of Science, 31

Brotherhood of the Screaming Abyss: My Life with Terence McKenna, The (memoir by Dennis McKenna), xviii, 13, 15–16, 112, 201–202, 415–416. *See also* McKenna, Dennis
Brotherhoods, as shams, 170
Brown, David Jay, 369
Brown, John, 104–107
Bruno, Giordano, 115
Bryant, Jacob, 383
Brzustowicz, Richard, 159, 167, 168
Buckley, William F., Jr., xiii
Burning Man, 246, 248
Burroughs, Edgar Rice, 11
Burroughs, William S., 10, 42, 99, 169, 305, 466–467n72
Burton, Pam, 215, 322
Butterflies and lepidoptery, and McKenna, 79–87
Butterfly Hunter, The (Klea McKenna), 82–83, 387, 388, 407
Butterfly, 242
Byron Bay Epicentre, 251

California Institute of Integral Studies (CIIS), 233–234, 304–305, 404
Calle, Horacio ("Alfredo Guzman" in *True Hallucinations*), 100, 109, 136, 137
Camden Centre, 242
Campbell, Joseph, 122, 220, 223, 225, 290–291, 323
Camp Shalom (retreat), 225
Camus, Albert, 19
Cancer, McKenna's brain tumor, ix, 368–369, 374, 483n7
  death from, 379–385
Cannabis
  a habit for McKenna, xx, 42, 198–199, 212
  indica, 58, 63
  legalization of, 77

  McKenna's first experiences, 30–31, 39
  and McKenna's tumor, 368
Cannon, Tim A. (Solly), 21
Captain Beefheart, 30
Captain Willard (film character), 203, 389
Carl Jung Society of greater Los Angeles, 46
Carlino, Jill, 222
Carlino, Lewis, 222, 371, 383
Carol Publishing Group, 235
Carroll, Lewis, 252
Carson, Rachel, 360
Casaubon, Meric, 383
Casement, Roger, 106
Cassady, Neal, 31
Castaneda, Carlos, 147
"Casting Nets in the Sea of Mind" (De Vosjoli and McKenna), 402
"Casting Nets" project, 292–295, 300
Catcher in the Rye, The (Salinger), 31
CDC 6400 (mainframe computer), 268
Cedar Hill Cemetery (Paonia), McKenna's gravesite at, 377–378
Celestine Prophecy (Redfield), 367
Chacruna (*Psychotria viridis*), 189, 190
Chagdud Rinpoche, 225
Chamberlain, Dean, 333, *334*
Chambers, Paul, 252, 413
Chang Chen Chi, 91
"Change and Becoming: Studies in a Fourth Dimensional Phenomenology of Mind" (McKenna), 127–142, 286, 309, 401, 436n31
Chan-Kah resort, 248
Chaos, Gaia, Eros (Abraham), 230
Chariots of the Gods (von Däniken), 323
Charlie Daniels Band, 286
Cherry Days festival (Paonia), 53
Chiapas, Mexico, 248
Childhood and early education, McKenna's, 12–23
Childhood's End (Clarke), 148
Chilton, Jeff, 164

Chislenko, Alexander, 359
Chomsky, Noam, xxiv, 24, 216, 320
Chousmer, Paul, 313
Christian cosmogony, 280
Chung Ta-Chen, 86
Cia, 103, 436n27. *See also* Solo Dark
CIA, 24, 34, 319
Cicero, 212
City and the Stars, The (Clarke), 12, 362
Civitas Dei, 91
Clark, Fraser, 239, 245
Clark, Leonard, 98–99, 110, 435n12
Clark, Walter Houston, 221
Clarke, Arthur C., 12, 90, 111, 148, 209, 345
Clooney, Rosemary, 19
Coast to Coast AM (radio program), 285–286, 322, 363
Coddington, Jack, 374
Coddington, Ricci, 374
Cognition Factor (film), 251, 415
Coil (band), 246, 461n104
Cole, Bill, 75–77, 96–97, 408
Cole, Tom, 243, 436n20
Coleridge, Samuel Taylor, 10, 347
Coleus scutellarioides, 379
Collected Works of Jung, 46, 60
Collector, The (film), 80
Colombia's Forgotten Frontier (Wylie), 106
Colorado Fuel and Iron, 74, 76
Comedy Central (cable network), 213
Coming of the Golden Age, The (Stent), 120
Comprehensive Drug Abuse Prevention and Control Act of 1970, 159
Compressionism, 262–263
Conference on Botanical Intelligence, Camp Shalom, *226*
Confessions of Aleister Crowley (Crowley), 129
Confessions of an English Opium-Eater (De Quincey), 159
Connelly, Joan, 59

Connett, Robert S., 191
Conrad, Joseph, 3, 4, 104, 106, 108
Contact (film), 359
Contact (Sagan), 285
Controlled Substances Act (1970), xxiii
Cooke, John Starr, 234–235
Cooper Union, 249
Coppola, Francis Ford, 3, 389
Córdova-Rios, Manuel, 167–168
Corso, Gregory, 385
Cosmic giggle, 84, 119, 278, 318, 440n94
Cosmic Trigger (Wilson), 268
Cosmos, desacralized, 48
Cosmos and History (Eliade), 48
Country Joe and the Fish (band), 39, 40
Crawford Market (Bombay), 72–73
Creative Commons, 396
"Cremation of Sam McGee, The" (Service), 368
Crick, Francis, 166
Criminalizing of illicit and maligned botanicals, xx
Crowley, Aleister, 129, 392
Crumb, R., 191
Crying of Lot 49, The (Pynchon), 39–40
"Crypto-Rap: Meta-Electrical Speculations on Culture" (McKenna), 58–59, 88, 96
Csicsery, George, 36, 44, 60–61, 119, 280, 408
Cthulu mythos (Lovecraft), 166
Cullenbine, Robert "Papa Elf" (Cully), 31–32
Cult of the Peacock Angel, The (Empson and Temple), xii–xiii
Curry, Ron
    in Berkeley after college, 146
    calls McKenna "a free agent, radical," 60
    Dennis McKenna's best friend in Paonia, 13
    first encounter with McKenna, 14–15

Curry, Ron (cont.)
  on protests at San Francisco State University, 61–62
  recalls McKenna near death, 376
  and shipments of hash from McKenna, 75–76
  on Terence's reading, 17
CU-SeeMe (software), 251
"Cyber Culture" (rap), 354
Cyberthon, 349, 354
Czechoslovakia, 246–247
  National Museum, Department of Mycology, 246–247

Dada, McKenna's interest in, 273
Damer, Bruce
  at All-Chemical Arts, 371, *372*
  creating of webcast with influence of McKenna, 362–363
  digitizes audio recordings of McKenna, 395–396
  on McKenna's aversion to psychotherapy, 198
  McKenna as a guiding influence on, 332–333
  on McKenna as typist, 352
  "Ode to Terence" and Dennis's memoir, 201–202, 203
  vision of McKenna departing in an elven limousine, 394
Dance of Life The (Ellis), 42
Darrow, Clarence, 17
Darwin, Charles, 22, 79–80, 433n79
Darwin among the Machines (Dyson), 360
Darwin's Pharmacy (Doyle), xxviii
Daryl Gates Show, The (KFI-AM), 301, 321
DataGlove, 349
Dave Bowman (character), 174
Dave. *See* Lasky, Michael (Dave)
Davis, Erik, xix, 409, 416
  butterfly print purchased from Klea, 388
  chat before McKenna's death, 376
  and the "cosmic giggle," 440n94
  on "Crypto-Rap," 58–59
  eulogy for McKenna, 367, 396
  and March Forth, 114
  on McKenna's collection of books, 382
  on McKenna's Hawaiian hideaway, 365
  names McKenna's futurist phenomenology "esoteritech," 92
Davis, Wade, 176
Death threats made toward McKenna, 367
Dee, John, 18, 309, 312, 317, 383
"Deep Dive" (podcast), 203–204
Demby, Constance, 372
"Dennis McKenna (with TMCK) La Chorrera original notes" (Dennis and Terence McKenna), 400
De Quincey, Thomas, 159, 383
Department of Entomology (UC Berkeley), 80
De Ropp, Robert S., 25
Dery, Mark, 249, 283–284
Descartes, René, 317, 391
Design for Evolution: Self-Organization and Planning in the Life of Human Systems (Jantsch), 146
Deus Ex McKenna ~ Terence McKenna Archive (YouTube channel), 406
"Devil Went Down to Georgia, The" (Charlie Daniels Band), 286
De Vosjoli, Philippe, 294–295, 402
Dharmapalas, Nepal, 53
"Diagram of Everything Living" (Gurdjieff), 267
Diaspora (Egan), 362, 479n30
Dick, Philip K., 126, 139, 150, 191, 275, 282, 354
Dick, Scotty, 63–64
DiJusto, Patrick, 355
Dire Straits (band), 72, 431n28
Djwal Khul (Madame Blavatsky), 312

Index

DMT (N,N-dimethyltryptamine), xi, xiv, xx, xxiv–xxv, xxix, 1–2
  and advanced civilizations, 165
  and Art Bell, 322
  articulating the experience, 54, 92, 93
  in Australia, 253
  at the Camden Centre, 242
  and the circus, 53
  crystal, 220
  and the dead or the Other, 310–312
  and Eliade, 50
  and elves, 312–313
  experience permeated with agency, 149
  Fellini and, 52
  flash, 44, 51, 71, 93, 171
  and Jung, 46, 50
  jungle source of, 96, 100
  and Kat Harrison, 56
  Leary's experiments with, 302
  McKenna listens to Stockhausen while on, 246
  in McKenna's psychedelic pedagogy, 304–308
  McKenna's response to, 27
  McKenna's stories about, 34
  and McKenna's UC Berkeley experience, 44–45
  and McLuhan, 50
  most radical unfolding of the hallucinogenic dimension, 107
  "Mothballs," 33
  oo-koo-hé paste, 99–100, 137, 175
  priming with LSD, 42
  and *Psilocybe* mushrooms, 3, 111
  research, 115
  singing on, 316
  restrictions on, in the United States, 335
  at retreat in Waimea, Hawaii, 227
  and Rick Watson, 9, 32–33
  and *Virola*, 176
  XDMT, 112, 120, 129, 315

DMT: The Spirit Molecule (Strassman), 307–308
"DMT, or, Spider Woman Comes to Town" (Watson), xxvii
DNA-year cycles, 123, 124, 127, 136, 140–141, 260, 465n42
Dobbs, J. R. "Bob," 282
Dobkin de Rios, Marlene, 173
Doblin, Rick, 241
Dolphin Tapes, 223, 404
Don Juan, 147
Donner Laboratory of Virology and Bacteriology (UC Berkeley), 119–120
Doré, Gustave, 17
Doubting Thomas, 439n66
"Down to Earth: A Treatment" (Humphrey), 402, 431n28, 459n67
"Down to Earth: Psilocybin and the UFOs" (McKenna), 401, 402
"Down to Earth: Story Breakdown and Draft" (McKenna), 402
Doyle, Richard, xxviii
Dracula (Stroker), 18
Dragonfly Records, 242
Dream Matrix Telemetry (Zuvuya), 313
Dreyfus, Hubert, 44
Drower, E. S., 54, 130
Drug Enforcement Administration, xxiii
Dr. Xaman (film character), 272–273
Duncan, Robert, xiii
Dune (Herbert), xxiii–xxiv
Durkheim, Emile, 36
"Dynamics of Hyperspace" (dialogue), 337
Dyson, George, 360

Earth Trust, 247
Earthwatch, 183
"Ebeneezer Goode" (the Shamen), 240
Ecodynamics: A New Theory of Societal Evolution (Boulding), 262
Ecstasis, 48–49
Edge-running, 4–5

Egan, Greg, 191, 362
Eigen, Manfred, 263
Einstein, Albert, 262, 273, 274, 341
Eisler, Riane, 225
Electric Kool-Aid Acid Test, The (Wolfe), 32
Electric Music for the Mind and Body (Country Joe and the Fish), 40
Elf Event, xxv, 10, 308
Elf realization, 48, 50–54
Eliade, Mircea, influences McKenna's thinking, xxviii, 36, 48–49, 45, 46, 50–51, 92, 89, 92, 260, 279, 303, 347
Elizabeth I, Queen of England, 18
Ellis, Havelock, 42
Ellul, Jacques, 36
Ely, Timothy C., 383, 486n55
Emmerich, Roland, 279
Encyclopaedia Psychedelica (magazine), 239
Encyclopedia (Horn), 67
Entangled Life (Sheldrake), 332
Entheobotany (conference), 206–207, 273
Entheogenesis, 330
Epstein, Brian, 236
Eranos circle, 49
Esalen Institute, 219–227
  Damer's "Ode to Terence" at, 201–203
  Finn at, 191
  McKenna at, 19, 138, 185–187, 204, 214, 216, 232, 239, 241, 245, 285, 301, 304, 309, 314, 318, 328, 331, 332, 335, 336, 342, 343, 348, 358, 359, 361, 362, 363
  McKenna bequeaths library to, xix, 383
  McKenna mentions Elf Event at, xxv
  McKenna's raps, 254–255
  outdoor baths, 249
  "Surfing on *Finnegan's Wake*" (McKenna), 52
  and Timewave Zero, 270

Escape Velocity (Dery), 283–284
Eschaton, xiii, 54, 116, 124, 125, 207, 265, 267, 279, 280, 282, 283, 293, 294, 345, 358, 360, 381, 385, 394, 396, 464n29
Eschatron, 125–126, 128–129, *133*, 138, 267, 268
Esoteritech, 92
Esquire (magazine), 231, 232, 282
"Essay on Mescaline Intoxication" (Mitchell), 42
"Ethnobotany and Chemistry of Psychoactive Plants" course, 248
"Ethnobotany of Shamanism" (course), 233–234
Etidorhpa (Lloyd), 441n8
EUQUINOM Gallery (San Francisco), 192
Evans-Wentz, Walter, 65, 91, 130–131, 310
Evergreen Review (journal), 19
Evolution (club), 239
Evolution (magazine), 239
Evolution Records, 242
Exegesis, The (Dick), 150, 275
Experimental College (Berkeley), 3, 10, 35, 36, 43–45, 153, 416
Experimental College (University of Wisconsin), 43
Explorations of the Upper Amazon (Whiffen), 437n36
Expo '70 (Osaka), 87

Fadiman, James, 28–29, 235, 423n69
Fairy Faith in Celtic Countries, The (Evans-Wentz), 310, 311
Far Eastern Mining and Minerals, xxii, 106
Fate (magazine), 17–18
Fear and Loathing in Las Vegas (Thompson), 251, 307
Federal Bureau of Narcotics and Dangerous Drugs, 75

Federal Youth Corrections Act, 76
Fellini, Federico, 52–53
Feyerabend, Paul, 44
Feynman, Richard, 217–218
Finnegans Wake (Joyce), xxiv, 52, 81, 91, 118, 126–127, 190, 215–216, 259, 309
Fitz Hugh Ludlow Memorial Library, 235
5-MEO-DMT, 99, 112, 196, 306
Flashback Books (Petaluma, California), 235
Flight into Egypt: Binding the Book, The (Ely), 383, 486n55
Florencia, Colombia, 103, 139, 151, 152, 446n28
Folsom State Prison, 166
Food of the Gods (McKenna), xiv, xxix, 241–242, 258, 323–327, 415
  addiction, 437n40
  Bantam publishes, 235, 236, 415
  "A Brief History of Psychedelics" chapter, 299, 304
  ecstasis, 48–49
  exemplifies a psychedelic utopia, 230
  humanity at a terminal phase, 202
  manifesto at the back of, 335
  and the scientific community, 298
  story arc, 317
  and vitalism, 222
Fort, Charles, 265
Forte, Robert, 222
FORTRAN, 268
Forward the Future, 251–252
Foster, Craig, 350–351
Foundation series (Asimov), 92, 148
Fourth Dimension, The (Hinton), 340
Fractal Time (Timewave Zero software for Windows), 268
Fractals, 269, 464n38
Frank Leslie's Illustrated Newspaper, 159
Frankenstein (Shelley), 18

Freaks in the Machine: Mondo 2000 in Late 20th Century Tech Culture, The (Sirius), 409
Free Speech Movement (Berkeley), 43
Freud, Sigmund, 1
"From Psychedelics to Cybernetics," 353
Fuller, Buckminster, 268
"Future of Art, The" (rap), 361–362
"Future of Humanity, The" (rap), 402
"Future of Magic in Electronic Societies, The" (McKenna), 45–46, 345, 400, 434n92, 479n32

Gallo, Philip, 486n55
Gandhi, Mahatma, 297
Garcia, Jerry, 181
Gates, Daryl, 301, 321
Gathering of the Tribes, The (be-in), 234
Genet, Jean, 19
George Malley (film character), 369
Gibson, William, 279, 349, 354
Gift, The (Nabokov), 52
Giger, H. R., 191
Gila, 55, 56
Gimbutas, Marija, 217–218
Ginsberg, Allen, 10, 23, 31, 99, 440n94
Giulietta degli spiriti (Fellini), 52–53
Glover, Martin, 242
"Gnome, The" (Pink Floyd), 89, 434n98
Gnostic and Hermetic sensibility, 260
Gnosticism, 54
  neo-gnosticism, 54, 303, 339, 362
Gnostic redemptionism, 178
Gnostic Religion, The (Jonas), 303
Gnostics, xiii–xiv
Goa trance, 242–243
Gödel, Kurt, xxvii
Godfrey-Smith, Peter, 350
"God Whistle Principle," 285
Goethe, Johann Wolfgang von, 383
Gordon, Janet, 112
Goswami, Amit, 219
Govinda, Lama, 65

Gracie and Zarkov, 304, 358
Grady, Tom, 235
Grateful Dead (band), xi, 181, 290–291, 350, 413, 457n34
Graves, Robert, 122, 161, 316
Great Compression, the, 134–139
Great Hall (Cooper Union), 249
"Great Timestream Bifurcation, The" (rap), 282, 284–285
Grey, Alex, 371
Grey, Zane, 11
Grof, Christina, 224, 235
Grof, Stanislav, xii, 219, 220, 222, 235
"Growing Metropolitan Evil, A" (*Frank Leslie's Illustrated Newspaper*), 159
Guadalupe, Point Sal Beach, 225
Guenther, Herbert V., 91
Gulf War, 248
Gurdjieff, G. I., 129, 267
Gutenberg, Johannes, 270
"Guzman, Alfredo" (Horacio Calle), 100
Gyaltsen, Tashi (Gelugpa Lama), 69, 70
Gyrus, 283

Hachten, Dhyana (Languedoc), 78–79, 82, 84, 87, 96–97
Haeckl, Ernst, 383
Hagerty, Lorenzo, 248, 396, 405, 409
HAL (computer), 174
Halifax, Joan, 219–220, 221, 225, *226*
Hall, Manly P., 1
"Hallucinogens: Before and after Psychology" (McKenna), 221
Hanegraaff, Wouter, 104
Hansen, Douglas, 4, 23–25, 32, 37, 42, 67
Hansen, Elizabeth, 30, 36–37, 43, 203, 206, 220, 222, 374, 421n33
Happy Valley Foundation, 225. *See also* Ojai Foundation
Hard Day's Night, A (film), 236

Hardenburg's Walter E., 437n36
Harman, Willis, 28
Harner, Michael, 104
HarperCollins, 104, 236
Harper San Francisco, 236
Harpignies, J. P., 249, 325, 395
Harris, Morgan, 415
Harrison, Kathleen LaPriel (Kat), x, xxii, 55–56, *218*, 407, 455n6
  and the Amazon, 159
  ardent Deadhead, 181
  and ayahuasca, 168–170, 188–190
  at Bioneers 1997, 173
  Botanical Dimensions, 183–188, 201, 348–349
  cottage in Santa Cruz, 59
  education, 428n77
  and Erich Jantsch, 146
  at Esalen, 222
  Hawaiian terror trip, 196–197, 201, 204–205
  in Israel, 55, 56
  life with McKenna and family, 181, *187*, 192, *193*, 194, 195, 197, 199, 206, 218
  love letters to McKenna, 157
  Lux Natura, 182, 451n14
  marries McKenna, 179, *180*
  on McKenna's character, 233, 330
  and McKenna's raps, 213, 217
  McKenna writes about, 156–157
  in Mexico, 171–172
  on Meyer and "time guys," 269
  and psilocybin, 158, 327
  Psychedelic Conference II, 221
  Quick Trading Press, 451n13
  and *Salvia divinorum*, 171–172
  Syzygy, 182
  and tripping, 158
  as trusting, 170
  visits McKenna in Berkeley, 59–60
Hart, Clive, 87
Hart, Harold, 60

Hartley, Sara, xxii, 402, 408
   Berkeley and the Experimental College, 42–43
   evacuates from La Chorrera, 118
   and Ganesha statue packed with hash, 74–75
   grand jury subpoena, 126
   in La Chorrera, 110, 116
   McKenna shares idea with, 95
   uncle Harold Hart finds a McKenna manuscript unreadable, 60
   in Victoria, British Columbia, 96–97
Hart Publishing, 60
Hasheesh (hash), xx, 129, 181, 301, 328
   as Finn's favorite scent, 190
   and international travel, 67
   in Kathmandu, 66
   Lebanese, 56
   Ludlow (and Randolph), 27, 51, 219
   McKenna seeks and finds the finest, 35, 42
   McKenna's federal importation charge, 76, 143, 320
   McKenna quits, 199
   McKenna ships from India to United States, 3, 74, 75
   and Ouspensky, 341, 342
   suppliers Horn and Dick, 63–64
   swamis as sources of, 72
Hasheesh Eater, The (Ludlow), xxviii
Hassall, Bernard "Neil," 184–185, 320, 349
Hawayahuasca. *See* Ayahuasca
Hawksworth, David L., 480n47
Hayakawa, Samuel, 61
Hayes, Charles, 51
Hazard, John, 365, 390–391
Heart of Darkness (Conrad), 3, 389
Heavy Metal (magazine), 191
Heidegger, Martin, 19, 43, 216
Heinlein, Robert A., 12, 63
Heintz, Karl, xxii, xxvii–xxviii, 83, 84, 483n11

Hells Angels, 32
"Hells bells" (Himalayan datura), 71
Heraclitus, 115, 199, 262, 309, 313
Heraclitus, RV (research vessel) 175–176
Herbert, Frank, xxiii–xxiv, 12, 324
Herbert, Nick, 353
Herbert, Paul, 223
Hermes Psychopompos, 19
Hermeticism, 150, 200
Hero-shaman, 48
Hicks, Bill, 325
Hicks, Dillon, 195, 253
Hierophany, 48
High Frontiers (newspaper), 217, 314, 351–353
High school years, McKenna's, 23–27
High Times (magazine), xii, 156, 282
High Weirdness: Drugs, Esoterica and Visionary Experiences in the Seventies (Davis), 409, 416
Hildebrand, Lee, 24–25
Himalayan datura, 71
Hinton, Charles H., 340
Hinton cubes, 340
Hirano, Satomi, 153–154
"History Ends in Green," 310–311
Hoffmann, Martina, 227, 371
Hofmann, Albert, 4, 41, 221, 303
"Ho Lo" (McKenna), 345, 400, 480n35
Holy People of the World (Jestice), 328
Horgan, John, 261
Horn, Richard, 63–64, 66–67, 430n6
Horowitz, Michael, 222, 234, 384
Houston, Jean, 229
How to Change Your Mind (Pollan), 326
How to Mutate & Take Over the World (DiJusto), 355
Hubbard, L. Ron, 234
Human Potential Audio Foundation, 457n35
Humphrey, Sheila, 402, 431n28, 459n67
Hunter, Robert, xi
Husserl, Edmund, 43, 89, 333

Hutchins, Bonnie, 18
Hutchins, Kris, 22, 23, 422n51
Huxley, Aldous, 10, 18, 19, 21, 23, 25, 28, 119, 213, 220, 223, 300, 396
Hyperborea, 357, 482n85
Hyper-carbolation, 111, 115, 435n8
HyperCard for Mac, and Timewave Zero software, 268
Hypercubes, 340
Hyperspace, 49, 51, 54, 100, 126, 137, 258, 337–343
Hyperspace, transit to, 266, 311

Ibogaine, 209
Icaros, 168, 178, 355
I Ching (*Book of Changes*), ix, xxvi, 120–125, 130, 135, 140, 233, 259, 260, 268, 275–276, 283
Idler, The, 247
i-D Magazine (magazine), 249
Idol, Billy, 245
Illich, Ivan, 360
Illusions and Delusions of the Supernatural and the Occult (Rawcliffe), 18
Immediatist vitalism, 333–336
Improvising, McKenna and the art of, xxvii–xxviii
Incapacitant 3-quinuclidinyl benzilate, 34
India, McKenna in, xxi, 72–73
Individuation (Jung), 47–48
Inferno, The, Doré's etchings of, 17
Ingram, Matthew, 222
Inn, Martin, 86, 146, 433n86, 437n31
Institute of Ecotechnics, 175
Institute for the Study of Consciousness (Berkeley), 219, 382
International Conference on Shamanism (1984), 177
International Federation for Internal Freedom (IFIF), 21
International Transpersonal Association Conference (Charles University, 1992), 247, 414

International Transpersonal Association Conference, 235, 248
Invisible College, The (Vallée), 310
Invisible Landscape, The (McKenna and McKenna), xxix, 103, 113, 115, 123, 140, 143, 148, 267–269, 278, 283, 287, 390, 414
and the Grateful Dead, 181
publishing history of, 104, 147, 182–183, 236–237, 276
"Shamanic Investigations" (McKenna and McKenna), 104, 112, 126, 127, 129, *141*, 146, 147, 219, 315, 401, 437n31, 443n47
and Timewave computer program, 153
Irwin, Jan, 319
Island (Huxley), 21

Jabberwock (club), 40, 41
"Jabberwocky" (Carroll), 216, 252
Jacobson, Mark, 200, 282, 283
Jacobson, Norman, 44
Jagger, Chris, 68
Jagger, Mick, 195
James, William, 19
Jantsch, Erich, 146, 263
Jarnow, Jesse, 181
Jarry, Alfred, 293, 397
Jaspers, Karl, 19
Jaynes, Julian, 215, 313–316
Jefferson Airplane (band), 32
Jenkins, John Major, 277
Jestice, Phyllis, 328
Jobs, Steve, 269
Joe Rogan Experience, The (radio program), 326
Joe's College. *See* Experimental College (UC Berkeley)
Johansson, Scarlett, 361
John Brockman Associates, 235
John of the Cross, Saint, 302
John the Apostle, 317
Jonas, Hans, xiii, 303, 316

Index

Joshua Tree, "Rites of Spring" (workshop, 1986), 225–226
Journal of Ethnopharmacology, 176
Journey to Everywhere (Kawitzky), 251
Journey to the Center of the Earth (Verne), 122–123
Joyce, James, 43, 52, 91, 118, 126–127, 260, 309, 385
Jung, Carl, influences McKenna's thinking, xxviii, 18, 36, 45, 49, 50–51, 89, 115, 150, 165, 167, 202–203, 211–212, 260, 279, 293, 302, 313
    alchemy in works by, 46, 47, 48, 132, 197, 287, 386
    McKenna's growing ambivalence, 46–48
Jurist, Steve, 35
Justicia pectoralis var. *stenophylla*, 115

Kaiser, Henry J., 12
Kant, Immanuel, 225
Karman (ex-soccer player), 140
Karmapa, HH Gyalwa, 16th, 70
Karolinska Institute, 444n70
Kassapa Buddha, 71–72
Kathmandu, Nepal, 65–66, 68, 73
Kawitzky, Mike (Schwann), xix, 19, 251, 359, 385–386, 409, 414
Keen, Sam, 235
Keep, Marcus, 368, 370, 483n7
Kelley, Edward, 312
Kelley, Royce, 35, 37, 97, 152–153, 268, 274, 436n20, 465n56
Kemp, Joseph (Dad), 12, 368
Kennedy, Alison, 354
Kennedy, John F., 23
Kenneth Shine (fictional character), 328
Kent, Stephen, 243
Kepler, Johannes, 32
Kesey, Ken, 32, 33, 34
Ketamine, xi, 241, 301

KFI-AM (Los Angeles), 301
Kierkegaard, Soren, 119
King Wen sequence (*I Ching*), 26, 122, 274
Kircher, Athanasius, 231
Kohoutek (comet), 142, 166
Kornfield, Jack, 235
Korzybski, Xandor, 245, 268
Krassner, Paul, 223, 249, 270, 271, 282
Krippner, Stanley, 220
Kubla Khan, 23
Kume. *See* Nietfeld, Erica (Kume)
Kunysz, Laura, 457n35
Kurtz (fictional character), 3–4, 388–389
Kurzweil, Ray, 266–267, 284, 468n107

Lachman, Gary, 341, 342
La Chorrera, McKenna in, 95–114, 118–120
    the experiment at, xviii, 96, 97, 103–104, 114–118, 123, 279, 314, 370, 381, 439n78
    and March Forth (March Fourth), 114, 116, 117, 121, 122, 129, 150, 303, 315, 318, 439n73, 439n78
La Chorrera, World Temporal Mechanics Institute, 285
La Honda, 32
Laing, R. D., 225
Lamb, F. Bruce, 167
Lamborn, Mount, 11
Lands of the Saracen, The (Taylor), 383
Lane, Tom, *226*
Lanier, Jaron, 349
Lanyon Gallery (Stanford), 31
Lasky, Michael (Dave), 96–97, 102, 116, 118
Latour, Bruno, 333
Lawler, Justus George, 147
League for Spiritual Discovery, 33
Leary, Timothy, xi, xii, xiv, xviii, 92, 320, 321, 354
    compared and contrasted with McKenna, 300–303, 352, 378

Leary, Timothy (cont.)
  and comet Kohoutek, 166
  in Europe, 353
  and glory seeds, 21
  introduces McKenna at Wilshire Ebell Theater in Los Angeles, 199
  and Kesey, 33
  and McKenna's thoughts on death, 379
  and McKenna's federal charge, 319
  and McKenna's "new fundamentalism," 119
  as populist demagogue, 396
  and "Prestonia," 305
  at Psychedelic Conference II, 221
  "SMI^{2}LE," 339
  and the War on Drugs, 301
  and the World Wide Web, 357
Lee, Martin, 234
Le Guin, Ursula K., 391
Lennon, John, 302
Lepidoptery, and McKenna, 79–87
Letters of Marshall McLuhan, The, McKenna's review of, 50, 354
Levinson, Richard, 76
Levy, Dan, 235–236, 295, 322
Lévy-Bruhl, Lucien, 90
Liber Novus (Jung), 132, 203, 212
Liberty cap (*Psilocybe semilanceata*), 161
Libido (journal), 191
Liechty, Mark, 65
Life (magazine), 111
Lilly, John C., 217–218, 219, 220
Linda (Rick Watson's girlfriend), 66
Little Fluffy Clouds (The Orb), 239
Livingston, Judy, *14*, 378
Livingston, Laddie, xxviii, 378
Logos, psilocybean, 46–47, 259
Logos, the, 116, 121, 139, 205, 212, 314–319, 474n80, 474n81
"Lord Dark" (a.k.a. Solo Dark), 167. See also Cia; Solo Dark
Los Angeles Times (newspaper), 249, 321

Lost at Last (ethno-trance act), 253
Losteks, 39
Lovecraft, H. P., xiii, 10, 12, 23, 111, 166, 191
LSD, xi, xx, xxv
  and Abraham, 228
  confirms Freud's dynamics of the psyche, 1
  and DMT, 42, 305
  and Harrison, 56
  and Hassell, 185
  and John Parker, 24
  Jung on, 48
  and Kesey, 32
  Lee and Shlain's social history of, 234
  McKenna's first experience with, 10, 16
  and McKenna's future phenomenology, 92
  and McKenna's literary choices, 19
  McKenna's research into, 99
  and McLuhan, 50
  and the International Federation for Internal Freedom's Zihuatanejo Project, 21
  and the International Foundation for Advanced Study (IFAS), 28, 29
  Orange Sunshine, 71
  Sandoz LSD, 39, 40, 41–42
  and 2012, 284
  and the war on drugs, 301
Lucy Ricardo (TV character), 318
Ludlow, Fitz Hugh, xxvii, 27, 42, 51, 219, 383
Luna, Luis Eduardo, 140, 188–189, 222, 370
Lunney-Wheeler, Nancy, 222, 228–229, 375
Lux Natura, 156, 182, 187–188, 451n14
Lux Natura: Ethnobotany Library, 184
Lux Natura: logo, *183*
Lyell, Charles, 79–80
Lysergic World (magazine), 235

Index 505

Machine elves (DMT elves), xxv, 10, 33, 53, 54, 108, 298, 308–314, 434n98
Macintosh Plus (computer), 188
MacLeish, Archibald, 215
Magical Blend (magazine), 224, 249, 316–317, 349
Mahoney, Kevin
 in Berkeley, 59, 74–75
 and Dennis McKenna, 50
 on Dhyana Hachten, 78
 and George Csicsery, 36
 jailed, 76
 and McKenna, 37–38, 80
Makua, Hale, 370
Malay Archipelago, The (Wallace), 80, 84, 85
Malcolm, Michael, xix, 20, 35, 67, 73, 87, 96–97, 119
Malibu, Camp Shalom (retreat), 225
"Man and Woman at the End of History," 225
Man in the Gray Flannel Suit, The (Wilson), 12
Man in the High Castle, The (Dick), 282
Mandaeism, 54
Mandel, William Marx, 26
Mandelbrot, Benoit, 269
Manson, Charles, 234–235
Manual of Evasion LX94 (film), 272–273, 415
MAO (monoamine oxidase), 99–100, 112, 119, 176
 inhibition, 119, 129, 136, 175, 253
March Forth, 114–118, 121, 150, 439n78
Marciniak, Barbara, 312
Marriage, between McKenna and Kat Harrison, 181, *187*, 192, *193*, 194, 195, 197, 199, 206, 218
Marijuana, 92. *See also* Cannabis
Maritime Hall (San Francisco), 253
Markoff, John, 348
Masks of God (Campbell), 323

Mason and Dixon (Pynchon), 359
Mathematically Illuminated Musical Instrument (MIMI), 338
Max, Peter, 236
Maxwell, Clerk, 273
Maxwell, Nicole, 225
Maya Cosmogenesis 2012 (Jenkins), 277
Mayan Conference, 225
Mayan Factor, The (Argüelles), 277–278
Maybeck, Bernard, 179
Mays, Chris, 403, 486n60
McIntire, Jon, 350
McKenna, Dennis (brother), xviii, xxi–xxii, xxiii, *102*, 415–416
 alternative intelligent design theory, 165–166, 167
 arrested, 75–76
 birth and childhood, 11, 12–15, 21
 and career as a scientist, 283
 co-discovery with Terence of a popular means of psilocybin cultivation, 5, 111, 154
 and compressionism, 135
 at Conference on Botanical Intelligence, *226*
 on "Crypto-Rap," 59
 and Damer's "Ode to Terence," 201–203
 at Esalen, 222
 as executor of Terence's estate, 383, 384, 385–386
 and the experiment at La Chorrera, 114–118
 idea that some hallucinogens "fit into the DNA," 95–96
 and *The Invisible Landscape* (see *Invisible Landscape, The*)
 and John Parker, 24, 95, 96
 moves to Berkeley, 146
 plant collecting in Peru, 175–176
 poor eyesight, 20
 in a psychotic break according to Hartley, 110

McKenna, Dennis (brother) (cont.)
  publication of memoir, 201–202
  and science fiction, 148
  and South America with Terence, 58, 97, 100, 107, 112, 113, 114, 118–120, 125–126, 127, 143
  Terence becomes protective of, 40
  and Terence's cancer and death, 369, 370–371, 373, 377, 394
  and Terence's childhood, 16, 22
  and Terence's legal problems in Colorado, 144
  writings and reflections, 150
McKenna, Finn (son), 190–191, 371, 407
  birth, 181
  and death of father, xviii, 391–392, 484n14
  and death threats toward father, 367
  and father's mood after learning of his tumor, 370
  splits time between parents' homes, 200
  Terence as a father to, 193–194
  3D modeling with Terence, 359
McKenna, Hazelle "Hadie," née Kemp (mother), 12
  ambitions for Dennis and Terence, 22–23
  children, Dennis and Terence, 12
  death, 98, 123, 266–267, 382, 465n42
  encourages Terence to read Huxley, 18
  health, 77
  marries Joe McKenna, 12
  reads to Terence, 17
McKenna, Joe (father), xxiii, 11–12
  ambitions for children, 22–23
  bookishness, 17–18
  death, 254
  McKenna's belief that parents were fascists, 22–23
  and McKenna's legal status, 144
  meets and marries Hazelle Kemp, 12

resemblance to Joseph Tussman, 44
  retirement, 253
  sends wired warning to McKenna, 77
  success as traveling salesman, 16
  and Truman (war buddy), 30
McKenna, Klea (daughter), xviii, *194*, *371*, 407
  and America in the 1980s, 190
  artistic work, 192–194
  birth, 181
  and *The Butterfly Hunter*, 82–83, 387–388, 407
  children, 452n33
  directs *Almost Visible*, 171
  How Forests Think series, 391
  and mediocrity, 190, 194
  Terence as a father to, 193–194
  on Terence's mood when learning of his tumor, 370
"McKenna's Law," 214
McLuhan, Marshall, influences McKenna's thinking, 36, 43, 44, 45, 46, 49–51, 89, 90, 91, 92, 119, 238, 260, 279, 238, 355, 357, 360, 361, 385, 397
McNally, Dennis, 181
MDMA, xi, 196, 222, 240, 241, 301–302
Medicine wheel, 226
Meditations (Descartes), 391
Megatripolis (London), 245, 291
Megatripolitan Utopia, 245
Meiklejohn, Alexander, 43
Melak Taus (Yezidi angel), xiii
Melton, Barry "the Fish," 39, 40, 41
Melville, Herman, 10, 51
Memories, Dreams, Reflections (Jung), 47, 212
Memory palace, 212–213
Mercurius, 19
Meredith, Leslie, 235
Merleau-Ponty, Maurice, 89, 225, 333
Merry Pranksters, The, 33
Messipia, SS, 55

Metzner, Ralph, 21, 189, *221*, 225, 233, 325
Meyer, Peter, 206, 268–269, 274, 393–394, 465n56
Michaux, André, 19
Michaux, Henri, 215
Microsoft Windows, and Timewave Zero software, 268
Milius, John, 3
Mills, Bud, 32
Mind Children (Moravec), 361–362
Minkowski, Hermann, 341
Minsky, Marvin, 355
Misuse of Drugs Act (UK 1971), 161
Mitchell, S. Weir, 42
Mixmaster Morris, 245
MKUltra, Project, (CIA), 34
Moby Dick (Melville), 215–216
Molecular Genetics (Stent), 120
Mondo 2000 (project), 49, 245, 354, 471n26
Mondo 2000 film crew, 271–272
Monkey Temple (Swayambhu), 66
Montgomery, Rob, 248
Moore, Michael, 32, 77–78, 403
More, Thomas, *Utopia*, 18, 91
Moravec, Hans, 361–362
Morgan, Richard K., 362
Morning glory seeds, xx, 21, 27–30, 416
Mosombite, Don Fidel, 168, 169
Mother Jones (magazine), 240
Mountain Girl, 32
Mountain View, California, 23–27, 28
Mountain View High School, 23. *See also* Awalt High School
Mount Tamalpais Mortuary, McKenna's body cremated at, 377
Munn, Henry, 466n71, 474n80
Murray, Michael H., 147
Mushroom Cultivator, The (Stamets and Chilton), 164
Mushrooms, xx, 196. *See also Psilocybe cubensis*

Mutts, the (garage band), 227
Mycologia (journal), 154
"Myconet," 480n47
MYCONET, 348–349
My Octopus Teacher (film), 350–351
Mysterium Coniunctionis (Jung), 46, 132
Mysterium cosmographicum (Kepler), 32
Mystery School in Hyperspace (St John), xi

Nabokov, Vladimir, 52, 115, 388
Nakano Academy of American English, 87
Naranjo, Claudio, 222
NASA's Apollo missions, 68, 107, 150
Naturphilosophie, McKenna's unique, 261
Nazca lines, 192
Necronomicon (Lovecraft), xiii
Neoplatonist, McKenna as a, 260
Nepal, McKenna and, xxi, 53, 65–71
"New and Old Maps of Hyperspace" (rap), 219, 286–287, 382
New Dimensions (radio series), 214–215
New Edge scene, 236
New Era of Thought, A (Hinton), 340
New Eschatology, 49
New Left, 96
New Science of Life, A (Sheldrake), 228
New York Times (newspaper), 248, 415
New York, NY, 31, 60, 78, 207, 236, 249–250, 325
Newton, Isaac, 115, 261
Nichols, David, 220
Nietfeld, Erica (Kume), 102, 130, 134, 153–153
  arrives in Berkeley with McKenna, 119
  in Colombia, 140
  and *Finnegans Wake*, 127
  in La Chorrera, 102, 103, 109, 110, 115, 117
  moves with McKenna in with Dennis, 144
  return to Berkeley in 1972, 146

Nietfeld, Erica (Kume) (cont.)
and Royce Kelley, 152, 274
and temporal elements of the *I Ching*, 123, 132
typing up *The Invisible Landscape*, 140
Nixon, Richard M., 61, 100
Nobody People, 13
Noffke, Will, 52, 216, 352
Norm (film character), 236
Norstrilia (Smith), xxiv
Nothing Lasts . . . But Nothing Is Lost (Shpongle), 395

Oasis (Chicago), 270
Occidental, California: McKenna in, 182, *187*, 192, 228, 239, 271–272
"Ode to Terence" (Damer), 201–202
Ojai Foundation (the Topa Institute), 10–11, 33–34, 225, 226, 457n39
Ojai Foundation, "Mayan Conference," 277
Olivier, Jacques, 226–227
Olsen, Ollie, 254
Omega Associates, xx
Omega Institute, 360
Omni (magazine), 299
One and the many, the, 91–93
One Flew over the Cuckoo's Nest (Kesey), 33
O'Neill, Gerard, 286
On the Edge (St. Aubyn), 328
Oo-koo-hé, 99, 100, 108, 111, 136–137, 175, 177, 308
Open Center (New York), 249–250, 311, 270
"Opium Den in Pell Street, Frequented by Working-Girls, An" (engraving), *159*
Orange Sunshine LSD, 71
Orb, The, 239
Oregon, legalization of psilocybin, 417–418n13

Origin of Consciousness in the Breakdown of the Bicameral Mind, The (Jaynes), 315–316
Orlovsky, Peter, 31
O'Shaughnessy, Katherine, 222
Osmond, Humphry, 221
Oss, O. T., 181
Ott, Jonathan, 248
"Our Man in Nirvana" (column), 233
Ouspensky, P. D., 129, 340–341, 342
Ozora Festival (Hungary), 33

Pacifica Radio (KPFK), 215, 322
Pagan Love Cult (band), 253
Palenque Norte speaker series (Burning Man), 248
Palenque, 248
Palmer, Cynthia, 222
Pangalacticspermia (ensemble), 253
Panpsychism, encapsulated in *concrescence*, 262
Panspermia, 166
Paonia, 11–23
Paonia High School, 12, 21
Papilio androcles, 85
Paradise Lost, Doré's etchings of, 17
Parallel YOUniversity lecture, 245
Parker, John, 23–24, 78, 95, 96, 435n8
Parmenides, 313
Paschal, Beverly Randolph, 51
Patrick, Saint, 312
Pavitt, Bruce, 333
Pease, RJ, 21
Pêra, Edgar, 272, 331, 343–344, 415
"Personality #2" (Jung) 212
Peruvian Amazonian Company, 104, 105
Pesce, Mark, 371
Phenomenon (film), 369
Phenomenon, the, 112, 118, 126–127, 128, 130, 135, 137, 138, 140
Phenomenon of Man, The (Teilhard de Chardin), 265, 464n23

Philo Judaeus, 316
Philo Judeus on the Logos (Bryant), 383
Philosophical Research Society (Los Angeles), 1, 262
Pickering, Phil, 313
Pike, Neil, 253
Pinkastares, 39
Pink Floyd (band), 89, 434n98
Planck's constant, 269, 465n40
Plato, xxvi, 18, 124, 309, 313
Playboy (magazine), 50
PlaySpace Gallery (San Francisco), 82
Pleiadians, The (Barbara Marciniak), 312
Plotinus, 28, 324
Plowman, Tim, 188–189
Poe, Edgar Allen, 383
Pohl, Frederik, 346
Poincaré, Henri, 340
Pollan, Michael, 326
Pollock, Jackson, 10, 17, 19, 20, 23
Posford, Simon, 460n91
"Post Electric Thought" (McKenna), 88–91, 108, 131, 307, 344–346, 402
Prague Gnosis (interviews), 247, 297
"Preliminary Report," 113, 120, 125, 138, 401
Price, David, 223, 224, 384, 457n35
Price, Dick, 219, 224
Prigogine, Ilya, xxvii, 263
Probation (McKenna's), 144
Process and Reality (Whitehead), 262
Process Church of the Final Judgment, 234–235
Psilocybe cubensis, xxii–xxiii, 5, 107–109, 111, 151, 154, 181, 182
  indoor cultivation of, 164
Psilocybe mexicana, 108
Psilocybe mushrooms, 3, 110–119
Psilocybe semilanceata (liberty cap), 161
Psilocybin, 418n13
Psilocybin: Magic Mushroom Grower's Guide (Oss and Oeric), 162–165, 167, 181
  revised edition, 182–183, 414–415

Psilocybin: Magic Mushroom Grower's Guide (Oss and Oeric) covers, *163*, *186*
Psychedelic Conference II, 221
Psychedelic Experience, The (Leary et al.), 69
Psychedelic fiction, 149
Psychedelic Illuminations (magazine), 357
"Psychedelic Luminaries" (exhibition), 333
Psychedelic Rangers, 234
Psychedelic Salon (podcast), 204, 396
Psychology and Alchemy (Jung), 18
Psychotria viridis, 189, 379
Psyharmonics Records, 253
Psytrance, 242–243
Ptolemy, 383
Putumayo: The Devil's Paradise: Travels to the Peruvian Amazon Region and an Account of the Atrocities Committed upon the Indians, The (Hardenburg), 437n36
Putumayo region, 100, 103–108, 121, 126, 437n36
Pynchon, Thomas, xxvii, 39, 181, 359
Pythagoras, xxvi, 115, 262

Quadripartite (Ptolemy), 383
Queen Mu (Alison Kennedy), 354
Quickening: Today's Trends, Tomorrow's World, The (Bell), 286
Quick Trading Press, 451n13

Radical MAO inhibition, 119
Ram, Raja, 242, 460n91
Ram Dass (Richard Alpert), xiv, 228, 235, 242, 297, 321, 440n94
Rand, Ayn, 31
Raps, McKenna's, 254–255, 404–406
  "Alien Love," 216, 446n21
  "Amazonian Shamanism," 225
  "Cyber Culture," 354
  "From Psychedelics to Cybernetics," 353

Raps, McKenna's (cont.)
"Future of Art, The," 361–362
"Great Timestream Bifurcation, The," 282, 284–285
"Hallucinogens: Before and after Psychology," 221
"History Ends in Green," 310–311
"Man and Woman at the End of History," 225
"New and Old Maps of Hyperspace," 219, 286–287, 382
"Rites of Spring," 202, 225–227"Shamanism, Alchemy, and the Millennium," 185, 222
"Shamanism: Before and beyond History," 225
"Shamanology," 178
"Sinking Submarine," 461n111
"SPLAT: Surprises in Art and Biology," 371–372
"Surfing on *Finnegans Wake*," 54
"Tao and the Timewave," 283
"Tryptamine Hallucinogens and Consciousness," 219
"Unfolding the Stone," 199–200
Rasputin, 103
Rätsch, Christian, 248
Raves, xi, 238–243
Ravi, 56, 57
Rawcliffe, D. H., 18
Reality Club, 249
Reality Hackers (magazine), 233, 353
Rebirth of Nature, The (Sheldrake), 230
Red Book, The (Jung), 132, 202–203
Redfield, James, 367
"Re:Evolution" (the Shamen), 173, 240, 242, 265, 459n79
Reid, Terry, 87, 96
Rembrandt, 262
Republic, The (Plato), xxvi, 18, 91, 124
Retreat: How the Counterculture Invented Wellness (Ingram), 222

Revolution and withdrawal, McKenna on, 68–69
Rim Institute (Payson, Arizona), 270
"Rites of Spring," 202, 225–227
Rivera, John Estacion, 106
Rivers Ran East, The (Clark), 98, 104, 435n12
Robbins, Tom, 371, 372–373
Roberts, Jane, 312
Rochlin, Maxine, 415
Rockwell, Norman, 19
Rolling Thunder, 219
Rommel, Erwin, 103
Rosemary, 42
Rose X, 243, 461n111
Rossman, Leslie, 236–238
Rucker, Rudy, 272
Rushkoff, Douglas, 354
Rustlers Valley, 251
Ryan, Sylvester J., 76

Sacred and Profane, The (Eliade), 48
Sacred Heart Catholic Church (Paonia), 17
Sagan, Carl, 285
Salinger, J. D., 31
Salvia divinorum, 171–172, 209, 379
San Francisco Chronicle (newspaper), 62
San Francisco Museum of Natural History, 146
San Francisco Oracle (newspaper), 96
San Francisco State University, 61
Sand, Nick, xi, 33, 305
Sandoz LSD, 39, 40, 41–42
Sandstead, Morris W., Jr. 144–146
Sartre, Jean-Paul, 21
Schmidt, Arthur, 37
Schorske, Carl E., 43
Schultes, Richard Evans, 99, 100, 175, 303, 325
Schwann (Mike Kawitzky), 251, 359, 363, 385–386
Scientology, Church of, 234

Scorpio, McKenna as a triple, 19, 421n33
Scottish Rite Masonic Temple (Los Angeles), 4, 222
"Screechpuke," 74–77, 257
Seabury Press, The, 103, 147
Seaholz, Mal, 353
Secret Adam: A Study of Nasoraean Gnosis, The (Drower), 54, 130
"Seeking the Magic Mushroom" (Wasson), 111
Self-Organizing Universe, The (Jantsch), 146
Sequenci, Nik, 242, 245
Seth (Jane Roberts), 312
Seychelles, McKenna in, 54–55, 57, 67–68, 91, 92, 430n11
"Shamanic Investigations." *See Invisible Landscape, The*
Shamanism, 49
"Shamanism, Alchemy, and the Millennium" (seminar), 185, 222
"Shamanism: Before and beyond History" (workshop 1988), 225
Shamanism, Colonialism, and the Wild Man (Taussig), 49, 106
"Shamanology," 178
Shamen, The (UK band), 173, 239–240, 241, 459n79
Shared Visions, 216, 353
  1983, 148
  1986, 187
Shared Visions (radio show), 216
Sharer, Robert, 466n71
"Shark, The," 179
Sharp, Jonah, 243, 460n96
Shastras, Tantra, 91
Sheldrake, Rupert, 228, 415
  and Catholicism, 281
  and compressionism, 289
  concept of "formative causation," 228–229
  and concrescence, 262
  and DMT, 307
  and fractals, 269
  and human history, 288, 290
  on McKenna, 327
  theory of "morphic resonance," 228–229, 241, 262
  Rebirth of Nature, The, 230
  son Merlin, 332
  and the transcendental object, 287
  on the World Wide Web, 356–358
Sheliak, John, 274
"Sheliak clarification," 274–275
Shelley, Mary, 360
Shine, Kenneth, 328–329
Shlain, Bruce, 234
Shpongle (band), 242, 308, 309, 395, 460n91
Shulgin, Alexander, 220, 221, 241, 248, 445n15
Shulgin, Ann, xiv, 248
Siebert, Daniel, 189
Silness, Christy, xii, xviii, 209, 367
  email to McKenna's supporters after his surgery, 373
  a fan of McKenna, 207
  and McKenna in the late 1990s, 4
  and McKenna's death, xviii, 376–377
  and McKenna's tumor, 367, 368, 373, 374
  in Mexico, 206–207
  photographed with McKenna in 1999, *375*
Silverman, Julian, 138–139
Sinology, 441n5
Sirens of Titan, The (Vonnegut), 265
Sirius, R. U. (Ken Goffman), 233, 352–353, 354, 392, 409
Siva-Sakti, 91
"Skateaway" (Dire Straits), 72, 431n28
Skelly (family hound), 37
"Sky" (online commenter), 205
Slaughterhouse-Five (Vonnegut), xxvii
Slick, Grace, 32
"SMI^{2}LE" (Leary), 339

Smith, Billy, 268
Smith, Cordwainer, xxiv, 324
Smith, Elvin D., 316
Smith, Harry, 82
Smithers, Leonard C., 383
Snyder, Gary, 65
Socrates, 315
Sogyal Rinpoche, 235, 376
Solar Quest, 245
Solo Dark, 102, 103, 109, 167. *See also* Cia
Soma: Divine Mushroom of Immortality (Wasson), 303–304
Somers, Kathi, 23
Somers, Ray, 23
Somers, Tress, 23, 30
Something's Happening (radio program), 217–219
Sound Photosynthesis, 217, 218
Source Telecomputing Corporation, 348
Space Time Continuum, 243
Spin Doctors (band), 236
Spiritual Emergency Network, 224
"SPLAT: Surprises in Art and Biology" (rap), 371–372
Squirrels, invocations of, 213–214
St. Aubyn, Edward, 328
Stamets, Paul, 164, 248, 326
Stanford Research Institute (SRI), 33–34
Stanford University, 248
Stanley, Owsley, 41
Star Trek, 148
Starr, Tama, 78, 146
Starseed (Leary), 166
Steele, John, *226*, 226–227
Stegner Fellowship program (Stanford), 33
Steiger, Rod, 318
Stent, Gunther, 119–120
Stephanie (Stefi), 35, 41, 55, 58
Sterling, Bruce, 191, 345, 354
Stevens, Wallace, 252
St John, Graham, x, xi, xii, xiv

Stockhausen, Karlheinz, 246
Stolaroff, Myron, 28, 220
"Stoned ape" hypothesis, 49, 222, 294, 304, 324–325, 415
Strange Attractor: The Hallucinatory Life of Terence McKenna (St John), xii
Strassman, Rick, 307–308
Structure and Motif in Finnegans Wake (Hart), 87
Students for a Democratic Society, 60
Sturgeon (sci-fi author), 12
Swayambhunath, Nepal, 66
Swiftdeer, Harley, 226
Sylvan, Robin, 225–226
Symington, Ken, 189, 248, 371
Synchronicities, 131–132
Synesthesia (Ely), 486n55
Syzygy, 182
Syzygy spore-print ad, *185*
Szwed, John, 82

Takayama, Masayasu, 87, 138, 153, 157, 181, 402, 442n35
Tales of the Inexpressible (record album), 308
"Tao and the Timewave," 283
Tao Lin, 190, 331–332
Tao Te Ching, 381
Tao, the, 262, 379
Tarnas, Richard, 235
Tarsius tarsier, 84
Taussig, Michael, 49, 106
Taylor, Bayard, 383
Techniques of Ecstasy, The (Eliade), 48
TechnoCalyps (documentary), 357, 379, 415
Teilhard de Chardin, Pierre, 36, 221, 265–266, 284, 356, 456n25, 464n23
Tempodrom, 353
Teotlnanácatl (*Psilocybe mexicana*), 108, 302
Terence McKenna Archive, 403
Terence McKenna Bibliography, 403

Terence McKenna Digital Revival (documentary series), 414
Terence K. McKenna Legacy Library, 404, 486n60
Terence McKenna Omnibus 2012, The (documentary series), 251, 414
Terence McKenna's True Hallucinations (documentary), 414
Teresa of Avila, 19
Ternate, 84, 433n79
Thangboche Monastery (Nepal), 66
Thangkas, xix, xxi, 10, 63, 73
Theater of All Possibilities, 175
Theys, Frank, 357, 379, 415
Thích Nhất Hạnh, 225
Thinking Allowed with Jeffrey Mishlove (TV series), 233
Third World Liberation Front (SFSU), 61
Thomas, Dylan, 23
Thompson, Hunter S., 307
Thompson, William Irwin, 250
Thought of Teilhard de Chardin, The (Murray), 147
Three Books of Occult Philosophy or Magic (Agrippa), 383
Tibet, 65, 66
Tibetan Book of the Dead, 381
Tibetan Book of Living and Dying, The (Sogyal Rinpoche), 376
Tibetan Mysterium (Guenther), 131
Tibetan Yoga and Secret Doctrines (Evans-Wentz), 130–131
Time Chamber, of the Newton Center (Harvard), 302
Time Explorer (Meyer), 274
Timewave, 259–261, 292–295. *See also* Eschaton; I Ching; The Transcendental Object at the End of Time; 2012
  as alchemy, 260, 287
  and apocalyptic religion and thought, 279–281, 284–287
  and chaos theory, 268
  as an occult device, ix
  and death, 381
  and the eschatron, 125
  evocative of an accelerated fall, xxix
  Finn McKenna's thoughts on, 391, 392
  fractal by nature, 269
  and the half twist, 274, 465n56
  as an instrument of McKenna's faith in "the concrescence," xxvi
  and Kohoutek (comet), 142
  as mathematical theory, 266
  and McKenna's legacy, 270–271, 281–284
  McKenna's pursuit of, 267–276, 287–290
  McKenna's theory of novelty, 261–267
  as McKenna's vision, 203
  Meyer on, 392–393
  as mythos, xxv–xxvi
  as party at the end of the world, 290–292
  as puzzle garden, 270
  seminars, workshops, and retreats on, 270–271
  as sustained meditation on death, 266–267
Time Wave Zero booklets, 182–183
Timewave Zero software, 268–270, 293
  and 2012, 276–279
Toffler, Alvin, 268
Tokyo, 88
Toms, Michael, 214–215
Torgoff, Martin, 424n85
Torres, C. Manuel, 248, 371
Towards 2012 (magazine), 283
Traherne, Thomas, 19
Transcendental Object at the End of Time, The, 2, 260, 264, 265, 287–288, 289, 292, 293–294, 324, 338. *See also* Timewave
Transcendental Object at the End of Time, The (documentary), 414
TrancElements 2 (festival), 171, 253

Transmigrations of the Mandarin Fum-Hoam, The (Smithers), 383
Transmission Theatre, The, 243, 312
Travels on the Amazon and Rio Negro (Wallace), 387
Travolta, John, 369
Trialogues (Sheldrake, Abraham, and McKenna), 227–230, 278, 280, 281, 287–290, 327, 356–357, 360, 415, 458n49
Tribal Energy, 245
TRIP (magazine), 362
Trip: Psychedelics, Alienation, and Change (Tao Lin), 331–332
Trips (magazine), 233
"Tryptamine Hallucinogens and Consciousness" (rap), 219
Trist, Alan, 181
True & Faithful Relation of What Passed for Many Yeers Between Dr. John Dee (A Mathematician of Great Fame in Q. Elizabeth and King James their Reigns) and Some Spirits, A (Casaubon), 383
True Hallucinations (McKenna), xxii, xxvii, xxix, xxx, 69–70, 119, 131, 213, 219, 414
 audiobook, 217
 audiobook cover, *218*
 book launch, 243
 frontispiece, *101*
 on Indonesia, 82
 "Kathmandu Interlude, 238"
 Leary's copy of, 300
 March Forth documented in, 114
 McKenna's goal to publish, 183
 mix of fact and fantasy in, 104
 published, 235–236
 "seeded genes" thesis in, 151, 165
 Solo Dark in, 103
True Hallucinations (film), 72
Truman (Joe McKenna's war buddy), 30, 31

Tryptamines, xxix, 113, 137, 155, 307, 308, 445n15
Tryptophan, 166
Tuckman, Roy, 217
Tussman, Joseph, 35, 43–44, 425n33
2001: A Space Odyssey (film), 59, 150, 174
2012, 276–279, 284–285, 392–394
2012 (film), 279
2012 doomsday prophecies, 279

Ulysses (Joyce), 52
Underhill, Evelyn, 19
Underhill, Linda, *86*, 146, 147
Understanding Media (McLuhan), 49–50
"Unfolding the Stone," 199–200
United States
 Army Chemical Corps, 34
 Customs, 74, 75
 Declaration of Independence, 90
 Only Afghani Restaurant in, The, 35
 versus Terence Kemp McKenna, *145*
United States of America v. Terence Kemp McKenna, 145
University of California, Berkeley, 80
 "Biochemical Markers for Individuality" (course), 445n15
 degree in Shamanic studies, 43–50
 entomology department, xxii
 Experimental College, 3, 10, 35, 36, 43–45, 153, 416
 lifelong interests formed in, 50–54
University of California, Los Angeles (UCLA), 321–322
University of California San Francisco (UCSF) Medical Center, 373
University of California, Santa Barbara, world psychedelic research community at, 221
University of California Santa Cruz, 230, 338
University of Sydney, 253

University of Wisconsin, Experimental College, 43
Upham, C., 159
US Psychotropic Substances Act (1978), xxiii
Utopia (More), 18, 91

Valde, Julio, 269
Valis (Dick), 282
Vallée, Jacques, 310, 440n94
Varela, Francisco, 225
Varieties of Religious Experience, The (James), 19
Vasulka, Steina, 247
Vasulka, Woody, 247
"Vegetalismo: Shamanism among the Mestizo Population of the Peruvian Amazon" (Luna), 140
Velikovsky, Immanuel, 323
Venosa, Robert, 227, 371, *372*, *394*
Verne, Jules, xxii, 12, 122–123
Veteran's Administration (VA) hospital, Los Angeles, 321–322
Vibrant Matter (Bennett), 333
Vibrations and Forms: Findings from Psychedelic Adventures (Abraham), 228
Vice (magazine), 190
Victorian Tales of Cannabis, 218–219, 455n6
Vietnam War, 100
Vighneshvara, the Lord of Obstacles, 74
Village Voice (newspaper), 19, 21
Ving, Vernor, 284
Virola theiodora, 99–100, 111, 176
Visible language, 216, 342–344
"Visionary" tourism, 449n89
Viviani, Arthur J., 76
von Bingen, Hildegard, 19
Vonnegut, Kurt, xxvii, 265
VR, 343, 344, 349. 350, 354, 355, 363

Wadsworth (venue), 321
Waldman, Anne, xxvii
Walken, Christopher, 236
Wallace, Alfred Russel, xxii, 79–80, 84–85, 218–219, 386–387, 433n79
Wallace, Brian, 217
Wallacea, 79
Wallace line, 79, 80–81
Wallin, David, 26
Warfield Theatre (San Francisco), 240
War on Drugs, 301
War of the Worlds (Wells), 91
Wasson, Robert G., 25, 28, 69, 103, 111, 170, 220, 303, 304–304, 323, 474n80
Waters, Frank, 466n67
Watkins, Matthew, xxvi, 273–275
Watkins objection, xxvi, 274
Watson, Ellen, 222
Watson, Rick, xix–xx, xxv, xxvi, xxvii, 86, *374*, 402–403, 414, 416, 448n77
  Amazonas, 448n77
  and DMT, 9, 32–33, 34
  escape from Palo Alto, 31–32
  in India, 78, 79
  on John Parker, 24
  and Kesey, 32
  and LSD, 41–42
  on McKenna, 4, 27, 51, 70
  and McKenna's childhood, 22
  McKenna encourages to join in the Amazon venture, 151, 153, 159, *160*, *161*, 167
  and McKenna's hash trades, 63–64
  as McKenna's lifelong pal, 11
  "Morning Glory," 27–30, 416, 423n69
  on Mountain View High School, 23
  in Nepal, 65–68, 73–78
  poems written to McKenna, 98, 435n11
  in San Francisco, 29–30
Watts, Alan, xi, 42, 373
Watts, Mark, 457n35
Waugh, Ernie, 35
Wave Chart, "Stage 5" (McKenna), *141*

Ways to Go Beyond and Why They Work (Sheldrake), 307
Weathermen, the, 60
Weber, Max, 36
Weed, Arthur H., 76
Weil, Andrew, 222, *226*
Weird Tales (magazine), 12
Welin, Britt, 238
Well, The (Whole Earth 'Lectronic Link), 251
Wells, H. G., 12, 91, 345
Wendigo, the, 13–15
West (comet), 167
West, Mick, 313
West, Richard, 239–240
Wetlands Preserve nightclub, 245, 249, 250, 285
What Do We Want? When Do We Want It! (film), 461n111
"What It Is That Evolves" (McKenna), 402
What the Dormouse Said (Markoff), 348
Wheeler, Gordon, 375, 384–385, 486n62
Whiffen, Thomas, 104–105, 437n36
White Goddess, The (Graves), 122, 161316
Whitehead, Alfred North, xxviii, 225, 261–262, 264, 333
Whole Life Expo (Austin), 143, 360
Whorf's law, "26n rule," xxiv
Wiener, Doris, 35
Wiener, Norbert, 361
Wilbert, Johannes, 226
Wilhelm, Richard, 121
Williams, Roger, 70
Wilshire Ebell Theatre (LA), 199
Wilson, Robert Anton, xiii, 268, 272, 354, 440n94
Wilson, Sloan, 12
Winterland (SF music venue), 181
Wired (magazine), xii, 367
Wise, Nina, 26–27, 68

acid trip in Santa Cruz, 59–60
in Israel, 55–56
on Kat and McKenna's marriage and family life, 194, 198, 201
on McKenna as celebrity, 206
McKenna encourages to join him in Nepal, 68
and McKenna's interest in Tibetan art, 73
Witoto, the, 99, 136–137, 176, 177
Wittgenstein, Ludwig, xxiv, 216, 225, 236
Wizard of the Upper Amazon (Lamb), 167
Wizard of Oz, The (film), 309
Wizards Camp (Ojai Foundation), 225
Wolfe, Beatie, 448n77
Wolfe, Tom, 32
Wollongong University, 254
Woodroffe, John, 91
Word for World Is Forest, The (Le Guin), 391
Worlds in Collision (Velikovsky), 323
World Temporal Mechanics Institute (La Chorrera), 285
World Wide Web, early, 358
World Wildlife Fund, 183
Wylie, Lesley, 106

Yagé, 444n80
Yage Letters, The (Burroughs), 99, 167
Yates, Francis, 19, 212
"Year of the Jackpot, The" (Heinlein), 63, 430n11
Yenches, John, 35, 42
Yezidi (Kurdish sect), xii–xiii
Young, Arthur M., 219
Young Republicans, LA County, 301
Youth (Martin Glover), 242
YouTube, 223
Y2K, 361

Zap (Crumb), 191
Zappa, Frank, 30

Publisher contact:
The MIT Press
Massachusetts Institute of Technology
77 Massachusetts Avenue, Cambridge, MA 02139
mitpress.mit.edu

EU Authorised Representative:
Easy Access System Europe, Mustamäe tee 50,
10621 Tallinn, Estonia
gpsr.requests@easproject.com

Printed by Integrated Books International,
United States of America

Zarkov and Gracie, 304, 358
Zebroski, Susan, 26
Zeff, Leo, 189, 222
Zerwic, Matthew, 403
Zerwic Library, 403
Ziegler, Mel, 233, 242
Ziegler, Patricia, 233, 242
Zihuatanejo Project (IFIF), 21
Zippy Pronoia Tour, 245
Zuvuya, 313